ADVANCED STRUCTURED COBOL AND PROGRAM DESIGN

Don Cass

Humber College
Rexdale, Ontario

PRENTICE HALL, Englewood Cliffs, New Jersey 07632

Library of Congress Cataloging-in-Publication Data

CASSEL, DON, (date)
   Advanced structured COBOL and program design.

   Includes index.
   1. COBOL (Computer program language)   2. Structured
programming.   I. Title.
QA76.73.C25C374 1988   005.1'33   87–25917
ISBN 0–13–011495–2

Editorial/production supervision: Joan McCulley
Interior design: Meryl Poweski
Cover design: Meryl Poweski
Manufacturing buyer: Ed O'Dougherty
Acquisitions editor: Marcia Horton

© 1988 by Prentice-Hall, Inc.
A Division of Simon & Schuster
Englewood Cliffs, New Jersey 07632

Printed in the United States of America
10 9 8 7 6 5 4 3 2 1

ISBN   0-13-011495-2

Prentice-Hall International (UK) Limited, *London*
Prentice-Hall of Australia Pty. Limited, *Sydney*
Prentice-Hall Canada Inc., *Toronto*
Prentice-Hall Hispanoamericana, S.A., *Mexico*
Prentice-Hall of India Private Limited, *New Delhi*
Prentice-Hall of Japan, Inc., *Tokyo*
Simon & Schuster Asia Pte. Ltd., *Singapore*
Editora Prentice-Hall do Brasil, Ltda., *Rio de Janeiro*

CONTENTS

8 SUBPROGRAMS AND THE LINKAGE SECTION   *291*

9 COBOL'S REPORT WRITER FEATURE   *325*

PREFACE

This book has been written to be used in a second-level course in COBOL. The preceding book of this pair, *Introduction to Structured COBOL and Program Design*, was written for the first-level course and presents an introduction to the COBOL language and structured problem solving. Thus, the current book picks up where the other left off and proceeds to the more advanced COBOL topics.

In this book, two main topics run concurrently throughout. One is the subject of files in COBOL and the other is the matter of structured program design. Files are COBOL's main strength and this book covers the subject in depth. A complete chapter is devoted to each of the subjects of sequential files (Chapter 3), relative files (Chapter 5), indexed sequential access method (ISAM) files (Chapter 6), and virtual storage access method (VSAM) files (Chapter 7). In addition to these chapters, separate chapters discuss the concepts of sequential files and I/O devices (Chapter 2) and nonsequential files and file concepts (Chapter 4).

Structured program design principles and tools are presented at the beginning of the book in Chapter 1. For some students this will be a review chapter, while others may possibly be learning these concepts for the first time. However, all students will find this material to be an important basis for developing the programs in the remainder of the book. The use of program specifications, input and output definition, structure charts, structured flowcharts, pseudo code, and good program style are all covered here.

Of even greater significance is the implementation of these program design concepts throughout the book. Each chapter contains one or more major application programs that demonstrate the use of the language features presented in that chapter. These programs are all developed with the use of these structured design tools. Every program is first presented with the program specifications and input/output definitions. Then the general solution is developed using a structure chart. Next, details of the solution are created with the aid of pseudo code and structured flowcharts. Finally, the program is written and tested. Each stage of this development is discussed, and details of the solution are explained so the reader may understand how to create similar solutions.

Because COBOL programming at this level is rarely limited only to file use, additional chapters are provided to cover other advanced topics. Included in these chapters are the use of subprograms and the LINKAGE SECTION (Chapter 8), the Report Writer (Chapter 9), character manipulation (Chapter 10), and interactive COBOL programming (Chapter 11). Appendixes are included on COBOL's SORT/MERGE feature, table handling, EBCDIC and ASCII conversion tables, reserved words, and COBOL language format notation.

Throughout the book are insert sections on program-style techniques to encourage the writing of programs that are clear and easy to read and maintain. Also included are debugging hint inserts. These entries show how to find your errors and fix them. The results of testing each program are given to encourage good program-testing practices.

Each chapter ends with a summary, a list of terms to study, and review questions, including multiple choice, true/false, and fill in the blanks. Finally, programming problems are supplied to put into practice the principles learned from the chapter. The first programming problem in each chapter suggests a revision to the program developed within that chapter. This exercise will give experience in program maintenance and also provide a gentle programming experience before attempting a more major project.

I trust this book will meet your needs for an advanced-level COBOL course. An expression of gratitude is in order for those who have contributed to this effort: Marcia Horton, my editor at Prentice Hall, who was a great encouragement and gave me the moral and editorial support when I needed it most, and the professors who took a great deal of their valuable time to review the manuscript and to give valuable suggestions and corrections to problems which I had missed. Thank you Frank T. Gergelyi, Metropolitan Technical Institute (Saddle Brook, NJ), Ann Houck, Department of Computer Science, Pima Community College (Tucson, AZ), James Payne, Department of Data Processing, Kellogg Community College (Battle Creek, MI), and Raymond Vogel, Department of Computer Science, Schenectady Community College (Schenectady, NY) for your contributions.

Finally, I appreciate the support of my production editor Joan McCulley and others at Prentice Hall who did their utmost to turn my efforts into a first-class production. Thank you each one.

Don Cassel

1

STRUCTURED PROGRAM DESIGN

INTRODUCTION

This book is addressed to students in an advanced or second-level COBOL programming course. It assumes that you have the background in COBOL programming that would typically be covered in an introductory COBOL course and would include the fundamentals of the COBOL language. This prerequisite knowledge includes the design, writing, testing, and debugging of programs that have sequential file input and printed output. Much of this programming includes creating reports containing headings, calculations, field editing, and totals; reports with one or more levels of control breaks; and programs using arrays or tables.

Programmers today are expected to have both a facility with the COBOL language and a working knowledge of the use of structured program design techniques. Applying these methods to the development of COBOL programs results in many positive consequences. One is improved programmer productivity. By using structured methodology, programmers become more productive, not because they are able to write COBOL code faster but because it is written more effectively and contains fewer errors. As a result, less time is spent debugging the program and the programmer can get on with more interesting work, thus increasing the programmer's job satisfaction. With reduced time spent on debugging and error correction, more projects will be completed on target, which will help to meet management's goals.

A second benefit of the structured techniques is a reduction in program-maintenance costs. If the program is written correctly and contains few errors, less time will be spent to maintain the program if the inevitable error is found. Naturally, this will reduce the cost of maintenance. A second component of maintenance is adding new features to an existing program. Updating to reflect changing needs in the business is more readily achieved if the program is structured. Again, the cost of maintenance will be less than for an unstructured program.

Another benefit of structured programming is improved program reliability. What we want are programs that will run correctly with a minimum of errors and abnormal program terminations. Naturally, we would prefer that there be no errors and that the program always terminate correctly, but this high goal does not always reflect real-life experience. By using structured design and programming techniques, we have a method that will substantially improve reliability and lead to greater user satisfaction.

For the remainder of this chapter, we will review the structured program design methods. These methods will be used throughout the book as we develop more advanced COBOL programming applications and will be required for the programming exercises that you will be doing as part of your studies.

STRUCTURED DESIGN METHODS

Numerous systems have been created for designing structured programs. These range from simple English statements to complex diagrams and charts. The intent in this chapter is not to present you with all the alternatives but to show a workable system that will help you to design your programs so that they are structured, contain a minimum of errors, and are easy to read and maintain. To achieve these objectives we will discuss the use of program specifications, structure charts, pseudo code, structured flowcharts, and a few other topics that relate to good structured design.

PROGRAM SPECIFICATIONS

To write a successful program, it is first necessary to define the program requirements. This definition includes a program **specifications** form, definition of input and output files, and report or screen layouts. Figure 1.1 shows a typical program specifications form that may be used to define the program requirements. This form will contain specifics about the processing, but will only identify the files (inputs and outputs) needed. Files have their own form, as we will see later.

Preparing the Specifications Form

The specifications form identifies the program by name and ID (identification code) as it will be referred to on the system. The programmer or analyst who prepares the document will include his or her name and the date when it was prepared.

```
                         PROGRAMMING SPECIFICATIONS
PROGRAM NAME:                                      PROGRAM ID:
PREPARED BY:                                       DATE:
_____

Program Description:



Input File(s):


Output File(s):


Program Requirements:




```

FIGURE 1.1   A program specification form

The form then contains a brief description of the program. This description is intended to convey a general understanding of the purpose of the program and will usually be anywhere from a single sentence to a paragraph in length.

Each input and output file that the program will use is identified. These entries may refer to tape, disk, printer, or other devices that are used by the program. The entry on this form will be descriptive in nature and serves to identify the file.

The last, and most major, section of the program specifications is the program requirements section. This part may run to several pages in length, depending on the complexity of the program requirements. Essentially, the requirements itemize in point form each operation that the program is required to do. These points are just a list of "to do" items and are not intended to represent program logic.

The requirements will list calculations that are to be done, what formulas should be used, and what functions or subroutines are available. Any decisions that affect calculations will be identified, as will tables that need to be used. This section of the program specifications also identifies fields that need to be validated, the types of tests to be done, and errors to be reported. It can also include the type of file updating or inquiries that the program needs to make.

Basically, this section is an opportunity to think about and make notes on the total requirements of the program. In some companies the systems analyst prepares the program specifications in consultation with the user department, and when the specs are complete, turns them over to the programmer for implementation. In other companies the programmer is fully involved with this process.

Figure 1.2 shows a completed program specifications form for a multiple-level control break report for budget analysis by division and department. (The analyst's name, Diane Quest, and later the programmer, Jonathan Youngman, are fictional characters from the first book in this series.) As this form shows, there is one input and one output file in use by the program. The requirements say a lot about what will be required in this program. We know that we are dealing with a sequential file and that the sequence of the file is to be checked. We know from it that a budget and actual amounts are given, but we will need to calculate a difference value. We know that totals are required for these amounts at the end of each department, division, and at the end of the report. There is to be group printing of the department and division numbers, meaning they are only printed once at the beginning of each group.

PROGRAMMING SPECIFICATIONS

PROGRAM NAME: Division/Dept Budget Analysis   PROGRAM ID: BUDGET

PREPARED BY: Diane Quest   DATE: September 3

Program Description:
    This program produces a budget analysis report with multiple control break totals at the end of each department and division.

Input File(s):
    Budget file

Output File(s):
    Division/Department Budget Analysis Report

Program Requirements:
1. Read and sequence check a file of budget records.
2. Prepare a report listing each input record, representing one account, on one line.
3. Single space each detail line.
4. For each account, calculate and print a difference amount that is the difference between the budget and actual amounts. If an actual amount exceeds the budget, show the difference as a negative value.
5. Print a total of the budget, actual, and difference amounts at the end of each department.
6. Also print these totals at the end of each division and at the end of the report as company totals.
7. Group print the division and department numbers.
8. Allow for a page overflow after 40 lines.

FIGURE 1.2   Program specifications for the budget analysis report

So we are able to understand a lot about the application from the specifications. If we are preparing the specs ourselves, this gives us an opportunity to think about the various steps required in the program without concerning ourselves with program logic.

The next stage of defining the program specifications is to identify the input and output files required by the program.

Input and Output Definitions

One of COBOL's main strengths is its file handling capability, and this ability is the reason it is the primary application language for business. Naturally, most COBOL programs will have files for both input and output of data. Some programs may even use more than one input and one output file.

Files, whether used for input or output, have important characteristics that must be defined by the program (**input and output definitions**). Depending on the hardware device and the way in which the file is used, these characteristics may vary widely. A disk input file that is only seen by the program would be expected to have a much different definition than a printed report that is sent to a user department.

Files that are only machine readable, such as disk or tape (and in some cases cards may still be used), will require one type of file definition. This information will be much the same whether the file is used for input or output. Some of the kinds of information that is needed for these types of files are as follows:

1. Device type or medium (such as disk, tape, cards).
2. Access method: sequential, direct, ISAM, VSAM.
3. Record layout showing the length and type of data in all fields.
4. For disk and tape, what blocking factor is used.
5. Is the file a transaction file, master, or updated file or is it simply input for other processing?

Figure 1.3 shows a completed definition for the input file to the division/department budget analysis program. This form shows all the information the programmer will need to know about this file to write the SELECT clause, FD entry, and record description entries in the COBOL program. The type field identifies specific usages such as N for numeric, A for alphabetic, A/N for alphanumeric, and P for packed decimal.

Specific values in the fields, such as codes and predefined ranges, may also appear here or in some cases will be a part of the program specifications form that we have seen earlier. In this example no codes are used in the input file. Before leaving the input and/or output design, walk through each entry in the form and confirm its accuracy and completeness. Thoroughness now can save much grief later in the program design and programming stages.

INPUT/OUTPUT RECORD DEFINITION				
File: Dept. Budget Record Length: 25 Sequence: Major—Division 　　　　　　Minor—Department			File Type: Disk Blocking Factor: 12 Access Method: Sequential	
COLUMNS	FIELD	TYPE	LENGTH	DECIMALS
1	Division	N	1	
2–3	Department	N	2	
4–6	Account	N	3	
7–12	Budget amount	N	6	2
13–18	Actual amount	N	6	2
19–25	Unused			

FIGURE 1.3 Budget input file definition

Output files also use the definition form shown for the input file except when the output is a report or screen. In that case, a special form will be used. For these kinds of output, different types of information will be required by the programmer. Some of the characteristics of human-readable output are as follows:

1. Device type.
2. Type of report or display. Often the terms detail, summary, or exception can be used.
3. Headings.
4. Definition of detail lines.
5. Control breaks and totals.
6. For screens, what prompts are used and what responses.

Figure 1.4 shows an output definition, really a report layout, for the budget analysis report. This layout shows the headings, detail lines, control totals, and report totals that the program will be required to produce. To simplify writing record description entries, the report layout shows specific columns and pictures for each field. The spacing of each line and its relationship to the heading and/or total lines are also shown. As

```
 Ø          1          2          3          4          5          6          7
 12345678901234567890123456789012345678901234567890123456789012345678901

              DIVISION/DEPARTMENT BUDGET ANALYSIS

 DIVISION    DEPT.    ACCOUNT      BUDGET        ACTUAL       DIFFERENCE

     9        99        999       Z,ZZ9.99     Z,ZZ9.99      --,---.99
                        999       Z,ZZ9.99     Z,ZZ9.99      --,---.99
                        999       Z,ZZ9.99     Z,ZZ9.99      --,---.99
                        999       Z,ZZ9.99     Z,ZZ9.99      --,---.99

              DEPARTMENT TOTALS  ZZ,ZZ9.99    ZZ,ZZ9.99      --,---.99*


     9        99        999       Z,ZZ9.99     Z,ZZ9.99      --,---.99
                        999       Z,ZZ9.99     Z,ZZ9.99      --,---.99
                        999       Z,ZZ9.99     Z,ZZ9.99      --,---.99

              DEPARTMENT TOTALS  ZZ,ZZ9.99    ZZ,ZZ9.99      --,---.99*


     9        99        999       Z,ZZ9.99     Z,ZZ9.99      --,---.99
                        999       Z,ZZ9.99     Z,ZZ9.99      --,---.99
                        999       Z,ZZ9.99     Z,ZZ9.99      --,---.99

              DEPARTMENT TOTALS  ZZ,ZZ9.99    ZZ,ZZ9.99      --,---.99*

              DIVISION TOTALS    ZZ,ZZ9.99    ZZ,ZZ9.99      --,---.99**


              COMPANY TOTALS     ZZ,ZZ9.99    ZZ,ZZ9.99      --,---.99***
```

FIGURE 1.4   Budget analysis report layout

with the input, accuracy and completeness are essential when defining a report or screen layout.

STRUCTURE CHARTS

The first step in solving a programming problem is to create a **structure chart.** Structure charts are used to organize the solution into **modules** by starting with a general definition or module and then proceeding to more detailed modules. This chart is sometimes called a **hierarchy chart** because at the top level the solution is very general, but as the chart goes down to lower levels in the hierarchy more detail is expressed. Other names that express much the same approach as the structure chart are visual table of contents (VTOC) and a functional decomposition diagram.

Figure 1.5 shows a structure chart for the budget analysis problem. Each box in the chart contains a descriptive name, and the boxes are connected by flow lines to show their relationship in the hierarchy. The chart starts at the top level with a description of the entire problem. Each lower level shows subsequent details representing modules in the solution. Numbers above these boxes represent module numbers that will eventually become paragraph numbers in the COBOL program.

The modules in a structure chart are drawn independently of their order of execution in the program. However, some programmers and analysts like to use a left-to-right pattern to define a certain order inherent in the chart. This tradition has been followed here as closely as possible. But, because of the frequent use of common modules, it is difficult to always follow this order.

Common Modules

Several other conventions are followed in structure charts to improve their usefulness. One is the small triangular symbol in the upper right corner of some boxes. This symbol is used to denote a common module that is used in two or more places in the chart. Ultimately, these modules will be performed paragraphs in the COBOL program.

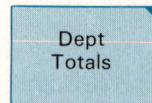

Selection

Another convention is the open-diamond symbol at the bottom of a box out of which one or more flow lines emerge. This symbol represents a decision where one or more modules are selected. Although the decision itself is not defined in the structure chart, the modules that are selected are shown.

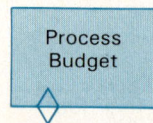

Repetition

The last symbol used is the circular arrow. It flows from the right side to the left side of a module to indicate that the code in that module is executed repetitively. The condition for continuing or terminating the repetition is not normally shown in the structure chart, but will be defined later in the pseudo code and of course in the program.

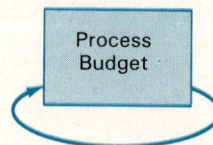

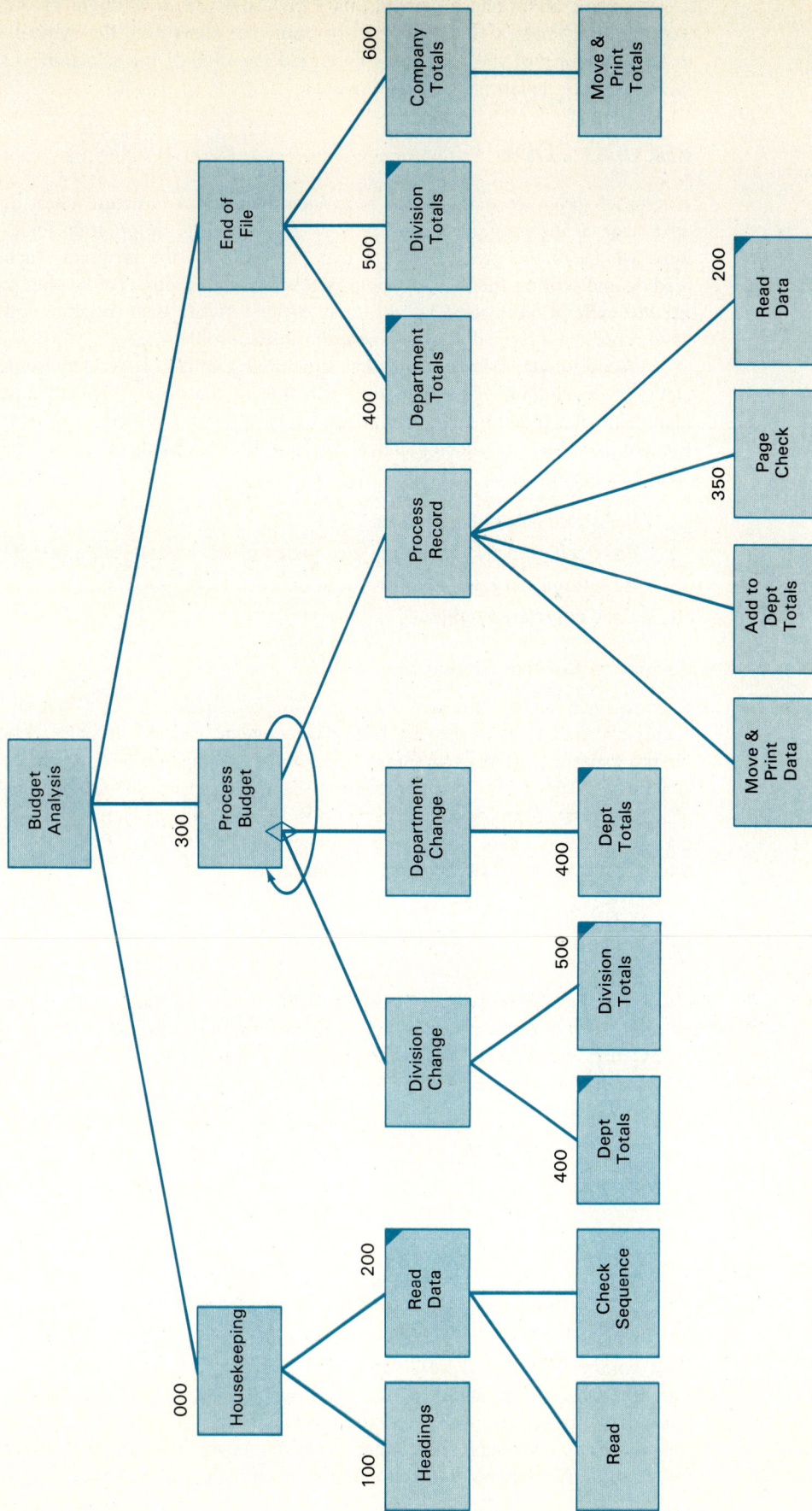

FIGURE 1.5 Structure chart for the budget analysis problem

Any or all of these symbols may be combined in a single module's box. For example, the Process Budget box in the structure chart used the symbol for repetition to show looping of the program's logic and the symbol for selection to choose either the division or department change module.

PSEUDO CODE

After each program module has been identified and a structure chart developed, the next stage in the program design process is to develop the program logic. By program logic we mean the precise actions that are taken by the program, such as opening, reading and writing files, calculations, decisions, and loops. To develop program logic, **pseudo code** is often used because it is easier to write than program code, but allows us to represent a logically correct solution to the problem.

Pseudo code, sometimes called structured English, is written from the structure chart by developing and expanding each box in the chart. While the structure chart identifies what functions are to be done by the program, pseudo code shows how each function is to be implemented. There are four different kinds of logical structures represented in pseudo code.

1. **Sequence control structure.**
2. **Selection control structure,** also called a decision structure or IF-THEN-ELSE.
3. **Repetition control structure,** also called a loop structure.
4. **Case control structure.**

Sequence Control Structure

The sequence control structure refers to a simple sequence of activities such as reading, printing, calculating, or moving data. The sequence control structure is fundamental to all programming. It does not make decisions or loop but simply proceeds from one statement to the next. Many statements in COBOL are sequence, including OPEN, CLOSE, ADD, SUBTRACT, READ, WRITE, and others. Here is an example of three pseudo-code statements that form a sequence control structure. To the right is a flowchart that graphically portrays the same structure.

1. Read Payroll Record
2. Calculate Tax
3. Print Tax

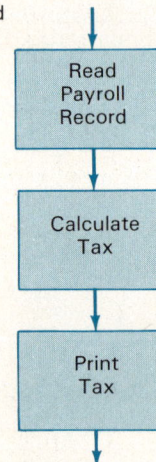

```
Read
Payroll
Record
```

```
Calculate
Tax
```

```
Print
Tax
```

Selection Control Structure

This control structure represents decision making in pseudo code. A decision has a condition that is evaluated. If the condition is determined to be true, one action is selected to be done. If the condition is determined to be false, the other action is selected. Only one action or the other is selected; never both. The IF statement implements selection in COBOL, as do other less obvious clauses such as AT END or ON INVALID KEY.

```
1. If Status = "Married"
      Calculate Married–Rate
   Else
      Calculate Single–Rate
   Endif
```

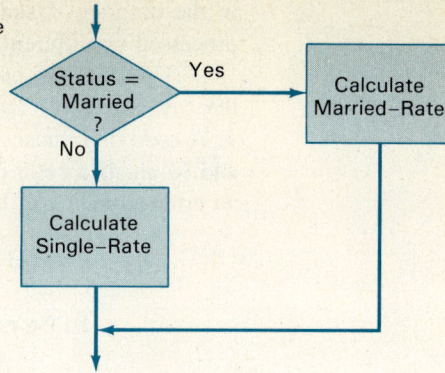

Status = Married ? — Yes → Calculate Married–Rate

No → Calculate Single–Rate

Repetition Control Structure

The repetition control structure also contains a decision, but the difference lies in the use of repetition. In this structure the decision determines if the action is to be repeated or if the program is to leave the control structure. This structure is implemented in COBOL with the PERFORM UNTIL statement.

```
1. Perform Count–Numbers
      Until Number > 10
2. Print Number
```

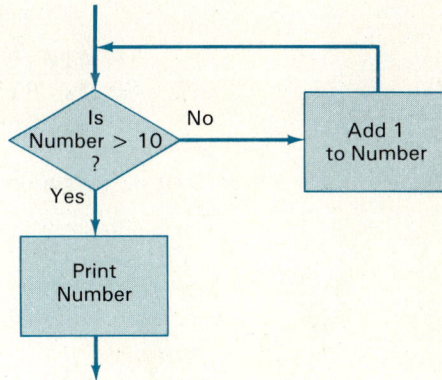

Is Number > 10 ? — No → Add 1 to Number

Yes → Print Number

```
Count Numbers

1. Add 1 to Number
```

Case Control Structure

The case control structure in COBOL, and therefore in our pseudo code, is a special form that may utilize COBOL's GO TO DEPENDING ON statement to reduce complexity

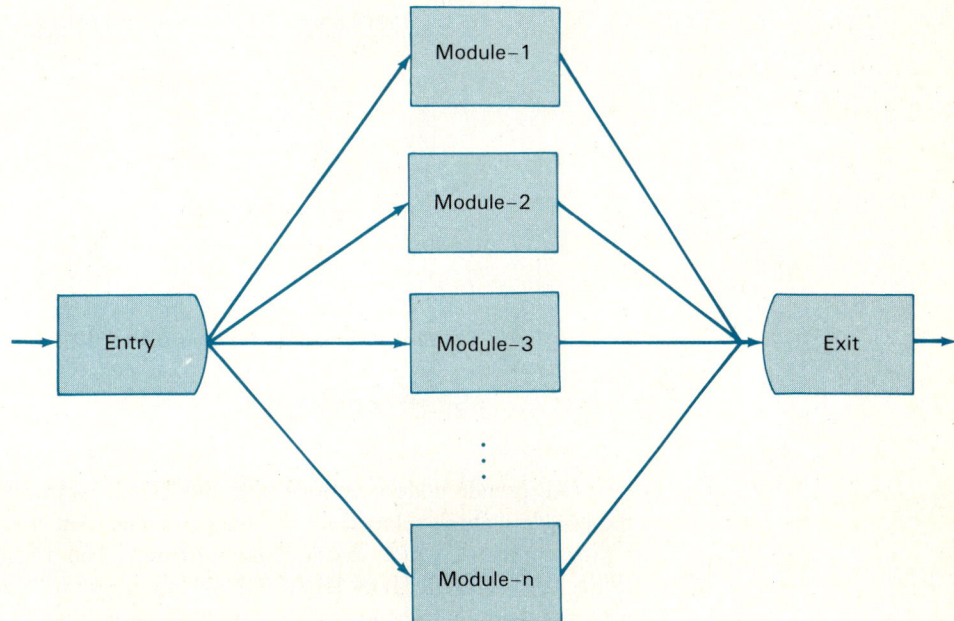

Entry → Module–1, Module–2, Module–3, ... Module–n → Exit

in the program. Usually, this form is used when several values for a code are to be processed by different paragraphs in the program.

This form of program logic depends on the value of a code that is analyzed by the case structure. Typically, the codes are consecutive integer values beginning with 1. A code of 1 causes a branch to the first module, a 2 branches to the second module, and so on. If a code is supplied that does not match the case structure's specifications, an error module will be executed.

```
Pseudo Code

1.Perform 400-Process.

400-Process

        Go to 420-Process-Add
              430-Process-Revise
              440-Process-Address-change
              450-Process-Delete
                   Depending On Input-Code.

410-Process-Error
1. Print error message.
2. Go to 490-Process-Exit.

420-Process-Add
              .
              .
              .
        Go to 490-Process-Exit.

430-Process-Revise
              .
              .
              .
        Go to 490-Process-Exit.

440-Process-Address-change
              .
              .
              .
        Go to 490-Process-Exit.

450-Process-Delete
              .
              .
              .
        Go to 490-Process-Exit.

490-Process-Exit
        Exit.
```

All pseudo code is written with these four control structures. Figure 1.6 contains the pseudo code developed for the budget application. Each pseudo-code form contains a program name, which is descriptive in nature, and a program ID, which will be used in the IDENTIFICATION DIVISION of the program. The programmer or analyst who prepared the pseudo code is also identified and the date it was written.

Pseudo code reflects the hierarchy developed in the structure chart. Each module will have a paragraph number and name with few exceptions. One such exception is when a box in the structure chart is simply used to identify a component of the solution but will not actually translate into code. Such is the case with the end of file box, which was used to clearly identify EOF activity.

PSEUDO CODE

PROGRAM NAME: Division/Dept Budget Analysis   PROGRAM ID: BUDGET
PREPARED BY: Jonathan Youngman   DATE: Sept 6   PAGE 1 of 4

000-Housekeeping
 1. Open input and output files
 2. Perform 100-Headings
 3. Perform 200-Read-Data
 4. Store sequence fields
010-Mainline
 1. Perform 300-Process-Budget
    until EOF-Flag = 1
 2. Perform 400-Dept-Totals
 3. Perform 500-Div-Totals
 4. Perform 600-Company-Totals
 5. Close files
 6. End of program
100-Headings
 1. Print heading line 1
 2. Print heading line 2
 3. Zero line count

FIGURE 1.6(a)   Pseudo code for the budget analysis report (1 of 4)

PSEUDO CODE

PROGRAM NAME: Division/Dept Budget Analysis   PROGRAM ID: BUDGET
PREPARED BY: Jonathan Youngman   DATE: Sept 6   PAGE 2 of 4

200-Read-Data
 1. Read Budget File
    At End Move 1 to EOF-Flag
 2. If EOF-Flag <> 1
       If Sequence Fields < Sequence Check Fields
          Display error message
          Close files
          Stop Run
       Else
          Store new sequence fields
       Endlf
    Else
          Next Sentence
    Endlf
300-Process-Budget
 1. If Division change
       Perform 400-Dept-Totals
       Perform 500-Div-Totals
    Else
       If Department change
          Perform 400-Dept-Totals
       Endlf
    Endlf
 2. If First line of a department
    2.1 Move division to print line
    2.2 Move department to print line
    2.3 Zero first line flag
 3. Calculate difference
 4. Move input data to print line

FIGURE 1.6(b)

Structured Program Design

   5. Add to department totals
       5.1 Add budget amount to total
       5.2 Add actual amount to total
       5.3 Add difference to total
   6. Write print line
       6.1 Write line
       6.2 Add 1 to line count
       6.3 Clear print line
       6.4 Perform 350-Page-Check
   7.   Perform 200-Read-Data
350-Page-Check
   1. If line count > 40
       Perform 100-Headings
    EndIf
400-Dept-Totals
   1. Move department totals to total line
   2. Write total line
       2.1 Write line double spaced
       2.2 Write blank lines
       2.3 Add 4 to line count
       2.4 Perform 350-Page-Check
   3. Add to division totals
       3.1 Add department budget amount to total
       3.2 Add department actual amount to total
       3.3 Add department difference to total
   4. Move zeros to department totals
   5. Store new department
   6. Set first line flag

FIGURE 1.6(c)

500-Div-Totals
   1. Move division totals to total line
   2. Write total line
       2.1 Write line single spaced
       2.2 Write blank lines
       2.3 Add 3 to line count
       2.4 Perform 350-Page-Check
   3. Add to company totals
       3.1 Add division budget amount to total
       3.2 Add division actual amount to total
       3.3 Add division difference to total
   4. Move zeros to division totals
   5. Store new division
   6. Set first line flag
600-Company-Totals
   1. Move company totals to total line
   2. Write total line double spaced

FIGURE 1.6(d)

Each step and decision required by the program will be identified here. Major steps are numbered for easy reference. Now is the time to begin thinking about identifier names. Although names in the pseudo code are not necessarily as formalized as in the program, these names should at least be used consistently.

STRUCTURED FLOWCHARTS

Flowcharts were once a popular tool for developing program logic. But, to be honest, they were often used by the programmer after a program was written to document the program logic. This tendency to do things in reverse came about because programmers often did not find flowcharts to be as useful a development tool as might be expected. Instead, it was often easier to write the program without the chart and then draw it after all the bugs had been corrected. Obviously, this practice did little to help improve the design and accuracy of programs.

A second problem with flowcharts is that they are not inherently structured. It is extremely easy to develop unstructured program logic, which leads to all the problems we had in the past with unstructured programs. As a result, most companies today are insisting that their programmers use the structured methods for developing program logic. By using structure charts and pseudo code or some variation of these tools, structured programs are a by-product with all the benefits of accurate code containing few errors. These programs are also easier to read and maintain because of their structured organization.

Because of this trend to minimize the use of flowcharts (structured or otherwise) in program design in the profession, we strongly encourage the student to use the structure chart and pseudo code when designing a program.

MODULES

MODULARITY

What is a module? From the viewpoint of a structure chart, a module can be thought of as a box in the chart. This module or box is a specific component of the solution to the problem. It may be as simple as a module for reading an input record or as complex as a module to calculate federal tax. In the pseudo code or program code, the module will be a paragraph that describes how to implement this component of the solution. Another way of expressing this concept is that a module is a series of statements designed and written to perform a specific function.

The purpose of a module, like the purpose for a structure chart, is to aid in reducing the complexity of a program. We do this by dividing the program into functional components (modules) that form the building blocks of the program. Each of these components, like each box in the structure chart, performs a specific function, and each function is much simpler to comprehend and write than the original problem.

A single function can invoke or perform other functions if necessary. This process may apply if the original function is too complex itself and needs to be further subdivided to reduce complexity. An example of this is shown in Figure 1.7 where the federal tax

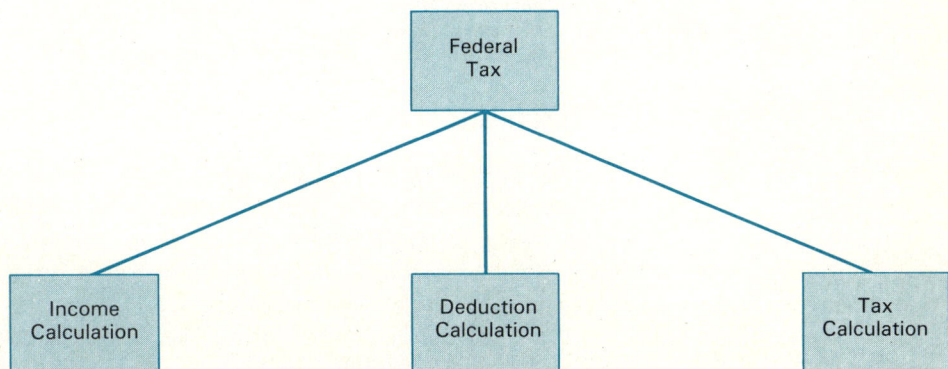

FIGURE 1.7 One module that invokes other modules

is broken down into modules that determine income, deductions, and the tax. Another reason why a function may call other functions is to use functions that already exist and therefore reduce the amount of coding necessary.

MODULE LENGTH

If a module can be as simple as reading an input file, then it would seem that the minimum length could be only one or two lines. That would seem to be true and in some cases a module will in fact be that short. But it is not the short modules that are troublesome, but rather modules that are too long. There is an interesting discovery in psychology that says that most people can on average memorize a random sequence of 7 digits when the numbers are read to them once. Some people can only manage 5 digits, while others, like we aspiring programmers of course, can handle up to 9 digits. This range of digits is called the magic number 7 plus or minus 2.

What this has to do with modules is related to the numbers we can recall. The larger the module is the more difficult it will be to understand the problem, solve it, and remember how it works. This length has implications for both problem solving and debugging modules in a program. Clearly, some of us will be able to handle longer modules than others, and some of us will even struggle with the shorter ones.

A commonly used standard in programming for module length is never to let a module exceed one page in length. The objective is to be able to see all the code in a single module at one time without the need for page flipping. A module that would ordinarily require more than a page would be split into parts, using a natural grouping of the statements, so that what might have been a very long module is now several shorter and more manageable ones.

Some modules are by nature very complex even though they may not be a page in length. Sometimes it will be helpful to split a module like this into several smaller ones just to reduce the complexity. Smaller, simpler modules are usually preferable to longer more complex ones.

INTERFACING

When a module is initiated, it will be expected to act on certain data in the program. It may help to think of these data as input to the module, even though there may not be an actual input operation involved. A module that calculates a gross salary may use an hourly rate and number of hours for the operation. Thus rate and hours may be thought of as input to the module. The module creates a value for gross salary, which may be used by other modules in the program. Therefore, gross may be thought of as output from the module.

These data are the **interface** between modules in the program. Because modules are rarely as simple as the one described above, with only two inputs and one output, the interface becomes more complex as the module is more complex. An objective, then, in designing a module is to minimize the amount of data passing to and from the module. The more data that are passed the more error prone the module will be.

COUPLING

Coupling is present in a module whenever data are passed to or from the module. Since modules usually have both input and output, coupling is virtually always present. A preferred level of coupling is low coupling. It exists when there is a minimum of data passing. Low coupling in a module makes it easier to write the module and to debug and maintain the code in the module.

High coupling exists when many data are passed between modules and should be avoided. With high coupling, there is a greater chance of error because of the inherently higher complexity of the module.

COHESION

Cohesion defines the degree to which the components of a module relate to each other. A highly cohesive module is one whose parts all relate to the same function. Modules with high levels of cohesion typically have low levels of coupling. By contrast, modules with low cohesion frequently have high levels of coupling.

A module that validates all 20 fields in an input record would tend toward low cohesion because of the complexity of the needs of these fields. However, 20 separate validation modules would each have high cohesion because each is solving only a small part of the problem. But here is where reality often raises its ugly head. The 20 separate modules may not always be practical. Perhaps there are different groups of fields with similar validation requirements, in which case maybe we can develop only a few modules and still retain high cohesion. Obviously, this is a decision that would be based on the program specifications.

INDEPENDENCE

Independence refers to how one module affects another module in the program. Although we cannot have total independence, we should strive to develop modules that are somewhat isolated from one another. As modules have greater dependence on other modules, program maintenance will become more difficult, because a change to the code in one module can adversely affect what happens in the dependent module. This relationship also has implications when debugging a program. An error in one module may create a subsequent error in a dependent module.

GENERALITY

Generality refers to a characteristic that renders a module useful in other sections of the program. This is often easier said than done, but by looking for similarities in the structure chart, pseudo code, and ultimately the program code, generality can be achieved.

For example, instead of using 20 WRITE statements to create error messages in a validation program, an alternative is to define 20 different error messages. These messages (one at a time) may be passed to a module containing a single WRITE to print the message.

In more complex situations, there may be subtle similarities between modules. The idea is to see if by modifying one module it can be made to satisfy the needs of both modules. Clearly, the more general a module becomes the more it is possible for it to increase in complexity. So it will be necessary to keep a sharp eye out for this trade-off and use some discernment in whether to become more general at the expense of added complexity. An interesting paradox is that sometimes generality results in *reduced* complexity.

STRUCTURED WALKTHROUGHS

The objective of a structured **walkthrough** is to find errors, potential problems, or omissions in the program and correct them before serious consequences result. A second objective is to ensure that the solution correctly implements the program specifications. The walkthrough procedure does not eliminate the need for testing our programs, but it may save us time in debugging them.

Walthroughs may be done at different times during program development. Unlike testing, a walkthrough is not simply done after the program is written, but rather it can be done to the structure chart, pseudo code, and program code. What we are looking for at each stage are errors. The earlier in the walkthrough that we find an error the better, because that error will not be carried forward to the more complex stages of the solution.

To do a walkthrough, it is best to have a second party present who is willing to examine your document (structure chart, pseudo code, or program) and point out errors, inconsistencies, or ambiguities. Although you can do your own walkthrough, a second person will not have a psychological mindset about your solution. When we create our own solution to a problem, we tend to see what we intend the solution to do and are often blinded by our own errors. A second person will have a fresh approach and can often see things we are totally oblivious to.

The basic procedure for a walkthrough is for the presenter to take a document, such as the structure chart, and explain it step by step to the second party or reviewer. The reviewer should be encouraged to ask questions frequently, and the presenter should not be defensive about his or her material. Any concerns that the reviewer has about the document should be explained or justified, and in many cases corrections will need to be made.

An error found in the structure chart must be corrected before proceeding to develop the pseudo code. If the error is of major significance, it may be necessary to completely redo the structure chart and perform another walkthrough before proceeding further with the design. It is essential to get things right at each level of the design before progressing to the next stage; otherwise, errors will tend to be compounded.

PROGRAM STYLE

The programmer's craft includes, first and foremost, the ability to write programs that solve the problem according to the specifications. But the program should also exhibit good style and create a visually pleasing appearance. Good style does not have any effect on the way the program runs, but it certainly enhances the appearance of the program. Style makes the program easier to read and hence to debug and maintain.

Most companies consider style to be of such importance that they have developed their own standards for ensuring that good style is used by each programmer. Many of these practices will be followed in this book.

STYLE IN THE IDENTIFICATION DIVISION

This is the easiest division for which to define style. There are few rules and these are easy to follow.

1. *Indent comment entries*: Good style in the IDENTIFICATION DIVISION would indent each comment entry to a common column of the coding sheet.
2. *Use two lines per entry*: Another technique to enhance readability is to place each comment entry on the line following the paragraph name.

Figure 1.8 shows these elements of style implemented in an IDENTIFICATION DIVISION.

STYLE IN THE ENVIRONMENT DIVISION

Good style in the ENVIRONMENT DIVISION is essentially the same as the techniques used in the IDENTIFICATION DIVISION. These techniques of style are as follows:

1. Indent entries within the paragraph to a common column on the coding form.
2. Place paragraph entries on one or more lines below the paragraph name.
3. If an entry such as a SELECT clause requires more than one line, indent second and subsequent lines to a common column.

```
      IDENTIFICATION DIVISION.
      PROGRAM-ID
          EXP01.
     *AUTHOR.
     *    JONATHAN YOUNGMAN.
     *INSTALLATION.
     *    SALES UNLIMITED CORPORATION.
     *DATE-WRITTEN.
     *    MARCH 7.
     *DATE-COMPILED.
     *    MARCH 12.
     *SECURITY.
     *    NONE.
     *REMARKS.
     *    THIS PROGRAM PRINTS THE PAYROLL REPORT.
```
FIGURE 1.8   IDENTIFICATION DIVISION with good style

```
ENVIRONMENT DIVISION.
CONFIGURATION SECTION.
SOURCE-COMPUTER.
    IBM-370.
OBJECT-COMPUTER.
    IBM-370.
SPECIAL-NAMES.
    C01 IS TO-TOP-OF-PAGE.
INPUT-OUTPUT SECTION.
FILE-CONTROL.
    SELECT DATA-IN       ASSIGN TO UR-2540R-S-INFILE.
    SELECT EMPLOYEE-FILE ASSIGN TO UT-3340-S-EMPFILE.
    SELECT SALARY-LIST   ASSIGN TO UR-1403-S-PRINTER.
```
FIGURE 1.9   Good style in the ENVIRONMENT DIVISION

By applying these methods, the division in Figure 1.9 is written using elements of good style.

STYLE IN THE DATA DIVISION

This division requires attention to style in FD entries and record description entries. Here are a few rules to apply:

1. Division names, section names, FD, and level number 01 all begin in area A (column 8). All other entries must be in area B, beginning in column 12.
2. Indent all entries that follow the FD to a common column using only one entry per line.
3. Indent all second-level entries in the record description entry by at least four columns. Indent each additional level four more columns. More than four may be used, but use the indenting consistently in the entire program.
4. Use descriptive data names.
5. Where appropriate, use a prefix and/or a suffix on the data name.
6. Align entries like PIC and VALUE on a single column.

Observe how these hints for good style in the DATA DIVISION are included in the COBOL statements shown in Figure 1.10.

```
DATA DIVISION.
FILE SECTION.

FD  SUB-FILE
    BLOCK CONTAINS 80 CHARACTERS
    LABEL RECORDS ARE OMITTED
    DATA RECORD IS RECORD-IN.

01  RECORD-IN.
    05  FILLER                      PIC X(80).

WORKING-STORAGE SECTION.

01  TOTALS.
    05  TOTAL-CUSTOMERS             PIC 9(05)     VALUE ZERO.
    05  TOTAL-PAID                  PIC 9(06)V99  VALUE ZERO.
    05  TOTAL-OWING                 PIC 9(06)V99  VALUE ZERO.

01  FLAGS.
    05  EOF-FLAG                    PIC X(03)     VALUE 'NO '.
    05  LINE-COUNT                  PIC 9(02)     VALUE ZERO.

01  SUBSCRIPTION-IN.
    05  ID-NUMBER-IN                PIC 9(10).
    05  CUSTOMER-IN.
        10  NAME-IN                 PIC X(15).
        10  ADDRESS-IN.
            15  STREET-IN           PIC X(15).
            15  CITY-IN             PIC X(15).
            15  POSTAL-IN           PIC X(07).
    05  DUE-DATE-IN                 PIC X(08).
    05  OWING-IN                    PIC 9(03)V99.
    05  PAID-IN                     PIC 9(03)V99.
```

FIGURE 1.10 Good style in the DATA DIVISION

STYLE IN THE PROCEDURE DIVISION

When coding this division, there can be many rules because of the many statement types available. Instead of attempting to create rules for every statement type, the following are general rules for coding the PROCEDURE DIVISION:

1. Write one statement per line.
2. Align common elements in statements.
3. Where possible, use one statement per sentence. Except where a logical grouping is needed, such as in the AT END phrase or IF statement, each statement should end with a period.
4. Start each new phrase on a new line. Statements like PERFORM, READ, or WRITE can contain two or more phrases. Write the second and subsequent phrase indented on a new line so that it will be clearly visible in the program.
5. Break long statements at the end of a word.
6. Use initialized data names instead of constants.
7. Label procedure names with a sequence number. Procedures or paragraphs in the program usually correspond to the functions defined in a structure chart. Since these functions form a hierarchy, the relationships are easier to visualize if each procedure is given a prefix number that reflects this hierarchy.

8. When optional phrases, such as ON SIZE ERROR, are used, place them on a separate line following the statement to which they belong.

9. Use line spacing for readability in the source listing.

10. Use the keywords EQUAL TO, GREATER THAN, or LESS THAN rather than the symbols =, >, or < for clarity.

11. Indent all actions to a common column within the IF and/or the ELSE.

12. If many statements are included with the IF or the ELSE, use a performed paragraph for each of these and place the statements in the performed paragraph.

13. Where possible, use a condition name rather than a nondescriptive relational condition.

14. Where possible, use the sign condition rather than the relational condition.

15. When compound conditions are used, align the AND and OR operators and write each new condition on separate lines.

16. Avoid the use of implicit subjects and relational operators.

17. When nested IF statements are used, write the ELSE under the same column as the IF to which it relates. Indent actions under the IF and ELSE by a consistent number of columns as used in the remainer of the program.

Figure 1.11 shows the program for the budget program. This is the program for the application discussed throughout the chapter. The elements of style discussed over the previous pages have also been incorporated here.

```
IDENTIFICATION DIVISION.

PROGRAM-ID.
      BUDGET.
*AUTHOR.
*      JOHNATHAN YOUNGMAN.
*INSTALLATION.
*      SALES UNLIMITED CORP.
*DATE-WRITTEN.
*      SEPTEMBER 11.
*DATE-COMPILED.
*      SEPTEMBER 13.
*SECURITY.
*      NONE.

ENVIRONMENT DIVISION.

CONFIGURATION SECTION.
SOURCE-COMPUTER.
      IBM-4381.
OBJECT-COMPUTER.
      IBM-4381.
SPECIAL-NAMES.
      C01 IS TO-TOP-OF-PAGE.

INPUT-OUTPUT SECTION.

FILE-CONTROL.
      SELECT BUDGET-FILE    ASSIGN TO UT-3340-S-BUDGET.
      SELECT BUDGET-REPORT ASSIGN TO UR-1403-S-SYSPRINT.

DATA DIVISION.

FILE SECTION.

FD   BUDGET-FILE
      BLOCK CONTAINS  12 RECORDS
      RECORD CONTAINS 25 CHARACTERS
      LABEL RECORDS ARE OMITTED
      DATA RECORD IS INPUT-REC.
```

FIGURE 1.11(a) Budget analysis program

```
01  INPUT-REC.
    05  FILLER                       PIC X(25).

FD  BUDGET-REPORT
    RECORD CONTAINS 133 CHARACTERS
    LABEL RECORDS ARE OMITTED
    DATA RECORD IS PRINT-LINE.
01  PRINT-LINE.
    05  FILLER                       PIC X(133).

WORKING-STORAGE SECTION.

01      OTHER-DATA.
        05  EOF-FLAG                 PIC 9(01) VALUE ZERO.
        05  LINE-COUNT               PIC 9(02) VALUE ZERO.
        05  FIRST-LINE-FLAG          PIC 9(01) VALUE 1.
            88  FIRST-LINE-FLAG-ON             VALUE 1.
            88  FIRST-LINE-FLAG-OFF            VALUE 0.
        05  CTL-BREAK-FIELDS.
            10  STORED-DIVISION      PIC 9(01).
            10  STORED-DEPT          PIC 9(02).
        05  SEQ-CHECK-FIELDS.
            10  PREV-DIVISION        PIC 9(01) VALUE ZERO.
            10  PREV-DEPT            PIC 9(02) VALUE ZEROS.

01      ACCUMULATORS.
        05  TOTALS USAGE COMP-3.
            10  DEPT-BUDGET-TOTAL    PIC  9(05)V99 VALUE ZEROS.
            10  DEPT-ACTUAL-TOTAL    PIC  9(05)V99 VALUE ZEROS.
            10  DEPT-DIFF-TOTAL      PIC S9(05)V99 VALUE ZEROS.
            10  DIV-BUDGET-TOTAL     PIC  9(05)V99 VALUE ZEROS.
            10  DIV-ACTUAL-TOTAL     PIC  9(05)V99 VALUE ZEROS.
            10  DIV-DIFF-TOTAL       PIC S9(05)V99 VALUE ZEROS.
            10  COMP-BUDGET-TOTAL    PIC  9(05)V99 VALUE ZEROS.
            10  COMP-ACTUAL-TOTAL    PIC  9(05)V99 VALUE ZEROS.
            10  COMP-DIFF-TOTAL      PIC S9(05)V99 VALUE ZEROS.
        05  DIFFERENCE               PIC S9(05)V99 USAGE COMP-3.

01      BUDGET-REC.
        05  SEQUENCE-FIELDS.
            10  DIVISION-IN          PIC 9(01).
            10  DEPT-IN              PIC 9(02).
        05  ACCOUNT-IN               PIC 9(03).
        05  BUDGET-IN                PIC 9(04)V99.
        05  ACTUAL-IN                PIC 9(04)V99.
        05  FILLER                   PIC X(07).

01      HEAD-1.
        05  FILLER                   PIC X(16) VALUE SPACES.
        05  FILLER                   PIC X(35)
            VALUE 'DIVISION/DEPARTMENT BUDGET ANALYSIS'.

01      HEAD-2.
        05  FILLER                   PIC X(34)
            VALUE ' DIVISION    DEPT.      ACCOUNT'.
        05  FILLER                   PIC X(34)
            VALUE 'BUDGET        ACTUAL        DIFFERENCE'.

01      DETAIL-LINE.
        05  FILLER                   PIC X(04) VALUE SPACES.
        05  DIVISION-OUT             PIC 9(01).
        05  FILLER                   PIC X(08) VALUE SPACES.
        05  DEPT-OUT                 PIC 9(02).
        05  FILLER                   PIC X(07) VALUE SPACES.
        05  ACCOUNT-OUT              PIC 9(03).
        05  FILLER                   PIC X(06) VALUE SPACES.
        05  BUDGET-OUT               PIC Z,ZZ9.99.
        05  FILLER                   PIC X(05) VALUE SPACES.
        05  ACTUAL-OUT               PIC Z,ZZ9.99.
        05  FILLER                   PIC X(04) VALUE SPACES.
        05  DIFFERENCE-OUT           PIC --,---.99.
```

FIGURE 1.11(b)

```
01   TOTAL-LINE.
     05  FILLER                        PIC X(12) VALUE SPACES.
     05  HEAD-TOTAL                    PIC X(18).
     05  BUDGET-TOTAL-OUT              PIC ZZ,ZZ9.99.
     05  FILLER                        PIC X(05) VALUE SPACES.
     05  ACTUAL-TOTAL-OUT              PIC Z,ZZ9.99.
     05  FILLER                        PIC X(04) VALUE SPACES.
     05  DIFFERENCE-TOTAL-OUT          PIC --,---.99.
     05  ASTERISK-OUT                  PIC X(03).

PROCEDURE DIVISION.

000-HOUSEKEEPING.
    OPEN INPUT  BUDGET-FILE
         OUTPUT BUDGET-REPORT.
    PERFORM 100-HEADINGS.
    PERFORM 200-READ-DATA.
    MOVE SEQUENCE-FIELDS TO CTL-BREAK-FIELDS.

010-MAINLINE.
    PERFORM 300-PROCESS-BUDGET
        UNTIL EOF-FLAG = 1.
    PERFORM 400-DEPT-TOTALS.
    PERFORM 500-DIV-TOTALS.
    PERFORM 600-COMPANY-TOTALS.
    CLOSE BUDGET-FILE
          BUDGET-REPORT.
    STOP RUN.

100-HEADINGS.
    WRITE PRINT-LINE FROM HEAD-1
        AFTER ADVANCING TO-TOP-OF-PAGE.
    WRITE PRINT-LINE FROM HEAD-2
        AFTER ADVANCING 2 LINES.
    MOVE SPACES TO PRINT-LINE.
    WRITE PRINT-LINE
        AFTER ADVANCING 1 LINES.
    MOVE ZEROS TO LINE-COUNT.

200-READ-DATA.
    READ BUDGET-FILE INTO BUDGET-REC
        AT END MOVE 1 TO EOF-FLAG.
    IF EOF-FLAG IS NOT EQUAL TO 1
        IF SEQUENCE-FIELDS IS LESS THAN SEQ-CHECK-FIELDS
            DISPLAY '**SEQUENCE ERROR**', SEQUENCE-FIELDS
            CLOSE BUDGET-FILE
                  BUDGET-REPORT
            STOP RUN
        ELSE
            MOVE SEQUENCE-FIELDS TO SEQ-CHECK-FIELDS
    ELSE
        NEXT SENTENCE.

300-PROCESS-BUDGET.
    IF DIVISION-IN IS GREATER THAN STORED-DIVISION
        PERFORM 400-DEPT-TOTALS
        PERFORM 500-DIV-TOTALS
    ELSE
        IF DEPT-IN IS GREATER THAN STORED-DEPT
            PERFORM 400-DEPT-TOTALS
        ELSE
            NEXT SENTENCE.
    IF FIRST-LINE-FLAG-ON
        MOVE DIVISION-IN    TO DIVISION-OUT
        MOVE DEPT-IN        TO DEPT-OUT
        MOVE ZERO           TO FIRST-LINE-FLAG.
    COMPUTE DIFFERENCE = BUDGET-IN - ACTUAL-IN.
    MOVE ACCOUNT-IN     TO ACCOUNT-OUT.
    MOVE BUDGET-IN      TO BUDGET-OUT.
    MOVE ACTUAL-IN      TO ACTUAL-OUT.
    MOVE DIFFERENCE     TO DIFFERENCE-OUT.
    ADD  BUDGET-IN      TO DEPT-BUDGET-TOTAL.
```

FIGURE 1.11(c)

Structured Program Design

21

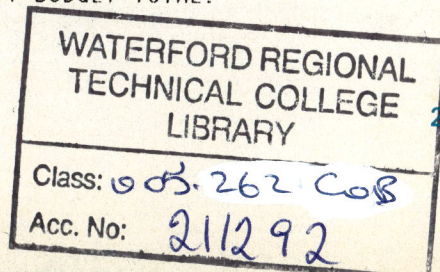

```
        ADD   ACTUAL-IN      TO DEPT-ACTUAL-TOTAL.
        ADD   DIFFERENCE     TO DEPT-DIFF-TOTAL.
        WRITE PRINT-LINE FROM DETAIL-LINE
            AFTER ADVANCING 1 LINES.
        ADD 1         TO LINE-COUNT.
        MOVE SPACES   TO DETAIL-LINE.
        PERFORM 350-PAGE-CHECK.
        PERFORM 200-READ-DATA.

    350-PAGE-CHECK.
        IF LINE-COUNT IS GREATER THAN 40
            PERFORM 100-HEADINGS.

    400-DEPT-TOTALS.
        MOVE 'DEPARTMENT TOTALS' TO HEAD-TOTAL.
        MOVE DEPT-BUDGET-TOTAL   TO BUDGET-TOTAL-OUT.
        MOVE DEPT-ACTUAL-TOTAL   TO ACTUAL-TOTAL-OUT.
        MOVE DEPT-DIFF-TOTAL     TO DIFFERENCE-TOTAL-OUT.
        MOVE '*'                 TO ASTERISK-OUT.
        WRITE PRINT-LINE FROM TOTAL-LINE
            AFTER ADVANCING 2 LINES.
        MOVE SPACES TO PRINT-LINE.
        WRITE PRINT-LINE
            AFTER ADVANCING 2 LINES.
        ADD 4 TO LINE-COUNT.
        PERFORM 350-PAGE-CHECK.
        ADD  DEPT-BUDGET-TOTAL   TO DIV-BUDGET-TOTAL.
        ADD  DEPT-ACTUAL-TOTAL   TO DIV-ACTUAL-TOTAL.
        ADD  DEPT-DIFF-TOTAL     TO DIV-DIFF-TOTAL.
        MOVE ZEROS TO DEPT-BUDGET-TOTAL
                      DEPT-ACTUAL-TOTAL
                      DEPT-DIFF-TOTAL.
        MOVE DEPT-IN TO STORED-DEPT.
        MOVE 1               TO FIRST-LINE-FLAG.

    500-DIV-TOTALS.
        MOVE 'DIVISION TOTALS' TO HEAD-TOTAL.
        MOVE DIV-BUDGET-TOTAL  TO BUDGET-TOTAL-OUT.
        MOVE DIV-ACTUAL-TOTAL  TO ACTUAL-TOTAL-OUT.
        MOVE DIV-DIFF-TOTAL    TO DIFFERENCE-TOTAL-OUT.
        MOVE '**'              TO ASTERISK-OUT.
        WRITE PRINT-LINE FROM TOTAL-LINE
            AFTER ADVANCING 1 LINES.
        MOVE SPACES TO PRINT-LINE.
        WRITE PRINT-LINE
            AFTER ADVANCING 2 LINES.
        ADD  3 TO LINE-COUNT.
        PERFORM 350-PAGE-CHECK.
        ADD  DIV-BUDGET-TOTAL   TO COMP-BUDGET-TOTAL.
        ADD  DIV-ACTUAL-TOTAL   TO COMP-ACTUAL-TOTAL.
        ADD  DIV-DIFF-TOTAL     TO COMP-DIFF-TOTAL.
        MOVE ZEROS TO DIV-BUDGET-TOTAL
                      DIV-ACTUAL-TOTAL
                      DIV-DIFF-TOTAL.
        MOVE DIVISION-IN TO STORED-DIVISION.
        MOVE 1               TO FIRST-LINE-FLAG.

    600-COMPANY-TOTALS.
        MOVE 'COMPANY TOTALS'    TO HEAD-TOTAL.
        MOVE COMP-BUDGET-TOTAL   TO BUDGET-TOTAL-OUT.
        MOVE COMP-ACTUAL-TOTAL   TO ACTUAL-TOTAL-OUT.
        MOVE COMP-DIFF-TOTAL     TO DIFFERENCE-TOTAL-OUT.
        MOVE '***'               TO ASTERISK-OUT.
        WRITE PRINT-LINE FROM TOTAL-LINE
            AFTER ADVANCING 2 LINES.
```

FIGURE 1.11(d)

SUMMARY

Using structured techniques for program design and implementation results in improved programmer productivity, fewer program bugs, reduced cost of maintenance, improved program reliability, and greater programmer and user satisfaction. Structured design begins with the program specifications and applies to all stages of development from input and output definition to structure charts, pseudo code or structured flowcharts, and structured program code.

Program specifications include a description of the program, a definition of each input and output file, and a list of program requirements, which is a point by point list of things to do in the program.

The input and output definitions expand on the files identified by the program specifications. File definitions include the device type or medium and the access method used, whether sequential, direct, ISAM, or VSAM. Each record format in the file is also described. This description includes a record layout, the length of each field, and the blocking factor for tape or disk files. Report definitions also show detail line layouts, headings, control breaks, and totals.

A structure chart is used to organize the solution into modules, beginning with a general definition and proceeding to more detailed lower-level definitions. This chart is sometimes called a hierarchy chart. Structure charts also use certain conventions to identify common modules (a filled-in triangular symbol), selection (a diamond symbol), and repetition (a curved line).

Pseudo code, sometimes called structured English, is used to develop the program logic. Pseudo code is written from the structure chart and proceeds by developing and expanding each module in the chart. The four logical structures used in pseudo code are the sequence, selection (also called IF-THEN-ELSE), repetition (also called a loop structure), and the case control structures.

Modules are a concept used in developing programs and may be thought of as a specific component of the solution to the problem. The purpose of a module is to reduce complexity by dividing the program into functional components. Modules should be restricted to a maximum length not to exceed the number of lines that fit on a single page. When one module interfaces with another, an objective is to minimize the amount of data that needs to pass between them. When many data are passed, there is a high level of coupling, which is to be avoided. Within the module we should strive for a high level of cohesion so that all components of the module relate to each other.

Modules that exhibit independence are least affected by changes to other areas of the program. A module that exhibits generality may often be used in other parts of the program or in other programs.

Structured walkthroughs are used to find errors and potential problems and to correct them before serious consequences result. A walkthrough involves a second party, who assists in examining your structure chart, pseudo code, and program code with the objective of finding potential problem areas.

Programming style is an essential part of writing effective programs. Style affects the appearance and readability of the program and hence makes the program easier to debug and maintain.

TERMS TO STUDY

Case control structure	Hierarchy chart
Cohesion	Independence
Coupling	Input definition
Generality	Interfacing

Module   Sequence control structure
Output definition   Specifications
Pseudo code   Structure chart
Repetition control structure   Style
Selection control structure   Walkthrough

1. The main objective in _____ program design is to create programs that will run correctly with a minimum of errors and abnormal program terminations.

2. The program _____ form will contain specifics about the processing steps but will only identify the files (inputs and outputs) needed.

3. An input/output _____ for a disk input file that is read by the program would be expected to have a much different content than a printed report that is sent to a user department.

4. The type field in a file definition identifies specific usages, such as P, for _____ _____ .

5. A _____ layout shows the headings, detail lines, control totals, and report totals that the program will be required to produce.

6. A structure chart is sometimes called a _____ chart because at the top level the solution is very general, but as the chart goes down to lower levels, more detail is expressed.

7. A small triangular symbol in the upper-right corner of some boxes in a structure chart is used to denote a _____ module that is used in two or more places in the chart.

8. The open-diamond symbol at the bottom of a box out of which one or more flow lines emerge represents a _____ where one or more modules are selected.

9. After a structure chart has been developed, the next stage in the program design process is to write the _____ _____ .

10. The _____ control structure refers to a simple sequence of activities, such as reading, printing, calculating, or moving data.

11. The _____ control structure represents decision making in pseudo code and may be an IF, AT END, or ON INVALID KEY statement in COBOL.

12. The repetition control structure also contains a decision that determines if the action is to be _____ or if the program is to leave the control structure.

13. The _____ control structure in COBOL is a special form that may utilize COBOL's GO TO DEPENDING ON statement to reduce complexity in the program.

14. A _____ that is a box in the structure chart is a specific component of the solution to the problem.

15. A commonly used standard in programming for module length is never to let a module exceed one _____ in length.

16. Data that are input or output to/from a module are called the _____ .

17. _____ is present in a module whenever data are passed to or from the module.

18. The term _____ defines the degree to which the components of a module relate to each other.

19. The term _____ refers to a characteristic that renders a module useful in other sections of the program.

20. The objective of a structured _____ is to find errors, potential problems, or omissions in the program and correct them.

21. Good _____ does not have any effect on the way the program runs, but it certainly enhances the appearance of the program, making it easier to read and hence to debug and maintain.

TRUE/FALSE

22. The program specifications form contains the logic to be followed by the program code.

23. An input definition will identify every field contained in the input record and the length of the field.

24. Another name for a structure chart is the vertical table of contents (VTOC).

25. In a structure chart, the operation of selection is shown by using a circular line with an arrow.

26. Pseudo code is formed by using a combination of four different control structures.

27. One purpose of a module is to help reduce the complexity of the program.

28. A module can be any length to be effective, providing it reduces program complexity in the process.

29. Walkthroughs are done at different stages of the program's development and are intended to find errors or omissions in the document.

MULTIPLE CHOICE

30. Select the item that would be found in an input definition for a sequential disk file.
    a. Access method.
    b. Record length.
    c. Blocking factor.
    d. All of the above.
    e. b and c.

31. Which statement best describes an output definition?
    a. It defines the characteristics of any type of output file.
    b. It is only used for defining report layouts.
    c. It is used to identify the basic structure of the program.
    d. None of the above.

32. How is a common module identified in a structure chart?
    a. With a small open-diamond symbol.
    b. With a small filled-in triangular symbol.
    c. With a circular arrow.
    d. No special symbol is used.

33. Where will the sequence, selection, repetition, and case control structures usually be found?
    a. Program specifications.
    b. Input/output definition.
    c. Pseudo code.
    d. All the above.
    e. None of the above.

34. Select the statement that is true for a selection control structure.
    a. Each action is done every time.
    b. A decision needs to be made before an action is taken.
    c. Looping is done.
    d. One of many different actions is taken.

35. Select the statement that is true for a case control structure.
    a. Each action is done every time.
    b. A decision needs to be made before an action is taken.
    c. Looping is done.
    d. One of many different actions is taken.

36. One of the following characteristics is present whenever data are passed between modules.

a. Interfacing.
b. Coupling.
c. Cohesion.
d. a and b.
e. b and c.

2

SEQUENTIAL FILE CONCEPTS

File processing is the primary topic of this book, but, before we look at COBOL's sequential file capabilities, this chapter discusses the concepts of sequential files. Sequential files, either on magnetic disk or tape, are used extensively in business information systems. Of course, the printer is sequential too, but this chapter is about tape and disk.

A RATIONALE FOR SEQUENTIAL FILES

The primary characteristic of a **sequential file** is that the records are stored in order or sequence from the first record in the file to the last. This sequence is particularly evident on tape, where records are recorded consecutively along the surface of the tape in a manner similar to recordings on a music cassette tape. Disk, as we will see later, also has a sequential property, although records are stored in quite a different manner.

Sequential files are typically used in batch processing, where all records of a file must be processed. For example, a payroll file would require pay checks for each employee on the file and so every record must be processed. This situation would call for sequential processing. Although this is an example of sequential processing, many state-of-the-art systems use a file organization that permits both sequential and direct access.

Another sequential situation could be a magazine company that has a file of subscribers to their publication. Each month mailing labels are required for the subscribers, and so all records in the file would be read and a label generated for each customer. This application would require sequential processing of the file. Another application for the magazine would be the need to produce reminders for those subscribers whose renewal date is almost due. By reading through the file sequentially, the program could produce reminders for only those customers who have reached the renewal date. Although only a small percentage may have reached the date this time, every record in the file would need to be read to determine those who require renewal.

Clearly, many more applications are suitable for sequential files and batch processing, but there are also interactive applications where a sequential file is useful. For example, transactions against a bank account are usually made directly from a terminal located in the bank. The deposit or withdrawal is made against the specific account without the need to access other accounts in the account file. Although this is an interactive environment and the account master file is accessed directly, the transactions are usually written onto a sequential file (tape or disk) to provide a backup file. This file provides a backup for the on-line activity in the event of a system failure and may also be used as a transaction log to record the activity against the account master file.

FILE TERMINOLOGY

When files for use in COBOL are discussed, invariably some terminology is needed to ensure that teacher and student are on the same wavelength. Some of the more common terms you will encounter are listed in Figure 2.1. Possibly you have already encountered these terms in a previous programming course or in an introductory computer or information systems course. If that is the case, a quick review of the terms will likely be enough. However, if these terms are new to you, it would be appropriate to refer to an introductory book on computers to get a more detailed definition.

In COBOL, we usually think of a byte consisting of 8 bits organized as an EBCDIC or ASCII value. An **item** or field may consist of one or more bytes as determined by the PICTURE clause. The USAGE clause will determine how these data are stored internally in the computer or externally on a file. Figure 2.2 shows the USAGE clause options for IBM COBOL.

A **record** consists of one or more fields, usually more. A transaction that specifies the addition of a new customer to the subscription master file would be a record. The data in the master file for that specific customer would also be a record. In COBOL,

FILE TERMINOLOGY

Term	Description
Data	A collection of facts in a manner suitable for processing.
Data base	An organized collection of related files.
File	An organized collection of data in the form of records.
Record	A unit of data comprising an element of a file. A record often pertains to an individual transaction.
Item	Also called a field. The smallest usable part of a record.
Group	In COBOL, a group of related fields or items.
Byte	The smallest addressable unit of storage usually containing a character or digit.
Bit	A binary digit, usually 8 bits per byte.

FIGURE 2.1   Basic terminology for file processing

USAGE	Storage Method	Field Length
DISPLAY	Zoned decimal	One byte per character or digit
COMPUTATIONAL	Binary	1–4 digits (2 bytes) 5–9 digits (4 bytes) 10–18 digits (8 bytes)
COMPUTATIONAL-1	Short-precision floating point	4 bytes
COMPUTATIONAL-2	Long-precision floating point	8 bytes
COMPUTATIONAL-3	Packed decimal	(Number of digits/2) + 1

FIGURE 2.2   USAGE clause storage allocations

these record formats are described by the record description entry in the DATA division. Then, of course, the file would be the records for all the customers. For the next two chapters, we will consider files to be sequential.

MAGNETIC TAPE

TAPE APPLICATIONS

Any sequential file application can use tape for storing its data. Tape has the advantage of being relatively inexpensive compared to disk, it is a compact form of storage, and the tape reel may be removed from the tape drive and stored in a tape library, thus providing an unlimited amount of storage. Tape is therefore ideal where large amounts of data need to be stored, especially when the data are not accessed frequently. For this reason, the federal government stores many of its tax records on tape because of the storage capabilities and infrequent access.

PHYSICAL STRUCTURE OF TAPE

Magnetic tape is a mylar-plastic-based tape with a coating of magnetic oxide material on one side. The tape is quite similar to tape used on a sound cassette or reel-to-reel recorder. The main difference is in the size of the tape. Computer tape, with the exception of some personal computers, is usually ½ in. (1¼ cm) in width and up to 2400 feet (732 m) in length (Figure 2.3). The thickness of the tape is roughly comparable to the thickness of a page in this book.

As shown in Figure 2.4, the tape is supplied on a reel that is up to 10½ in. (26.7 cm) in diameter. Shorter lengths of tape will be supplied on smaller reels, but most systems use one standard size for easy storage in the tape library. Although the data on the tape are identified magnetically on its surface by the program, external identification is also important. For this reason, an adhesive-backed paper label is placed on the surface of the reel with appropriate identification, such as the file name and creation date.

To mount the tape on a tape drive requires a leader of blank tape at the beginning of the tape. Because of the way computer tapes are read and the great precision required, it is necessary for the tape drive to know precisely where the data begin. To identify this position on the tape, a reflective marker is placed on the tape at this location during manufacturing. This marker (Figure 2.5) is called the **load point marker** because

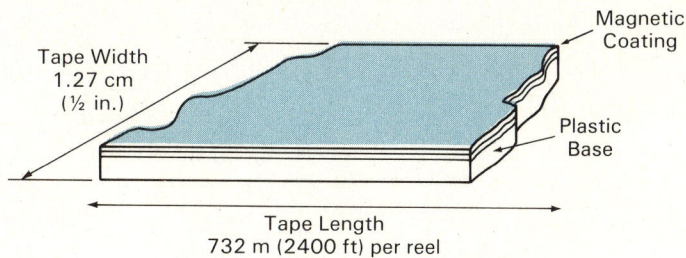

FIGURE 2.3 Composition of magnetic tape

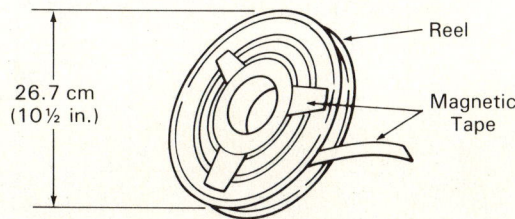

FIGURE 2.4 Plastic reel containing magnetic tape

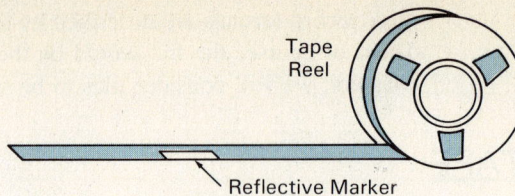

FIGURE 2.5   Position of the load point marker

it identifies the point where the tape is loaded on the drive mechanism. A similar marker is placed near the end of the tape to identify when the end of the reel is about to be reached. For extra-long files, data may be continued on a second or subsequent reel of tape as required.

TAPE DRIVES

To read or write tape requires that a tape drive be used. A reel of tape is mounted in the drive's mechanism as shown in Figure 2.6. The leader of tape is placed through the drive capstan and read/write head assembly and onto the machine or take-up reel. More sophisticated tape drives (meaning more costly, too) will do this procedure automatically. When the tape is to be read or written on, the capstan moves the tape past the read/write heads. The tape only moves when it is being read or written on and then stops while the record is processed, thus requiring the stopping and starting of the tape.

When the end of the file has been reached, the tape is rewound at high speed back onto the file reel. However, because it is possible to have more than one file on a reel, the program can decide whether to rewind the tape when end of file is reached or to continue on and read or write the next file.

DENSITY

As data are written on the tape surface, they are translated into magnetic spots in the pattern of EBCDIC or ASCII bits. Figure 2.7 shows a nine-track tape with the EBCDIC coding system. Each track represents one of the 9 bits required in the EBCDIC coding system, and so all nine across the width of the tape represent a single character. Each

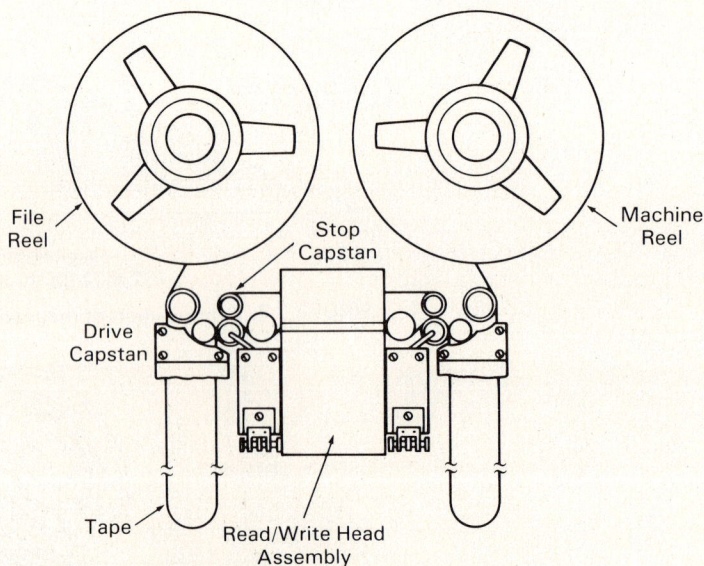

FIGURE 2.6   Tape drive mechanism and head assembly

Chapter 2

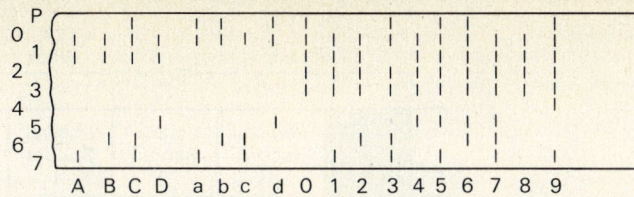

FIGURE 2.7 Data recorded as magnetic bits on a nine-track tape

of the nine tracks receives the magnetic coding simultaneously, something like a nine-track stereo with all channels sounding at once.

The number of characters or bytes that can be recorded along the surface of the tape depends on the size of the magnetic spots. The smaller they are and the less space between them, the more data that can be packed into a given amount or length of the tape. This measurement is known as **density** and is expressed in bytes per inch (or centimeter). Density is determined by the tape drive and may vary from one machine to another. A typical density on magnetic tape is 1600 bytes per inch (BPI) or 630 bytes per centimeter. To use an analogy, suppose each byte were a car on the thruway. Then 1600 cars would be a line-up about 5 miles (8 km) long. Quite a traffic jam!

A practical consideration with density is that it is a major factor in determining how much data may be stored on a reel of tape. Conversely, density will partly determine the length of tape required to store a specific file. The other factor that determines tape use is the length of the interblock gap, which will be discussed shortly.

TAPE SPEED

The speed at which the tape is moved past the read/write heads is called the **tape speed** and is measured in inches or centimeters per second. A typical speed is 200 in./s (IPS) (508 cm/s), but can vary from one machine to another. A higher speed will result in faster reading or writing of data and, of course, a lower speed will result in slower reading or writing.

By multiplying the tape speed by the density, we get a number called the data rate. This value is expressed as the number of bytes per second (BPS) and is a significant factor in determining how fast the program can process the data on the file. A tape with 1600-BPI density and a drive with a 200-IPS speed will have a data rate of 320,000 BPS.

BLOCKING

As tape is being read, it must be moved at a constant speed across the read/write heads. But once the record has been read, the tape stops temporarily until the computer can process the record. Then it accelerates up to speed once again to read the next record. This stopping and starting results in a space or gap on the tape between records where no data are stored. This gap is called an interblock gap or **IBG.** (Sometimes it is called an interrecord gap or IRG.) Figure 2.8 shows this gap in relation to the records on a tape. The record stored between gaps is called a physical record or block.

The length of this gap will depend on the model of tape drive in use, but a

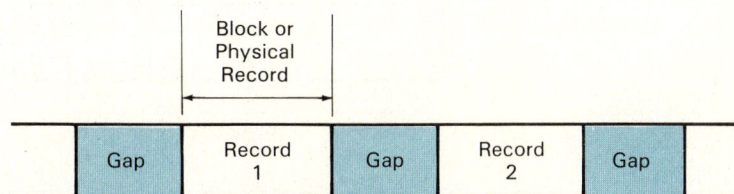

FIGURE 2.8 Interblock gap on a magnetic tape

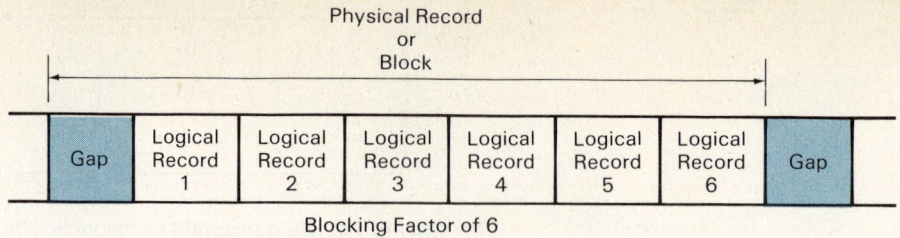

Physical Record
or
Block

| Gap | Logical Record 1 | Logical Record 2 | Logical Record 3 | Logical Record 4 | Logical Record 5 | Logical Record 6 | Gap | |

Blocking Factor of 6

FIGURE 2.9   Using a blocking factor of 6 on tape

common length is 0.6 in. (1.5 cm). If the tape has a density of 1600 BPI as discussed earlier, an 80-byte record would occupy only 0.05 in. (0.127 cm). Obviously, the diagram is not proportional because the IBG actually requires 12 times as much space on the tape than does the record. This does not bode well for the efficient use of magnetic tape.

The solution to this problem is shown in Figure 2.9. By having the program block several logical records together before creating a physical record on the tape, we can reduce the number of IBGs and increase the efficient use of tape.

In the diagram, a **blocking factor** of 6 is used. This means that six 80-byte (or other length as required) logical records are grouped together to form a block or physical record. This block is then written on the tape. Now our calculations show that the block is 6 × 80 or 480 bytes long. This block would occupy 0.3 in. (0.76 cm) on the tape, which is only half the length of the IBG.

For even greater efficiency, a blocking factor of 12 could be used. Now the block is 12 × 80, which is 960 bytes in length. This block will require 0.6 in., which is exactly the length of the gap. Thus the higher the blocking factor is the more efficiently the tape file will be used by the program. However, practical limitations to the length of a block are imposed by the memory available in the computer for both the program and the storing of a physical record in the program. The higher the blocking factor is the more memory that is required in the program for the input/output area assigned to the file.

COBOL identifies the blocking factor in the FD entry with the BLOCK CONTAINS clause.

FIXED- AND VARIABLE-LENGTH RECORDS

The previous example used logical records of 80 bytes in length for each record in the file. When all records in a file are of the same length, they are called **fixed-length records.** Figure 2.10 shows fixed-length records of 133 bytes per record such as might be used when printer records are temporarily stored on tape prior to being printed.

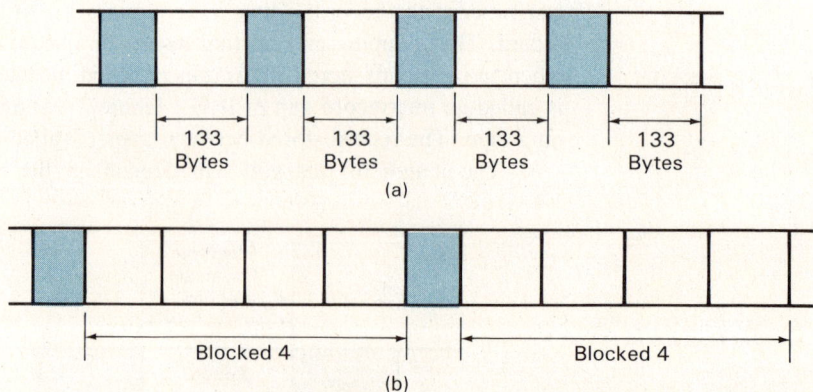

133 Bytes   133 Bytes   133 Bytes   133 Bytes

(a)

Blocked 4   Blocked 4

(b)

FIGURE 2.10   Fixed-length records on tape. (a) Fixed-length records (b) Fixed-length blocked records

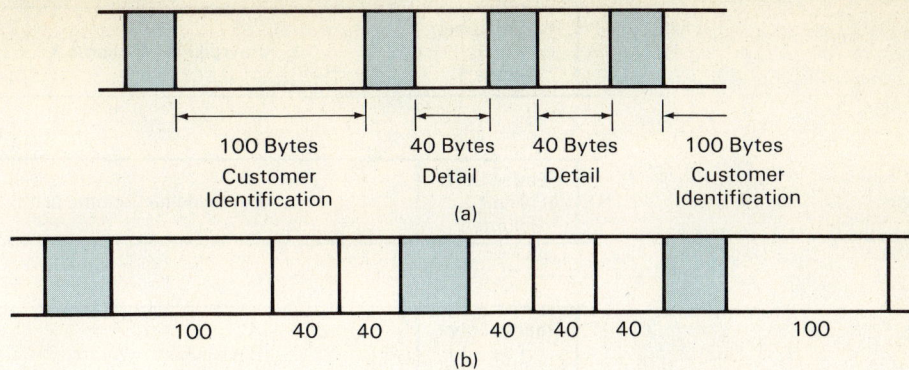

FIGURE 2.11   Variable-length records on tape. (a) Variable-length records (b) Variable-length blocked records

Fixed-length records may be any length, such as 30, 60, 80, or even 200 bytes or more, providing that every record in the file is of the same length.

Fixed-length records are usually blocked for more efficient use of the tape. As the figure shows, when fixed-length records are blocked, the blocking factor will be constant for each block and therefore so will the length of the block. The only exception is the last block in the file, which could be a short block if the blocking factor and the number of records do not divide evenly. This situation is handled by the operating system and so does not need to be a concern of the COBOL programmer.

Variable-length records may be used for applications where a variety of record sizes are needed. For example, a purchase order file may require a record type that identifies a particular customer by account number, name, address, order number, order date, and so on. This record may require 100 bytes of data. Following this customer identification are a number of shorter records that supply the item number, quantity, and cost for each item purchased. These records may only require 40 bytes apiece.

Figure 2.11 shows both variable-length unblocked records of this type and variable-length blocked records. The unblocked records result in physical blocks that are either 100 bytes or 40 bytes in length, depending on whether a customer identification record or a detail item purchase is recorded. Naturally, this results in inefficient use of the tape, so blocking the tape will improve storage efficiency.

When variable-length records are blocked, a maximum block size is chosen for the file. In the figure, a block size of 180 could result in a 100-byte customer record followed by two 40-byte detail records. But the next group consists of three 40-byte records (120 bytes) only, because the next record of 100 bytes will not fit into the maximum block size of 180 bytes. Therefore, the actual block size for variable-length records will vary depending on the size of the logical records. Because of this variability, the term blocking factor is not meaningful with variable-length records.

HEADER AND TRAILER LABELS

Each tape file will contain a magnetically recorded **header label** at the beginning of the file and a **trailer label** at the end of the file. These labels may be omitted by using the FD entry LABEL RECORDS ARE OMITTED in the DATA DIVISION. However, labels are used to ensure the integrity of data in the file and should not normally be omitted when creating a tape file.

Header labels are created on the tape when an OPEN is used for an output file and checked when an input file is opened. The exact content of the label depends on the system, but it usually contains file identification, a creation date, and a volume number. The volume number is necessary when a large file occupies more than one reel of tape, which is called a **multivolume file.** Figure 2.12 shows a payroll file that requires three reels of tape to contain all the records. This figure shows a single file,

Header Label File 1 Volume 1	Payroll File — Volume 1	Trailer Label End of Volume 1	

Header Label File 1 Volume 2	Payroll File — Volume 2	Trailer Label End of Volume 2	

Header Label File 1 Volume 3	Payroll File — Volume 3	Trailer Label End of Volume 3	

FIGURE 2.12   Multivolume payroll file

Header Label File 1 Volume 1	Purchase File	Trailer Label End of File 1	Header Label File 2 Volume 1	Returns File	Trailer Label End of File 2	

FIGURE 2.13   Multifile volume with two files on one tape

the payroll file, which consists of three volumes. Volume number in some systems is called reel number.

When more than one file is recorded on a single reel of tape, the label also contains a file number to identify the specific file in use. Several files on a single tape are called **multifile volumes,** as shown in Figure 2.13. Files in this situation are numbered consecutively.

Trailer labels are created when the file is closed on output and checked when an input file is closed. This label usually contains a block count, which is used to determine if all records have been processed from the file. This count ensures that no data have been lost or gained in the file.

OTHER TYPES OF TAPE

In this chapter we have been primarily discussing reel-to-reel tapes because they are the type used in most computer applications. However, a few other types of tape are available for limited use.

One of these is the cassette tape. The cassette is inexpensive, but slow and inefficient for large amounts of data. It was once used for data-entry applications, but it has mostly been replaced by the floppy disk, although some cassette systems still exist. Some inexpensive personal computers also use cassettes, but these are not usually adequate for business applications.

Another, more popular type of tape is the streamer tape, or stringy floppy as it is sometimes called. This is a high-speed tape which is used for backing up hard disk data to guard against the loss of data due to a hardware failure. Streamer tapes do not start and stop between physical records and therefore have no provision for the processing of the data. Instead, they simply record a copy of disk data and retain that copy as a backup. If a machine failure occurs, the streamer can be read very quickly and the data restored on the hard disk.

MAGNETIC DISK

Disk has no contenders for first place in the most widely used storage device for computers. Personal computers use floppy disks or hard disk for virtually all their storage requirements with few exceptions. Mainframe and minicomputers invariably use one or more varieties of hard disk with storage capacity into the billions of bytes of data. Disk is generally much faster than tape and has a greater storage capacity. Although these are important advantages, the main benefit to be received from using disk is the ability to access data either sequentially or directly as required.

DISK APPLICATIONS

Because of the disk's ability to access data either sequentially or directly, it has become an important alternative to tape. In many systems, particularly personal computers, disk has almost totally replaced tape because of the ease of use and reliability of the floppy disk. Almost anything you can do on tape you can also do on disk. Therefore, the applications we discussed for tape apply equally to disk.

Any application that requires only sequential access, and these are becoming fewer each day, can use disk. Transaction logging files, then, can use disk for storage rather than tape. Disk is also useful for temporary files such as those used for sorting.

Applications that require direct access or a combination of sequential and direct may be implemented successfully using disk, and we will be writing many programs for this type of application in this book. A payroll system may require sequential access for producing pay checks, but direct access when changing an employee's address or department. A hotel reservation system will require direct access to records when a customer reserves a room for the night and when the customer pays the bill upon leaving. Direct access of files is an important concept, which will be discussed in depth beginning in Chapter 4.

Virtually any application that can be named would find disk to be an appropriate storage medium. However, one area where tape still excels over disk is in off-line storage, which we mentioned earlier. Remember the federal tax department? Although some disk drives have removable disk packs that can be used for off-line storage, tape is still a superior method because it is considerably less costly than disk for this purpose.

PHYSICAL STRUCTURE OF DISK

Disks are constructed of one or more circular metal platters with a magnetic coating on both sides of the platter. This coating is similar to the coating on the surface of a magnetic tape. Floppy disks are similar to hard disks except they do not use a metal platter, but just a Mylar disk enclosed in a stiff cardboard container. Because COBOL is primarily a mainframe language, we will concentrate on hard disks and their function.

The disk platter is mounted on a central hub that is motor driven to rotate the disk. When there is more than one platter, these are stacked one above the other on the central hub. Figure 2.14 shows a disk drive with six platters mounted on the central hub. On the magnetic surface of each disk are **tracks** for recording data. These tracks

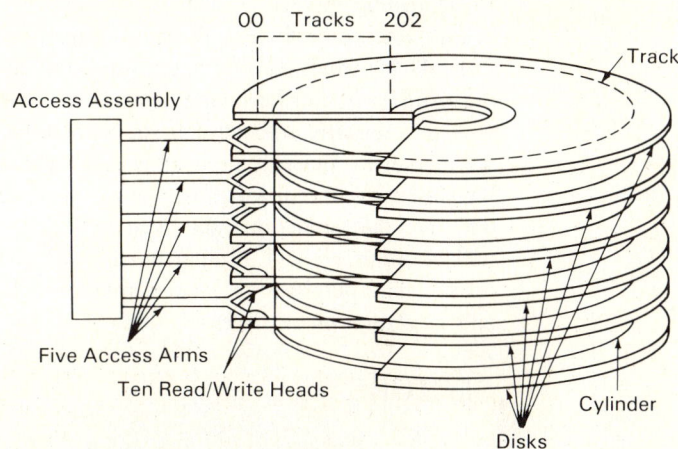

FIGURE 2.14   Disk drive assembly

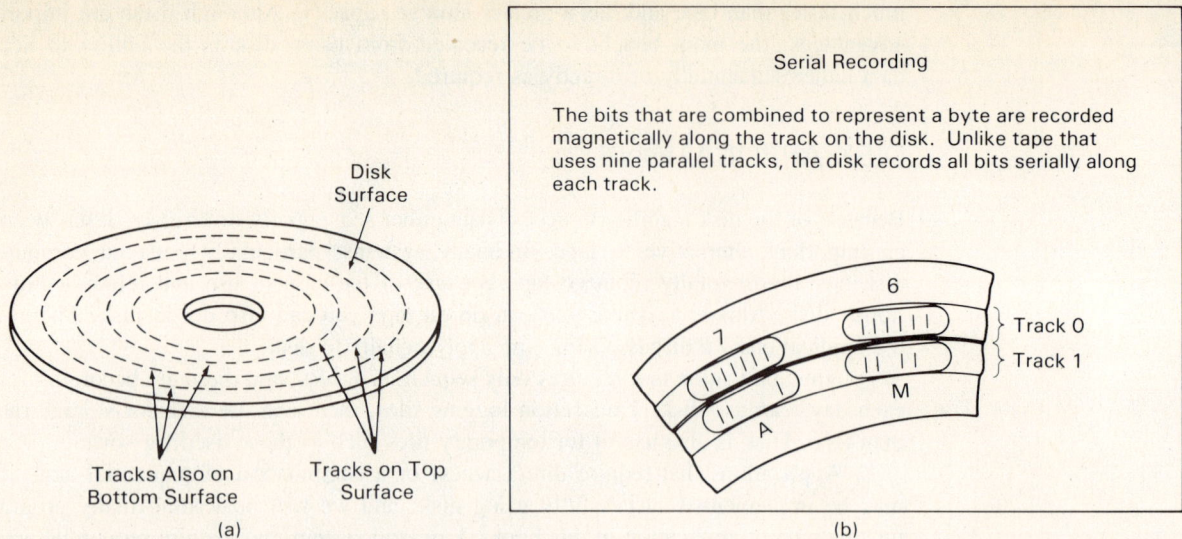

FIGURE 2.15 Recording of bits and bytes along a disk track

are concentric, meaning that they do not spiral in toward the center of the disk like the tracks of an LP record, but instead each track is a separate and independent track. One measurement of the storage capacity of a disk is the number of bytes per track that may be recorded.

To read or write data on the surface of the disk, the entire disk is rotated on the hub. The data are read or written by the read/write heads that are mounted on access arms and positioned in close proximity to the surface of the disk. Usually, there is one head per disk surface, although very high speed disks may have one head per track. Unlike tape, which stops and starts, the disk is rotated at a constant speed and data are read on the fly as they pass the head.

DISK TRACKS

When a disk **file** is created, each byte of data is written magnetically along a track on the disk's surface. Because there is only one head over the track at the time of writing (or reading), the byte is written as a serial row of bits. This method of recording is shown in Figure 2.15, where each track shows a few bytes recorded as a series of magnetic spots along the track.

Because the disk does not start and stop like tape, there must be another method for determining where the data begin on the track. The most commonly used technique is to record a magnetic marker on each track, which is detected by the disk drive when reading or writing. This marker tells the drive where the first record on the track begins. Each record along the track is then positioned relative to this marker.

At the time the program issues a command to read a record from disk, the drive must first wait for the track marker to be detected. Then, as the disk rotates, the head will, in a specific amount of time, become positioned to the record. The time taken for the marker to rotate to the head is called **rotational delay.**

Because the disk is always rotating when a read or write command is issued, the odds are that sometimes the head will be close to the record required and the delay will be minimal, and at other times it will need to wait for almost a full rotation. So for practical purposes an average rotational delay is used, which is the time needed for half a rotation of the disk.

SECTORS

Some disks that use fixed-block architecture organize their data into sectors or blocks. A **sector** (Figure 2.16) is a part of a track and can store a given amount of data. The

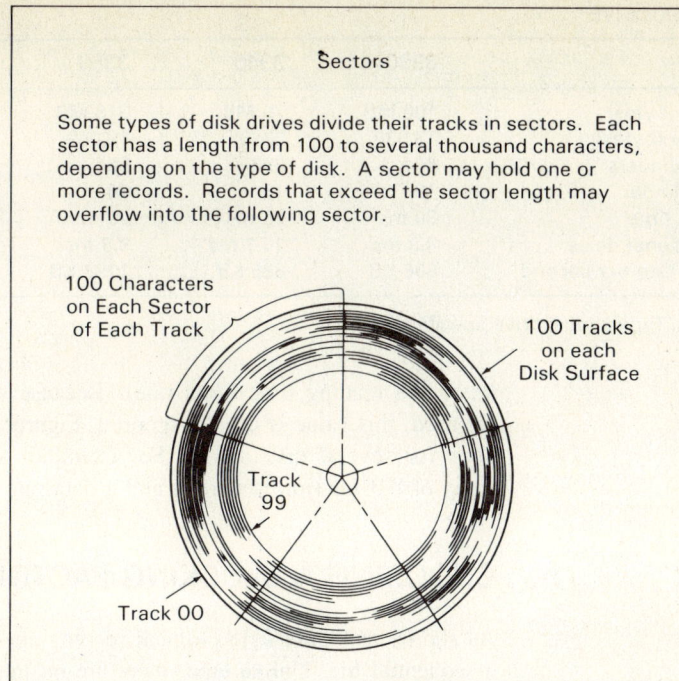

Sectors

Some types of disk drives divide their tracks in sectors. Each sector has a length from 100 to several thousand characters, depending on the type of disk. A sector may hold one or more records. Records that exceed the sector length may overflow into the following sector.

100 Characters on Each Sector of Each Track

100 Tracks on each Disk Surface

Track 99

Track 00

FIGURE 2.16 Sectors on the surface of a disk

capacity of a sector depends on the type of disk drive but can range from as low as 100 bytes to several thousands of bytes. Floppy disks that identify sectors magnetically are called soft-sectored disks. Disks that use a series of physical holes in the disk are hard-sectored disks.

SEEK TIME

When there is only one head per surface (the usual case), the head must be moved back and forth to be positioned over the correct track prior to reading or writing. Because a disk surface may have several hundred tracks, there may be a lot of movement of the heads. The time it takes to move the head to an adjacent track, say from track 12 to track 13, is called track-to-track **seek time.** If more than a single track is covered, an average seek time is used to calculate the time for head movement.

CYLINDERS

When several disks are stacked on a single drive hub, each surface will have a track and a read/write head that are accessible without head movement. If there are 10 surfaces that contain recording tracks, each surface will have a track 0 located in a vertical column. Then when the head for one surface is positioned to track 0, all other heads will also be at track 0 on their respective surfaces. This feature of disk is called the **cylinder,** because the shape of the tracks forms a cylinderlike object.

To save time when reading or writing sequential files, records are stored along a track until the track is filled. Then the data are stored on the next track in the same cylinder, and so on, until all tracks in the cylinder contain data. If the cylinder contains 10 tracks, then all 10 tracks of sequential data may be read or written without the need to move the heads. This approach to sequential access reduces seek time to an insignificant factor.

ACCESS TIME

Access time refers to the time it takes to access a record on the file. Access time considers all aspects of the functions of the disk drive, including rotational delay, seek

	3330	3340	3350	3370	3375	3380
Disk capacity (bytes)	100 MB	70 MB	318 MB	571 MB	820 MB	1260 MB
Track capacity (bytes)	13,030	8368	19,069	31,744	35,616	47,476
Number of cylinders	404	696	555	1,500	1,918	1,770
Tracks per cylinder	19	12	30	12	12	15
Average seek time	30 ms	25 ms	25 ms	30 ms	19 ms	16 ms
Average rotational delay	8.3 ms	10.1 ms	8.3 ms	10.1 ms	10.1 ms	8.3 ms
Data transfer rate per second	806 KB	885 KB	1198 KB	1859 KB	1859 KB	3000 KB

FIGURE 2.17 Typical disk drive specifications

time, and reading time (data rate). Because seek time is insignificant when cylinders are used, this value is usually ignored. Figure 2.17 shows some representative specifications for several disk drives. For example, the IBM 3380 has an average rotational delay of 8.3 ms (milliseconds) and a data rate of 3000 KB (kilobytes).

CHOOSING A BLOCKING FACTOR

As shown in Figure 2.18, logical records are written along the track consecutively for a sequential file. Unlike tape, there are no interblock gaps for starting and stopping on disk, but there are areas of control information that occupy space. This control data identifies the record, its position on the track, and error-checking information. Because this control information requires space on the track, it reduces the number of bytes available for storing data.

For example, the 3340 disk drive has a track capacity of 8368 bytes. If we created a file consisting of 100-byte records, then it would appear that we could store 8368/100 = 83 records on a single track. But, instead, the capacity of the track is reduced by the control information, and so fewer records may be recorded on the track. To determine the number of records that the track will hold, we need to use a formula supplied by the disk manufacturer. For the 3340 the formula is

$$\frac{8535}{\text{block length} + 167} = \text{no. of physical records per track}$$

For the previous example, the formula tells us how many 100-byte logical records (unblocked and therefore 100 bytes per block) will fit on a track.

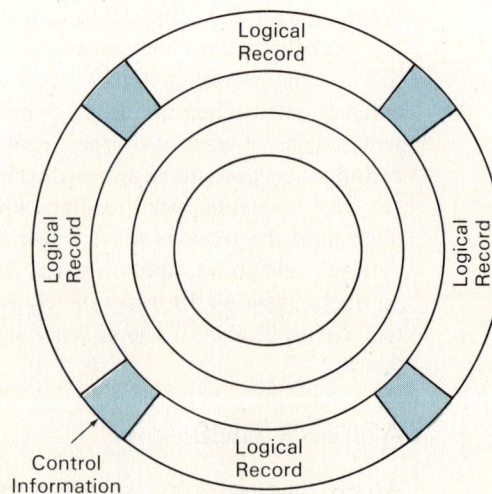

FIGURE 2.18 Position of logical records on a track

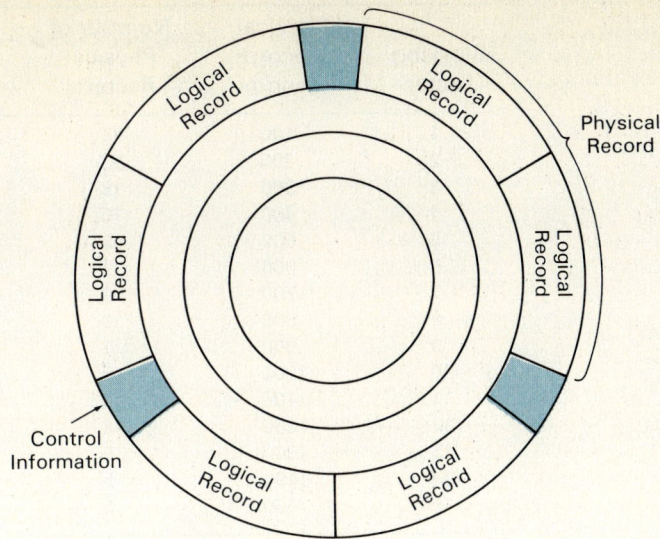

FIGURE 2.19 Use a blocking factor of 2

$$\frac{8535}{100 + 167} = 31 \text{ physical records}$$

Because the records are unblocked, a physical record is the same as a logical record, so in this case only 31 records will fit on a track. Whatever happened to the 83 records we started with? Because of all the control data, a considerable amount of space was used and not available for records. This is a parallel situation to tape. There we solved the problem by blocking the records, and that's what we do on disk as well.

If we used a blocking factor of 2, as shown in Figure 2.19, there is then a 200-byte physical block. Using this value in the formula gives

$$\frac{8535}{200 + 167} = 23 \text{ physical records}$$

The disk stores 23 physical records per track, but each physical record contains 2 logical records. This gives $2 \times 23 = 46$ logical records per track. Clearly, the use of a blocking factor of 2 gives a significant improvement over an unblocked file.

To find the best blocking factor requires us to try several values until an optimum is found. Figure 2.20 shows blocking factors from 1 to 15 for this file of 100-byte records. Normally, the higher the blocking factor is the better the utilization of the track. However, as an optimum factor is reached, this argument does not necessarily hold true. For example, a blocking factor of 10 gives 70 records per track, yet blocking 13 gives only 65 records. The best choice depends on the size of the physical record the program can comfortably handle. As for a blocked tape file, blocking a disk file also requires additional memory. From the chart, we can see that a blocking factor of 15 is best, but choosing 12 is a good compromise if a shorter block is required.

The calculation done here was based on the formula for an IBM-compatible 3340 disk drive. Each model of disk drive will have a unique formula for its calculations and would be substituted for the one used here. Computer installations have one or more manuals that are supplied with the disk drive hardware, which will contain the appropriate formula for that disk.

ACCESS METHODS

Files are stored on disk under one of several available access methods. When a file is first created, it will be stored under a specific access method. In the future, each access

Blocking Factor	Physical Record Length	Number of Physical Records	Number of Logical Records
1	100	31	31
2	200	23	46
3	300	18	54
4	400	15	60
5	500	12	60
6	600	11	66
7	700	9	63
8	800	8	64
9	900	7	63
10	1000	7	70
11	1100	6	66
12	1200	6	72
13	1300	5	65
14	1400	5	70
15	1500	5	75

FIGURE 2.20   Optimum blocking factors for 100-byte logical records

of that file must be with the same access method by which it was created. The choice of an access method must then be carefully made because once the file is created you are stuck with that access method. However, the decision is not entirely irreversible. By writing a special program, a file could be converted from one access method to another. Naturally, this is something that should be avoided by making good decisions in the first place.

The access methods that are available will depend on the computer system in use (mainframe systems usually have a greater variety than smaller computers) and on the COBOL compiler that is used on the system. The variety is normally limited to four types of access methods. These are summarized briefly.

1. *Sequential*: Records are stored sequentially and may only be processed sequentially.
2. *Relative*: This access method is also known as direct or random. Records stored in this manner are accessed directly by the use of a key field that identifies each record. Frequently, relative files may only be accessed directly, but some systems provide sequential access capabilities.
3. *Indexed sequential access method* (ISAM): This method stores records sequentially but uses indexes to point to records within the file. This way the entire file may be read sequentially, or by use of the index and a key, a specific record may be accessed.
4. *Virtual storage access method* (VSAM): This method is similar to ISAM but offers improved storage of records and updating of the file. With VSAM files, records may be accessed either sequentially or directly.

This chapter and the next concentrate on sequential files, and so the other three access methods will not be explained more fully right now. Starting with Chapter 4, the nonsequential methods will be discussed.

SEQUENTIAL ACCESS

To the COBOL programmer, a sequential disk file looks pretty much like a sequential tape file. But there is a physical difference as we have seen already. Now we want to take a look at the difference between the logical and physical organization of a sequential file on disk. Remember that the term logical refers to the order or way in which the program sees the records. Physical refers to how it is physically located on the disk.

Surface	Cylinder 1		Cylinder 2	
1	123 125 127 130 131	Records 1–5	352 354 357 360 362	Records 51–55
2	133 135 136 138 140		367 370 371 377 378	
3	142 143 147 151 152			
4	153 158 163 170 175			
5	198 208 209 231 244			
6	250 251 252 253 258			
7	262 265 267 270 271			
8	278 281 285 286 296			
9	303 307 319 327 330			
10	344 346 347 348 351	Records 46–50		

FIGURE 2.21 Physical organization of a sequential file

Logical records on a sequential disk file may, like tape, be either fixed or variable in length.

Figure 2.21 shows how we can think about this physical organization and how it relates to the logical. The three-digit numbers represent records. If it helps to think of the numbers as an account number or part number, then so much the better.

As we know, records are stored on both sides of the disk, which are called surfaces in Figure 2.21. Depending on the record size and blocking factor chosen, a specific number of records may be stored on each track. Each cylinder in the figure consists of 10 tracks, one per surface. So on surface 1 there are five records: 123, 125, 127, 130, and 131. These records are in sequential order by the record identification and are also in the same physical order around the track.

Surface 2 (track 2 on cylinder 1) contains the next five records in sequence. The read/write heads do not need to be moved to read these records because they are in the same logical and physical sequence. This pattern is continued for each surface within the cylinder.

If there are enough records to fill the cylinder, the next cylinder will be used to continue this sequential pattern. Usually, a file will not require all the cylinders on a disk drive, and so several files may occupy the one drive. To locate each file's starting location on the disk, a directory or volume table of contents (VTOC) is used. This VTOC (pronounced vee-tock) contains entries for each file, its name, and its location on the disk. When an OPEN statement is issued in a program, the operating system searches the VTOC for the file requested and returns its location to the program in preparation for reading the first record.

In the next chapter we will examine the use of COBOL's input and output features for creating and using sequential files.

SUMMARY

Sequential files are typically tape or disk files. Records on a sequential file are stored in order from the first record in the file to the last. Sequential files are frequently used in batch applications where all records of a file must be processed. Interactive applications may use sequential files as backup or for a transaction log.

Magnetic tape contains records that are recorded consecutively along the magnetic oxide-coated Mylar surface. Tapes have both external (paper) and internal (magnetic) labels to identify the contents. The density of the tape drive determines the amount of data in bytes that may be stored in 1 in. of tape length. A typical density is 1600 bytes/in. (630 bytes/cm). Both the density and the tape speed (inches or centimeters per second) determine the data rate (bytes per second) of the tape. A high density or a higher tape speed both result in a higher data rate.

Blocking several logical records on tape into a physical record results in a significant improvement in storage space on the tape. Higher blocking factors result in greater storage capacity and in faster data rates. Blocking is identified in COBOL in the FD entry.

Header and trailer labels on tape are recorded magnetically at the beginning and end of each file. The header label is processed when the OPEN statement is issued and the trailer label when the CLOSE is given in the program. Header labels identify the file, give a creation date, and give a volume number. Trailer labels provide a block count to ensure that all data in the file have been processed.

A multivolume file contains several volumes of data in a single file requiring several reels of tape. A multifile volume contains more than one file on a single reel of tape.

Magnetic disk may also store sequential files, but the data need not be in a consecutive order physically on the disk. Any application that may be done on tape may alternately be done on disk. Today, many applications require both sequential and direct access, which makes disk a more generally suitable medium. Data are recorded along tracks on the disk, and the disk spins at a high rate while data are read or written.

Disk does not start and stop while reading and so interblock gaps are not a problem. However, blocking disk records will result in improved efficiency and higher speed. Seek time is the time taken for the read/write head to move to a required track. Cylinders are created when a disk drive consists of several platters stacked one on top of the other. For effective sequential file processing, records are recorded down the tracks on a complete cylinder before the heads are moved to the next cylinder. Access time refers to the time it takes to access a record in the file, including the seek time, rotational delay, and read time.

In addition to sequential files, disk may use relative organization, indexed sequential access method (ISAM), or virtual storage access method (VSAM).

TERMS TO STUDY

Blocking factor	Record
Cylinder	Reflective marker
Density	Rotational delay
File	Sector
Fixed-length record	Seek time
Header label	Sequential file
IBG	Tape speed
ISAM	Track
Item	Trailer label
Load point marker	Variable-length record
Multifile volume	VSAM
Multivolume file	VTOC

1. The type of file stored on the tape is identified magnetically by a _____ label, which is processed by the program.

2. For external identification a _____ _____ is placed on the surface of the reel with appropriate identification, such as the file name and creation date.

3. To identify the beginning of data on the tape, a reflective marker is placed on the tape during manufacturing. This marker is called the _____ _____ marker.

4. A measurement known as _____ is expressed in bytes per inch (or centimeter) and refers to the amount of data that can be stored in a given length of tape.

5. The speed at which the tape is moved past the read/write heads is called the _____ _____ and is measured in inches or centimeters per second.

6. The value called a _____ _____ is expressed as the number of bytes per second (BPS) with which data are read or written on tape. It is a significant factor in determining how fast the program can process the data on the file.

7. Stopping and starting during the writing on tape results in a space or gap on the tape between records where no data are stored. This gap is called an _____.

8. By using a _____ factor, several logical records are grouped together before creating a physical record on the tape, and we can reduce the number of gaps between blocks.

9. _____-length records are used when all records in a file are of the same length.

10. _____-length records may be used for applications where a variety of record sizes are needed.

11. _____ labels are created on the tape when an OPEN is used for an output file and checked when an input file is opened.

12. The magnetic surface of each disk contains concentric _____ for recording the data.

13. An _____ _____ _____ is used to identify the time needed for half a rotation of the disk.

14. Some disks that use fixed-block architecture organize their data into _____ or blocks.

15. When the heads are moved over two or more tracks on the disk, a value called the _____ _____ time is used to calculate the time for head movement.

16. When the head for one surface is positioned to track 0, and all other heads are also on track 0 for their respective surfaces, we have what is called the _____ concept.

TRUE/FALSE

17. Magnetic tape may only contain sequentially organized files.

18. The only method for identifying the contents of a tape file is by the adhesive label on the outside of the reel.

19. The larger the blocking factor used on a tape file the less is the length of tape that will be required for storing the file.

20. One reason disk is faster than tape is because the disk rotates at a constant speed and is not required to start and stop.

21. Blocking is not required on disk files for efficient storage of the data.

22. An indexed sequential access method (ISAM) permits reading a file either sequentially or directly.

23. In COBOL, a sequential disk file is read essentially in the same manner as a sequential tape file.

MULTIPLE CHOICE

24. What is the result of starting and stopping the tape between records?
   a. A blocking factor.   c. A sequential file.
   b. An interblock gap.   d. Header and trailer labels.

25. Which factor affects the length of tape required for storing a specific logical record?
   a. Density.   d. a and b.
   b. Record length.   e. b and c.
   c. Blocking factor.

26. A multivolume tape file means that:
   a. One reel of tape will contain several files.
   b. One file will require two or more reels of tape.
   c. A file will not contain header or trailer labels.

27. What factor is implemented on a disk file to improve the time needed to read or write a sequential file.
   a. The cylinder concept is used.
   b. Disk uses the average seek time.
   c. Records are blocked.
   d. All the above.

28. Blocking records on a disk file has the effect of:
   a. Minimizing start and stop time.
   b. Maximizing the use of the storage space.
   c. Creating a variable-length record.
   d. Creating a sequential file.

29. Which disk access method provides the ability for accessing a required record directly?
   a. Relative.   d. All the above.
   b. ISAM.   e. None of the above.
   c. VSAM.

30. Which disk access method provides the ability for accessing a required file sequentially?
   a. Sequential.   d. a and b.
   b. ISAM.   e. All the above.
   c. VSAM.

3

PROGRAMMING FOR SEQUENTIAL FILES

Sequential tape or disk file programming in COBOL is based on records that are stored in a consecutive order within the file. As we have seen in the previous chapter, records in a sequential file are ordered one after the other from the beginning to the end of the file. The contents of each record do not need to bear any relationship to the order of these records because sequential refers to the physical sequence of the records. In other words, record 1 is followed by record 2, and so on. These records must always be read in this order whenever a sequential file is in use. This order corresponds to the physical order of records on tape discussed in the previous chapter.

SEQUENCE FIELDS

However, records on a sequential file are often stored in a logical sequence. For example, accounting records would be stored in order by account number on the sequential file (Figure 3.1). The first record in the file would contain the lowest account number, the

Record Number	Account Number	Amount	Date
1	120	145.85	04/26/86
2	122	35.86	05/19/86
3	125	145.72	09/18/86
4	126	456.82	01/14/87
5	130	143.88	06/03/87
6	137	6.45	01/09/88
7	141	195.20	04/30/86
8	143	295.90	07/19/87

FIGURE 3.1   Records stored in sequence on account number in a sequential file

second record the next highest account, and so on. The last record on the file would be the highest account number. The account number is called the **sequence field.** Notice that there are often gaps between the account numbers. Account number 120 is first, but the next account on the file is account 122. This is a usual characteristic of sequential files and has some implications when we begin to write programs for updating files.

Figure 3.1 showed records in sequence by account number. Other files may use a customer number or an employee number. In some cases several fields may be involved in the sequence. If there are two sequence fields such as salesperson number within region, we would have a major (region) and minor (salesperson) sequence. There could be more fields involved in the sequence depending on the type of data and the characteristics of the application.

SEQUENTIAL FILES AND BATCH PROCESSING

Generally, data stored on sequential files are processed in a batch environment. Thus records are accumulated over a given time period and then processed as a batch rather than processed interactively as they are received. The time frame could be as short as a day or as long as a week, month, or quarter. A sequential file can also be created as a result of an on-line application, such as the logging of transactions discussed earlier, and then processed later in a batch system.

When a system, or part of a system, uses batch processing, it is usually because of efficiency considerations. When a large percentage of the records in a file are affected by the transactions, then batch processing will be faster than direct processing. For example, if an account file has more than 40 percent activity against its records, a sequential update of that file will be the most efficient in terms of computer usage. However, if only 5 percent of the records are affected, then direct updating is a better choice.

This percentage is called the **file activity ratio.** Higher activity ratios suggest using sequential files and batch processing. Obviously, there is a gray area where choices are not so clear-cut. Also, an application that requires immediate feedback may be interactive and use direct updating, although there is a high file activity ratio. The need for immediate response in the system may override the efficiency consideration of batch processing of sequential files.

SELECT CLAUSES FOR SEQUENTIAL FILES

INPUT-OUTPUT SECTION.

FILE-CONTROL.
    SELECT filename
        ASSIGN TO system-name
        [ORGANIZATION IS SEQUENTIAL]
        [ACCESS MODE IS SEQUENTIAL].

The FILE-CONTROL paragraph for sequential files contains one or more SELECT clauses similar to the following device-independent statement for an IBM OS/VS system. This statement could select either a tape or disk file depending on job control language parameters.

```
SELECT MASTER
    ASSIGN TO UT-S-MAST101
    ORGANIZATION IS SEQUENTIAL
    ACCESS MODE  IS SEQUENTIAL.
```

```
ASSIGN TO SYSnnn-class-device-org[-name]
```

Symbolic unit   Class   Hardware   Organization   External
SYS000 to   indicator   device   indicator   file
SYS221   (UR, UT, DA) number   (S, D or I)   name

```
Examples:   ASSIGN TO SYS001-UT-2400-S.
            ASSIGN TO SYS010-UT-3340-S-MASTER.
            ASSIGN TO SYS025-UT-3375-S-FILE1.
```

FIGURE 3.2   ASSIGN clause for IBM DOS/VS systems

```
ASSIGN TO class-org-name
```

Class   Organization   External
indicator   indicator   file
(UR, UT, DA)   (S, D or I)   name

```
Examples:   ASSIGN TO UT-S-LOGFILE.
            ASSIGN TO UT-S-TRANS.
            ASSIGN TO UT-S-MASTER.
```

FIGURE 3.3   ASSIGN clause for IBM OS/VS systems

The file-name entry (MASTER) is the name that will be used in the COBOL program to refer to the file. A file-name, like other names in COBOL, may have up to 30 characters consisting of alphabetic, numeric, and hyphens. The name may not begin or end with a hyphen and may not include spaces within it.

The system-name entry (UT-S-MAST101) defines the hardware device to which the file is associated. This name is system dependent, meaning that its format and content will depend on the computer on which it is used. In addition to being dependent on the computer, it can also depend on the operating system in use on that computer. Figure 3.2 shows the format for IBM DOS/VS systems and Figure 3.3 shows the IBM OS/VS system format. Other manufacturers will have different formats, which will be defined in the COBOL manual for that system. For examples of complete SELECT clauses, see Figures 3.4 and 3.5.

The entries ORGANIZATION IS SEQUENTIAL and ACCESS MODE IS SEQUENTIAL are optional. Because the defaults for these entries are both SEQUENTIAL, they are frequently omitted for sequential file definitions. The following entry is equivalent to the one above.

```
SELECT MASTER
     ASSIGN TO UT-S-MAST101.
```

The class indicator entry in the system name is a two-character code that identifies the class of device. There are three possible classes:

- UR: Unit record refers to devices such as card readers, printers, and card punch units.
- UT: The utility class refers to devices that read or write data sequentially, like magnetic tape and disk files.
- DA: Direct access is a class used for devices containing files that are directly accessed. This class will be used later for relative, ISAM, and VSAM files.

```
        INPUT-OUTPUT SECTION.
        FILE-CONTROL.
            SELECT PURCHASE-FILE
                ASSIGN TO SYS080-UT-2400-S.
            SELECT MASTER-FILE
                ASSIGN TO SYS001-UT-3380-S-MAST101.
```

FIGURE 3.4 An INPUT-OUTPUT SECTION for a tape and disk file, respectively, in a DOS/VS system

```
        INPUT-OUTPUT SECTION.
        FILE-CONTROL.
            SELECT EMPLOYEE-FILE
                ASSIGN TO UT-S-EMPFILE.
            SELECT TRANSACTION
                ASSIGN TO UT-S-TRANSFLE.
```

FIGURE 3.5 An INPUT-OUTPUT SECTION for a disk and tape file on an IBM OS/VS system

The organization indicator is used to specify the method of access used for the file:

- S: Sequential is used for all unit record and utility class files.
- D: Direct is used for direct-access files.
- I: Indexed sequential (ISAM) files are indicated by this organization indicator.
- Blank: Organization is blank for VSAM files.

The external file-name specifies the name allocated to the file by the operating system. It is not necessarily the same as the file-name used in the program. The external name is a permanent one, which will be used by any program that references the file. By contrast, the file-name used in the COBOL program is a programmer supplied name that does not need to be the same in each program, although many shops recommend standard file-names also.

FILE DESCRIPTION (FD) ENTRY

DATA DIVISION.

FILE SECTION.

FD file-name

    BLOCK CONTAINS [integer-1 TO] integer-2 $\begin{Bmatrix} \text{CHARACTERS} \\ \text{RECORDS} \end{Bmatrix}$

    RECORD CONTAINS [integer-3 TO] integer-4 CHARACTERS

    LABEL $\begin{Bmatrix} \text{RECORD IS} \\ \text{RECORDS ARE} \end{Bmatrix}$ $\begin{Bmatrix} \text{STANDARD} \\ \text{OMITTED} \end{Bmatrix}$

    DATA $\begin{Bmatrix} \text{RECORD IS} \\ \text{RECORDS ARE} \end{Bmatrix}$ data-name-1 [data-name-2]... .

01   data-name.

    02–49 $\begin{Bmatrix} \text{data-name} \\ \text{FILLER} \end{Bmatrix}$ $\begin{Bmatrix} \text{PICTURE} \\ \text{PIC} \end{Bmatrix}$ IS string   VALUE is literal.

Each file used by the COBOL program will require a SELECT clause in the ENVIRONMENT DIVISION and an FD entry in the DATA DIVISION. The FD entry names the file using the same file-name identified in the SELECT clause. The BLOCK CONTAINS clause identifies the number of logical records contained in a physical record. This value is the blocking factor for the file. RECORD CONTAINS identifies the number of bytes (CHARACTERS) in each logical record. This value must correspond to the length of the record that follows the FD entry.

For sequential tape or disk files, LABEL RECORDS are usually the standard system labels and so the STANDARD option will be used. Unit record files would not contain labels. Finally, a record is defined for the FD where the data will be read or written from. This record description entry defines a logical record, not a physical one. Based on the BLOCK CONTAINS clause, the compiler sets up an area in storage where the block is read or written. In COBOL, we need only be concerned about processing a logical record and the system will take care of the physical records.

Example 1 The FD and record for a disk file with a blocking factor of 10 and a 100-byte record size.

```
     A    B
1  4 78   12                                                              72
───────────────────────────────────────────────────────────────────────────
     DATA DIVISION.
     FILE SECTION.
     FD  INVOICE-MASTER-IN
         BLOCK  CONTAINS 10 RECORDS
         RECORD CONTAINS 100 CHARACTERS
         LABEL RECORDS ARE STANDARD
         DATA RECORD IS INVOICE-IN.

     01  INVOICE-IN.
         05  FILLER          PIC X(100).
```

Example 2 An FD for a tape file with a blocking factor of 15 and logical record length of 50 bytes.

```
     A    B
1  4 78   12                                                              72
───────────────────────────────────────────────────────────────────────────
     DATA DIVISION.
     FILE SECTION.
     FD  SALES-DATA-IN
         BLOCK  CONTAINS 15 RECORDS
         RECORD CONTAINS 50 CHARACTERS
         LABEL RECORDS ARE STANDARD
         DATA RECORD IS SALES-REC-IN.

     01  SALES-REC-IN.
         05  FILLER          PIC X(50).
```

PROGRAM STYLE AND THE FD ENTRY

- Write each clause on a separate line indented four columns from the FD line. These are B margin entries and so this indenting will come naturally.
- Because disk or tape files can use a blocking factor, always use the BLOCK CONTAINS clause, even when a file is unblocked.
- Use the format BLOCK CONTAINS integer RECORDS, rather than the CHARACTERS option. In this way the blocking factor will always be clearly identified.
- Use a simple record description entry with the FD and, for input files, use the READ INTO format. For output use the WRITE FROM.

PROCEDURE DIVISION STATEMENTS

File processing, like all other processing in COBOL, occurs in the PROCEDURE DIVISION. While all statements in this division are candidates for use when processing file data, a few primary statements relate specifically to files. These statements are the OPEN, READ, WRITE, and CLOSE.

OPEN STATEMENT

$$\underline{OPEN} \left\{ \begin{array}{l} [\ \underline{INPUT}\ \{\text{file-name}\}\ .\ .\ .\ ] \\ [\ \underline{OUTPUT}\ \{\text{file-name}\}\ .\ .\ .\ ] \end{array} \right\}\ .\ .\ .$$

Each sequential file must be opened before being used in the PROCEDURE DIVISION. Issuing the OPEN positions the read/write mechanism to the beginning of the file. Opening an input file results in the header label on that file being read and checked. A header label is written on an output file when it is opened.

Usually, all files for use in a program are opened at the beginning of the program (Figure 3.6) with a single OPEN statement. However, more complex applications may use a file as both output and later as input in the same program. In such a situation the file is only opened initially for its current use. Later it will be closed and then opened for other use within the program.

```
    A   B
1   4  78  12                                                                72
─────────────────────────────────────────────────────────────────────────────
        OPEN INPUT   INVOICE-MASTER-IN
                     SALES-DATA-IN
             OUTPUT  INVOICE-MASTER-OUT
                     LOG-FILE
                     REPORT-OUT.
```

FIGURE 3.6   Opening input and output files

READ STATEMENT

READ file-name RECORD [<u>INTO</u> identifier]

    AT <u>END</u>   imperative-statement.

A logical record from a sequential input file is accessed by the READ statement. All unblocking of records is handled by the operating system externally to the program. The file named in the READ must be opened before the READ is executed in the program. For the sake of good program organization, it is preferable to use the INTO format and process the input record in WORKING-STORAGE (Figure 3.7). All sequential files will at some point return an AT END condition when no more data are available on the file. Usually, we will set an end-of-file flag in the AT END clause and test for it in the program logic.

```
    A   B
1   4  78  12                                                                72
─────────────────────────────────────────────────────────────────────────────
        READ INVOICE-MASTER-IN INTO MASTER-RECORD
            AT END MOVE 'YES' TO EOF-FLAG.
```

FIGURE 3.7   Reading a master file into WORKING-STORAGE

WRITE STATEMENT

WRITE record-name [FROM identifier-1].

The WRITE statement is used to place a logical record on an output file. The operating system will take care of any blocking that may have been identified in the FD entry, so only logical records are handled here. Good program organization and style suggest that the output record will be formed in WORKING-STORAGE and written from this area. A WRITE to the LOG-FILE could be written as follows:

```
WRITE LOG-RECORD-OUT FROM WORKING-LOG.
```

CLOSE STATEMENT

CLOSE file-name-1 [file-name-2] . . .

When the program is finished with a file, a CLOSE statement must be used. The CLOSE checks the record counts on the trailer label for input files to ensure file integrity. For output files, a trailer label will be created.

The statement in Figure 3.8 closes the files opened at the beginning of a program.

```
      A    B
 1  4  78  12                                                        72
            CLOSE  INVOICE-MASTER-IN
                   SALES-DATA-IN
                   INVOICE-MASTER-OUT
                   LOG-FILE
                   REPORT-OUT.
```

FIGURE 3.8 Closing input and output files

CREATING A SEQUENTIAL MASTER FILE

Before we can get into the concepts of sequential file updating, a master file is required. Creating this master is an activity that is only done at the beginning of the life of an application. Later in the chapter we will be updating an inventory master file. The frequency of updating depends on the amount of activity against the inventory, but creating the file, as we will be doing here, only occurs once in the lifetime of the file. After the file has been created, it can be updated as frequently as needed for the application.

SOURCE DATA FOR A MASTER FILE

Data for creating a master file must be available in some form that can be read by the program. Any device that can be defined as an input to a COBOL program can provide the data for a master file. Thus the data may come from a tape or disk file, document reader, or terminal keyboard. The source file may contain the exact fields in each record that are required for the master file, or it may contain additional data that are not required on the master. This situation is often true when an existing file is used to create a new master. And, of course, there may be several files that must be combined to create a master file.

Whatever the source of the data, there are two important considerations to think about when writing the create program: (1) the records must contain valid data, and (2) they must be in the sequence required for the master file. Thus data validation and sequence checking are usually a necessary part of the create program logic.

DATA VALIDATION

When a master file is created, it is essential that each transaction used to create a master record be valid. Each field in the record must contain appropriate data, with certain possible restrictions on the contents of some field. Careful data validation when creating a master file will ensure the integrity of the master, which is important for later updating of the file. If errors are permitted to get into the master when it is created, further, more serious problems can result when an update is done to the master.

Validation is not a specific topic in this book, but some of the types of data validation that should be considered are the following:

1. Field check: field missing or not numeric.
2. Range test: such as month 01 to 12.
3. Limit check: such as a minimum purchase of $15.00.
4. Reasonableness check: is an amount of $100,000 reasonable for the price of a car.
5. Justification check: for example, a left justified alphanumeric field.
6. Valid code check: such as code M for male, F for female.
7. Relationship check: for example, a region 3 entry may only have departments 100 to 300.
8. Date check: are month, day, and year in the correct positions in the field and in the right range.
9. Check digit (modulus-11): a check digit used to detect key entry errors.

Not every create program will need to use all these tests. Which ones to use will be determined by the nature of the data and its source. A more detailed discussion of each of these validation checks and sample program code can be found in our previous volume, *Introduction to Structured COBOL and Program Design*.

SEQUENCE CHECKING

A master file must be in a predefined sequence if updating to it is to be orderly and complete. Updating logic, as we will see later, is dependent on the sequence of the records in the file. Thus the transactions used to create the master must also be in this sequence. To ensure that transaction records are in the correct order, it will be necessary for the create program to perform a **sequence check.** Out-of-sequence records will be identified on an error report and not included on the master file.

CREATING THE INVENTORY MASTER: AN APPLICATION

The inventory master file is to be created in this application. As shown in the system flowchart in Figure 3.9, the transaction records come from a tape input file. The master will be a sequential disk file, which will be used for the update application later in the chapter. A validation report is a second output. The report will list each transaction and either identify errors that were found in the record or show that it was used to create a master record.

If errors are found in the transaction file, the report will identify them, and they can be corrected before another computer run is done to create the master. In such a case, the first master file would be discarded in favor of a new and correct one. Because this is an operational concern, the program will not be required to consider the number of runs and corrections needed before a valid master file has been produced.

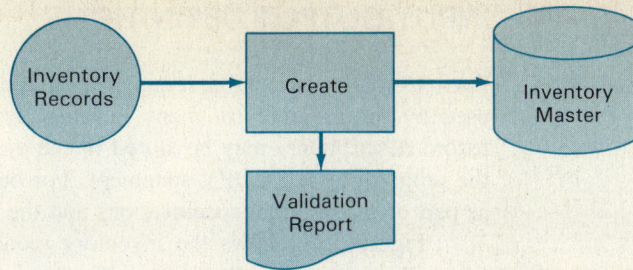

FIGURE 3.9 System flowchart for creating a master file

PROGRAM SPECIFICATIONS

The specifications for the creation of the inventory master are given in Figure 3.10. This information represents the first draft of the program requirements and is the basis for all further design of the program. In addition to the specifications, the input and output definitions are needed for a complete set of requirements. Each program developed in this book will have program specifications so that it will be clear what the program is intended to accomplish.

This program will create a sequential disk master file from the transactions provided on a tape file. Each record is validated prior to writing a master record, and an error report is produced giving the status of each record. The specifications give the details for error checking each field and sequence checking the file. Now let's look at the input/output definitions.

PROGRAMMING SPECIFICATIONS

PROGRAM NAME: Create Inventory Master   PROGRAM ID: CREATE3

PREPARED BY: Diane Quest   DATE: May 1, 1986

Program Description:

     This program reads the inventory records transaction file, validates the records, and creates an inventory master file.

Input File(s):

     Inventory records file

Output File(s):

     Inventory master file

     Inventory master validation report

Program Requirements:

     1. Read a tape file containing inventory transactions.

     2. Validate each record from the inventory records file to ensure correctness of the record. The following checks are to be made:

         a) Item number must be all numeric.

         b) Unit cost must be numeric.

         c) Stock quantity numeric.

         d) Reorder quantity numeric.

         e) Stock location numeric. Row in the range of 01–49. Shelf in the range 01–09.

     3. Inventory transaction records must be in ascending sequence on item number.

     4. All errors occurring for each record are to be printed on the validation report. These records will not be included on the master file.

     5. Group print records in the report. Print the record only once, but use a separate line for each error found.

     6. Write correct transaction records on the master file. Include today's date as the date of last activity on the master record. Write this same record on the validation report, indicating that it has been added to the inventory master file.

     7. Provide the following counts at the end of the report:

         a) Number of transaction records containing errors.

         b) Number of records created on the master file.

         c) The total number of transactions processed. This should be the sum of the two previous totals.

FIGURE 3.10 Program specifications for the inventory create program

INPUT/OUTPUT DEFINITIONS

Each COBOL application requires a detailed definition of the input and output files used by the program. In many business systems, these file formats (FD entries and record descriptions) may be stored in the system source image library and accessed in the program by the COPY statement. For our purposes, each file will be fully defined as part of the program specifications and the detailed entries made in the program.

Figure 3.11 shows the inventory records file. This is the file that provides the transactions to create the master. Each transaction consists of one record containing the fields required for the master file. The definition for the inventory records file identifies the type of file (tape), the logical record length (40 bytes), the blocking factor (12), and the access method used.

Figure 3.12 gives the inventory master file's format. Its fields are the same as the transaction file, the only exception being the activity date, which will be provided by the program. The inventory master is a sequential disk file with a record length of 45 and a blocking factor of 20. A difference in record length or blocking between the transaction and master file is quite consistent with information-system practices. Each file is organized on the basis of its own merits, depending on data requirements, the type of device, and the access method used.

INPUT/OUTPUT RECORD DEFINITION				
File: Inventory Records Record Length: 40 Sequence: Item No.		File Type: Tape Blocking Factor: 12 Access Method: Sequential		
COLUMNS	FIELD	TYPE	LENGTH	DECIMALS
1–5	Item no.	N	5	
6–20	Description	A/N	15	
21–25	Unit cost	N	5	2
26–28	Stock quantity	N	3	
29–31	Reorder quantity	N	3	
32–35	Stock location			
	Row	N	2	
	Shelf	N	2	
36–40	Unused		5	

FIGURE 3.11   Inventory transaction file definition

INPUT/OUTPUT RECORD DEFINITION				
File: Inventory Masters Record Length: 45 Sequence: Item No.		File Type: Disk Blocking Factor: 20 Access Method: Sequential		
COLUMNS	FIELD	TYPE	LENGTH	DECIMALS
1–5	Item no.	N	5	
6–20	Description	A/N	15	
21–25	Unit cost	N	5	2
26–28	Stock quantity	N	3	
29–31	Reorder quantity	N	3	
32–35	Stock location			
	Row	N	2	
	Shelf	N	2	
36–43	Last activity date	A/N	8	
44–45	Unused		2	

FIGURE 3.12   Inventory master file definition

```
      Ø           1           2           3           4           5           6           7           8           9
      123456789012345678901234567890123456789012345678901234567890123456789012345678901234567890123456789012345
```

```
                  INVENTORY MASTER VALIDATE AND CREATE

      ITEM    DESCRIPTION         UNIT COST   STOCK    REORDER    LOCATION     MESSAGES

      XXXXX   X-------------X     XXX.XX      XXX       XXX       XX XX        ** MASTER RECORD CREATED **

      XXXXX   X-------------X     XXX.XX      XXX       XXX       XX XX        ITEM NOT NUMERIC
                                                                              UNIT COST NOT NUMERIC
                                                                              STOCK QTY NOT NUMERIC
                                                                              REORDER QTY NOT NUMERIC
                                                                              STOCK LOCATION NOT NUMERIC
                                                                              ROW NOT IN RANGE Ø-49
                                                                              SHELF NOT IN RANGE Ø1-Ø9
                                                                              OUT OF SEQ OR DUP RECORD



      RECORDS CONTAINING ERRORS: ZZZ9

      RECORDS ON MASTER FILE:    ZZZ9

      TOTAL TRANSACTIONS:        ZZZ9
```

FIGURE 3.13   Inventory master validate and create report layout

The output from this program is the report in Figure 3.13. Each transaction that is a candidate for creating a master record will be listed in this report. A message on the report will show that the record has either been added to the master file or it will list the reasons why it was not added. Because these transaction records may contain errors, each field is printed with an alphanumeric format as indicated by the X's in the layout. If a numeric picture were used, data errors would occur on the output operation.

STRUCTURE CHART

The top-level consideration when developing a solution for this problem is to take care of the preliminaries such as initialization, a process loop, and a summary module to print the final totals. Here is the top-level design of the structure chart:

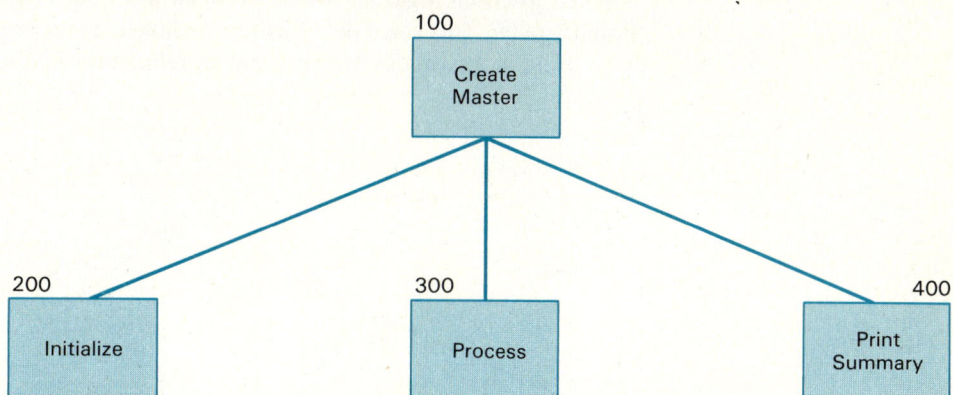

Initialize simply does the preliminary operations, such as opening files, printing headings, and reading the initial input record. The real meat to this problem is in the process loop, which contains two important parts of the solution. These two parts are required for each record for the validation and printing of the record and creating a master record.

The last module at the top level is the printing of the summary totals when end of file has been reached.

The Process Module

The processing of a single record requires that, first, each record be validated. If any errors are found, the record is printed with appropriate error messages. If there are no errors, the record is also printed and then written on the inventory master file. These modules under the process box in the structure chart are developed as follows:

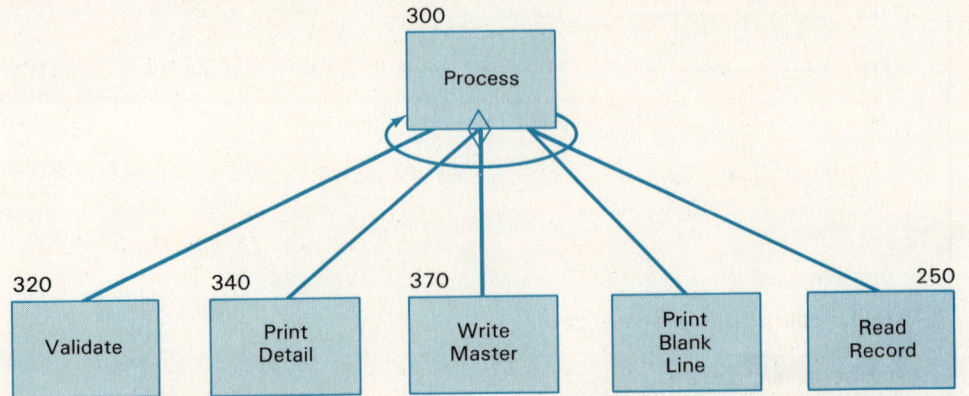

The module Validate is to be executed for every input record. However, what happens during validation (there may or may not be an error) determines whether the modules Print Detail and Write Master are to be executed. These modules are identified in the structure chart with the selection symbol to show that their execution is conditional.

Printing a blank line is necessary to get an extra space between records on the report, regardless of whether or not an error was printed. Then, of course, the next input record is read and the process is repeated.

The Validate Module

This module examines each field in the transaction file for correctness. It bears repeating that, because these records are used to create the master, it is important that no errors be introduced to the master file from the transactions. There are only five fields that need to be checked and, for the most part, the checking done is simply to determine if the fields are numeric. In each case, if an error is discovered, an error message is printed. The only addition to this checking is the location field, which must also be checked to ensure that the row is between the values 01 to 49 inclusive and the shelf from 01 to 09. This small detail will be included later when the pseudo code is designed.

Here is the validate module and its refinement into lower-level modules:

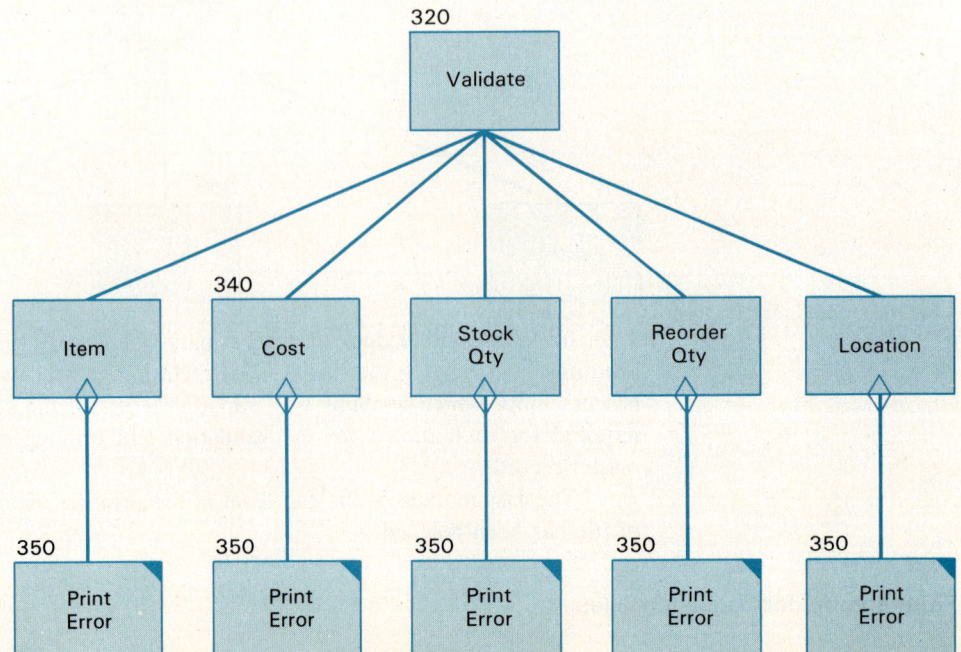

Finalizing the Structure Chart

Now that each component of the structure chart has been developed, a walkthrough of it would be in order to ensure that the hierarchy is correct. We also want to be sure that nothing of importance is missing before proceeding to more detailed logic development. As the chart is considered, it might be useful to break down the Initialize module into several parts, including a heading and a read module.

The Print Detail module could also be expanded to show a module to print a line, which in turn may require the use of the heading module if a page overflow is detected. After ensuring that all these details are taken care of, the complete structure chart is developed as shown in Figure 3.14.

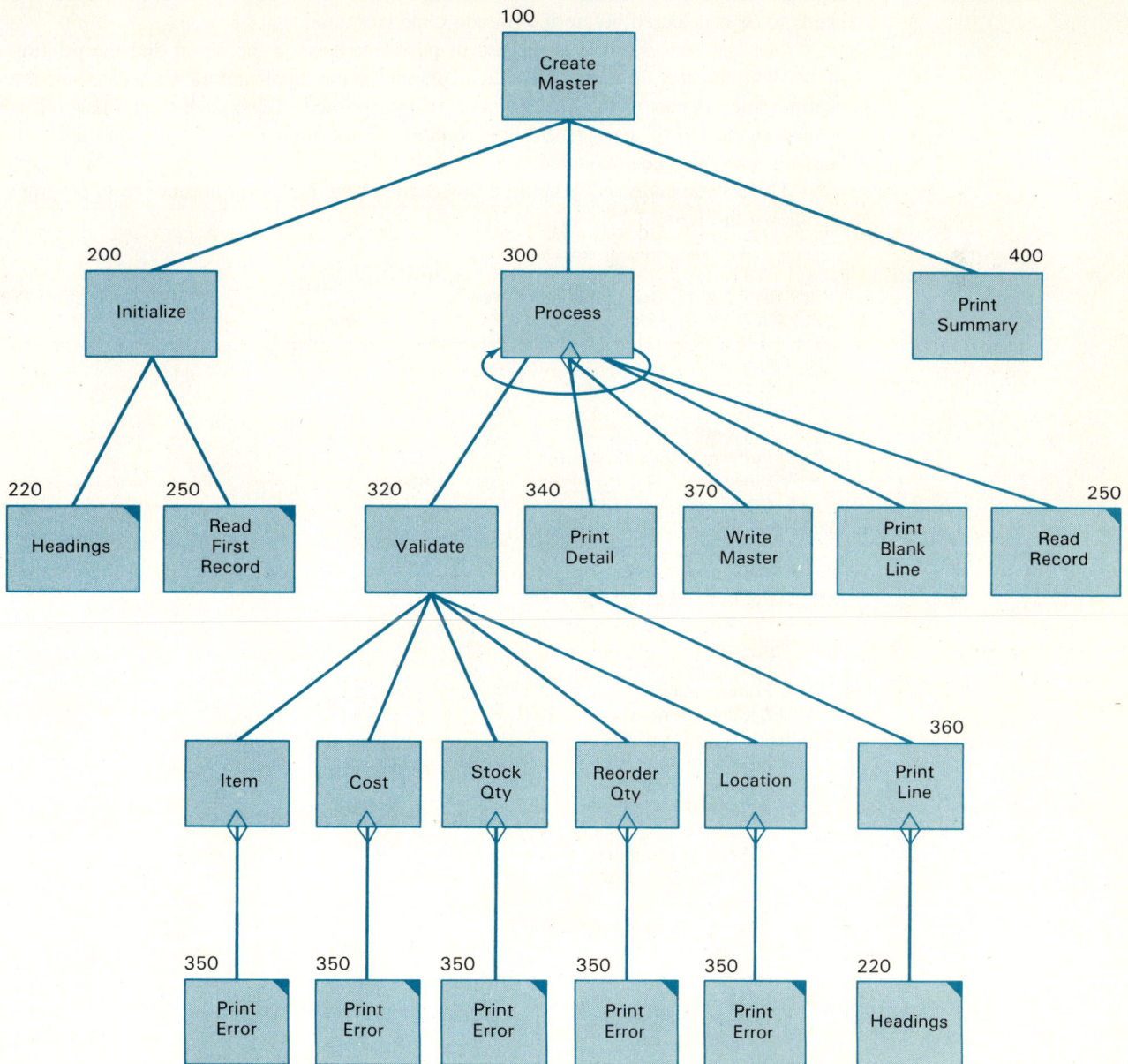

FIGURE 3.14 Structure chart for creating inventory master

PSEUDO CODE

When writing the pseudo code, several more detailed decisions need to be made that were not necessary considerations in the structure chart. One consideration is the use of flags in the logic. A flag for end-of-file detection is appropriate, and so is a flag to tell us when an error has been detected. This error flag will be used to determine if the record should be written on the new master file.

Another concern is the handling of an out-of-sequence record. Because we want to get the most information possible about the transactions file, a sequence error will only create an error message. It will not terminate the program.

Error messages will be set up in a table to simplify the writing of the error report and to improve the organization and maintenance of the program. This decision, while a programming one, will have some bearing on how the pseudo code is developed and needs to be considered before the pseudo code is written.

One last consideration is the use of page overflow on the report and the printing of headings on the first and subsequent pages. In this application, we will count the heading lines as part of the total number of lines printed. Thus, each time a heading is printed at the top of a page, the line counter will be reset to 4 to show that the four heading lines have been counted.

The pseudo code and structured flowchart for the inventory master create program are shown in Figure 3.15.

PSEUDO CODE

PROGRAM NAME: Create Inventory Master   PROGRAM ID: CREATE3
PREPARED BY: Jonathan Youngman   DATE: May 2   PAGE 1 of 2

100-Mainline
    1. Perform 200-Initialize.
    2. Perform 300-Process
        Until EOF.
    3. Perform 400-Print-Summary.
    4. Close files.
    5. Stop Run
200-Initialize
    1. Open input and output files.
    2. Get current date.
    3. Perform 220-Headings.
    4. Perform 250-Read.
220-Headings
    1. Print heading 1.
    2. Print heading 2.
    3. Set line count to 4.
250-Read
    1. Read inventory
        at end move 'yes' to EOF-Flag.
    2. If Not EOF
      Add 1 to total transactions
      If Not in sequence
        Perform 350-Print-Error
      Else
        Store item in previous item
      EndIf
    EndIf
300-Process
    1. Perform 320-Validate.
    2. If No errors
      Perform 340-Print-Detail
      Perform 350-Write-Master
    Else
      Add 1 to total errors
    EndIf

FIGURE 3.15(a)   Pseudo code for creating an inventory master

    3. Print blank line.

    4. Perform 250-Read.

320-Validate

    1. Move inventory data to detail line.

    2. Reset error flag to 'no'.

    3. If item not numeric

       Move message to detail line

       Perform 350-Print-Error

      EndIf

    4. If cost not numeric

       Move message to detail line

       Perform 350-Print-Error

      EndIf

    5. If stock quantity not numeric

       Move message to detail line

       Perform 350-Print-Error

      EndIf

    6. If reorder quantity not numeric

       Move message to detail line

       Perform 350-Print-Error

      EndIf

    7. If item not numeric

       Move message to detail line

       Perform 350-Print-Error

     Else

       Perform 330-Check-Location

     EndIf

330-Check-Location

    1. If row is not 01 to 49 inclusive

       Move message to detail line

       Perform 350-Print-Error

      EndIf

    2. If shelf is not 01 to 09 inclusive

       Move message to detail line

       Perform 350-Print-Error

      EndIf

340-Print-Detail

    1. Move numeric unit cost to detail line.

    2. Move O.K. message to detail line.

    3. Perform 360-Print-Line.

    4. Blank out the detail line to prepare for the next record.

350-Print-Error

    1. Perform 360-Print-Line.

    2. Blank out detail line so the record prints only once.

    3. Set error flag to 'yes'.

360-Print-Line

    1. Write the detail line.

    2. Add 1 to line count.

    3. If line count > 35

       Perform 220-Headings

     EndIf

370-Write-Master

    1. Move transaction fields to master fields.

    2. Move current date to master.

    3. Write inventory master record.

    4. Add 1 to total master records.

400-Print-Summary

    1. Print count of records with errors.

    2. Print count of records on the master file.

    3. Print count of transactions read.

FIGURE 3.15(b)

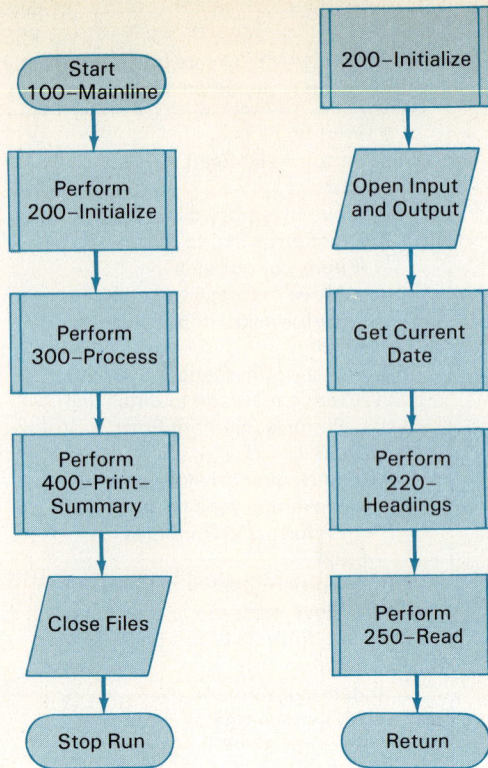

FIGURE 3.15(c) Structured flowchart for creating an inventory master

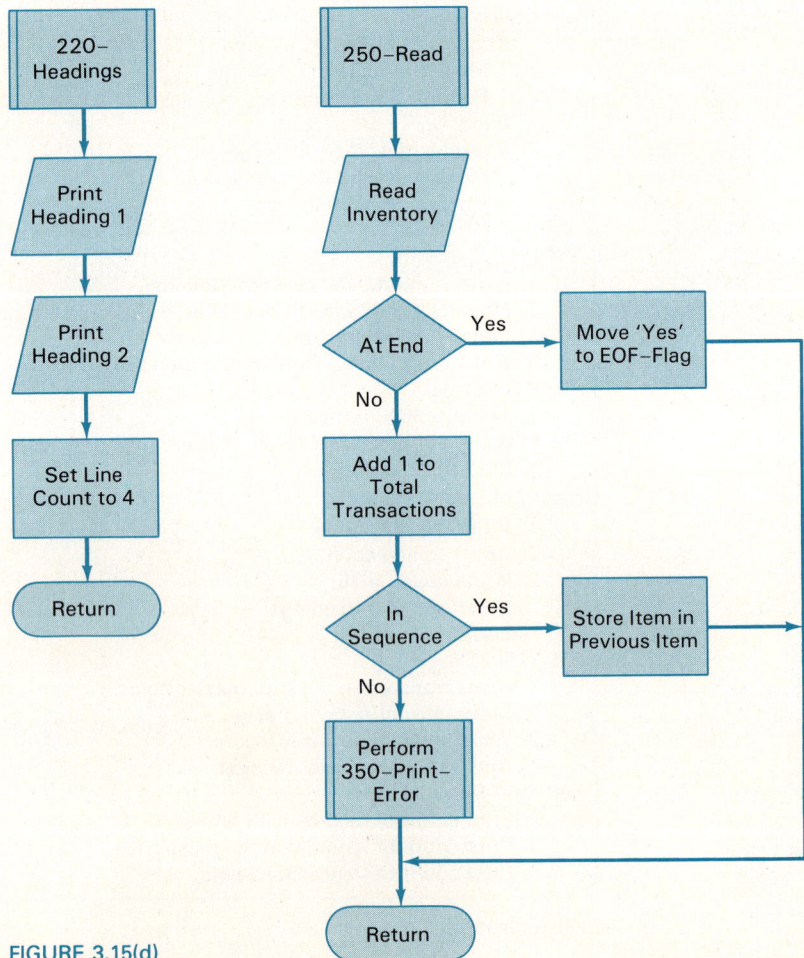

FIGURE 3.15(d)

Chapter 3

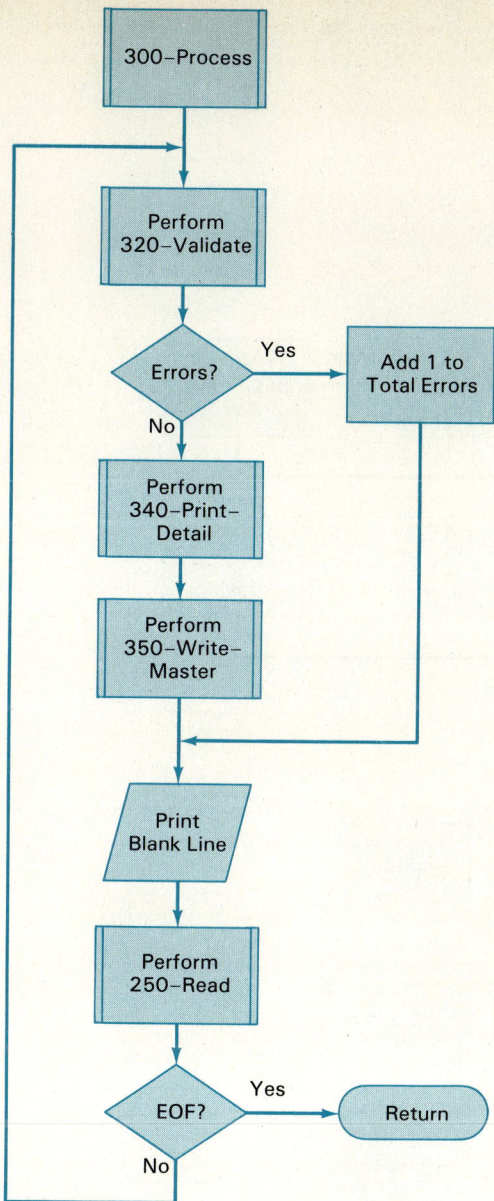

FIGURE 3.15(e)

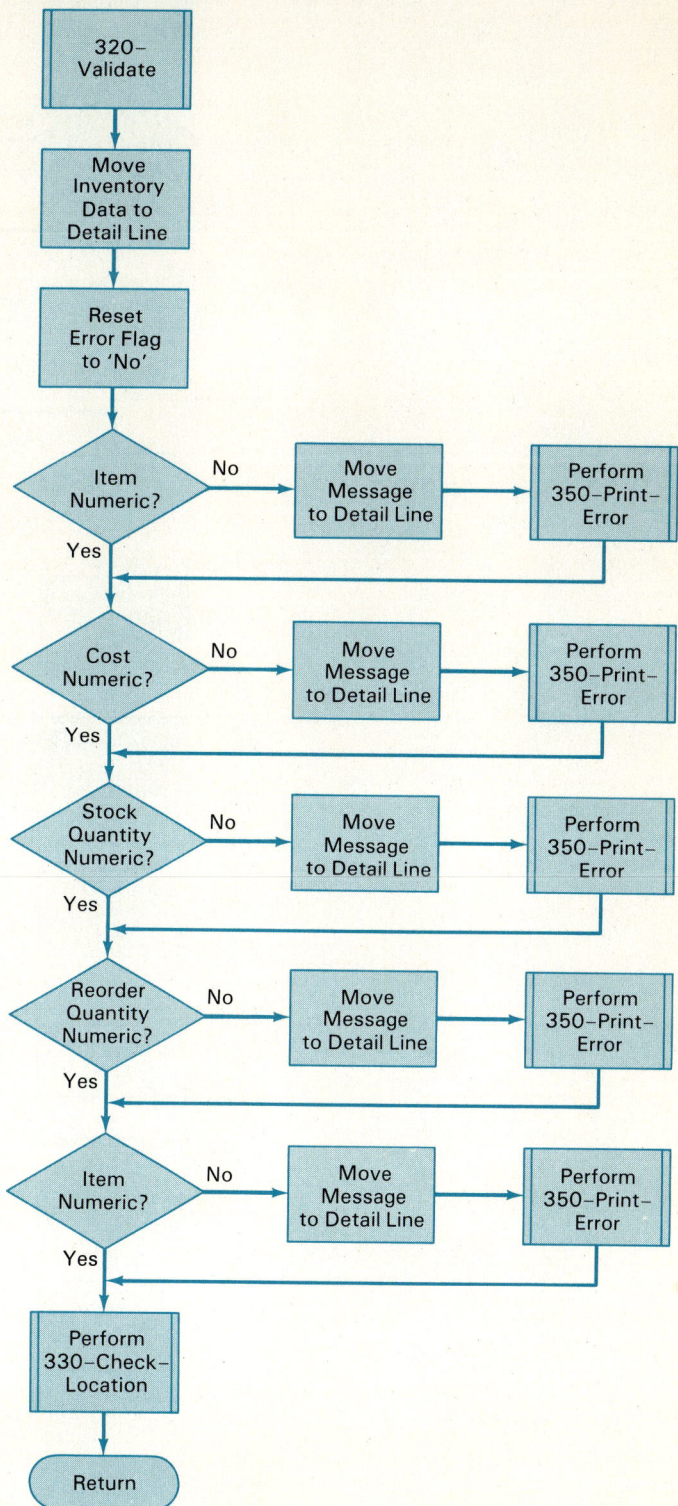

FIGURE 3.15(f)

Programming for Sequential Files

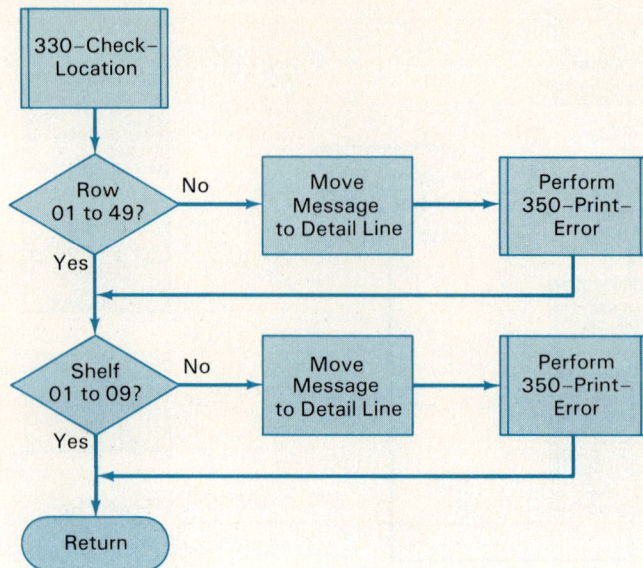

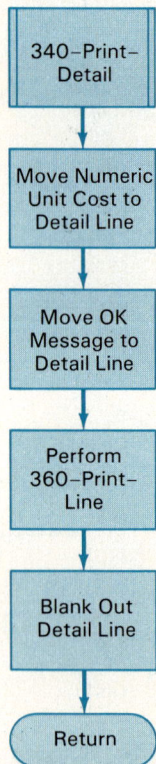

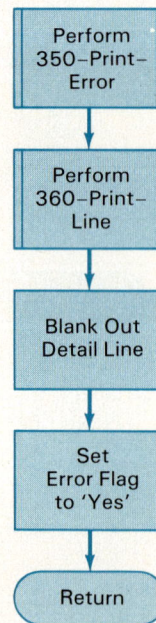

FIGURE 3.15(g)

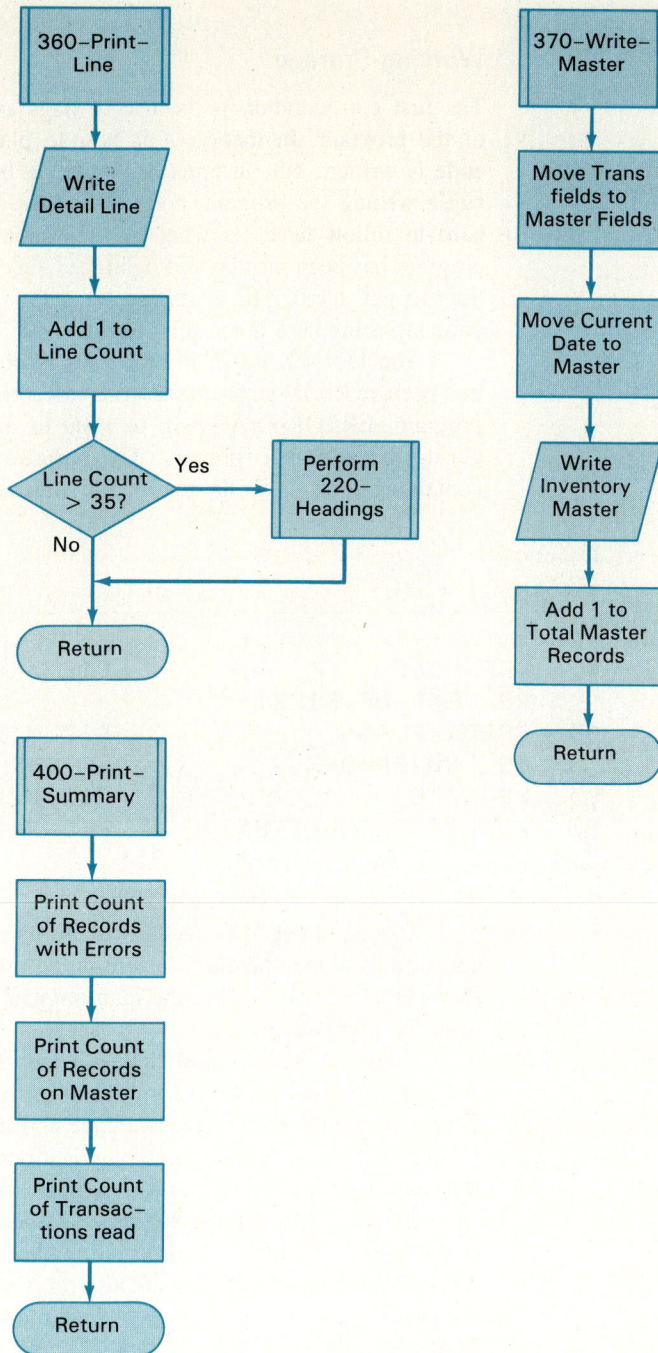

FIGURE 3.15(h)

PROGRAM CODING

The program for the inventory create application is shown in its entirety at the end of this section. But, first, let's look at some of the main features beginning with the use of WORKING-STORAGE. Some of these needs were considered prior to developing the pseudo code, but now it is necessary to finalize our plans for the program.

Working-Storage

The first consideration is the use of flags and other items necessary for the operation of the program. In theory, it is best to plan all these entries before the first line of code is written, but, in practice, we often become aware of specific needs only as we begin writing the program code. However, that kind of mental process would be too hard to follow here, so what we will look at are the entries as they exist after the program has been written and debugged successfully. Remember, if you require several tries to get a program working, the author goes through the same process and what you are seeing here is the final result.

The EOF-FLAG in Figure 3.16 is obviously used to indicate when end of file has been reached on the transaction file, because it is the only input file used by the program. ERROR-FLAG will be used to indicate when an error has been discovered during the validation process. The purpose of this flag is to bypass writing a record containing an error on the master file after all validation has been completed.

```
      A    B
1   4 78   12                                                              72
_____
        01   FLAGS.
             05   EOF-FLAG                 PIC X(03)    VALUE 'NO'.
                  88   END-OF-FILE                      VALUE 'YES'.
             05   ERROR-FLAG               PIC X(03)    VALUE 'NO'.
                  88   NO-ERRORS                         VALUE 'NO'.
             05   WS-DATE                  PIC X(08).
             05   PREVIOUS-INV-ITEM        PIC X(05)    VALUE SPACES.
```
FIGURE 3.16 Flags and other items in WORKING-STORAGE

The identifier WS-DATE will be used to store the current date, which will be accessed from the operating system in the initialization paragraph. Finally, PREVIOUS-INV-ITEM is used to store the item number for sequence checking of the input records from the transaction file.

Figure 3.17 show how the error messages have been organized for this program. Although they are in table form, they are not defined as an array. An array could be used here, but there is little advantage and the use of subscripting in the PROCEDURE DIVISION would add further complications that are really unnecessary. Simplicity in the solution is a good rule to follow in this situation.

Figure 3.18 contains the record description entry for the inventory record. This is the source of our data for creating the master file and is the record that must be validated. When doing data validation, it is usually important to avoid program interrupts because of data errors by using alphanumeric fields. Thus PIC X fields have been used in this record.

One exception to this is the redefinition of unit cost. The field is available as both alphanumeric or numeric. The alphanumeric name will be used for error checking and printing the error report if an error is found. The numeric name is used for creating the master record (although this is not strictly necessary in this case). It is also used for printing the unit cost on the report when the record is found to contain no errors. By providing an edited numeric picture in the detail line, the unit cost can be printed with a decimal point to enhance its readability.

```
          01    MESSAGES.
                05    MESSAGE-01                   PIC X(30)
                             VALUE 'ITEM NOT NUMERIC'.
                05    MESSAGE-02                   PIC X(30)
                             VALUE 'UNIT COST NOT NUMERIC'.
                05    MESSAGE-03                   PIC X(30)
                             VALUE 'STOCK QTY NOT NUMERIC'.
                05    MESSAGE-04                   PIC X(30)
                             VALUE 'REORDER QTY NOT NUMERIC'.
                05    MESSAGE-05                   PIC X(30)
                             VALUE 'STOCK LOCATION NOT NUMERIC'.
                05    MESSAGE-06                   PIC X(30)
                             VALUE 'ROW NOT IN RANGE 01 - 49'.
                05    MESSAGE-07                   PIC X(30)
                             VALUE 'SHELF NOT IN RANGE 01 - 09'.
                05    MESSAGE-08                   PIC X(30)
                             VALUE 'OUT OF SEQ OR DUP RECORD'.
                05    MESSAGE-09                   PIC X(30)
                             VALUE '** MASTER RECORD CREATED **'.
```

FIGURE 3.17 Table of error messages

```
          01    WS-INV-REC.
                05    INV-ITEM                     PIC X(05).
                05    INV-DESC                     PIC X(15).
                05    INV-UNIT-COST                PIC 9(03)V99.
                05    INV-ERROR-COST REDEFINES INV-UNIT-COST
                                                   PIC X(05).
                05    INV-STOCK-QTY                PIC X(03).
                05    INV-REORDER-QTY              PIC X(03).
                05    INV-LOCATION.
                      10    INV-ROW                PIC X(02).
                      10    INV-SHELF              PIC X(02).
                05    FILLER                       PIC X(05).
```

FIGURE 3.18 Record description for the inventory record

Coding the PROCEDURE DIVISION

100-MAINLINE   This paragraph controls the beginning of the program, processing of each input record, and performing the summary totals. Essentially, this is the implementation of the top level as seen in both the structure chart and pseudo code.

200-INITIALIZE   This paragraph, as you might expect, get things started in the program by opening the input and output files. It also accesses the current date from the operating system (this step is unique to IBM systems and may require a different approach on other systems). Finally, the headings are printed and the first input transaction is read.

220-HEADINGS   As the name suggests, this paragraph prints headings at the top of each new page. It also initializes the line counter to 4 each time, thus including the heading lines in the count.

250-READ Each transaction record is read by this paragraph and end of file is checked by the READ statement. Two additional activities are necessary for each input record, but these must not be done if end of file has been reached. So, first, the paragraph checks the end-of-file flag and, if it was not detected, the transaction read is counted in the counter TOTAL-TRANS. Then the sequence of the record is checked as follows to ensure it is in ascending sequence on the item number:

```
      A   B
1  4  78  12                                                          72
_____
      IF INV-ITEM IS NOT GREATER THAN PREVIOUS-INV-ITEM
         MOVE MESSAGE-08      TO DTL-MESSAGE
         PERFORM 350-PRINT-ERROR
      ELSE
         MOVE INV-ITEM        TO PREVIOUS-INV-ITEM.
```

MESSAGE-08 contains the sequence error message, which is moved to DTL-MESSAGE, and then the paragraph 350-PRINT-ERROR is performed to print the message. This approach is followed throughout the program whenever an error is found. If there is no sequence error (the usual case), the item number from the current record is moved to PREVIOUS-INV-ITEM in preparation for the next input record.

300-PROCESS This paragraph (Figure 3.19) is the main process loop executed for each record. Its main function is to validate the record and, if there are no errors (NO-ERRORS, the error flag evaluates true), create a detail line and a master record. In the event that there was one or more errors, a 1 is added to TOTAL-ERRORS, which represents the total number of records containing errors. This is not to be confused with the total number of errors, which could be more than one in a given record.

The last three lines of the paragraph first cause a blank line to be printed to get a space between records on the report. Then the next input record is read before the loop is repeated.

```
      A   B
1  4  78  12                                                          72
_____
   300-PROCESS.
      PERFORM 320-VALIDATE.
      IF NO-ERRORS
         PERFORM 340-PRINT-DETAIL
         PERFORM 370-WRITE-MASTER
      ELSE
         ADD 1 TO TOTAL-ERRORS.
      MOVE SPACES TO DETAIL-LINE.
      PERFORM 360-PRINT-LINE.
      PERFORM 250-READ.
```

FIGURE 3.19   The main process paragraph

320-VALIDATE All the data validation is done in this paragraph. First, the data from the input record are moved to the detail line. These moves are done before any errors are printed so that the transaction is printed only the one time. After the first error is printed, the line is cleared to spaces, thus removing the record. If there are subsequent errors, only the error message will be printed.

The error flag is also reset here with the following statement:

```
         MOVE 'NO'    TO ERROR-FLAG.
```

It will be set to 'YES' when an error is found.

Each field in the input record is checked to ensure that it contains only numeric information. These checks are quite straightforward and follow the pattern of the following statements for checking the item number:

```
        A    B
1   4   78   12                                                              72
```

```
       IF INV-ITEM NOT NUMERIC
          MOVE MESSAGE-01     TO DTL-MESSAGE
          PERFORM 350-PRINT-ERROR.
```

The last field to be checked is location, which has the unique requirement of a range limitation in the row and shelf subfields. This need is handled by performing the paragraph 330-CHECK-LOCATION when it has been determined that the location is numeric.

```
        A    B
1   4   78   12                                                              72
```

```
       IF   INV-LOCATION NOT NUMERIC
          MOVE MESSAGE-05     TO DTL-MESSAGE
          PERFORM 350-PRINT-ERROR
       ELSE
          PERFORM 330-CHECK-LOCATION.
```

330-CHECK-LOCATION This paragraph checks the range of row between 01 and 49 and shelf from 01 to 09. Because these fields and values are independent of each other, the checks are done separately. If an error is found, the appropriate message is moved to the detail line and 350-PRINT-ERROR is performed.

```
        A    B
1   4   78   12                                                              72
```

```
       330-CHECK-LOCATION.
          IF    (INV-ROW IS LESS THAN '01')
             OR (INV-ROW IS GREATER THAN '49')
                MOVE MESSAGE-06     TO DTL-MESSAGE
                PERFORM 350-PRINT-ERROR.
          IF    (INV-SHELF IS LESS THAN '01')
             OR (INV-SHELF IS GREATER THAN '09')
                MOVE MESSAGE-07     TO DTL-MESSAGE
                PERFORM 350-PRINT-ERROR.
```

340-PRINT-DETAIL This paragraph is invoked only when a record is found that contains no errors. Because all fields from the record have previously been moved to the detail line, it is only necessary to move the numeric unit cost field now that we know it is numeric. MESSAGE-09 indicates that the record is OK and that it will be added to the master file. Paragraph 360-PRINT-LINE does the actual printing of the line.

```
        A    B
1   4   78   12                                                              72
```

```
       340-PRINT-DETAIL.
          MOVE INV-UNIT-COST       TO DTL-UNIT-COST.
          MOVE MESSAGE-09          TO DTL-MESSAGE.
          PERFORM 360-PRINT-LINE.
          MOVE SPACES              TO DETAIL-LINE.
```

350-PRINT-ERROR All error messages are printed from this paragraph. After printing the line, the detail line is cleared to spaces so that the record it contained will not be printed again for subsequent errors if they occur on the same record. Finally, the ERROR-FLAG is set to indicate that an error has been found. It may seem like an odd place to set the error flag, but this paragraph is one place in the program that is common to all errors found.

```
         A    B
1    4   78   12                                                         72

         350-PRINT-ERROR.
             PERFORM 360-PRINT-LINE.
             MOVE SPACES              TO DETAIL-LINE.
             MOVE 'YES'               TO ERROR-FLAG.
```

360-PRINT-LINE Every line, except for heading lines, printed by this program will be printed from this paragraph. This use of a common printing paragraph requires the line to be printed to be available in the record DETAIL-LINE. The line printed is also counted, and if the maximum number of lines per page is reached, the heading paragraph will also be performed.

```
         A    B
1    4   78   12                                                         72

         360-PRINT-LINE.
             WRITE PRINT-REC FROM DETAIL-LINE
                 AFTER ADVANCING 1 LINE.
             ADD 1                       TO LINE-COUNT.
             IF LINE-COUNT IS GREATER THAN 35
                 PERFORM 220-HEADINGS.
```

370-WRITE-MASTER This paragraph, although quite important, is also quite simple. It moves each of the input fields to the master record area and writes the record on the master file. After the record has been written, a 1 is added to the TOTAL-MASTERS counter, which counts the number of records on the master file.

```
         A    B
1    4   78   12                                                         72

         370-WRITE-MASTER.
             MOVE INV-ITEM          TO   MST-ITEM.
             MOVE INV-DESC          TO   MST-DESC.
             MOVE INV-UNIT-COST     TO   MST-UNIT-COST.
             MOVE INV-STOCK-QTY     TO   MST-STOCK-QTY.
             MOVE INV-REORDER-QTY   TO   MST-REORDER-QTY.
             MOVE INV-LOCATION      TO   MST-LOCATION.
             MOVE WS-DATE           TO   MST-LAST-DATE.
             WRITE MST-REC FROM WS-MST-REC.
             ADD 1 TO TOTAL-MASTERS.
```

400-PRINT-SUMMARY The last paragraph in the program prints the summary of totals that have been accumulated during processing. For each total (there are three of them), a message is moved to the SUMMARY-MESSAGE, the total is also moved to the line, and the line is printed with double spacing. This process is repeated for each total in the summary.

```
      400-PRINT-SUMMARY.
          MOVE ' RECORDS CONTAINING ERRORS:'  TO SUMMARY-MESSAGE.
          MOVE TOTAL-ERRORS              TO SUMMARY-AMT.
          WRITE PRINT-REC FROM SUMMARY-LINE
              AFTER ADVANCING 2 LINES.
          MOVE ' RECORDS ON MASTER FILE:' TO SUMMARY-MESSAGE.
          MOVE TOTAL-MASTERS             TO SUMMARY-AMT.
          WRITE PRINT-REC FROM SUMMARY-LINE
              AFTER ADVANCING 2 LINES.
          MOVE ' TOTAL TRANSACTIONS:'   TO SUMMARY-MESSAGE.
          MOVE TOTAL-TRANS              TO SUMMARY-AMT.
          WRITE PRINT-REC FROM SUMMARY-LINE
              AFTER ADVANCING 2 LINES.
```

This ends the discussion of each module in the program. The complete program to implement the solution to create the inventory file is given in Figure 3.20.

```
      IDENTIFICATION DIVISION.

      PROGRAM-ID.
          CREATE3.
     *AUTHOR.
     *     JOHNATHAN YOUNGMAN.
     *INSTALLATION.
     *     SALES UNLIMITED CORP.
     *DATE-WRITTEN.
     *     APRIL 23.
     *DATE-COMPILED.

     *SECURITY.
     *     NONE.

      ENVIRONMENT DIVISION.

      CONFIGURATION SECTION.
      SOURCE-COMPUTER.
          IBM-370.
      OBJECT-COMPUTER.
          IBM-370.
      SPECIAL-NAMES.
          C01 IS TO-TOP-OF-PAGE.

      INPUT-OUTPUT SECTION.

      FILE-CONTROL.
          SELECT INVENTORY ASSIGN TO UT-S-TRANS.
          SELECT MASTER    ASSIGN TO UT-S-FILEA.
          SELECT LISTING   ASSIGN TO UR-S-PRINTER.

      DATA DIVISION.

      FILE SECTION.

      FD  INVENTORY
          BLOCK  CONTAINS 12 RECORDS
          RECORD CONTAINS 40 CHARACTERS
          LABEL RECORDS ARE STANDARD
          DATA RECORD IS INV-REC.
      01  INV-REC.
          05  FILLER                 PIC X(40).
```

FIGURE 3.20(a) Program for creating the inventory master file

```
        FD   MASTER
             BLOCK  CONTAINS 20 RECORDS
             RECORD CONTAINS 45 CHARACTERS
             LABEL RECORDS ARE STANDARD
             DATA RECORD IS MST-REC.
        01   MST-REC.
             05  FILLER                    PIC X(40).

        FD   LISTING
             RECORD CONTAINS 133 CHARACTERS
             LABEL RECORDS ARE OMITTED
             DATA RECORD IS PRINT-REC.
        01   PRINT-REC.
             05  PRINT-LINE                PIC X(133).

        WORKING-STORAGE SECTION.

        01   FLAGS.
             05  EOF-FLAG                  PIC X(03)   VALUE 'NO'.
                 88  END-OF-FILE                       VALUE 'YES'
             05  ERROR-FLAG                PIC X(03)   VALUE 'NO'.
                 88  NO-ERRORS                          VALUE 'NO'.
             05  WS-DATE                   PIC X(08).
             05  PREVIOUS-INV-ITEM         PIC X(05)   VALUE SPACES

        01   TOTALS.
             05  LINE-COUNT                PIC 9(02)   VALUE ZERO.
             05  TOTAL-ERRORS              PIC 9(04)   VALUE ZERO.
             05  TOTAL-MASTERS             PIC 9(04)   VALUE ZERO.
             05  TOTAL-TRANS               PIC 9(04)   VALUE ZERO.

        01   MESSAGES.
             05  MESSAGE-01                PIC X(30)
                     VALUE 'ITEM NOT NUMERIC'.
             05  MESSAGE-02                PIC X(30)
                     VALUE 'UNIT COST NOT NUMERIC'.
             05  MESSAGE-03                PIC X(30)
                     VALUE 'STOCK QTY NOT NUMERIC'.
             05  MESSAGE-04                PIC X(30)
                     VALUE 'REORDER QTY NOT NUMERIC'.
             05  MESSAGE-05                PIC X(30)
                     VALUE 'STOCK LOCATION NOT NUMERIC'.
             05  MESSAGE-06                PIC X(30)
                     VALUE 'ROW NOT IN RANGE 01 - 49'.
             05  MESSAGE-07                PIC X(30)
                     VALUE 'SHELF NOT IN RANGE 01 - 09'.
             05  MESSAGE-08                PIC X(30)
                     VALUE 'OUT OF SEQ OR DUP RECORD'.
             05  MESSAGE-09                PIC X(30)
                     VALUE '** MASTER RECORD CREATED **'.

        01   WS-INV-REC.
             05  INV-ITEM                  PIC X(05).
             05  INV-DESC                  PIC X(15).
             05  INV-UNIT-COST             PIC 9(03)V99.
             05  INV-ERROR-COST REDEFINES INV-UNIT-COST
                                           PIC X(05).
             05  INV-STOCK-QTY             PIC X(03).
             05  INV-REORDER-QTY           PIC X(03).
             05  INV-LOCATION.
                 10  INV-ROW               PIC X(02).
                 10  INV-SHELF             PIC X(02).
             05  FILLER                    PIC X(05).

        01   WS-MST-REC.
             05  MST-ITEM                  PIC X(05).
             05  MST-DESC                  PIC X(15).
             05  MST-UNIT-COST             PIC 9(03)V99.
             05  MST-STOCK-QTY             PIC X(03).
             05  MST-REORDER-QTY           PIC X(03).
             05  MST-LOCATION.
                 10  MST-ROW               PIC X(02).
                 10  MST-SHELF             PIC X(02).
             05  MST-LAST-DATE             PIC X(08).
             05  FILLER                    PIC X(02).
```

FIGURE 3.20(b)

70

Chapter 3

```
01  HEAD-1.
    05  FILLER                      PIC X(20)    VALUE SPACES.
    05  FILLER                      PIC X(36)
            VALUE 'INVENTORY MASTER VALIDATE AND CREATE'.
01  HEAD-2.
    05  FILLER                      PIC X(37)
            VALUE ' ITEM     DESCRIPTION      UNIT COST'.
    05  FILLER                      PIC X(40)
            VALUE 'STOCK    REORDER    LOCATION     MESSAGES'.

01  DETAIL-LINE.
    05  FILLER                      PIC X(01)    VALUE SPACES.
    05  DTL-ITEM                    PIC X(05).
    05  FILLER                      PIC X(03)    VALUE SPACES.
    05  DTL-DESC                    PIC X(15).
    05  FILLER                      PIC X(03)    VALUE SPACES.
    05  DTL-UNIT-COST               PIC 9(03).99.
    05  DTL-ERROR-COST REDEFINES DTL-UNIT-COST
                                    PIC X(05).
    05  FILLER                      PIC X(05)    VALUE SPACES.
    05  DTL-STOCK-QTY               PIC X(03).
    05  FILLER                      PIC X(06)    VALUE SPACES.
    05  DTL-REORDER-QTY             PIC X(03).
    05  FILLER                      PIC X(06)    VALUE SPACES.
    05  DTL-LOCATION.
        10  DTL-ROW                 PIC X(02).
        10  FILLER                  PIC X(01)    VALUE SPACES.
        10  DTL-SHELF               PIC X(02).
    05  FILLER                      PIC X(07)    VALUE SPACES.
    05  DTL-MESSAGE                 PIC X(30).

01  SUMMARY-LINE.
    05  SUMMARY-MESSAGE             PIC X(28)    VALUE SPACES.
    05  SUMMARY-AMT                 PIC Z(03)9.
PROCEDURE DIVISION.

100-MAINLINE.
    PERFORM 200-INITIALIZE.
    PERFORM 300-PROCESS
        UNTIL END-OF-FILE.
    PERFORM 400-PRINT-SUMMARY.
    CLOSE INVENTORY
        MASTER
        LISTING.
    STOP RUN.

200-INITIALIZE.
    OPEN INPUT  INVENTORY
        OUTPUT MASTER
               LISTING.
    MOVE CURRENT-DATE TO WS-DATE.
    PERFORM 220-HEADINGS.
    PERFORM 250-READ.

220-HEADINGS.
    WRITE PRINT-REC FROM HEAD-1
        AFTER ADVANCING TO-TOP-OF-PAGE.
    WRITE PRINT-REC FROM HEAD-2
        AFTER ADVANCING 2 LINES.
    MOVE SPACES TO PRINT-REC.
    WRITE PRINT-REC
        AFTER ADVANCING 1 LINE.
    MOVE 4 TO LINE-COUNT.

250-READ.
    READ INVENTORY INTO WS-INV-REC
        AT END MOVE 'YES' TO EOF-FLAG.
    IF NOT END-OF-FILE
        ADD 1 TO TOTAL-TRANS
        IF INV-ITEM IS NOT GREATER THAN PREVIOUS-INV-ITEM
            MOVE MESSAGE-08      TO DTL-MESSAGE
            PERFORM 350-PRINT-ERROR
        ELSE
            MOVE INV-ITEM        TO PREVIOUS-INV-ITEM.
```

FIGURE 3.20(c)

Programming for Sequential Files   71

```
300-PROCESS.
    PERFORM 320-VALIDATE.
    IF NO-ERRORS
        PERFORM 340-PRINT-DETAIL
        PERFORM 370-WRITE-MASTER
    ELSE
        ADD 1 TO TOTAL-ERRORS.
    MOVE SPACES TO DETAIL-LINE.
    PERFORM 360-PRINT-LINE.
    PERFORM 250-READ.

320-VALIDATE.
    MOVE INV-ITEM             TO DTL-ITEM.
    MOVE INV-DESC             TO DTL-DESC.
    MOVE INV-ERROR-COST       TO DTL-ERROR-COST.
    MOVE INV-STOCK-QTY        TO DTL-STOCK-QTY.
    MOVE INV-REORDER-QTY      TO DTL-REORDER-QTY.
    MOVE INV-ROW              TO DTL-ROW.
    MOVE INV-SHELF            TO DTL-SHELF.
    MOVE 'NO'                 TO ERROR-FLAG.
    IF INV-ITEM NOT NUMERIC
        MOVE MESSAGE-01       TO DTL-MESSAGE
        PERFORM 350-PRINT-ERROR.
    IF INV-ERROR-COST NOT NUMERIC
        MOVE MESSAGE-02       TO DTL-MESSAGE
        PERFORM 350-PRINT-ERROR.
    IF INV-STOCK-QTY NOT NUMERIC
        MOVE MESSAGE-03       TO DTL-MESSAGE
        PERFORM 350-PRINT-ERROR.
    IF INV-REORDER-QTY NOT NUMERIC
        MOVE MESSAGE-04       TO DTL-MESSAGE
        PERFORM 350-PRINT-ERROR.
    IF INV-LOCATION NOT NUMERIC
        MOVE MESSAGE-05       TO DTL-MESSAGE
        PERFORM 350-PRINT-ERROR
    ELSE
        PERFORM 330-CHECK-LOCATION.

330-CHECK-LOCATION.
    IF    (INV-ROW IS LESS THAN '01')
       OR (INV-ROW IS GREATER THAN '49')
        MOVE MESSAGE-06       TO DTL-MESSAGE
        PERFORM 350-PRINT-ERROR.
    IF    (INV-SHELF IS LESS THAN '01')
       OR (INV-SHELF IS GREATER THAN '09')
        MOVE MESSAGE-07       TO DTL-MESSAGE
        PERFORM 350-PRINT-ERROR.

340-PRINT-DETAIL.
    MOVE INV-UNIT-COST        TO DTL-UNIT-COST.
    MOVE MESSAGE-09           TO DTL-MESSAGE.
    PERFORM 360-PRINT-LINE.
    MOVE SPACES               TO DETAIL-LINE.

350-PRINT-ERROR.
    PERFORM 360-PRINT-LINE.
    MOVE SPACES               TO DETAIL-LINE.
    MOVE 'YES'                TO ERROR-FLAG.

360-PRINT-LINE.
    WRITE PRINT-REC FROM DETAIL-LINE
        AFTER ADVANCING 1 LINE.
    ADD 1                     TO LINE-COUNT.
    IF LINE-COUNT IS GREATER THAN 35
        PERFORM 220-HEADINGS.

370-WRITE-MASTER.
    MOVE INV-ITEM             TO   MST-ITEM.
    MOVE INV-DESC             TO   MST-DESC.
    MOVE INV-UNIT-COST        TO   MST-UNIT-COST.
    MOVE INV-STOCK-QTY        TO   MST-STOCK-QTY.
    MOVE INV-REORDER-QTY      TO   MST-REORDER-QTY.
    MOVE INV-LOCATION         TO   MST-LOCATION.
    MOVE WS-DATE              TO   MST-LAST-DATE.
    WRITE MST-REC FROM WS-MST-REC.
    ADD 1 TO TOTAL-MASTERS.
```

FIGURE 3.20(d)

Chapter 3

```
400-PRINT-SUMMARY.
    MOVE ' RECORDS CONTAINING ERRORS:'  TO SUMMARY-MESSAGE.
    MOVE TOTAL-ERRORS               TO SUMMARY-AMT.
    WRITE PRINT-REC FROM SUMMARY-LINE
        AFTER ADVANCING 2 LINES.
    MOVE ' RECORDS ON MASTER FILE:' TO SUMMARY-MESSAGE.
    MOVE TOTAL-MASTERS              TO SUMMARY-AMT.
    WRITE PRINT-REC FROM SUMMARY-LINE
        AFTER ADVANCING 2 LINES.
    MOVE ' TOTAL TRANSACTIONS:'     TO SUMMARY-MESSAGE.
    MOVE TOTAL-TRANS               TO SUMMARY-AMT.
    WRITE PRINT-REC FROM SUMMARY-LINE
        AFTER ADVANCING 2 LINES.
```

FIGURE 3.20(e)

PROGRAM TESTING

The final step remaining is to test the create program and be sure that it functions correctly. To do this will require a set of test data for the transaction file. Because the program validates the input data before creating the master, the test file should contain both good and bad data. There should be a record containing each type of error and also one or more records containing several errors in a single record to be sure the program finds them all. Finally, enough data should be provided to test the page overflow logic for the report.

Test data that include these considerations are shown in Figure 3.21.

The two pages of the report printed by the create program are shown in Figure 3.22. This report identifies the records that were added to the master file with the message ** MASTER RECORD CREATED **. Ideally, most records should receive this flag. The others will have one or more error messages to tell us why the record was not acceptable for creating the master file.

At the end of the report are totals to summarize the actions taken on the input records. The sum of the records containing errors and the records added to the master should be equal to the number of transaction records. If these amounts do not tally, we would have a problem with the program.

```
12000DISTRIBUTOR      045981000251203
12100WIRE SET         012950500201204
12210A/C RELAY        018000050101101
12220VALVE            007950000202005
12240STEM             002950750300501
13005CLEANER          R45981000251203
13100HARNESS          012050500201204
13220RUBBER INSERT    01800005AB01101
13250CLAMP            00795000020%005
13340STEM A           002950750305510
13341STEM B           0W2R50R50TTA110
14200WHEEL 14"        087290050022701
15000WHEEL 15"        095980090052703
15200POLISH           003350500153204
15210RELAY AB         010100150203101
15420ANTENNA          018950020104101
15640LIGHT KIT        057950120033501
```

- Item number
- Description
- Unit cost
- Stock quantity
- Reorder quantity
- Stock location

FIGURE 3.21 Test data for the inventory create program

```
                  INVENTORY MASTER VALIDATE AND CREATE

   ITEM    DESCRIPTION      UNIT COST  STOCK   REORDER   LOCATION   MESSAGES

   12000   DISTRIBUTOR      045.98     100     025       12 03      ** MASTER RECORD CREATED **

   12100   WIRE SET         012.95     050     020       12 04      ** MASTER RECORD CREATED **

   12210   A/C RELAY        018.00     005     010       11 01      ** MASTER RECORD CREATED **

   12220   VALVE            007.95     000     020       20 05      ** MASTER RECORD CREATED **

   12240   STEM             002.95     075     030       05 01      ** MASTER RECORD CREATED **

   13005   CLEANER          R4598      100     025       12 03      UNIT COST NOT NUMERIC

   13100   HARNESS          01205      050     020       12 04      STOCK QTY NOT NUMERIC

   13220   RUBBER INSERT    01800      005     AB0       11 01      REORDER QTY NOT NUMERIC

   13250   CLAMP            00795      000     020       %0 05      STOCK LOCATION NOT NUMERIC

   13340   STEM A           00295      075     030       55 10      ROW NOT IN RANGE  01 - 49
                                                                    SHELF NOT IN RANGE 01 - 09

   13341   STEM B           0W2R5      0R5     0TT       A1 10      UNIT COST NOT NUMERIC
                                                                    STOCK QTY NOT NUMERIC
                                                                    REORDER QTY NOT NUMERIC
                                                                    STOCK LOCATION NOT NUMERIC

   14200   WHEEL 14"        087.29     005     002       27 01      ** MASTER RECORD CREATED **

   15000   WHEEL 15"        095.98     009     005       27 03      ** MASTER RECORD CREATED **

   15200   POLISH           003.35     050     015       32 04      ** MASTER RECORD CREATED **
   - - - - - - - - - - - - - - - - - - - - - - - - - - - - - - - - - - - - - - - - - - - - - -
   ITEM    DESCRIPTION      UNIT COST  STOCK   REORDER   LOCATION   MESSAGES

   15210   RELAY AB         010.10     015     020       31 01      ** MASTER RECORD CREATED **

   15420   ANTENNA          018.95     002     010       41 01      ** MASTER RECORD CREATED **

   15640   LIGHT KIT        057.95     012     003       35 01      ** MASTER RECORD CREATED **

   RECORDS CONTAINING ERRORS:      6

   REORDS ON MASTER FILE:         11

   TOTAL TRANSACTIONS:            17
```

FIGURE 3.22   The inventory validate and create report

SEQUENTIAL FILE UPDATING

To update the contents of a sequential file requires a program that reads a transaction file containing the changes to be made. The program also reads the master file and creates a second, updated master as a new sequential file, because the original file cannot be overwritten. This updating process is shown in the system flowchart in Figure 3.23, where an activity report is also shown as an output from the update.

Updating occurs on a regular basis; the frequency could be daily, weekly, biweekly, or monthly, depending on the application. When an update is done, the updated master

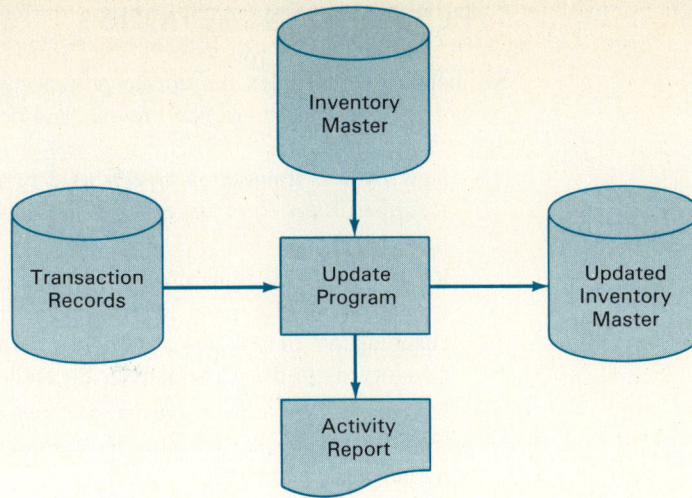

FIGURE 3.23 System flowchart for updating a sequential master file

becomes the master file for the next update run. The previous master then is a history file because it is no longer current. However, to guard against possible system failure, several old masters are retained in the library as **backup files.**

As an update occurs, the new master file that is created is called the son. The old master file is now a father. But next week (assuming a weekly update cycle), the son is used for updating, thus creating a new son. The file that we had called a son now becomes a father, and the previous father file is now a grandfather (see Figure 3.24). This sequence of history files is called a **grandfather, father, son sequence.** Usually, at least these three files are retained as backup. In some cases, where updating is frequent, more history files can be retained.

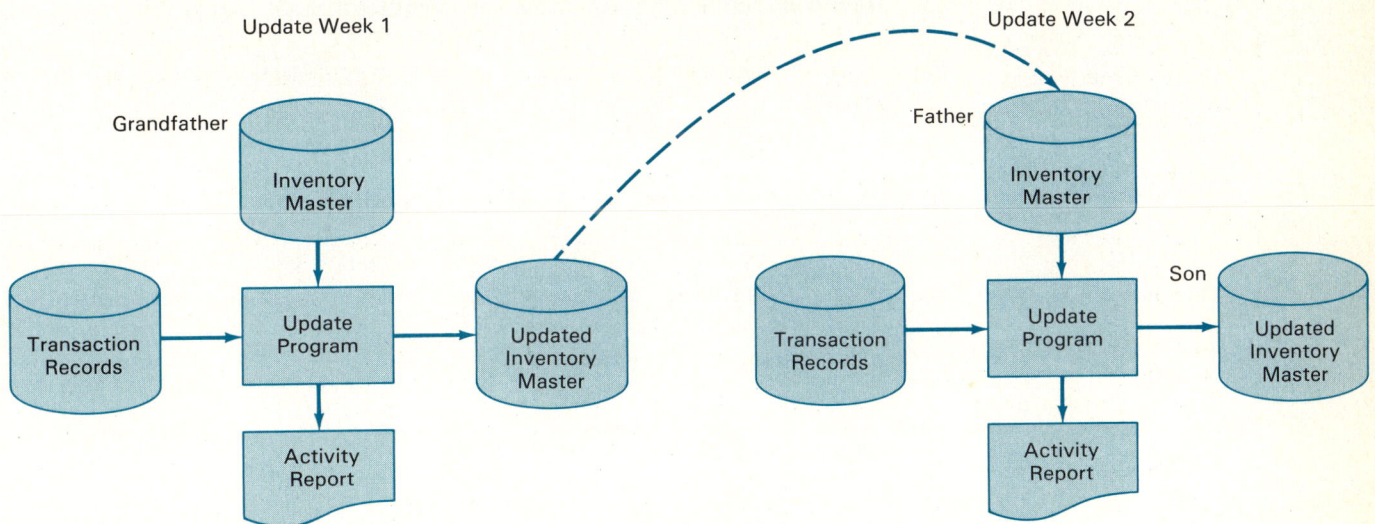

FIGURE 3.24 History of sequential file updating

TRANSACTION FILE VERSUS THE MASTER FILE

When doing a sequential update, a very important consideration is the sequence of the master file. The master file we created earlier was in ascending sequence on item number. This sequence is the basis for all updating activity, and the transaction file must also be ordered in the same sequence. Usually, the transactions are sorted prior to doing the update. For our purposes we will assume that the transaction file has been sorted prior to the update program, although in some applications the update could begin by first sorting the transaction file.

TYPES OF TRANSACTIONS

No matter how complex the update program may be, transactions fall into three basic categories. These three are new, revise, and delete transactions:

- New: A new transaction type is used to add a record to the master file. This new record will not correctly exist on the master, but will be included on the updated master.
- Revise: A revise transaction type is used to change the contents of an existing master record. Revision may mean increasing or reducing a quantity in stock or changing an item's description or location. Most updating types fall into this category, with the exact activity depending on the application.
- Delete: As this term suggests, this transaction type is used to delete an existing record from the master file. The deleted record will not appear on the updated master file.

RELATIONSHIP BETWEEN THE KEYS

With reference to the sequence fields in both the master and transaction files, if the file sequence is on item number, then the item number field is called a key. Updating logic depends on the relationship between the key in the current record of the transaction file and the key in the current master record. This relationship may be expressed in three ways as follows:

1. **Equal transaction key:** transaction key is equal to the master key.
2. **Low transaction key:** transaction key is less than the master key.
3. **High transaction key:** transaction key is greater than the master key.

Each of these relationships determines a specific type of action to be taken by the update program.

REVISING OR DELETING A MASTER RECORD

Figure 3.25 shows the relationship when the transaction key is equal to the master key. This condition occurs when a transaction that affects an existing master record has been read by the program. A transaction type of **revise record** or **delete record** would be appropriate in this situation.

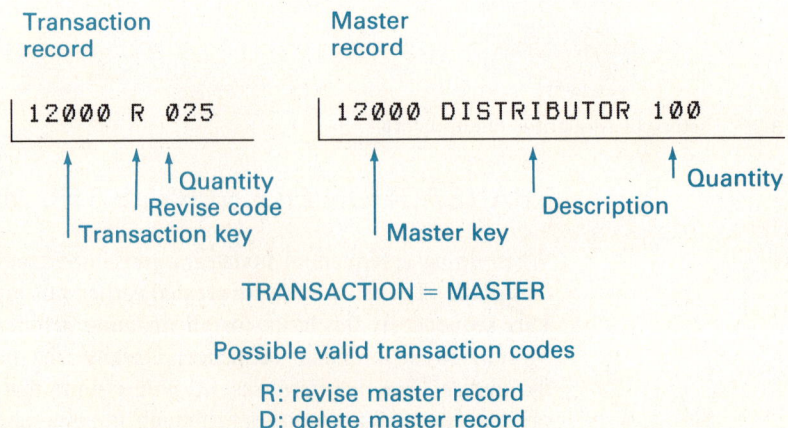

FIGURE 3.25   Transaction key equals master key

When an equal transaction is found, the program would next examine the type of transaction. If it was other than a revise or delete, an error message would be issued and the next transaction read from the input file. Providing the transaction is valid, the program would then proceed to take the appropriate action.

ADDING A NEW RECORD TO THE MASTER

Figure 3.26 shows a second relationship where, in this case, the transaction key is less than the master key. When this condition occurs, the only valid transaction type is the new record, or **add record,** which is to be added to the master. A new record is added to the master by writing the data from the transaction onto the updated master file. The current master record is held in its input area for possible future updating from a subsequent transaction.

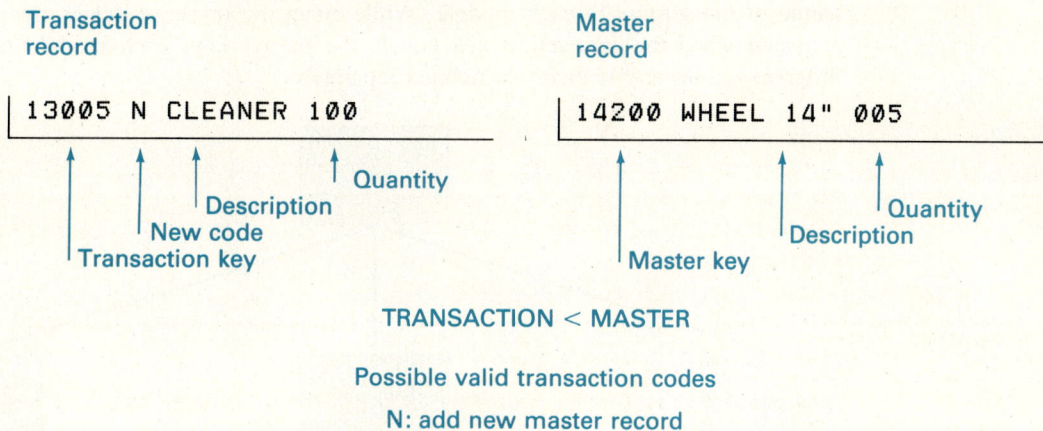

Transaction
record

Master
record

```
13005 N CLEANER 100            14200 WHEEL 14" 005
```

Quantity   Quantity

Description   Description

New code

Transaction key   Master key

TRANSACTION < MASTER

Possible valid transaction codes

N: add new master record

FIGURE 3.26   Transaction key is less than the master key

NO UPDATING OR UPDATING IS COMPLETED

The last type of relationship between the transaction and the master is the greater than relation. When the transaction key is greater than the master key, as shown in Figure 3.27, this can mean one of two things. First, it can indicate that the current master record requires no updating and can thus be written directly to the updated master with no changes necessary. This situation will happen frequently in applications where there is a low frequency of activity against the master.

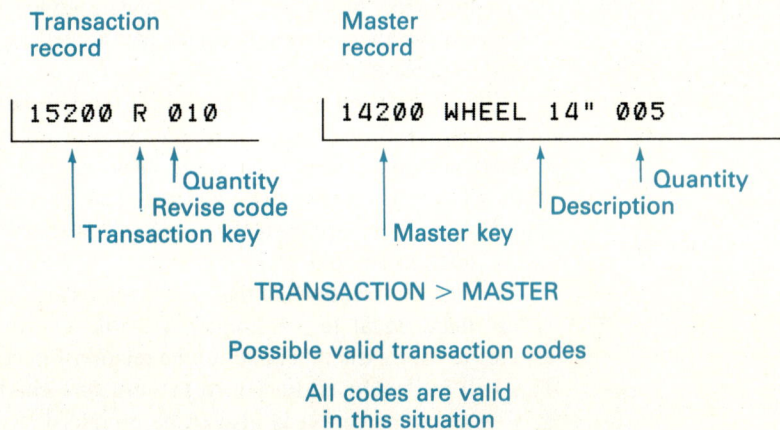

Transaction
record

Master
record

```
15200 R 010            14200 WHEEL 14" 005
```

Quantity   Quantity

Revise code   Description

Transaction key   Master key

TRANSACTION > MASTER

Possible valid transaction codes

All codes are valid
in this situation

FIGURE 3.27   Transaction key is greater than the master key

The second situation, when the transaction is greater than the master, occurs when the master record has been updated by one or more transactions, but now a transaction has been read for the next master record. In this case, the current master has received all the updating it is going to get, and so it is now time to write it on the updated master.

A BASIC STRUCTURE CHART FOR UPDATING

Figure 3.28 shows the top level of a structure chart for an updating program. Although this is just a skeleton of the final chart for a complete update, this version represents the fundamental requirements of an updating program. Much of the detail at the lower levels will depend on the specific requirements of the program.

In this chart, processing is divided into four components rather than the three discussed in the preceding material. The reason for using four modules hinges on the nature of the activity in each module. While either the revise or delete module can be activated when the transaction key equals the master key, each module takes quite different actions and is therefore defined separately.

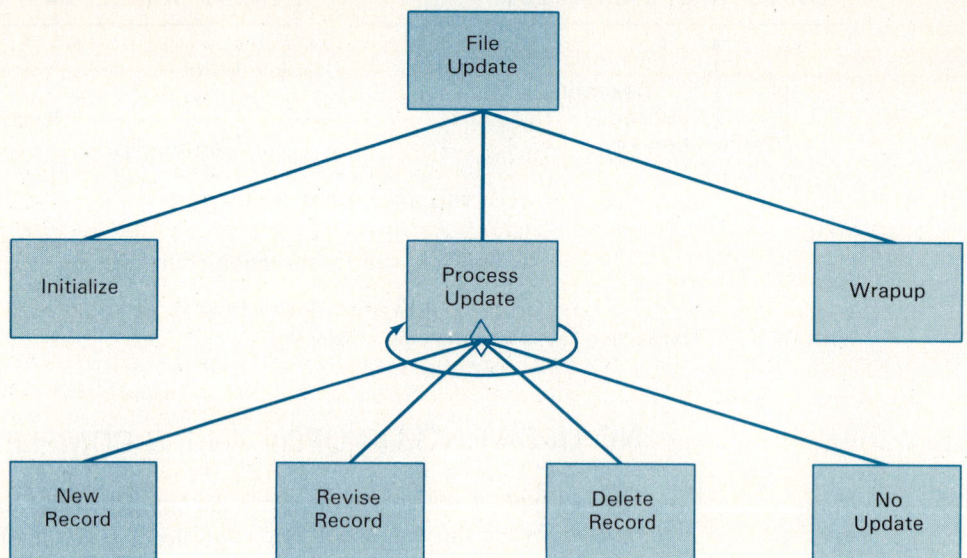

FIGURE 3.28   Basic structure chart for sequential file updating

INVENTORY MASTER UPDATE: AN APPLICATION

PROGRAM SPECIFICATIONS

This application builds on the file update concepts presented on the previous pages. We are to use the inventory master file created earlier and process a file of transaction records against this master.

The specifications in Figure 3.29 outline the processing to be done for each type of transaction. As we know, there are three basic categories of transactions in a sequential update, and this is true of this application. One variation here is that there are two types of revise transactions, codes 2 and 3. Code 2 is used when items are being added to stock to replenish the supplies, whereas code 3 is used when items are taken out of stock to be sold.

Further instructions in the specifications are given for processing when a transaction is less than, equal to, or greater than the existing master record. These instructions also relate the transaction codes to the relationship between the master and the transaction. This will be developed further in the structure chart and pseudo code.

An activity report is also to be produced by this program. This report shows all the activity generated by the transactions, the transaction itself, and any errors that

PROGRAMMING SPECIFICATIONS
PROGRAM NAME: Inventory Master Update   PROGRAM ID: UPDATE3
PREPARED BY: Diane Quest   DATE: May 7, 1986

Program Description:

This program reads a file of transactions and updates the inventory master file. Both files are in sequence on item number. The program will apply transactions to add new records, revise existing records, and delete records from the master. An activity report is printed as a by-product of the update.

Input File(s):

Transaction file

Inventory master file

Output File(s):

Updated inventory master file

Inventory activity report

Program Requirements:

1. Read the inventory master file and update it with records from the transaction file.
2. For each transaction record with an item number less than the master, process an add (code 1). All other codes are invalid. To add a new record to the master, move the data from the transaction to the updated master area and write an updated master record. Write a line on the activity report and then read a new transaction and continue processing.
3. For each transaction that has an item equal to the master item number, check for a revise (code 2 or 3) or a delete (code 4). Process each of these codes as follows. Other codes are invalid here.
   a) Code 2—Add to stock. If a stock quantity is present in the transaction, add its amount to the stock quantity field in the master record. The other fields (description, unit cost, reorder quantity, and stock location) may be present in the transaction. For each field present, replace the equivalent field in the master with the new data from the transaction.
   b) Code 3—Remove from stock. If a stock quantity is present in the transaction, subtract its amount from the stock quantity field in the master record. As for a code 2, other fields present in the transaction replace existing data in the master.
   c) After processing a code 2 or 3, do not write the updated master as there could be more than one transaction against a master record. Write an activity report line for the transaction and then read another transaction for processing.
   d) Code 4—Delete a master record. To delete a master record, issue a read for the next master input record without writing the master to be deleted. However, a line must be printed on the activity report showing the record deleted.
4. When a transaction contains an item number that is greater than the master item, there is either no updating for this master or updating has been completed. Write the current master on the updated master file and read a new master record. Do not read another transaction at this time, and do not write an activity report line.
5. Each transaction must appear on the activity report with an indication of the processing done or an error message if the transaction could not be processed. Master records do not appear on the activity report.
6. When an end of file is reached on either the transaction or master file, move high values to the key field (item number) so that records on the other file will continue to be processed. When both files contain high values, this indicates that all updating is completed, so the totals can be printed and the files closed.
7. At the end of the activity report, print totals for the following:
   a) Total number of transaction records.
   b) Total number of master records.
   c) Total number of updated master records.

FIGURE 3.29 Program specifications for the inventory update

may have been detected during processing. Master records are not printed by this program, just the activity against the master.

When end of file is reached on either of the input files, it indicates that this file has completed processing. For example, if the transaction file is finished first, then we know that no more transactions need to be processed; however, there may still be records on the old master that need to be transferred to the updated master. By moving high values to the transaction's item number field, the transaction will always compare high to the master, thus causing the master record to be written directly on the updated master.

Conversely, if the master reaches end of file first, then high values are moved to the master item number. Now all transactions will compare low to the master, which means the transaction must be a new record to be added to the updated master; otherwise, the transaction is an error.

Finally, the activity report shows a count of transactions, old master records, and updated master records. These counts appear as a summary at the end of the report.

INPUT/OUTPUT DESIGN

The program requires four different files for its operation. First, of course, are the transaction (Figure 3.30) and master (Figure 3.31) files, which have already been discussed in this chapter. The master file is created earlier, but the transaction file is defined in more detail here than in our previous discussion.

INPUT/OUTPUT RECORD DEFINITION				
File: Transactions Record Length: 40 Sequence: Item No.	File Type: Disk Blocking Factor: 10 Access Method: Sequential			
COLUMNS	FIELD	TYPE	LENGTH	DECIMALS
Codes 1, 2, and 3				
1–5	Item no.	N	5	
6	Transaction code 1—New record 2—Add to stock 3—Subtract	N	1	
7–21	* Description	A/N	15	
22–26	* Unit cost	N	5	2
27–29	* Stock quantity	N	3	
30–32	* Reorder quantity	N	3	
33–36	* Stock location			
	Row	N	2	
	Shelf	N	2	
37–40	Unused		2	
* Optional fields on codes 2 and 3.				
Code 4—Delete				
1–5	Item no.	N	5	
6	Transaction code	N	1	
7–40	Unused			

FIGURE 3.30   Transaction file definition

INPUT/OUTPUT RECORD DEFINITION				
File: Inventory Master Record Length: 45 Sequence: Item No.	File Type: Disk Blocking Factor: 20 Access Method: Sequential			
COLUMNS	FIELD	TYPE	LENGTH	DECIMALS
1–5	Item no.	N	5	
6–20	Description	A/N	15	
21–25	Unit cost	N	5	2
26–28	Stock quantity	N	3	
29–31	Reorder quantity	N	3	
32–35	Stock location			
	Row	N	2	
	Shelf	N	2	
36–43	Last activity date	A/N	8	
44–45	Unused		2	

FIGURE 3.31   Inventory master file definition

Most notable in the transaction file is the fact that there are different record formats used, depending on the transaction type. In this application the differences are minor, but some applications will have a wide variety of transaction types. Another consideration about the transaction file is the presence of the transaction code in column 6. This causes all fields to be shifted one column to the right relative to their position in the master file. This will not cause any problem, providing we define the record description entries accordingly in the program.

The third file is the updated master (Figure 3.32). This file has an identical format to the master file, except that it is an output file that will receive all updated master records. When designing and coding an update program, it is essential that the updated master contain the same fields, record length, and blocking factor as the old master file. The reason for this precaution is that the updated master becomes the master file on the next update cycle. Remember the grandfather, father, and son concept?

The fourth file is the activity report shown in Figure 3.33.

INPUT/OUTPUT RECORD DEFINITION				
File: Updated Inventory Master Record Length: 45 Sequence: Item No.	File Type: Disk Blocking Factor: 20 Access Method: Sequential			
COLUMNS	FIELD	TYPE	LENGTH	DECIMALS
1–5	Item no.	N	5	
6–20	Description	A/N	15	
21–25	Unit cost	N	5	2
26–28	Stock quantity	N	3	
29–31	Reorder quantity	N	3	
32–35	Stock location			
	Row	N	2	
	Shelf	N	2	
36–43	Last activity date	A/N	8	
44–45	Unused		2	

FIGURE 3.32   Updated inventory master file

```
     0          1          2          3          4          5          6          7          8          9
     1234567890123456789012345678901234567890123456789012345678901234567890123456789012345

              INVENTORY MASTER ACTIVITY REPORT

     ITEM   DESCRIPTION        UNIT COST  STOCK   REORDER   LOCATION    MESSAGES

     XXXXX  X-------------X    ZZ9.99     ---9     ZZ9       99 99

     XXXXX  X-------------X    ZZ9.99     ---9     ZZ9       99 99       TRANSACTION OUT OF SEQUENCE
                                                                        MASTER OUT OF SEQUENCE
                                                                        NEW MASTER RECORD CREATED
                                                                        MASTER UPDATED
                                                                        NO MASTER FOUND
                                                                        MASTER DELETED
                                                                        INVALID TRANSACTION CODE




     TOTAL TRANSACTIONS:       ZZZ9

     TOTAL MASTER RECORDS:     ZZZ9

     UPDATED MASTER RECORDS:   ZZZ9
```

FIGURE 3.33   Inventory master update activity report layout

STRUCTURE CHART

Top-down design for the inventory update program is based on the structure-chart skeleton used to introduce the concepts of sequential file updating. First, let's consider the expansion of the initialization box. Because this module gets things started, it will open the files and print the headings for the report. Also keep in mind that update logic requires a record from the transaction file and a record from the master file so that their key fields can be compared. Reading these initial records is an important part of the initialization module. Here is the expansion:

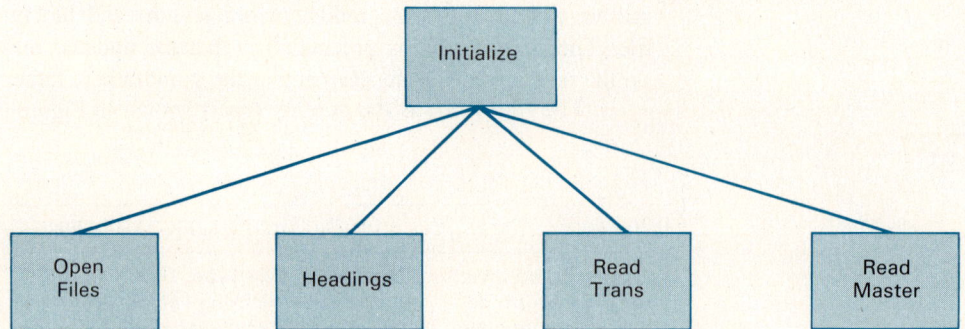

```
                          ┌────────────┐
                          │ Initialize │
                          └────────────┘
           ┌──────────────────┼──────────────────┐
   ┌────────────┐     ┌────────────┐     ┌────────────┐     ┌────────────┐
   │    Open    │     │  Headings  │     │    Read    │     │    Read    │
   │   Files    │     │            │     │   Trans    │     │   Master   │
   └────────────┘     └────────────┘     └────────────┘     └────────────┘
```

The next steps to developing the solution are to expand each of the four components of the process update module. These components are (1) add a new record, (2) revise the master, (3) delete a master record, and (4) no update to process.

First, the module to add a new record to the master is expanded. When a new record is added to the updated master, the data come from a transaction. It is first necessary to move these data to the updated master record area and then write the new record on the new master file. This transaction must then supply a line for the report and, finally, a new transaction needs to be read. Here is the result:

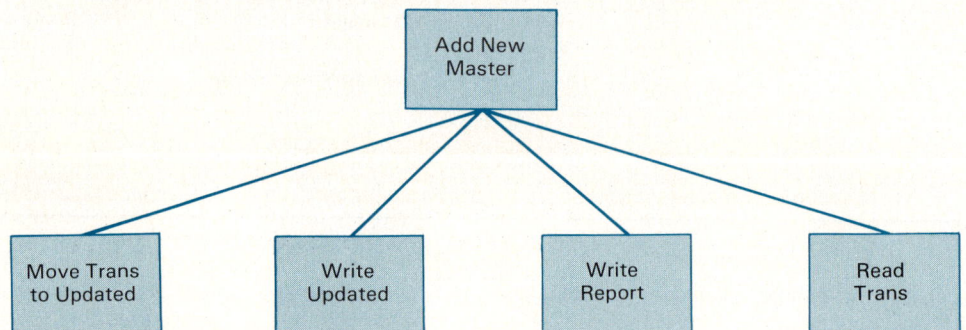

```
                          ┌────────────┐
                          │  Add New   │
                          │   Master   │
                          └────────────┘
           ┌──────────────────┼──────────────────┐
   ┌────────────┐     ┌────────────┐     ┌────────────┐     ┌────────────┐
   │ Move Trans │     │   Write    │     │   Write    │     │    Read    │
   │ to Updated │     │  Updated   │     │   Report   │     │   Trans    │
   └────────────┘     └────────────┘     └────────────┘     └────────────┘
```

To revise a master module requires that the master record be updated with the data contained in the transaction. Either a code 2 or 3 can cause a revision, but the only significant difference is whether to add or subtract the stock quantity. This consideration is too detailed to include in the structure chart. After processing, the transaction record requires that a report line be printed and then the next transaction read.

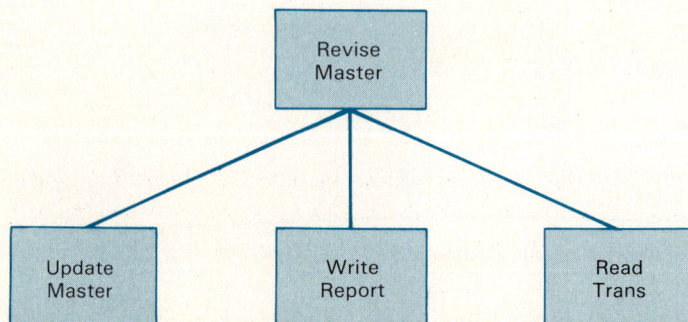

```
                          ┌────────────┐
                          │   Revise   │
                          │   Master   │
                          └────────────┘
                ┌──────────────┼──────────────┐
         ┌────────────┐  ┌────────────┐  ┌────────────┐
         │   Update   │  │   Write    │  │    Read    │
         │   Master   │  │   Report   │  │   Trans    │
         └────────────┘  └────────────┘  └────────────┘
```

To delete a master record, the program must simply read another master without writing the current record on the updated master. The transaction that activates the delete goes on the report like all other transactions, and a new transaction must also be read before leaving the module.

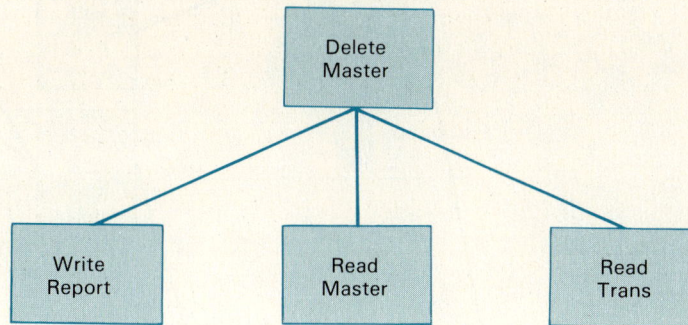

The last module of this group of four under the process loop is the module required when a master does not need updating. Remember that a master may have been updated previously, but now all transactions have been processed against the master. This module writes the current master record on the updated master and reads a new master record.

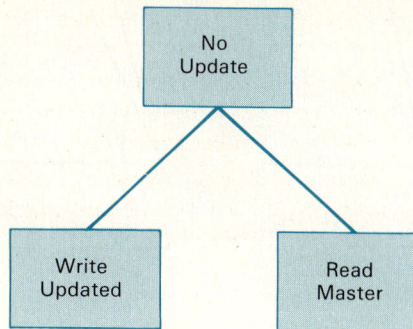

That covers the processing of transactions and master records. The last module in this program is the wrap-up module, which does all the end-of-file activities, including printing the summary totals and closing the files. Although we have previously closed files as part of the mainline, this activity is sometimes included in a wrap-up module, as has been done in this case.

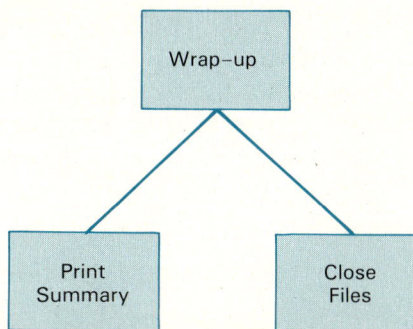

All these modules are combined into the total solution shown in Figure 3.34. Note the addition of module numbers, the indication for looping, and modules that are used in more than one location in the structure chart.

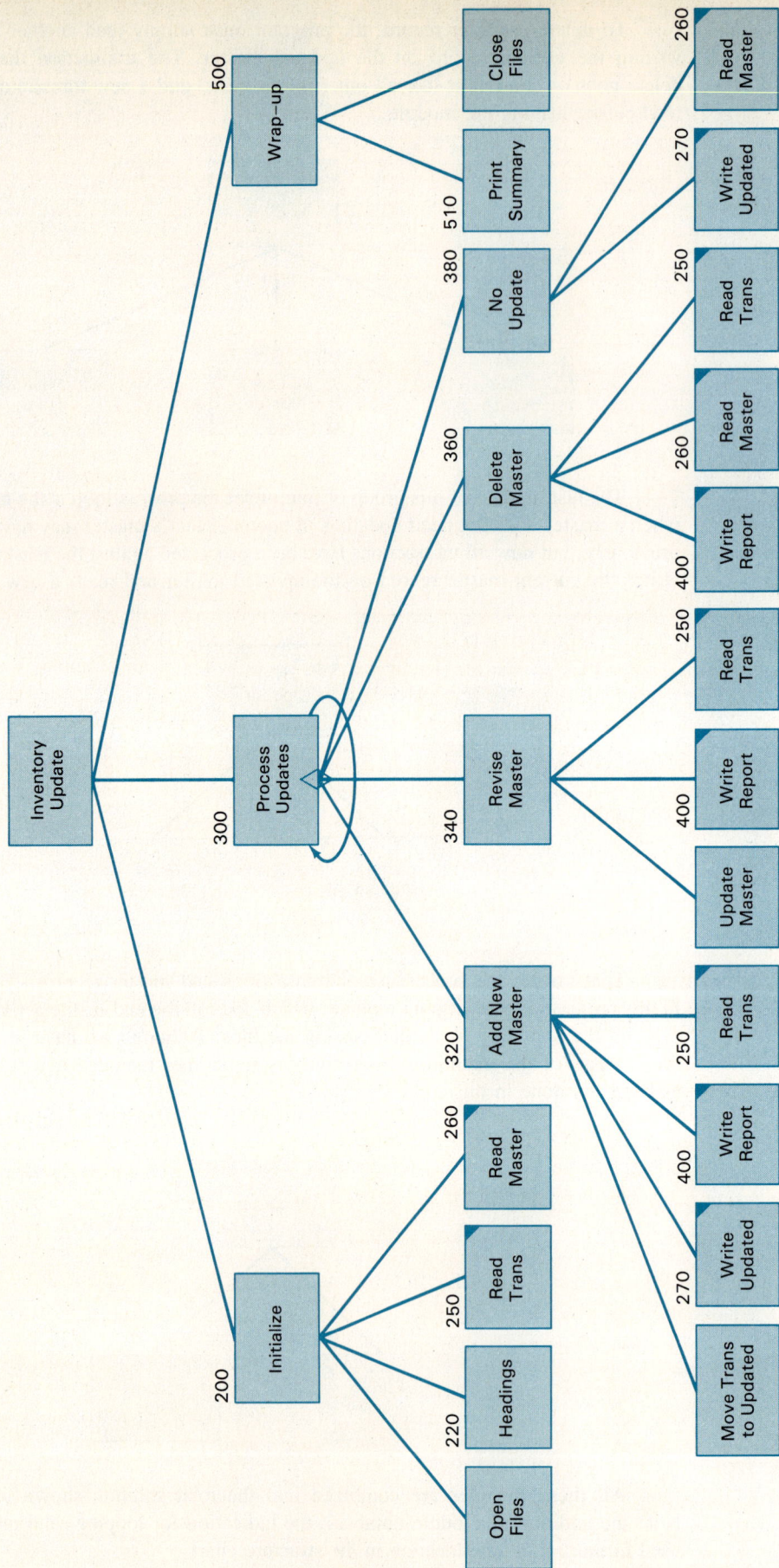

FIGURE 3.34 Structure chart for the inventory update

PSEUDO CODE

Figure 3.35 shows the pseudo code and structured flowchart for the inventory update. There are a few significant points to consider with the pseudo code, beginning with the read modules for the transaction and master files. In each of these modules, an end-of-file test is made in the usual manner. But, in addition to setting an end of file flag (each file has its own flag), high values is moved to the item number of the file. By using high values, the records in the opposite file will continue to be processed normally until end of file is reached there also. For example, if end of file is reached first in the transaction file, then the transaction item number will be set to high values as follows.

```
1. Read Trans
      at end move 'yes' to EOF-Trans
              move high-values to trans-item.
```

Now, whenever the transaction is compared to the master, it will be greater than the master, causing the master to be processed with no updates. Each master record is then written to the updated master with no activity recorded on the record. End of file in the master is handled in a similar fashion.

Both the transaction and master files are sequence checked to ensure the integrity of the update. Sequence checking occurs in the same way as for other sequential files. It is important to note that each file requires its own previous item field because it is not possible to check sequence on two files by using a single previous item number.

The paragraph 300-Process implements the logic to check the relationship between the transaction and master files. This decision is only alluded to in the structure chart, but it is developed fully as follows in the pseudo code:

```
300-Process
      1. If trans-item < mast-item
              Perform 320-New-Master
          Else
              If trans-item = mast-item
                      Perform 310-Equal
              Else
                      Perform 380-No-Update
              EndIf
          EndIf
```

At this point in the logic development, it is important to clearly implement the three relationships represented between the two files. Because the equal condition can require several actions depending on the transaction code, an additional paragraph 310-Equal is developed as follows to determine the type of processing required:

```
1. If add or subtract (codes 2 or 3)
      Perform 340-Revise-Master
  Else
      If delete (code 4)
              Perform 360-Delete-Master
      Else
              Move error message to line
              Perform 400-Print-Line
      EndIf
  EndIf
```

```
                              PSEUDO CODE
PROGRAM NAME: Update Inventory Master        PROGRAM ID: UPDATE3
PREPARED BY: Jonathan Youngman    DATE: May 6    PAGE 1 of 3
```

<u>100-Mainline</u>

    1. Perform 200-Initialize.
    2. Perform 300-Process
           Until EOF-Trans and EOF-Mast.
    3. Perform 500-Wrap-up.
    4. Stop Run

<u>200-Initialize</u>

    1. Open input and output files.
    2. Get current date.
    3. Perform 220-Headings.
    4. Perform 250-Read-Trans.
    5. Perform 260-Read-Mast.

<u>220-Headings</u>

    1. Print heading 1.
    2. Print heading 2.
    3. Set line count to 4.

<u>250-Read-Trans</u>

    1. Read Trans
        at end move 'yes' to EOF-Trans
            move high-values to trans-item.
    2. If Not EOF-Trans
       Add 1 to total transactions
       If Not in sequence
           Move error message to line
           Perform 400-Print-Line
       Else
           Store trans-item in previous-trans-item
       EndIf
      EndIf

<u>260-Read-Mast</u>

    1. Read Mast
        at end move 'yes' to EOF-Mast
            move high-values to mast-item.
    2. If Not EOF-Mast
       Add 1 to total master
       If Not in sequence
           Move error message to line
           Perform 400-Print-Line
       Else
           Store mast-item in previous-mast-item
       EndIf
      EndIf

<u>270-Write-Updated</u>

    1. Add 1 to total updated.
    2. Write updated master.

<u>300-Process</u>

    1. If trans-item < mast-item
       Perform 320-New-Master
      Else
       If trans-item = mast-item
           Perform 310-Equal
       Else
           Perform 380-No-Update
       EndIf
      EndIf

<u>310-Equal</u>

    1. If add or subtract (codes 2 or 3)
       Perform 340-Revise-Master

FIGURE 3.35(a)   Pseudo code for the inventory update

```
            Else
                If delete (code 4)
                        Perform 360-Delete-Master
                Else
                        Move error message to line
                        Perform 400-Print-Line
                EndIf
            EndIf
```

320-New-Master

```
    1. If not a new record (not code 1)
            Move error message to line
        Else
            Move new message to line
            Move trans to updated master and to line
            Perform 270-Write-Updated
        EndIf
    2. Perform 400-Print-Line.
    3. Perform 250-Read-Trans.
```

340-Revise-Master

```
    1. Move transaction to detail line.
    2. If add (code 2) and stock quantity numeric
            add stock quantity to master
        EndIF
    3. If subtract (code 3) and stock quantity numeric
            subtract stock quantity from master
        EndIf
    4. If transaction contains a description
            move description to master
        EndIf
    5. If transaction contains a unit cost
            move unit cost to master
        EndIf
    6. If transaction contains a reorder quantity
            move reorder quantity to master
        EndIf
    7. If transaction contains a location
             move location to master
        EndIf
    8. Move activity date to master.
    9. Move updated message to line.
   10. Perform 400-Print-Line.
   11. Perform 250-Read-Trans.
```

360-Delete-Master

```
    1. Move master to detail line.
    2. Move deleted message to line.
    3. Perform 400-Print-Line.
    4. Perform 260-Read-Mast.
    5. Perform 250-Read-Trans.
```

380-No-Update

```
    1. Move master to updated master.
    2. Perform 270-Write-Updated.
    3. Perform 260-Read-Mast.
```

400-Print-Line

```
    1. Write detail line
            after advancing 2 lines.
    2. Add 2 to line count.
    3. If line count exceeds page limit
            Perform 220-Headings
        EndIf
    4. Move spaces to detail line.
```

FIGURE 3.35(b)

Programming for Sequential Files

```
                              PSEUDO CODE
PROGRAM NAME: Update Inventory Master          PROGRAM ID: UPDATE3
PREPARED BY: Jonathan Youngman      DATE: May 6    PAGE 3 of 3

500-Wrap-Up
     1. Perform 510-Print-Summary.
     2. Close files.
510-Print-Summary
     1. Print total transactions.
     2. Print total master records.
     3. Print total updated master records.
```

FIGURE 3.35(c)

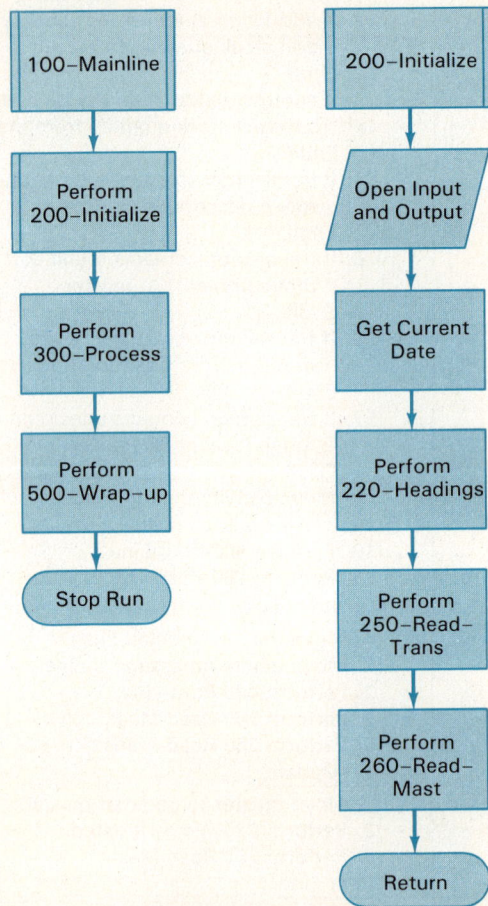

FIGURE 3.35(d) Structured flowchart
for the inventory update

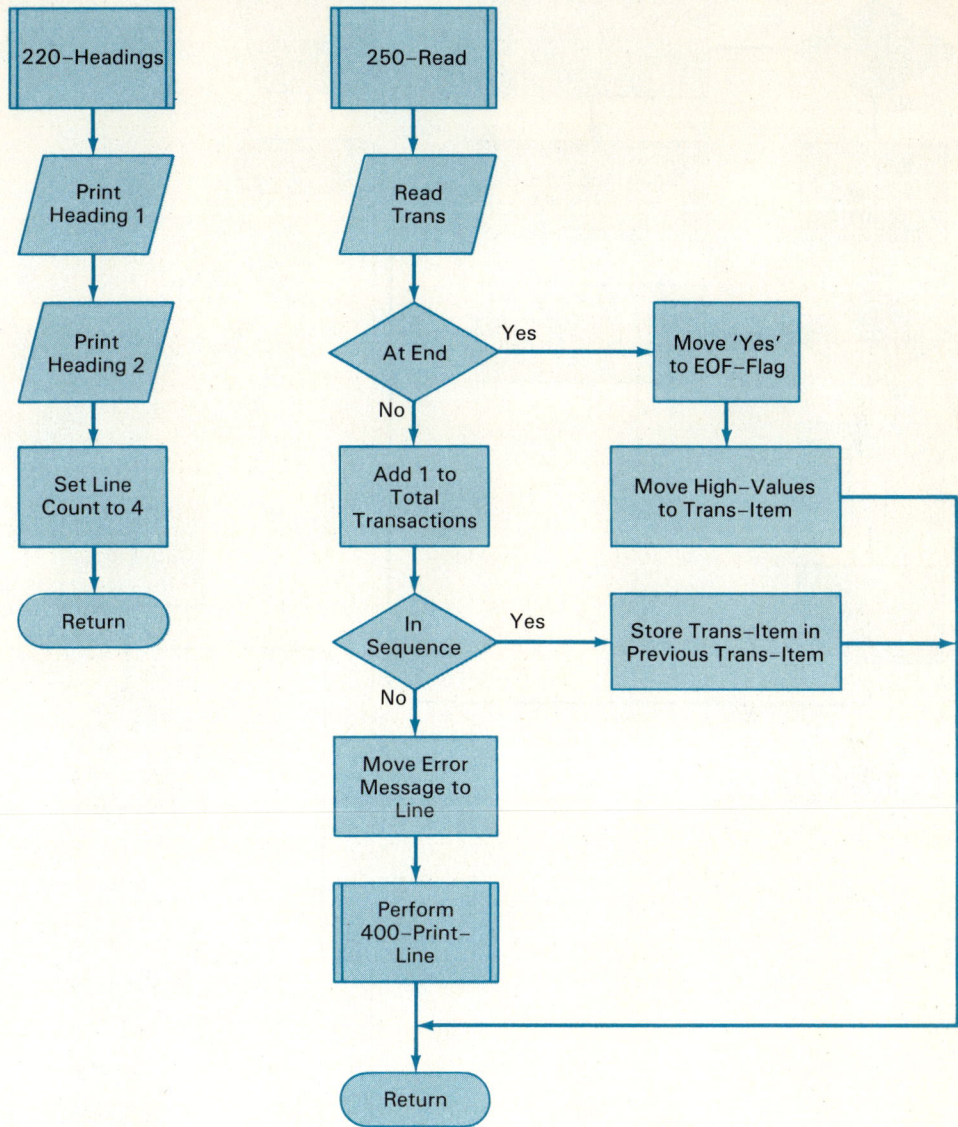

FIGURE 3.35(e)

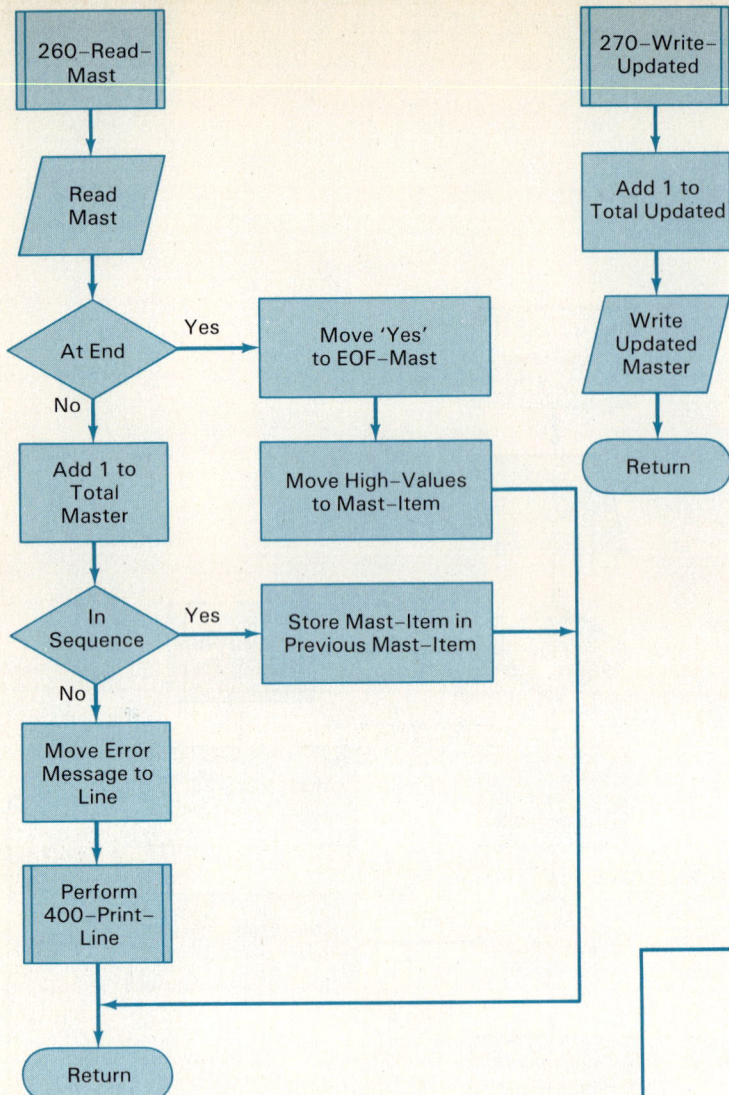

FIGURE 3.15(f)

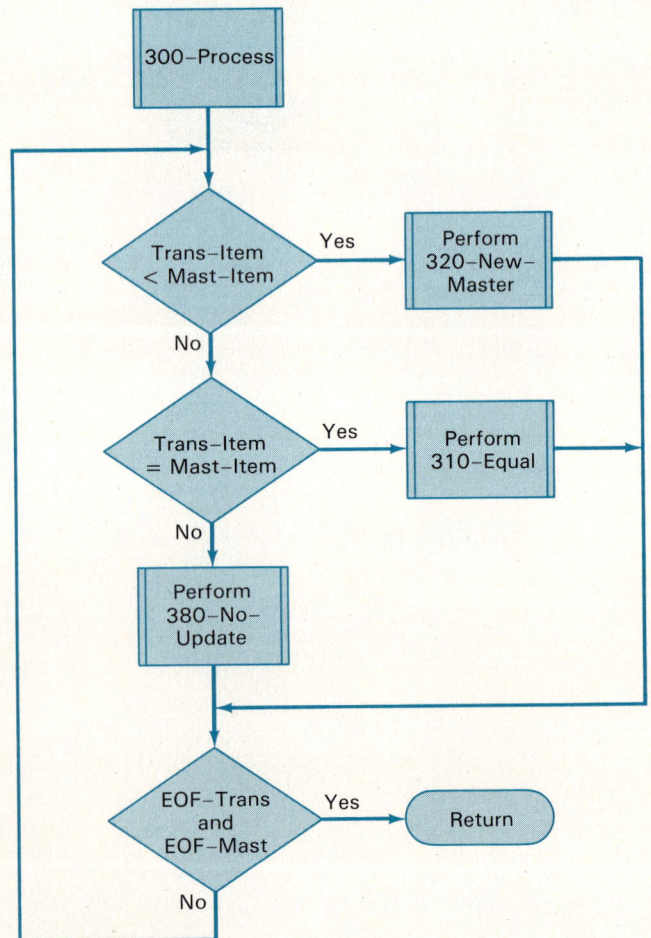

FIGURE 3.35(g)

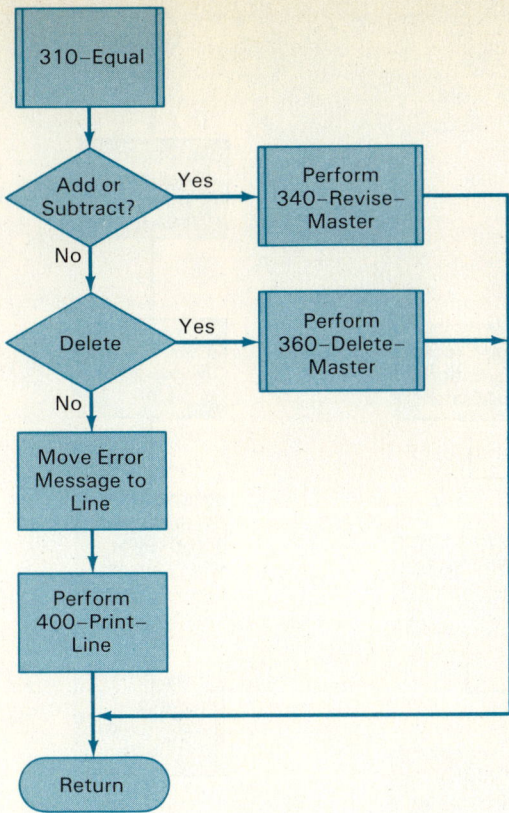

FIGURE 3.35(h)

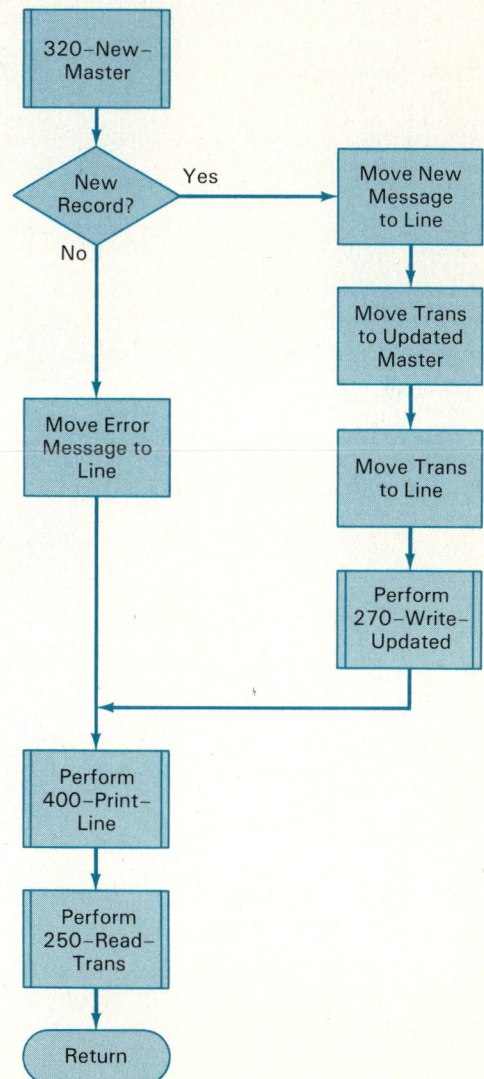

FIGURE 3.35(i)

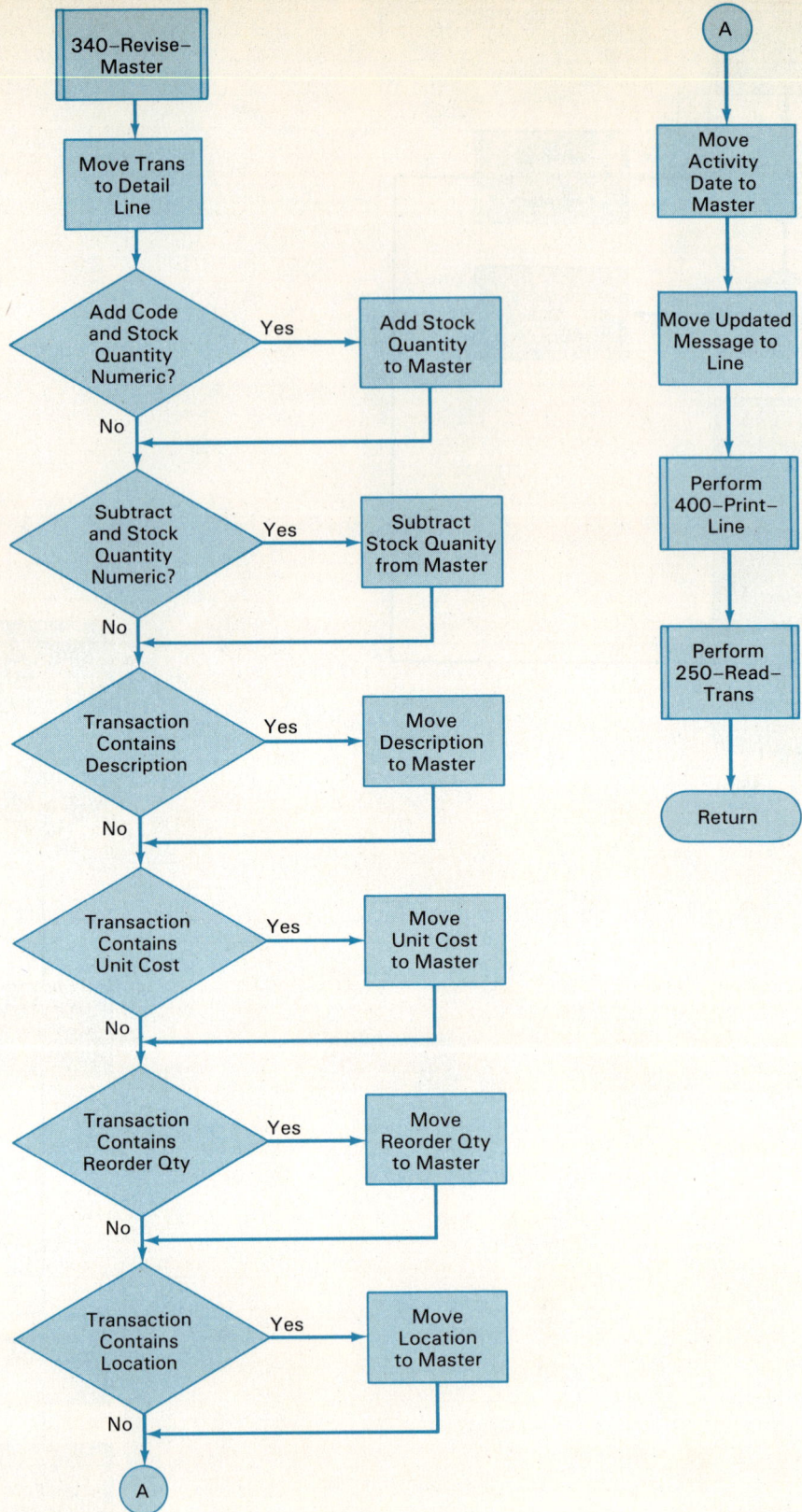

FIGURE 3.35(j)

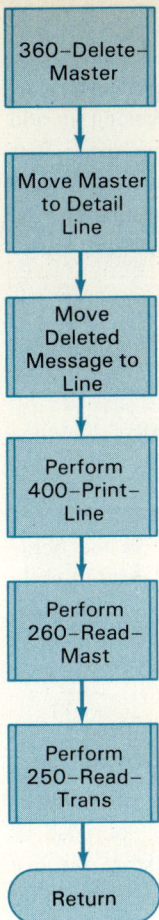

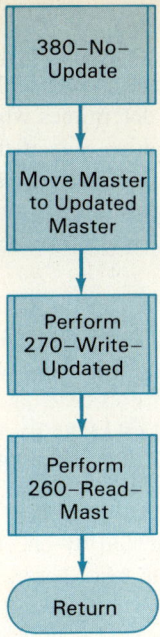

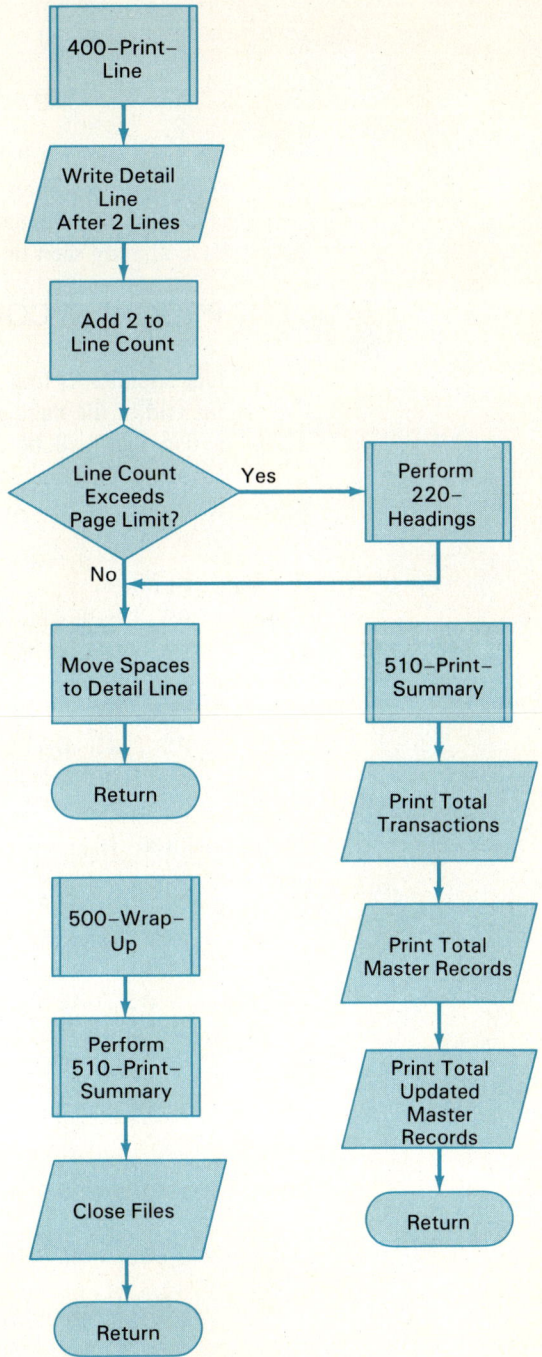

FIGURE 3.35(k)

FIGURE 3.35(l)

Codes 2 and 3 are handled by 340-Revise-Master and a code 4 is processed in the paragraph 360-Delete-Master. All other codes that might arrive at this module are errors and are handled by the module 400-Print-Line, which prints error messages.

The paragraph 340-Revise-Master first determines whether it is processing an add or subtract quantity and then the activity is done only if the quantity is numeric. It is possible that a transaction is used to update a field other than the stock quantity, and either a code 2 or 3 can be used for this purpose. Other than adding or subtracting, the stock quantity, if it is present, represents the only difference between the processing of codes 2 and 3.

Next the module must examine each field in the transaction to determine if it is to be updated. The approach taken is to check whether the file contains any data. For example, the description field is handled in the following way:

```
4. If transaction contains a description
      move description to master
   EndIf
```

An alphanumeric field check can be implemented by checking for spaces in the field. A numeric field can be checked by a numeric test. The remainder of the pseudo code is fairly self-explanatory and is developed on the basis of the structure chart that we have already seen in this chapter.

PROGRAM CODING

Our attention is first given to the WORKING-STORAGE entries for this program where the end of file flags are defined. Both input files, the transaction and the master, require a flag that will be set when end of file is reached on the file. For the purpose of sequence checking, each input file will require a previous item field to store the last item number read from the file. These fields are also defined in the entries in Figure 3.36.

```
01   FLAGS.
     05   EOF-TRANS-FLAG            PIC X(03)   VALUE 'NO'.
          88   END-OF-FILE-TRANS                VALUE 'YES'.
     05   EOF-MAST-FLAG             PIC X(03)   VALUE 'NO'.
          88   END-OF-FILE-MAST                 VALUE 'YES'.
     05   WS-DATE                   PIC X(08).
     05   PREVIOUS-TRN-ITEM         PIC X(05)   VALUE SPACES.
     05   PREVIOUS-MST-ITEM         PIC X(05)   VALUE SPACES.
```

FIGURE 3.36   Flags and previous item fields

```
01   MESSAGES.
     05   MESSAGE-01                PIC X(30)
                   VALUE 'TRANSACTION OUT OF SEQUENCE'.
     05   MESSAGE-02                PIC X(30)
                   VALUE 'MASTER OUT OF SEQUENCE'.
     05   MESSAGE-03                PIC X(30)
                   VALUE 'NEW MASTER RECORD CREATED'.
     05   MESSAGE-04                PIC X(30)
                   VALUE 'MASTER UPDATED'.
     05   MESSAGE-05                PIC X(30)
                   VALUE 'NO MASTER FOUND'.
     05   MESSAGE-06                PIC X(30)
                   VALUE 'MASTER DELETED'.
     05   MESSAGE-07                PIC X(30)
                   VALUE 'INVALID TRANSACTION CODE'.
```

FIGURE 3.37   Program messages

Another important need is to define the error messages that are to be printed in the report. Also included are messages that tell the user when an activity such as creating a new master or updating an existing master is done. These messages were generally identified in the pseudo code, but we need to be very specific in the program. Figure 3.37 shows these messages and their related message number to be used by the program. These messages will be defined in WORKING-STORAGE.

That covers the less obvious entries in the DATA DIVISION. Of course, there are many more. Each file requires an FD entry and a detail record description entry. This program defines the records for each input and output file, including the report, in WORKING-STORAGE, where they will be read into or written from as the file requires. Totals are also required for the final report summary and so is a record entry for the summary lines. One record will be adequate for the summary, although there are three different summary lines to be printed.

Now let's examine the coding for each paragraph in the PROCEDURE DIVISION in Figure 3.38.

```
        IDENTIFICATION DIVISION.
*
 PROGRAM-ID.
     UPDATE3.
*AUTHOR.
*    JOHNATHAN YOUNGMAN.
*INSTALLATION.
*    SALES UNLIMITED CORP.
*DATE-WRITTEN.
*    MAY 10.
*DATE-COMPILED.
*
*SECURITY.
*    NONE.
*
 ENVIRONMENT DIVISION.
*
 CONFIGURATION SECTION.
 SOURCE-COMPUTER.
     IBM-370.
 OBJECT-COMPUTER.
     IBM-370.
 SPECIAL-NAMES.
     C01 IS TO-TOP-OF-PAGE.
*
 INPUT-OUTPUT SECTION.
*
 FILE-CONTROL.
     SELECT TRANSACTIONS ASSIGN TO UT-S-FILET.
     SELECT MASTER       ASSIGN TO UT-S-FILEM.
     SELECT UPDATED      ASSIGN TO UT-S-FILEU.
     SELECT LISTING      ASSIGN TO UR-S-PRINTER.
*
 DATA DIVISION.
*
 FILE SECTION.
*
 FD  TRANSACTIONS
     BLOCK  CONTAINS 10 RECORDS
     RECORD CONTAINS 40 CHARACTERS
     LABEL RECORDS ARE STANDARD
     DATA RECORD IS TRN-REC.
 01  TRN-REC.
     05  FILLER                  PIC X(40).
*
 FD  MASTER
     BLOCK  CONTAINS 20 RECORDS
     RECORD CONTAINS 45 CHARACTERS
     LABEL RECORDS ARE STANDARD
     DATA RECORD IS MAST-REC.
 01  MST-REC.
     05  FILLER                  PIC X(40).
```

FIGURE 3.38(a) Inventory master update program

```
     *
     FD  UPDATED
         BLOCK  CONTAINS 20 RECORDS
         RECORD CONTAINS 45 CHARACTERS
         LABEL RECORDS ARE STANDARD
         DATA RECORD IS UPD-REC.
     01  UPD-REC.
         05  FILLER                    PIC X(40).
     *
     FD  LISTING
         RECORD CONTAINS 133 CHARACTERS
         LABEL RECORDS ARE OMITTED
         DATA RECORD IS PRINT-REC.
     01  PRINT-REC.
         05  PRINT-LINE                PIC X(133).
     *
     WORKING-STORAGE SECTION.
     *
     01  FLAGS.
         05  EOF-TRANS-FLAG            PIC X(03)    VALUE 'NO'.
             88  END-OF-FILE-TRANS                  VALUE 'YES'.
         05  EOF-MAST-FLAG             PIC X(03)    VALUE 'NO'.
             88  END-OF-FILE-MAST                   VALUE 'YES'.
         05  WS-DATE                   PIC X(08).
         05  PREVIOUS-TRN-ITEM         PIC X(05)    VALUE SPACES.
         05  PREVIOUS-MST-ITEM         PIC X(05)    VALUE SPACES.
     *
     01  TOTALS.
         05  LINE-COUNT                PIC 9(02)    VALUE ZERO.
         05  TOTAL-TRANS               PIC 9(04)    VALUE ZERO.
         05  TOTAL-MASTER              PIC 9(04)    VALUE ZERO.
         05  TOTAL-UPDATED             PIC 9(04)    VALUE ZERO.
     *
     01  MESSAGES.
         05  MESSAGE-01                PIC X(30)
                 VALUE 'TRANSACTION OUT OF SEQUENCE'.
         05  MESSAGE-02                PIC X(30)
                 VALUE 'MASTER OUT OF SEQUENCE'.
         05  MESSAGE-03                PIC X(30)
                 VALUE 'NEW MASTER RECORD CREATED'.
         05  MESSAGE-04                PIC X(30)
                 VALUE 'MASTER UPDATED'.
         05  MESSAGE-05                PIC X(30)
                 VALUE 'NO MASTER FOUND'.
         05  MESSAGE-06                PIC X(30)
                 VALUE 'MASTER DELETED'.
         05  MESSAGE-07                PIC X(30)
                 VALUE 'INVALID TRANSACTION CODE'.
     *
     01  WS-TRN-REC.
         05  TRN-ITEM                  PIC X(05).
         05  TRN-CODE                  PIC X.
             88 NEW-REC    VALUE '1'.
             88 ADD-QTY    VALUE '2'.
             88 SUBT-QTY   VALUE '3'.
             88 DELETE-REC VALUE '4'.
         05  TRN-DESC                  PIC X(15).
         05  TRN-UNIT-COST             PIC 9(03)V99.
         05  TRN-STOCK-QTY             PIC 9(03).
         05  TRN-REORDER-QTY           PIC 9(03).
         05  TRN-LOCATION              PIC 9(04).
         05  FILLER                    PIC X(04).
     *
     01  WS-MST-REC.
         05  MST-ITEM                  PIC X(05).
         05  MST-DESC                  PIC X(15).
         05  MST-UNIT-COST             PIC 9(03)V99.
         05  MST-STOCK-QTY             PIC 9(03).
         05  MST-REORDER-QTY           PIC 9(03).
         05  MST-LOCATION              PIC X(04).
         05  MST-LAST-DATE             PIC X(08).
         05  FILLER                    PIC X(02).
```

FIGURE 3.38(b)

```
01  WS-UPD-REC.
    05  UPD-ITEM                    PIC X(05).
    05  UPD-DESC                    PIC X(15).
    05  UPD-UNIT-COST               PIC 9(03)V99.
    05  UPD-STOCK-QTY               PIC 9(03).
    05  UPD-REORDER-QTY             PIC 9(03).
    05  UPD-LOCATION                PIC X(04).
    05  UPD-LAST-DATE               PIC X(08).
    05  FILLER                      PIC X(02).
*
01  HEAD-1.
    05  FILLER                      PIC X(20)    VALUE SPACES.
    05  FILLER                      PIC X(36)
                VALUE 'INVENTORY MASTER ACTIVITY REPORT'.

01  HEAD-2.
    05  FILLER                      PIC X(37)
            VALUE ' ITEM      DESCRIPTION     UNIT COST'.
    05  FILLER                      PIC X(40)
            VALUE 'STOCK   REORDER   LOCATION     MESSAGES'.
*
01  DETAIL-LINE.
    05  FILLER                      PIC X(01)    VALUE SPACES.
    05  DTL-ITEM                    PIC X(05).
    05  FILLER                      PIC X(03)    VALUE SPACES.
    05  DTL-DESC                    PIC X(15).
    05  FILLER                      PIC X(03)    VALUE SPACES.
    05  DTL-UNIT-COST               PIC ZZ9.99.
    05  FILLER                      PIC X(04)    VALUE SPACES.
    05  DTL-STOCK-QTY               PIC ---9.
    05  FILLER                      PIC X(06)    VALUE SPACES.
    05  DTL-REORDER-QTY             PIC ZZ9.
    05  FILLER                      PIC X(06)    VALUE SPACES.
    05  DTL-LOCATION                PIC 99B99.
    05  FILLER                      PIC X(07)    VALUE SPACES.
    05  DTL-MESSAGE                 PIC X(30).
*
01  SUMMARY-LINE.
    05  SUMMARY-MESSAGE             PIC X(28)    VALUE SPACES.
    05  SUMMARY-AMT                 PIC Z(03)9.
*
PROCEDURE DIVISION.
*
100-MAINLINE.
    PERFORM 200-INITIALIZE.
    PERFORM 300-PROCESS
        UNTIL END-OF-FILE-TRANS
            AND END-OF-FILE-MAST.
    PERFORM 500-WRAP-UP.
    STOP RUN.
*
200-INITIALIZE.
    OPEN INPUT   TRANSACTIONS
                 MASTER
          OUTPUT UPDATED
                 LISTING.
    MOVE CURRENT-DATE TO WS-DATE.
    MOVE SPACES       TO DETAIL-LINE.
    PERFORM 220-HEADINGS.
    PERFORM 250-READ-TRANS.
    PERFORM 260-READ-MAST.
*
220-HEADINGS.
    WRITE PRINT-REC FROM HEAD-1
        AFTER ADVANCING TO-TOP-OF-PAGE.
    WRITE PRINT-REC FROM HEAD-2
        AFTER ADVANCING 2 LINES.
    MOVE SPACES TO PRINT-REC.
    WRITE PRINT-REC
        AFTER ADVANCING 1 LINE.
    MOVE 4 TO LINE-COUNT.
```

FIGURE 3.38(c)

```
*
  250-READ-TRANS.
       READ TRANSACTIONS INTO WS-TRN-REC
            AT END MOVE 'YES'        TO EOF-TRANS-FLAG
                 MOVE HIGH-VALUES TO TRN-ITEM.
       IF NOT END-OF-FILE-TRANS
            ADD 1 TO TOTAL-TRANS
            IF TRN-ITEM IS NOT GREATER THAN PREVIOUS-TRN-ITEM
                 MOVE MESSAGE-01        TO DTL-MESSAGE
                 PERFORM 400-PRINT-LINE
            ELSE
                 MOVE TRN-ITEM          TO PREVIOUS-TRN-ITEM.
*
  260-READ-MAST.
       READ MASTER INTO WS-MST-REC
            AT END MOVE 'YES'        TO EOF-MAST-FLAG
                 MOVE HIGH-VALUES TO MST-ITEM.
       IF NOT END-OF-FILE-MAST
            ADD 1 TO TOTAL-MASTER
            IF MST-ITEM IS NOT GREATER THAN PREVIOUS-MST-ITEM
                 MOVE MESSAGE-02        TO DTL-MESSAGE
                 PERFORM 400-PRINT-LINE
            ELSE
                 MOVE MST-ITEM          TO PREVIOUS-MST-ITEM.
*
  270-WRITE-UPDATED.
       ADD 1                        TO TOTAL-UPDATED.
       WRITE UPD-REC
            FROM WS-UPD-REC.
*
  300-PROCESS.
       IF TRN-ITEM < MST-ITEM
            PERFORM 320-NEW-MASTER
       ELSE
            IF TRN-ITEM = MST-ITEM
                 PERFORM 310-EQUAL
            ELSE
                 PERFORM 380-NO-UPDATE.
*
  310-EQUAL.
       IF ADD-QTY OR SUBT-QTY
            PERFORM 340-REVISE-MASTER
       ELSE
            IF DELETE-REC
                 PERFORM 360-DELETE-MASTER
            ELSE
                 MOVE MESSAGE-07        TO DTL-MESSAGE
                 MOVE TRN-ITEM          TO DTL-ITEM
                 PERFORM 400-PRINT-LINE.
*
  320-NEW-MASTER.
       IF NOT NEW-REC
            MOVE MESSAGE-07         TO DTL-MESSAGE
            MOVE TRN-ITEM           TO DTL-ITEM
       ELSE
            MOVE MESSAGE-03         TO DTL-MESSAGE
            MOVE TRN-ITEM           TO UPD-ITEM          DTL-ITEM
            MOVE TRN-DESC           TO UPD-DESC          DTL-DESC
            MOVE TRN-UNIT-COST      TO UPD-UNIT-COST     DTL-UNIT-COST
            MOVE TRN-STOCK-QTY      TO UPD-STOCK-QTY     DTL-STOCK-QTY
            MOVE TRN-REORDER-QTY    TO UPD-REORDER-QTY   DTL-REORDER-QTY
            MOVE TRN-LOCATION       TO UPD-LOCATION      DTL-LOCATION
            MOVE WS-DATE            TO UPD-LAST-DATE
            PERFORM 270-WRITE-UPDATED.
       PERFORM 400-PRINT-LINE.
       PERFORM 250-READ-TRANS.
*
  340-REVISE-MASTER.
       MOVE TRN-ITEM                        TO DTL-ITEM.
       IF  ADD-QTY AND TRN-STOCK-QTY NUMERIC
            MOVE TRN-STOCK-QTY      TO DTL-STOCK-QTY
            ADD TRN-STOCK-QTY       TO MST-STOCK-QTY.
       IF  SUBT-QTY AND TRN-STOCK-QTY NUMERIC
            MOVE TRN-STOCK-QTY      TO DTL-STOCK-QTY
            SUBTRACT TRN-STOCK-QTY  FROM MST-STOCK-QTY.
```

FIGURE 3.38(d)

```
        IF   TRN-DESC NOT = SPACES
             MOVE TRN-DESC              TO DTL-DESC
             MOVE TRN-DESC              TO MST-DESC.
        IF   TRN-UNIT-COST NUMERIC
             MOVE TRN-UNIT-COST         TO DTL-UNIT-COST
             MOVE TRN-UNIT-COST         TO MST-UNIT-COST.
        IF   TRN-REORDER-QTY NUMERIC
             MOVE TRN-REORDER-QTY       TO DTL-REORDER-QTY
             MOVE TRN-REORDER-QTY       TO MST-REORDER-QTY.
        IF   TRN-LOCATION NOT = SPACES
             MOVE TRN-LOCATION          TO DTL-LOCATION
             MOVE TRN-LOCATION          TO MST-LOCATION.
        MOVE WS-DATE                    TO UPD-LAST-DATE.
        MOVE MESSAGE-04                 TO DTL-MESSAGE.
        PERFORM 400-PRINT-LINE.
        PERFORM 250-READ-TRANS.

   *
    360-DELETE-MASTER.
        MOVE MST-ITEM                   TO DTL-ITEM.
        MOVE MST-DESC                   TO DTL-DESC.
        MOVE MST-UNIT-COST              TO DTL-UNIT-COST.
        MOVE MST-STOCK-QTY              TO DTL-STOCK-QTY.
        MOVE MST-REORDER-QTY            TO DTL-REORDER-QTY.
        MOVE MST-LOCATION               TO DTL-LOCATION.
        MOVE MESSAGE-06                 TO DTL-MESSAGE
        PERFORM 400-PRINT-LINE.
        PERFORM 260-READ-MAST.
        PERFORM 250-READ-TRANS.

   *
    380-NO-UPDATE.
        MOVE WS-MST-REC                 TO WS-UPD-REC.
        PERFORM 270-WRITE-UPDATED.
        PERFORM 260-READ-MAST.

   *
    400-PRINT-LINE.
        WRITE PRINT-REC FROM DETAIL-LINE
             AFTER ADVANCING 2 LINES.
        ADD 2                           TO LINE-COUNT.
        IF LINE-COUNT IS GREATER THAN 35
             PERFORM 220-HEADINGS.
        MOVE SPACES                     TO DETAIL-LINE.

   *
    500-WRAP-UP.
        PERFORM 510-PRINT-SUMMARY.
        CLOSE TRANSACTIONS
             MASTER
             UPDATED
             LISTING.

   *
    510-PRINT-SUMMARY.
        MOVE ' TOTAL TRANSACTIONS:'     TO SUMMARY-MESSAGE.
        MOVE TOTAL-TRANS                TO SUMMARY-AMT.
        WRITE PRINT-REC FROM SUMMARY-LINE
             AFTER ADVANCING 2 LINES.
        MOVE ' TOTAL MASTER RECORDS:'   TO SUMMARY-MESSAGE.
        MOVE TOTAL-MASTER               TO SUMMARY-AMT.
        WRITE PRINT-REC FROM SUMMARY-LINE
             AFTER ADVANCING 2 LINES.
        MOVE ' UPDATED MASTER RECORDS:' TO SUMMARY-MESSAGE.
        MOVE TOTAL-UPDATED              TO SUMMARY-AMT.
        WRITE PRINT-REC FROM SUMMARY-LINE
             AFTER ADVANCING 2 LINES.
```

FIGURE 3.38(e)

100-MAINLINE   This paragraph implements the main or top-level structure of the design documents. Through it, the paragraphs to initialize, process each input record, and wrap up the end of the application are executed. Although this is a simple paragraph, it has overall control of program execution.

200-INITIALIZE   Initialization involves opening the files, printing the headings, and reading the first record from the transaction and master files. Other details are included in this paragraph, such as getting the current date and storing it in WS-DATE. Another need that this paragraph takes care of is to move spaces to the detail line. This step was not identified earlier, and whether it is needed may not be noticed by most programmers until a test run is done.

If spaces are not moved to the detail line and the first record to be printed does not contain all the fields, then unused fields will print with random characters (better known as garbage). So issuing this move in the initialize paragraph ensures that the line is clear of unwanted characters prior to printing the first line.

220-HEADINGS   This paragraph is fairly self-explanatory. It prints the heading lines and sets the line count to 4, showing the number of lines currently printed.

250-READ-TRANS   Clearly, this paragraph reads a record from the transaction file. It also sets EOF-TRANS-FLAG when end of file is reached and moves HIGH-VALUES to the item number. If end of file has not been reached (notice the extra test here that uses the flag), then the record count is increased and the record is checked for sequence.

260-READ-MAST   This paragraph is almost a carbon copy of the previous paragraph that reads a transaction. Often, when writing code, we try to look for modules that are similar in order to combine them into a single module. Here is a case where two modules are quite similar and yet cannot be combined. However, if you took great care when writing the first module, then this one is virtually a duplicate in terms of logic. Only the names have been changed to make it functional.

270-WRITE-UPDATED   All this module does is to write a record on the updated master from WS-UPD-REC and to count the record for the report totals. The reason for making this a paragraph is primarily because writing the updated master is done in two places in the program. A good rule of style is to use only one READ or WRITE statement for a specific sequential file.

300-PROCESS   This paragraph determines the relationship between the transaction item number and the master. If TRN-ITEM is less than MST-ITEM, paragraph 320-NEW-MASTER is performed. If the fields are equal in value, 310-EQUAL is performed. A greater than condition, which is the default if the other two conditions are not true, causes 380-NO-UPDATE to be performed.

One more word about the paragraph 310-EQUAL. It is possible to take the logic in this paragraph and include it in 300-PROCESS. Both of these paragraphs are quite short, so length does not present a problem. But, if they are combined, the result will be two more levels of nested IFs in addition to the current nesting. This much nesting can be difficult to manage, yet by using two paragraphs the difficulty seems to vanish. So the moral is to attempt to keep nesting of IF statements to a minimum and your logic will be easier to write and debug.

310-EQUAL   As we have already suggested, this paragraph is an extension of 300-PROCESS. Now the program checks the transaction type. Three types are valid here, an add or subtract on the stock quantity (handled by paragraph 340-REVISE-MASTER) and a delete (360-DELETE-MASTER). Otherwise, an error message is printed.

320-NEW-MASTER   This paragraph is performed when the transaction item number is less than the master item. Only in this situation is the addition of a new record appropriate. However, the addition to the updated master should only take place if the transaction is a code 1 (NEW-REC). Any other transaction type would be an error. Recognizing this need, the code tests for a new transaction record and if it is not moves an error message to the detail line.

Notice that the line is not printed when there is an error, but will be printed later in the paragraph. If a good transaction was provided, a "new master record created" message is moved to the line. Now all the transaction fields are also moved to the updated master record and to the print line. Then the updated master record is written by performing paragraph 270-WRITE-UPDATED.

After either the error activity or writing the updated master activity has been done, the detail line is printed by performing paragraph 400-PRINT-LINE. This line will either contain an error message or a new record added to the master.

Finally, 250-READ-TRANS is performed to get the next transaction from the file.

340-REVISE-MASTER   This paragraph does all the hard work associated with revising a master record. First, the transaction file's item number is moved to the detail line because this is the only field we can be sure is contained in the record. Next is a series of If statements that examines each field in turn and determines what needs updating. If an add transaction (ADD-QTY) is present and the transaction contains a stock quantity value (TRN-STOCK-QTY), then this amount is added to the master record's stock quantity. Similarly, if the transaction is a subtract (SUBT-QTY) and there is a stock quantity (TRN-STOCK-QTY), then this quantity is subtracted from the master record's stock quantity.

The other fields in the transaction, TRN-DESC, TRN-UNIT-COST, TRN-REORDER-QTY, and TRN-LOCATION, are checked to see if they are present. For TRN-DESC, this is done by testing for SPACES. Anything other than SPACES means that the description is present and will update the master. All other fields are tested for numeric. A numeric field indicates that an amount is present and that field is updated in the master record.

If a field is updated, that field is also moved to the detail line for printing. In this way, only fields that reflect appropriate updating for the master are included on the activity report.

After updating the master record, the date of last activity is also updated in the master. Then an "updated" message is moved to the detail line and the line is printed. Finally, a new transaction is read before leaving the paragraph.

360-DELETE-MASTER   Deleting a master requires only that a new master be read. But we will need to print a line on the activity report to show the deleted record, and so each field from the master is moved to the detail line and printed before the next master is read. A new transaction is also read before leaving this paragraph.

380-NO-UPDATE   This paragraph will be performed either because updating has been completed for a master record or there was no updating in the first place. The current master record (WS-MST-REC) is moved to the updated master record (WS-UPD-REC) and written on the updated master file. Then a new master record is read by 260-READ-MAST.

400-PRINT-LINE   With the exception of headings and the summary, all printing is done by the paragraph. Prior to coming here, the performing module will have moved all necessary data to DETAIL-LINE. So it only remains for this paragraph to print the line, using double spacing, and then check for page overflow.

500-WRAP-UP   The last major activity after end of file has been reached on both the transaction and master files is to print the summary. Paragraph 510 is performed for that purpose, and then all files are closed prior to returning control to 100-MAINLINE, where the program is terminated.

510-PRINT-SUMMARY   The three summary lines are built one at a time and printed from this paragraph. This is the same technique used earlier in the master file create program for printing the summary of activities. Each line is printed double-spaced and containing a message and a total.

PROGRAM TESTING

To test this update program requires that we have both a master file and a transaction file present. The master was created earlier in the chapter and is shown in its current form in Figure 3.39. It is imperative that this master be created with only valid records with all fields in the correct location in the record. Many problems with file updating are a result of incorrectly creating the master file.

Next, a transaction file is needed. This file must be available in the format defined in the program specifications. For an initial test, it is best not to include many error records, but mostly records that test each transaction type (codes 1, 2, 3, and 4) and each relationship between the transaction and master file item numbers. The transaction file is shown in Figure 3.40.

With the transaction and master files in place on disk, the update program may now be compiled and executed. Assuming there are no compile errors, the program will produce two output files. One will be the report shown in Figure 3.41, and the second will be the updated master file in Figure 3.42. To see the updated master, you will need to write a small program to read and display the records. If you are fortunate to have a system that gives you access to files through an editor, then examining the updated master will be quite easy.

Each line of the report should be examined to ensure that it contains the correct information, indicating that the updates were processed as expected. The updated master should also be examined to ensure it contains the correct records and that the right records were revised, new records were added, or old ones were deleted as defined by the transactions.

```
12000DISTRIBUTOR      04598100025120304/28/86
12100WIRE SET         01295050020120404/28/86
12210A/C RELAY        01800005010110104/28/86
12220VALVE            00795000020200504/28/86
12240STEM             00295075030050104/28/86
14200WHEEL 14''       08729005002270104/28/86
15000WHEEL 15''       09598009005270304/28/86
15200POLISH           00335050015320404/28/86
15210RELAY AB         01010015020310104/28/86
15420ANTENNA          01895002010410104/28/86
15640LIGHT KIT        05795012003350104/28/86
```

(Item number, Description, Unit cost, Stock quantity, Reorder quantity, Location, Date of last activity)

FIGURE 3.39 Master file records before updating

```
120002                             025
122103                             002
122204
130051CLEANER         045981000251203
152002RUST INHIBITOR  013500100201301
156403                             3502
```

(Item number, Code, Description, Unit cost, Stock quantity, Reorder quantity, Location)

FIGURE 3.40 Transaction file for testing the update program

```
                 INVENTORY MASTER ACTIVITY REPORT

ITEM   DESCRIPTION        UNIT COST  STOCK   REORDER   LOCATION    MESSAGES

12000                                  25                          MASTER UPDATED

12210                                  -2                          MASTER UPDATED

12220   VALVE               7.95        0      20      20 05       MASTER DELETED

13005   CLEANER            45.98      100      25      12 03       NEW MASTER RECORD CREATED

15200   RUST INHIBITOR     13.50       10      20      13 01       MASTER UPDATED

15640                                   0              35 02       MASTER UPDATED

TOTAL TRANSACTIONS:          6

TOTAL MASTER RECORDS:       11

UPDATED MASTER RECORDS:     11
```

FIGURE 3.41   Update activity report

```
12000DISTRIBUTOR       04598125025120305/09/86
12100WIRE SET          01295050020120404/28/86
12210A/C RELAY         01800003010110105/09/86
12240STEM              00295075030050104/28/86
13005CLEANER           04598100025120305/09/86
14200WHEEL 14"         08729005002270104/28/86
15000WHEEL 15"         09598009005270304/28/86
15200RUST INHIBITOR    01350060020130105/09/86
15210RELAY AB          01010015020310104/28/86
15420ANTENNA           01895002010410104/28/86
15640LIGHT KIT         05795012003350205/09/86
```

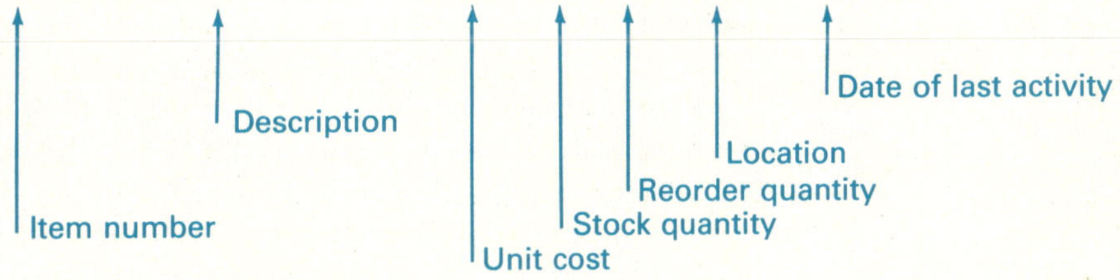

Item number · Description · Unit cost · Stock quantity · Reorder quantity · Location · Date of last activity

FIGURE 3.42   Updated master file

DEBUGGING HINTS

Most problems associated with debugging a sequential file update program can be avoided by careful attention to the program design. By taking the time to understand the program specifications and to develop fully the structure chart and pseudo code, problems will be detected before they are incorporated into the program code. An essential part of this process is the walkthrough, which should be engaged in at each stage of the design. If problems still occur, some of the following items may help to discover the reason for the bug.

1. Each input file must have its own end-of-file flag, which is set independently of other files.

2. Each input file must also have its own sequence check and its own previous item number (or other field) for comparison. Sharing a single field between files will not work.

3. Make sure that transactions do not contain errors or, if they do, that the error is intentional and that the program tests for it. It is best to avoid error transactions for initial testing, but use them in a later test after good data are processing correctly.

4. The logic that tests the relationship between a transaction and a master (such as in 300-PROCESS) is critical to the success of an update program. Make sure this logic is correct. As mentioned earlier, avoiding too many levels of nesting in this logic will minimize coding and logic errors.

5. If the last group of transactions fails to be processed after a master end of file or you lose all master records after the transactions run out, take a look at your end of file activities. Be sure that HIGH-VALUES are moved to the comparison fields of the file that has reached the end. If your system does not support HIGH-VALUES, use 9's in each position of the field and the effect will be the same.

6. If a transaction seems to be processing over and over again, you probably missed a perform to read a transaction record after one has been processed. As a result, this transaction is still in the record description area and will be processed ad infinitum.

SUMMARY

Sequential files usually contain data recorded in a specific sequence. This sequence is determined by the values of one or more sequence fields in each record. A file that contains records with a high activity ratio is best suited for sequential processing.

In COBOL, a sequential file is defined by a SELECT clause in the FILE-CONTROL paragraph of the INPUT-OUTPUT SECTION. The ORGANIZATION and ACCESS MODE clauses define the file here as SEQUENTIAL. Sequential files are typically UR or UT device types.

Next the file is defined in detail in the FILE SECTION of the DATA DIVISION with an FD and record description entry. The FD defines the record length and blocking factor, whether labels are used, and gives the name of the record description entry. The record description, which may be expanded on in WORKING-STORAGE, describes each field in the record and gives the field name, a PICTURE for its format, and a USAGE.

The file is opened for either INPUT or OUTPUT in the PROCEDURE DIVISION. A READ statement is used to access a record from an input file, whereas a WRITE statement places a record on an OUTPUT file. When a file is no longer required by the program, a CLOSE statement is issued.

To create a sequential file source, data are needed, which can come from another file or a document reader or are entered at a terminal keyboard. When creating a file, it is often necessary to validate the data to ensure that a "clean" file is the result. Validation may consist of a field check, range test, limit check, reasonableness check, justification check, valid code check, relationship check, date check, and a check digit check.

When updating a master file, records in both the master and transaction files must be in the same sequence. Transactions generally fall into one of three categories: a new transaction, a revision, and a deletion. Updating begins by comparing the transaction key to the master key. Differing actions are taken depending on the relationship between these keys and the transaction type. When the transaction key equals the master key, two actions are possible. A revision to the current master is one possibility and the deletion of a master record is the other.

When the transaction key is less than the master key, a transaction to add a new record to the master file is the only valid possibility. Finally, when the transaction key is greater than the master key, there is no updating to be done, and so the master record is written to the updated master file and a new master record is read.

Add record   High transaction key
Backup file   Low transaction key
Delete record   Revise record
Equal transaction key   Sequence check
File activity ratio   Sequence field
Grandfather, father, son sequence

REVIEW QUESTIONS

FILL IN THE BLANK

1. Records in a sequential tape or disk file are stored in _____ order within the file.

2. Accounting records may be stored in ascending order on a _____ field such as account number.

3. Records stored in a sequential file are frequently processed in a _____ rather than an interactive environment.

4. The ORGANIZATION entry in the SELECT clause identifies the file as _____ .

5. LABEL RECORDS on a sequential tape or disk file are usually defined as _____ .

6. When creating a sequential master file, it is important to first _____ the data that are the source for the master.

7. When end of file is reached in a sequential file, a _____ is set in the AT END clause of the READ statement.

8. Sequential file updating requires two input files, a _____ file and a _____ file.

9. Updating creates a second master file called the _____ master.

10. The relationship between the _____ in the transaction and master files determines the type of updating that may be done.

11. Revising or deleting the master record may be done when the transaction _____ the master.

12. When the master reaches end of file, the end-of-file flag is set and _____ are moved to the master key field.

13. A master record is deleted by simply _____ the next master.

TRUE/FALSE

14. A file that has two sequence fields will have both a major and a minor sequence.

15. When there is a high file activity ratio, interactive processing will be the most efficient processing method.

16. Tape and disk use a class indicator of UT in the SELECT clause.

17. A disk file with a blocking factor of 10 can, at the programmer's option, be coded in the FD without a BLOCK CONTAINS clause.

18. Detailed record description entries for input files should be coded in the FILE SECTION for efficiency and ease of coding.

19. Data validation and sequence checking are important features of a master file creation program.

20. A sequential file update program requires that all records from the transaction file be read until end of file is reached prior to reading the master file.

21. The frequency of sequential updating is always on a weekly basis.

22. When the transaction key is less than the master key, only a delete transaction may be processed.

MULTIPLE CHOICE

23. Sequential files and batch processing are best used when:
   a. A system does not have enough terminals for the users.
   b. There is a high file activity ratio.
   c. There is a low file activity ratio.
   d. Only disk files are available.

24. The default value for ACCESS MODE in the SELECT clause is:
   a. SEQUENTIAL.   **c.** ISAM.
   b. RANDOM.   **d.** VASM.

25. One of these statements would not be used for the processing of sequential disk or tape files.
   a. OPEN   **d.** DISPLAY
   b. READ   **e.** CLOSE
   c. WRITE

26. When a master file is being created for the first time, what activity would not be a concern of the create program?
   a. Validation of the source data.
   b. Sequence checking of the source data file.
   c. Comparing the transaction key to the master key.
   d. Writing a sequential output file.

27. After two program runs to update a master file have been completed, there are several versions of the master available. Which of the following is not available?
   a. Great-grandfather.   **c.** Father.
   b. Grandfather.   **d.** Son.

28. In question 27, which version of the master will be used for the next update?
   a. Great-grandfather.   **c.** Father.
   b. Grandfather.   **d.** Son.

29. Three basic types of transactions are used for sequential file updating. Which of the following is correct for these types?
   a. New.   **d.** All the above.
   b. Revise.   **e.** None of the above.
   c. Delete.

30. When a new transaction record is to be added to the master file, what must be the relationship between the transaction key and the master key?
   a. Transaction < master.   **c.** Transaction > master.
   b. Transaction = master.   **d.** Any condition is acceptable.

31. If there are remaining master records after the transactions have reached end of file, what action is taken in an update program?
   a. Move high values to the master key.
   b. Move high values to the transaction key.
   c. Close the master file.
   d. All the above.
   e. None of the above.

32. When an update program has two input files and two output files, how many different end-of-file flags will be required in the program?
   a. One   **c.** Three
   b. Two   **d.** Four

1. Using the inventory update program in this chapter, make the following revisions as a program-maintenance exercise. Then create a transaction file for testing your changes and use the updated master for your master file.

   a. If a sequence error occurs on either the transaction or master file, print the error message; then close the files and terminate the program.

   b. Add totals to the report summary to show records added, records deleted, and master records revised.

   c. Include a column in the report for the updated master stock quantity to print when an update occurs to the master record.

2. PART I: The College Credit Union maintains a sequential master file of accounts for its customers. For the first part of this assignment, write a program to create the master file. Use a file of source data you have designed that is in the format of the master file. Validate each record.

   PART II: Prepare a structure chart, write the pseudo code, and write a program to update the master file. Prepare your own test data for this application. The following statements should be considered when writing the program.

   a. A new account is created on the master with a code 1 transaction. All fields in the transaction must be present; otherwise, an error output is generated.

   b. A deposit or withdrawal is made by a transaction supplied to update the account balance in the master file.

   c. Only a code 4 transaction may be used to modify the contents of the master file. Any field, including branch, surname, initials, and balance, may be changed if present in this transaction.

   d. A withdrawal is not permitted to place an account in a negative balance. If this is possible, produce an error and do not process the transaction.

   e. Codes 2 and 3 must contain a branch that compares equal to the master branch field. If the accounts are equal but the branch is not, do not process the transaction but create an error message.

INPUT/OUTPUT RECORD DEFINITION				
File: Account Transactions Record Length: 40 Sequence: Account Number		File Type: Tape Blocking Factor: 20 Access Method: Sequential		
COLUMNS	FIELD	TYPE	LENGTH	DECIMALS
1–5	Account number	N	5	
6–7	Branch	N	2	
8–22	Surname	A/N	15	
23–24	Initials	A/N	2	
25–31	Balance	N	7	2
32–39	Date	N	8	
40	Type of update	N	1	
	1—New account			
	2—Deposit			
	3—Withdrawal			
	4—Revise master			
	5—Close account			

INPUT/OUTPUT RECORD DEFINITION

File: Account Master
Record Length: 40
Sequence: Account Number

File Type: Disk
Blocking Factor: 15
Access Method: Sequential

COLUMNS	FIELD	TYPE	LENGTH	DECIMALS
1–5	Account number	N	5	
6–7	Branch	N	2	
8–22	Surname	A/N	15	
23–24	Initials	A/N	2	
25–31	Balance	N	7	2
32–39	Date of last update	N	8	

```
 Ø         1         2         3         4         5         6         7         8
1234567890123456789012345678901234567890123456789012345678901234567890123456789Ø
```

```
                         COLLEGE CREDIT UNION

ACCOUNT   BRCH   NAME                        BALANCE   DATE      MESSAGES
99999     99     X-------------X  XX         ZZZZ9.99  99/99/99  X------------

99999     99     X-------------X  XX         ZZZZ9.99  99/99/99  X------------

99999     99     X-------------X  XX         ZZZZ9.99  99/99/99  X------------
```

3. A program is required to be run once a month against the credit union master file. This program will apply an interest amount to the balance of each account, providing the account contains a balance. Provide a transaction that permits a variable interest rate and prorate it for a monthly calculation.

4

NONSEQUENTIAL FILE CONCEPTS

A significant disadvantage of sequential files is the need to read through the file from beginning to end, even if only a few records are required for processing. As we discussed previously, files with a high activity ratio will benefit from sequential organization and batch processing. But what about files that have a low activity ratio?

Systems may have a need for files with a low activity ratio, where only a small number of records in the file need to be accessed. For example, an exmployee personnel file may need to be accessed regularly to change an employee's address, basic salary, tax deduction, or department. But these changes occur infrequently for most employees, so at any one time possibly less than 1% of the file will be affected. A low activity such as this will benefit from the use of a nonsequential file organization.

There are basically three types of nonsequential organizations used in COBOL. These are **relative files, indexed sequential access method** (ISAM), and **virtual storage access method** (VSAM). Depending on the computer system, other types of files may be used, but for the most part they will share similar features with these three file types.

RELATIVE FILES

Consider an application where 1000 employee records are to be maintained on a disk file with direct-access capability. For some uses the file needs to be read sequentially, but most of the time only the record affected by the processing needs to be accessed due to a low file activity ratio. Conveniently, these employees each have a unique employee number from 0001 to 1000, which could act as a key. In such a situation a relative file would be an appropriate file organization method to use.

RELATIVE FILE ORGANIZATION

In a relative file, records are stored consecutively as shown in Figure 4.1. Each record in the file has a **key** that identifies the record and permits direct access to the record. The first record in the file has a key of 0001, the second record's key is 0002, and so

Track

0	0001 Employee 1	0002 Employee 2	0003 Employee 3	0004 Employee 4

1	0005 Employee 5	0006 Employee 6	0007 Employee 7	0008 Employee 8

2	0009 Employee 9	0010 Employee 10	0011 Employee 11	0012 Employee 12

3	0013 Employee 13	0014 Employee 14	0015 Employee 15	0016 Employee 16

4	0017 Employee 17	0018 Employee 18	0019 Employee 19	0020 Employee 20

:

n	0997 Employee 997	0998 Employee 998	0999 Employee 999	1000 Employee 1000

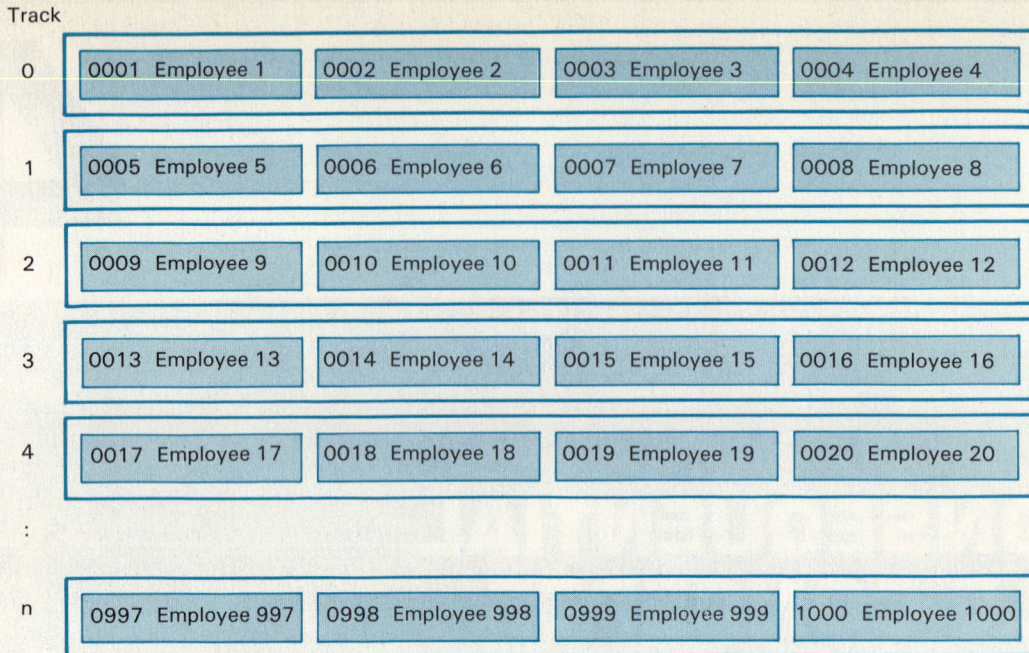

FIGURE 4.1   Relative record organization on disk

on. Record one thousand would have a key of 1000. For random accessing of the file, the program supplies the key, called a relative key, and the record specified is supplied to the program.

In addition to the benefits of the access method, a relative file uses disk space efficiently. Records are stored consecutively from the beginning of the file. Each disk address contains a record, so no space is wasted between records other than what the disk drive needs for its operation. This space efficiency, however, would not apply if some of the keys were not needed. Suppose there were no employees with numbers 0500 to 0549. These 50 records would still occupy space on disk although they are not needed by the application. Thus relative files are most useful in applictions where there are few gaps in the keys.

RELATIVE RECORD ACCESSING

Records in a relative file are accessed directly when the file is used in random mode. Although the term random is used as the access method, it refers to direct access of the record. If a key of 0012 is supplied by the program, the record with that key is read into storage. The record may then be processed, values in it may be changed if necessary, and then the record may be rewritten back into its original location on the disk. The modified record then replaces the original one. A record that has not been changed by the program does not need to be rewritten back to disk because the program works with a copy of the record.

RELATIVE FILE LIMITATIONS

Relative file organization has surfaced predominately on personal computers although it is available as an option in 1985 ANS COBOL for mainframe systems. One clear limitation is the use of consecutive keys and records. This is fine if the application uses consecutive numbers, such as the employee file mentioned already. But many applications do not fit so neatly into this pattern.

What about the organization that stocks parts from several suppliers and must record them under the supplier's number? These numbers may not be consecutive or may have many gaps between groups of numbers. Part numbers can also be alphanumeric, which creates other problems.

Even though the employee file, discussed before, looks foolproof, it could be changed over time. Employees quit and their numbers are discontinued after a reasonable time period. New employees are hired and must be given new numbers. The company expands and so on. Of course, we could suggest that employee numbers get recycled, but this may then cause excessive work to keep track of unused numbers.

So relative files have limited use. Mathematical and other methods are available that let the program find a record without the use of consecutive keys. One such method retains an index of, say, part numbers. When a part number such as 12A34 is supplied, it is looked up in the index, which says that this part is at address 0457. Then it is a simple matter of reading the file using this number as the key.

Another method for finding an address uses a formula. This method works with numeric keys and basically uses a random method of determining the location of each record when it is initially stored on the file. For example, if we know there are 1000 records in the file, then dividing each key by 1000 will give a remainder between 0 and 999, or 1000 different values. This remainder can then be used as the key. The only problem with this method is that more than one record could conceivably get the same remainder. Then more complex methods need to be used to find a different key for one of these records.

Because of the inherent problems with relative files, other methods such as ISAM and VSAM have become more popular and, in their own way, have resolved these problems with keys and storage efficiency.

INDEXED SEQUENTIAL ACCESS METHOD (ISAM)

Many information system applications require the capability to access data from a file either sequentially or directly. Payroll is an excellent example of this type of requirement. On a weekly, biweekly, or monthly basis, a payroll file needs to be accessed sequentially to generate pay checks for each employee in the company. In this situation there is a high file activity ratio, and direct accessing of the records would be inefficient and would not make it easier to generate the checks.

At other times, new employees may be hired by the company and existing employees may require changes to their records, such as a change of address, income level, or the department in which they work. Because these types of changes are usually minor and represent a low file activity ratio, direct accessing is a much more efficient way to access the records.

Most systems today also use terminals for interactive on-line processing. Inquiries may be made to the payroll file to determine the current status of an employee's record. For interactive applications such as this, direct-access capabilities are a must.

One method used for achieving the capability of both sequential and direct access to the same file is the indexed sequential access method (ISAM).

INDEXED FILE ORGANIZATION

Records in an ISAM file are stored sequentially in the prime data area on each track as shown in Figure 4.2. Each record in the file contains a record key that uniquely identifies the record and is used for directly accessing it. But because records are stored in record key sequence, ordered from the lowest key to the highest key in the file, the file can be read sequentially from the beginning to the end of the file.

Unlike relative files, ISAM does not require a record for each key value. If there is no record for a specific key, such as record 0003, it simply does not exist in the file, and the missing record will not occupy any space on the file. Thus gaps in record sequence have no adverse effect on storage efficiency in ISAM.

Track Index	0007 0	0018 1	0030 2	0038 3	0056 4

Track   Prime Data Area

Track				
0	0001 – data –	0002 – data –	0005 – data –	0007 – data –
1	0011 – data –	0012 – data –	0015 – data –	0018 – data –
2	0021 – data –	0023 – data –	0024 – data –	0030 – data –
3	0032 – data –	0034 – data –	0035 – data –	0038 – data –
4	0040 – data –	0048 – data –	0053 – data –	0056 – data –

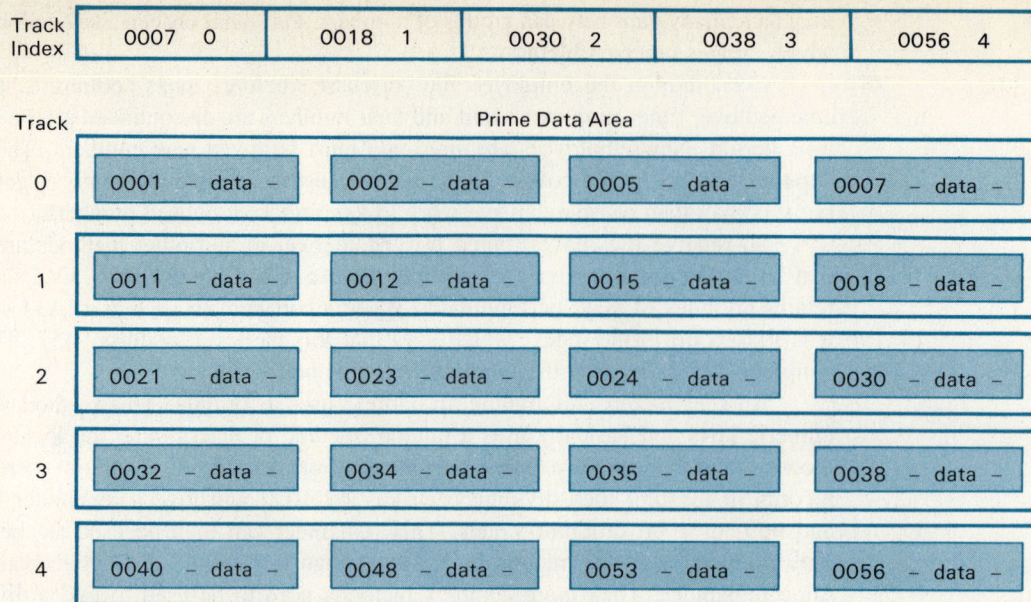

FIGURE 4.2 Indexed sequential organization on disk

TRACK INDEX

For direct accessing of the ISAM file an index is used. The **track index** contains an entry for the highest key of each track and a pointer to the track. The first entry contains the key 0007 and a pointer value of 0 identifying track zero. This means that the highest key on track 0 is 0007 and that any records with this key or lower, such as 0001, 0002, and so on, will also be on track zero.

When a record is to be read directly from the ISAM file, a key is provided by the program. If the key was the value 0034, then a search is first made of the track index for a key that is greater than or equal to the search key. The first key value in the track index that satisfies this requirement is the entry 0038. This entry points to track 3, and so the record for 0034 will be located on track 3 if it exists. In this case the record does exist, and so it will be transferred to the program.

If the key had been the value 0033 (see Figure 4.2), this compares as less than or equal to the track index entry 0038. But this time when a search is made on track 3, no record 0033 is found. This situation is called an *invalid key* and will result in an error indicator being sent to the program, where appropriate action may be taken.

OVERFLOW

When new records need to be added to an ISAM file, the file is organized with one or more overflow tracks in addition to the prime data area tracks. Figure 4.3 shows what happens when a new record with key 0003 is added to the file. First, space is made available on the prime data track and the last record on the track (record 0007) is bumped to an **overflow area,** usually located at the end of the cylinder. Initially, the overflow track is empty, but gradually space is used as new records are added to the file.

To locate the record in overflow, an additional overflow index entry is required for each track in the file. In Figure 4.3, all tracks contain an overflow entry, which is identical to the prime index entry except for the track 0, which contains an overflow record. Because record 0007 is now located on overflow track 5, the overflow index entry contains a key of 0007 and a pointer to track 5. But record 0003 was inserted on track 0, causing record 0005 to be moved to the last position on the track. As a result,

Track Index	0005	0	0018	1	0030	2	0038	3	0056	4
Overflow Entries	0007	5	0018	1	0030	2	0038	3	0056	4

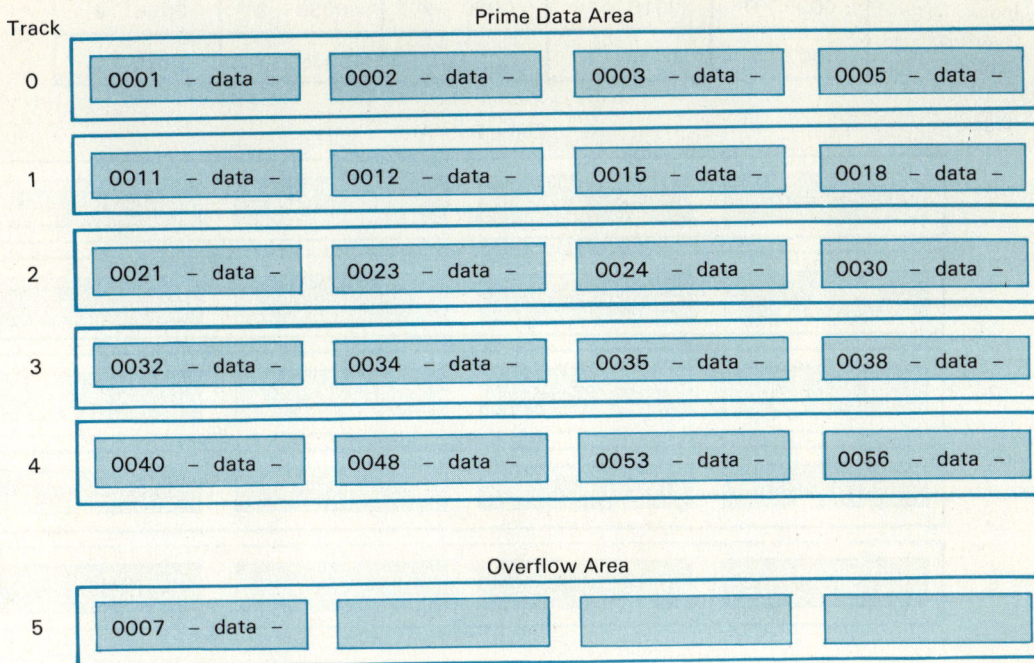

Track

Prime Data Area

Track				
0	0001 – data –	0002 – data –	0003 – data –	0005 – data –
1	0011 – data –	0012 – data –	0015 – data –	0018 – data –
2	0021 – data –	0023 – data –	0024 – data –	0030 – data –
3	0032 – data –	0034 – data –	0035 – data –	0038 – data –
4	0040 – data –	0048 – data –	0053 – data –	0056 – data –

Overflow Area

5	0007 – data –			

FIGURE 4.3 Adding a record to an ISAM file using the overflow area

the track index entry for track 0 is changed to 0005, thus reflecting the current status of the track.

The amount of space allocated for overflow must be determined when an ISAM file is originally created. Part of the analysis task is to determine the amount of activity of new additions that will be added to the file. The percentage of additions will determine the amount of overflow space that should be allocated.

If a file contains 10,000, and 2000 new records are expected to be added to the file, then a minimum of 20% of the file space will need to be set up as overflow tracks. These tracks will initially be empty, but will gradually receive new records as they are added to the file. Eventually, this overflow space will be filled and the ISAM file will need to be reorganized by running a program to copy all the records and overflow records into a new ISAM file. When this procedure is followed, a new ISAM file is created and all the records will be in the prime data area. This activity is an essential part of file maintenance when ISAM files are used.

CYLINDER INDEX

When an ISAM file occupies more than one cylinder of disk space, a **cylinder index** is also used in addition to the track index. The cylinder index is a higher-level index that contains the highest key for each cylinder in the file. Figure 4.4 shows the ISAM file defined previously with additional cylinders of data and a cylinder index for accessing the records in the file.

The cylinder index entry contains a key that identifies the highest key on the cylinder and a cylinder number. To search for a record such as key 0074, the cylinder index is searched for an entry greater than or equal to the key. The search key 0074 is less than the cylinder index entry 0110, which indicates that record 0074 is located somewhere on cylinder 2.

Cylinder Index	0056	1	0110	2	0163	3	0206	4

Cylinder 1

Track Index	0005	0	0018	1	0030	2	0038	3	0056	4
Overflow Entries	0007	5	0018	1	0030	2	0038	3	0056	4

Track

Prime Data Area

Track				
0	0001 – data –	0002 – data –	0003 – data –	0005 – data –
1	0011 – data –	0012 – data –	0015 – data –	0018 – data –
2	0021 – data –	0023 – data –	0024 – data –	0030 – data –
3	0032 – data –	0034 – data –	0035 – data –	0038 – data –
4	0040 – data –	0048 – data –	0053 – data –	0056 – data –

Overflow Area

5	0007 – data –			

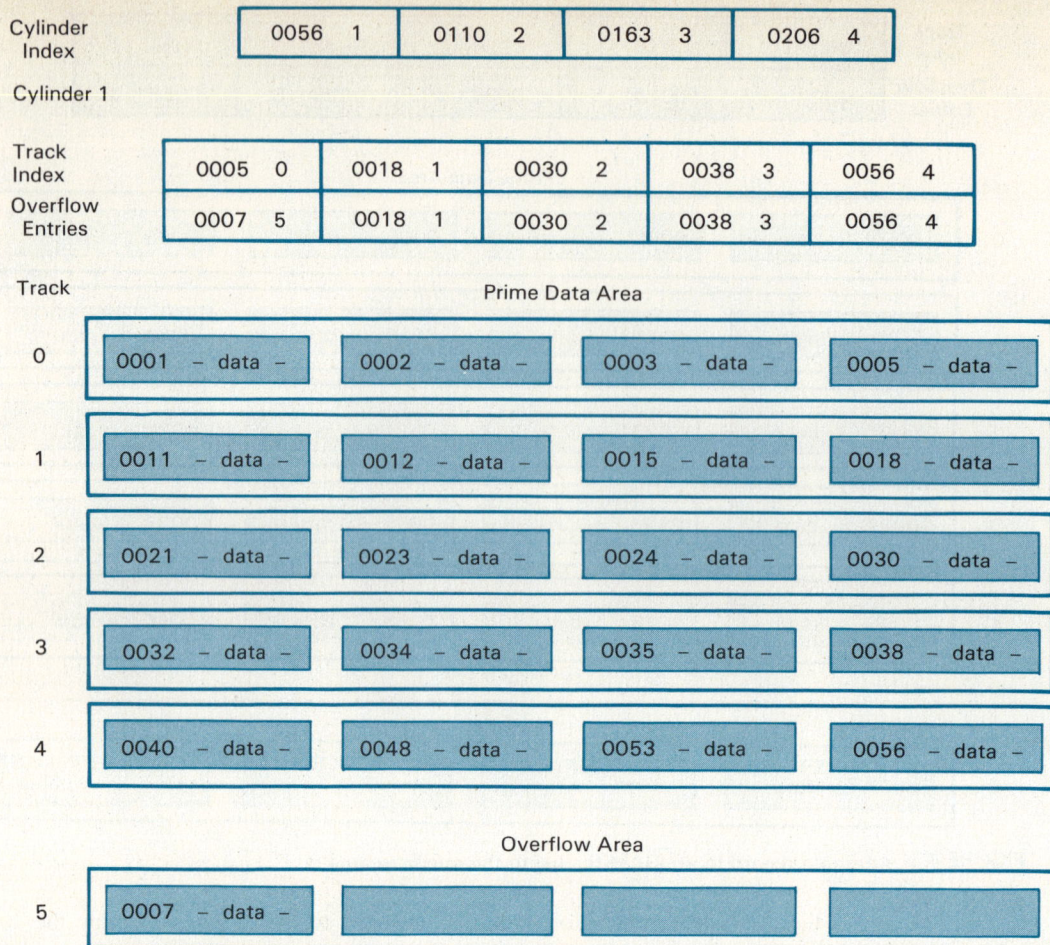

FIGURE 4.4 Using the cylinder index on an ISAM file showing prime data in two of four cylinders

Next the track index on cylinder 2 is searched for an entry greater than or equal to 0074. The second entry (0075) in the track index of cylinder 2 satisfies this requirement, and so the search goes to track 1 of cylinder 2, where the record is found. By searching the cylinder index and then the appropriate track index, the number of searches is reduced and the record is found efficiently even on quite large files.

MASTER INDEX

For some applications, files will be extremely large and require all the space on a disk or even several disks to hold the data. When files become this large an additional index, the **master index,** may be used for improved efficiency. The master index permits the use of several cylinder indexes so that search time is reduced. Figure 4.5 shows the organization of an ISAM file when a master index is used in addition to cylinder and track indexes.

LIMITATIONS OF AN ISAM FILE

While ISAM provides an effective means for accessing records either sequentially or directly, it does not do so as efficiently as a relative file. Yet it is a reasonably efficient access method. Another benefit of ISAM is that keys do not need to exist without gaps

Cylinder 2

Track Index	0067	0	0075	1	0087	5	0097	3	0110	4
Overflow Entries	0068	5	0075	1	0087	2	0098	5	0110	4

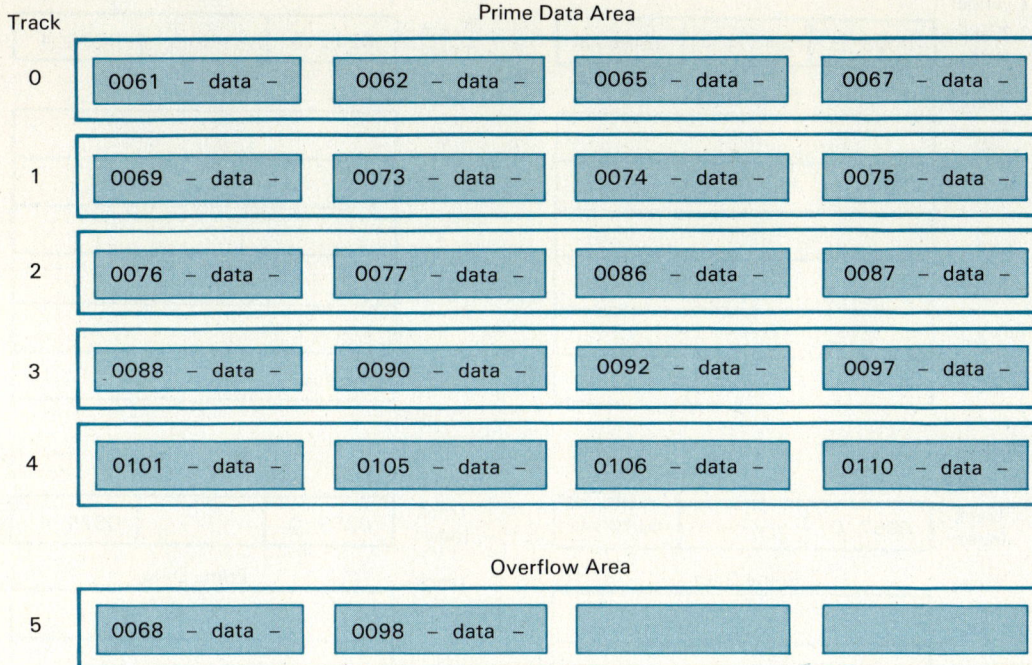

Track   Prime Data Area

0	0061 – data –	0062 – data –	0065 – data –	0067 – data –
1	0069 – data –	0073 – data –	0074 – data –	0075 – data –
2	0076 – data –	0077 – data –	0086 – data –	0087 – data –
3	0088 – data –	0090 – data –	0092 – data –	0097 – data –
4	0101 – data –	0105 – data –	0106 – data –	0110 – data –

Overflow Area

5	0068 – data –	0098 – data –		

FIGURE 4.4 (*Continued*)

between them and thus do not waste space. It might then seem that ISAM is the ideal form of storage and its use should be encouraged.

Where problems occur with ISAM is when records need to be added to the file and the overflow area must be used. First, the overflow area is totally wasted space until records are added to the file. Then, when records are added, the indexes become more complex due to the overflow pointers that are needed. Searching now becomes less efficient and it takes longer to find a record. As more records are added, the less efficient the searches become until it is necessary to reorganize the file. This process temporarily eliminates the overflow by moving these records back into the prime data areas, but as new records are again added to the file, the cycle continues.

Because of this reduction in efficiency as records are added and the need for regular reorganization of the ISAM file, a new, more effective system of file organization has been developed. VSAM is a system that has effectively resolved the problems inherent in ISAM and has become a widely used replacement.

VIRTUAL STORAGE ACCESS METHOD (VSAM)

To address the problems of speed, access methods, and file maintenance, the virtual storage access method (VSAM) was introduced on many mainframe systems. VSAM gives the ability to access records either directly or sequentially like ISAM or randomly

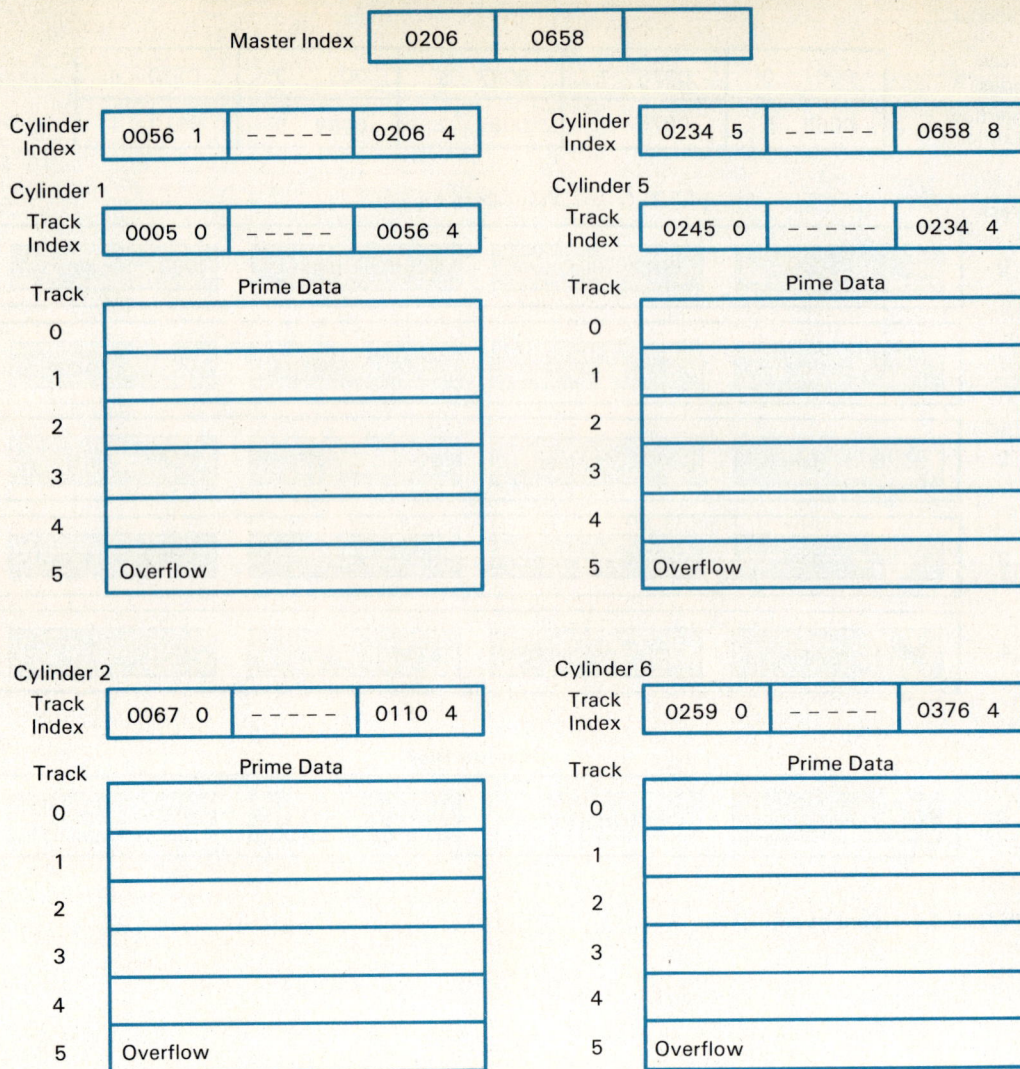

FIGURE 4.5 Using a master index on an ISAM file

like a relative file. It is a faster access method than ISAM because of its unique design, which also practically eliminates the need for periodic file maintenance. Another advantage of VSAM is its **device independence,** which permits data storage on any type of direct-access storage device without the need for special consideration in the program.

VSAM DATA SETS

A VSAM file is called a **data set,** which consists of groups of records that are arranged into one of three file organizations. These data sets are either key sequenced, entry sequenced, or relative record.

KEY-SEQUENCED DATA SET (KSDS)

The **key-sequenced data set** is the most commonly used organization method for VSAM files. It is most like the organization of an ISAM file because records are stored in the sequence of a key field and may be accessed directly by providing the key or the file may be read sequentially. With the key sequence, data-set records may be revised, added to the file, or deleted as required. Key-sequenced VSAM files are the type of organization that will be used in this book.

ENTRY-SEQUENCED DATA SET (ESDS)

The **entry-sequenced data set** refers to a VSAM file where the records are stored sequentially in the order they are received. Entry sequence files are most like sequential files; records are read or written sequentially. As far as VSAM is concerned, these records do not contain keys and may not be accessed directly.

RELATIVE RECORD DATA SET (RRDS)

A file using a **relative record data set** is essentially like a relative file. Records are stored in order with the first record having a key of 1, the second 2, and so on. Record n is identified by a relative key of n. Like relative files, each record is assumed to be present and will occupy space in the file. Records may be added, providing the position is available in the data set. Deletion simply makes the record space available without physically removing it from the file. A relative record data set may be read sequentially or directly.

CONTROL INTERVALS

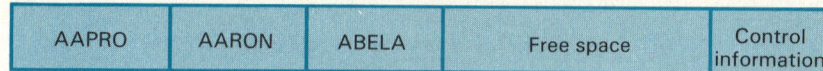

Logical records in a VSAM file are organized into groups called **control intervals** (Figure 4.6). A control interval contains three fundamental types of information:

1. One or more logical records as defined by the application.
2. Control information, which points to the records in the control interval and identifies available free space.
3. Free space, the area available for adding new records to the file.

Control Interval

AAPRO	AARON	ABELA	Free space	Control information

FIGURE 4.6   A control interval in VSAM

The control interval's size is based on a number of factors, including logical record size, program buffer size, the hardware device used for the data set, and the amount of free space required. Defining these requirements is a task for the systems programmer and will not be dealt with in greater depth here.

A control interval uses a contiguous area on the direct-access storage device, such as a full track on a disk. This allocation makes for efficient and fast operation when reading and writing records.

CONTROL AREA

Whereas records are grouped into a control interval, control intervals are further grouped into **control areas** (Figure 4.7). Each control interval has its own free space for the addition of new records, and the control area also has free space reserved. This additional

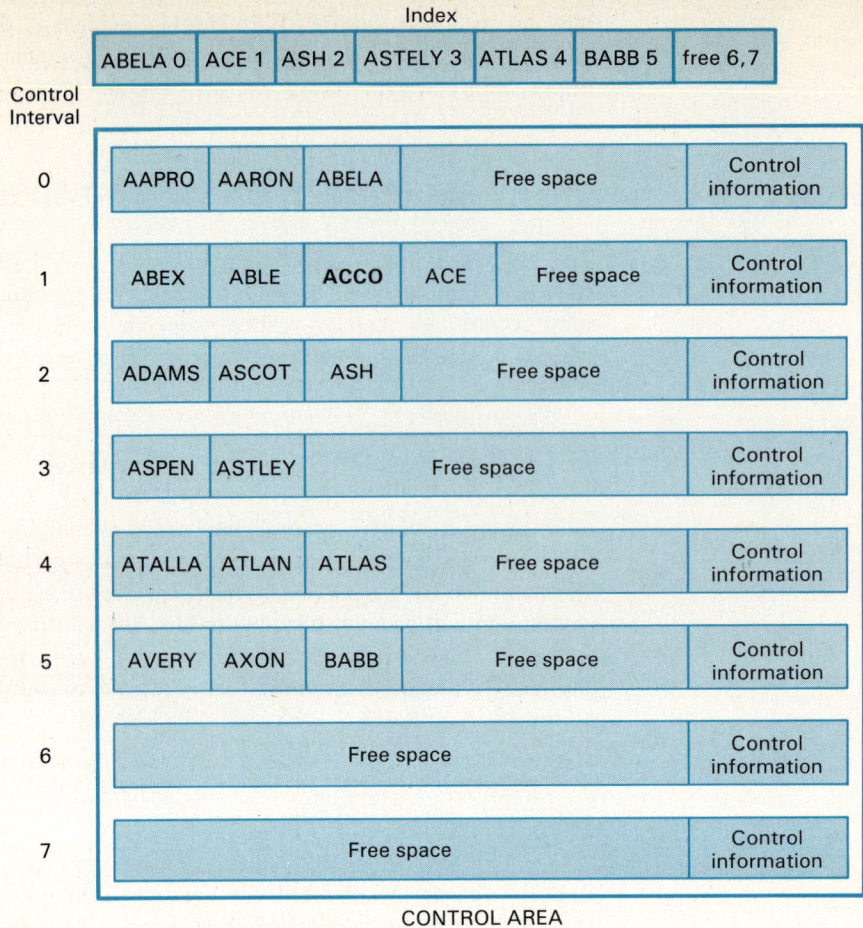

FIGURE 4.7 Inserting record ACCO in a VSAM control area

free space is used for overflow from the control interval when one of its free space areas is filled.

The control area also has an index that identifies the location of records within the control area. This index is similar to the index used in an ISAM file and has much the same function. To find a record such as ABLE directly, a search is made of the index for a less than or equal to entry. Because ABLE is less than ACE, a further search is made in the second control interval (control interval 1) where the record for ABLE is found.

CONTROL INTERVAL OVERFLOW

A new record is added to a VSAM file by inserting it in the appropriate position in the control interval (Figure 4.8). Because each control interval contains free space, an overflow will not usually occur, unlike an ISAM file. For example, when ACCO is inserted in control interval 1, the free space is used to make room and no other change to the file is necessary.

In the case of adding both ATEGA and ATKIN to control interval 4, more space is required. This time the former records in the control interval, ATLAN and ATLAS, are split and form a new control interval in the free space reserved in the control area. The index is then updated to reflect the new position of these records and the inserted records.

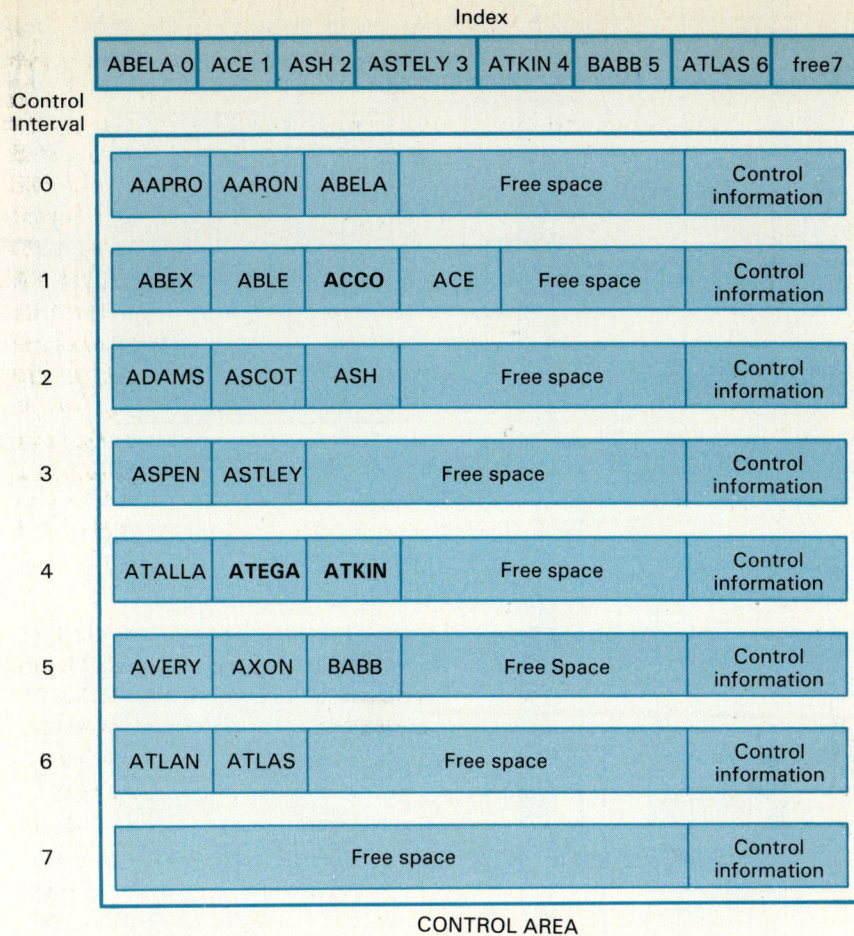

Index

| ABELA 0 | ACE 1 | ASH 2 | ASTELY 3 | ATKIN 4 | BABB 5 | ATLAS 6 | free7 |

Control Interval

0	AAPRO	AARON	ABELA	Free space	Control information
1	ABEX	ABLE	**ACCO**	ACE	Free space	Control information
2	ADAMS	ASCOT	ASH	Free space	Control information
3	ASPEN	ASTLEY	Free space	Control information
4	ATALLA	**ATEGA**	**ATKIN**	Free space	Control information
5	AVERY	AXON	BABB	Free Space	Control information
6	ATLAN	ATLAS	Free space	Control information
7	Free space	Control information

CONTROL AREA

FIGURE 4.8 A control interval split in a VSAM control area

A COMPLETE VSAM DATA SET

A fully operational VSAM data set will consist of several, even many, control areas. These control areas are tied together by another level of index called an **index set.** There may be several levels of index sets as shown in Figure 4.9 in order for the entire VSAM file to be accessed effectively. Depending on the size of the file, VSAM will maintain a hierarchy of these indexes, control areas, and control intervals. Unlike ISAM, which requires occasional reorganization of the file to maintain an efficient operation, this is never needed in VSAM. As records are added or deleted, VSAM maintains the file in good order for optimal efficiency.

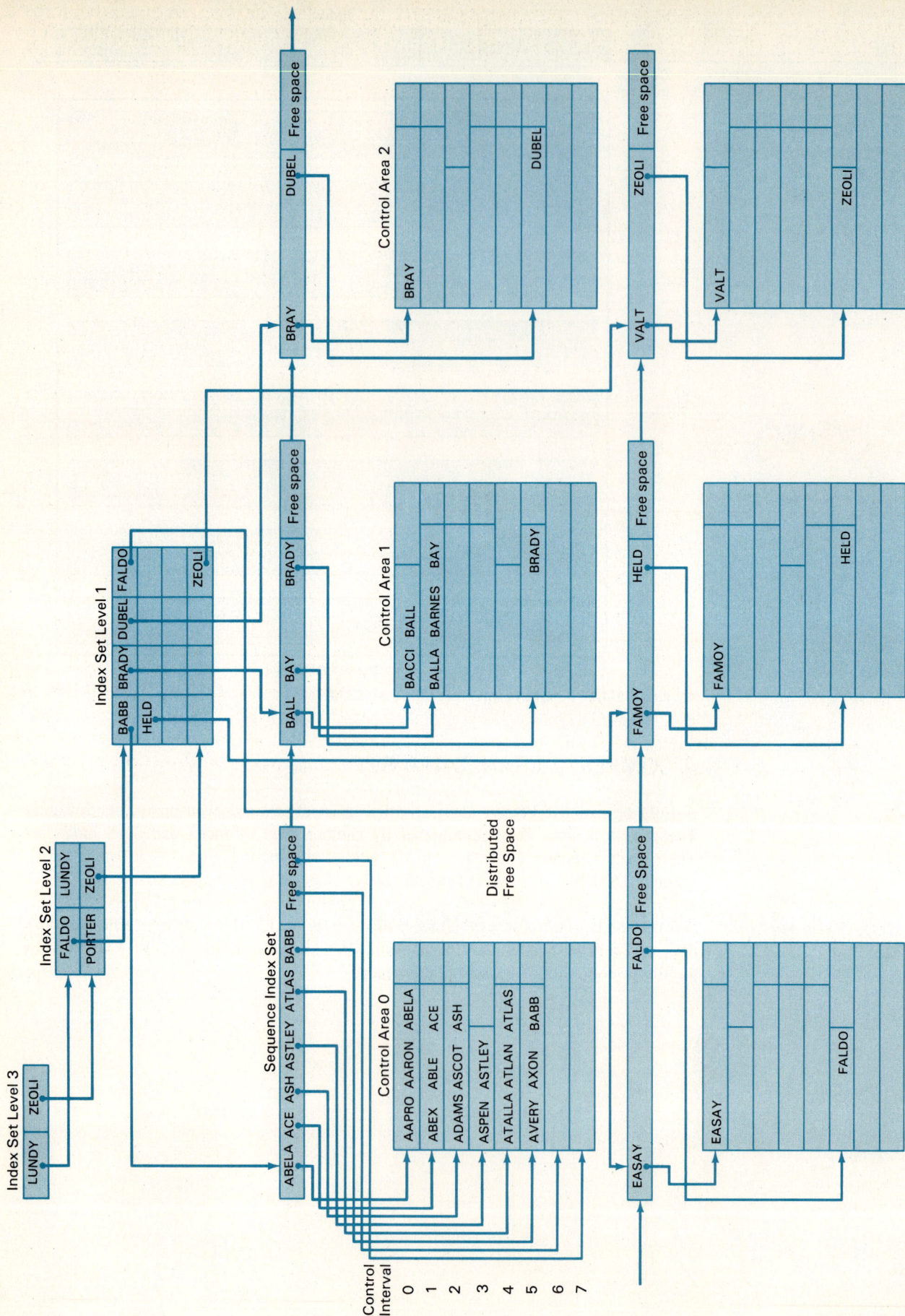

FIGURE 4.9 A complete VSAM data set

SUMMARY

Nonsequential files are best used for applications that have a low file activity ratio. Three types of nonsequential files available in COBOL are relative, indexed sequential access method (ISAM), and virtual storage access method (VSAM).

In a relative file, records are stored consecutively. Each record has a key that specifies its relative position within the file. The first record has key 0001, the second 0002, and so on. Relative files are useful if records have identifiers that are consecutively numbered, but may waste valuable disk space if this is not the case.

Indexed sequential files provide for both sequential and direct access of records within the file, thus permitting a range of applications. An ISAM file stores the records sequentially, but provides an index of record locations within the file so that a record may be directly accessed. Each record has a key, but consecutive values are not required. Overflow space is also provided to permit the addition of new records to the file. Large ISAM files may use a hierarchy of indexes for efficient retrieval of records. These indexes range from the track index to the cylinder index to a master index on the largest files.

ISAM is limited because it does not access records sequentially as efficiently as a sequential file, nor does it retrieve records directly as efficiently as a direct file. As new records are added to the file, the organization of the prime data and overflow areas becomes less efficient, and eventually a reorganization of the file is needed.

The virtual storage access method organizes records into data sets in one of three organizations: key sequenced, entry sequenced, and relative record. A key-sequenced data set (KSDS) is most like an ISAM file. Records may be accessed sequentially or directly with a key. Entry-sequenced data sets (ESDS) store records in the order they are received and are essentially like sequential files. A relative record data set (RRDS) is essentially like a relative file with similar capabilities.

VSAM deals with the file organization problem of ISAM by organizing records into a control interval. Each control interval has free space where new records may be added. Control intervals are further grouped into control areas where there is additional free space for use in the event that a control interval's free space overflows. Control area splits may also occur as an area fills with data. As a result, no file reorganization is required for VSAM files.

TERMS TO STUDY

Control area
Control interval
Cylinder index
Data set
Device independence
Entry-sequenced data set
Indexed sequential access method
Index set
Key

Key-sequenced data set
Master index
Overflow area
Relative file
Relative record accessing
Relative record data set
Track index
Virtual storage access method

TRUE/FALSE

1. A significant disadvantage of sequential files is the need to read through the file from beginning to end, even if only a few records need to be read.

2. A high file activity ratio suggests that the application would benefit from the use of a nonsequential file organization.

3. In a relative file, records are stored randomly.

4. Each record in a relative file has a key that identifies the record and permits direct access to the record.

5. For random accessing of a relative file, the program supplies a key, called a relative key.

6. One clear limitation of relative files is the use of consecutive keys and records.

7. For interactive applications where terminals are used, direct-access capabilities are not normally needed.

8. When ISAM files become very large, an additional index, the master index, may be used for improved efficiency.

9. ISAM provides the most effective means for accessing records either sequentially or directly from a file.

10. A disadvantage of VSAM is its device independence, which permits data storage on any type of direct-access storage device.

FILL IN THE BLANK

11. The first record in a _____ file has a key of 0001, the second record's key is 0002, and so on. Record one thousand would have a key of 1000.

12. A relative file uses disk space efficiently because records are stored _____ from the beginning of the file.

13. Records in a relative file are accessed directly when the file is used in _____ mode.

14. Many information-system applications require the capability to access data from a file either sequentially or _____ .

15. Unlike relative files, _____ does not require a record for each key value.

16. When new records need to be added to an ISAM file, the file is organized with one or more _____ tracks.

17. The lowest level of index in an ISAM file is called a _____ index.

18. Regular _____ of an ISAM file is required because of the reduction in efficiency as records are added to the file.

19. A VSAM file is called a _____ _____ , which consists of groups of records that are arranged into one of three file organizations.

20. The _____ data set is the most commonly used organization method for VSAM files, which is most like the organization of an ISAM file.

MULTIPLE CHOICE

21. There are basically three types of nonsequential organizations used in COBOL. Which of the following is not one of these?
   a. Relative files.
   b. Indexed sequential access method (ISAM).

c. Virtual storage access method (VSAM).

d. Data-set files.

22. Relative file organization has surfaced predominately on _____ _____ although it is available as an option in 1985 ANS COBOL for mainframe systems.

a. Personal computers.   c. Telecommunications.

b. Minicomputers.   d. Cable television.

23. What method or methods are sometimes used to improve the access of records in relative files?

a. Use of an index.   c. Both a and b.

b. Use of a remainder after dividing.   d. Neither a nor b.

24. For direct accessing of the ISAM file, an index is used. The track index contains an entry for what value?

a. Each logical record.   c. The lowest key of each track.

b. The highest key of each track.   d. None of the above.

25. When an ISAM file occupies more than one cylinder of disk space, what index is used to point to the cylinder?

a. Master index.   c. Track index.

b. Cylinder index.

26. VSAM gives the ability to access records in what way?

a. Directly like ISAM.   c. Randomly like a relative file.

b. Sequentially like ISAM.   d. All the above.

27. A VSAM file is organized in one of three types of file organization schemes. Which of the following is not one of these organizations?

a. Index sequenced.   c. Entry sequenced.

b. Key sequenced.   d. Relative record.

28. What fundamental types of information are found in a control interval?

a. One or more logical records.   d. None of the above.

b. Control information.   e. All the above.

c. Free space.

5

PROGRAMMING WITH RELATIVE FILES

Relative files are files on a direct-access device that may be accessed sequentially or randomly. We know that for random (or direct) access the records are organized consecutively with a record number. The first record is record number 0001, the second 0002, and so on to the end of the file. Record content may be designed in the same manner as records for a sequential file with one new consideration: the key field.

KEY FIELDS

Because each record in a relative file is positioned in the file and identified by a consecutive record number, the question arises whether the key needs to be stored in the record. Let's face it, if record 0005 is read, we don't need the number to be in the record to know which record it is.

However, there are times when having a key in the record can be useful. One of these times is when an error occurs and we want to **dump** (print) the record that caused the error. Having a **key field** in the record (Figure 5.1) makes for easy identification in this situation.

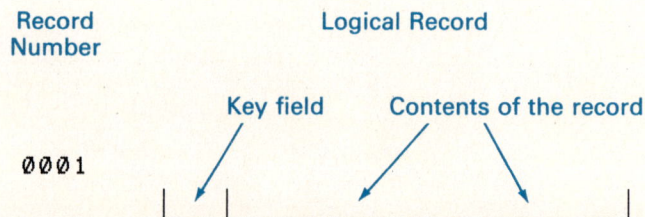

FIGURE 5.1   Position of the key field in a relative file's record

Another time when the key is needed in the record is for more sophisticated relative file applications. In the previous chapter we discussed using an index file for accessing a relative record when there are known gaps in the keys. Another technique was a mathematical one by which the record number was derived from another field.

This other field is the real key to the record and must be a part of the record. Admittedly, if files are recorded in either of these ways, then probably an ISAM or VSAM file would be a better choice than a relative file. But there may be other reasons, such as efficiency or availability, why a relative file is chosen, and so these uses of the key field would be significant.

DELETE BYTE

Records on a relative-access file for 1968 ANS COBOL do not have the capability of being deleted from the file. Instead they may be flagged as inactive by using a one-byte (**delete byte**) field at the beginning of the record (Figure 5.2). If this byte contains a space or a LOW-VALUE, the record is considered active. HIGH-VALUE or 9's or the letter D indicates a deleted or inactive record. It is the programmer's responsibility to monitor and set this flag as required by the application. Installations with 1972 or later ANS COBOL may use the DELETE statement to delete a record from the file.

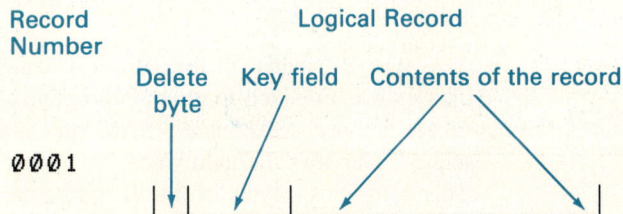

FIGURE 5.2   Position of the delete byte in a relative file's record

SELECT CLAUSE FOR RELATIVE FILES

```
INPUT-OUTPUT SECTION.

FILE-CONTROL.
      SELECT filename
           ASSIGN TO system-name
           ORGANIZATION IS RELATIVE
                             SEQUENTIAL      [RELATIVE KEY IS data-name-1]
      [ACCESS MODE IS        RANDOM
                             DYNAMIC         RELATIVE KEY IS data-name-1
      [FILE STATUS IS data-name-2].
```

The preceding general format shows the available entries for the relative file SELECT clause. The first new entry in the SELECT is the ORGANIZATION clause, which defines the file as RELATIVE. This entry will be required in all SELECTs written for relative files.

A significant entry, for relative files, is the ACCESS MODE clause. This entry has three possible options: **SEQUENTIAL, RANDOM,** or **DYNAMIC ACCESS.** Choosing the appropriate entry depends on the way the file is to be used in the application program.

```
                       SEQUENTIAL      [RELATIVE KEY IS data-name-1]
[ACCESS MODE IS        RANDOM
                       DYNAMIC         RELATIVE KEY IS date-name-1
```

Here is a description of each of the ACCESS MODE options.

- SEQUENTIAL: As the name suggests, this entry is used when the relative file is to be accessed sequentially. In this situation, records are read in the same manner as a sequential file until the end of the file is reached. A second use for SEQUENTIAL is when a relative file is created. Records are written sequentially on the file in key sequence, identified by the **RELATIVE KEY** entry, to initially create the relative file.
- RANDOM: This entry is used in the SELECT clause when the file is to be accessed directly. When RANDOM is used, a RELATIVE KEY entry is required to identify the record that is to be accessed. RANDOM permits reading, writing, rewriting, and deleting records on the relative file.
- DYNAMIC: This third option is similar to RANDOM except that it permits switching from random to sequential operation of the file as required by the program. All features of random processing are available in DYNAMIC mode.

```
[FILE STATUS IS data-name-2].
```

The last entry in the SELECT clause is an optional one; the **FILE STATUS** clause. It is provided to give the program access to system information about the status of file activity. ISAM and VSAM files may also access this status information. Data-name-2 identifies the field where the status information is stored after an I/O operation. This field is two bytes in length and contains the values shown in Figure 5.3. Some of this is system dependent information and will vary in different implementations.

Status	Meaning
00	Successful completion of the operation.
10	End of file.
21	Invalid key: sequence error.
22	Invalid key: duplicate key.
23	Invalid key: no matching record found.
24	Invalid key: file boundary exceeded.
30	Permanent error such as a data check or parity check.
34	Invalid key: file boundary exceeded.
9n	System defined error.

FIGURE 5.3 File status values

The following examples show how SELECT clauses may be written for different applications of relative files.

Example 1 A SELECT such as this one may be used to access a relative file sequentially or for creating a new relative file.

```
       A    B
1   4  78   12                                                          72
_____
       SELECT PRODUCT-FILE
          ASSIGN TO PRODUCT
          ORGANIZATION IS RELATIVE
          ACCESS MODE IS SEQUENTIAL
          RELATIVE KEY IS WS-PRODUCT-KEY.
```

Example 2 This SELECT clause may be used when a relative file is to be accessed randomly. The RELATIVE KEY will provide the key of the record to be accessed by the program. Notice that the only difference between the previous example and this one is the ACCESS MODE entry.

```
      A   B
1   4 78  12                                                      72

         SELECT PRODUCT-FILE
            ASSIGN TO PRODUCT
            ORGANIZATION IS RELATIVE
            ACCESS MODE IS RANDOM
            RELATIVE KEY IS WS-PRODUCT-KEY.
```

FILE DESCRIPTION (FD) ENTRY

DATA DIVISION.

FILE SECTION.
FD   file-name

$$\left[\underline{\text{BLOCK}} \text{ CONTAINS integer-1} \left\{ \begin{array}{l} \text{CHARACTERS} \\ \text{RECORDS} \end{array} \right\} \right]$$

[RECORD CONTAINS integer-2 CHARACTERS]

$$\underline{\text{LABEL}} \left\{ \begin{array}{l} \underline{\text{RECORD IS}} \\ \underline{\text{RECORDS ARE}} \end{array} \right\} \left\{ \begin{array}{l} \underline{\text{STANDARD}} \\ \underline{\text{OMITTED}} \end{array} \right\}$$

$$\left[\underline{\text{DATA}} \left\{ \begin{array}{l} \underline{\text{RECORD IS}} \\ \underline{\text{RECORDS ARE}} \end{array} \right\} \quad \text{data-name-1 [data-name-2]. . .} \right].$$

01   data-name.

$$02\text{--}49 \left\{ \begin{array}{l} \text{data-name} \\ \underline{\text{FILLER}} \end{array} \right\} \left\{ \begin{array}{l} \underline{\text{PICTURE}} \\ \underline{\text{PIC}} \end{array} \right\} \text{IS string [}\underline{\text{VALUE}}\text{ IS literal].}$$

In the FD the BLOCK CONTAINS clause is available only for users of 1985 ANS COBOL. Other relative file applications may not use blocked records. Entries in the FD are independent of the access method used. The data record used for the file may contain a deleted byte as the first byte of the file if this is required by the level of COBOL used. A typical FD may be written as follows:

```
      A   B
1   4 78  12                                                      72

      FD   PRODUCT-FILE
           RECORD CONTAINS 60 CHARACTERS
           LABEL RECORDS ARE STANDARD
           DATA RECORD IS PRODUCT-RECORD-IN.
      01   PRODUCT-RECORD-IN.
           05 FILLER      PIC X(70).
```

In addition to the data record defined after the FD entry, a relative key field must be defined in WORKING-STORAGE. The following entry would identify a four-byte relative key for the product file. This is the key field identified in the SELECT clause.

```
      A   B
1   4 78  12                                                      72

      WORKING-STORAGE SECTION.
              :
           05 WS-PRODUCT-KEY PIC X(04).
```

Programming with Relative Files   127

PROCEDURE DIVISION STATEMENTS

Like sequential files, relative files use a variety of statements in the PROCEDURE DIVISION for input and output activity. The usual OPEN, CLOSE, READ, and WRITE statements are used, but not always in the same sense as for sequential files, as we will see shortly. In addition to these more common statements, statements unique to nonsequential files are also available. These new statements include a READ for random access of the file, START, REWRITE, and DELETE for users of post 1968 ANS COBOL.

OPEN STATEMENT

$$
\underline{\text{OPEN}}\begin{Bmatrix} [\ \underline{\text{INPUT}}\ \{\text{file-name}\}\ \ldots\ ] \\ [\ \underline{\text{OUTPUT}}\ \{\text{file-name}\}\ \ldots\ ] \\ [\ \underline{\text{I-O}}\ \{\text{file-name}\}\ \ldots\ ] \end{Bmatrix}\ \ldots
$$

OPEN is used to identify the file used in the program prior to issuing statements to read or write the file. The INPUT entry is used to prepare the file for use as either a sequential or random input to the program. Only the READ statement may be used in this mode. For sequential access, START may also be used to position the file.

OUTPUT is used when a new relative file is being created. When an output is being used, the SELECT clause will have an ACCESS MODE entry of SEQUENTIAL. Only the WRITE statement may be used with an OUTPUT file.

I-O means input/output. This option in the OPEN may be used when the relative file is to be used for both input and output operations. On input the READ statement will be used, and on output the WRITE or REWRITE statements are available. To delete a record, the DELETE statement is used for an I-O file. ACCESS MODE may be either RANDOM or DYNAMIC.

Example Open the PRODUCT-FILE for use as a randomly accessible file to be read and updated as needed.

```
     A    B
1    4    78   12                                                        72
──────────────────────────────────────────────────────────────────────────
         OPEN I-O PRODUCT-FILE.
```

READ STATEMENT

READ file-name RECORD [INTO identifier]

$$
\begin{Bmatrix} \underline{\text{AT END}} \\ \underline{\text{INVALID}}\ \text{KEY} \end{Bmatrix}\ \text{imperative-statement.}
$$

The READ statement may be used in the program for either a sequential read of a relative file or a random access to a specific record.

Sequential Reading

For sequential reading, the file must first be opened as INPUT. Then the file is read in the same manner as a sequential file by issuing a READ statement such as the following:

```
         READ PRODUCT-FILE INTO PRODUCT-RECORD
             AT END MOVE 'YES' TO EOF-FLAG.
```

Normally, the file will be read from beginning to end unless a START statement had been issued prior to the read. When end of file is reached, the program logic should handle this in the same manner as a sequential file by setting and testing an end-of-file flag.

Random Reading

When a random read is required, the key of the record needed must first be moved to the relative key field in WORKING-STORAGE. Then a READ with the **INVALID KEY** clause is used to access the record. The INVALID KEY will be activated if the record is not found during the read operation.

```
MOVE PRODUCT-NUMBER-IN   TO WS-PRODUCT-KEY.
READ PRODUCT-FILE INTO  PRODUCT-RECORD
     INVALID KEY PERFORM 450-KEY-ERROR.
```

START STATEMENT

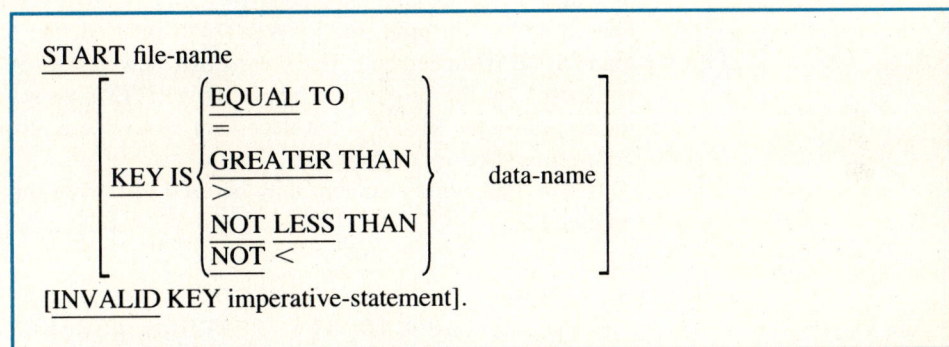

START file-name
```
      ┌     ⎧ EQUAL TO          ⎫              ⎤
      │     ⎪ =                 ⎪              │
      │     ⎪ GREATER THAN      ⎪              │
      │ KEY IS⎨ >              ⎬  data-name    │
      │     ⎪ NOT LESS THAN     ⎪              │
      └     ⎩ NOT <             ⎭              ┘
```
[INVALID KEY imperative-statement].

Start is used for a sequentially active relative file to begin the read at a specific record. Using the KEY IS EQUAL clause causes a search for the record with a key equal to that specified in the data name. Then, by using the READ statement, the file may be read sequentially beginning at that record in the file.

The other logical operators may be used when the exact key in the file is unknown, but positioning of the file is required before reading. For example, if the first record available is at 1000, this value may be supplied in the data name and the KEY IS NOT LESS THAN clause is used. The first available record beginning at 1000 will then be the starting point of the read. Here is the full statement for this last example:

```
MOVE 1000 TO WS-PRODUCT-KEY.
START PRODUCT-FILE
      KEY IS NOT LESS THAN WS-PRODUCT-KEY
      INVALID KEY PERFORM 450-KEY-ERROR.
```

WRITE STATEMENT

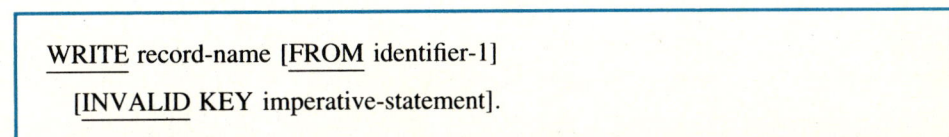

WRITE record-name [FROM identifier-1]

[INVALID KEY imperative-statement].

The WRITE statement is used when creating a new relative file. Each record is placed on the file by moving it to the identifier and then issuing the WRITE statement. An INVALID KEY is activated when a record is written that is not in key sequence or if the file becomes filled with records. Before issuing a WRITE, the relative key field must be assigned a value of the key for the record being written. This value normally comes from a transaction file that supplies the data to create the file, or it is generated by the program.

```
MOVE TR-PRODUCT-NUMBER TO WS-PRODUCT-KEY.
WRITE PRODUCT-RECORD-OUT FROM PRODUCT-RECORD
    INVALID KEY PERFORM 450-KEY-ERROR.
```

REWRITE STATEMENT

REWRITE record-name [FROM identifier-1]

    [INVALID KEY imperative-statement].

REWRITE is used in either RANDOM or DYNAMIC mode to rewrite a record onto the relative file after the record has been modified. The file must have been previously opened as I-O. In order for REWRITE to be used, the record must first be read by a random READ statement. The record that now resides in the program's memory may be revised by the program. Then a REWRITE is issued to place the new version of the record on the file. It is not necessary to rewrite a record that has been read but has not been revised by the program.

The following statement may be used to rewrite the product record back onto the product file:

```
REWRITE PRODUCT-RECORD-OUT FROM PRODUCT-RECORD
    INVALID KEY PERFORM 450-KEY-ERROR.
```

This example assumes the record has been previously read by the program. The relative key field would have been set up prior to the READ and must contain the same key value when the REWRITE is issued.

DELETE STATEMENT

DELETE file-name RECORD

    [INVALID KEY imperative-statement].

Except for 1968 ANS COBOL, which uses a delete byte, the **DELETE** statement is issued to render a current record inactive on a relative file. If an attempt is made to read this record after the DELETE has been issued, an INVALID KEY error will result. To delete a record, first move the key of the record to the relative key field, and then issue the DELETE statement as follows.

```
DELETE PRODUCT-FILE
    INVALID KEY PERFORM 450-KEY-ERROR.
```

Before a record is deleted, a good practice is to read it to ensure its presence in the file. The record may also be printed to show its contents at the time of deletion. If an invalid key occurs during the read, the record is already deleted and the DELETE should not then be issued.

CLOSE STATEMENT

CLOSE file-name-1 [file-name-2] . . .

When the program is finished with a relative file, the file must be closed. The CLOSE is used for relative files in the same way as for a sequential file discussed earlier in the book. All file types may be closed with the one CLOSE statement, as follows:

```
CLOSE PRODUCT-FILE
      TRANSACTION-FILE
      UPDATE-REPORT.
```

PROGRAM STYLE AND RELATIVE FILES

USE OF INPUT AND OUTPUT STATEMENTS

Because there is much file activity associated with the processing of relative files, the program may contain a lot of READ, WRITE, REWRITE, and DELETE statements. To minimize coding errors, simplify debugging, and enhance program organization, each disk operation should occupy its own paragraph. As a result, one paragraph will be needed to read the file, unless both sequential and random reads are required in the one program; then there would be two read paragraphs.

Using a performed paragraph also minimizes logic problems associated with the INVALID KEY clause when an I/O operation is done as the result of an IF statement.

USE OF FLAGS

At any time in programming, the use of flags should be kept to a minimum. This is also true of relative file processing. However, it is reasonable to expect that a flag may be required at times to indicate the result of a disk operation. For example, a record should not be deleted if a previous read has indicated the record to be deleted does not exist. Setting a flag in this case can be helpful for the delete code logic to detect whether to issue the delete statement.

Whenever flags are used, it is preferred to use 88-level entries to make the flag more descriptive and easier to check in the program.

CREATING A RELATIVE FILE: AN APPLICATION PROGRAM

A relative master file is required in this application for the employee records. To create this master, a transaction file exists in employee number sequence, which will be read by the create program. The employee number is a consecutive value beginning at 0001 and increasing by 1 for each employee's record. A system flowchart for this application is shown in Figure 5.4, where the transaction file is the input and the relative master is an output of the create process. This master file will further be updated in the next application in the chapter.

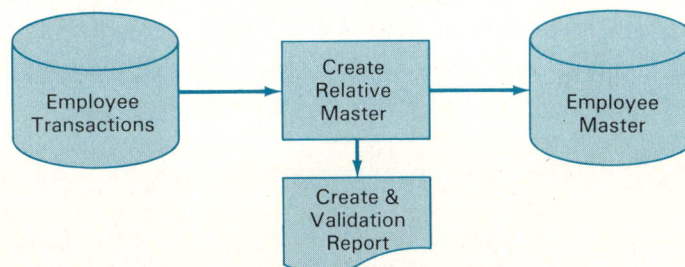

FIGURE 5.4 System flowchart for creating a relative master file

```
                    PROGRAMMING SPECIFICATIONS
PROGRAM NAME: Employee Master Create          PROGRAM ID: CREATE5
PREPARED BY: Diane Quest                       DATE: May 19, 1986
```

Program Description:
  The program defined here creates a relative record employee master file.
Input File(s):
  Employee transaction file
Output File(s):
  Relative employee master file
  Error and create report
Program Requirements:
  1. Read a disk file of employee transaction records in employee number sequence.
  2. Validate the transactions according to the following criteria:
     a) All fields in each record must contain numeric values, with the exception of name.
     b) Normally, previous department in the transaction will be blank, but any numeric value is considered correct.
     c) Education code must be in the range 1 to 7.
     d) Job code must be in the range 10 to 55 inclusive.
     e) Income is not to exceed $60,000.

FIGURE 5.5(a)   Program specifications for creating the relative employee master

```
                    PROGRAMMING SPECIFICATIONS
PROGRAM NAME: Employee Master Create          PROGRAM ID: CREATE5
PREPARED BY: Diane Quest                       DATE: May 19, 1986
```

  3. Print an error message for each error found. Do not create a master record for any transaction containing an error.
  4. Transactions begin with employee number 0001 and increase by 1 for each record. Records must be in ascending sequence.
  5. Check for an invalid key on the master and if one occurs print an appropriate error message. In this case, the master record will not have been created.
  6. At the end of the report, print the following totals:
     a) The number of transaction records with errors.
     b) The number of records written on the master.
     c) The total number of transactions read.

FIGURE 5.5(b)

SPECIFICATIONS

The specifications for this program are listed in Figure 5.5. These requirements are a lot like the ones we defined for the creation of the sequential master file earlier in the book. The reason for this similarity is that a relative file is also created sequentially, and so the need for valid records that are in ascending sequence still exists.

Alternative Methods for Creating a Relative File

When a relative file is created, the position of the record in the file is of vital importance. Reading the error report will indicate whether all records were written to the master or if some were rejected because of errors. An error in even one record can throw off the position of the relative record in the master, and so each error must be corrected and the file re-created. An alternative to this approach is to write a master file containing all blank records coded as deleted. Then read the transactions into the update program as adds to the file.

INPUT/OUTPUT DESIGN

Transaction records used to create the master are located on a sequential disk file as shown in Figure 5.6. These records are in the same format as the master, which simplifies creating the master and producing the report. Although most of the fields are defined

	INPUT/OUTPUT RECORD DEFINITION			

File: Create transactions   **File Type:** Disk
Record Length: 60   **Blocking Factor:** 10
Sequence: Employee number   **Access Method:** Sequential

COLUMNS	FIELD	TYPE	LENGTH	DECIMALS
1	Delete byte *	A/N	1	
2–5	Employee number	N	4	
6–25	Name	A/N	20	
26–28	Current dept.	A/N	3	
29–31	Previous dept.	A/N	3	
32–35	Year employed	A/N	4	
36–41	Birth date	A/N	6	
42	Education code	A/N	1	
43–44	Job code	A/N	2	
45–52	Income	N	8	2

* The delete byte is necessary only on 1968 ANS COBOL.

FIGURE 5.6 Definition for the transaction file

here as numeric, they will be defined as alphanumeric in the create program because of the need for validation.

Figure 5.7 gives the file layout for the master. This file is virtually identical to the transaction file, but it is a relative file with no blocking and therefore requires a separate definition. Both the master and the transaction files contain a delete byte in column 1. This field is not strictly necessary unless you are using pre-1974 ANS COBOL, in which case the employee number could begin in column 1 and each field would be positioned one byte to the left of the current position.

The master is a relative file that refers to its file type. But when it is created, it is accessed sequentially. This difference is especially important when a file definition is made and is why both items are included in the record definition form.

	INPUT/OUTPUT RECORD DEFINITION			

File: Employee master   **File Type:** Relative disk
Record Length: 60   **Blocking Factor:** 1
Sequence: Employee number   **Access Method:** Sequential

COLUMNS	FIELD	TYPE	LENGTH	DECIMALS
1	Delete byte*	A/N	1	
2–5	Employee number**	N	4	
6–25	Name	A/N	20	
26–28	Current dept.	A/N	3	
29–31	Previous dept.	A/N	3	
32–35	Year employed	A/N	4	
36–41	Birth date	A/N	6	
42	Education code	A/N	1	
43–44	Job code	A/N	2	
45–52	Income	N	8	2

* The delete byte is necessary only on 1968 ANS COBOL.
** Relative key field.

FIGURE 5.7 Definition for the employee master file

Programming with Relative Files

```
        0         1         2         3         4         5         6         7         8         9
        1234567890123456789012345678901234567890123456789012345678901234567890123456789012345678901234567890123

                        EMPLOYEE MASTER VALIDATE AND CREATE
        X-----------------------------------------------------------X    ** MASTER RECORD CREATED **
        X-----------------------------------------------------------X    ** MASTER RECORD CREATED **
        X-----------------------------------------------------------X    EMPLOYEE NO NOT NUMERIC
                                                                         CURRENT DEPT NOT NUMERIC
                                                                         YEAR EMPLOYED NOT NUMERIC
                                                                         YEAR EMPLOYED NOT IN RANGE
                                                                         BIRTH DATE NOT NUMERIC
                                                                         BIRTH DATE NOT IN RANGE
                                                                         EDUCATION NOT IN RANGE 01-07
                                                                         JOB CODE NOT IN RANGE 10-55
                                                                         INCOME EXCEEDS $60,000
                                                                         OUT OF SEQ OR DUP RECORD
                                                                         MASTER RECORD KEY ERROR


        RECORDS CONTAINING ERRORS:  ZZZ9
        RECORDS ON MASTER FILE:     ZZZ9
        TOTAL TRANSACTIONS:         ZZZ9
```

FIGURE 5.8 Create employee master report layout.

Figure 5.8 shows the report to be generated by the create program. This report is much like the one created for the sequential file create and validation program written earlier, and so its content should be self-explanatory. One difference of note, however, is the way the record is printed. Because this record is used to affirm the creation of the master or show an error that was detected, it is printed without formatting. This technique is sometimes used when only the programmer will be reading and acting on the results of this type of report. It is usually not recommended if the user department will be working with the results.

STRUCTURE CHART

Program Stubs

Because we are creating a relative file by writing the records sequentially, the hierarchy chart is quite similar to the one for creating a sequential file. However, in this program there is a new concept to be introduced, **program stubs.** Note the use of the entry STUB in the following process loop for the validation module:

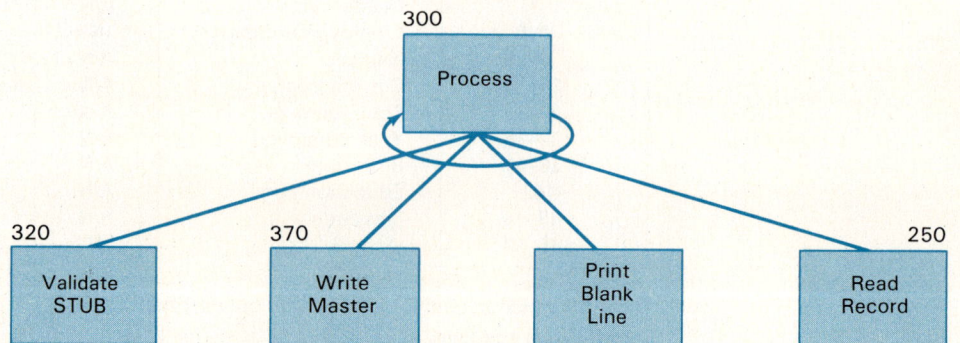

A stub is used when we are not ready to develop the entries for a particular module. There may be several reasons why a module might not be developed at this time in the application. One reason can be that the detailed specifications for the module are not yet available, and so we do not have sufficient information to create the module.

Another reason for using a stub is to temporarily reduce program complexity. Let's face it, for some of us the validation module is the most complex part of the program, and so, by making it a stub, we can concentrate on developing the rest of the program and come back to the validation part later. For very complex programs, the programmer might initially develop only the top levels of the program and make all lower-level modules stubs. Then as the top level is debugged, lower-level modules are written and testing proceeds. This process is repeated until all modules are included in the final product.

Considering a Key Error

Another different situation with this program is the need to test for an invalid key when writing a master record. An invalid key error can occur if a record is written out of sequence or if the file is filled before the last record has been written. This error is taken care of in the structure chart by showing a selection module under the write master module to either process a key error or print the record that has been correctly added to the master file.

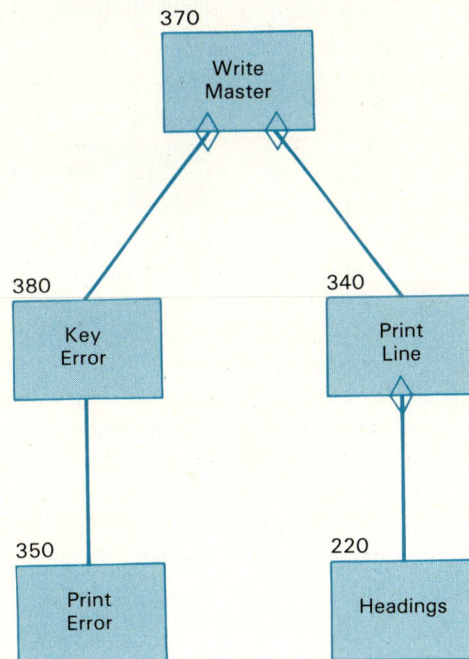

The complete structure chart for the creation of the relative master file is shown in Figure 5.9. Notice in the final chart that the validate stub is identified but not developed further at this time. Ultimately, the stub would be developed and the structure chart updated to show the contents of the validate module.

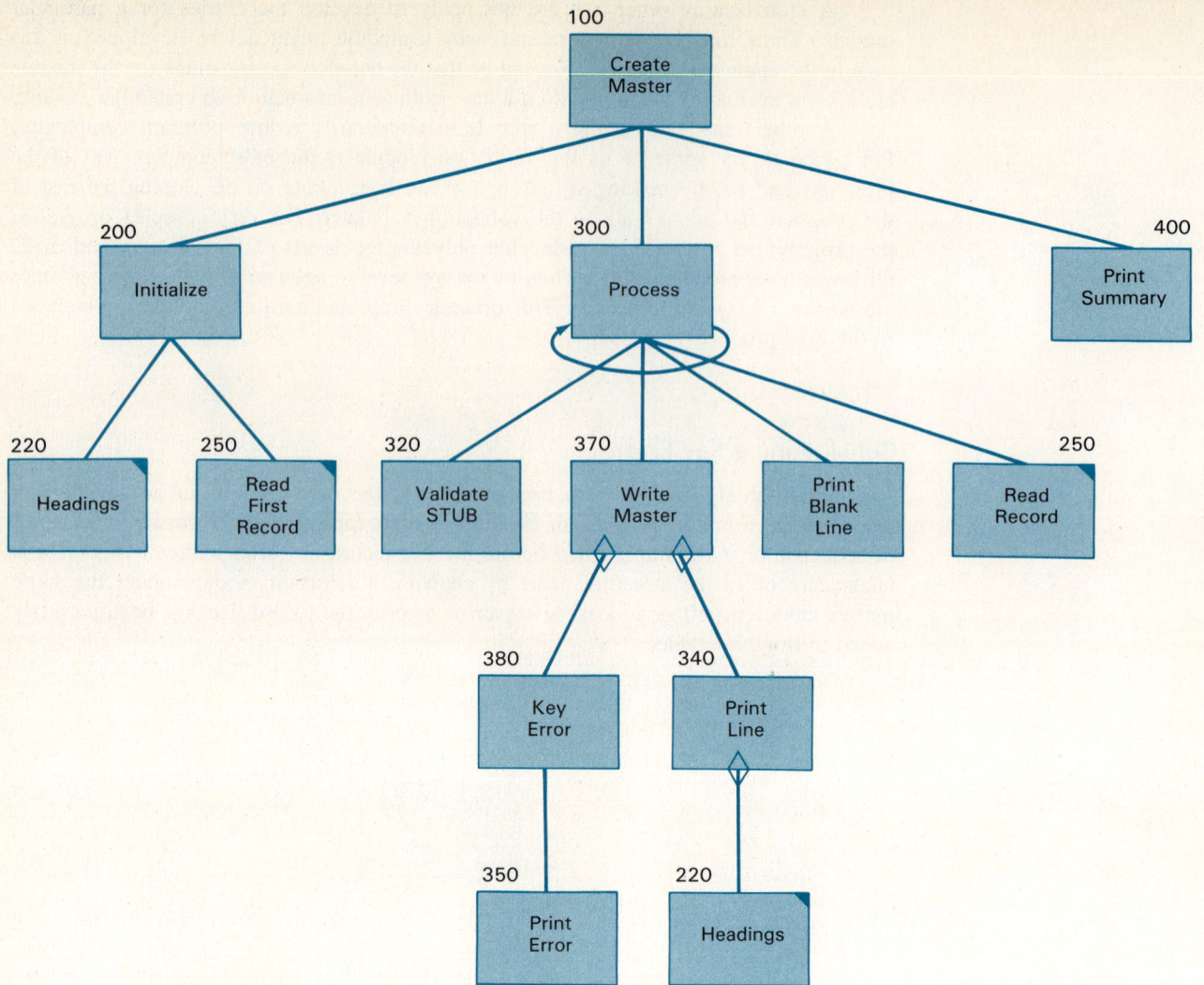

FIGURE 5.9 Structure chart for creating the relative master

PSEUDO CODE

The major difference in program logic between this and the previous file-creation program is the write logic for the relative file. First, a write statement for a direct-access (random) file requires the use of an invalid key clause. This clause will identify the action to be taken if a key error is detected during the writing of the new master file. Therefore, a statement in the pseudo code such as this is used:

```
Write inventory master record
     invalid key Perform 380-Key-error.
```

The performed paragraph will set a flag that will determine whether a line should be printed showing that the record has been successfully added to the master. Checking the key error flag can be handled as follows:

```
If key error
   next sentence
else
   Perform 340-Print-detail
   Add 1 to total master records
EndIf
```

The paragraph that is performed when an invalid key is detected begins by setting the flag as follows:

```
380-Key-error
        1. Move 'Yes' to error flag.
        2. Perform 350-Print-Error.
        3. Add 1 to total errors.
```

It continues by printing an error message and counting this record as an error. Key errors should be the exception rather than the rule. If there are many key errors, something is terribly wrong with the data or, worse, there is a program bug that has yet to be corrected.

We also should look at the implementation of the program stub in the pseudo code. The validate module is to be implemented here without its complete error-checking logic. An important consideration when implementing a stub is to ask the question, what does the remainder of the program need as a result of this module being a stub? In other words, does any part of the program require data or a flag setting that this module would normally set? Although the validate module is not written in full, it must contain some code to let it function as a stub.

One activity that the module will do is to set up the print line in case an error message needs to be printed. Also, an error flag will be set if there is an error, and so it should be initialized at the beginning of the module. These activities can be done in the stub without the need to write all the other code, which is to be developed at a later time.

```
320-Validate - STUB
        1. Move transaction to detail line.
        2. Reset error flag to 'no'.
```

Figure 5.10 shows the complete pseudo code and structured flowchart for creating the relative employee master file.

PSEUDO CODE

PROGRAM NAME: Employee Master Create   PROGRAM ID: CREATE5

PREPARED BY: Jonathan Youngman   DATE: May 22   PAGE 1 of 3

100-Mainline
  1. Perform 200-Initialize.
  2. Perform 300-Process
          Until EOF.
  3. Perform 400-Print-Summary.
  4. Close files.
  5. Stop Run.
200-Mainline
  1. Open input and output files.
  2. Perform 220-Headings.
  3. Perform 250-Read.
220-Headings
  1. Print heading 1.
  2. Print blank line.
  3. Set line count to 2.
250-Read
  1. Read transactions
        at end move 'yes' to EOF-Flag.
  2. If Not EOF
        Add 1 to total transactions
        If Not in sequence
            Perform 350-Print-Error
        Else
            Store employee no. in previous employee no.
        EndIf
      EndIf

FIGURE 5.10(a) Pseudo code for creating the relative master

300-Process
1. Perform 320-Validate.
2. If No errors
    Perform 370-Write-Master
   Else
    Add 1 to total errors
   EndIf
3. Print blank line.
4. Perform 250-Read.

320-Validate—STUB
1. Move transaction to detail line.
2. Reset error flag to 'no'.

340-Print-Detail
1. Move master created message to detail line.
2. Perform 360-Print-Line.
3. Blank out the detail line to prepare for the next record.

350-Print-Error
1. Perform 360-Print-Line.
2. Blank out detail line so the record prints only once.
3. Set error flag to 'yes'.

FIGURE 5.10(b)

360-Print-Line
1. Write the detail line.
2. Add 1 to line count.
3. If line count > 35
    Perform 220-Headings
   EndIf

370-Write-Master
1. Move spaces to master record.
2. Move transaction fields to master fields.
3. Set key error flag to 'NO'.
4. Move employee number to relative key.
5. Write inventory master record
    invalid key Perform 380-Key-error.
6. If key error
    next sentence
   else
    Perform 340-Print-detail
    Add 1 to total master records
   EndIf

380-Key-error
1. Move 'Yes' to error flag.
2. Perform 350-Print-Error.
3. Add 1 to total errors.

400-Print-Summary
1. Print count of records with errors.
2. Print count of records on the master file.
3. Print count of transactions read.

FIGURE 5.10(c)

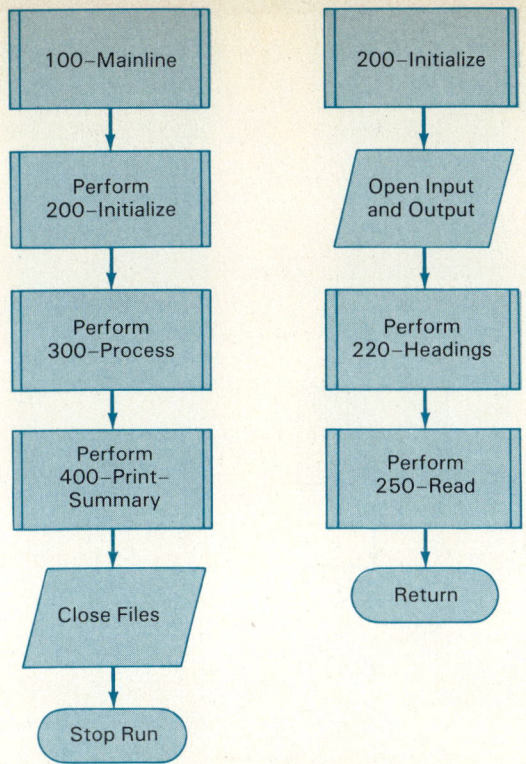

FIGURE 5.10(d) Structured flowchart for creating the relative master

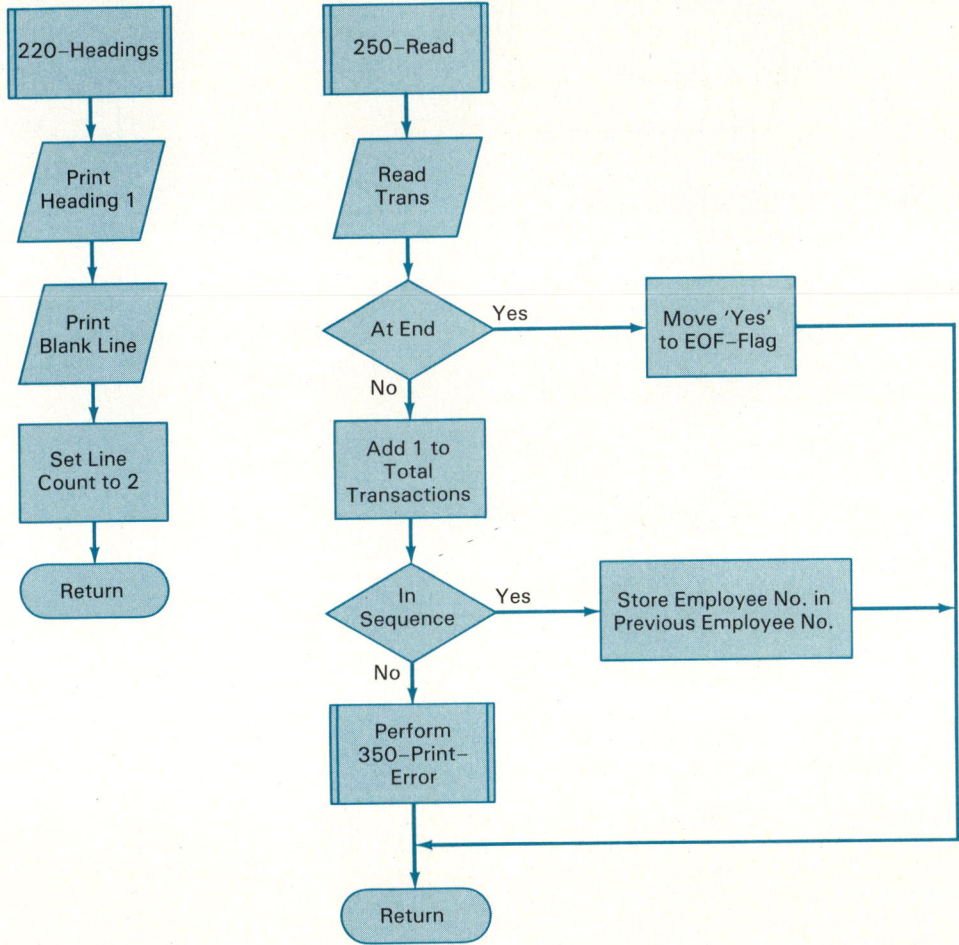

FIGURE 5.10(e)

Programming with Relative Files

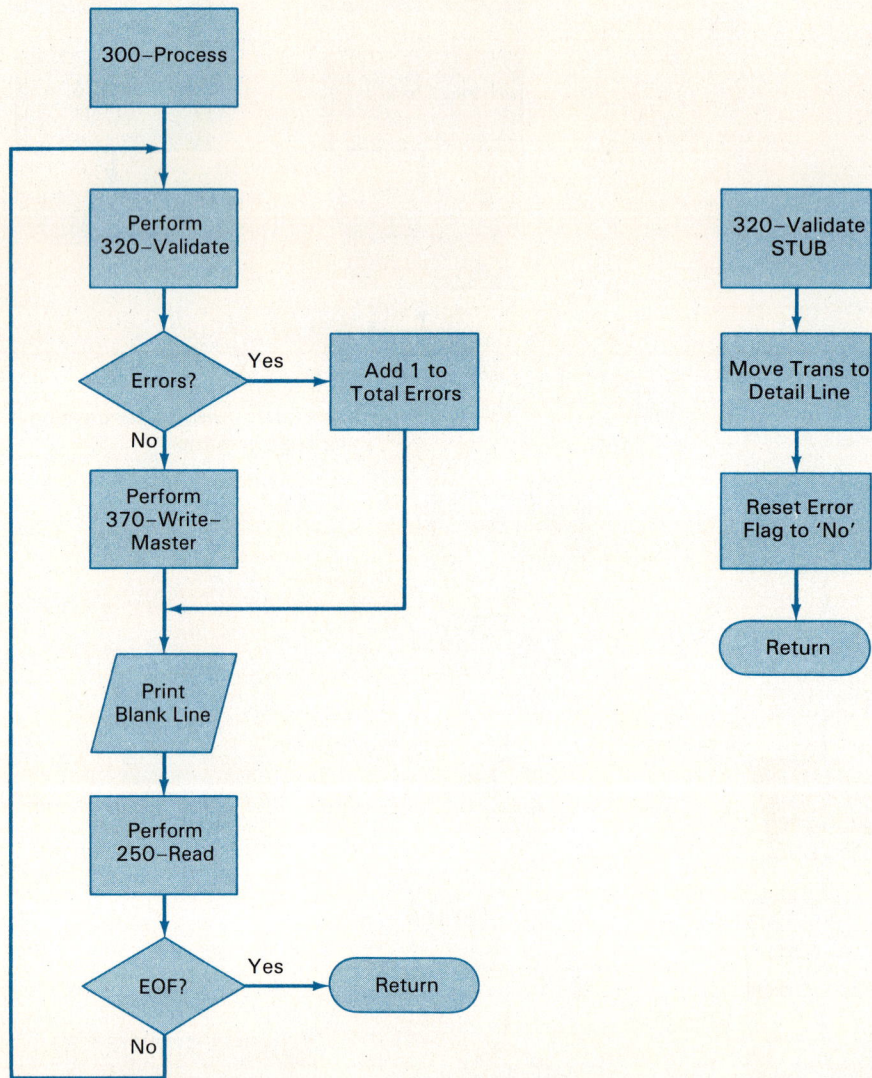

FIGURE 5.10(f)

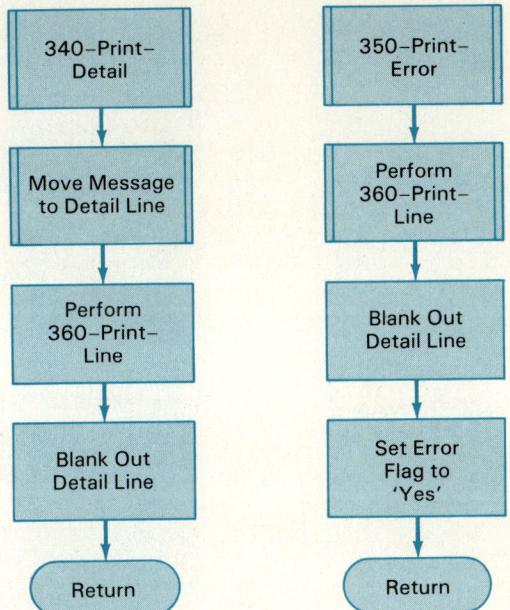

FIGURE 5.10(g)

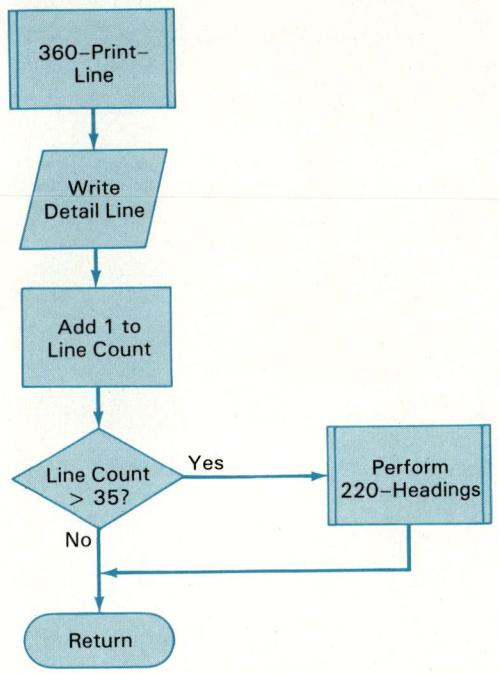

FIGURE 5.10(h)

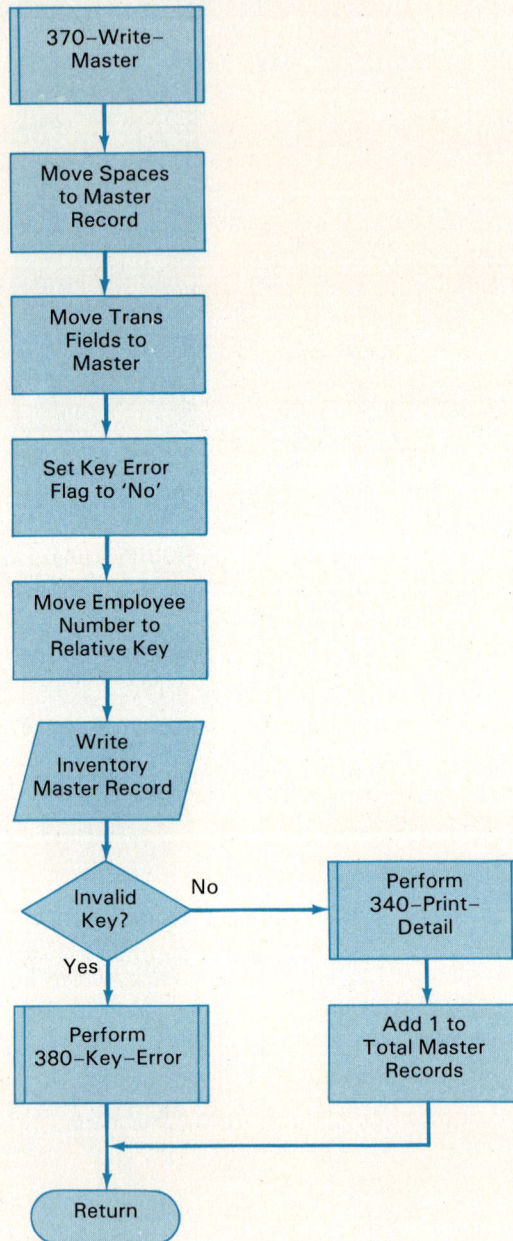

FIGURE 5.10(i)

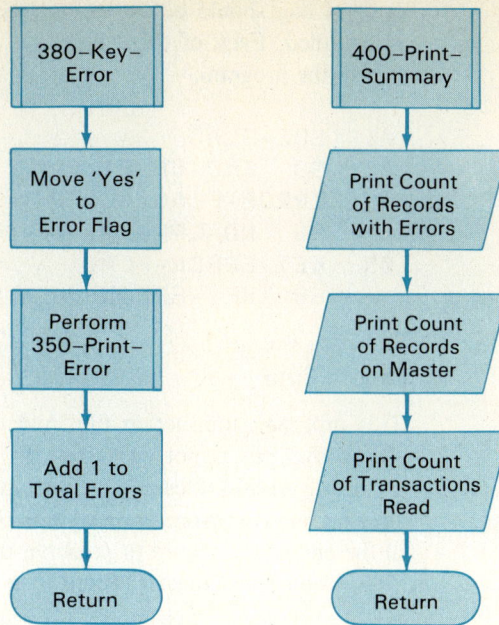

380–Key–Error

Move 'Yes' to Error Flag

Perform 350–Print–Error

Add 1 to Total Errors

Return

400–Print–Summary

Print Count of Records with Errors

Print Count of Records on Master

Print Count of Transactions Read

Return

FIGURE 5.10(j)

PROGRAM CODING

SELECT Clause

The program in Figure 5.11 is the first we have written that defines a nonsequential file in the SELECT clause. The entries are similar to those used as examples earlier in the chapter, but this time we have a real file that is to be created by a COBOL program. First, let's look at the SELECT.

```
SELECT EMPLOYEE-MASTER  ASSIGN TO MASTER
       ORGANIZATION IS RELATIVE
       ACCESS IS SEQUENTIAL
       RELATIVE KEY IS WS-EMPLOYEE-NO.
```

As usual, the file name used by the program is assigned to the name associated with the external device (in this case a disk). The ORGANIZATION, as we know, is RELATIVE, and therefore this entry is required; otherwise, the system would default to a sequential file. Although the organization of the file is relative, to create it the records will be written sequentially. So the ACCESS entry chooses SEQUENTIAL as its option. Finally, the RELATIVE KEY is defined as WS-EMPLOYEE-NO. The name of this key is up to us to choose, but it must correspond to the identifier specified in WORKING-STORAGE. Some systems do not require the relative key to be specified when the file is being created.

Flags

Most programs require the use of some flags, and this one is no exception. Because a sequential transaction file is read, an end-of-file flag is required to detect the end of this file. Second, validation of the transactions is to be done. Although the validation module is a stub, an intelligent guess would suggest that an error flag will be needed to control the printing of error records and to ensure that an error record is not transmitted to the relative master file.

Finally, the write logic for the relative file will test for an invalid key. Because the presence of an invalid key changes the activity for the record that caused the key error, a flag should be set to identify this error. So the identifier KEY-ERROR-FLAG is specified. Each of these flags has 88-level entries as follows to simplify testing the flag in the program:

```
05    EOF-FLAG                    PIC X(03)    VALUE 'NO'.
      88   END-OF-FILE                         VALUE 'YES'.
05    ERROR-FLAG                  PIC X(03)    VALUE 'NO'.
      88   NO-ERRORS                           VALUE 'NO'.
05    KEY-ERROR-FLAG              PIC X(03)    VALUE 'NO'.
      88   KEY-ERROR                           VALUE 'YES'.
```

Delete Byte

This program, transaction file, and master file have been defined with a delete byte. Recall that this is not necessary for 1974 and later versions of ANS COBOL. If you are using one of these implementations, the entry MAST-DELETE as shown below may be removed from the program. An additional byte should be added to the FILLER at the end of the record to preserve the correct record length.

The current master record is as follows:

```
01 WS-MAST-REC.
   05    MAST-DELETE            PIC X(01).
   05    MAST-EMPLOYEE-NO       PIC X(04).
   05    MAST-NAME              PIC X(20).
         :
   05    FILLER                 PIC X(08).
```

To eliminate the delete byte, change the record as follows:

```
01   WS-MAST-REC.  ←──────────────────────── Delete removed
     05    MAST-EMPLOYEE-NO     PIC X(04).
     05    MAST-NAME            PIC X(20).
           :
     05    FILLER               PIC X(09). ←─── X(08) becomes
                                               X(09).
```

Procedure Division

100-MAINLINE   This module controls all the activity of the program at the top level of the program logic.

200-INITIALIZE   Paragraph 200 opens the input and output files. Notice that the relative master file is opened as OUTPUT because in this program it is being created, which requires sequential output. The module also activates the printing of the heading and reading of the first input record from the transaction file.

220-HEADINGS   This paragraph prints the heading and blank line that follows it. Because headings may be printed at the beginning of the program and also if page overflow occurs, this paragraph is performed from more than one location. It also resets LINE-COUNT each time a heading is printed.

250-READ   Each transaction for creating the master file is read by this paragraph. If end of file is not detected, the record is checked for sequence and counted as one transaction. A sequence error would result in an error message.

300-PROCESS This is the process loop that controls the processing of each transaction. Essentially, each record is first validated, and if no errors are found, the module 370-WRITE-MASTER is performed to write the record on the relative master. A blank line is then printed to get double spacing between records, but retains the single spacing of multiple error messages that could print for some records. Finally, the next transaction is read by performing 250-READ.

320-VALIDATE This paragraph is the validate program stub we discussed in the sections on the structure chart and pseudo code. Assuming that a record will be printed whether or not it contains an error, it is in any case moved to the detail line. The error flag is also initialized in this module to indicate that currently no error has been found. This obviously assumes that all records processed at this time are error free. It is the programmer's responsibility to ensure that this is indeed the case; otherwise, the results of the program will not be as expected.

340-PRINT-DETAIL This small paragraph prints each record that has been added to the relative master file. MESSAGE-11 is included with this record to indicate that an add to the master took place successfully.

350-PRINT ERROR This module initiates printing of an error message by performing the paragraph 360-PRINT-LINE. The detail line is then cleared by moving spaces to it to ensure that the record prints only once, even if there are more errors. The error flag is also set here to indicate that the current record contains one or more errors.

360-PRINT-LINE All printing, except for the heading, occurs in this paragraph. Other paragraphs may set up the record to be printed, but the printing is done by performing this module. After the line is printed, a value of 1 is added to the line counter and it is checked to see if it has reached the page limit. If the page is full, the heading module is performed to take care of the page eject, printing the heading, and resetting the line count.

370-WRITE-MASTER Each valid transaction is written on the relative master file by this paragraph. First, the contents of the fields in the transaction record are moved to the corresponding fields in the master record. Then the key error flag is set off (NO) to prepare for writing the master. The relative key (WS-EMPLOYEE-NO) is given the value of the transaction's employee number, and then the record is written on the master file. Note that a write to a relative file uses the record name, not the file name, just as it does for the printer or any other output file.

A key error, if detected, causes 380-KEY-ERROR to be performed, which will print an error message and set the KEY-ERROR-FLAG. At the end of the paragraph, 340-PRINT-DETAIL is activated if there was no key error. This paragraph will print the record and the message to indicate it was added to the master file. The record is also counted before leaving the module.

380-KEY-ERROR When an invalid key is detected while writing a record on the master file, this paragraph will be performed. It sets the KEY-ERROR-FLAG and then moves the record and an error message to the print line. The line is then printed, and 1 is added to the error count.

400-PRINT-SUMMARY This paragraph is performed when all transactions have been processed and the master is complete. It prints the counts of transactions read, number of error records detected, and the number of records written to the master file.

Figure 5.11 shows the program to create a relative file.

```
        IDENTIFICATION DIVISION.

        PROGRAM-ID.
            CREATE5.
       *AUTHOR.
       *    JOHNATHAN YOUNGMAN.
       *INSTALLATION.
       *    SALES UNLIMITED CORP.
       *DATE-WRITTEN.
       *    MAY 26.
       *DATE-COMPILED.

       *SECURITY.
       *    NONE.

        ENVIRONMENT DIVISION.

        CONFIGURATION SECTION.
        SOURCE-COMPUTER.
            IBM-PC.
        OBJECT-COMPUTER.
            IBM-PC.

        INPUT-OUTPUT SECTION.

        FILE-CONTROL.
            SELECT TRANSACTIONS     ASSIGN TO TRANS5.
            SELECT EMPLOYEE-MASTER  ASSIGN TO MASTER
                    ORGANIZATION IS RELATIVE
                    ACCESS IS SEQUENTIAL
                    RELATIVE KEY IS WS-EMPLOYEE-NO.
            SELECT ERROR-REPORT     ASSIGN TO PRINTER.

        DATA DIVISION.

        FILE SECTION.

        FD  TRANSACTIONS
            BLOCK  CONTAINS 10 RECORDS
            RECORD CONTAINS 60 CHARACTERS
            LABEL RECORDS ARE STANDARD
            DATA RECORD IS TRANS-REC.
        01  TRANS-REC.
            05  FILLER              PIC X(60).

         FD  EMPLOYEE-MASTER
            RECORD CONTAINS 60 CHARACTERS
            LABEL RECORDS ARE STANDARD
            DATA RECORD IS MASTER-REC.
        01  MASTER-REC.
            05  FILLER              PIC X(60).

        FD  ERROR-REPORT
            RECORD CONTAINS 133 CHARACTERS
            LABEL RECORDS ARE OMITTED
            DATA RECORD IS PRINT-REC.
        01  PRINT-REC.
            05  PRINT-LINE          PIC X(133).

        WORKING-STORAGE SECTION.

        01  OTHER-ITEMS.
            05  WS-EMPLOYEE-NO      PIC 9(04).
            05  EOF-FLAG            PIC X(03)   VALUE 'NO'.
                88  END-OF-FILE                 VALUE 'YES'.
            05  ERROR-FLAG          PIC X(03)   VALUE 'NO'.
                88  NO-ERRORS                   VALUE 'NO'.
            05  KEY-ERROR-FLAG      PIC X(03)   VALUE 'NO'.
                88  KEY-ERROR                   VALUE 'YES'.
            05  PREV-EMPLOYEE-NO    PIC 9(04)   VALUE ZERO.
```

FIGURE 5.11(a) Program to create a relative file

```
01   TOTALS.
     05   LINE-COUNT               PIC 9(02)   VALUE ZERO.
     05   TOTAL-ERRORS             PIC 9(04)   VALUE ZERO.
     05   TOTAL-MASTERS            PIC 9(04)   VALUE ZERO.
     05   TOTAL-TRANS              PIC 9(04)   VALUE ZERO.

01   MESSAGES.
     05   MESSAGE-01               PIC X(30)
                 VALUE 'EMPLOYEE NO. NOT NUMERIC'.
     05   MESSAGE-02               PIC X(30)
                 VALUE 'CURRENT DEPT. NOT NUMERIC'.
     05   MESSAGE-03               PIC X(30)
                 VALUE 'YEAR EMPLOYED NOT NUMERIC'.
     05   MESSAGE-04               PIC X(30)
                 VALUE 'YEAR EMPLOYED NOT IN RANGE'.
     05   MESSAGE-05               PIC X(30)
                 VALUE 'BIRTH DATE NOT NUMERIC'.
     05   MESSAGE-06               PIC X(30)
                 VALUE 'BIRTH DATE NOT IN RANGE'.
     05   MESSAGE-07               PIC X(30)
                 VALUE 'EDUCATION NOT IN RANGE 01 - 07'.
     05   MESSAGE-08               PIC X(30)
                 VALUE 'JOB CODE NOT IN RANGE 10 - 55'.
     05   MESSAGE-09               PIC X(30)
                 VALUE 'INCOME EXCEEDS $60,000'.
     05   MESSAGE-10               PIC X(30)
                 VALUE 'OUT OF SEQ OR DUP RECORD'.
     05   MESSAGE-11               PIC X(30)
                 VALUE '** MASTER RECORD CREATED **'.
     05   MESSAGE-12               PIC X(30)
                 VALUE 'MASTER RECORD KEY ERROR'.

01   WS-TRANS-REC.
     05   TRANS-DELETE             PIC X(01).
     05   TRANS-EMPLOYEE-NO        PIC X(04).
     05   TRANS-NAME               PIC X(20).
     05   TRANS-CURRENT-DEPT       PIC X(03).
     05   TRANS-PREV-DEPT          PIC X(03).
     05   TRANS-YEAR-EMPLOYED      PIC X(04).
     05   TRANS-BIRTH-DATE.
          10   TRANS-MONTH         PIC X(02).
          10   TRANS-DAY           PIC X(02).
          10   TRANS-YEAR          PIC X(02).
     05   TRANS-EDUCATION          PIC X(01).
     05   TRANS-JOB-CODE           PIC X(02).
     05   TRANS-INCOME             PIC X(08).
     05   FILLER                   PIC X(08).

01   WS-MAST-REC.
     05   MAST-DELETE              PIC X(01).
     05   MAST-EMPLOYEE-NO         PIC X(04).
     05   MAST-NAME                PIC X(20).
     05   MAST-CURRENT-DEPT        PIC X(03).
     05   MAST-PREV-DEPT           PIC X(03).
     05   MAST-YEAR-EMPLOYED       PIC X(04).
     05   MAST-BIRTH-DATE.
          10   MAST-MONTH          PIC X(02).
          10   MAST-DAY            PIC X(02).
          10   MAST-YEAR           PIC X(02).
     05   MAST-EDUCATION           PIC X(01).
     05   MAST-JOB-CODE            PIC X(02).
     05   MAST-INCOME              PIC X(08).
     05   FILLER                   PIC X(08).

01   HEAD-1.
     05   FILLER                   PIC X(20)   VALUE SPACES.
     05   FILLER                   PIC X(36)
                 VALUE 'EMPLOYEE MASTER VALIDATE AND CREATE'.
```

FIGURE 5.11(b)

```
01  DETAIL-LINE.
    05  FILLER                      PIC X(01)   VALUE SPACES.
    05  DETAIL-RECORD               PIC X(60)   VALUE SPACES.
    05  FILLER                      PIC X(05)   VALUE SPACES.
    05  DETAIL-MESSAGE              PIC X(30)   VALUE SPACES.

01  SUMMARY-LINE.
    05  SUMMARY-MESSAGE             PIC X(28)   VALUE SPACES.
    05  SUMMARY-AMT                 PIC Z(03)9.

PROCEDURE DIVISION.

100-MAINLINE.
    PERFORM 200-INITIALIZE.
    PERFORM 300-PROCESS
        UNTIL END-OF-FILE.
    PERFORM 400-PRINT-SUMMARY.
    CLOSE TRANSACTIONS
          EMPLOYEE-MASTER
          ERROR-REPORT.
    STOP RUN.

200-INITIALIZE.
    OPEN INPUT   TRANSACTIONS
         OUTPUT  EMPLOYEE-MASTER
                 ERROR-REPORT.
    PERFORM 220-HEADINGS.
    PERFORM 250-READ.

220-HEADINGS.
    WRITE PRINT-REC FROM HEAD-1
        AFTER ADVANCING TO-TOP-OF-PAGE.
    MOVE SPACES TO PRINT-REC.
    WRITE PRINT-REC
        AFTER ADVANCING 1 LINE.
    MOVE 2 TO LINE-COUNT.

250-READ.
    READ TRANSACTIONS INTO WS-TRANS-REC
        AT END MOVE 'YES' TO EOF-FLAG.
    IF NOT END-OF-FILE
        ADD 1 TO TOTAL-TRANS
        IF TRANS-EMPLOYEE-NO IS NOT GREATER THAN PREV-EMPLOYEE-NO
            MOVE MESSAGE-10     TO DETAIL-MESSAGE
            PERFORM 350-PRINT-ERROR
        ELSE
            MOVE TRANS-EMPLOYEE-NO TO PREV-EMPLOYEE-NO.

300-PROCESS.
    PERFORM 320-VALIDATE.
    IF NO-ERRORS
        PERFORM 370-WRITE-MASTER
    ELSE
        ADD 1 TO TOTAL-ERRORS.
    MOVE SPACES TO DETAIL-LINE.
    PERFORM 360-PRINT-LINE.
    PERFORM 250-READ.


 320-VALIDATE.
************************************************************
*    *** VALIDATION STUB - TO BE IMPLEMENTED ***    *
************************************************************
    MOVE WS-TRANS-REC       TO DETAIL-RECORD.
    MOVE 'NO'               TO ERROR-FLAG.

 340-PRINT-DETAIL.
    MOVE MESSAGE-11         TO DETAIL-MESSAGE.
    PERFORM 360-PRINT-LINE.
    MOVE SPACES             TO DETAIL-LINE.
```

FIGURE 5.11(c)

```
350-PRINT-ERROR.
    PERFORM 360-PRINT-LINE.
    MOVE SPACES              TO DETAIL-LINE.
    MOVE 'YES'               TO ERROR-FLAG.

360-PRINT-LINE.
    WRITE PRINT-REC FROM DETAIL-LINE
        AFTER ADVANCING 1 LINE.
    ADD 1                    TO LINE-COUNT.
    IF LINE-COUNT IS GREATER THAN 35
        PERFORM 220-HEADINGS.

370-WRITE-MASTER.
    MOVE   SPACES               TO  WS-MAST-REC.
    MOVE   TRANS-DELETE         TO  MAST-DELETE.
    MOVE   TRANS-EMPLOYEE-NO    TO  MAST-EMPLOYEE-NO.
    MOVE   TRANS-NAME           TO  MAST-NAME.
    MOVE   TRANS-CURRENT-DEPT   TO  MAST-CURRENT-DEPT.
    MOVE   TRANS-PREV-DEPT      TO  MAST-PREV-DEPT.
    MOVE   TRANS-YEAR-EMPLOYED  TO  MAST-YEAR-EMPLOYED.
    MOVE   TRANS-BIRTH-DATE     TO  MAST-BIRTH-DATE.
    MOVE   TRANS-EDUCATION      TO  MAST-EDUCATION.
    MOVE   TRANS-JOB-CODE       TO  MAST-JOB-CODE.
    MOVE   TRANS-INCOME         TO  MAST-INCOME.
    MOVE   'NO'                 TO  KEY-ERROR-FLAG.
    MOVE   TRANS-EMPLOYEE-NO    TO  WS-EMPLOYEE-NO.
    WRITE MASTER-REC FROM WS-MAST-REC
        INVALID KEY PERFORM 380-KEY-ERROR.
    IF KEY-ERROR
        NEXT SENTENCE
    ELSE
        PERFORM 340-PRINT-DETAIL
        ADD 1 TO TOTAL-MASTERS.

380-KEY-ERROR.
    MOVE 'YES'               TO KEY-ERROR-FLAG.
    MOVE WS-TRANS-REC        TO DETAIL-RECORD.
    MOVE MESSAGE-12          TO DETAIL-MESSAGE.
    PERFORM 350-PRINT-ERROR.
    ADD 1 TO TOTAL-ERRORS.

400-PRINT-SUMMARY.
    MOVE ' RECORDS CONTAINING ERRORS:'  TO SUMMARY-MESSAGE.
    MOVE TOTAL-ERRORS              TO SUMMARY-AMT.
    WRITE PRINT-REC FROM SUMMARY-LINE
        AFTER ADVANCING 2 LINES.
    MOVE ' RECORDS ON MASTER FILE:' TO SUMMARY-MESSAGE.
    MOVE TOTAL-MASTERS            TO SUMMARY-AMT.
    WRITE PRINT-REC FROM SUMMARY-LINE
        AFTER ADVANCING 2 LINES.
    MOVE ' TOTAL TRANSACTIONS:'   TO SUMMARY-MESSAGE.
    MOVE TOTAL-TRANS              TO SUMMARY-AMT.
    WRITE PRINT-REC FROM SUMMARY-LINE
        AFTER ADVANCING 2 LINES.
```

FIGURE 5.11(d)

PROGRAM TESTING

A crucial part of this application is adequate testing of the create program. Because this program creates a master file that will be used by the following program for updating purposes, the master must be clean, error free, and correctly organized as a relative access file. Any errors introduced in the create process will often be magnified when an update program attempts to use the file.

The first step, then, is to ensure that the transactions used to create the master are themselves free of errors. Because we are using a validation stub in the program, it will be necessary to manually check each transaction to make sure it satisfies the needs of the program. These transactions are shown in Figure 5.12. Each field is supplied, except for the previous department in columns 29–31, which is intentionally blank as defined by the program specifications.

```
0001Falcon, Lloyd          140    19500325323420425000
0002Carney, Jim            130    19630404444350356000
0003Chambers, JK           130    19650715433420421300
0004Gallagher, Angelo      120    19661111453260315000
0005Ellis, Mike            140    19680105462230259000
0006Dawson, Mary           140    19721230553270301000
0007Arbor, Noel            105    19740401532230273458
0008DaCosta, Michael       105    19750629575450527500
0009Eagle, Wilfred         190    19770518311140234000
0010Assad, James           110    19780918463250294530
0011Baird, Joan            105    19831011592210168000
0012Gallagher, Pat         115    19831231622210168000
0013Baird, Joan            105    19830101622210168000
0014Cantoone, Phil         120    19840827544370124000
0015Harris, Jim            105    19840321564210167000
```

FIGURE 5.12 Transaction file used to create the employee master

The next step is to run the create program using these transactions and create the relative master file. The results you see in Figure 5.13 show that each record has been successful in creating a master file. If any errors occur in the first run, they will be because of compile diagnostics or an invalid key on the master file. In either case a correction would be necessary, and the program would then be rerun. This process will be repeated until the master is successfully created with no errors indicated on the report.

The totals at the end of the report are helpful in confirming a correct run. If the number of errors is zero, and the numbers of transactions and master records are equal, then at least all the records are processing correctly. A second check requires us to visually observe the contents of each field on the report and confirm its accuracy. Because each record is printed in the transaction format, it is relatively easy to check these values.

```
              EMPLOYEE MASTER VALIDATE AND CREATE

0001Falcon, Lloyd        140   19500325323420425000   ** MASTER RECORD CREATED **
0002Carney, Jim          130   19630404444350356000   ** MASTER RECORD CREATED **
0003Chambers, JK         130   19650715433420421300   ** MASTER RECORD CREATED **
0004Gallagher, Angelo    120   19661111453260315000   ** MASTER RECORD CREATED **
0005Ellis, Mike          140   19680105462230259000   ** MASTER RECORD CREATED **
0006Dawson, Mary         140   19721230553270301000   ** MASTER RECORD CREATED **
0007Arbor, Noel          105   19740401532230273458   ** MASTER RECORD CREATED **
0008DaCosta, Michael     105   19750629575450527500   ** MASTER RECORD CREATED **
0009Eagle, Wilfred       190   19770518311140234000   ** MASTER RECORD CREATED **
0010Assad, James         110   19780918463250294530   ** MASTER RECORD CREATED **
0011Baird, Joan          105   19831011592210168000   ** MASTER RECORD CREATED **
0012Gallagher, Pat       115   19831231622210168000   ** MASTER RECORD CREATED **
0013Baird, Joan          105   19830101622210168000   ** MASTER RECORD CREATED **
0014Cantoone, Phil       120   19840827544370124000   ** MASTER RECORD CREATED **
0015Harris, Jim          105   19840321564210167000   ** MASTER RECORD CREATED **


RECORDS CONTAINING ERRORS:     0
RECORDS ON MASTER FILE:        15
TOTAL TRANSACTIONS:            15
```

FIGURE 5.13 Report from creating the employee master

DUMPING THE MASTER FILE

Although the report suggests that the master file has been created successfully and correctly, it is no guarantee that the master is in fact correct. That may seem like a strong statement to make, but all the report really does is tell us the program detected no errors in the transactions and that no key errors were found. Important as this may be, the master itself is a relative disk file that to this point we have not seen.

Another important part of testing a program that creates a disk file is to dump the file that was created. Dumping simply means to print the contents of the file as the data appear on the disk without regard for formatting or editing of the fields. Utility programs are available in most systems that may be used for dumping a file by supplying a few parameter records to the utility. For our purposes, a short COBOL program has been written in Figure 5.14 to read the relative file sequentially and print the contents of each record.

```
IDENTIFICATION DIVISION.

PROGRAM-ID.
    DUMP5.
*AUTHOR.
*    JOHNATHAN YOUNGMAN.
*INSTALLATION.
*    SALES UNLIMITED CORP.
*DATE-WRITTEN.
*    MAY 26.
*DATE-COMPILED.

*    DUMPS CONTENTS OF RELATIVE MASTER FILE

ENVIRONMENT DIVISION.

CONFIGURATION SECTION.
SOURCE-COMPUTER.
    IBM-PC.
OBJECT-COMPUTER.
    IBM-PC.

INPUT-OUTPUT SECTION.

FILE-CONTROL.
    SELECT EMPLOYEE-MASTER  ASSIGN TO MASTER
            ORGANIZATION IS RELATIVE
            ACCESS IS SEQUENTIAL
            RELATIVE KEY IS WS-EMPLOYEE-NO.
    SELECT DUMP-REPORT      ASSIGN TO PRINTER.

DATA DIVISION.

FILE SECTION.

FD  EMPLOYEE-MASTER
    RECORD CONTAINS 60 CHARACTERS
    LABEL RECORDS ARE STANDARD
    DATA RECORD IS MASTER-REC.
01  MASTER-REC.
    05  FILLER                  PIC X(60).

FD  DUMP-REPORT
    RECORD CONTAINS 133 CHARACTERS
    LABEL RECORDS ARE OMITTED
    DATA RECORD IS PRINT-REC.
01  PRINT-REC.
    05  PRINT-LINE              PIC X(133).
```

FIGURE 5.14(a)   Program to dump the relative master file

```
WORKING-STORAGE SECTION.

    01  OTHER-ITEMS.
        05  WS-EMPLOYEE-NO          PIC 9(04).
        05  EOF-FLAG                PIC X(03)    VALUE 'NO'.
            88  END-OF-FILE                      VALUE 'YES'.
        05  LINE-COUNT              PIC 9(02)    VALUE ZERO.

    01  WS-MAST-REC.
        05  MAST-DELETE             PIC X(01).
        05  MAST-EMPLOYEE-NO        PIC X(04).
        05  MAST-NAME               PIC X(20).
        05  MAST-CURRENT-DEPT       PIC X(03).
        05  MAST-PREV-DEPT          PIC X(03).
        05  MAST-YEAR-EMPLOYED      PIC X(04).
        05  MAST-BIRTH-DATE.
            10  MAST-MONTH          PIC X(02).
            10  MAST-DAY            PIC X(02).
            10  MAST-YEAR           PIC X(02).
        05  MAST-EDUCATION          PIC X(01).
        05  MAST-JOB-CODE           PIC X(02).
        05  MAST-INCOME             PIC 9(06)V99.
        05  FILLER                  PIC X(08).

    01  HEAD-1.
        05  FILLER                  PIC X(20)    VALUE SPACES.
        05  FILLER                  PIC X(36)
                    VALUE 'EMPLOYEE MASTER FILE DUMP'.

    01  DETAIL-LINE.
        05  FILLER                  PIC X(01)    VALUE SPACES.
        05  DETAIL-RECORD           PIC X(60)    VALUE SPACES.

PROCEDURE DIVISION.

100-MAINLINE.
    PERFORM 200-INITIALIZE.
    PERFORM 300-PROCESS
        UNTIL END-OF-FILE.
    CLOSE EMPLOYEE-MASTER
        DUMP-REPORT.
    STOP RUN.

200-INITIALIZE.
    OPEN INPUT  EMPLOYEE-MASTER
        OUTPUT DUMP-REPORT.
    PERFORM 220-HEADINGS.
    PERFORM 250-READ.

220-HEADINGS.
    WRITE PRINT-REC FROM HEAD-1
*       AFTER ADVANCING TO-TOP-OF-PAGE.
    MOVE SPACES TO PRINT-REC.
    WRITE PRINT-REC
*       AFTER ADVANCING 1 LINE.
    MOVE 2 TO LINE-COUNT.

250-READ.
    READ EMPLOYEE-MASTER INTO WS-MAST-REC
        AT END MOVE 'YES' TO EOF-FLAG.

300-PROCESS.
    MOVE SPACES          TO DETAIL-LINE.
    MOVE WS-MAST-REC     TO DETAIL-RECORD.
    PERFORM 360-PRINT-LINE.
    PERFORM 250-READ.

360-PRINT-LINE.
    WRITE PRINT-REC FROM DETAIL-LINE
*       AFTER ADVANCING 1 LINE.
    ADD 1               TO LINE-COUNT.
    IF LINE-COUNT IS GREATER THAN 35
        PERFORM 220-HEADINGS.
```

FIGURE 5.14(b)

For this dump program, the SELECT clause is written as follows:

```
SELECT EMPLOYEE-MASTER  ASSIGN TO MASTER
       ORGANIZATION IS RELATIVE
       ACCESS IS SEQUENTIAL
       RELATIVE KEY IS WS-EMPLOYEE-NO.
```

Again, the ORGANIZATION IS RELATIVE and ACCESS IS SEQUENTIAL. But this time the EMPLOYEE-MASTER will be opened as an input file:

```
OPEN INPUT  EMPLOYEE-MASTER
     OUTPUT DUMP-REPORT.
```

Because the relative file is to be read sequentially from the beginning to the end of the file, it is simply handled in the same manner as any other sequential disk file. The only difference is in the SELECT clause, which we have already seen. When the file is read sequentially, it is not necessary to move a value to the relative key field unless a START statement were used to begin reading other than at the beginning of the file.

When this program is run, the report in Figure 5.15 is printed showing the contents of the relative file. Again, these records should be checked against the transactions to ensure that all records are accounted for and that the data are accurate.

```
                    EMPLOYEE MASTER FILE DUMP

       0001Falcon, Lloyd      140      19500325323420425000
       0002Carney, Jim        130      19630404444350356000
       0003Chambers, JK       130      19650715433420421300
       0004Gallagher, Angelo  120      19661111453260315000
       0005Ellis, Mike        140      19680105462230259000
       0006Dawson, Mary       140      19721230553270301000
       0007Arbor, Noel        105      19740401532230273458
       0008DaCosta, Michael   105      19750629575450527500
       0009Eagle, Wilfred     190      19770518311140234000
       0010Assad, James       110      19780918463250294530
       0011Baird, Joan        105      19831011592210168000
       0012Gallagher, Pat     115      19831231622210168000
       0013Baird, Joan        105      19830101622210168000
       0014Cantoone, Phil     120      19840827544370124000
       0015Harris, Jim        105      19840321564210167000
```

FIGURE 5.15   A dump of the master file after creation

UPDATING THE EMPLOYEE MASTER: AN APPLICATION PROGRAM

Updating a relative master is quite different from the program to update a sequential master file. First, there is only one master file to be used, unlike the sequential update, which requires a master file and an updated master file. With the relative file, records are read directly and, if they are revised, are rewritten back onto the master. No new master file is created as a result of the update (see Figure 5.16). An important consideration here is that the master contents will be different after the update, but a backup is not a normal by-product of the update. Because of this, many applications create a backup file before the update program is run.

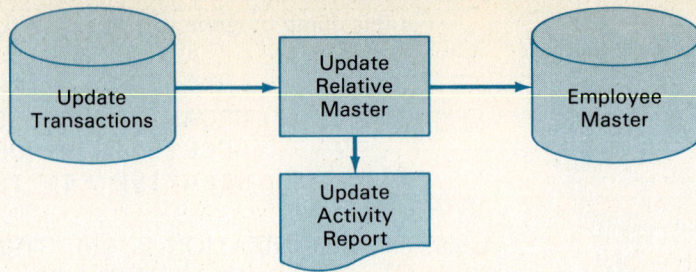

FIGURE 5.16 System flowchart for updating a relative master file

SPECIFICATIONS

The specifications for a relative update do not look much different from those for a sequential update. There are transactions to add new records, revise records, and delete unwanted records. A report is usually required to show the update activity and any error messages if something goes wrong during the update. The difference with a relative file update program comes in the logic required to implement a solution.

In this logic, we need to contend with the possibility of key errors when doing any activity against the master file. Key errors can mean different things in different situations, as we will see later. For now, take a look at the specifications in Figure 5.17.

PROGRAMMING SPECIFICATIONS

PROGRAM NAME: Employee Master Update   PROGRAM ID: UPDATE5
PREPARED BY: Diane Quest   DATE: May 29, 1986

Program Description
    The program defined here updates the relative record employee master file.
Input File(s):
    Transaction file
Input/Output File(s):
    Relative employee master file
Output File(s):
    Update activity report
Program Requirements:
1. Read a disk file of update transaction records identified by the following transaction codes:

Code	Type of transaction
1	New—add a new record to the master file.
2	Revise—modify an existing record on the master file.
3	Delete—remove a record from the master.

2. As the master contains a delete code in the first byte of the record, it will be necessary to test for this code. A value of 9 indicates the record has been previously deleted and should not be considered currently active. To delete an active record, move a 9 to this field and rewrite the master record.
3. Validate the transactions according to the following criteria:
    a) The employee number supplies the relative key for accessing the master record. This field must be numeric.
    b) Only transaction codes 1, 2, or 3 are acceptable.
    c) Other validations are to yet be defined, so use a program stub for the remainder of this module.
4. Print a message for each error found. Some likely errors that may occur during the update are:
    a) A master record cannot be found.
    b) A master already exists for a new add to the file.
    c) A key error occurs on a rewrite. This indicates a system problem, but it should not be ignored.

FIGURE 5.17(a) Program specifications for updating the relative employee master

5. Also print a message for successful processing of each transaction, including the following:
   a) When the master record is revised.
   b) When a new master record is created.
   c) When a master record has been deleted.
   Every transaction must appear on the report with a message indicating its status.
6. Updates (revision code 2) occur to a field if that field is supplied in the transaction. A blank (nonnumeric for income) field indicates no activity. If the current department is to be revised, first move the master's current department field to the previous department and then revise the current field.
7. Check for an invalid key on the master, and if one occurs, print an appropriate error message. The exception to this is when an invalid key occurs for a new record to be added. In this case the record can be written to the master.

FIGURE 5.17(b)

INPUT/OUTPUT DEFINITION

Like all update programs, this one uses a transaction file (Figure 5.18). Unlike a sequential update, a relative update program does not require the transactions to be in key sequence. Transactions are usually in the order they are received from their source. However, for testing purposes later, we will have them in sequence to simplify checking the results of the update.

The relative master file (Figure 5.19) is defined exactly as it was for creating the file. This is an important check in a walkthrough, because if we are to read a master file in an update program, its specifications must be the same as when it was created. All programs that use this file will use the same specifications; otherwise, errors will occur that may not be the fault of the programmer, but rather of the file definition.

Because the relative file is used in a random update, it will be used for both input and output. In COBOL terminology, it is called an I/0 file. To access records from the file, the program will issue a read statement, and the file becomes an input to

INPUT/OUTPUT RECORD DEFINITION				
File: Transactions Record Length: 60 Sequence: None required		File Type: Disk Blocking Factor: 10 Access Method: Sequential		
COLUMNS	FIELD	TYPE	LENGTH	DECIMALS
1–4	Employee number 1—new 2—revise 3—delete	N	4	
5	Type code	N	1	
6–25	Name	A/N	20	
26–28	Current dept.	A/N	3	
29–31	Previous dept.	A/N	3	
32–35	Year employed	A/N	4	
36–41	Birth date	A/N	6	
42	Education code	A/N	1	
43–44	Job code	A/N	2	
45–52	Income	N	8	2

FIGURE 5.18   Definition for the transaction file

Programming with Relative Files

INOUT/OUTPUT RECORD DEFINITION				
File: Employee master Record Length: 60 Sequence: Employee number		File Type: Relative disk Blocking Factor:1 Access Method: Sequential		
COLUMNS	FIELD	TYPE	LENGTH	DECIMALS
1	Delete byte*	A/N	1	
2–5	Employee number**	N	4	
6–25	Name	A/N	20	
26–28	Current dept.	A/N	3	
29–31	Previous dept.	A/N	3	
32–35	Year employed	A/N	4	
36–41	Birth date	A/N	6	
42	Education code	A/N	1	
43–44	Job code	A/N	2	
45–52	Income	N	8	2
* The delete byte is necessary only on 1968 ANS COBOL. ** Relative key field.				

FIGURE 5.19   Definition for the employee master file

the program. After a record has been changed, it will be placed back on the file with a rewrite and therefore becomes an output from the program.

One other output from the program is the update report (Figure 5.20). This report lists each transaction read and the activity taken for the record. This activity could be a list of errors, if they occur, or it can show the action taken against the master by the processing of the transaction. The report does not show any totals, although that is a distinct possibility as a future requirement.

The report layout shows the position of each field, which seems to imply that every field will always be present. This is not always the case, because a revision will only include the fields that need to be revised. Similarly, a delete only needs the employee number of the record to be deleted.

```
                                                                    1       1       1
     0       1       2       3       4       5       6       7       8       9       0       1       2
     1234567890123456789012345678901234567890123456789012345678901234567890 123456789012345678901234567890

                      EMPLOYEE MASTER UPDATE
     EMPLOYEE  NAME                    DEPARTMENT    YEAR        BIRTH        CODES     INCOME     MESSAGES
     NUMBER                            CURR PREV   EMPLOYED      DATE        ED   JOB

      9999     X------------------X    XXX  XXX      XXXX       XXBXXBXX      X    XX    ZZZZ9.99   MASTER RECORD REVISED

      9999                                                                                         MASTER RECORD DELETED

      9999     X------------------X    XXX  XXX      XXXX       XXBXXBXX      X    XX    ZZZZ9.99   MASTER RECORD NOT FOUND

      9999     X------------------X    XXX  XXX      XXXX       XXBXXBXX      X    XX    ZZZZ9.99   NEW MASTER RECORD CREATED

      9999     X------------------X    XXX  XXX      XXXX       XXBXXBXX      X    XX    ZZZZ9.99   NON-NUMERIC EMPLOYEE NO.
                                                                                                   TRANS CODE NOT 1, 2 OR 3


                                                                                                   *** END OF FILE UPDATE **
```

FIGURE 5.20   Update report layout

STRUCTURE CHART

When developing the structure chart for the relative update, we need to consider that two basic file types are in use. One file contains the transactions and is in sequential order. This sequence suggests a need for routine logic that handles the reading of input records until end of file has occurred.

The second file type is the relative master. This file may be accessed randomly by supplying the relative key of the record required. Rather than reading the master, as we did in a sequential update, we only read the record that needs to be processed based on the transaction currently in storage. Therefore, the master is processed directly by each module that does the updating.

How does this approach affect the structure chart? To understand this method, let's first develop the process module as follows:

```
                            300
                       Process
                       Updates

    320           400           360           250
Move          Validate    Update      Print     Read
Fields                    Master      Line
```

The first step in processing, assuming a transaction has already been read by the initialization module, is to move the fields to the report. Then the record is validated before further processing is considered. If every field checks out, then the master may be updated by performing module 400. Finally, the detail line is printed to give a blank line between records on the report and the next transaction is read. The key to doing the updating of the master lies within module 400, so let's look at its refinement.

```
                400
            Update
            Master

    410         420         430
Add New    Revise    Delete
Master     Master    Master
```

Essentially, like any update, there are three fundamental types of activities against the master; add, revise, and delete. In each of these modules, the activity against the master, including reading and rewriting, will be done. First, the add module is expanded.

```
                410
            Add New
            Master

  450       350       415       460
Read    Print    Create    Rewrite
Master  Error    New       Master
```

To add a new master record, it is necessary to read the master file to ensure this record does not already exist. If it exists, but the delete code has been set, then we can revise this previously deleted record, make it active, and rewrite it to the master file. If the master record was currently active, then an error message is created to indicate the master already exists.

The next module to develop is the revise. It is similar to the new module except, of course, we expect to get a currently active record. Again, a master record is read, revised according to the transaction's contents, and rewritten to the master file. Here is the expanded portion of the structure chart for the revision.

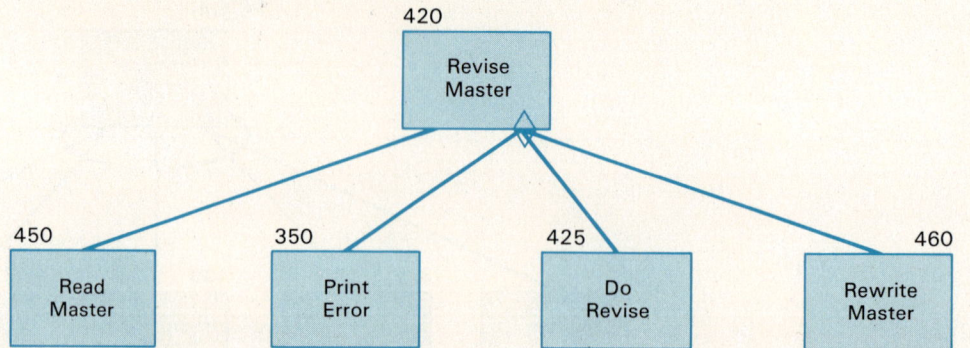

The third type of update to the master is a delete transaction. This processing also reads a master and checks to see if it is currently active. If the record is active, the delete byte is set on and the record is rewritten. Otherwise, the record is already deleted and an error message is produced.

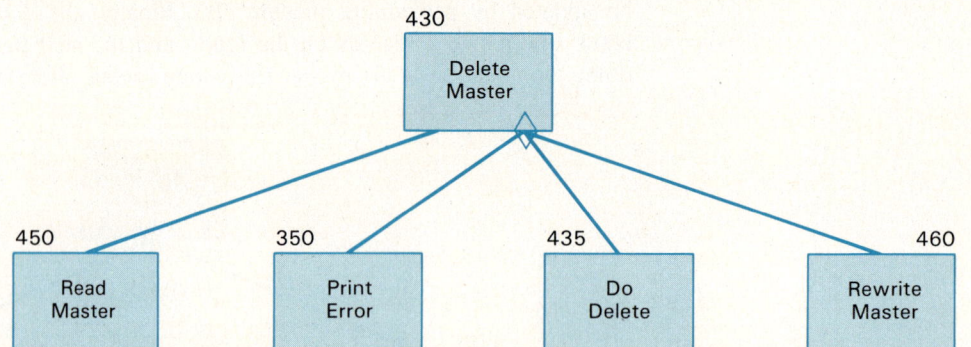

Figure 5.21 shows the complete structure chart for the update to the relative employee master file.

PSEUDO CODE

To develop the pseudo code, more attention is paid to the details of the checking of flags that relate to errors or invalid key detection when accessing the master. For example, in the process module, the transaction is validated to make sure its fields contain correct data before attempting an update. Therefore, the logic in the pseudo code must have a dependency on the results of the validation. This test is handled as follows in the process module:

```
4. Perform 320-Validate.

5. If no errors were found
      Perform 400-Update-Master
   EndIf
```

Next the validation steps need to be defined in more detail than the structure chart gave. In particular, the method for checking employee number and the transaction

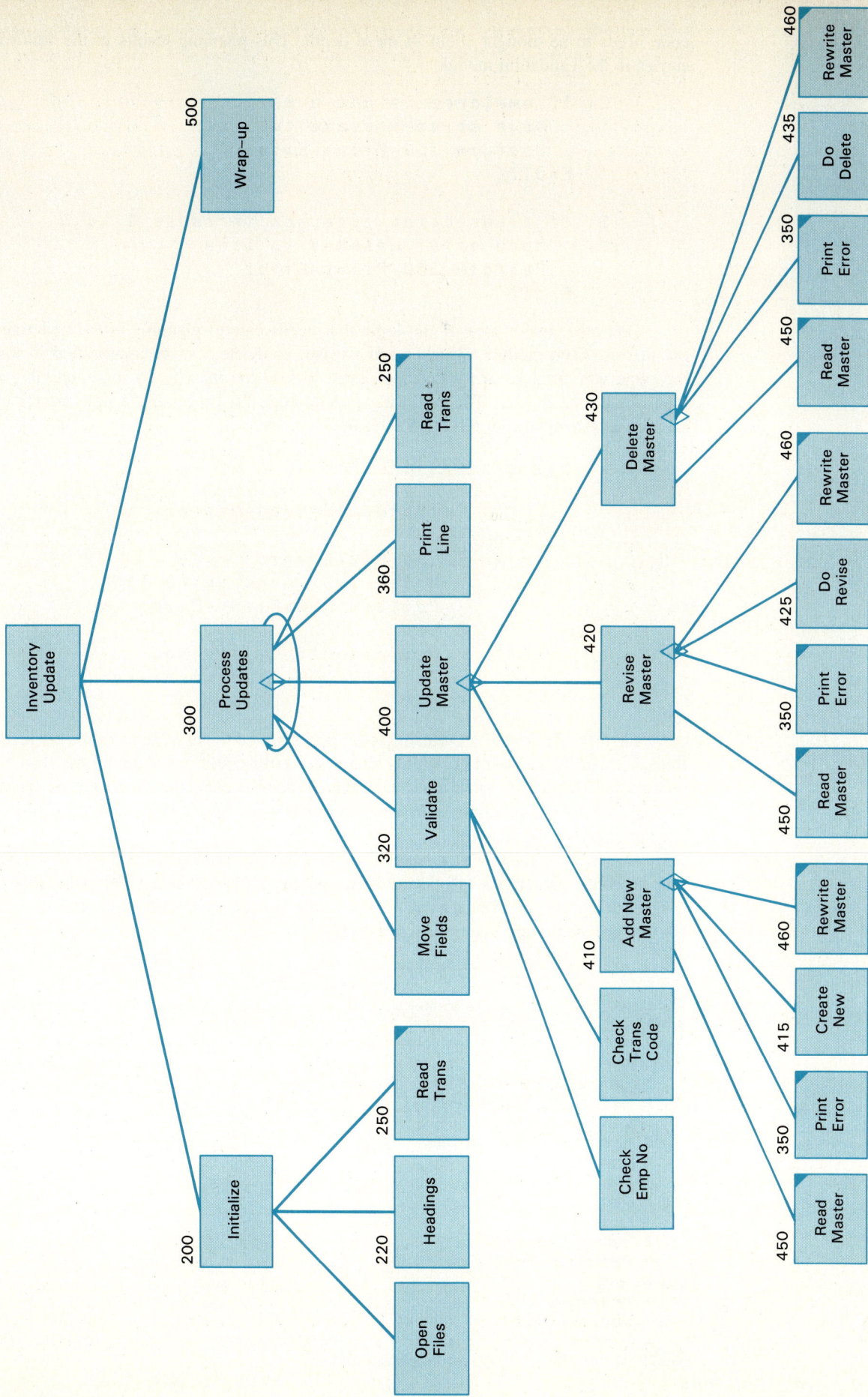

FIGURE 5.21 Structure chart for the inventory update

159

code needs to be thought about in more depth. This planning results in the following entries in the validation module:

```
2. If employee is not numeric
     Move error message to line
     Perform 350-Print-Error
   EndIf

3. If transaction code not in range 1 to 3
     Move error message to line
     Perform 350-Print-Error
   EndIf
```

One other major area of the logic that needs careful planning is the updating of the master. Each module, whether add, revise, or delete, can be approached in much the same way because of the common need to read the master, do some activity, and then rewrite the master. The following pseudo code for processing a new master may be used as a template for the other modules:

```
410-New-Master

   1. Perform 450-Read-Master.

   2. If no key error
        Move error message to line
        Perform 350-Print-Error
      Else
        Perform 415-Create-New
        Perform 460-Rewrite-Master
      EndIf
```

First, the paragraph 450-Read-Master is performed to get access to a master record. Because there is a distinct possibility that a key error could occur during the read, this module must check for such an occurrence. If none occurs, then a master exists and, in this case, the transaction is in error because it is attempting to add a record that already exists on the master.

However, if there was a key error, then we can proceed to add the new record by performing paragraphs 415-Create-New and 460-Rewrite-Master. Following this pattern, each update module is written. The entire pseudo code and structured flowchart for this application are given in Figure 5.22.

PSEUDO CODE		
PROGRAM NAME: Employee Master Update		PROGRAM ID: UPDATE5
PREPARED BY: Jonathan Youngman	DATE: May 30	PAGE 1 of 5

100-Mainline
   1. Perform 200-Initialize.
   2. Perform 300-Process
      Until end of file.
   3. Perform 500-End-of-Update.
   4. Close files.
   5. Stop run.
200-Initialize
   1. Open files.
   2. Perform 220-Headings.
   3. Perform 250-Read.
220-Headings
   1. Write heading 1.
   2. Write heading 2.

FIGURE 5.22(a) Pseudo code for employee update

    3. Write blank line.
    4. Set line count to 5.

250-Read
    1. Read transaction
        At end move 'yes' to Eof-Flag.

300-Process
    1. Move spaces to detail line.
    2. Move transaction fields to detail line.
    3. If income is numeric
        Move income to detail line
      EndIf
    4. Perform 320-Validate.
    5. If no errors were found
        Perform 400-Update-Master
      EndIf
    6. Perform 360-Print-Line (blank line).
    7. Perform 250-Read.

320-Validate
    1. Move 'no' to error flag.
    2. If employee is not numeric
        Move error message to line
        Perform 350-Print-Error
      EndIf
    3. If transaction code not in range 1 to 3
        Move error message to line
        Perform 350-Print-Error
      EndIf
    *** remainder of this module is a stub ***

FIGURE 5.22(b)

340-Print-Detail
    1. Perform 360-Print-Line.
    2. Move spaces to detail line.

350-Print-Error
    1. Perform 360-Print-Line.
    2. Move spaces to detail line.
    3. Move 'yes' to error flag.

360-Print-Line
    1. Write detail line.
    2. Add 1 to line count.
    3. If line count > 35
        Perform 220-Headings
      EndIf

400-Update-Master
    1. Move employee number to relative key.
    2. If add transaction
        Perform 410-New-Master
      Else
        If revise transaction
            Perform 420-Revise-Master
        Else
            Perform 430-Delete-Master
        EndIf
      EndIf

FIGURE 5.22(c)

PROGRAM NAME: Employee Master Update   PROGRAM ID: UPDATE5
PREPARED BY: Jonathan Youngman   DATE: May 30   PAGE 3 of 5

410-New-Master
1. Perform 450-Read-Master.
2. If no key error
   Move error message to line
   Perform 350-Print-Error
   Else
      Perform 415-Create-New
      Perform 460-Rewrite-Master
   EndIf

415-Create-New
1. Clear master delete code.
2. Move transaction fields to master and detail line.
3. Perform 360-Print-Line.

420-Revise-Master
1. Move message to line.
2. Perform 450-Read-Master.
3. If key error
   Move error message to line
   Perform 350-Print-Error
   Else
      Perform 425-Do-Revise
      Perform 460-Rewrite-Master
   EndIf

FIGURE 5.22(d)

PSEUDO CODE
PROGRAM NAME: Employee Master Update   PROGRAM ID: UPDATE5
PREPARED BY: Jonathan Youngman   DATE: May 30   PAGE 4 of 5

425-Do-Revise
1. If name present
   Move name to master
   End If
2. If current dept present
   Move master current dept to master previous dept
   Move current dept to master
   End If
3. If birth date present
   Move birth date to master
   End If
4. If education code present
   Move education code to master
   End If
5. If job code present
   Move job code to master
   End If
6. If income present
   Move income to master
   End If
7. Move message to line.
8. Perform 360-Print-Line.

430-Delete-Master
1. Perform 450-Read-Master.
2. If key error
   Move error message to line
   Perform 350-Print-Error
   Else
      Perform 435 Do-Delete
   End If

FIGURE 5.22(e)

PROGRAM NAME: Employee Master Update   PROGRAM ID: UPDATE5
PREPARED BY: Jonathan Youngman   DATE: May 30   PAGE 5 of 5

435-Do-Delete
1. Move '9' to master delete code.
2. Perform 460-Rewrite-Master.
3. Move message to line.
4. Perform 360-Print-Line.

450-Read-Master
1. Read Employee Master
    Invalid key move 'yes' to key error flag.
2. If Master delete code = '9'
    Move 'yes' to key error flag
    End If

460-Rewrite-Master
1. Rewrite Employee Master
    Invalid key move message to line
        Perform 350-Print-Error.

500-End-Of-Update
1. Print *end of update* message.

FIGURE 5.22(f)

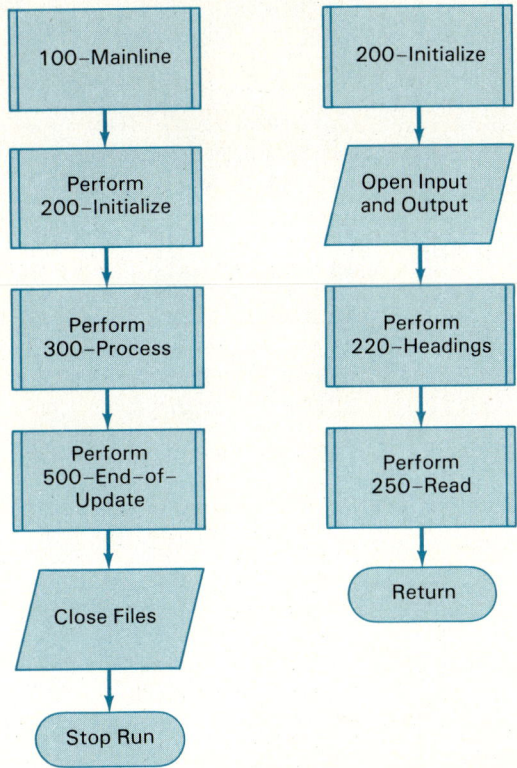

FIGURE 5.22(g)   Structured flowchart for employee update

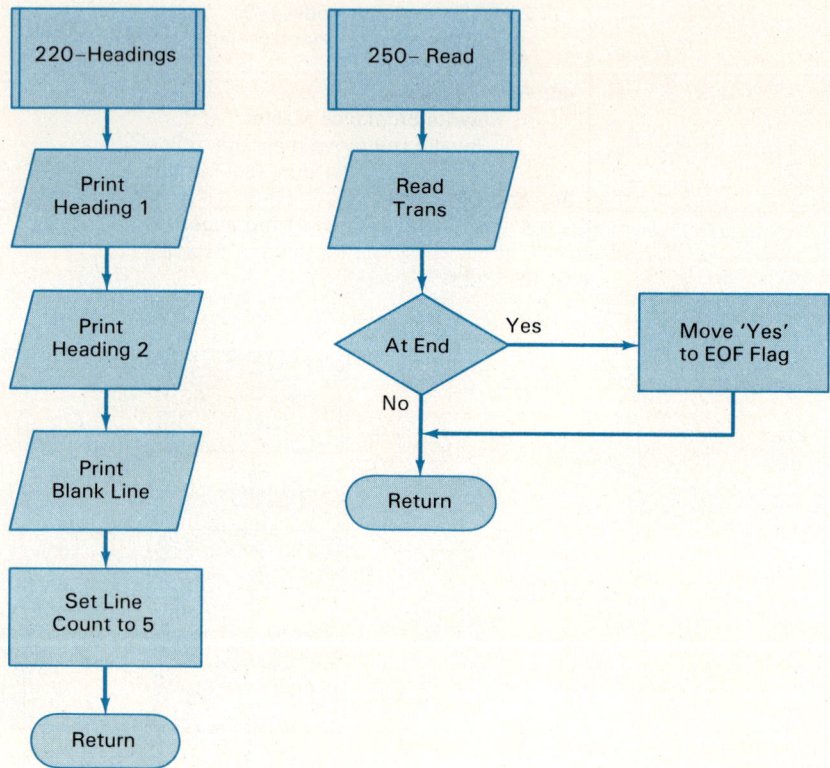

FIGURE 5.22(h)

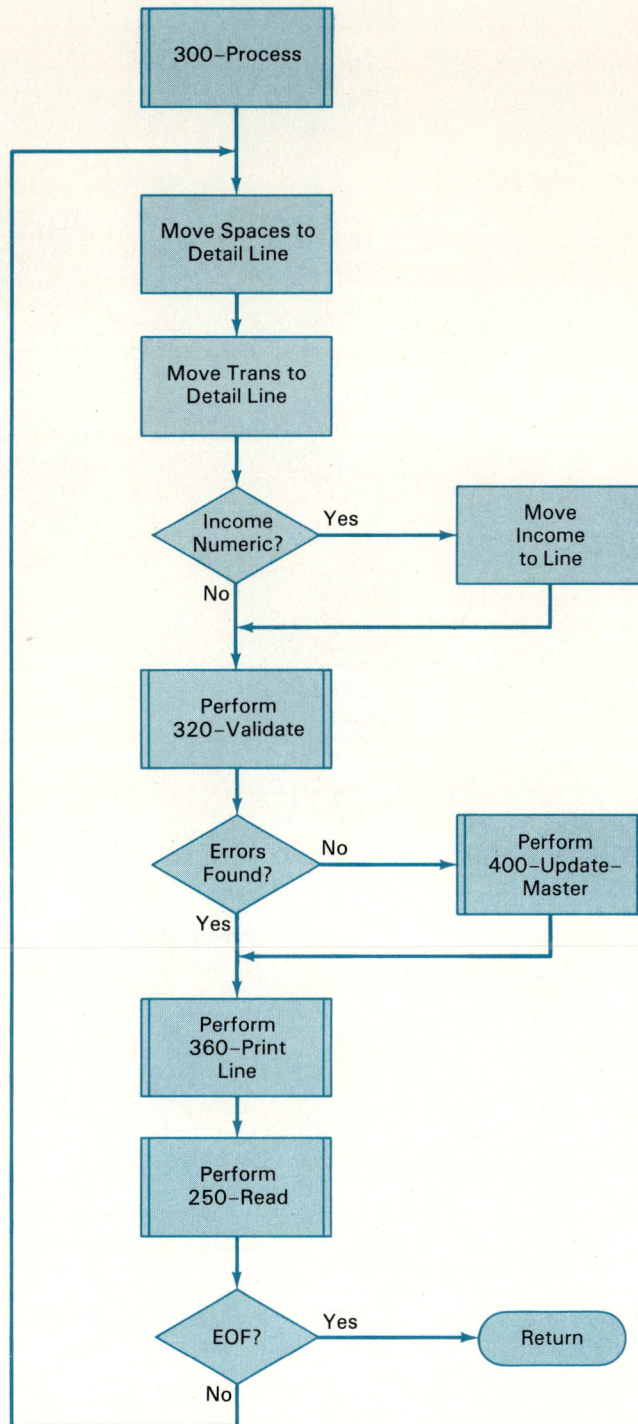

FIGURE 5.22(i)

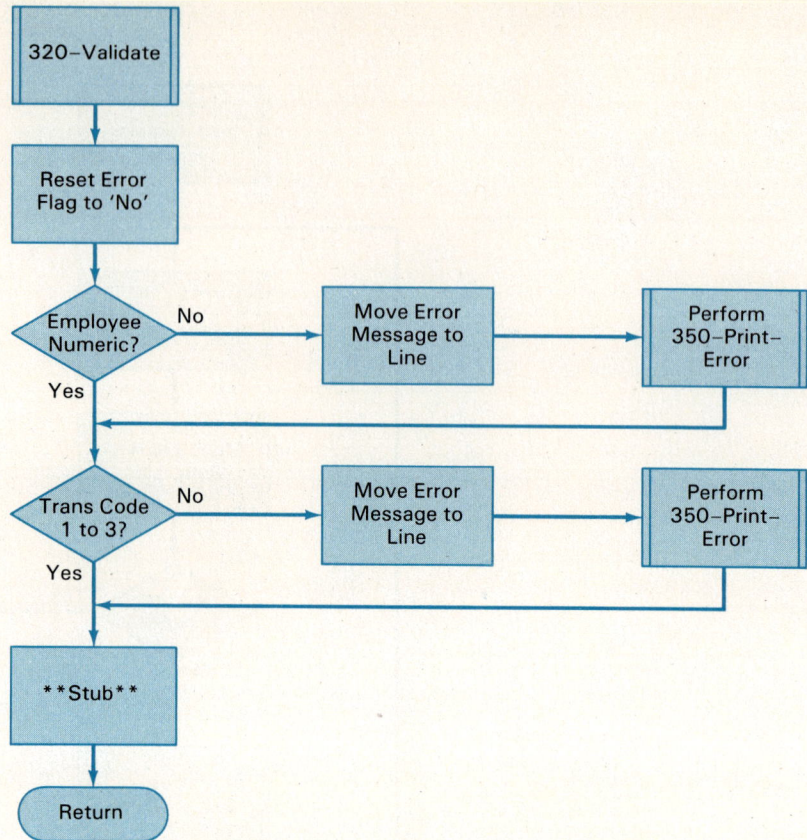

FIGURE 5.22(j)

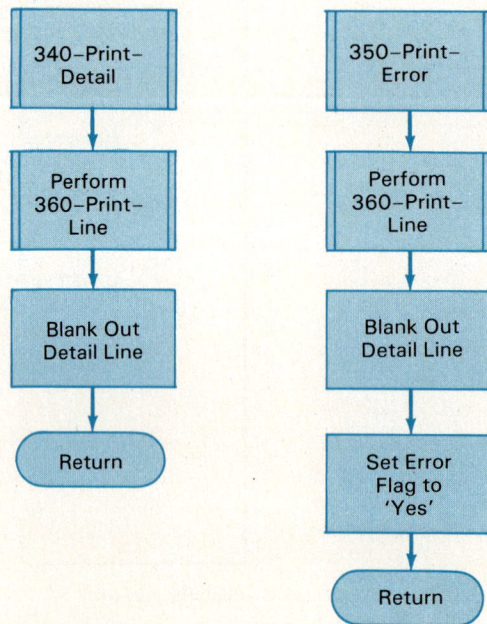

FIGURE 5.22(k)

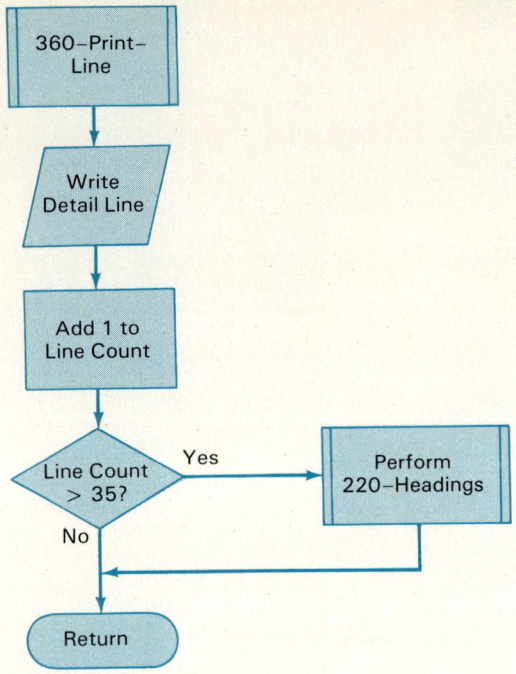

FIGURE 5.22(l)

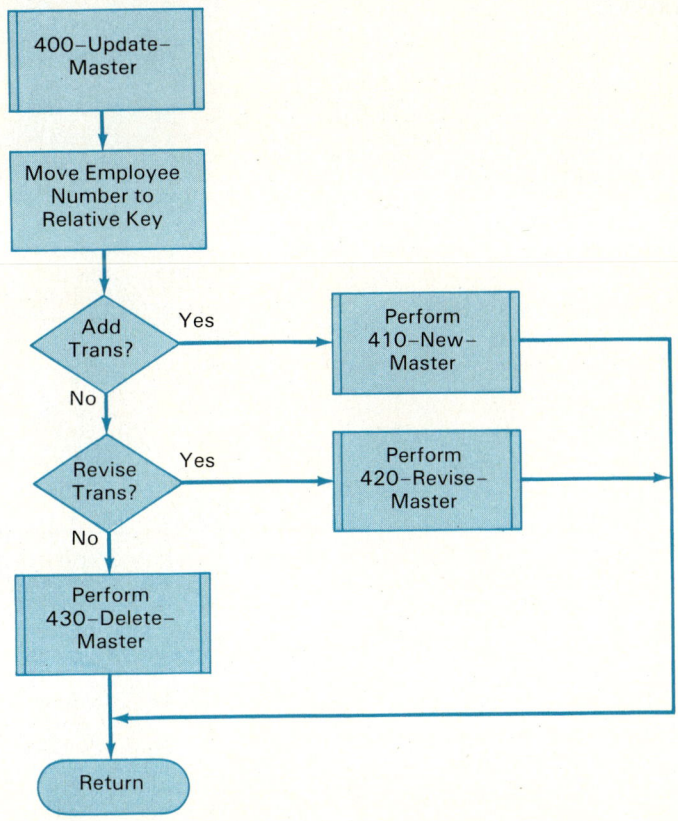

FIGURE 5.22(m)

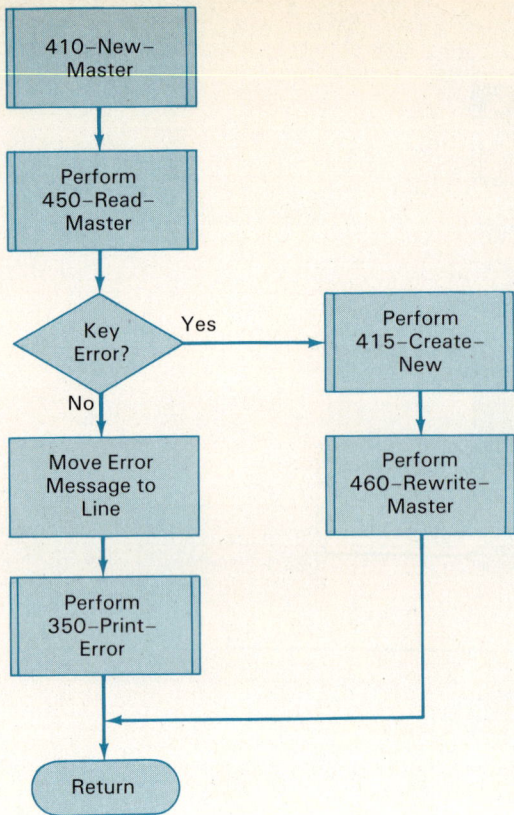

FIGURE 5.22(n)

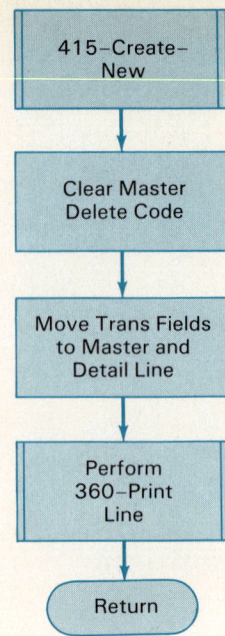

FIGURE 5.22(o)

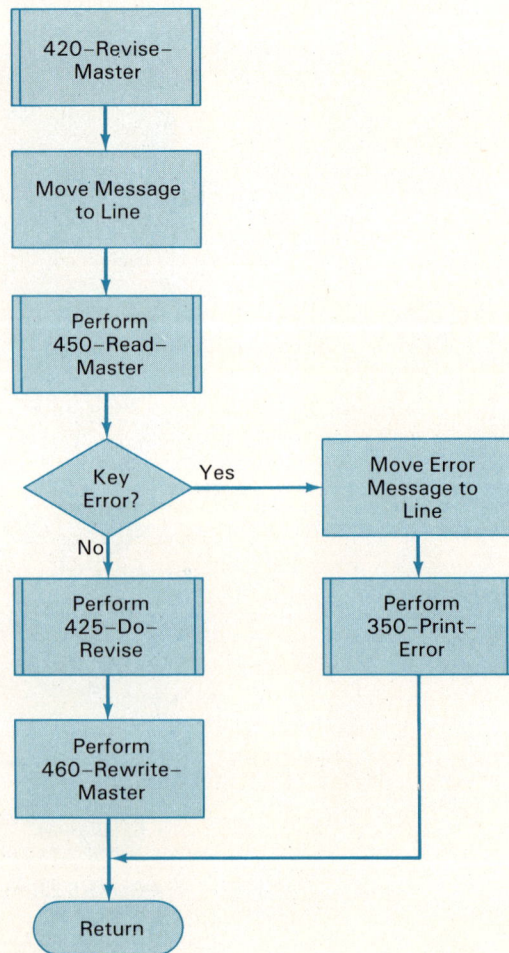

FIGURE 5.22(p)

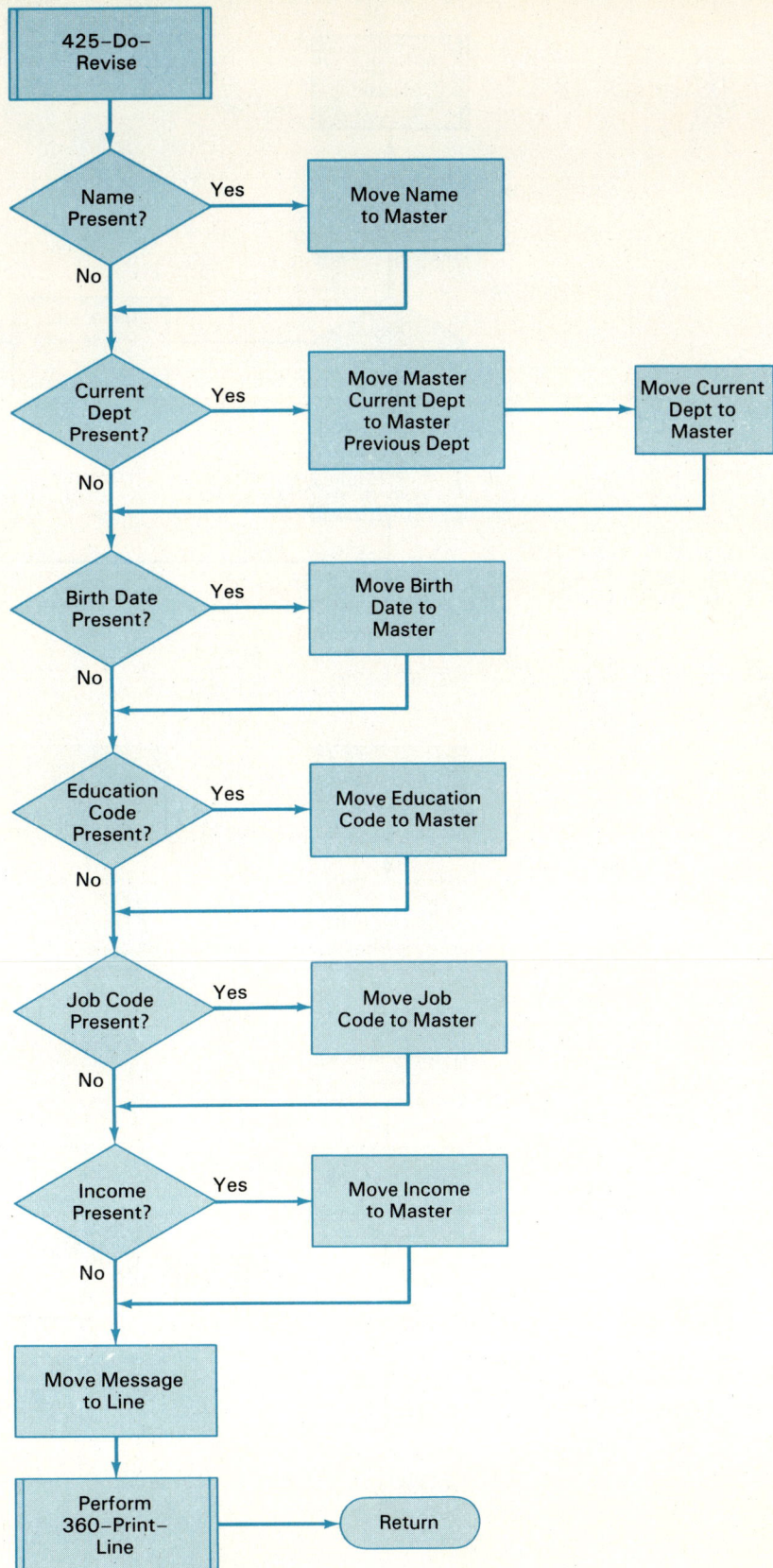

FIGURE 5.22(q)

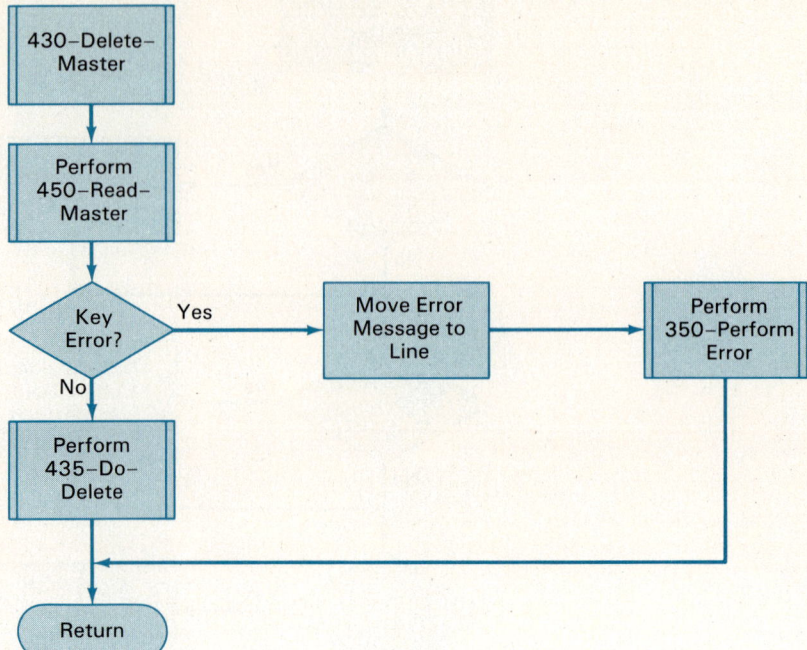

FIGURE 5.22(r)

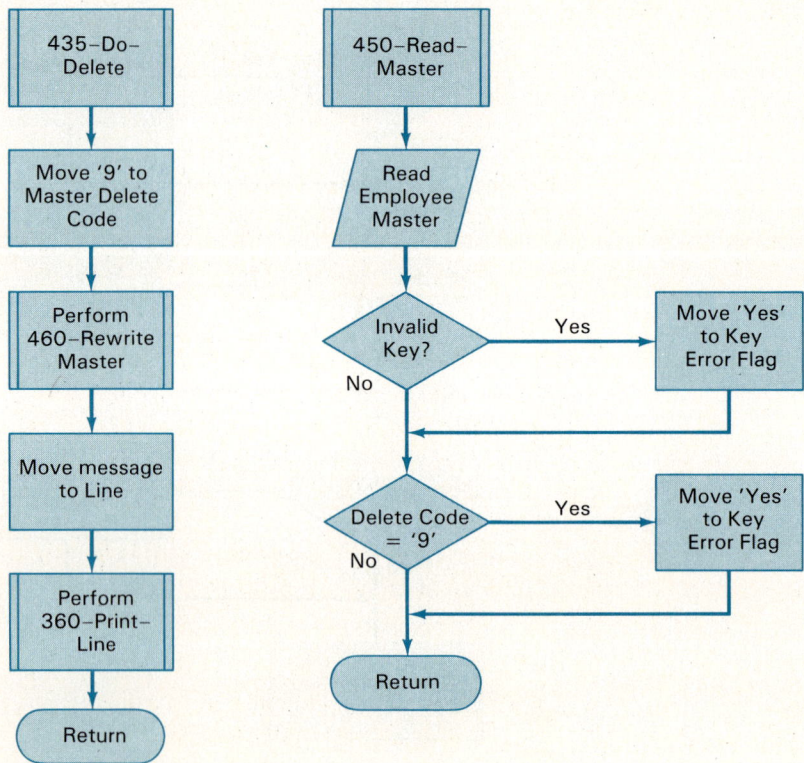

FIGURE 5.22(s)

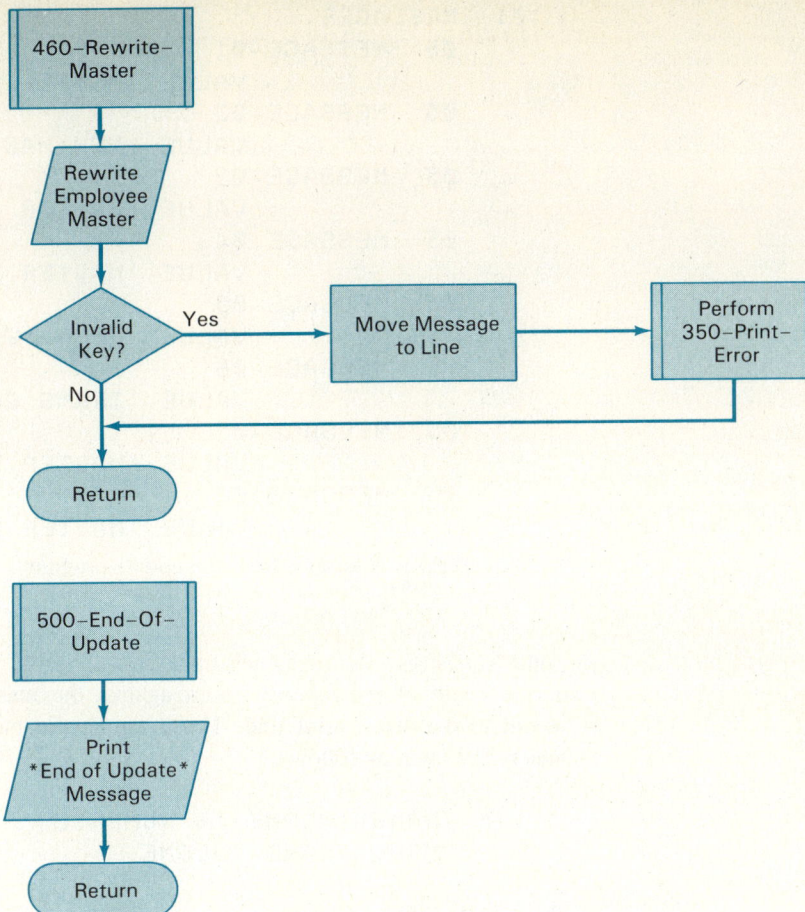

FIGURE 5.22(t)

PROGRAM CODING

When the first three divisions of this program are considered, we will realize that it begins much the same way as the create program written earlier. There are three files here: the transaction file, master file, and a report. Because of the transactions being sequential, an end of file flag is needed, and to check for key errors on the master, a key error flag will be required. Record formats are quite similar, the one difference being the transaction code in each transaction record, and of course the report layout is different in this program.

One important area where the update has new requirements is the list of errors that may be encountered. Figure 5.23 itemizes these messages, which will be coded in WORKING-STORAGE.

You might want to reference the complete program in Figure 5.24 as we discuss some of the paragraphs it contains.

100-MAINLINE   This is the top level of the program and, as in our previous programs, it performs the initialization module, the process loop, and any end-of-program activities before the program is terminated.

200-INITIALIZE   This paragraph opens files, performs the module that prints the headings, and reads the first transaction record. Because this is a relative update program, the first master record is not read here, but rather it will be read when the type of update has been determined.

```
01   MESSAGES.
     05   MESSAGE-01              PIC X(25)
               VALUE 'MASTER RECORD REVISED'.
     05   MESSAGE-02              PIC X(25)
               VALUE 'NEW MASTER RECORD CREATED'.
     05   MESSAGE-03              PIC X(25)
               VALUE 'MASTER RECORD DELETED'.
     05   MESSAGE-04              PIC X(25)
               VALUE 'MASTER RECORD NOT FOUND'.
     05   MESSAGE-05              PIC X(25)
               VALUE 'NONNUMERIC EMPLOYEE NO.'.
     05   MESSAGE-06              PIC X(25)
               VALUE 'TRANS CODE NOT 1, 2 OR 3'.
     05   MESSAGE-07              PIC X(25)
               VALUE 'MASTER REWRITE ERROR'.
     05   MESSAGE-08              PIC X(25)
               VALUE 'MASTER ALREADY EXISTS'.
```

FIGURE 5.23 Messages from the update program

300-PROCESS Because each transaction is to be printed, with either error messages or the result of the activity taken against the master, the first step is to move the record to the detail print line. These are simple move statements except for income, which is written as follows:

```
IF TRANS-INCOME IS NUMERIC
     MOVE TRANS-INCOME              TO DET-INCOME.
```

The need to check for numeric on this field is because of the numeric pictures used in both records. Sometimes income will be blank in the transaction, which would result in an error if it were moved to a numeric picture. To avoid this problem, income is moved only if it contains a numeric value. Otherwise, the income field in the report will be blank.

Next, the transaction is validated. If no errors are found, paragraph 400 is performed to update the master file. If there was an error, no updating to the master is possible. Finally, a blank line is printed to get double-spacing between transactions on the report, and the next input record is read.

320-VALIDATE Each transaction is passed to this module for error checking. Part of the module is a stub, but the existing logic checks for a valid employee number to ensure that a numeric key will be provided to the relative file operation. The transaction code is also tested to ensure it is in the range of 1 to 3 inclusive. Any other value will be handled as an error.

350-PRINT-ERROR Any error that is detected by the program (primarily by the validate module) will be processed by this paragraph. The primary purpose here is to print the message supplied by the performing paragraph. Before leaving this module, the error flag is set as follows:

```
MOVE 'YES'                    TO ERROR-FLAG.
```

400-UPDATE-MASTER The first step here is to recognize that whatever transaction we are about to process will require an access of the master. So this module begins by initializing the relative key field as follows:

```
MOVE   TRANS-EMPLOYEE-NO        TO   WS-EMPLOYEE-NO.
```

The remainder of this paragraph checks the transaction code to determine what type of update is required. This is a sequence of IF statements, as follows, that performs the necessary paragraph for the appropriate updating.

```
IF ADD-TRANS
      PERFORM 410-NEW-MASTER
ELSE
      IF REVISE-TRANS
            PERFORM 420-REVISE-MASTER
      ELSE
            PERFORM 430-DELETE-MASTER.
```

410-NEW-MASTER and 415-CREATE-NEW   These paragraphs operate together to create a new master record. First the master is read to see if there is an existing record (there should be, but with a delete code of 9). If there isn't, an error message is created.

If a record is available for the new master, the second paragraph (415-CREATE-NEW) is performed. This paragraph clears the delete code and moves all transaction fields to the master. These fields are also moved to the detail line for the report. A rewrite from paragraph 460-REWRITE-MASTER is then issued to place the new record on the master file.

420-REVISE-MASTER and 425-DO-REVISE   These paragraphs work together also to revise a master record when a transaction code 2 is being processed. Again, the master record is read, and if an invalid key is detected, an error message is produced and processing of the transaction is discontinued.

When a valid master is successfully read, paragraph 425-DO-REVISE is entered. Each field, as necessary, is revised by checking for its presence in the transaction and making this necessary revision to the corresponding master field. For example, the name field is handled as follows:

```
IF TRANS-NAME IS NOT EQUAL TO SPACES
      MOVE  TRANS-NAME              TO  MAST-NAME.
```

When all fields have been revised that need revising, the master is rewritten with the changes onto the relative file.

430-DELETE-MASTER and 435-DO-DELETE   This final pair of paragraphs deletes a master record. Again, a master is read, and if currently active (it does not contain a delete code), paragraph 435-DO-DELETE moves a '9' to the master delete code and the record is rewritten to the master file.

This process is much simpler with 1985 ANS COBOL. It is essentially a matter of using the DELETE statement, and the rest is done by the operating system. With the DELETE statement, it is not necessary to first read the master file. A key error this time means that no record exists to be deleted.

```
DELETE EMPLOYEE-MASTER
      INVALID KEY MOVE 'YES' to KEY-ERROR-FLAG.
```

450-READ-MASTER   To read a master record requires that the relative key first be set to the key of the record you wish to read. This was done previously in paragraph 400-UPDATE-MASTER. Now a READ can be issued against the master. If a key error occurs, the record does not exist and the key error flag is set.

```
READ EMPLOYEE-MASTER INTO WS-MAST-REC
      INVALID KEY MOVE 'YES' TO KEY-ERROR-FLAG.
```

Because a delete code is used in the master, it must also be checked to ensure that the master is not inactive. This is done as follows, and if the delete code contains a '9', the key error flag is also set.

```
IF MAST-DELETE IS EQUAL TO '9'
    MOVE 'YES' TO KEY-ERROR-FLAG.
```

The effect of this statement is for the program to act as if a key error had occurred, although the real reason was the value in the delete code. 1985 ANS COBOL would not require the use of this extra IF statement to detect a deleted record.

460-REWRITE-MASTER   After a master record has been modified, either because of a revise transaction or a delete, it must be rewritten back onto the master file. This paragraph does the rewrite. The invalid key clause is supplied, although normally it should not be executed by the program. A key error here suggests a program error, such as inadvertently destroying the relative key field or writing a record of the wrong length.

500-END-OF-UPDATE   This paragraph prints a message to show the user that the program came to successful completion. This approach is important when there are no totals to be printed and it is not clear whether the program was actually finished or if it terminated prematurely because of some error.

```
IDENTIFICATION DIVISION.

PROGRAM-ID.
    UPDATE5.
*AUTHOR.
*    JOHNATHAN YOUNGMAN.
*INSTALLATION.
*    SALES UNLIMITED CORP.
*DATE-WRITTEN.
*    JUNE 8.
*DATE-COMPILED.

*SECURITY.
*    NONE.

ENVIRONMENT DIVISION.

CONFIGURATION SECTION.
SOURCE-COMPUTER.
    IBM-PC.
OBJECT-COMPUTER.
    IBM-PC.
SPECIAL-NAMES.
    C01 IS TO-TOP-OF-PAGE.

INPUT-OUTPUT SECTION.

FILE-CONTROL.
    SELECT TRANSACTIONS    ASSIGN TO TRANS52.
    SELECT EMPLOYEE-MASTER  ASSIGN TO MASTER
        ORGANIZATION IS RELATIVE
        ACCESS IS RANDOM
        RELATIVE KEY IS WS-EMPLOYEE-NO.
    SELECT UPDATE-REPORT    ASSIGN TO PRINTER.

DATA DIVISION.

FILE SECTION.
```

FIGURE 5.24(a)   Relative file update program for the employee master

```
FD  TRANSACTIONS
    BLOCK  CONTAINS 10 RECORDS
    RECORD CONTAINS 60 CHARACTERS
    LABEL RECORDS ARE STANDARD
    DATA RECORD IS TRANS-REC.
01  TRANS-REC.
    05  FILLER                      PIC X(60).

FD  EMPLOYEE-MASTER
    RECORD CONTAINS 60 CHARACTERS
    LABEL RECORDS ARE STANDARD
    DATA RECORD IS MASTER-REC.
01  MASTER-REC.
    05  FILLER                      PIC X(60).

FD  UPDATE-REPORT
    RECORD CONTAINS 133 CHARACTERS
    LABEL RECORDS ARE OMITTED
    DATA RECORD IS PRINT-REC.
01  PRINT-REC.
    05  PRINT-LINE                  PIC X(133).

WORKING-STORAGE SECTION.

01  OTHER-ITEMS.
    05  WS-EMPLOYEE-NO              PIC 9(04).
    05  EOF-FLAG                    PIC X(03)    VALUE 'NO'.
        88  END-OF-FILE                          VALUE 'YES'.
    05  ERROR-FLAG                  PIC X(03)    VALUE 'NO'.
        88  NO-ERRORS                            VALUE 'NO'.
    05  KEY-ERROR-FLAG              PIC X(03)    VALUE 'NO'.
        88  KEY-ERROR                            VALUE 'YES'.

01  TOTALS.
    05  LINE-COUNT                  PIC 9(02)    VALUE ZERO.

01  MESSAGES.
    05  MESSAGE-01                  PIC X(25)
            VALUE 'MASTER RECORD REVISED'.
    05  MESSAGE-02                  PIC X(25)
            VALUE 'NEW MASTER RECORD CREATED'.
    05  MESSAGE-03                  PIC X(25)
            VALUE 'MASTER RECORD DELETED'.
    05  MESSAGE-04                  PIC X(25)
            VALUE 'MASTER RECORD NOT FOUND'.
    05  MESSAGE-05                  PIC X(25)
            VALUE 'NON-NUMERIC EMPLOYEE NO.'.
    05  MESSAGE-06                  PIC X(25)
            VALUE 'TRANS CODE NOT 1, 2 OR 3'.
    05  MESSAGE-07                  PIC X(25)
            VALUE 'MASTER REWRITE ERROR'.
    05  MESSAGE-08                  PIC X(25)
            VALUE 'MASTER ALREADY EXISTS'.

01  WS-TRANS-REC.
    05  TRANS-EMPLOYEE-NO           PIC X(04).
    05  TRANS-CODE                  PIC X(01).
        88  ADD-TRANS                            VALUE '1'.
        88  REVISE-TRANS                         VALUE '2'.
        88  DELETE-TRANS                         VALUE '3'.
    05  TRANS-NAME                  PIC X(20).
    05  TRANS-CURRENT-DEPT          PIC X(03).
    05  TRANS-PREV-DEPT             PIC X(03).
    05  TRANS-YEAR-EMPLOYED         PIC X(04).
    05  TRANS-BIRTH-DATE.
        10  TRANS-MONTH             PIC X(02).
        10  TRANS-DAY               PIC X(02).
        10  TRANS-YEAR              PIC X(02).
    05  TRANS-EDUCATION             PIC X(01).
    05  TRANS-JOB-CODE              PIC X(02).
    05  TRANS-INCOME                PIC 9(06)V99.
    05  FILLER                      PIC X(08).
```

FIGURE 5.24(b)

```
01  WS-MAST-REC.
    05  MAST-DELETE              PIC X(01).
    05  MAST-EMPLOYEE-NO         PIC X(04).
    05  MAST-NAME                PIC X(20).
    05  MAST-CURRENT-DEPT        PIC X(03).
    05  MAST-PREV-DEPT           PIC X(03).
    05  MAST-YEAR-EMPLOYED       PIC X(04).
    05  MAST-BIRTH-DATE.
        10  MAST-MONTH           PIC X(02).
        10  MAST-DAY             PIC X(02).
        10  MAST-YEAR            PIC X(02).
    05  MAST-EDUCATION           PIC X(01).
    05  MAST-JOB-CODE            PIC X(02).
    05  MAST-INCOME              PIC 9(06)V99.
    05  FILLER                   PIC X(08).

01  HEAD-1.
    05  FILLER                   PIC X(40)    VALUE SPACES.
    05  FILLER                   PIC X(24)
            VALUE 'EMPLOYEE MASTER UPDATE'.

01  HEAD-2.
    05  FILLER                   PIC X(34)
            VALUE ' EMPLOYEE   NAME'.
    05  FILLER                   PIC X(37)
            VALUE 'DEPARTMENT    YEAR       BIRTH'.
    05  FILLER                   PIC X(30)
            VALUE 'CODES      INCOME     MESSAGES'.

01  HEAD-3.
    05  FILLER                   PIC X(34)
            VALUE '  NUMBER'.
    05  FILLER                   PIC X(36)
            VALUE 'CURR PREV   EMPLOYED    DATE'.
    05  FILLER                   PIC X(30)
            VALUE 'ED  JOB'.

01  DETAIL-LINE.
    05  FILLER                   PIC X(01)    VALUE SPACES.
    05  DET-EMPLOYEE-NO          PIC X(04).
    05  FILLER                   PIC X(05)    VALUE SPACES.
    05  DET-NAME                 PIC X(20).
    05  FILLER                   PIC X(03)    VALUE SPACES.
    05  DET-CURRENT-DEPT         PIC X(03).
    05  FILLER                   PIC X(02)    VALUE SPACES.
    05  DET-PREV-DEPT            PIC X(03).
    05  FILLER                   PIC X(06)    VALUE SPACES.
    05  DET-YEAR-EMPLOYED        PIC X(04).
    05  FILLER                   PIC X(06)    VALUE SPACES.
    05  DET-BIRTH-DATE           PIC XXBXXBXX.
    05  FILLER                   PIC X(04)    VALUE SPACES.
    05  DET-EDUCATION            PIC X(01).
    05  FILLER                   PIC X(04)    VALUE SPACES.
    05  DET-JOB-CODE             PIC X(02).
    05  FILLER                   PIC X(04)    VALUE SPACES.
    05  DET-INCOME               PIC Z(05)9.99.
    05  FILLER                   PIC X(03)    VALUE SPACES.
    05  DET-MESSAGE              PIC X(25).

PROCEDURE DIVISION.

100-MAINLINE.
    PERFORM 200-INITIALIZE.
    PERFORM 300-PROCESS
        UNTIL END-OF-FILE.
    PERFORM 500-END-OF-UPDATE.
    CLOSE TRANSACTIONS
        EMPLOYEE-MASTER
        UPDATE-REPORT.
    STOP RUN.
```

FIGURE 5.24(c)

```
200-INITIALIZE.
    OPEN INPUT  TRANSACTIONS
         I-O    EMPLOYEE-MASTER
         OUTPUT UPDATE-REPORT.
    PERFORM 220-HEADINGS.
    PERFORM 250-READ.

220-HEADINGS.
    WRITE PRINT-REC FROM HEAD-1
        AFTER ADVANCING TO-TOP-OF-PAGE.
    WRITE PRINT-REC FROM HEAD-2
        AFTER ADVANCING 2 LINES.
    WRITE PRINT-REC FROM HEAD-3
        AFTER ADVANCING 1 LINE.
    MOVE SPACES TO PRINT-REC.
    WRITE PRINT-REC
        AFTER ADVANCING 1 LINE.
    MOVE 5 TO LINE-COUNT.

250-READ.
    READ TRANSACTIONS INTO WS-TRANS-REC
        AT END MOVE 'YES' TO EOF-FLAG.

300-PROCESS.
    MOVE SPACES              TO DETAIL-LINE.
    MOVE TRANS-EMPLOYEE-NO   TO DET-EMPLOYEE-NO.
    MOVE TRANS-NAME          TO DET-NAME.
    MOVE TRANS-CURRENT-DEPT  TO DET-CURRENT-DEPT.
    MOVE TRANS-PREV-DEPT     TO DET-PREV-DEPT.
    MOVE TRANS-YEAR-EMPLOYED TO DET-YEAR-EMPLOYED.
    MOVE TRANS-BIRTH-DATE    TO DET-BIRTH-DATE.
    MOVE TRANS-EDUCATION     TO DET-EDUCATION.
    MOVE TRANS-JOB-CODE      TO DET-JOB-CODE.
    IF TRANS-INCOME IS NUMERIC
        MOVE TRANS-INCOME            TO DET-INCOME.

    PERFORM 320-VALIDATE.
    IF NO-ERRORS
        PERFORM 400-UPDATE-MASTER.
    MOVE SPACES TO DETAIL-LINE.
    PERFORM 360-PRINT-LINE.
    PERFORM 250-READ.

320-VALIDATE.
    MOVE 'NO'                    TO ERROR-FLAG.
    IF TRANS-EMPLOYEE-NO IS NOT NUMERIC
        MOVE MESSAGE-05          TO DET-MESSAGE
        PERFORM 350-PRINT-ERROR.

    IF    (TRANS-CODE IS LESS THAN '0')
       OR (TRANS-CODE IS GREATER THAN '3')
        MOVE MESSAGE-06          TO DET-MESSAGE
        PERFORM 350-PRINT-ERROR.

********************************************************
*    *** PARTIAL STUB - TO BE IMPLEMENTED ***    *
********************************************************

340-PRINT-DETAIL.
    PERFORM 360-PRINT-LINE.
    MOVE SPACES              TO DETAIL-LINE.

350-PRINT-ERROR.
    PERFORM 360-PRINT-LINE.
    MOVE SPACES              TO DETAIL-LINE.
    MOVE 'YES'               TO ERROR-FLAG.

360-PRINT-LINE.
    WRITE PRINT-REC FROM DETAIL-LINE
        AFTER ADVANCING 1 LINE.
    ADD 1                    TO LINE-COUNT.
    IF LINE-COUNT IS GREATER THAN 35
        PERFORM 220-HEADINGS.
```

FIGURE 5.24(d)

Programming with Relative Files

```
400-UPDATE-MASTER.
    MOVE  TRANS-EMPLOYEE-NO        TO  WS-EMPLOYEE-NO.
    IF ADD-TRANS
        PERFORM 410-NEW-MASTER
    ELSE
        IF REVISE-TRANS
            PERFORM 420-REVISE-MASTER
        ELSE
            PERFORM 430-DELETE-MASTER.


410-NEW-MASTER.
    PERFORM 450-READ-MASTER.
    IF NOT KEY-ERROR
        MOVE MESSAGE-08    TO DET-MESSAGE
        PERFORM 350-PRINT-ERROR
    ELSE
        PERFORM 415-CREATE-NEW
        PERFORM 460-REWRITE-MASTER.


415-CREATE-NEW.
    MOVE  SPACES                   TO  MAST-DELETE.
    MOVE  TRANS-EMPLOYEE-NO        TO  MAST-EMPLOYEE-NO
                                       DET-EMPLOYEE-NO.
    MOVE  TRANS-NAME               TO  MAST-NAME
                                       DET-NAME.
    MOVE  TRANS-CURRENT-DEPT       TO  MAST-CURRENT-DEPT
                                       DET-CURRENT-DEPT.
    MOVE  TRANS-PREV-DEPT          TO  MAST-PREV-DEPT
                                       DET-PREV-DEPT.
    MOVE  TRANS-YEAR-EMPLOYED      TO  MAST-YEAR-EMPLOYED
                                       DET-YEAR-EMPLOYED.
    MOVE  TRANS-BIRTH-DATE         TO  MAST-BIRTH-DATE
                                       DET-BIRTH-DATE.
    MOVE  TRANS-EDUCATION          TO  MAST-EDUCATION
                                       DET-EDUCATION.
    MOVE  TRANS-JOB-CODE           TO  MAST-JOB-CODE
                                       DET-JOB-CODE.
    MOVE  TRANS-INCOME             TO  MAST-INCOME
                                       DET-INCOME.
    MOVE  MESSAGE-02               TO  DET-MESSAGE.
    PERFORM 360-PRINT-LINE.

420-REVISE-MASTER.
    PERFORM 450-READ-MASTER.
    IF KEY-ERROR
        MOVE MESSAGE-04    TO DET-MESSAGE
        PERFORM 350-PRINT-ERROR
    ELSE
        PERFORM 425-DO-REVISE
        PERFORM 460-REWRITE-MASTER.


425-DO-REVISE.
    IF TRANS-NAME IS NOT EQUAL TO SPACES
        MOVE  TRANS-NAME                TO  MAST-NAME.
    IF TRANS-CURRENT-DEPT IS NOT EQUAL TO SPACES
        MOVE  MAST-CURRENT-DEPT         TO  MAST-PREV-DEPT
        MOVE  TRANS-CURRENT-DEPT        TO  MAST-CURRENT-DEPT.
    IF TRANS-YEAR-EMPLOYED IS NOT EQUAL TO SPACES
        MOVE  TRANS-YEAR-EMPLOYED       TO  MAST-YEAR-EMPLOYED.
    IF TRANS-BIRTH-DATE IS NOT EQUAL TO SPACES
        MOVE  TRANS-BIRTH-DATE          TO  MAST-BIRTH-DATE.
    IF TRANS-EDUCATION IS NOT EQUAL TO SPACES
        MOVE  TRANS-EDUCATION           TO  MAST-EDUCATION.
    IF TRANS-JOB-CODE IS NOT EQUAL TO SPACES
        MOVE  TRANS-JOB-CODE            TO  MAST-JOB-CODE.
    IF TRANS-INCOME IS NUMERIC
        MOVE  TRANS-INCOME              TO  MAST-INCOME.
    MOVE MESSAGE-01                     TO  DET-MESSAGE.
    PERFORM 360-PRINT-LINE.
```

FIGURE 5.24(e)

```
430-DELETE-MASTER.
    PERFORM 450-READ-MASTER.
    IF KEY-ERROR
        MOVE MESSAGE-04      TO DET-MESSAGE
        PERFORM 350-PRINT-ERROR
    ELSE
        PERFORM 435-DO-DELETE.

435-DO-DELETE.
    MOVE '9'                 TO MAST-DELETE.
    PERFORM 460-REWRITE-MASTER.
    MOVE MESSAGE-03          TO DET-MESSAGE.
    PERFORM 360-PRINT-LINE.

450-READ-MASTER.
    READ EMPLOYEE-MASTER INTO WS-MAST-REC
        INVALID KEY MOVE 'YES' TO KEY-ERROR-FLAG.
    IF MAST-DELETE IS EQUAL TO '9'
        MOVE 'YES' TO KEY-ERROR-FLAG.

460-REWRITE-MASTER.
    REWRITE MASTER-REC FROM WS-MAST-REC
        INVALID KEY MOVE MESSAGE-07 TO DET-MESSAGE
                    PERFORM 350-PRINT-ERROR.

500-END-OF-UPDATE.
    MOVE SPACES                       TO DETAIL-LINE.
    MOVE '*** END OF FILE UPDATE ***' TO DET-MESSAGE.
    PERFORM 360-PRINT-LINE.
```

FIGURE 5.24(f)

PROGRAM TESTING

Figure 5.25 contains the transaction file test data used for the first run of the update program. This file contains transactions to revise records (code 1), add a new record to the master (code 2), and delete records (code 3). For the delete, only the employee number and transaction code are supplied, as the other fields are irrelevant to a delete operation.

Most of the transactions are revisions so that different fields may be supplied to test for the updating of these fields. Just as important, we need to ensure that fields that are not supplied in the transaction are not changed in the master file. One update of particular importance is the handling of the change to current department. The old value in the master must be moved to the previous department field and the new value in the transaction moved to the master's current department field.

```
00012Falcone, Lloyd T.      210
00032                             1966
00043
00061Wilson, Mary           120      19861024675230230000
00122                                         01720000
00133
00142                                       53901410000
00192Conseca, Jill          175
```

FIGURE 5.25 Transactions used to update the employee master

Figure 5.26 shows the current master file as it appears before updating occurs. It is important when testing a relative update program to be familiar with the contents of the existing master. Then a comparison can be made to the updated master to see that all updates were correctly implemented.

```
0001Falcon, Lloyd           140      19500325323420425000
0002Carney, Jim             130      19630404444350356000
0003Chambers, JK            130      19650715433420421300
0004Gallagher, Angelo       120      19661111453260315000
0005Ellis, Mike             140      19680105462230259000
0006Dawson, Mary            140      19721230553270301000
0007Arbor, Noel             105      19740401532230273458
0008DaCosta, Michael        105      19750629575450527500
0009Eagle, Wilfred          190      19770518311140234000
0010Assad, James            110      19780918463250294530
0011Baird, Joan             105      19831011592210168000
0012Gallagher, Pat          115      19831231622210168000
0013Baird, Joan             105      19830101622210168000
0014Cantoone, Phil          120      19840827544370124000
0015Harris, Jim             105      19840321564210167000
```

FIGURE 5.26   A dump of the master file before the update

Now the test run is done, which produces the report shown in Figure 5.27. Each transaction is listed here, showing the fields that were involved in the update process. At the end of each line is a message that confirms the action taken or error discovered by the program. Take note of the message on the last line, indicating successful completion of the update run.

The last step in evaluating the success of the test run is to obtain a dump of the updated master file. This listing can be obtained by running the same dump program used when the master was first created. Results are shown in Figure 5.28.

One characteristic of a good programmer is to pay attention to the details of the output from a test run. This can get a bit wearying; but if followed systematically, it can be done with a minimum of agony. Really, part of the joy of programming is discovering that your program works and, if there are bugs, that you have the ability to find and eliminate them. This program is no exception and requires some time to examine the output, both the report and the master file dump, to ensure that all the updating was done correctly.

```
                              EMPLOYEE MASTER UPDATE

EMPLOYEE  NAME                 DEPARTMENT    YEAR      BIRTH    CODES     INCOME    MESSAGES
NUMBER                         CURR PREV   EMPLOYED    DATE    ED   JOB
  0001    Falcone, Lloyd T.    210                                                 MASTER RECORD REVISED

  0003                                      1966                                   MASTER RECORD REVISED

  0004                                                                             MASTER RECORD DELETED

  0006    Wilson, Mary         120         1986       102467   5    23   23000.00  MASTER ALREADY EXITS

  0012                                                                   17200.00  MASTER RECORD REVISED

  0013                                                                             MASTER RECORD DELETED

  0014                                                          5    39   14100.00  MASTER RECORD REVISED

  0019    Conseca, Jill        175                                                 MASTER RECORD NOT FOUND

                                                                         *** END OF FILE UPDATE **
```

FIGURE 5.27   Report generated from updating the employee master file

```
    0001Falcone, Lloyd T.      2101401950032532342042500000
    0002Carney, Jim            130   1963040444435035600000
    0003Chambers, JK           130   1966071543342042130000
 90004Gallagher, Angelo        120   1966111145326031500000
    0005Ellis, Mike            140   1968010546223025900000
    0006Dawson, Mary           140   1972123055327030100000
    0007Arbor, Noel            105   1974040153223027345877
    0008DaCosta, Michael       105   1975062957545052750000
    0009Eagle, Wilfred         190   1977051831114023400000
    0010Assad, James           110   1978091846325029453000
    0011Baird, Joan            105   1983101159221016800000
    0012Gallagher, Pat         115   1983123162221017200000
 90013Baird, Joan              105   1983010162221016800000
    0014Cantoone, Phil         120   1984082754539014100000
    0015Harris, Jim            105   1984032156421016700000
```

FIGURE 5.28 Dump of updated employee master file

DEBUGGING HINT

Another important strategy for testing an update to the relative file is to make a copy of the original master. This copy can then be used to restore the master file's contents in the event that something goes wrong during the update test run. Invariably, some error will occur that will incorrectly affect the master. The backup may then be used to easily restore the master, and the program is then corrected and the test rerun.

SUMMARY

Relative files are files stored on a direct-access device that may be accessed randomly or sequentially. Each record in the file is identified by a consecutive record key. In 1968 ANS COBOL, records must contain a delete byte that is used as a flag to identify deleted records. Later versions of COBOL may use the DELETE statement to delete a relative record.

Relative files are defined in a SELECT statement with the ORGANIZATION IS RELATIVE entry. ACCESS MODE must also indicate whether a SEQUENTIAL, RANDOM, or DYNAMIC access is required. In each case, a RELATIVE KEY field must also be specified. An optional FILE STATUS field may be defined to retain system information about the file activity.

FD entries for a relative file are like any other file except that the BLOCK CONTAINS clause may only be used in ANS 1985 COBOL. In the PROCEDURE DIVISION, relative files may be opened as INPUT, OUTPUT, or I-O. A READ statement is used to access a record from the file. If a random read is done, a relative key field must be given the value of the key of the record to be read prior to issuing the READ statement. The START statement may also be used to indicate the first record in the file where reading is to begin.

To create a new record on the file, a WRITE statement is issued. Before issuing the WRITE, the relative key field must be assigned the value of the key for the record being written. REWRITE is used to rewrite a record onto the relative file after the record has been modified. For this operation, the file must have previously been opened as I-O and the record read by a random READ.

An INVALID KEY may be used on the READ, WRITE, REWRITE, and DELETE statements when random processing is done. Usually, a flag is set when an invalid key is detected and then, depending on the circumstances, appropriate action may be taken by the program after testing the value of the flag. When testing an update program for relative files, it will be necessary to dump the contents of the file before and after the update to verify the changes that have occurred in the file as a result of the update.

TERMS TO STUDY

DELETE
Delete byte
Dump
DYNAMIC access
FILE STATUS
INVALID KEY
Key field
OPEN
Program stub
RANDOM access
Relative file
RELATIVE KEY
REWRITE
SEQUENTIAL access
START

REVIEW QUESTIONS

TRUE/FALSE

1. A relative file does not require the relative key to be a part of the record.
2. When a relative file contains a delete byte in each record, the DELETE command is used in the program to delete a logical record.
3. File status is an indicator used to tell the program the reason for a key error occurring.
4. To create a relative file, the file would be opened as an output from the program.
5. Reading a relative file sequentially requires the use of the AT END clause on the read statement.
6. Reading a relative file randomly requires the use of the AT END clause on the read statement.
7. The START statement is always necessary to get the process of reading a relative file started.
8. When an invalid key occurs on the REWRITE operation, it is likely because the record was not found on the master file.
9. A program stub is a temporarily empty or almost empty paragraph that will be developed later in the programming and testing cycle.
10. When writing a relative update program, the master file is usually opened as an output file.

FILL IN THE BLANK

11. A record is identified on the relative file by a _____ _____ field that is normally defined in the WORKING-STORAGE SECTION of the program.

12. A relative file may be defined with ACCESS MODE _____ when the file is created and when all records are to be read from the file.

13. OPEN _____ is used when a relative file is to be used for both input and output operations, such as when updating the file.

14. A READ statement with the _____ _____ clause would be used for random reading.

15. The _____ statement is used for file operations in a program to place records on a newly created relative file.

16. In an update program, the _____ statement is used to update the master record on the relative file after the record has been read and revised by the program.

17. When the relative key used on a random read is not found on the master file, a (an) _____ error results.

18. In an application where a delete byte is used on the master file, a record is deleted by moving a '9' or a 'D' to the byte and _____ the record.

19. When all the specifications are not available for a specific module, a program _____ may be used temporarily to aid in writing and testing the program.

20. To read a master record requires that the _____ key first be set to the key of the record you wish to read.

MULTIPLE CHOICE

21. One of the following is not an acceptable entry for the ACCESS MODE clause in the SELECT statement.
    a. DIRECT
    b. DYNAMIC
    c. RANDOM
    d. SEQUENTIAL

22. Which access method is used when creating a relative file for the first time?
    a. DIRECT
    b. DYNAMIC
    c. RANDOM
    d. SEQUENTIAL

23. Which access method is used when reading 15% of the records in the file for the purpose of updating them?
    a. DIRECT
    b. DYNAMIC
    c. RANDOM
    d. SEQUENTIAL

24. A program requires many uses of the READ statement to access a relative file. What is the best strategy for implementing these reads?
    a. Use one read in each place that a read is required.
    b. If possible, use only one read for the entire program.
    c. Use different groups of reads according to the location of their use.

25. Which of the following are reasons for using a stub in the program?
    a. We are not ready to develop the logic in this part of the program.
    b. Detailed specifications are not yet available.
    c. To temporarily reduce program complexity.
    d. All the above.
    e. None of the above.

26. What document is best used to confirm the accuracy of the master file after it has been updated?
   a. Program listing.
   b. Report generated by the update program.
   c. Dump of the updated master.
   d. A list of invalid key errors.

27. How can we be sure that a relative record exists on the file?
   a. After a READ there is no key error detected by the program.
   b. After a READ there is no key error, but the delete byte contains a value of '9'.
   c. Only if we have issued a WRITE to put it there.
   d. In a relative file, all records are always present.

28. Under what circumstances should a record on a relative file be updated?
   a. The record exists on the master.
   b. There are no errors in the transaction.
   c. The transaction is error free, the master record exists, and it is currently in active status.
   d. Relative records should not normally be updated.

PROGRAMMING EXERCISES

1. Modify the create program in this chapter to include the validate and additional specifications given next. Revise the transaction file so that it contains a few error records and then test your modifications to the program with this file.

PROGRAMMING SPECIFICATIONS

PROGRAM NAME: Employee Master Create   PROGRAM ID: CREATE
PREPARED BY: DATE:

Program Description:
   These represent additional specifications to the create program for the employee master file.
Input File(s):
   Employee transaction file
Output File(s):
   Relative employee master file
   Error and create report
Program Requirements:
   1. Update the validate stub to include the following criteria.
      a) All fields in each record must contain numeric values, with the exception of name.
      b) Normally, previous department in the transaction will be blank, but any numeric value is considered correct.
      c) Education code must be in the range 1 to 7.
      d) Job code must be in the range 10 to 55 inclusive.
      e) Income is not to exceed $60,000.
   2. Ensure that all records written to the master are accounted for. If a record is rejected because of an error, a blank record is to be written to the master file containing a delete code of '9'. Identify this action in the report.

---

2. A relative master file is to be created for subscribers to the Cassette Music Box Company. The transactions for creating the master are in the same format as the master definition given next, but may be considered to be on a sequential disk file. Consider the following program specifications when writing this program.

PROGRAM NAME: Cassette Subscribers   PROGRAM ID: SUBSCR1
PREPARED BY: DATE:

Program Description:
    The program defined here creates the cassette subscriber master file.
Input File(s):
    Subscriber transactions file
Output File(s):
    Subscriber master file
    Create and validate report
Program Requirements:
    1. Read a file of transactions in sequence by subscriber number and create the relative
       subscriber master file.
    2. Validate each transaction according to the following criteria.
        a) Subscriber number must be numeric.
        b) A name and two address lines must be included.
        c) Date of last order will be today's date to start.
        d) Music type must be a numeric digit representing the following categories:
            1—Country
            2—Classical
            3—Jazz
            4—Rock

PROGRAM NAME: Cassette Subscribers   PROGRAM ID: SUBSCR1
PREPARED BY: DATE:

        e) The field agreement type may be a value from 1 to 5, indicating the number of
           selections the customer has agreed to purchase.
        f) The number-of-orders field will be initially set to 1 because the creating of the record
           implies the first order.
        g) The balance field will be set to the value in the transaction, providing it is numeric
           and less than $30.00. This value represents the amount of the first order. It must
           provide a sign to permit negative values.
    3. Print each transaction processed with appropriate messages.
    4. It is possible that some subscriber records will be missing in the transaction file or
       that they will be rejected because of an error. In either case, create a master record for
       that number. The record will contain blank fields and a delete code of 'D'.

INPUT/OUTPUT RECORD DEFINITION

File: Subscriber file   File Type: Disk-Relative
Record Length: 80   Blocking Factor: 1
Sequence: Subscriber number   Access Method: Sequential

COLUMNS	FIELD	TYPE	LENGTH	DECIMALS
1	Delete byte	A/N	1	
2–4	Subscriber no.	N	4	
5–24	Name	A/N	20	
25–44	Address line 1	A/N	20	
45–64	Address line 2	A/N	20	
65–70	Date of last order	N	6	
71	Music type	N	1	
72	Agreement type	N	1	
74	Number of orders	N	2	
75–80	Account balance	N	6	2

3. Write an update program to process orders, payments, and cancellations against
   the subscriber file created in the previous assignment. The transaction file is in
   the same format as the master except that column 1 of the transactions contains
   the update code. The following specifications outline the appropriate activities to
   be considered in the program.

PROGRAM NAME: Cassette Subscribers   **PROGRAM ID:** SUBSCR2
PREPARED BY: **DATE:**

Program Description:
   The program defined here updates the cassette subscriber master file.
Input File(s):
   Subscriber transactions file
Input-Output File(s):
   Subscriber master file
Output File(s):
   Subscriber update report
Program Requirements:
   1. Read a file of transactions and update the subscriber master file randomly according to the contents of the transaction.
   2. Transactions may be any of the following types and are processed as described in the next 4 steps.
   3. Code 1—New subscriber. This type of transaction is handled like the create transaction in the previous program. All fields must be validated as discussed previously; however, a blank record is not created if an error is found.

PROGRAM NAME: Cassette Subscribers   **PROGRAM ID:** SUBSCR2
PREPARED BY: **DATE:**

   4. Code 2—Order. This is a customer ordering a cassette. In addition to the subscriber number, the quantity and amount fields will be included. The quantity is added to the number-of-orders field in the master. The amount is added to the account balance field. If the total number of orders in the master exceeds 10, then the amount is first reduced by 5%. If an address is included in the transaction, change the same field in the master.
   5. Code 3—Payment. A customer is making a payment for a previous order. The amount in the transaction is subtracted from the account balance field in the master. A payment may also include an address change.
   6. Code 4—Cancel. Remove a customer from the file if the number of orders in the master is greater than the agreement field. Otherwise, a cancellation is not acceptable.
   7. Design your own report for this program. Include each transaction, and if a record is deleted because of a cancellation, include the data from the master record being deleted in the report. Include all necessary error messages and messages identifying other activity.

INPUT/OUTPUT RECORD DEFINITION

File: Transactions—FORMAT 1   File Type: Disk
Record Length: 80   Blocking Factor: 12
Sequence: None   Access Method: Sequential

COLUMNS	FIELD	TYPE	LENGTH	DECIMALS
1	Update code	N	1	
	1—New subscriber			
2–4	Subscriber no.	N	4	
5–24	Name	A/N	20	
25–44	Address line 1	A/N	20	
45–64	Address line 2	A/N	20	
65–70	Date of last order	N	6	
71	Music type	N	1	
72	Agreement type	N	1	
74	Number of orders	N	2	
75–80	Account balance	N	6	2

INPUT/OUTPUT RECORD DEFINITION

File: Transactions—FORMAT 2　　　　　**File Type: Disk**
Record Length: 80　　　　　　　　　　**Blocking Factor: 12**
Sequence: None　　　　　　　　　　　**Access Method: Sequential**

COLUMNS	FIELD	TYPE	LENGTH	DECIMALS
1	Update code	N	1	
	2—Order			
	3—Payment			
	4—Cancel			
2–4	Subscriber no.	N	4	
5–24	Name	A/N	20	
25–44	Address line 1	A/N	20	
45–64	Address line 2	A/N	20	
74	Quantity ordered	N	2	
75–80	Amount	N	6	2

INPUT/OUTPUT RECORD DEFINITION

File: Subscriber master file　　　　　**File Type: Disk—Relative**
Record Length: 80　　　　　　　　　　**Blocking Factor: 1**
Sequence: Subscriber number　　　　**Access Method: Sequential**

COLUMNS	FIELD	TYPE	LENGTH	DECIMALS
1	Delete byte	A/N	1	
2–4	Subscriber no.	N	4	
5–24	Name	A/N	20	
25–44	Address line 1	A/N	20	
45–64	Address line 2	A/N	20	
65–70	Date of last order	N	6	
71	Music type	N	1	
72	Agreement type	N	1	
74	Number of orders	N	2	
75–80	Account balance	N	6	2

6

PROGRAMMING WITH ISAM FILES

Indexed sequential files have been more widely used for disk storage than have the relative files discussed in the preceding chapter. ISAM provides for sequential and especially direct access of records in the file, which is an essential characteristic of on-line interactive systems where a low activity ratio of records is common.

Unlike relative files, ISAM does not require records to have consecutive key values. Records in ISAM must be stored in sequence, but there may be any number of unused keys between each record. When a key is not used, for example existing record 2301 is followed by record 2303, no space exists on the file for record 2302. Thus ISAM makes effective use of disk space when no record is available. As we saw in Chapter 4, a new record is added to the file by using an overflow area, which is located on a separate track on the disk and is not part of the data area.

For many years, ISAM was the favored method for file organization on mainframe computers when sequential and direct access was needed. However, because ISAM requires occasional reorganization of records on the file, VSAM is becoming a more widely used system. In this chapter we will look at programming with ISAM for two reasons. One is that ISAM systems still exist, and it is important for the future programmer to be knowledgeable on their use. Second, a programmer who has mastered ISAM will easily learn to use VSAM, because programming in COBOL for the two file organization methods is quite similar.

RECORD KEY FIELD

A key field in a relative file was an optional item because the record number was equivalent to the key of the record. With ISAM, things are not so simple. In reality, there is no such thing as a record number in an ISAM file, but each record is identified by a record key. When the file is created, each record contains a key, and the records must be written in sequence on the file by this key.

Figure 6.1 shows a format of the ISAM record and the location of the record key field. The key is usually located at the beginning of the record and is called the record key. Each record must contain a unique value for the key; no two records may share the same key. The record is identified by this key, which is used to access the record when called for by the COBOL program. Refer to Chapter 4 for more detail on the use of the key for the various indexes used by ISAM.

Logical Record

Record key field   Contents of the record

FIGURE 6.1   Position of the key field in an ISAM file's record

DELETE BYTE

Records on an indexed file for 1968 ANS COBOL (like relative files) are not capable of being deleted from the file. Instead, they may be flagged as inactive by using a one-byte **(delete byte)** field at the beginning of the record (Figure 6.2). If this byte contains a space or a LOW-VALUE, the record is considered active. HIGH-VALUE would indicate a deleted or inactive record. If 1972 or later ANS COBOL is used, the **DELETE** statement is available to delete a record from the file.

Logical Record

Delete byte   Record key field   Contents of the record

FIGURE 6.2   Position of the delete byte in an ISAM record (1968 COBOL)

FILE BACKUP

Update of an indexed sequential file does not require the use of a second (updated) file as we used for sequential updating. Instead, updating is done to the current file by adding new records, revising existing ones, or deleting records from the file. All changes as a result of the update are reflected in the file, and thus no backup file occurs as a natural byproduct of the update.

Because on-line systems tend to update their files frequently, the ISAM master could quickly change as processing occurs on a regular basis. If the file is lost or damaged, no backup can be called upon to recreate the lost master file. As a result, a copy of the ISAM master is made on a regular basis (sometimes daily or even more frequently) and stored as a sequential **backup file** (Figure 6.3). By creating this file sequentially, all records from the ISAM file are stored in the order of their record key, including records from the overflow tracks.

If the updated file is lost, it can then be re-created from the backup, as explained in the next section on file reorganization. When the new file is created after a system failure, it may be necessary to update the file with any transactions that were in process on the system between the time the backup file was created and the system failure occurred.

FILE REORGANIZATION

When records have been added to or deleted from an ISAM file, the organization of the file gradually becomes less efficient. In Chapter 4 we saw that adding new records to the file required the use of an overflow area, which had a limited amount of space.

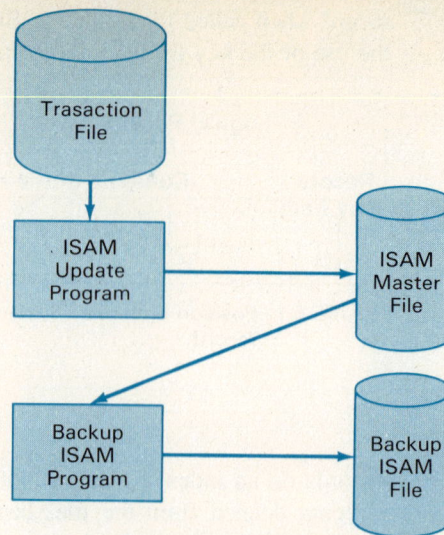

FIGURE 6.3 Creating a backup for an ISAM file.

Eventually, this area is filled, and the file will then need to be reorganized if more records are to be added. Because of these characteristics of an ISAM file, occasional **reorganization** of the file will be necessary. How frequently this process is done depends on the amount of activity against the file.

To reorganize an ISAM file requires the use of the backup file discussed previously. It is really a very simple procedure. By reading the sequential backup, the records are written to a new ISAM file (Figure 6.4) as if a file were being created for the first time. The records will be stored sequentially in the data area of the ISAM file, thus

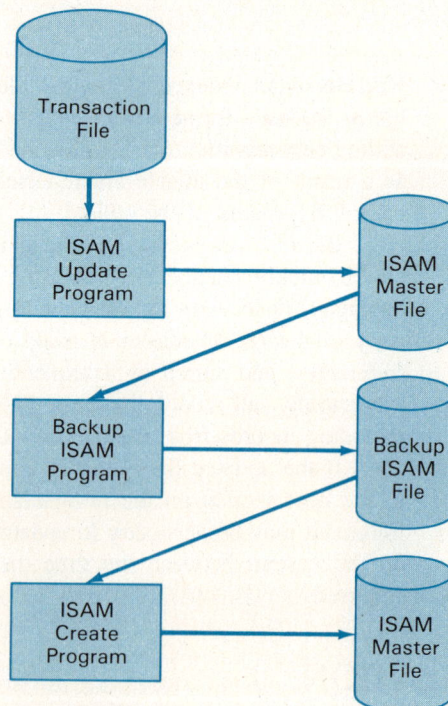

FIGURE 6.4 Doing a reorganization of an ISAM file

SELECT CLAUSE FOR ISAM FILES

```
INPUT-OUTPUT SECTION.

FILE-CONTROL.
     SELECT filename
          ASSIGN TO system-name
          ⎡ RESERVE integer ⎡ AREA  ⎤ ⎤
          ⎣                 ⎣ AREAS ⎦ ⎦
          [ORGANIZATION IS INDEXED]
          ⎡                    ⎧ SEQUENTIAL ⎫ ⎤
          ⎢ ACCESS MODE IS     ⎨ RANDOM     ⎬ ⎥
          ⎣                    ⎩ DYNAMIC    ⎭ ⎦
          RECORD KEY IS data-name-1
          [FILE STATUS IS data-name-2].
```

leaving the overflow area empty for new records that can be added during later updating runs.

This general format shows the options available in the **SELECT** clause for ISAM files. Most entries are required, with the exception of **FILE STATUS,** which is optional. The first entry is system name, which is system dependent as we have seen earlier in previous programs. Next is the ORGANIZATION entry, which identifies the file as INDEXED.

The ACCESS MODE clause contains three options: **SEQUENTIAL, RANDOM,** and **DYNAMIC.** These may be used under the following conditions:

- SEQUENTIAL: Used when records are to be processed from the beginning to the end of the file or from a specific starting location by using the **START** statement. In either case the file will be handled as an INPUT file. The ISAM file will also be SEQUENTIAL when it is first created, in which case it will be an OUTPUT file.
- RANDOM: Used when only selected records are to be processed in the file. When RANDOM is used, a key is provided by the program to identify the record to be processed. Most processing against an ISAM file is typically done in this mode, which permits accessing, revising, deleting, and adding new records to the file.
- DYNAMIC: Used when both sequential and random processing are needed against the same file in the one program. This mode might be used when a file requires random updating followed by a sequential printing of the records on the file or the creating of a backup file.

The **RECORD KEY** entry is used to identify the field in the record used as the key for the indexes. Usually this field will be the first field in the record, unless a delete byte is used, in which case the delete byte will be the first field.

The last entry in the SELECT clause is for the FILE STATUS. It is an optional entry, but can be used to give useful information in the event of an incomplete operation against the ISAM file. Figure 6.5 lists the codes that the system provides and includes an explanation of them. These codes are system dependent and will vary depending on the hardware and operating system in use.

Status	Meaning
00	Successful completion of the input/output operation.
10	End of file. This code will occur when the end is reached during the reading of a sequential file.
21	Invalid key: sequence error. Normally occurs when a key is found to be out of sequence on a sequential WRITE.
22	Invalid key: duplicate key. Can occur when a new record is being written with the WRITE statement and the record already exists.
23	Invalid key: no matching record found. Occurs when an operation requires a record that is not found on the file.
24	Invalid key: the file boundary of the disk space is exceeded.
30	Permanent error such as a data check or parity check.
9n	System-defined error.

FIGURE 6.5 File status codes

Each different use of an ISAM file will require a SELECT clause to identify that use. The following examples show a variety of SELECT clauses used in different situations.

Example 1 This SELECT clause may be used when an ISAM file is to be created or if it needs to be read sequentially.

```
      A    B
1   4 78   12                                                              72

      SELECT ACCOUNT-MASTER
          ASSIGN TO ACCOUNT-MST
          ORGANIZATION IS INDEXED
          ACCESS MODE IS SEQUENTIAL
          RECORD KEY IS MS-ACCOUNT-NUMBER
          FILE STATUS IS WS-STATUS-CODE.
```

Example 2 The SELECT may be used when an ISAM file is to be accessed randomly for the purpose of inquiry or updating records within the file. Before a record is read or written, the key of the record required must be moved to the RECORD KEY field and then the READ, WRITE, REWRITE, and so on, may be issued.

```
      A    B
1   4 78   12                                                              72

      SELECT ACCOUNT-MASTER
          ASSIGN TO ACCOUNT-MST
          ORGANIZATION IS INDEXED
          ACCESS MODE IS RANDOM
          RECORD KEY IS MS-ACCOUNT-NUMBER
          FILE STATUS IS WS-STATUS-CODE.
```

Example 3 When an ISAM file is to be updated directly and then read sequentially, the DYNAMIC access method may be used. Some systems may not be able to use the DYNAMIC option.

```
      A    B
1   4 78   12                                                              72

      SELECT ACCOUNT-MASTER
          ASSIGN TO ACCOUNT-MST
          ORGANIZATION IS INDEXED
          ACCESS MODE IS DYNAMIC
          RECORD KEY IS MS-ACCOUNT-NUMBER.
```

NOMINAL KEY FOR 1968 ANS COBOL

Users of the 1968 version of ANS COBOL will also require the use of the **NOMINAL KEY** entry in the SELECT clause. This entry defines a WORKING-STORAGE identifier, which must contain the key of the record to be accessed randomly from the ISAM file. Functionally, the NOMINAL KEY field operates like the RECORD KEY field for later versions of COBOL. Here is an example of a SELECT clause with the NOMINAL KEY entry.

```
      A    B
1   4  78  12                                                          72

        SELECT CUSTOMER-MASTER
            ASSIGN TO CUSTOMER-MST
            ORGANIZATION IS INDEXED
            ACCESS MODE IS RANDOM
            RECORD KEY IS MS-CUSTOMER-NUMBER
            NOMINAL KEY IS WS-CUSTOMER-NUMBER
            FILE STATUS IS WS-STATUS-CODE.

        :

        WORKING-STORAGE SECTION.
        01  WS-KEY-FIELDS.
            05 WS-CUSTOMER-NUMBER   PIC 9(12).
```

FILE DESCRIPTION (FD) ENTRIES

DATA DIVISION.

FILE SECTION.
FD file-name

$$\left[\text{BLOCK CONTAINS} \quad \text{integer-1} \begin{Bmatrix} \underline{\text{CHARACTERS}} \\ \underline{\text{RECORDS}} \end{Bmatrix} \right]$$

$$[\text{RECORD CONTAINS integer-2} \quad \underline{\text{CHARACTERS}}]$$

$$\underline{\text{LABEL}} \begin{Bmatrix} \text{RECORD IS} \\ \underline{\text{RECORDS ARE}} \end{Bmatrix} \begin{Bmatrix} \underline{\text{STANDARD}} \\ \underline{\text{OMITTED}} \end{Bmatrix}$$

$$\left[\underline{\text{DATA}} \begin{Bmatrix} \text{RECORD IS} \\ \underline{\text{RECORDS ARE}} \end{Bmatrix} \quad \text{data-name-1 [data-name-2]...} \right].$$

01   data-name

$$02\text{--}49 \begin{Bmatrix} \text{data-name} \\ \underline{\text{FILLER}} \end{Bmatrix} \begin{Bmatrix} \underline{\text{PICTURE}} \\ \underline{\text{PIC}} \end{Bmatrix} \text{IS string [}\underline{\text{VALUE}}\text{ IS literal]}.$$

File description entries for indexed sequential files are similar to the entries for other disk files. All the same options are available to the COBOL programmer and are selected based on the file characteristics. The data record used here is unique to ISAM only in the need to include the RECORD KEY field as part of the record description entry. For 1968 ANS COBOL, a delete code will also be included as the first byte of the record. Here is a typical FD entry for an ISAM file.

```
      A    B
1   4  78  12                                                          72

        FD  ACCOUNT-MASTER
            RECORD CONTAINS 100 CHARACTERS
            LABEL RECORDS ARE STANDARD
            DATA RECORD IS MS-ACCOUNT-RECORD.
```

```
01   MS-ACCOUNT-RECORD.
     05 MS-ACCOUNT-NUMBER          PIC 9(07).  ←——Record
     05 FILLER                     PIC X(93).       key
```

The field MS-ACCOUNT-NUMBER in the record description entry is the record key that would be identified in the SELECT clause with the RECORD KEY entry. This field will be used to identify the record when accessed randomly from the ISAM file and will be supplied as part of the PROCEDURE DIVISION code.

PROCEDURE DIVISION STATEMENTS

ISAM file processing requires the use of **OPEN, CLOSE, READ, WRITE, REWRITE, DELETE,** and **START** statements similar to those used for relative files. The statements used depend on whether the file is to be created, is to be read sequentially or randomly, and whether updating is to occur. Naturally, not all these actions will occur in a single program, and so only some of these statements will be required for a given application.

OPEN STATEMENT

$$\underline{\text{OPEN}} \begin{Bmatrix} [\underline{\text{INPUT}} \ \{\text{file-name}\} \ . \ . \ . \ ] \\ [\underline{\text{OUTPUT}} \ \{\text{file-name}\} \ . \ . \ . \ ] \\ [\underline{\text{I-O}} \ \{\text{file-name}\} \ . \ . \ . \ ] \end{Bmatrix} \ . \ . \ .$$

The OPEN statement must be issued in the PROCEDURE DIVISION prior to the first operation against an ISAM file. INPUT is used when the file is to be read either sequentially or randomly (the SELECT clause will identify which in the ACCESS MODE option) with the READ statement. If the file is to be read sequentially, the START statement may also be used in the program to identify the key of the record where reading is to begin. If START is not used, reading will begin at the first record in the file.

OUTPUT is chosen for an ISAM file that is being created by the program. This option requires records to be written sequentially, beginning with the record containing the lowest key and proceeding to the highest one.

The third option is I-O meaning input/output. This option is chosen when records are to be read from the file, modified, and then rewritten back to the file. Usually, this mode means the file is read randomly with the program supplying the key of each record to be read. With I-O, an ISAM file is updated when the REWRITE is used to place the revised record on the disk. Other statements that may be used in the program are READ, to access the record from the file, WRITE, to place a new record on the file, and DELETE, to delete a record that is no longer required on the file.

Example 1 Open the ACCOUNT-MASTER file to be read as input. This open may be used for either a sequential or random READ operation.

```
    A    B
1   4  78  12                                                          72
─────────────────────────────────────────────────────────────────────────
        OPEN INPUT ACCOUNT-MASTER.
```

Example 2 Open the ACCOUNT-MASTER file for random updating of the records. The program will be revising records, adding new records, and deleting records from the file.

```
        OPEN I-O ACCOUNT-MASTER.
```

READ STATEMENT

```
READ file-name RECORD [ INTO identifier ]

⎰ AT END     ⎱
⎱ INVALID KEY ⎰     imperative-statement .
```

A READ statement will be used in the program to access a record from the ISAM file. When READ is used for sequential access, the AT END clause will be used to detect when end of file has been reached. Usually, a flag is set when AT END occurs in the same manner as for a sequential file.

```
        READ ACCOUNT-MASTER
            AT END MOVE 'YES' TO MST-EOF-FLAG.
```

The **INVALID KEY** clause will be used when the ISAM file is accessed randomly. Prior to the READ statement, the key of the required record must be moved to the RECORD KEY field (also to the NOMINAL KEY field for 1968 ANS COBOL) located in the record description entry. The INVALID KEY clause will be invoked if an error occurs during the read operation. To determine the type of error, the file status code may be checked, but the basic effect in the program will be that the record being read was not found and therefore it cannot be processed.

```
        MOVE TRN-ACCOUNT-NUMBER TO MS-ACCOUNT-NUMBER.
        READ ACCOUNT-MASTER INTO WS-ACCOUNT-MASTER
            INVALID KEY MOVE 'YES' TO MS-KEY-ERROR-FLAG.
```

START STATEMENT

```
START file-name

⎡       ⎧ EQUAL TO       ⎫       ⎤
⎢       ⎪ =              ⎪       ⎥
⎢ KEY IS⎨ GREATER THAN   ⎬ data-name ⎥
⎢       ⎪ >              ⎪       ⎥
⎢       ⎪ NOT LESS THAN  ⎪       ⎥
⎣       ⎩ NOT <          ⎭       ⎦
[INVALID KEY imperative-statement].
```

START is used for ISAM files in the same manner as for relative files. When the file is being accessed sequentially, START may be used to specify the record to begin the read operation. Depending on the KEY IS option used, the precise record key or a range of key may be specified. Review the section on the START statement for relative files for additional details.

WRITE STATEMENT

> <u>WRITE</u> record-name [<u>FROM</u> identifier-1]
>
> [<u>INVALID</u> KEY imperative-statement].

The WRITE statement is used in two basic situations for ISAM files. The first use is for when the file is created and the WRITE will be used to place records in key sequence on the file. WRITE may also be used when updating an ISAM file to add a new record to the file. For both of these uses, the fields in the record must be supplied the data that are to be written on the file before the WRITE is issued. Of great importance is the need to supply the value for the key in the record key field, which must be a part of this record.

INVALID KEY on the WRITE statement will be activated for several reasons. One is an out-of-sequence key in a record being written on the file when it is first created. Another reason for a key error is attempting to write a new record randomly when a record already exists with that key on the file. In both of these situations the record will not be written on the file. To determine the precise nature of the error, the file status code may be checked by the program.

Example

```
    A   B
1   4   78  12                                                          72
─────────────────────────────────────────────────────────────────────────
        WRITE ACCOUNT-RECORD FROM WS-ACCOUNT-RECORD
            INVALID KEY MOVE 'YES' TO MS-KEY-ERROR-FLAG.
```

REWRITE STATEMENT

> <u>REWRITE</u> record-name [<u>FROM</u> identifier-1]
>
> [<u>INVALID</u> KEY imperative-statement].

The REWRITE is used for files that are opened as I-O. REWRITE is issued in an update program after a record has been read from the file and modified. The newly revised record must then be rewritten back on the file, replacing the old record with the new one. A REWRITE statement is composed in the same way as a WRITE statement, the difference being that a record already exists with that key, whereas the WRITE is used when there was no previous record.

Example

```
    A   B
1   4   78  12                                                          72
─────────────────────────────────────────────────────────────────────────
        REWRITE ACCOUNT-RECORD FROM WS-ACCOUNT-RECORD
            INVALID KEY MOVE 'YES' TO MS-KEY-ERROR-FLAG.
```

The INVALID KEY clause should not normally be activated by a REWRITE. If a key error does occur, this usually indicates some kind of program error, such as the record key being changed between the time of the READ and the REWRITE.

When a random READ is used in an update program, but the master record is not changed as a result of the processing, it is not necessary to REWRITE the record. The original record will still exist on the file without any change to its content.

DELETE STATEMENT

<u>DELETE</u> file-name RECORD

[<u>INVALID</u> KEY imperative-statement].

DELETE is used to remove a record from active status on the ISAM file. 1968 ANS COBOL programmers use the delete code in the record for this purpose. The DELETE statement is used in much the same way as the random READ. First, the key of the record to be deleted is moved to the record key field. Then the DELETE statement is issued. A record will be successfully deleted unless the INVALID KEY clause has been activated, in which case a record with a matching key may not have been found. To prevent this problem, a READ statement could first be used to confirm the existence of the record to be deleted, and then the DELETE will be issued if the record exists.

CLOSE STATEMENT

<u>CLOSE</u> file-name-1 [file-name-2] . . .

Each file that has been opened during execution of a COBOL program must be closed before the program is terminated. The CLOSE statement is used after all records in an input file have been read or all output records have been written. Normally, the CLOSE will be placed just prior to the STOP RUN statement that terminates the program, but it may be logically placed anywhere after the file has finished its operation.

The CLOSE statement, unlike the OPEN, does not distinguish between input or output. You simply name the file or files to be closed, using the name previously defined in the SELECT and FD entries. Buffers that may have been allocated by the program for the file will be released when the CLOSE is issued.

Example Three files are closed with a single CLOSE statement. The filenames each occupy a separate line for good style.

```
     A    B
1  4 78   12                                                        72
─────────────────────────────────────────────────────────────────────
         CLOSE MASTER
               TAPE-A
               INVENTORY.
```

CREATING AN ISAM FILE

The procedure to **create** an ISAM file is quite similar to that for creating a relative file. The only major difference is the record key used by the ISAM file. Records must be in sequence by this key, but they need not be consecutive values. In fact, a key may consist of several fields grouped together as a group item. The name of the group item would then be the RECORD KEY.

In the following program we are going to create an ISAM customer name and

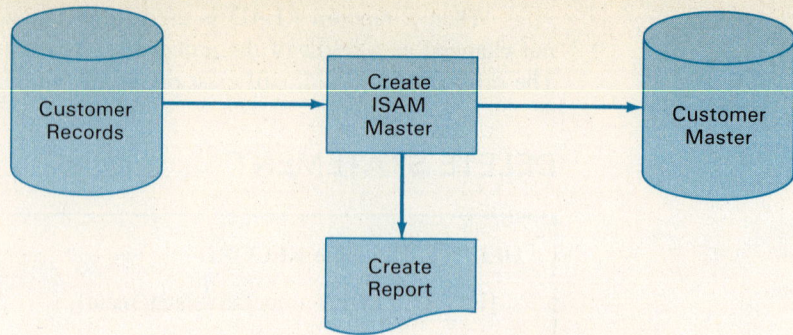

FIGURE 6.6 System flowchart for creating an ISAM master file

address file. Initially, a sequential file of transactions will be used to create the ISAM file, as shown in Figure 6.6. Each record from this file is read, and if it is error free, the record is written on the ISAM master file. A create report is printed as a by-product of the creation program.

The program to create this master file is shown in Figure 6.7. In it, the transactions

```
IDENTIFICATION DIVISION.

PROGRAM-ID.
    CREATE6.
*AUTHOR.
*    JOHNATHAN YOUNGMAN.
*INSTALLATION.
*    SALES UNLIMITED CORP.
*DATE-WRITTEN.
*    JULY 30.
*DATE-COMPILED.

ENVIRONMENT DIVISION.

CONFIGURATION SECTION.
SOURCE-COMPUTER.
    IBM-4381.
OBJECT-COMPUTER.
    IBM-4381.

INPUT-OUTPUT SECTION.

FILE-CONTROL.
    SELECT CUSTOMERS        ASSIGN TO CUST6.
    SELECT CUSTOMER-MASTER  ASSIGN TO MASTER
            ORGANIZATION IS INDEXED
            ACCESS MODE IS SEQUENTIAL
            RECORD KEY IS MST-CUSTOMER-NO.
    SELECT ERROR-REPORT     ASSIGN TO PRINTER.

DATA DIVISION.

FILE SECTION.

FD  CUSTOMERS
    RECORD CONTAINS 70 CHARACTERS
    LABEL RECORDS ARE STANDARD
    DATA RECORD IS CUSTOMER-REC.
01  CUSTOMER-REC.
    05  FILLER              PIC X(70).

FD  CUSTOMER-MASTER
    RECORD CONTAINS 70 CHARACTERS
    LABEL RECORDS ARE STANDARD
    DATA RECORD IS MASTER-REC.
01  MASTER-REC.
    05  MST-CUSTOMER-NO     PIC X(05).
    05  FILLER              PIC X(65).
```

FIGURE 6.7(a) Program to create an ISAM file

```
FD  ERROR-REPORT
    RECORD CONTAINS 133 CHARACTERS
    LABEL RECORDS ARE OMITTED
    DATA RECORD IS PRINT-REC.
01  PRINT-REC.
    05  PRINT-LINE              PIC X(133).

WORKING-STORAGE SECTION.

01  OTHER-ITEMS.
    05  WS-CUSTOMER-NO          PIC 9(05).
    05  EOF-FLAG                PIC X(03)    VALUE 'NO'.
        88  END-OF-FILE                      VALUE 'YES'.
    05  ERROR-FLAG              PIC X(03)    VALUE 'NO'.
        88  NO-ERRORS                        VALUE 'NO'.
    05  KEY-ERROR-FLAG          PIC X(03)    VALUE 'NO'.
        88  KEY-ERROR                        VALUE 'YES'.
    05  PREV-CUSTOMER-NO        PIC 9(05)    VALUE ZERO.

01  TOTALS.
    05  LINE-COUNT              PIC 9(02)    VALUE ZERO.
    05  TOTAL-ERRORS            PIC 9(04)    VALUE ZERO.
    05  TOTAL-MASTERS           PIC 9(04)    VALUE ZERO.
    05  TOTAL-TRANS             PIC 9(04)    VALUE ZERO.

01  MESSAGES.
    05  MESSAGE-01              PIC X(30)
            VALUE 'OUT OF SEQ OR DUP RECORD'.
    05  MESSAGE-02              PIC X(30)
            VALUE '** MASTER RECORD CREATED **'.
    05  MESSAGE-03              PIC X(30)
            VALUE 'MASTER RECORD KEY ERROR'.

01  WS-TRANS-REC.
    05  TRANS-CUSTOMER-NO       PIC X(05).
    05  TRANS-NAME              PIC X(20).
    05  TRANS-ADDRESS-01        PIC X(20).
    05  TRANS-ADDRESS-02        PIC X(20).
    05  TRANS-CREDIT-RATING     PIC X(01).
    05  FILLER                  PIC X(04).

01  WS-MAST-REC.
    05  MAST-CUSTOMER-NO        PIC X(05).
    05  MAST-NAME               PIC X(20).
    05  MAST-ADDRESS-01         PIC X(20).
    05  MAST-ADDRESS-02         PIC X(20).
    05  MAST-CREDIT-RATING      PIC X(01).
    05  FILLER                  PIC X(04).

01  HEAD-1.
    05  FILLER                  PIC X(20)    VALUE SPACES.
    05  FILLER                  PIC X(22)
            VALUE 'CUSTOMER MASTER CREATE'.

01  DETAIL-LINE.
    05  FILLER                  PIC X(01)    VALUE SPACES.
    05  DETAIL-RECORD           PIC X(66)    VALUE SPACES.
    05  FILLER                  PIC X(05)    VALUE SPACES.
    05  DETAIL-MESSAGE          PIC X(30)    VALUE SPACES.

01  SUMMARY-LINE.
    05  SUMMARY-MESSAGE         PIC X(28)    VALUE SPACES.
    05  SUMMARY-AMT             PIC Z(03)9.
```

FIGURE 6.7(b)

```
PROCEDURE DIVISION.

    100-MAINLINE.
        PERFORM 200-INITIALIZE.
        PERFORM 300-PROCESS
            UNTIL END-OF-FILE.
        PERFORM 400-PRINT-SUMMARY.
        CLOSE CUSTOMERS
            CUSTOMER-MASTER
            ERROR-REPORT.
        STOP RUN.

    200-INITIALIZE.
        OPEN INPUT  CUSTOMERS
            OUTPUT CUSTOMER-MASTER
                ERROR-REPORT.
        PERFORM 220-HEADINGS.
        PERFORM 250-READ.

    220-HEADINGS.
        WRITE PRINT-REC FROM HEAD-1
            AFTER ADVANCING TO-TOP-OF-PAGE.
        MOVE SPACES TO PRINT-REC.
        WRITE PRINT-REC
            AFTER ADVANCING 1 LINE.
        MOVE 2 TO LINE-COUNT.

    250-READ.
        READ CUSTOMERS INTO WS-TRANS-REC
            AT END MOVE 'YES' TO EOF-FLAG.
        IF NOT END-OF-FILE
            ADD 1 TO TOTAL-TRANS
            MOVE WS-TRANS-REC TO DETAIL-RECORD.
            IF TRANS-CUSTOMER-NO IS NOT GREATER THAN PREV-CUSTOMER-NO
                MOVE MESSAGE-01     TO DETAIL-MESSAGE
                PERFORM 350-PRINT-ERROR
            ELSE
                MOVE TRANS-CUSTOMER-NO TO PREV-CUSTOMER-NO.

    300-PROCESS.
        IF NO-ERRORS
            PERFORM 370-WRITE-MASTER
        ELSE
            ADD 1 TO TOTAL-ERRORS.
        MOVE SPACES TO DETAIL-LINE.
        PERFORM 360-PRINT-LINE.
        PERFORM 250-READ.

    340-PRINT-DETAIL.
        MOVE MESSAGE-02         TO DETAIL-MESSAGE.
        PERFORM 360-PRINT-LINE.
        MOVE SPACES             TO DETAIL-LINE.

    350-PRINT-ERROR.
        PERFORM 360-PRINT-LINE.
        MOVE SPACES             TO DETAIL-LINE.
        MOVE 'YES'              TO ERROR-FLAG.

    360-PRINT-LINE.
        WRITE PRINT-REC FROM DETAIL-LINE
            AFTER ADVANCING 1 LINE.
        ADD 1                   TO LINE-COUNT.
        IF LINE-COUNT IS GREATER THAN 35
            PERFORM 220-HEADINGS.
```

FIGURE 6.7(c)

```
370-WRITE-MASTER.
    MOVE   SPACES                  TO  WS-MAST-REC.
    MOVE   TRANS-CUSTOMER-NO       TO  MST-CUSTOMER-NO.
    MOVE   TRANS-CUSTOMER-NO       TO  MAST-CUSTOMER-NO.
    MOVE   TRANS-NAME              TO  MAST-NAME.
    MOVE   TRANS-ADDRESS-01        TO  MAST-ADDRESS-01.
    MOVE   TRANS-ADDRESS-02        TO  MAST-ADDRESS-02.
    MOVE   TRANS-CREDIT-RATING     TO  MAST-CREDIT-RATING.
    MOVE   WS-MAST-REC             TO  DETAIL-RECORD.
    MOVE   'NO'                    TO  KEY-ERROR-FLAG.
    WRITE MASTER-REC FROM WS-MAST-REC
        INVALID KEY PERFORM 380-KEY-ERROR.
    IF KEY-ERROR
        NEXT SENTENCE
    ELSE
        PERFORM 340-PRINT-DETAIL
        ADD 1 TO TOTAL-MASTERS.

380-KEY-ERROR.
    MOVE 'YES'            TO KEY-ERROR-FLAG.
    MOVE WS-TRANS-REC     TO DETAIL-RECORD.
    MOVE MESSAGE-03       TO DETAIL-MESSAGE.
    PERFORM 350-PRINT-ERROR.
    ADD 1 TO TOTAL-ERRORS.

400-PRINT-SUMMARY.
    MOVE ' RECORDS CONTAINING ERRORS:'  TO SUMMARY-MESSAGE.
    MOVE TOTAL-ERRORS             TO SUMMARY-AMT.
    WRITE PRINT-REC FROM SUMMARY-LINE
        AFTER ADVANCING 2 LINES.
    MOVE ' RECORDS ON MASTER FILE:' TO SUMMARY-MESSAGE.
    MOVE TOTAL-MASTERS            TO SUMMARY-AMT.
    WRITE PRINT-REC FROM SUMMARY-LINE
        AFTER ADVANCING 2 LINES.
    MOVE ' TOTAL CUSTOMERS:'     TO SUMMARY-MESSAGE.
    MOVE TOTAL-TRANS             TO SUMMARY-AMT.
    WRITE PRINT-REC FROM SUMMARY-LINE
        AFTER ADVANCING 2 LINES.
```

FIGURE 6.7(d)

are read from a sequential disk file (CUST6) where they are checked for sequence before writing on the ISAM master file. Because most of the record contains nonnumeric data (name and address fields), no validation is done. It would be possible to check the customer number and credit-rating fields for a correct range; but in the interest of concentrating on creating an ISAM file, this was not done.

The SELECT clause for the master file is written as follows:

```
SELECT CUSTOMER-MASTER  ASSIGN TO MASTER
       ORGANIZATION IS INDEXED
       ACCESS MODE IS SEQUENTIAL
       RECORD KEY IS MST-CUSTOMER-NO.
```

This is an indexed file, which explains the ORGANIZATION entry, and because it is being created, the ACCESS MODE is SEQUENTIAL. The RECORD KEY refers to the field in the data record that follows the FD for the master file. This record contains the field MST-CUSTOMER-NO as follows:

```
01  MASTER-REC.
    05  MST-CUSTOMER-NO      PIC X(05).
    05  FILLER               PIC X(65).
```

Because we are using a more recent version of COBOL than 1968 ANS, the delete code is not included as part of this record.

The master record is quite simply defined for this application. It contains the customer number, which is ISAM's key field, followed by name and address fields.

The only other field in the record is the credit-rating field. Here is the record description entry for the master file. The transaction file uses an identical format.

```
01   WS-MAST-REC.
     05   MAST-CUSTOMER-NO        PIC X(05).
     05   MAST-NAME               PIC X(20).
     05   MAST-ADDRESS-01         PIC X(20)
     05   MAST-ADDRESS-02         PIC X(20).
     05   MAST-CREDIT-RATING      PIC X(01).
     05   FILLER                  PIC X(04).
```

Figure 6.8 shows the master file dump after the create program has been run. This dump can be easily created by reading the master file sequentially and printing the contents of each record until end of file has been reached. Notice that, unlike a relative file, the key field has gaps between records, but this does not require extra space on the disk file when ISAM is used.

```
00100THE LOFT COMPANY    1609 HAIG ST.       TORONTO, ONT.         5
00101STATIONERY GRAPHICS 2118 FOWLER AVE.    HAMILTON, ONT.        3
00105MERIT PRINTING CO.  3330 SOUTH MILLWAY  BUFFALO, NY           5
00107WOOD PRINTING       1650CARRINGTON DR.  ROCHESTER, NY         4
00108ERIN GRAPHICS       2689 BATTLEFORD     FORT ERIE, ONT.       5
00109ENGLISH PRINTING    18 KENTWOOD RD.     ERIE, PA              5
00110THE INKSPOT         1333 BLOOR ST.      TORONTO, ONT.         2
00201ACE PRINTING        123 FLAGSHIP DR.    LEWISTON, NY          4
00202ELEGANT STATIONERY  1 10TH AVE.         BUFFALO, NY           5
00203ONE DAY PRINTING    70 PARK AVE.        NIAGARA FALLS, ONT.   3
00205FORMS FORMS FORMS   2222 NOIR ROAD      TORONTO, ONT.         4
00210THE GRAPHIC EDGE    3220 CAWTHRA        MISSISSAUGA, ONT.     5
00220S AND M PRINTING    10 SOUTH MAIN ST.   ROCHESTER, NY         5
00221GRAPHICS 2000       3175 KIRWIN DR.     BATAVIA, NY           3
00223MULTIGRAPHICS DESIGN18 S. 11TH ST.      BUFFALO, NY           4
```

FIGURE 6.8   ISAM Customer master file dump.

UPDATING THE CUSTOMER MASTER: AN APPLICATION PROGRAM

This application takes the ISAM customer master file previously created and applies updating transactions against the file. The systems flowchart for this program is shown in Figure 6.9. In it, the transaction file is a sequential input disk file that provides the transactions for updating the master file. The transactions will be of three types to provide for adding new records to the master, revising existing ones, and deleting records from the master. Transactions are an input file to the update.

The ISAM master file provides for both input and output operations. It will be input when records are to be read for revision and output when new records are created or existing ones are rewritten with changes. Finally, there is the delete operation, which

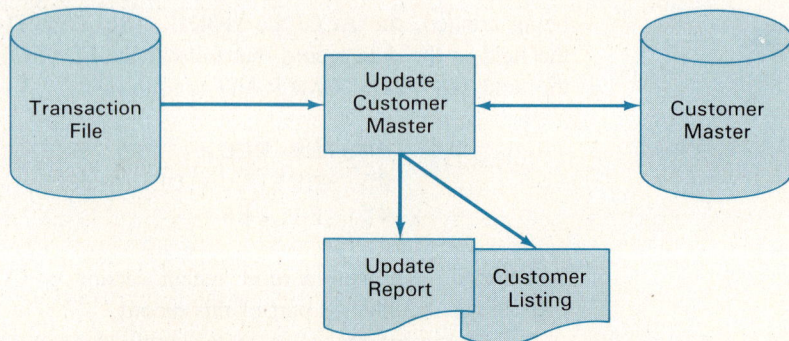

FIGURE 6.9   System flowchart for updating the customer master file

is also a form of output from the program. The importance of this discussion is to determine how the file will be opened (as I-O) and accessed in the COBOL program.

Finally, the program produces two reports. The first report shows the activity of the transactions against the master. Messages will be included to indicate if successful processing occurred or, if there was an error, to identify it. Each transaction will be listed on this report in the order that it was read and processed by the program.

The second report will be implemented, for now, as a program stub. Later we will discuss how the ISAM file can be read sequentially to produce a listing of all records contained in the file. The implementation of the report code will be left as an assignment for the end of the chapter.

SPECIFICATIONS

Figure 6.10 outlines the program specifications for the update program. Special attention is given to the types of updating to be done and to the types of error checking that will be necessary for the ISAM program logic. Many of the errors will result from key errors that occur during ISAM file operations, but some will require data validation of the transactions. Some additional requirements for the report are supplied in the specifications and will be detailed further in the report layout.

PROGRAMMING SPECIFICATIONS

PROGRAM NAME: Update Customer Master   PROGRAM ID: UPDATE6

PREPARED BY: Diane Quest   DATE: July 21, 1986

Program Description:
> This program updates the ISAM customer master file, producing an update report and a customer listing.

Input File(s):
> Transaction file
> Customer Master (output for new and updated records)

Output File(s):
> Update report
> Customer Listing

Program Requirements:
1. Read a transaction file and update the customer master randomly with each transaction. Three update codes are available, as follows:
   1—Create a new record on the master.
   2—Revise the master containing the same customer number as the transaction. Only fields present in the transaction are to be revised.
   3—Delete the master record with the same customer number.

FIGURE 6.10(a)   Program specifications for the customer file update

---

PROGRAMMING SPECIFICATIONS

PROGRAM NAME: Update Customer Master   PROGRAM ID: UPDATE6

PREPARED BY: Diane Quest   DATE: July 21, 1986

---

2. List each transaction on the update report, indicating the action taken. This may be a message indicating the successful processing of the transaction or the reason why processing was unsuccessful.
3. Validate each transaction for the following. The customer number must be numeric. Transaction update codes must be values 1, 2, or 3, and the credit rating, if it is present, must be in the range 1 to 5.
4. Other errors may be found during processing that require special handling and an appropriate error message on the update report. These errors are:
   —The master record for a matching key is not found during the processing of a revise or delete transaction.
   —A master record already exists for a new transaction type.
   —A key error occurs during a rewrite operation. This likely indicates a program error, but should be identified if it occurs.

FIGURE 6.10(b)

5. When successful processing of a transaction has been completed, indicate in the report the action taken. These actions will include:
—Master record is revised.
—New master record created.
—Master record deleted from the file.
6. At the end of the update report, print totals indicating the number of good transactions processed, the number of transactions in error, and the total number of transactions.
7. Supply a program stub that will later be coded to print a second report listing all customer records in customer number sequence by reading the ISAM file as a sequential file.

FIGURE 6.10(c)

INPUT/OUTPUT DEFINITIONS

Figure 6.11 shows the input definition for the transaction file. This is a sequential file on disk that has a blocking factor of 10. Although the file is sequential, the records themselves do not need to be in any specific sequence to be processed directly against the ISAM master.

INPUT/OUTPUT RECORD DEFINITION				
File: Transactions Record Length: 80 Sequence: N/A			File Type: Sequential disk Blocking Factor: 10 Access Method: Sequential	
COLUMNS	FIELD	TYPE	LENGTH	DECIMALS
1	Update code 1—New record 2—Revise 3—Delete	N	1	
2–6	Customer number	N	5	
7–26	Name	A/N	20	
27–46	Address line 1	A/N	20	
47–66	Address line 2	A/N	20	
67	Credit rating	N	1	
68–80	Unused	A/N	13	

FIGURE 6.11 Input definition for the transaction file

Figure 6.12 shows the customer master file. This is the ISAM file created earlier and has the same format. This file provides the master data and will be updated as a result of this program. Changes to the file will occur during the running of the program, and so it would be a good idea to create a backup of the file prior the first run of the update program.

The update report (Figure 6.13) is printed from the update program to show the results of processing each transaction. Transactions are printed double-spaced for readability. If there is more than one message for a transaction, single spacing is used. At the end of the report are totals to show the number of transactions, the number that were successfully processed, and the number that contained errors.

INPUT/OUTPUT RECORD DEFINITION					
File: Customer master Record Length: 70 Sequence: Customer no.			File Type: ISAM Blocking Factor: None Access Method: Random		
COLUMNS	FIELD	TYPE	LENGTH	DECIMALS
1–5	Customer number	N	5	
6–25	Name	A/N	20	
26–45	Address line 1	A/N	20	
46–65	Address line 2	A/N	20	
66	Credit rating	N	1	
67–70	Unused	A/N	13	

FIGURE 6.12 ISAM customer master file.

```
                        CUSTOMER MASTER UPDATE

CUST.   NAME                    ADDRESS                                      CREDIT   MESSAGE
NUM.                                                                         CODE

99999   XXXXXXXXXXXXXXXXXXXX    XXXXXXXXXXXXXXXXXXXX    XXXXXXXXXXXXXXXXXXXX   X      MASTER RECORD CREATED

99999   XXXXXXXXXXXXXXXXXXXX    XXXXXXXXXXXXXXXXXXXX    XXXXXXXXXXXXXXXXXXXX   X      MASTER RECORD CREATED

99999   XXXXXXXXXXXXXXXXXXXX    XXXXXXXXXXXXXXXXXXXX    XXXXXXXXXXXXXXXXXXXX   X      MASTER RECORD REVISED


                                                                                    NON-NUMERIC CUSTOMER NO.
                                                                                    UPDATE CODE NOT 1, 2 OR 3
                                                                                    MASTER RECORD DELETED
                                                                                    MASTER RECORD NOT FOUND
                                                                                    MASTER ALREADY EXISTS




GOOD RECORDS:           ZZZ9
ERROR RECORDS:          ZZZ9
TOTAL TRANSACTIONS:     ZZZ9
```

FIGURE 6.13 Update report layout

STRUCTURE CHART

Functionally, an ISAM update program is a lot like a relative file update. Each will require modules for processing transactions, adding a new record to the master, revising a record, and deleting one. Once we understand the basic concepts of random updating, we can apply these principles to relative files, ISAM files, and, in the next chapter, VSAM files.

At the top level of the structure chart, we get the following four modules: initialize, process, wrap-up, and the master listing.

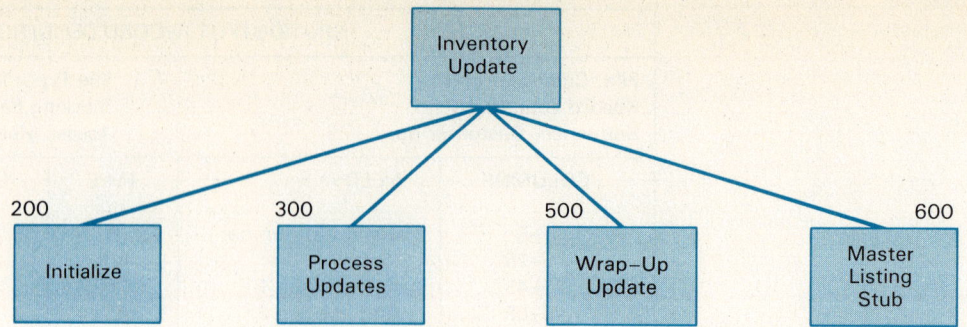

You might have come up with a different structure and you might have been right in doing so. As problems have more components and greater complexity (although this one is not much more complex than ones we have done before), there is room for different approaches to solving the problem. Any one of these approaches could work. In fact, a good programmer would consider several different solutions and then choose the best. Of course, what is best is also, at times, an open question.

Next we will expand the process module. Because transactions come from a sequential file, the first record from this file is read in the initialization module, which is not shown here but will be included in the complete structure chart. So, when the process module is expanded, it first moves the data from the transaction file to the report's detail line. This is the move module. Then the transaction is validated to ensure it contains no errors. Finally, a good transaction will proceed to the module for updating the master file.

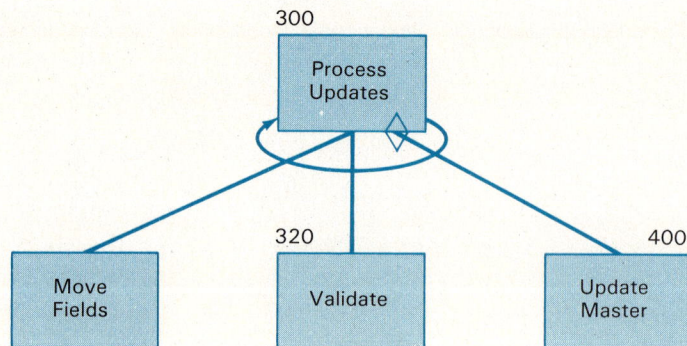

The validate module is expanded next. Because the customer number is used as a key to access records from the ISAM customer master file, it must be checked for numeric. If this field is not numeric, no updating activity may be done against the master for this record. The credit rating is also checked for a range of 1 to 5. All other fields in the transaction do not require validating.

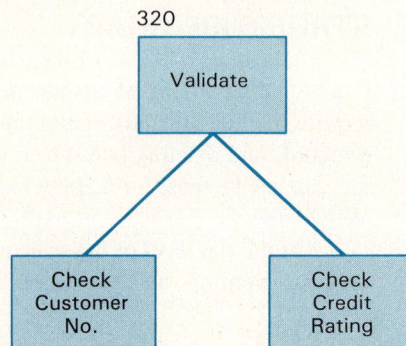

Once validation is completed, module 400 may be expanded to show the functions needed to update the master. These are the three functions common to file updating and ISAM is no exception: add, revise, and delete. Only one of these modules is selected for each transaction, depending on the value of the transaction code.

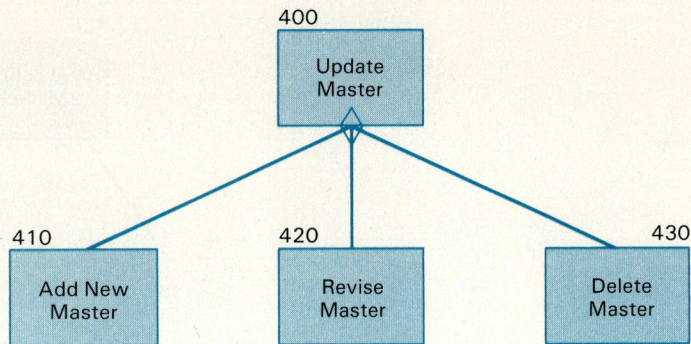

```
                        400
                    ┌─────────┐
                    │ Update  │
                    │ Master  │
                    └────◇────┘
            ┌──────────┼──────────────┐
   410      │     420  │         430  │
┌─────────┐ │  ┌─────────┐    ┌─────────┐
│ Add New │   │ Revise  │    │ Delete  │
│ Master  │   │ Master  │    │ Master  │
└─────────┘   └─────────┘    └─────────┘
```

A code 1 will select the Add module to add a new record to the master file. First, the program needs to read a master record. If one is found with the matching customer number, then the record already exists and an error message is printed. However, a key error on this read is what we want to indicate that no master exists, and then the program may proceed to create a new master record, as the following part of the structure chart shows.

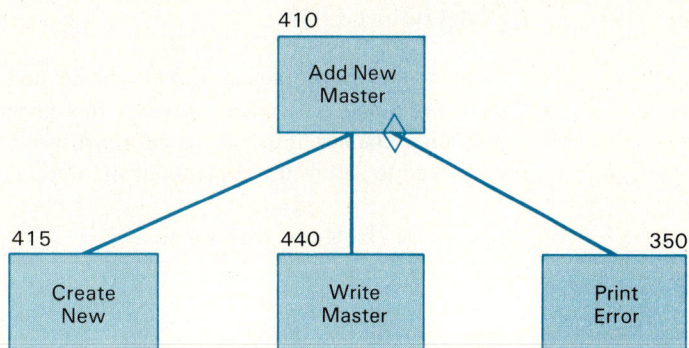

```
                        410
                    ┌─────────┐
                    │ Add New │
                    │ Master  │
                    └────◇────┘
            ┌──────────┼──────────────┐
   415      │     440  │         350  │
┌─────────┐ │  ┌─────────┐    ┌─────────┐
│ Create  │   │ Write   │    │ Print   │
│ New     │   │ Master  │    │ Error   │
└─────────┘   └─────────┘    └─────────┘
```

To revise the master, we need modules to read an existing master record, revise the record with the contents of the transaction, and then rewrite the revised master on the ISAM master file. If no master was found with an equal key, an error message needs to be printed and the revise (not the program) is aborted.

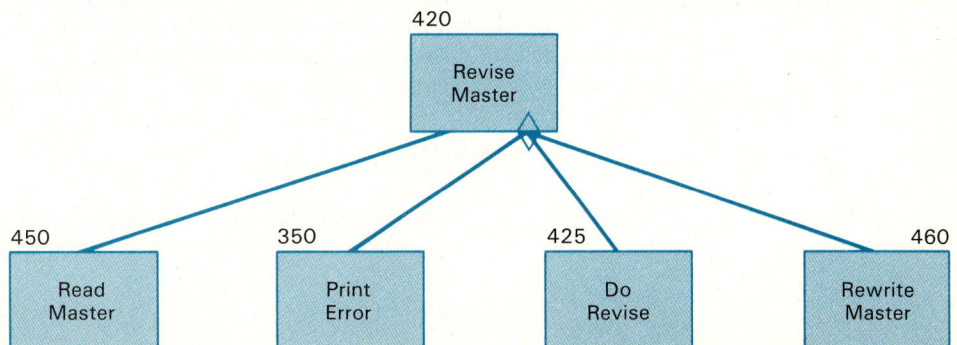

```
                        420
                    ┌─────────┐
                    │ Revise  │
                    │ Master  │
                    └────◇────┘
        ┌───────┬───────┼────────────────┐
  450   │   350 │  425  │           460  │
┌─────────┐ ┌─────────┐ ┌─────────┐ ┌─────────┐
│ Read    │ │ Print   │ │ Do      │ │ Rewrite │
│ Master  │ │ Error   │ │ Revise  │ │ Master  │
└─────────┘ └─────────┘ └─────────┘ └─────────┘
```

In this application, we will assume a later version of ANS COBOL than 1968. This level will provide us with the DELETE statement and eliminate the necessity of using a delete byte in the master file's record. For 1968 versions, the procedure will require the use of the delete byte as described for relative files. In this solution, an error will occur on the delete operation if there is no record on the master file to be deleted. Otherwise, the record will be deleted from the file.

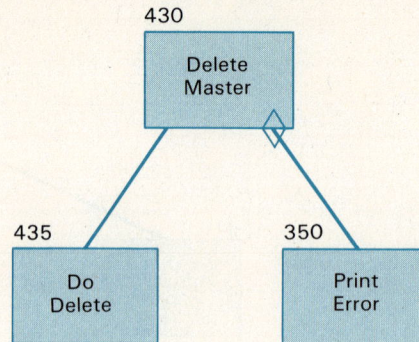

Figure 6.14 combines these elements of the structure chart with the other loose ends that we did not discuss. This solution looks very much like the solution for the relative update, and so it should. Random updating logic is quite similar in COBOL, regardless of the file type being used, so once you have mastered one type of file, moving to a new file type is not very difficult.

PSEUDO CODE

Because we are doing an ISAM update and using a recent level of ANS COBOL, there are some differences between this program and the relative update done in the preceding chapter. First is the approach used to create a new master. With ISAM we only need to set up the contents of the master record and then write it to the file.

```
410-New-Master

    1. Perform 415-Create-New.

    2. Perform 440-Write-Master.

    3. If key error
          Move error message to detail line
          Perform 350-Print-Error
       EndIf
```

Because there is no existing master record, the new one is written directly on the disk. However, if a record existed with the same key as the transaction, a key error would occur, which is detected in the WRITE statement as follows.

```
440-Write-Master

    1. Move 'no' to key error flag.

    2. Write customer record
          Invalid Key move 'yes' to key error flag.
```

Notice that the error flag is set to 'no' before the write is issued to ensure that no previous setting in the flag will interfere with this operation. This technique is used in each ISAM file operation.

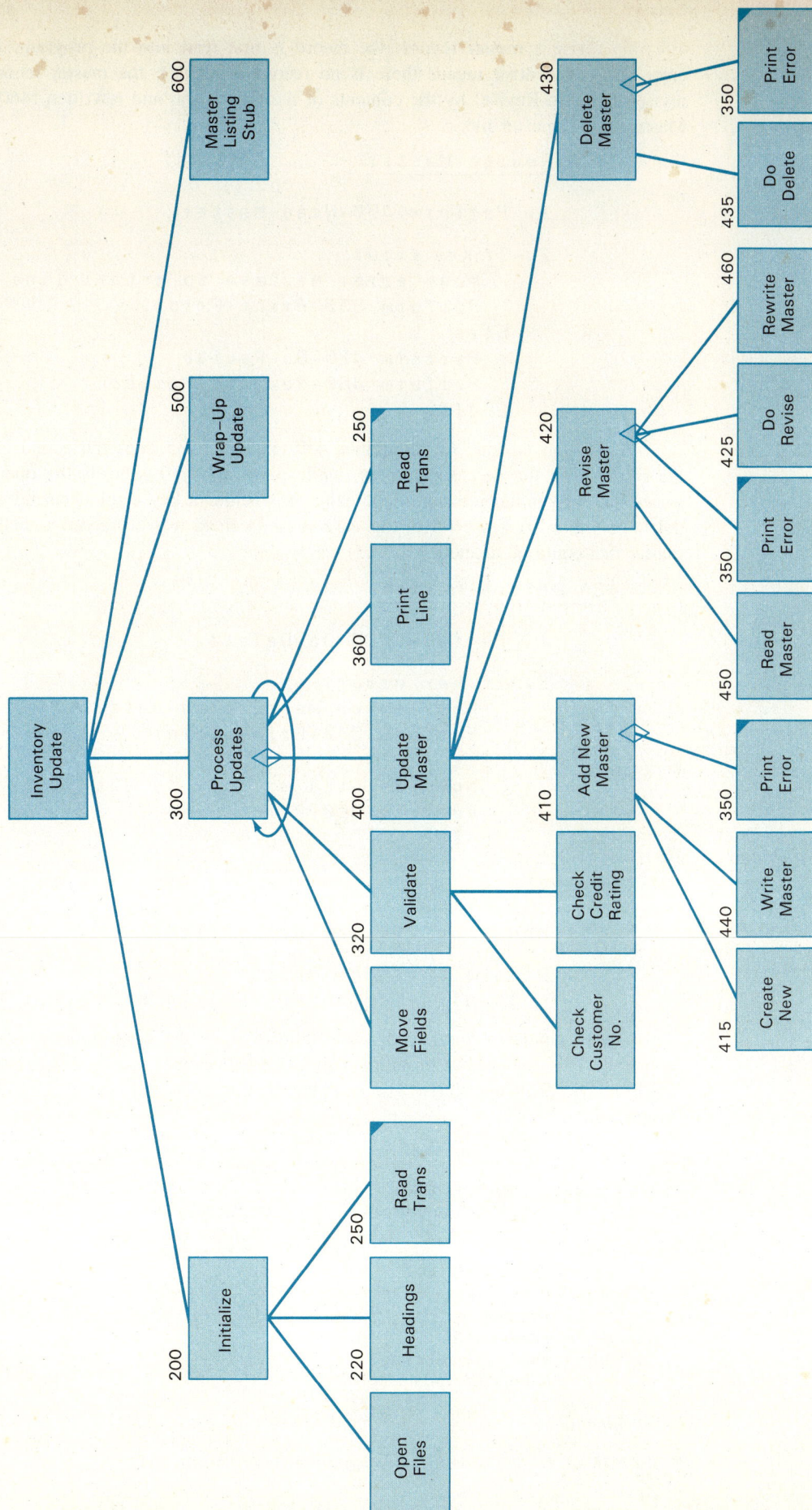

FIGURE 6.14 Structure chart for updating the ISAM customer master file

To revise a master record, the record is first read into the program. If no key error occurs (an error means there is no record available), the master record can be revised (425-Do-Revise) by the contents of the transaction and rewritten (460-Rewrite-Master) to the master file.

```
420-Revise-Master

    1. Perform 450-Read-Master.

    2. If key error
           Move error message to detail line
           Perform 350-Print-Error
       Else
           Perform 425-Do-Revise
           Perform 460-Rewrite-Master
       EndIf
```

A deletion is done in paragraphs 430 and 435. 435 does the actual deletion of the record with the delete statement, while paragraph 430 controls the operation and issues the appropriate message depending on whether a key error occurred during the delete operation. A key error in this case suggests there was no record available on the master that could be deleted.

```
430-Delete-Master

    1. Perform 435-Do-Delete.

    2. If key error
           Move error message to detail line
           Perform 350-Print-Error
       Else
           Move deleted message to detail line
           Perform 360-Print-Line
       EndIf
```

```
435-Do-Delete

    1. Move 'no' to key error flag.

    2. Delete customer master
           Invalid Key move 'yes' to key error flag.
```

The remainder of the pseudo code follows much the same logic as other update programs. This one has a program stub for the customer listing in paragraph 600, which will be dealt with later. The complete pseudo code and structured flowchart are given in Figure 6.15.

PSEUDO CODE		
PROGRAM NAME: Customer Master Update		PROGRAM ID: UPDATE6
PREPARED BY: Jonathan Youngman	DATE: Aug 5	PAGE 1 of 4

100-Mainline
   1. Perform 200-Initialize.
   2. Perform 300-Process
              Until EOF.
   3. Perform 500-Wrap-Up.
   4. Perform 600-Customer-Listing.
   5. Perform 700-End-Of-Update.
   6. Close files.
   7. Stop run.

FIGURE 6.15(a) Pseudo code for updating the customer master file

200-Initialize
1. Open input, I-O, and output files.
2. Perform 220-Headings.
3. Perform 250-Read.

220-Headings
1. Print heading 1 at top of page.
2. Print heading 2.
3. Print heading 3.
4. Print blank line.
5. Set line count to 5.

250-Read
1. Read transactions
    at end move 'yes' to EOF-Flag.
2. If Not EOF
    Add 1 to total transactions
   EndIf

300-Process
1. Move transaction fields to detail line.
2. Perform 320-Validate.
3. If no errors
    Perform 400-Update-Master
   EndIf
4. If no errors and no key error
    Add 1 to total good transactions
   Else
    Add 1 to total error transactions
   EndIf
5. Print blank line.
6. Perform 250-Read.

320-Validate
1. Move 'no' to error flag.
2. If customer no. is not numeric
    Move error message to detail line
    Perform 350-Print-Error
   EndIf
3. If transaction code not in range 1 to 3
    Move error message to detail line
    Perform 350-Print-Error
   EndIf

350-Print-Error
1. Perform 360-Print-Line.
2. Move spaces to detail line.
3. Move 'yes' to error flag.

360-Print-Line
1. Write print line
    advancing 1 line.
2. Add 1 to line count.
3. If line count > 50
    Perform 220-Headings.

400-Update-Master
1. Move customer number to record key.
2. If add
    Perform 410-New-Master
   Else
    If revise
        Perform 420-Revise-Master
    Else
        Perform 430-Delete-Master
    EndIf
   EndIf

FIGURE 6.15(b)

410-New-Master
1. Perform 415-Create-New.
2. Perform 440-Write-Master.
3. If key error
    Move error message to detail line
    Perform 350-Print-Error
    EndIf

415-Create-New
1. Move transaction fields to master record.
2. Move transaction fields to detail line.
3. Move created message to detail line.
4. Perform 360-Print-Line.

420-Revise-Master
1. Perform 450-Read-Master.
2. If key error
    Move error message to detail line
    Perform 350-Print-Error
    Else
    Perform 425-Do-Revise
    Perform 460-Rewrite-Master
    EndIf

425-Do-Revise
1. If name is present
    Move name to master
    EndIf
2. If address-01 is present
    Move address-01 to master
    EndIf
3. If address-02 is present
    Move address-02 to master
    EndIf
4. If credit rating is present
    Move credit rating to master
    EndIf
5. Move revised message to detail line.
6. Perform 360-Print-Line.

430-Delete-Master
1. Perform 435-Do-Delete.
2. If key error
    Move error message to detail line
    Perform 350-Print-Error
    Else
    Move deleted message to detail line
    Perform 360-Print-Line
    EndIf

435-Do-Delete
1. Move 'no' to key error flag.
2. Delete customer master
    Invalid Key move 'yes' to key error flag.

440-Write-Master
1. Move 'no' to key error flag.
2. Write customer record
    Invalid Key move 'yes' to key error flag.

450-Read-Master
1. Move 'no' to key error flag.
2. Read customer master
    Invalid Key move 'yes' to key error flag.

460-Rewrite-Master
1. Move 'no' to key error flag.

FIGURE 6.15(c)

2. Rewrite customer master
   Invalid Key move error message to detail line.
      Perform 350-Print-Error.

500-Wrap-Up
   1. Move message to summary line.
   2. Move total good to summary line.
   3. Perform 360-Print-Line.
   4. Move message to summary line.
   5. Move total errors to summary line.
   6. Perform 360-Print-Line.
   7. Move message to summary line.
   8. Move total transactions to summary line.
   9. Perform 360-Print-Line.

600-Customer-Listing
   1. *** Program Stub ***

700-End-Of-Update
   1. Move end of update message to detail line.
   2. Perform 360-Print-Line.

FIGURE 6.15(d)

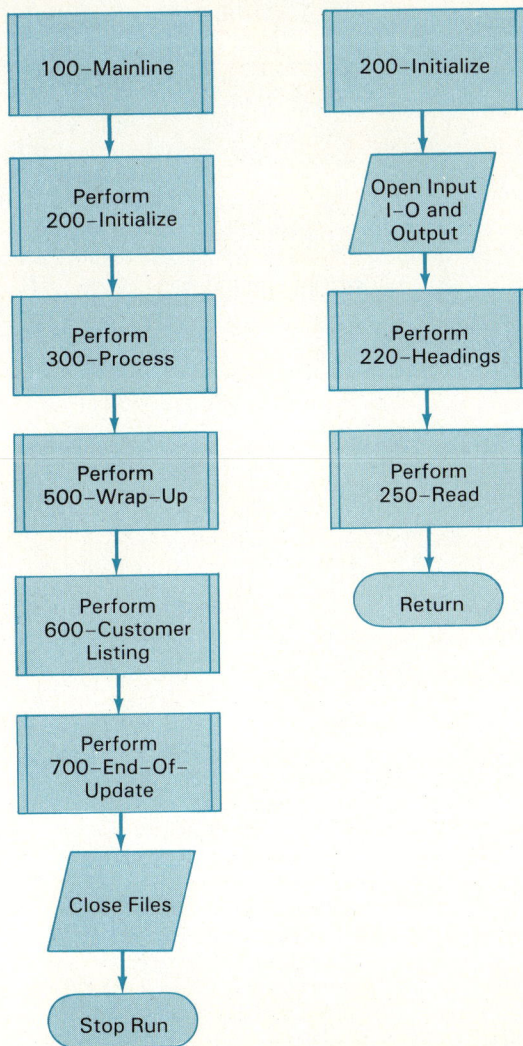

FIGURE 6.15(e) Structured flowchart for updating the customer master file

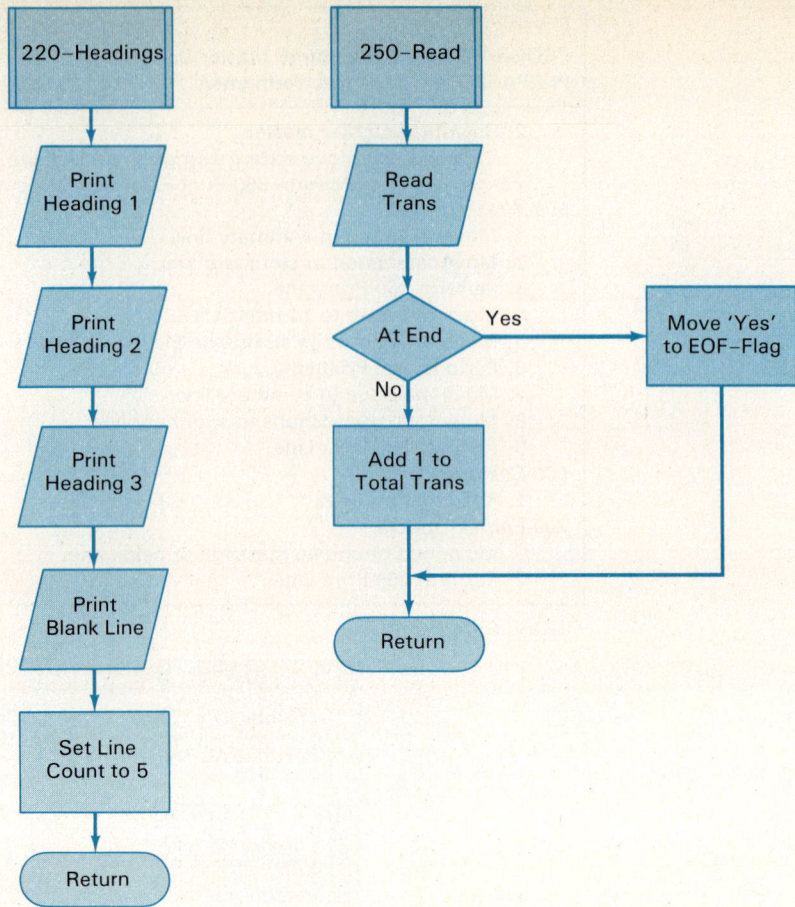

FIGURE 6.15(f)

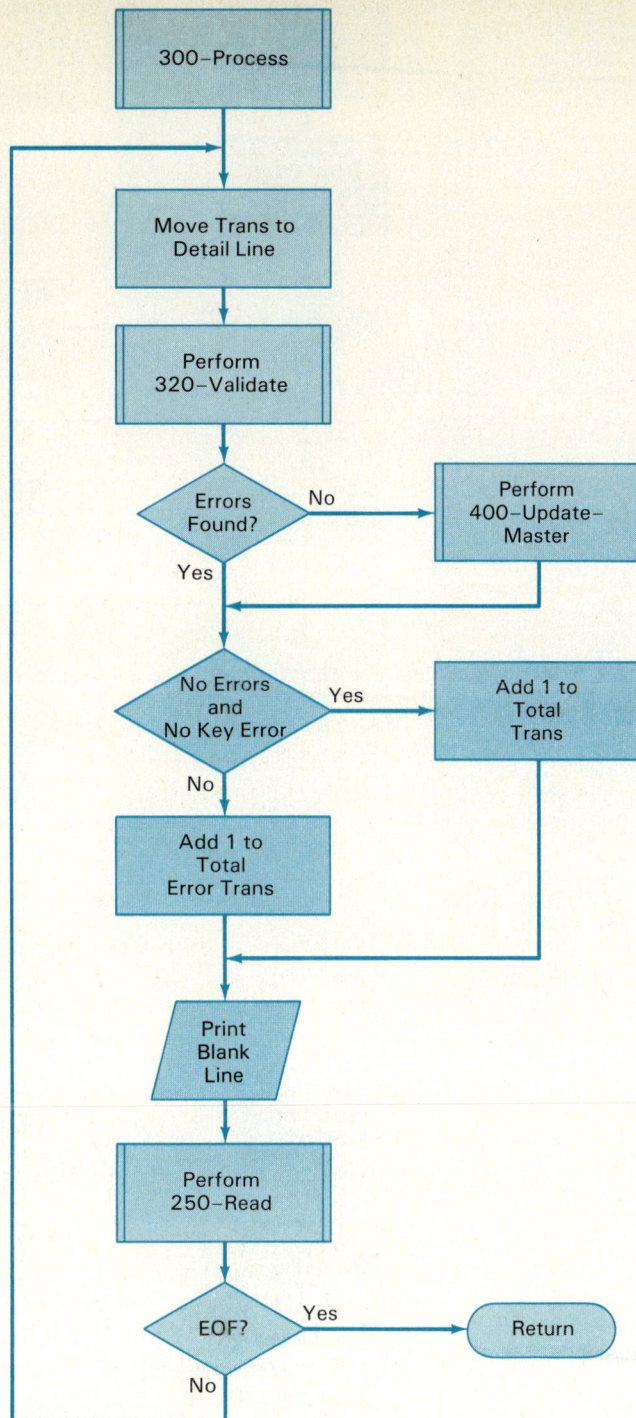

FIGURE 6.15(g)

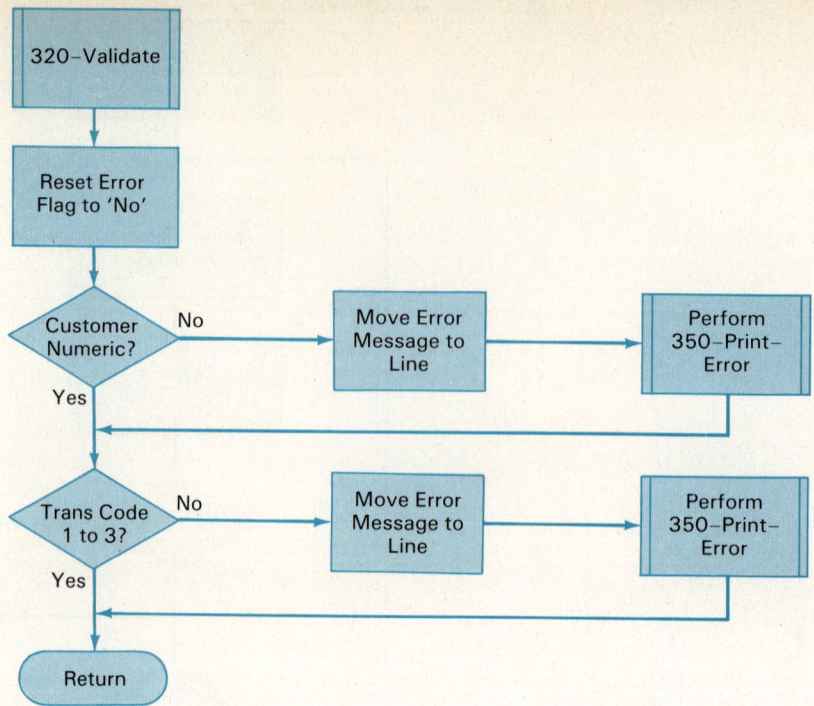

FIGURE 6.15(h)

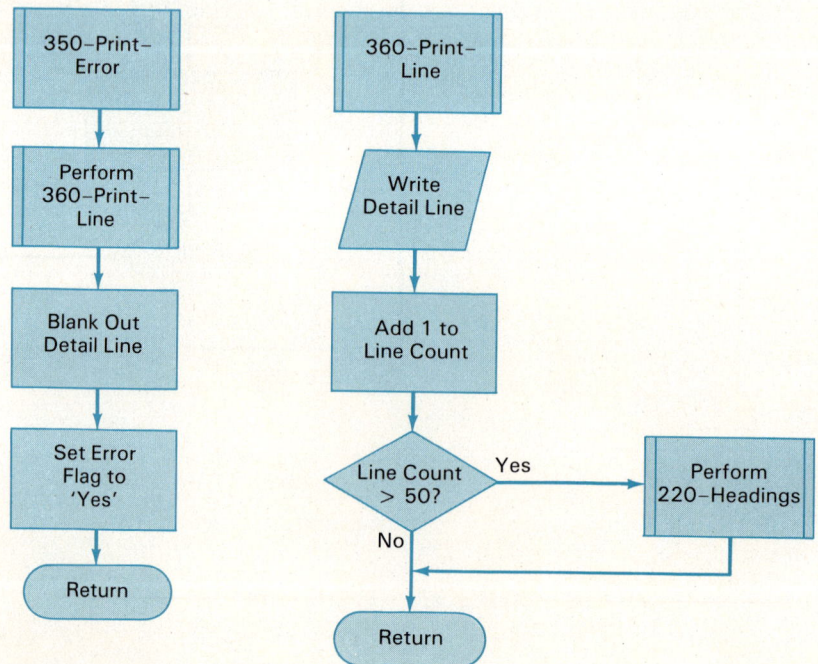

FIGURE 6.15(i)

Chapter 6

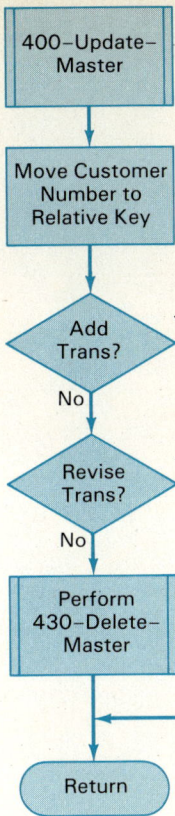

FIGURE 6.15(j)

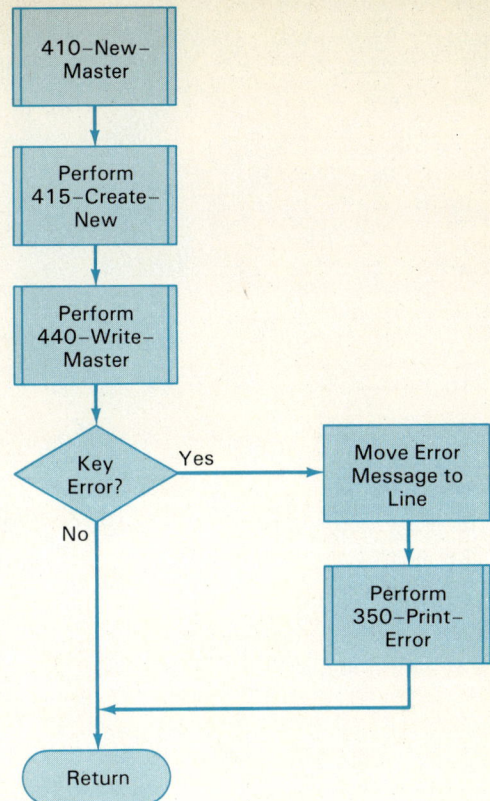

FIGURE 6.15(k)

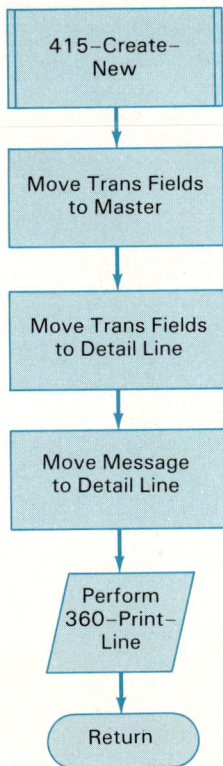

FIGURE 6.15(l)

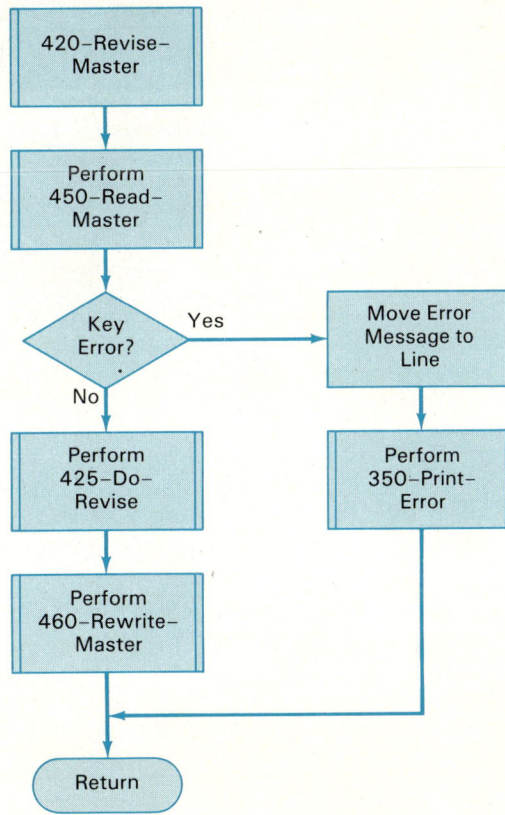

FIGURE 6.15(m)

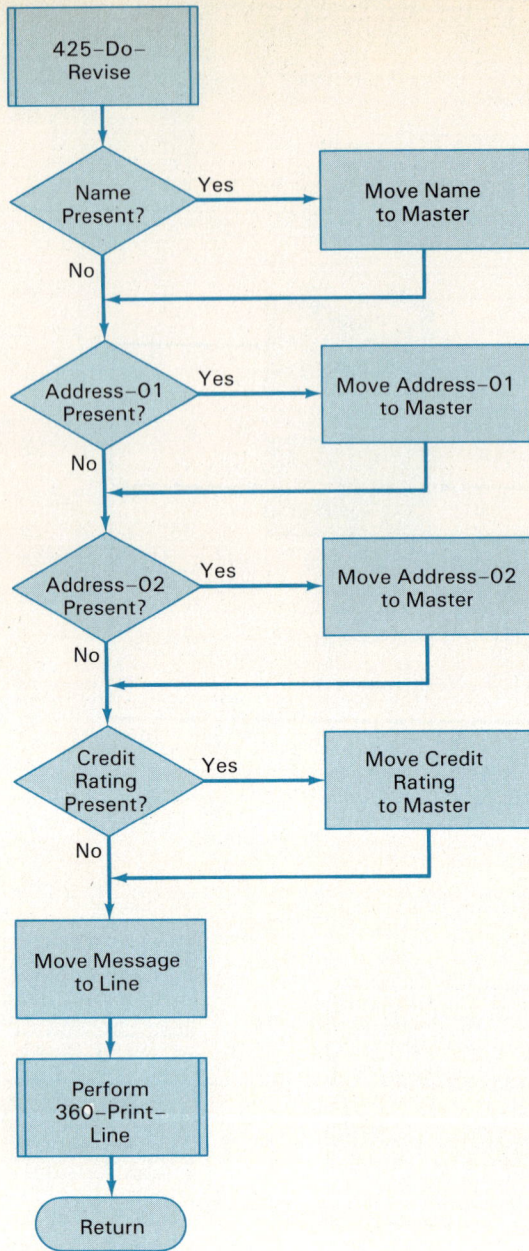

FIGURE 6.15(n)

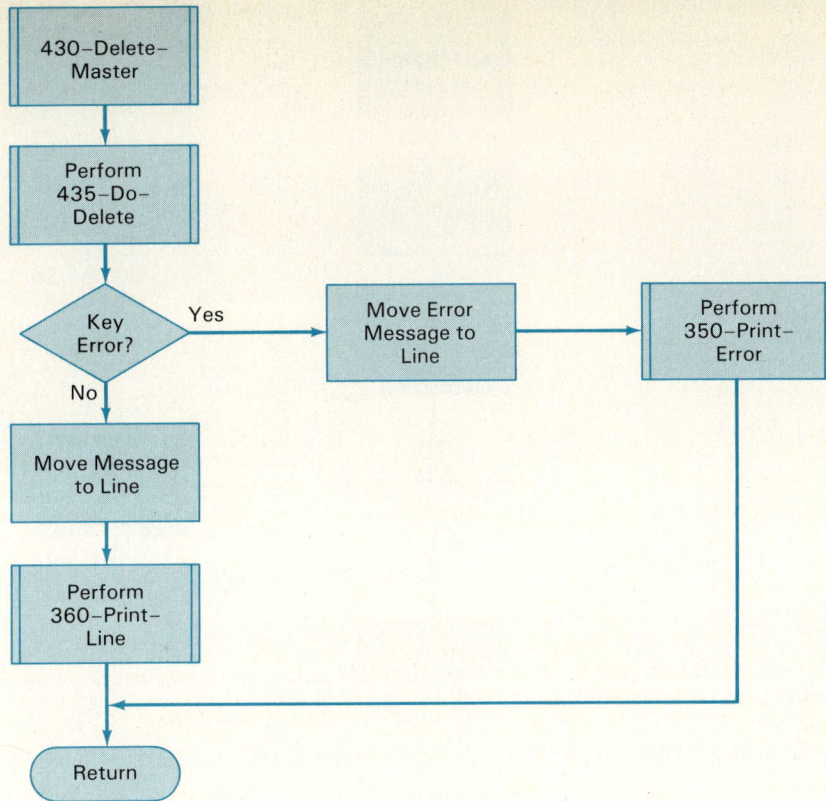

FIGURE 6.15(o)

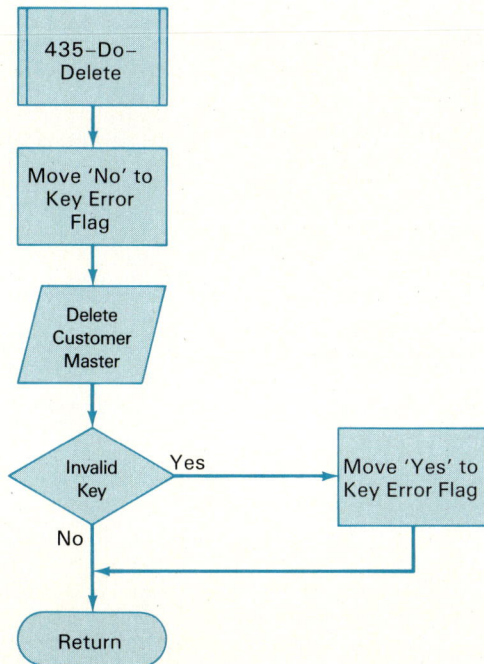

FIGURE 6.15(p)

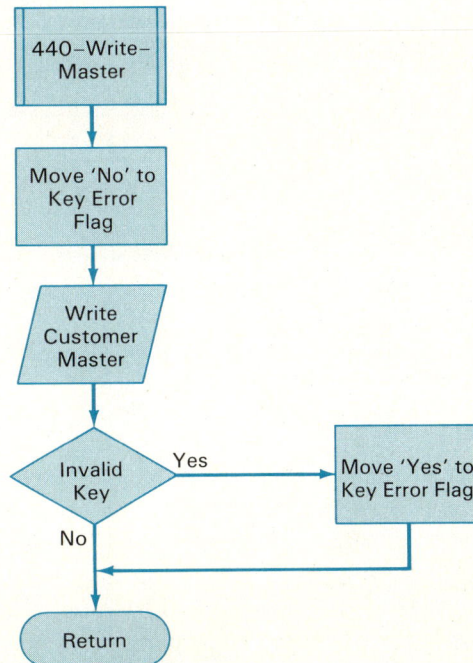

FIGURE 6.15(q)

Programming with ISAM Files

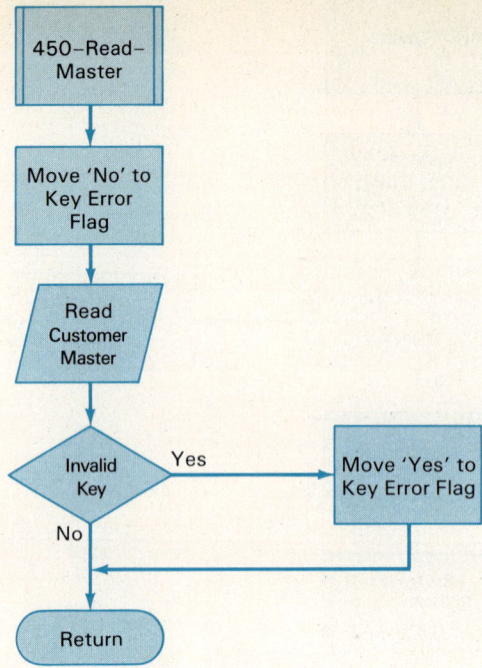

FIGURE 6.15(r)

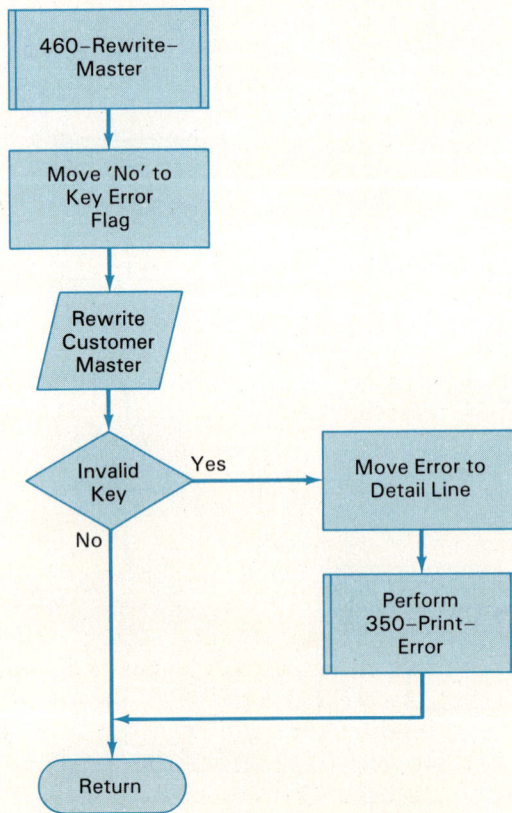

FIGURE 6.15(s)

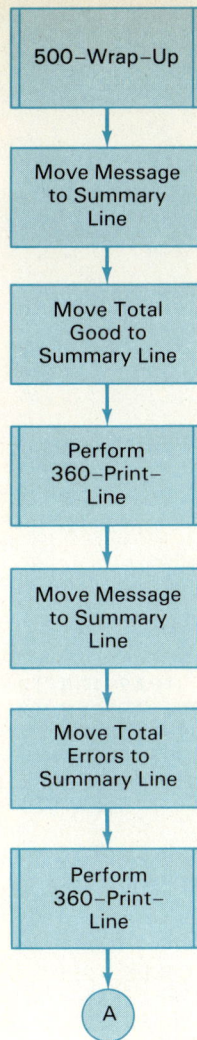

FIGURE 6.15(t)

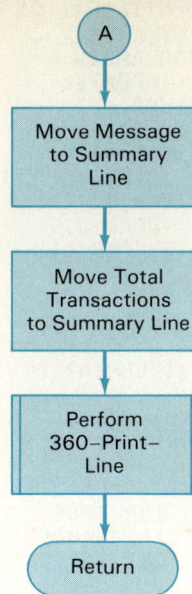

FIGURE 6.15(u)

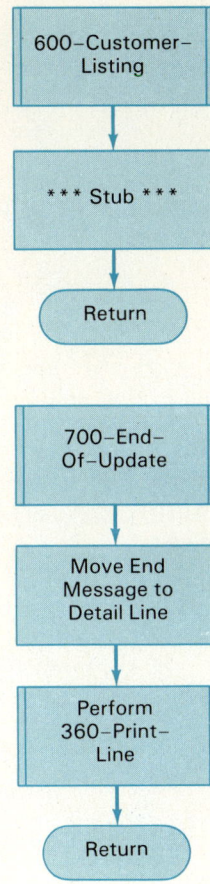

PROGRAM CODING

The complete program for updating the customer master file is shown in Figure 6.16. Because this program will eventually access the ISAM file randomly for updating and sequentially to produce the customer listing, the access mode in the following SELECT clause is DYNAMIC.

```
SELECT CUSTOMER-MASTER  ASSIGN TO MASTER
       ORGANIZATION IS INDEXED
       ACCESS MODE IS DYNAMIC
       RECORD KEY IS MST-CUSTOMER-NO.
```

The program we are writing for now will only update the file, and so it is opened as an I-O file. When the report module is implemented, the customer file must first be closed and then opened as an input file.

The FD entries for the customer file are common to both uses of the file. The file is unblocked, so there is no BLOCK CONTAINS clause, although the RECORD CONTAINS is included. The entry MST-CUSTOMER-NO identifies the RECORD KEY field that was specified in the SELECT clause.

```
        IDENTIFICATION DIVISION.

        PROGRAM-ID.
           UPDATE6.
       *AUTHOR.
       *    JOHNATHAN YOUNGMAN.
       *INSTALLATION.
       *    SALES UNLIMITED CORP.
       *DATE-WRITTEN.
       *    JULY 31.
       *DATE-COMPILED.

       *SECURITY.
       *    NONE.

        ENVIRONMENT DIVISION.

        CONFIGURATION SECTION.
        SOURCE-COMPUTER.
           IBM-4381.
        OBJECT-COMPUTER.
           IBM-4381.
        SPECIAL-NAMES.
           C01 IS TO-TOP-OF-PAGE.

        INPUT-OUTPUT SECTION.

        FILE-CONTROL.
           SELECT TRANSACTIONS      ASSIGN TO TRANS6.
           SELECT CUSTOMER-MASTER   ASSIGN TO MASTER
                 ORGANIZATION IS INDEXED
                 ACCESS MODE IS DYNAMIC
                 RECORD KEY IS MST-CUSTOMER-NO.
           SELECT UPDATE-REPORT     ASSIGN TO PRINTER.

        DATA DIVISION.

        FILE SECTION.

        FD  TRANSACTIONS
            BLOCK  CONTAINS 10 RECORDS
            RECORD CONTAINS 80 CHARACTERS
            LABEL RECORDS ARE STANDARD
            DATA RECORD IS TRANS-REC.
        01  TRANS-REC.
            05  FILLER                 PIC X(80).

        FD  CUSTOMER-MASTER
            RECORD CONTAINS 70 CHARACTERS
            LABEL RECORDS ARE STANDARD
            DATA RECORD IS MASTER-REC.
        01  MASTER-REC.
            05  MST-CUSTOMER-NO        PIC X(05).
            05  FILLER                 PIC X(65).

        FD  UPDATE-REPORT
            RECORD CONTAINS 133 CHARACTERS
            LABEL RECORDS ARE OMITTED
            DATA RECORD IS PRINT-REC.
        01  PRINT-REC.
            05  PRINT-LINE             PIC X(133).

        WORKING-STORAGE SECTION.

        01  OTHER-ITEMS.
            05   WS-CUSTOMER-NO        PIC 9(05).
            05   EOF-FLAG              PIC X(03)    VALUE 'NO'.
                 88  END-OF-FILE                .  VALUE 'YES'.
            05   ERROR-FLAG            PIC X(03)    VALUE 'NO'.
                 88  NO-ERRORS                      VALUE 'NO'.
            05   KEY-ERROR-FLAG        PIC X(03)    VALUE 'NO'.
                 88  KEY-ERROR                      VALUE 'YES'.
                 88  NO-KEY-ERROR                   VALUE 'NO'.
```

FIGURE 6.16(a) Customer master update program

```
01  TOTALS USAGE IS COMP-3.
    05  LINE-COUNT                  PIC 9(03)    VALUE ZERO.
    05  TOTAL-GOOD                  PIC 9(05)    VALUE ZERO.
    05  TOTAL-ERRORS                PIC 9(05)    VALUE ZERO.
    05  TOTAL-TRANS                 PIC 9(05)    VALUE ZERO.

01  MESSAGES.
    05  MESSAGE-01                  PIC X(30)
            VALUE 'CUSTOMER RECORD REVISED'.
    05  MESSAGE-02                  PIC X(30)
            VALUE 'NEW CUSTOMER RECORD CREATED'.
    05  MESSAGE-03                  PIC X(30)
            VALUE 'CUSTOMER RECORD DELETED'.
    05  MESSAGE-04                  PIC X(30)
            VALUE 'CUSTOMER RECORD NOT FOUND'.
    05  MESSAGE-05                  PIC X(30)
            VALUE 'NON-NUMERIC CUSTOMER NO.'.
    05  MESSAGE-06                  PIC X(30)
            VALUE 'UPDATE CODE NOT 1, 2 OR 3'.
    05  MESSAGE-07                  PIC X(30)
            VALUE 'FILE REWRITE ERROR'.
    05  MESSAGE-08                  PIC X(30)
            VALUE 'CUSTOMER ALREADY EXISTS'.
    05  MESSAGE-09                  PIC X(30)
            VALUE 'CREDIT RATING NOT 1 TO 5'.

01  WS-TRANS-REC.
    05  TRANS-CODE                  PIC X(01).
        88  ADD-CUSTOMER                         VALUE '1'.
        88  REVISE-CUSTOMER                      VALUE '2'.
        88  DELETE-CUSTOMER                      VALUE '3'.
    05  TRANS-CUSTOMER-NO           PIC X(05).
    05  TRANS-NAME                  PIC X(20).
    05  TRANS-ADDRESS-01            PIC X(20).
    05  TRANS-ADDRESS-02            PIC X(20).
    05  TRANS-CREDIT-RATING         PIC X(01).
    05  FILLER                      PIC X(04).

01  WS-MAST-REC.
    05  MAST-CUSTOMER-NO            PIC X(05).
    05  MAST-NAME                   PIC X(20).
    05  MAST-ADDRESS-01             PIC X(20).
    05  MAST-ADDRESS-02             PIC X(20).
    05  MAST-CREDIT-RATING          PIC X(01).
    05  FILLER                      PIC X(04).

01  HEAD-1.
    05  FILLER                      PIC X(52)    VALUE SPACES.
    05  FILLER                      PIC X(22)
            VALUE 'CUSTOMER MASTER UPDATE'.

01  HEAD-2.
    05  FILLER                      PIC X(01)    VALUE SPACES.
    05  FILLER                      PIC X(70)
            VALUE 'CUST.  NAME                        ADDRESS'.
    05  FILLER                      PIC X(16)
            VALUE 'CREDIT    MESSAGE'.

01  HEAD-3.
    05  FILLER                      PIC X(01)    VALUE SPACES.
    05  FILLER                      PIC X(70)
            VALUE 'NUM.'.
    05  FILLER                      PIC X(16)
            VALUE ' CODE'.
```

FIGURE 6.16(b)

```
01  DETAIL-LINE.
    05  FILLER                      PIC X(01)   VALUE SPACES.
    05  DET-CUSTOMER-NO             PIC X(05).
    05  FILLER                      PIC X(02)   VALUE SPACES.
    05  DET-NAME                    PIC X(20).
    05  FILLER                      PIC X(02)   VALUE SPACES.
    05  DET-ADDRESS-01              PIC X(20).
    05  FILLER                      PIC X(02)   VALUE SPACES.
    05  DET-ADDRESS-02              PIC X(20).
    05  FILLER                      PIC X(02)   VALUE SPACES.
    05  DET-CREDIT-RATING           PIC X(01).
    05  FILLER                      PIC X(05)   VALUE SPACES.
    05  DET-MESSAGE                 PIC X(25).

01  SUMMARY-LINE.
    05  SUMMARY-MESSAGE             PIC X(23)   VALUE SPACES.
    05  SUMMARY-AMT                 PIC Z(03)9.

PROCEDURE DIVISION.

100-MAINLINE.
    PERFORM 200-INITIALIZE.
    PERFORM 300-PROCESS
        UNTIL END-OF-FILE.
    PERFORM 500-WRAP-UP.
    PERFORM 600-CUSTOMER-LISTING.
    PERFORM 700-END-OF-UPDATE.
    CLOSE TRANSACTIONS
        CUSTOMER-MASTER
        UPDATE-REPORT.
    STOP RUN.

200-INITIALIZE.
    OPEN INPUT  TRANSACTIONS
         I-O    CUSTOMER-MASTER
         OUTPUT UPDATE-REPORT.
    PERFORM 220-HEADINGS.
    PERFORM 250-READ.

220-HEADINGS.
    WRITE PRINT-REC FROM HEAD-1
        AFTER ADVANCING TO-TOP-OF-PAGE.
    WRITE PRINT-REC FROM HEAD-2
        AFTER ADVANCING 2 LINES.
    WRITE PRINT-REC FROM HEAD-3
        AFTER ADVANCING 1 LINE.
    MOVE SPACES TO PRINT-REC.
    WRITE PRINT-REC
        AFTER ADVANCING 1 LINE.
    MOVE 5 TO LINE-COUNT.

250-READ.
    READ TRANSACTIONS INTO WS-TRANS-REC
        AT END MOVE 'YES' TO EOF-FLAG.
     IF NOT END-OF-FILE
        ADD 1 TO TOTAL-TRANS.

300-PROCESS.
    MOVE SPACES                 TO DETAIL-LINE.
    MOVE TRANS-CUSTOMER-NO       TO DET-CUSTOMER-NO.
    MOVE TRANS-NAME              TO DET-NAME.
    MOVE TRANS-ADDRESS-01        TO DET-ADDRESS-01.
    MOVE TRANS-ADDRESS-02        TO DET-ADDRESS-02.
    MOVE TRANS-CREDIT-RATING     TO DET-CREDIT-RATING.
    PERFORM 320-VALIDATE.
    IF NO-ERRORS
        PERFORM 400-UPDATE-MASTER.
    IF NO-ERRORS AND NO-KEY-ERROR
        ADD 1 TO TOTAL-GOOD
    ELSE
        ADD 1 TO TOTAL-ERRORS.
    MOVE SPACES TO DETAIL-LINE.
    PERFORM 360-PRINT-LINE.
    PERFORM 250-READ.
```

FIGURE 6.16(c)

```
320-VALIDATE.
    MOVE 'NO'                        TO ERROR-FLAG.
    IF TRANS-CUSTOMER-NO IS NOT NUMERIC
        MOVE MESSAGE-05          TO DET-MESSAGE
        PERFORM 350-PRINT-ERROR.

    IF      (TRANS-CODE IS LESS THAN '1')
        OR (TRANS-CODE IS GREATER THAN '3')
        MOVE MESSAGE-06          TO DET-MESSAGE
        PERFORM 350-PRINT-ERROR.

    IF      (TRANS-CREDIT-RATING IS LESS THAN '1')
        OR (TRANS-CREDIT-RATING IS GREATER THAN '5')
        MOVE MESSAGE-09          TO DET-MESSAGE
        PERFORM 350-PRINT-ERROR.

350-PRINT-ERROR.
    PERFORM 360-PRINT-LINE.
    MOVE SPACES                  TO DETAIL-LINE.
    MOVE 'YES'                   TO ERROR-FLAG.

360-PRINT-LINE.
    WRITE PRINT-REC FROM DETAIL-LINE
        AFTER ADVANCING 1 LINE.
    ADD 1                        TO LINE-COUNT.
    IF LINE-COUNT IS GREATER THAN 50
        PERFORM 220-HEADINGS.

400-UPDATE-MASTER.
    MOVE  TRANS-CUSTOMER-NO        TO  MST-CUSTOMER-NO.
    IF ADD-CUSTOMER
        PERFORM 410-NEW-MASTER
    ELSE
        IF REVISE-CUSTOMER
            PERFORM 420-REVISE-MASTER
        ELSE
            PERFORM 430-DELETE-MASTER.

410-NEW-MASTER.
    PERFORM 415-CREATE-NEW.
    PERFORM 440-WRITE-MASTER.
    IF KEY-ERROR
        MOVE MESSAGE-08      TO DET-MESSAGE
        PERFORM 350-PRINT-ERROR.

415-CREATE-NEW.
    MOVE    TRANS-CUSTOMER-NO      TO   MAST-CUSTOMER-NO
                                       DET-CUSTOMER-NO.
    MOVE    TRANS-NAME            TO   MAST-NAME
                                       DET-NAME.
    MOVE    TRANS-ADDRESS-01      TO   MAST-ADDRESS-01
                                       DET-ADDRESS-01.
    MOVE    TRANS-ADDRESS-02      TO   MAST-ADDRESS-02
                                       DET-ADDRESS-02.
    MOVE    TRANS-CREDIT-RATING   TO   MAST-CREDIT-RATING
                                       DET-CREDIT-RATING.
    MOVE    MESSAGE-02            TO   DET-MESSAGE.
    PERFORM 360-PRINT-LINE.

420-REVISE-MASTER.
    PERFORM 450-READ-MASTER.
    IF KEY-ERROR
        MOVE MESSAGE-04      TO DET-MESSAGE
        PERFORM 350-PRINT-ERROR
    ELSE
        PERFORM 425-DO-REVISE
        PERFORM 460-REWRITE-MASTER.
```

FIGURE 6.16(d)

```
425-DO-REVISE.
    IF TRANS-NAME IS NOT EQUAL TO SPACES
        MOVE  TRANS-NAME              TO  MAST-NAME.
    IF TRANS-ADDRESS-01 IS NOT EQUAL TO SPACES
        MOVE  TRANS-ADDRESS-01        TO  MAST-ADDRESS-01.
    IF TRANS-ADDRESS-02 IS NOT EQUAL TO SPACES
        MOVE  TRANS-ADDRESS-02        TO  MAST-ADDRESS-02.
    IF TRANS-CREDIT-RATING IS NOT EQUAL TO SPACES
        MOVE  TRANS-CREDIT-RATING     TO  MAST-CREDIT-RATING
    MOVE MESSAGE-01                    TO  DET-MESSAGE.
    PERFORM 360-PRINT-LINE.

430-DELETE-MASTER.
    PERFORM 435-DO-DELETE.
    IF KEY-ERROR
        MOVE MESSAGE-04      TO DET-MESSAGE
        PERFORM 350-PRINT-ERROR
    ELSE
        MOVE MESSAGE-03      TO DET-MESSAGE
        PERFORM 360-PRINT-LINE.

435-DO-DELETE.
    MOVE 'NO' TO KEY-ERROR-FLAG.
    DELETE CUSTOMER-MASTER
        INVALID KEY MOVE 'YES' TO KEY-ERROR-FLAG.

440-WRITE-MASTER.
    MOVE 'NO' TO KEY-ERROR-FLAG.
    WRITE MASTER-REC FROM WS-MAST-REC
        INVALID KEY MOVE 'YES' TO KEY-ERROR-FLAG.

450-READ-MASTER.
    MOVE 'NO' TO KEY-ERROR-FLAG.
    READ CUSTOMER-MASTER INTO WS-MAST-REC
        INVALID KEY MOVE 'YES' TO KEY-ERROR-FLAG.

460-REWRITE-MASTER.
    MOVE 'NO' TO KEY-ERROR-FLAG.
    REWRITE MASTER-REC FROM WS-MAST-REC
        INVALID KEY MOVE MESSAGE-07 TO DET-MESSAGE
                    PERFORM 350-PRINT-ERROR.

500-WRAP-UP.
    MOVE ' GOOD RECORDS:'        TO SUMMARY-MESSAGE.
    MOVE TOTAL-GOOD              TO SUMMARY-AMT.
    MOVE SUMMARY-LINE            TO DETAIL-LINE.
    PERFORM 360-PRINT-LINE.
    MOVE ' ERROR RECORDS:'       TO SUMMARY-MESSAGE.
    MOVE TOTAL-ERRORS            TO SUMMARY-AMT.
    MOVE SUMMARY-LINE            TO DETAIL-LINE.
    PERFORM 360-PRINT-LINE.
    MOVE ' TOTAL TRANSACTIONS:'  TO SUMMARY-MESSAGE.
    MOVE TOTAL-TRANS             TO SUMMARY-AMT.
    MOVE SUMMARY-LINE            TO DETAIL-LINE.
    PERFORM 360-PRINT-LINE.

600-CUSTOMER-LISTING.
    DISPLAY '***** CUSTOMER LISTING STUB *****'.

700-END-OF-UPDATE.
    MOVE SPACES                     TO DETAIL-LINE.
    MOVE '*** END OF FILE UPDATE ***' TO DET-MESSAGE.
    PERFORM 360-PRINT-LINE.
```

FIGURE 6.16(e)

```
FD  CUSTOMER-MASTER
    RECORD CONTAINS 70 CHARACTERS
    LABEL RECORDS ARE STANDARD
    DATA RECORD IS MASTER-REC.
01  MASTER-REC.
    05  MST-CUSTOMER-NO          PIC X(05).
    05  FILLER                   PIC X(65).
```

100-MAINLINE This paragraph is the top level of the program and controls the activity of all major modules within it. Each of these modules is performed, including 600-CUSTOMER-LISTING, which is a temporary stub, from this level of the program.

200-INITIALIZE This paragraph opens the files to be used for updating the customer master, performs the print headings module, and reads the first transaction record.

220-HEADINGS Paragraph 220 prints the heading lines at the top of each page for the update report. It is accessed from both the initialization paragraph and when page overflow occurs during the printing of report lines.

250-READ Each time a transaction is required, this paragraph will be performed by the program. In it, the transaction is read, end of file is checked because this is a sequential file, and a count is made of the number of transactions.

300-PROCESS The process paragraph controls the processing of each transaction read by the program. Fields from each transaction are moved to the detail line in preparation for printing. Paragraph 320-VALIDATE is then performed to check the transaction for errors. If there are no errors, 400-UPDATE-MASTER is performed to begin the update process against the master file. Counts are also updated here to indicate the number of transactions that have been correctly processed and those that were in error. Two fundamental reasons for errors may exist. One error is the result of an invalid field in the transaction that was caught by the validation module. If there is no validation error, it will be reflected in the condition name NO-ERRORS.

The other reason why a transaction may be considered in error is if an error occurred during the processing against the master file. If processing went without a hitch, this condition is indicated by the name NO-KEY-ERROR.

320-VALIDATE As the name suggests, this module checks the transaction for errors. There can be three error types detected here: a nonnumeric customer number, an update code that is not a value of 1, 2, or 3, and a credit rating that is not in the range of 1 to 5 inclusive. In each case, an error will produce an appropriate error message, and it is possible that up to three messages could be printed for a single transaction.

350-PRINT-ERROR This paragraph is performed each time an error is detected. The error message is printed from here, and the error flag is also set to ensure that no further processing is attempted for that transaction.

360-PRINT-LINE All lines, except for headings, are printed from this paragraph. This means that other areas of the program must first set up the necessary information in the detail line and then the printing is done in paragraph 360. The paragraph also counts the number of lines printed and checks for page overflow.

400-UPDATE-MASTER When the program arrives at this paragraph, a valid transaction will be ready for processing. The first step is to move the customer number from the transaction to the record-key field located in the master record (MST-CUSTOMER-NO). Then the type of transaction is determined and the appropriate paragraph is performed to process that transaction.

410-NEW-MASTER and 415-CREATE-NEW These paragraphs work together to create a new master record by processing an add new record (code 1) transaction. 415 is responsible for setting up the contents of the master record from the transaction. Then 410 performs the write module and checks for any errors that could result on disk if the record was not successfully written. Either a message indicating a successful add to the file or an error message will be printed.

420-REVISE-MASTER and 425-DO-REVISE A revise transaction (code 2) is processed here. First, the master record is read, and if a record was successfully retrieved, paragraph 425 applies the changes to the master record from the transaction. The record is then rewritten back to the master file, and a message is printed to indicate successful updating. Any key errors here will result in an error message being printed, and the transaction processing will be aborted without an update to the master.

430-DELETE-MASTER and 435-DO-DELETE Code 3 transactions are processed here by issuing a delete operation against the master file. An invalid key here can indicate that the record with the transaction's customer number was not found and therefore could not be deleted. In this case, an error message is printed. If there is no invalid key, the record was successfully deleted and the delete message is printed.

440-WRITE-MASTER This paragraph does the actual writing of a record to the master file.

450-READ-MASTER Paragraph 450 reads each record from the master file based on the value contained in the record key field.

460-REWRITE-MASTER This paragraph will be performed after a revision has been made to the master record and it is ready to be rewritten back onto the master field. Normally, a key error will not occur here unless there is a program logic problem or a problem with the disk.

500-WRAP-UP This paragraph prints the summary totals for the end of the update report. These totals show the number of transactions read, the number that were correctly processed, and the number containing errors.

600-CUSTOMER-LISTING This is the program stub for the customer listing to be implemented at the end of the chapter.

700-END-OF-UPDATE When the program has been successfully completed, this paragraph will print a message to indicate that all updating is completed. The program will then return to the top-level mainline and terminate operation.

PROGRAM TESTING

Test data for the customer master update program are shown in Figure 6.17. To the right of each record is a comment to indicate the purpose of the transaction and how it

```
200100THE LOFT CCMPANY    1200 YORK ST,      TORONTO, ONT,    5    revise
100102DYNAMIC GRAPHICS    2121 FOWLER AVE,   HAMILTON, ONT,   2    add new master
200108ERIN GRAPH CS                          ERIN, ONT,       5    revise
200109KLEAR PRIN NG                                                revise
300201                                                             delete master
100202ELEGANT ST TIONERY  1 10TH AVE,        BUFFALO, NY      5    already on master
200204THE PAPER'S EDGE    83 MENTOR          LOCKPORT, NY     3    master not found
300207                                                             master not found
200221GRAPHICS 2000                                          4    update credit
2001@9ALL PRINTING        18 MELITTA ST,     OLEAN, NY        6    validation errors
```
FIGURE 6.17 Transaction file (TRANS6) for updating the customer master

should affect the master during the update process. If a test record is long enough, these comments can be entered in the record, because they would simply exist in the FILLER field used to end the record description in the program. Failing this, the comments could be entered on your coding sheet, but not keyed into the transaction file when it is prepared.

READING THE ISAM MASTER FILE SEQUENTIALLY

Before and after the update, we will need to have a dump of the master file to determine if the updating was correct. One way to dump the file is to use a utility program, but for this case a COBOL program is provided in Figure 6.18. This program may be used to dump the master both before and after the update occurs.

```
IDENTIFICATION DIVISION.

PROGRAM-ID.
    DUMP6.

ENVIRONMENT DIVISION.

CONFIGURATION SECTION.
SOURCE-COMPUTER.
    IBM-4381.
OBJECT-COMPUTER.
    IBM-4381.

INPUT-OUTPUT SECTION.

FILE-CONTROL.
    SELECT CUSTOMER-MASTER  ASSIGN TO MASTER
            ORGANIZATION IS INDEXED
            ACCESS MODE IS SEQUENTIAL
            RECORD KEY IS MST-CUSTOMER-NO.
    SELECT DUMP-UPDATE    ASSIGN TO PRINTER.

DATA DIVISION.

FILE SECTION.

FD  CUSTOMER-MASTER
    RECORD CONTAINS 70 CHARACTERS
    LABEL RECORDS ARE STANDARD
    DATA RECORD IS MASTER-REC.
01  MASTER-REC.
    05  MST-CUSTOMER-NO         PIC X(05).
    05  FILLER                  PIC X(65).

FD  DUMP-UPDATE
    RECORD CONTAINS 133 CHARACTERS
    LABEL RECORDS ARE OMITTED
    DATA RECORD IS PRINT-REC.
01  PRINT-REC.
    05  FILLER                  PIC X.
    05  PRINT-LINE              PIC X(132).

WORKING-STORAGE SECTION.

01  OTHER-ITEMS.
    05  EOF-FLAG                PIC X(03)    VALUE 'NO'.
        88  END-OF-FILE                      VALUE 'YES'.

01  WS-MAST-REC.
    05  MAST-CUSTOMER-NO        PIC X(05).
    05  MAST-NAME               PIC X(20).
    05  MAST-ADDRESS-01         PIC X(20).
    05  MAST-ADDRESS-02         PIC X(20).
    05  MAST-CREDIT-RATING      PIC X(01).
    05  FILLER                  PIC X(04).
```

FIGURE 6.18(a)   Program to dump the master file

```
01  HEAD-1.
    05  FILLER                    PIC X(23)   VALUE SPACES.
    05  FILLER                    PIC X(22)
                    VALUE 'CUSTOMER MASTER DUMP'.

PROCEDURE DIVISION.

100-MAINLINE.
    PERFORM 200-INITIALIZE.
    PERFORM 300-DUMP
        UNTIL END-OF-FILE.
    CLOSE CUSTOMER-MASTER
            DUMP-UPDATE.
    STOP RUN.

200-INITIALIZE.
    OPEN INPUT  CUSTOMER-MASTER
            OUTPUT DUMP-UPDATE.
    PERFORM 220-HEADINGS.
    PERFORM 250-READ.

220-HEADINGS.
    WRITE PRINT-REC FROM HEAD-1
        AFTER ADVANCING 2 LINES.
    MOVE SPACES TO PRINT-REC.
    WRITE PRINT-REC
        AFTER ADVANCING 1 LINE.

250-READ.
    READ CUSTOMER-MASTER INTO WS-MAST-REC
        AT END MOVE 'YES' TO EOF-FLAG.

300-DUMP.
    MOVE SPACES                TO PRINT-REC.
    MOVE MASTER-REC            TO PRINT-LINE.
    WRITE PRINT-REC FROM DETAIL-LINE
        AFTER ADVANCING 1 LINE.
    PERFORM 250-READ.
```

FIGURE 6.18(b)

The program may also be used as a model to develop the module 600-CUSTOMER-LISTING. Because this module is part of the update program, the master was defined with an ACCESS of DYNAMIC so that it could be accessed sequentially. However, the dump defines the file with SEQUENTIAL access.

The result of running the dump program before the update is run is shown in Figure 6.19. Although this program does not print each field separately, it is quite

CUSTOMER MASTER DUMP

```
00100THE LOFT COMPANY      1609 HAIG ST.        TORONTO, ONT.         5
00101STATIONERY GRAPHICS 2118 FOWLER AVE.       HAMILTON, ONT.        3
00105MERIT PRINTING CO.    3330 SOUTH MILLWAY   BUFFALO, NY           5
00107WOOD PRINTING         1650 CARRINGTON DR.  ROCHESTER, NY         4
00108ERIN GRAPHICS         2689 BATTLEFORD      FORT ERIE, ONT.       5
00109ENGLISH PRINTING      18 KENTWOOD RD.      ERIE, PA              5
00110THE INKSPOT           1333 BLOOR ST.       TORONTO, ONT.         2
00201ACE PRINTING          123 FLAGSHIP DR.     LEWISTON, NY          4
00202ELEGANT STATIONERY    1 10TH AVE.          BUFFALO, NY           5
00203ONE DAY PRINTING      70 PARK AVE.         NIAGARA FALLS, ONT.   3
00205FORMS FORMS FORMS     2222 NOIR ROAD       TORONTO, ONT.         4
00210THE GRAPHIC EDGE      3220 CAWTHRA         MISSISSAUGA, ONT.     5
00220S AND M PRINTING      10 SOUTH MAIN ST.    ROCHESTER, NY         5
00221GRAPHICS 2000         3175 KIRWIN DR.      BATAVIA, NY           3
00223MULTIGRAPHICS DESIGN18 S. 11TH ST.         BUFFALO, NY           4
```

FIGURE 6.19 Master file dump prior to the update

readable because of the alphanumeric fields, which inherently provide for some spacing. Caution is needed when dumping files that contain many numeric fields and especially when those fields are packed decimal. In such a case, each field must be moved separately to the print line in order for them to be in display format.

RESULTS OF THE UPDATE

Running the update program results in the printing of the update report (Figure 6.20). This report shows the activity against the master file and the action taken with each transaction processed. Records are double-spaced as required by the specifications, with single spacing when more than one message is printed for a single record.

```
                        CUSTOMER MASTER UPDATE

CUST.  NAME                ADDRESS                          CREDIT  MESSAGE
NUM.                                                        CODE
00100  THE LOFT COMPANY    1200 YORK ST.      TORONTO, ONT.    5    MASTER RECORD REVISED
00102  DYNAMIC GRAPHICS    2121 FOWLER AVE.   HAMILTON, ONT.   2    MASTER RECORD CREATED
00108  ERIN GRAPHICS                          ERIN, ONT.       5    MASTER RECORD REVISED
00109  KLEAR PRINTING                                               MASTER RECORD REVISED
00201                                                               MASTER RECORD DELETED
00202  ELEGANT STATIONERY  1 10TH AVE.        BUFFALO, NY      5    MASTER ALREADY EXISTS
00204  THE PAPER'S EDGE    83 MENTOR          LOCKPORT, NY     3    MASTER RECORD NOT FOUND
00207                                                               MASTER RECORD NOT FOUND
00221  GRAPHICS 2000                                          4    MASTER RECORD REVISED
001@9  ALL PRINTING        18 MELITTA ST.     OLEAN, NY        6    NONNUMERIC CUSTOMER NO.
                                                                    UPDATE CODE NOT 1, 2, OR 3

GOOD RECORDS:          6
ERROR RECORDS:         4
TOTAL TRANSACTIONS:   10
```

FIGURE 6.20   Update report from the customer file update

The end of the report shows the summary totals required. These totals are for the number of transactions read, the number of good transactions, and the number containing errors.

The final step in testing this program is to once again dump the master file. Figure 6.21 shows this dump of the master after the updates have revised it. Changes to the file will be reflected here, including new records, revised records, and the absence of records that have been deleted.

```
00100THE LOFT COMPANY       1200 YORK ST.        TORONTO, ONT.          5
00101STATIONERY GRAPHICS    2118 FOWLER AVE.      HAMILTON, ONT.         3
00102DYNAMIC GRAPHICS       2121 FOWLER AVE.      HAMILTON, ONT.         2
00105MERIT PRINTING CO.     3330 SOUTH MILLWAY    BUFFALO, NY            5
00107WOOD PRINTING          1650 CARRINGTON DR.   ROCHESTER, NY          4
00108ERIN GRAPHICS          2689 BATTLEFORD       ERIN, ONT.             5
00109KLEAR PRINTING         18 KENTWOOD RD.       ERIE, PA               5
00110THE INKSPOT            1333 BLOOR ST.        TORONTO, ONT.          2
00202ELEGANT STATIONERY     1 10TH AVE.           BUFFALO, NY            5
00203ONE DAY PRINTING       70 PARK AVE.          NIAGARA FALLS, ONT.    3
00205FORMS FORMS FORMS      2222 NOIR ROAD        TORONTO, ONT.          4
00210THE GRAPHIC EDGE       3220 CAWTHRA          MISSISSAUGA, ONT.      5
00220S AND M PRINTING       10 SOUTH MAIN ST.     ROCHESTER, NY          5
00221GRAPHICS 2000          3175 KIRWIN DR.       BATAVIA, NY            3
00223MULTIGRAPHICS DESIGN18 S. 11TH ST.          BUFFALO, NY            4
```

FIGURE 6.21   Dump of the updated customer master file.

If errors are detected in this dump, corrections will need to be made to the update program and the test of the program run once again. This will create a unique problem, because the master now reflects the changes from the first test run. If these were incorrect (that's why we need to do a further test run), the master file must be restored to its original values before a second test can be run. For this reason, a backup copy of this file is essential before testing an update to an ISAM file, as we discussed in the debugging hint for relative files.

DEBUGGING HINT   Many of the problems associated with ISAM files will be because of invalid keys. This is also true of relative and VSAM files. The best way to cope with the occurrence of an invalid key is to check the **file status code** in the program before taking further action. To do this requires that we specify the file status code in the SELECT clause for the ISAM file in the update program as follows:

```
INPUT-OUTPUT SECTION.

FILE-CONTROL.
     SELECT CUSTOMER-MASTER  ASSIGN TO MASTER
               ORGANIZATION IS INDEXED
               ACCESS MODE IS DYNAMIC
               RECORD KEY IS MST-CUSTOMER-NO
               FILE STATUS IS WS-STATUS-CODE.
```

The field WS-STATUS-CODE must also be defined in WORKING-STORAGE as follows:

```
     05 WS-STATUS-CODE          PIC X(02).
```

Now when any operation is done against the ISAM file, the field WS-STATUS-CODE will be set to a two-character value (values for this code were given earlier in the chapter), indicating the result of the operation. For example, if the following READ statement is issued, the field WS-STATUS-CODE can be checked to determine the result of the operation. A value of '00' indicates a successful read, but a value of '23' would indicate that no record was found.

```
     450-READ-MASTER.
          READ CUSTOMER-MASTER INTO WS-MAST-REC
               INVALID KEY MOVE 'YES' TO KEY-ERROR-FLAG.
          IF WS-STATUS-CODE IS EQUAL TO '00'
               MOVE 'NO' TO KEY-ERROR-FLAG.
```

The IF statement shows how a single condition for a successful operation could be tested. Similarly, other status code values could be checked to determine if unexpected disk problems were encountered. A message could be printed or the status code itself could be part of the output from the program. Each READ, WRITE, REWRITE, and DELETE statement in the program should have a test of the status code.

SUMMARY

ISAM files are used where data must be accessed both sequentially and directly. Each record in an ISAM file contains a record key that is not required to have a consecutive value, but it must uniquely identify the record. 1968 ANS COBOL files will also require a delete byte at the beginning of each record to be used as a flag when a record is deleted. Because a second file is not required for file updating in ISAM, it is useful to have a backup file that can be used to restore the file in the event of system failure. Doing a backup requires a special program, which may also double as a file reorganization program.

An ISAM file is defined with the SELECT clause, which may contain a RESERVE clause for alternate input/output buffers. ORGANIZATION IS INDEXED defines the file type, and the ACCESS clause defines the access method to be used in the program, whether SEQUENTIAL, RANDOM, or DYNAMIC. A RECORD KEY entry is used to identify the key field. 1968 ANS COBOL users will also specify a NOMINAL KEY.

The FD entry for the ISAM file is written in the same way as for other disk files. BLOCK, RECORD, LABEL, and DATA entries are all available for ISAM. In the PROCEDURE DIVISION, the file may be opened as INPUT, OUTPUT, or I-O depending on how data are to be accessed. A record is read from the file with a READ statement. If the access is sequential, the READ functions like a sequential READ and uses an AT END clause. START may be used to identify the first record of the file to be read for a sequential operation. If access is RANDOM or DYNAMIC, the READ uses an INVALID KEY clause. A record key value must also be supplied prior to the read operation.

The WRITE statement places a new record on the ISAM file. Unless a new file is being created, the WRITE operates in random mode and requires a record key to be specified for each record prior to writing the record on the file. WRITE always uses the INVALID KEY clause.

When a file is being updated, each record that has been revised will be rewritten with the changes onto the file with a REWRITE statement. REWRITE is used in I-O mode and requires the record to have been previously read directly from the file. REWRITE always uses an INVALID KEY clause. However, when a record is to be deleted from the file, the DELETE statement will be used, unless a 1968 version of ANS COBOL is used.

ISAM files are commonly created sequentially, but updated randomly. File dumps are essential for testing an ISAM update program to determine if the updates have been successful. Dumps are done sequentially even when the update was random. After a period of time when updates, additions, and deletions have been applied to the ISAM file, a file reorganization will be necessary to maintain file efficiency.

TERMS TO STUDY

Backup file	RANDOM
CLOSE	READ
Create	RECORD KEY
DELETE	Reorganization
Delete byte	REWRITE
DYNAMIC	SELECT
FILE STATUS	SEQUENTIAL
File status code	START
INVALID KEY	Update
NOMINAL KEY	WRITE
OPEN	

TRUE/FALSE

1. The term ISAM means indexed sequential access method.
2. The record key field associated with an ISAM file will be located in the transaction file.
3. A new and separate file is created as a result of updating an ISAM master file.
4. Reorganization of an ISAM file usually makes use of a backup file.
5. To create an ISAM file for the first time, the ACCESS MODE clause would contain the SEQUENTIAL entry.
6. A file status value of 00 normally means that a disk operation was successfully completed.
7. Because an ISAM file can be used for both input and output in the same program, an OPEN statement is not necessary.
8. Prior to a random READ, the key of the required record must be moved to the record key field.
9. The WRITE statement is used to write a record that has been revised back onto the ISAM file.
10. Testing an ISAM update program requires that the transaction file be in ascending key sequence.

FILL IN THE BLANK

11. Each record in an ISAM file is identified by a _____ field.
12. A _____ file is created to protect against loss of data when an ISAM file is frequently updated.
13. The _____ code indicates the result of an I/O operation on an ISAM file.
14. When an ISAM file is used both randomly and sequentially, an ACCESS MODE of _____ is used.
15. When the file is used for updating (input and output are required), the OPEN statement will use the _____ entry.
16. A random READ statement will require an _____ clause to determine if the disk operation was successful.
17. The _____ statement is used to place a new record on an ISAM file.
18. When testing an ISAM update program, a _____ of the master file should be taken before and after the program is run.

MULTIPLE CHOICE

19. ISAM records are stored sequentially but do not require the keys to be:
    a. Stored in the record.
    b. Consecutive values.
    c. Used in the application.
20. What level of ANS COBOL uses a delete byte?
    a. 1968
    b. 1974
    c. 1985
21. Eventually, after records have been added to and deleted from an ISAM file, it will be necessary to _____ the file.
    a. dump
    b. list
    c. reorganize
    d. erase

22. Which entry is used in the ACCESS MODE clause when only updating is done to the file?
    a. SEQUENTIAL   c. DYNAMIC
    b. RANDOM   d. UPDATE

23. An ISAM file SELECT clause entry that is only needed for 1968 ANS COBOL is:
    a. RECORD KEY   c. NOMINAL KEY
    b. ORGANIZATION   d. FILE STATUS

24. When an ISAM file is created, it will be opened as:
    a. INPUT   c. I-O
    b. OUTPUT   d. NEW

25. A READ that is used for sequential input from an ISAM file will use which clause?
    a. AT END   b. INVALID KEY

26. When a READ is issued for a record that is not on the ISAM file, what happens?
    a. No record is read.   d. a and b.
    b. An invalid key occurs.   e. a, b, and c.
    c. The program aborts.

27. Except for 1968 ANS COBOL, which statement or method is used to remove a record from active status on the ISAM file?
    a. DELETE   c. REMOVE
    b. ERASE   d. The delete byte is used.

PROGRAMMING EXERCISES

1. The program UPDATE6 from this chapter contained a stub for the customer listing that was to be produced after the updating of the master file and the update report were completed. Modify the program to produce this report by first closing the master file and then opening it as INPUT to be read sequentially. The customer listing layout follows the master file definition. A second requirement of this exercise is to modify the program to include the file status code as part of the message printed for each transaction in the update report. This code is not required when the message is a validation error in the transaction, but must be included for all messages that represent ISAM file activity.

INPUT/OUTPUT RECORD DEFINITION				
File: Customer master Record Length: 70 Sequence: Customer no.	File Type: ISAM Blocking Factor: None Access Method: Sequential			
COLUMNS	FIELD	TYPE	LENGTH	DECIMALS
1–5	Customer number	N	5	
6–25	Name	A/N	20	
26–45	Address line 1	A/N	20	
46–65	Address line 2	A/N	20	
66	Credit rating	N	1	
67–70	Unused	A/N	13	

```
                    CUSTOMER MASTER LISTING

CUST.  NAME                   ADDRESS                ADDRESS                CREDIT
NUM.                          LINE 1                 LINE 2                 CODE

99999  XXXXXXXXXXXXXXXXXXXX   XXXXXXXXXXXXXXXXXXXX   XXXXXXXXXXXXXXXXXXXX   X

99999  XXXXXXXXXXXXXXXXXXXX   XXXXXXXXXXXXXXXXXXXX   XXXXXXXXXXXXXXXXXXXX   X

99999  XXXXXXXXXXXXXXXXXXXX   XXXXXXXXXXXXXXXXXXXX   XXXXXXXXXXXXXXXXXXXX   X




NUMBER OF MASTER RECORDS:     ZZZ9
```

2. Create an ISAM master file based on the following file definition. Write a minimum of 20 records on the disk file, making sure they are in key sequence (account number) and that there are no duplicate keys. Produce a report listing each record created on the master file and appropriate error messages if for any reason a master record cannot be written.

INPUT/OUTPUT RECORD DEFINITION				
File: Account master Record Length: 90 Sequence: Account no.		File Type: ISAM Blocking Factor: None Access Method: Sequential		
COLUMNS	FIELD	TYPE	LENGTH	DECIMALS
1–7	Account number	N	7	
8–27	Name	A/N	20	
28–47	Address	A/N	20	
48–62	City and state or province	A/N	15	
63–69	Zip or postal code	A/N	7	
70–75	Account balance	N	6	2
76–81	Charges last month	N	6	2
82–87	Credit limit	N	6	2

```
                        ACCOUNT MASTER CREATE

ACCOUNT   NAME                    ADDRESS                  ACCOUNT   CHARGES   CREDIT    MESSAGES
NUMBER                                                     BALANCE             LIMIT

9999999   XXXXXXXXXXXXXXXXXXXX    XXXXXXXXXXXXXXXXXXXX     ZZZ9.99   ZZZ9.99   ZZZ9.99   XXXXXXXXXXXXX
                                  XXXXXXXXXXXXXXXXXXXX
                                  XXXXXXX

9999999   XXXXXXXXXXXXXXXXXXXX    XXXXXXXXXXXXXXXXXXXX     ZZZ9.99   ZZZ9.99   ZZZ9.99   XXXXXXXXXXXXX
                                  XXXXXXXXXXXXXXXXXXXX
                                  XXXXXXX

9999999   XXXXXXXXXXXXXXXXXXXX    XXXXXXXXXXXXXXXXXXXX     ZZZ9.99   ZZZ9.99   ZZZ9.99   XXXXXXXXXXXXX
                                  XXXXXXXXXXXXXXXXXXXX
                                  XXXXXXX



NUMBER OF MASTER RECORDS CREATED:    ZZZ9

NUMBER OF ERROR RECORDS:             ZZZ9
```

3. Write a COBOL program to dump the master file created in problem 2. Retain this program to be used for testing the following program, which will update the master file.

4. Write a program with complete program specifications, input/output definitions, structure chart, pseudo code, test data, and file dumps. This program will update the Account Master file created in problem 2 by applying the following transactions to the master.

INPUT/OUTPUT RECORD DEFINITION				
File: Account transactions Record Length: 90 Sequence: Account no.		File Type: Sequential disk Blocking Factor: 12 Access Method: Sequential		
COLUMNS	FIELD	TYPE	LENGTH	DECIMALS
1–7	Account number	N	7	
8	Transaction code N-new account D-delete account P-payment C-charge	A	1	
9–28	Name	A/N	20	
29–48	Address	A/N	20	
49–63	City and state or province	A/N	15	
64–70	Zip or postal code	A/N	7	
71–76	Account balance	N	6	2
77–82	Charges last month	N	6	2
83–88	Credit limit	N	6	2

There are four types of transactions:

New account (N): This type adds a new record to the master file. All fields must be present in the transaction for this code. Normally, account balance and charges last month will contain zero values.

Delete account (D): This transaction will delete a matching record from the master file. Only the account number and transaction code need be present in a delete transaction. To be deleted, a master record must have an account balance of zero; otherwise, the transaction is an error.

Payment (P): When a payment is made, only the account number, transaction code, and balance field need be present in the transaction. The balance field in this case represents the payment amount, which will be subtracted from the amount in the master record. Any other fields that are present in the transaction simply replace the corresponding field in the master.

Charge (C): Account number, code, and the charge amount are the only fields present in the transaction. A charge is made by adding the balance field in the transaction (which now represents a charge) to the balance in the master. However, if it will cause the balance to exceed the credit limit, it cannot be accepted and an error message should be produced. If the charge is OK, then it is also moved to the charges-last-month field in the master record.

PROGRAMMING WITH VSAM FILES

As we discussed in Chapter 4, the virtual storage access method **(VSAM)** is becoming widely used on mainframe computers. The most significant reason for this is that the organization method used permits addition and deletion of records without the necessity to reorganize the file after a certain volume of activity has occurred. Remember, this need to reorganize the file periodically was a major disadvantage of ISAM files.

A second benefit of using a VSAM file is the capability of defining an alternate key to the primary one. Like ISAM, the VSAM file if defined with a key field that may be used for random access of the file. But a second key field, called the alternate key, may also be defined, giving the file more than one way of being accessed. For more complex files, this gives added flexibility to how the file may be used.

VSAM files also share some of the benefits of ISAM. They permit both sequential and random access to the records and, with the DYNAMIC option, can also achieve this access in the same program. VSAM permits the use of the DELETE statement, which removes the record from the file, thus leaving room for a new addition. We have seen that some ISAM systems also use DELETE, while others require the delete byte, which only flags the record and does not physically delete it.

KEY FIELDS

A key field (Figure 7.1) in VSAM is defined in the same way as an ISAM file. Usually the **key** is the first field in the record, as shown by the customer number in the figure, but this position is not mandatory. The value of the key may be either numeric or alphanumeric as required by the application. Keys in each record do not need to be consecutive in value and, like ISAM, there are no empty spaces between records except the control areas required for file manipulation.

Keys may also be formed of group items when several fields are used to identify a record. For example, a customer may be identified uniquely by a customer number, region, and country number. These three fields are grouped together into a single key field, as shown in Figure 7.2, which is used as the key for the VSAM file. Any key activity would refer to this composite field, while other activities in the program, such as printing a report, can refer to the individual fields.

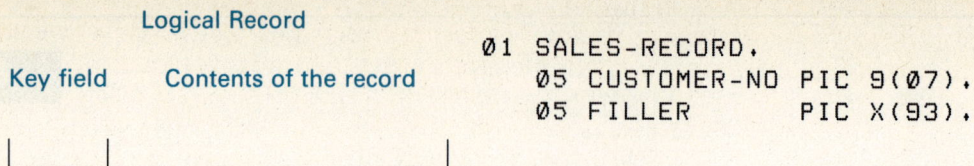

FIGURE 7.1   The key field in a VSAM file's record

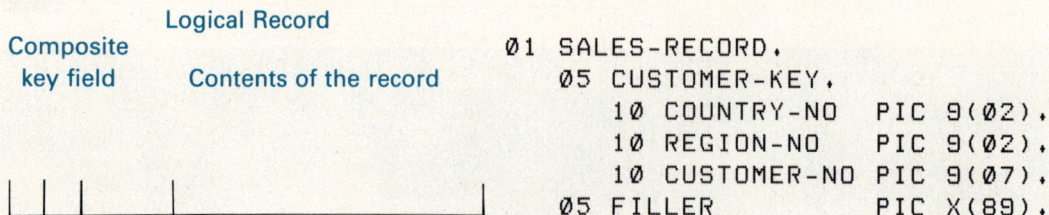

FIGURE 7.2   Using a composite key field in a VSAM record

ALTERNATE KEYS

Only VSAM permits the use of one or more **alternate keys** in addition to the record key. The alternate key is different in the sense that it permits duplicate keys to exist. For example, in the composite key field there are likely to be several, perhaps many, customers with the same region number. If region number were specified as the alternate key, then the first read issued for, say, a region 05 would provide the first customer for region 05. Subsequent reads would get succeeding region 05 customer's records until there were no more to access.

Similarly, a field such as customer name could be specified as an alternate key. It's not as likely that there would be duplicate records for customers with the same name, but no doubt there would be some. Usually, the alternate key is used for accessing the file for display or reporting purposes. Updating would be done by referring to the primary record key to ensure the correct record was updated.

SELECT CLAUSE FOR VSAM FILES

```
INPUT-OUTPUT SECTION.

FILE-CONTROL.
     SELECT filename
          ASSIGN TO system-name
          [RESERVE integer ⎡ AREA  ⎤ ]
                          ⎣ AREAS ⎦
          ORGANIZATION is INDEXED
                          ⎧ SEQUENTIAL ⎫
          [ACCESS MODE IS ⎨ RANDOM     ⎬      ]
                          ⎩ DYNAMIC    ⎭
          RECORD KEY IS data-name-1
          [ALTERNATE RECORD KEY IS data-name   [ WITH DUPLICATES ] ] . . .
          [FILE STATUS IS data-name-2].
```

The SELECT clause for VSAM files follows all the same rules discussed in the previous chapter for ISAM. Note that, although we are defining a virtual file, the ORGANIZATION entry is still INDEXED. In this sense, COBOL does not distinguish between

ISAM and VSAM, which is to your benefit as a programmer. Once you understand ISAM, the concepts are transferrable to VSAM programming.

There is one important difference in the SELECT clause between ISAM and VSAM and that is the **ALTERNATE KEY** entry. This entry is not available on all systems, but where it is used it can define one or more alternate keys for accessing the file. Each of these keys, like the record key, must be contained within the master record description.

```
ALTERNATE KEY IS CUSTOMER-NO
```

Fields like the customer number in certain applications may contain duplicate numbers. Certainly, a region number as an alternate key would contain many duplicates. In these situations the **WITH DUPLICATES** option must also be used.

```
ALTERNATE KEY IS CUSTOMER-NO WITH DUPLICATES
```

The following examples show how SELECT clauses may be written for different applications of relative files.

Example 1 Select a VSAM file for random accessing on the record key and return the file status value after each operation.

```
       A   B
1   4  78  12                                                         72
_____

     SELECT CUSTOMER-FILE
         ASSIGN TO DA-3340-SYS001
         ORGANIZATION IS INDEXED
         ACCESS MODE IS RANDOM
         RECORD KEY IS CUSTOMER-KEY
         FILE STATUS IS WS-STATUS-FLAG.
```

Example 2 The CUSTOMER-FILE is to be available both sequentially and randomly to the program. This need requires the use of the **DYNAMIC** option in the ACCESS MODE clause.

```
       A   B
1   4  78  12                                                         72
_____

     SELECT CUSTOMER-FILE
         ASSIGN TO DA-3340-SYS001
         ORGANIZATION IS INDEXED
         ACCESS MODE IS DYNAMIC
         RECORD KEY IS CUSTOMER-KEY
         FILE STATUS IS WS-STATUS-FLAG.
```

Example 3 Access the customer file on the alternative key of REGION-NO, which can have duplicate values in the file. In this situation the RECORD KEY entry must still be used in the SELECT clause.

```
       A   B
1   4  78  12                                                         72
_____

     SELECT CUSTOMER-FILE
         ASSIGN TO DA-3340-SYS001
         ORGANIZATION IS INDEXED
         ACCESS MODE IS DYNAMIC
         RECORD KEY IS CUSTOMER-KEY
         ALTERNATE KEY IS REGION-NO WITH DUPLICATES.
```

Programming with VSAM Files

FILE DESCRIPTION (FD) ENTRY

```
DATA DIVISION.

FILE SECTION.
FD file-name
      [RECORD CONTAINS integer-2 CHARACTERS]
      LABEL  ⎰RECORD IS  ⎱  ⎰STANDARD⎱
             ⎱RECORDS ARE⎰  ⎱OMITTED ⎰
             ⎰RECORD IS  ⎱
      [DATA  ⎱RECORDS ARE⎰      data-name-1 [data-name-2 . . .].
 01  data-name.
           02-49  ⎰data-name⎱  ⎰PICTURE⎱  IS string [VALUE IS literal].
                  ⎱FILLER    ⎰  ⎱PIC    ⎰
```

The FD for VSAM files provides the same entries as for other direct-access files with one important difference. VSAM files cannot be blocked, and therefore the BLOCK CONTAINS clause is not available. COBOL programs (other languages too) cannot specify blocking because, with the VSAM file organization, the operating system determines the most effective organization of the file based on the device used for storing the VSAM file. This approach actually relieves the programmer of an added responsibility of knowing the most effective blocking for the device used.

The record description entry that follows the FD will contain the record key entry and, if used, the alternate key(s) as well. Records may be read into or written from working storage, as has ben our usual practice.

Example

```
        A    B
1   4   78   12                                                          72

        FD   CUSTOMER-FILE
             RECORD CONTAINS 100 CHARACTERS
             LABEL RECORDS ARE STANDARD
             DATA RECORD IS SALES-RECORD.

        01   SALES-RECORD.
             05 CUSTOMER-KEY.
                10 COUNTRY-NO    PIC 9(02).
                10 REGION-NO     PIC 9(02).
                10 CUSTOMER-NO   PIC 9(07).
             05 FILLER           PIC X(89).
```

PROCEDURE DIVISION STATEMENTS

PROCEDURE DIVISION coding for VSAM files closely follows that for ISAM file processing. Whether you are adding a new record to the file, updating a record, or deleting one (only for 1974 and 1985 ANS) from the file, the procedure and logic are the same. Although the organization of the VSAM file on a disk is different from the indexes and overflow areas of an ISAM file, COBOL sees these two types of files in the same way.

The statement format of all statements to be used for VSAM file activity are shown in Figure 7.3. These statements are consistent with ISAM, and so there is little that is new here from the previous chapter. Instead of reviewing these statements, let's look at some typical activities that would be done in a VSAM program.

```
        ⎧INPUT     file-name-1 [file-name-2] . . .⎫
OPEN⎨OUTPUT    file-name-5 [file-name-4] . . .⎬ . . .
        ⎩I-O       file-name-5 [file-name-6] . . .⎭
```

```
READ file-name RECORD [ INTO identifier ]
    ⎧AT END      ⎫
    ⎨INVALID KEY⎬        imperative-statement.
    ⎩             ⎭
```

```
START file-name
    ⎡       ⎧EQUAL TO       ⎫          ⎤
    ⎢       ⎪=              ⎪          ⎥
    ⎢       ⎪GREATER THAN   ⎪          ⎥
    ⎢KEY IS⎨>              ⎬ data-name ⎥
    ⎢       ⎪NOT LESS THAN  ⎪          ⎥
    ⎢       ⎩NOT <          ⎭          ⎥
    ⎣                                  ⎦
    [INVALID KEY imperative-statement].
```

```
WRITE record-name [FROM identifier-1]
    [INVALID KEY imperative-statement].
```

```
REWRITE record-name [FROM identifier-1]
    [INVALID KEY imperative-statement].
```

```
DELETE file-name RECORD
    [INVALID KEY imperative-statement].
```

```
CLOSE file-name-1 [file-name-2] . . .
```

FIGURE 7.3 Statement formats for use with VSAM file operations

CREATING A VSAM FILE

To create a VSAM file, the file will be defined as **SEQUENTIAL** and used as an OUTPUT file. Initial records may be read from a transaction file, as we have done to create previous files, and written in key sequence on the VSAM file. Alternatively, the file could be created with one record (or even no records), and then all additional records could be added to it in an update program as new records. Because there is no organizational or reorganization problem with VSAM, this second method is sometimes used.

Figure 7.4 shows a few selected statements that would be used in a program to create a VSAM file. In the SELECT clause, the ACCESS MODE entry is SEQUENTIAL because records will be written in key sequence to the file. The RECORD KEY specified in the SELECT clause is CUSTOMER-KEY, which references this entry in the record description following the FD.

This file is opened as an OUTPUT file that is written to with a WRITE statement after the WS-SALES-RECORD has been set up with data from the transaction. If an INVALID KEY occurs during the write operation, a flag is set that can be tested by the program. An INVALID key in this situation will likely result from a duplicate key in the record being written to the VSAM file. More detail can be found by specifying the FILE STATUS field and examining its contents.

```
ENVIRONMENT DIVISION.
INPUT-OUTPUT SECTION.
FILE-CONTROL.
    SELECT CUSTOMER-FILE
        ASSIGN TO DA-3340-SYS001
        ORGANIZATION IS INDEXED
        ACCESS MODE IS SEQUENTIAL
        RECORD KEY IS CUSTOMER-KEY.

DATA DIVISION.
FILE SECTION.
FD  CUSTOMER-FILE
    RECORD CONTAINS 100 CHARACTERS
    LABEL RECORDS ARE STANDARD
    DATA RECORD IS SALES-RECORD.

01 SALES-RECORD.
    05 CUSTOMER-KEY.
        10 COUNTRY-NO    PIC 9(02).
        10 REGION-NO     PIC 9(02).
        10 CUSTOMER-NO   PIC 9(07).
    05 FILLER           PIC X(89).

                :

PROCEDURE DIVISION.
    OPEN INPUT  TRANSACTION-FILE
        OUTPUT CUSTOMER-FILE.

            :

        WRITE SALES-RECORD FROM WS-SALES-RECORD
            INVALID KEY MOVE 'YES' TO KEY-FLAG.
```

FIGURE 7.4   Selected COBOL statements used to create a VSAM file

RANDOMLY UPDATING A VSAM RECORD

Figure 7.5 shows some of the program code needed to update a record on the VSAM file. In this example, the ACCESS MODE used is **RANDOM;** it could have been DYNAMIC if the same program needed to read the file sequentially. Again, in this example the record key is CUSTOMER-KEY, which is really a composite of three fields, as shown in the record description entry.

The CUSTOMER-FILE IS OPENED AS I-O because records will be both read and rewritten according to the update requirements. To READ the required record from the VSAM file, the values for the **composite key** field must be set up in the RECORD KEY field. Therefore, there is a move from the transaction data to the field CUSTOMER-KEY. If a record is not found on the master file, an INVALID KEY occurs.

The record is then updated by the program (not shown) and finally is rewritten back to the VSAM file. Like ISAM, an INVALID KEY at this time can only mean one thing, a program error.

```
ENVIRONMENT DIVISION,
INPUT-OUTPUT SECTION,
FILE-CONTROL,
    SELECT CUSTOMER-FILE
        ASSIGN TO DA-3340-SYS001
        ORGANIZATION IS INDEXED
        ACCESS MODE IS RANDOM
        RECORD KEY IS CUSTOMER-KEY,

DATA DIVISION,
FILE SECTION,
FD  CUSTOMER-FILE
    RECORD CONTAINS 100 CHARACTERS
    LABEL RECORDS ARE STANDARD
    DATA RECORD IS SALES-RECORD,

01 SALES-RECORD,
    05 CUSTOMER-KEY,
        10 COUNTRY-NO     PIC 9(02),
        10 REGION-NO       PIC 9(02),
        10 CUSTOMER-NO     PIC 9(07),
    05 FILLER             PIC X(89),

            :

PROCEDURE DIVISION,
    OPEN INPUT  TRANSACTION-FILE
         I-O    CUSTOMER-FILE,

            :

    MOVE TRANS-CUSTOMER-KEY    TO CUSTOMER-KEY,
    READ CUSTOMER-FILE INTO WS-SALES-RECORD
        INVALID KEY MOVE 'YES' TO KEY-FLAG,

            :

    REWRITE SALES-RECORD FROM WS-SALES-RECORD
        INVALID KEY MOVE 'YES' TO KEY-FLAG,
```

FIGURE 7.5   Selected COBOL statements to update a VSAM record

READING A VSAM FILE SEQUENTIALLY

Figure 7.6 shows the skeleton code reading a VSAM file in sequential order. In this example, the ACCESS MODE entry is DYNAMIC, which would also permit direct accessing of the file in this same program. The purpose of the transaction file in this code is to provide a starting key for the START statement. Issuing the START will

```
ENVIRONMENT DIVISION.
INPUT-OUTPUT SECTION.
FILE-CONTROL.
      SELECT CUSTOMER-FILE
           ASSIGN TO DA-3340-SYS001
           ORGANIZATION IS INDEXED
           ACCESS MODE IS DYNAMIC
           RECORD KEY IS CUSTOMER-KEY.

DATA DIVISION.
FILE SECTION.
FD  CUSTOMER-FILE
      RECORD CONTAINS 100 CHARACTERS
      LABEL RECORDS ARE STANDARD
      DATA RECORD IS SALES-RECORD.

01 SALES-RECORD.
      05 CUSTOMER-KEY.
          10 COUNTRY-NO    PIC 9(02).
          10 REGION-NO     PIC 9(02).
          10 CUSTOMER-NO   PIC 9(07).
      05 FILLER            PIC X(89).


           :


PROCEDURE DIVISION.
      OPEN INPUT  TRANSACTION-FILE
                  CUSTOMER-FILE.


           :


      START CUSTOMER-FILE KEY IS EQUAL TO TRANS-CUSTOMER-KEY
           INVALID KEY MOVE 'YES' TO KEY-FLAG.


           :


      READ CUSTOMER-FILE INTO WS-SALES-RECORD
           AT MOVE 'YES' TO EOF-FLAG.
```

FIGURE 7.6 Reading a VSAM file sequentially

position the file to a specific record in the file. Subsequent reads will read from this position until end of file is reached or the program determines that enough records have been read. For example, a new region number may be identified, and the reading could stop at this point.

A similar program, but without the START statement, would begin reading at the first record in the file. Reading continues through the file until end of file is reached.

If both sequential and random reading are required, first close the file after the sequential operation is complete. Then open it as I-O and now random reads may be issued for specific keys.

```
           CLOSE CUSTOMER-FILE.
           OPEN I-O CUSTOMER-FILE.


                :


           MOVE TRANS-CUSTOMER-KEY    TO CUSTOMER-KEY.
           READ CUSTOMER-FILE INTO WS-SALES-RECORD
                INVALID KEY MOVE 'YES' TO KEY-FLAG.
```

Of course, the file could first be opened as I-O and read randomly. Then it may be closed and opened for sequential reading. Which comes first is not important to COBOL, but only to the application that uses these techniques. The important part of this discussion is that the file may only be opened for one type of operation at one time. It cannot be opened for both sequential and random processing simulataneously.

USING AN ALTERNATE KEY

In the example shown in Figure 7.7, the field CUSTOMER-NAME is defined as an ALTERNATE KEY field in the VSAM master. With this definition, records may be

```
ENVIRONMENT DIVISION.
INPUT-OUTPUT SECTION.
FILE-CONTROL.
     SELECT CUSTOMER-FILE
          ASSIGN TO DA-3340-SYS001
          ORGANIZATION IS INDEXED
          ACCESS MODE IS RANDOM
          RECORD KEY IS CUSTOMER-KEY
          ALTERNATE RECORD KEY IS CUSTOMER-NAME
               WITH DUPLICATES.

DATA DIVISION.
FILE SECTION.
FD  CUSTOMER-FILE
     RECORD CONTAINS 100 CHARACTERS
     LABEL RECORDS ARE STANDARD
     DATA RECORD IS SALES-RECORD.

01 SALES-RECORD.
     05 CUSTOMER-KEY.
        10 COUNTRY-NO    PIC X(02).
        10 REGION-NO     PIC X(02).
        10 CUSTOMER-NO   PIC X(07).
     05 CUSTOMER-NAME    PIC X(12).
     05 FILLER           PIC X(77).


          :


PROCEDURE DIVISION.
     OPEN INPUT  TRANSACTION-FILE
          I-O    CUSTOMER-FILE.


          :


     MOVE SPACES                 TO CUSTOMER-KEY.
     MOVE TRANS-CUSTOMER-NAME     TO CUSTOMER-NAME.
     READ CUSTOMER-FILE INTO WS-SALES-RECORD
          INVALID KEY MOVE 'YES' TO KEY-FLAG.


          :


     REWRITE SALES-RECORD FROM WS-SALES-RECORD
          INVALID KEY MOVE 'YES' TO KEY-FLAG.
```

FIGURE 7.7 Using an alternate key to randomly access a VSAM record

retrieved by either the primary key (CUSTOMER-KEY) or by the alternate key field by supplying the customer name as a key. The SELECT clause entry

```
ALTERNATE RECORD KEY IS CUSTOMER-NAME
            WITH DUPLICATES.
```

specifies that there is the possibility of records that contain duplicate customer names. In such a situation, a sequential READ will continue to access consecutive records containing the same key value.

PROGRAMMING STYLE: OPEN AND CLOSE STATEMENTS

Both OPEN and CLOSE statements will operate more efficiently in virtual storage if several files are opened or closed at one time. When opening the files for use in a program, all files should be opened in a single statement,

```
   A    B
1  4 78 12                                                           72
────────────────────────────────────────────────────────────────────────
      OPEN INPUT   TRANSACTION-FILE
           I-O     CUSTOMER-FILE
           OUTPUT  REPORT.
```

rather than using separate open statements:

```
   A    B
1  4 78 12                                                           72
────────────────────────────────────────────────────────────────────────
      OPEN INPUT   TRANSACTION-FILE.
      OPEN I-O     CUSTOMER-FILE.
      OPEN OUTPUT  REPORT.
```

Similarly, a single CLOSE statement should close all the files that are no longer active in the program rather than using several statements:

```
   A    B
1  4 78 12                                                           72
────────────────────────────────────────────────────────────────────────
      CLOSE   TRANSACTION-FILE
              CUSTOMER-FILE
              REPORT.
```

An exception to this rule of style is when a VSAM file has been used in one mode such as sequential INPUT and then needs to be closed and opened as I-O. In this case, it is quite permissible, and necessary, to close this one file and open the new one without referring to other files in the program.

INVENTORY UPDATE: AN APPLICATION PROGRAM

The inventory master file (Figure 7.8) used in this program is a VSAM file using an item number as a key. Each record in the master represents an inventory item and shows the current in-stock status of the item. A sequential transaction file provides updating data to be processed against the master file. Items are taken out of stock or placed in stock by processing these transactions. New items may be added to the file and existing ones may be deleted as required by the application.

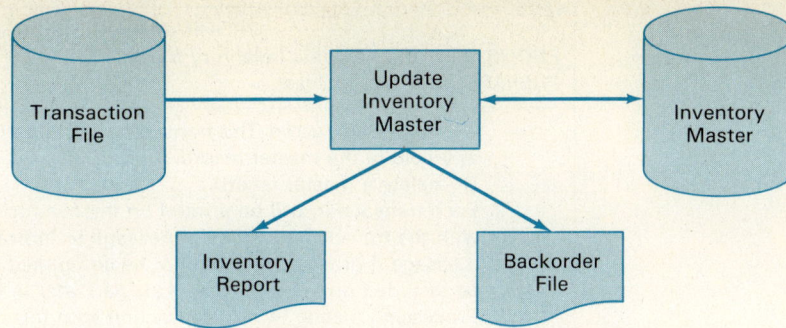

FIGURE 7.8 System flowchart for updating a VSAM inventory file

When an order for a part is processed, there is a possibility that there will be an insufficient quantity in stock to cover the order. Or there may be adequate stock, but the quantity may be reduced to the reorder point. In either case, **backorder** record is generated on the backorder file shown in the system flowchart.

A report is also printed by the inventory update program to show the activity of each transaction against the master.

SPECIFICATIONS

A program of this complexity will quite naturally have a lengthy set of specifications to define its requirements. The number of operations to organize and develop into a structured program underscores the need to use all the tools available to us for program development. Not only does this program do updating of a VSAM, file, but it also creates another output (in addition to the report), a sequential file for the backorder items.

At first glance, this may seem to add considerably to the program complexity. But, in reality, it is more like printing another line of output that is written on a different file. But more on this subject later.

The program specifications in Figure 7.9 explain that there are five transaction codes. These are an add (A), order (O), stock update (S), update (U), and delete (D). Each of these codes is explained separately in the specifications.

Also of interest (to say nothing of its importance) is the explanation of when a backorder is to be created. This process, which does get somewhat complex, is explained

---

PROGRAMMING SPECIFICATIONS

PROGRAM NAME: Update Inventory Master   PROGRAM ID: INVENTORY
PREPARED BY: Diane Quest   DATE: Aug. 14, 1986

Program Description:
    This program updates the VSAM inventory master file, creating a backorder file for items
    where there is not sufficient stock and producing a report of updating activity.
Input File(s):
    Transaction file
    Inventory master file
Output File(s):
    Backorder file
    Inventory report
Program Requirements:
    1. Read a transaction file, which has been previously validated, and update the customer
       master randomly with each transaction. Five update codes are available as follows:
       A—add a new record to the master.
       O—order an item. This transaction reduces the quantity in stock and if necessary creates
       a backorder.
       S—stock update. This transaction places new items in stock.

FIGURE 7.9(a) Specifications for the inventory file update

U—update the record. This transaction provides for corrections to the master by updating any field in the master record.

D—delete a master record.

2. Each transaction will be printed on the inventory report as it is processed. Included with the transaction will be a message to indicate successful processing or an error message if processing could not be completed. Other data from the master file may be included on the report as explained later in the specifications.

3. Processing a code 'A'—A transaction with this code adds a new item to the inventory master. Stock and order quantities will be zero, although the reorder point may be specified. No validation is necessary because error checking has been done in a previous program (not specified in this exercise).

   Write this record on the master file, and if an invalid key is detected, create an error message on the report. If there is no error, print a message to indicate the record has been added to the master.

4. Processing a code 'O'—This transaction represents an order that requires a quantity of an item to be removed from stock. The only transaction fields used for this code are the transaction code, item number, and quantity (stock). Read the master and, if it is present, reduce the stock quantity by the quantity in the transaction.

   If there is insufficient stock in the master, add the difference between the in-stock quantity in the master and the transaction-order quantity to the quantity on order field and reduce the stock quantity to zero. This amount is also written as a backorder quantity on the backorder file.

5. Processing a code 'S'—When items are placed into stock (i.e., an order for part was received), this transaction will update the quantity-in-stock field of the master record. The quantity will also be reduced from the order-quantity field in the master. Code 'S' records will contain a code, item number, and quantity (stock) fields.

6. Processing a code 'U'—Provides for changing the contents of any field in the master record. Any field that is present in the transaction simply replaces that field in the master

7. Processing a code 'D'—Deletes the existing master. This transaction will only contain a code and an item number. The report should inclue fields from the master for a successful deletion.

8. Whenever the quantity-in-stock field is reduced by any value, it must be checked against the reorder point. If the stock is less than or equal to the reorder point, write a backorder record for the reorder amount. Add this amount to the quantity-on-order field.

9. Any time a master record is updated successfully, the activity date on the master will be updated to show the current date.

10. The inventory report shows a line for each transaction processed. For a new record (code 'A'), all fields will be supplied by the transaction. For codes 'O', 'S', 'U', and 'D', move description, unit cost, stock quantity, order quantity, and reorder point from the master. Other fields are provided by the transaction as necessary.

FIGURE 7.9(b)

in step 4 and again in step 8 of the specifications. There are other rationales for determining when a backorder should be produced and in what quantity. But that is a topic for a different business discipline.

INPUT/OUTPUT DEFINITION

There are four files to be defined for this application, a transaction file, the VSAM inventory master, a backorder file, and the report. Figure 7.10 shows a sequential transaction file that will be used as input to the program. This file contains records for updating the master. The first field in the record contains a letter that is the transaction code. Next is the item number that will supply the key for accessing the master file. Remaining fields may or may not be present, depending on the type of transaction. Figure 7.11 shows fields that may be present for each transaction type.

To simplify things somewhat in this application, we will assume that the transaction file has been processed previously by a validation program. The file we are using here will contain only the accepted records that were not rejected during the validation process.

INPUT/OUTPUT RECORD DEFINITION				
File: Transactions Record Length: 50 Sequence: N/A		File Type: Sequential disk Blocking Factor: 20 Access Method: Sequential		
COLUMNS	FIELD	TYPE	LENGTH	DECIMALS
1	Transaction code A—New item O—Order S—Stock update U—Update D—Delete	A/N	1	
2–6	Item number	N	5	
7–21	Description	A/N	15	
22–27	Unit cost	N	6	2
28–30	Qty in stock	N	3	
31–33	Qty on order	N	3	
34–36	Reorder point	N	3	
37–44	Activity date	N	8	
45–50	Unused	A/N	6	

FIGURE 7.10   Input definition for the transaction file

Field	A	O	S	U	D
Transaction code	*	*	*	*	*
Item number	*	*	*	*	*
Description	*			O	
Unit cost	*			O	
Qty in stock	*	*	*	O	
Qty on order	*			O	
Reorder point	*			O	
Activity date				O	
* Field must be present. O Optional field.					

FIGURE 7.11   Key to fields used in the transaction file

The VSAM inventory master defined in Figure 7.12 will be used for random input and output operations. The records on the master use the same format as the transaction file, except that column 1 is unused in the master record. Cost and quantity fields are all numeric in the master because they will be used for calculations in the program. An IBM or compatible system could define these fields as USAGE COMP-3 for improved storage and operational efficiency. In this case, the quantity fields would occupy only two bytes each in the record while unit cost would occupy four bytes and could permit up to seven digits. We'll look at the contents of this file later in the application.

The backorder file (Figure 7.13) is a sequential output from the program. Its format is quite simple, containing an item number, description, backorder quantity, and the date. Each field will always be present for every record in the file. The backorder quantity is calculated by the program according to the algorithm described in the program specifications.

Although this file is sequential, the records will not necessarily be in item number sequence. Rather, the sequence of the records will depend on the order of the records in the transaction file. Clearly, the backorder file will require further processing after

INPUT/OUTPUT RECORD DEFINITION

File: Inventory master
Record Length: 50
Sequence: Item no.

File Type: VSAM
Blocking Factor:
Access Method: Random

COLUMNS	FIELD	TYPE	LENGTH	DECIMALS
1	Unused	A/N	1	
2–6	Item number	N	5	
7–21	Description	A/N	15	
22–27	Unit cost	N	6	2
28–30	Qty in stock	N	3	
31–33	Qty on order	N	3	
34–36	Reorder point	N	3	
37–44	Activity date	N	8	
45–50	Unused	A/N	6	

FIGURE 7.12   File definition for the inventory master file

INPUT/OUTPUT RECORD DEFINITION

File: Backorder file
Record Length: 32
Sequence: N/A

File Type: Sequential disk
Blocking Factor: 20
Access Method: Sequential

COLUMNS	FIELD	TYPE	LENGTH	DECIMALS
1	Unused	A/N	1	
2–6	Item number	N	5	
7–21	Description	A/N	15	
22–24	Backorder qty	N	3	
25–32	Date	N	8	

FIGURE 7.13   File definition for the backorder file

the update run is complete. However, the nature of this processing is not defined by the current specifications.

Figure 7.14 gives the layout for the inventory report. This report is unusual because it gets some of its data from the transaction, and other data come from the master as indicated in the specifications. When a new record is created for a stock item, all the information for the report must come from the transaction because no master as yet exists.

```
                                                                              1          1          1
    Ø          1          2          3          4          5          6          7          8          9          0          1          2
    1234567890123456789012345678901234567890123456789012345678901234567890123456789012345678901234567890123456789012345678901234567890


                                        INVENTORY REPORT


    TRANS    ITEM    DESCRIPTION          UNIT    TRANSACTION      MASTER        REORDER    BACKORDER    MESSAGES
    CODE     NO.                          COST    STOCK   ORDER    STOCK  ORDER   POINT        QTY

     U      ØØ85Ø    MAILER               2.19    5ØØ       Ø      5ØØ      Ø       2Ø                    INVENTORY RECORD REVISED
     X      99999    XXXXXXXXXXXXXXX     ZZZ9.99   ZZ9      ZZ9    ZZ9     ZZ9     ZZ9         ZZ9         XXXXXXXXXXXXXXXXXXXXXXXX
     X      99999    XXXXXXXXXXXXXXX     ZZZ9.99   ZZ9      ZZ9    ZZ9     ZZ9     ZZ9         ZZ9         XXXXXXXXXXXXXXXXXXXXXXXX
     X      99999    XXXXXXXXXXXXXXX     ZZZ9.99   ZZ9      ZZ9    ZZ9     ZZ9     ZZ9         ZZ9         XXXXXXXXXXXXXXXXXXXXXXXX
```

FIGURE 7.14   Inventory update report layout

But, for other transactions, only the transaction code and item number are certain to be supplied. For the order and stock update, there is also a quantity supplied by the transaction. Other fields will come from the master record after the update has been successfully completed. For example, the master stock and order quantity and the reorder point come from the master. If a backorder is generated, its quantity will also appear on the report.

STRUCTURE CHARTS AND PROBLEM COMPLEXITY

A structure chart for a problem of this complexity presents a dilemma for the program's designer. The problem appears when you attempt to fit all the modules into the limited space available on an ordinary-sized sheet of paper. The solution is quite simple and, we hope, obvious. By using several pages, the complete structure chart may be developed.

The key to using several pages successfully without losing the flow of the **top-down design** is to develop specific **structure chart modules** on each page. Let's face it! Most real-life business applications are more complex than most of the applications in this book, which are intended to demonstrate concepts. So developing an application in parts is a usual procedure for the analyst or programmer.

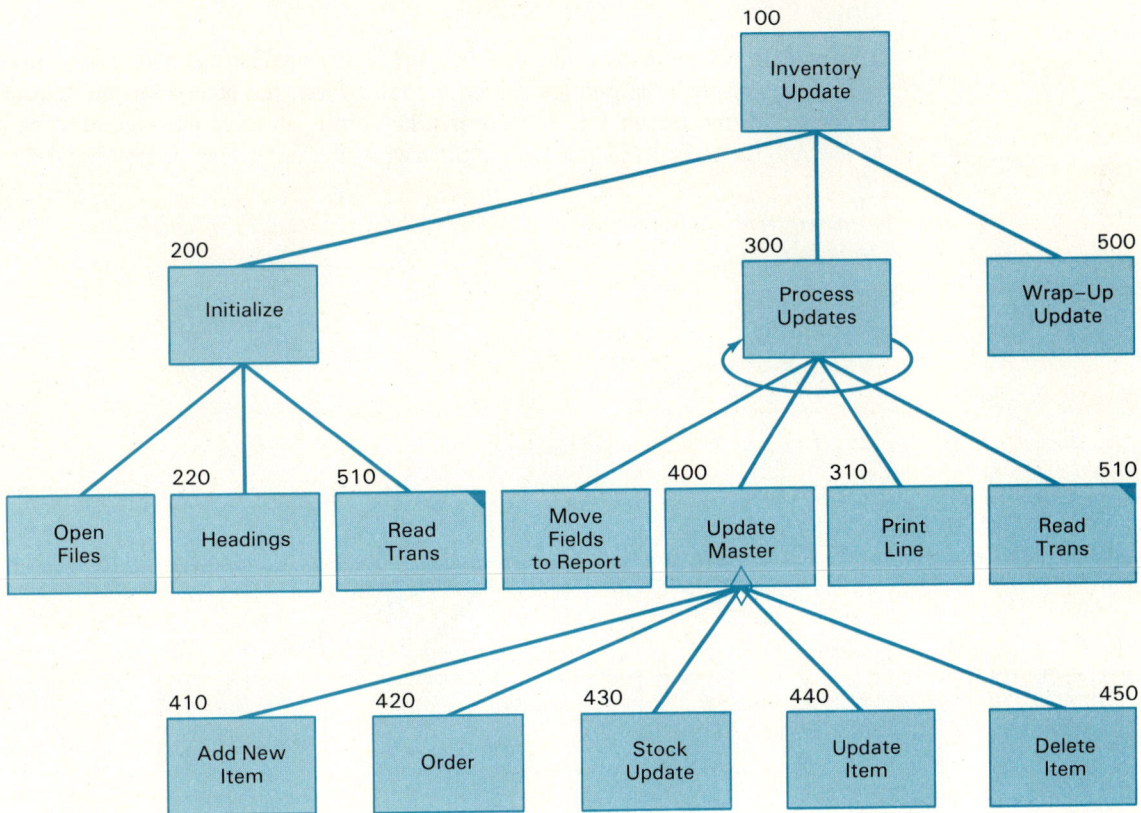

FIGURE 7.15 Top level of the inventory update structure chart

The top few levels of the VSAM inventory update program are developed in Figure 7.15. Here we can see the basic structure of the solution and have some idea of how we expect the update to function. The real complexity begins to show as we approach the development of each of the update modules, which are a refinement of module 400 Update Master. This is a natural place to break the top-down development into smaller parts. And so each of these update modules is developed on separate pages, in this case separate figures.

New Item Module

The module in Figure 7.16 is the structure chart for adding a new item to the inventory file. First, the module sets up the record by moving the fields from the transaction to

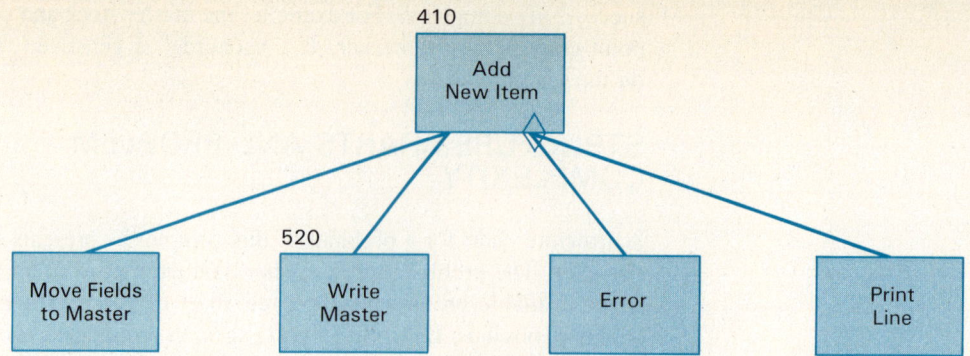

FIGURE 7.16   Structure chart module for adding an item to the master

the master record area. Then the record is written onto the VSAM master file. If a key error is detected, an error message is generated; otherwise, a message to indicate that an add to the file has been completed successfully is provided.

Order Processing Module

The module for processing an order (Figure 7.17) against the master is considerably more involved than the one for adding an item. First, the record for the item needs to be read from the master file. If there is a key error, an error message must be printed to indicate the record was not found. Otherwise, the order may be processed.

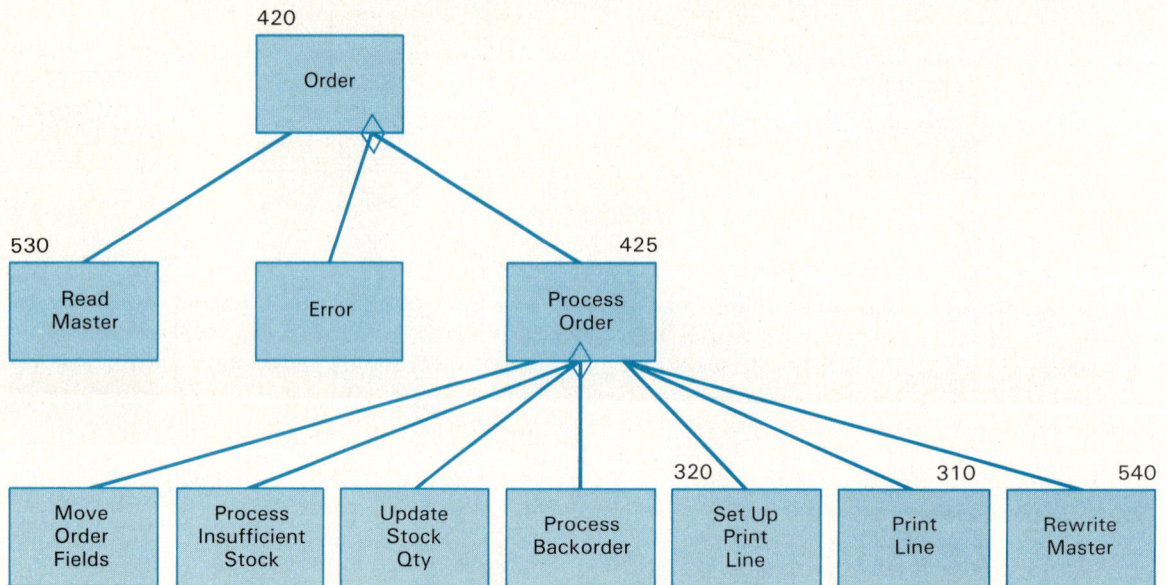

FIGURE 7.17   Structure chart module for processing an order

To process an order requires that several fields be moved in preparation for the processing, fields such as the activity date and quantities in the event a backorder is needed. The need to move these fields may not be all that evident this early in the program design stage, but will become more obvious as we proceed.

The next step is to determine if processing is necessary for insufficient stock and whether a backorder is required. These modules are indicated with decisions on the structure chart because they will not necessarily apply to every order. Next the print line is set up with values and then the line is printed. Finally, the master record is rewritten to reflect the changes that have been made to it.

Stock-update Module

This module (Figure 7.18) is used whenever an item is placed into stock. Assuming that a quantity of an item has been received, it must be reflected in the stock quantity

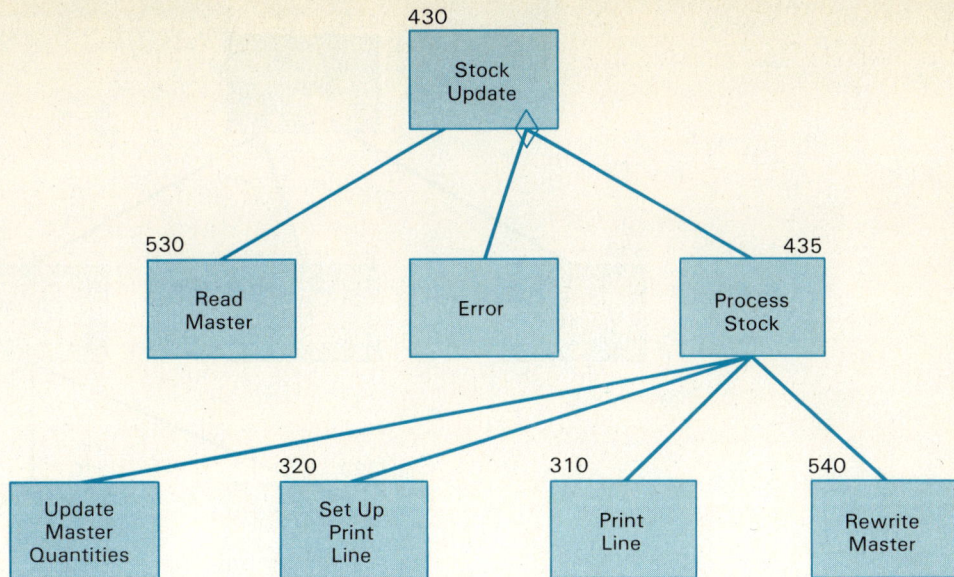

FIGURE 7.18   Structure chart module for updating stock

in the master file. And, because the item is received as the result of a previous order, the order field must also be updated.

First, the master record for the item is read. A key error results only if the record is not found, in which case no further processing will be necessary. If a record is received, then the stock update is processed. The stock and order quantities in the master are updated, and then the print line is set up with data from the master. Next the line is printed and the master is rewritten with the changes.

Update Module

Unlike the stock update, which only updates quantities, this module (Figure 7.19) processes a transaction to update any field in the corresponding master record. This procedure may be used to make changes or corrections to the master.

First, the master record to be updated is read. A key error, if it occurs, is processed in the usual manner. To update a record, each field in the transaction is checked to see

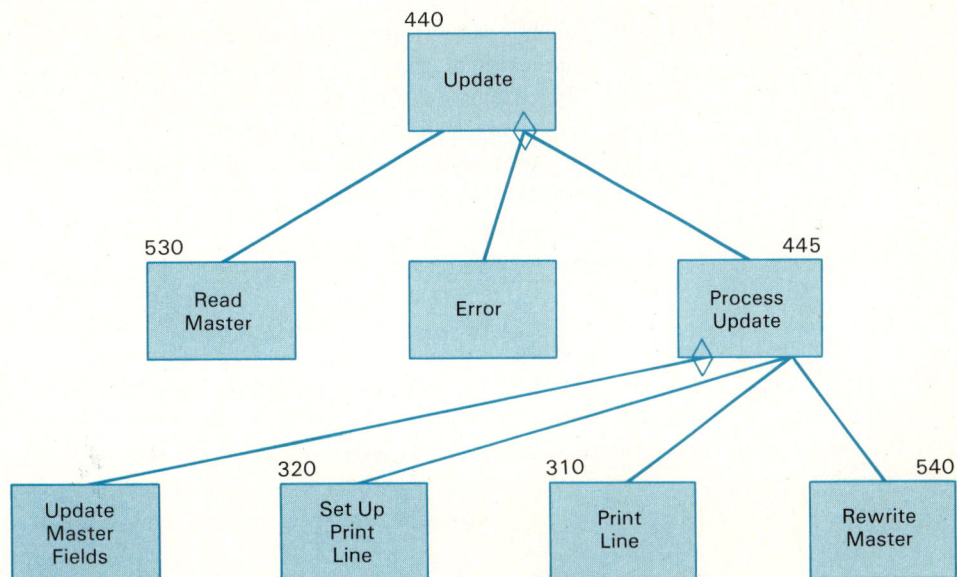

FIGURE 7.19   Structure chart module for updating a record

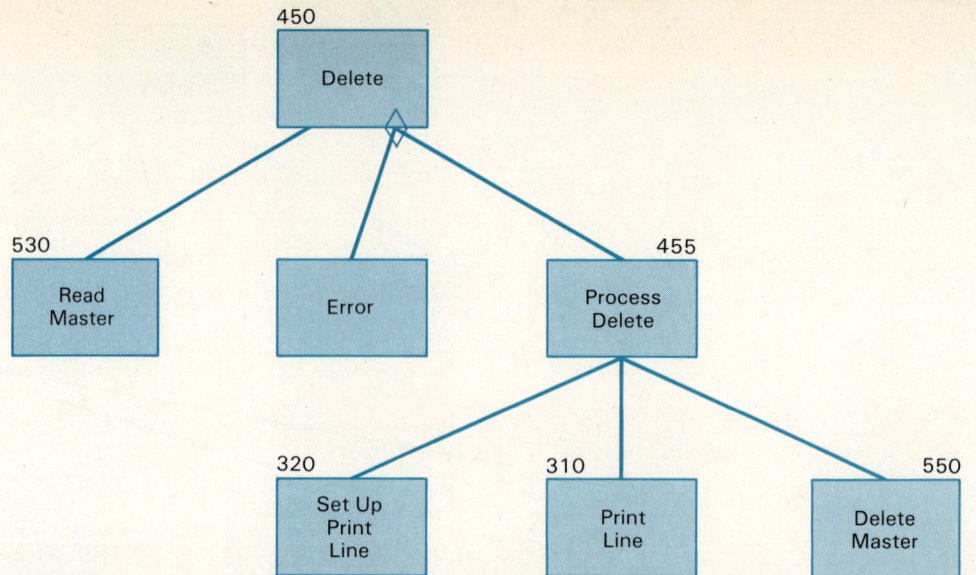

FIGURE 7.20 Structure chart module to delete a master record

if it contains a field, which is then used to update the equivalent master field. This process is represented by one box in the structure chart. After updating is completed, the print line is set up with data from the master, the line is printed on the report, and the master record is rewritten onto the VSAM file.

Delete Module

The last module to be developed is the one for deleting a record from the master. This module, in Figure 7.20, begins by reading a master to ensure that it exists. The master record is also used to provide data for the report that are not available on the transaction. After the print line has been set up, it is printed, and the delete command is issued to remove the record from the master file. Notice that the actual delete is only done after all other activities have been successfully completed.

PSEUDO CODE

Our pseudo code will follow the modular pattern of the structure chart, but, because of the complexity of this application, significantly more detail will be included in the code. For example, in the module 300-Process, we should now give some thought to the specific fields that are to be moved from the transaction record to the detail line. We must also keep in mind that not all the transactions will contain every field. So the pseudo code will develop all along these lines.

```
300-Process
    1. Move spaces to detail line.
    2. Move transaction code to    detail line.
    3. If unit cost is present in transaction
         Move to detail line
       EndIf
    4. If stock quantity is present in transaction
         Move to detail line
       EndIf
```

This pattern is repeated for each field in the transaction that is optional and may not always be present.

Another module that is used is 320-Set up-Print-Line. This code is developed to move the master fields to the print line when a master record contains data that the transaction does not or the master is changed as a result of the update. Rather than using this code each place it is needed in the program, we place it in a single module and thus enhance the cohesion of our program.

```
320-Set up-Print-Line
     1. Move master stock, order, reorder point,
        and description to detail line.
```

Processing Orders and Backorders

A particularly complex part of this problem is the module (425) for processing an order. The reason for the difficulty is the need to determine whether there is sufficient stock to fill the order and, second, whether a backorder will be needed as a result of processing the order.

First, it is necessary to initialize a few fields in preparation for processing the order. Other fields, such as the item number and description, will need to be moved to the backorder record.

```
425-Process-Order
     1. Initialize backorder fields.
     2. Move fields to backorder record.
```

These steps are done in anticipation of the need for a backorder. The reason for this approach is again to reduce the amount of program code necessary. Because a backorder can be created in several different situations, the fields are set up in advance and then they will be ready as they are needed.

The next step for processing an order is to determine if there is enough stock to fill the order. If there isn't adequate stock, then a backorder must be generated for the missing quantity, as follows:

```
3. If master stock quantity < transaction stock quantity
     Compute backorder quantity = trans qty - master qty
     Add backorder quantity to master order quantity
     Zero master stock quantity
     Move backorder quantity to backorder record
     Move backorder quantity to detail line
     Perform 560-Write-Backorder
```

The backorder quantity is added to the on-order quantity on the master and also moved to the backorder record and written on the backorder file. Stock quantity is also set to zero because all stock has now been exhausted.

If there was sufficient stock, the preceding if statement would evaluate false as follows,

```
Else
     Subtract transaction stock quantity from master
```

and the stock quantity on the order would be subtracted from the master's stock quantity. Now, because the quantity in stock has been reduced, there is another possibility that a backorder is necessary. Therefore, the stock quantity is compared against the reorder point to determine if a backorder must be generated.

```
If master stock quantity <= reorder point
    Set backorder quantity to reorder point
    Move backorder quantity to detail line
    Add reorder point to order quantity
    Perform 560-Write-Backorder
    EndIf
EndIf
```

Stock Update

The stock-update module first reads a master record based on the key supplied by the transaction. If a record is found, the processing of the update proceeds (by performing module 435-Process-Stock), but if there is no record with a matching key, an error message is printed and the module is terminated.

```
430-Stock-Update
    1. Perform 530-Read-Master.
    2. If key error
        Move 'record not found' message to detail line
        Perform 310-Print-Line
    Else
        Perform 435-Process-Stock
    EndIf
```

Both of the modules 440-Update-Item and 450-Delete-Item follow the pattern set by paragraph 430-Stock-Update described above. In each case it is necessary to first establish the presence of a master record before further updating can proceed. This process is even necessary for the delete, because data are needed from the master record for the report.

Record Updating

Module 445-Process-Update does the updating of individual fields in the record. Because each field may be revised by a code 'U' transaction, it is necessary to examine the field's content to determine if updating is necessary. Remember that a previous program does the validation of the transaction, and so just the presence of data in the field means that the corresponding master field will be updated. Here is the pseudo code.

```
445-Process-Update
    1. Move date to activity date.
    2. If transaction description is present
        Move description to master
    EndIf
    3. If transaction unit cost is present
        Move unit cost to master
    EndIf
    4. If transaction stock quantity is present
        Move stock quantity to master
    EndIf
    5. If transaction order quantity is present
        Move order quantity to master
    EndIf
    6. If transaction reorder point is present
        Move reorder point to master
    EndIf
```

After each field has been updated as necessary in this module, the print line is set up (from the master) and a message is moved to the line to indicate the record has been updated. Then the record is printed. Finally, the updated master record is rewritten to the master file.

```
 7. Perform 320-Set up-Print-Line.
 8. Move 'master revised' message to detail line.
 9. Perform 310-Print-Line.
10. Perform 540-Rewrite-Master.
```

Figure 7.21 shows the complete pseudo code and structured flowchart for the update program. Notice that each of the five modules for processing a transaction type is developed on separate pages of pseudo code, just as their structure charts were developed separately.

PSEUDO CODE

PROGRAM NAME: Update Inventory Master   PROGRAM ID: INVENTORY
PREPARED BY: Jonathan Youngman   DATE: Aug 22   PAGE 1 of 4

100-Mainline
   1. Perform 200-Initialize.
   2. Perform 300-Process
         Until EOF.
   3. Perform 600-Wrap-Up.
   4. Close files.
   5. Stop Run
200-Initialize
   1. Open input, I-O, and output files.
   2. Get current date.
   3. Perform 220-Headings.
   4. Perform 510-Read.
220-Headings
   1. Print heading 1.
   2. Print heading 2.
   3. Print heading 3.
   4. Set line count to 5.
300-Process
   1. Move spaces to detail line.
   2. Move transaction code to   detail line.
   3. If unit cost is present in transaction
      Move to detail line
    EndIf
   4. If stock quantity is present in transaction
      Move to detail line
    EndIf
   5. If order quantity is present in transaction
      Move to detail line
    EndIf
   6. If reorder quantity is present in transaction
      Move to detail line
    EndIf
   7. Perform 400-Update-Master.
   8. Perform 310-Print-Line (blank line).
   9. Perform 510-Read.
310-Print-Line
   1. Write print-rec from detail line
      advancing one line.
   2. Add 1 to line count.
   3. Move spaces to detail line.
   4. If line count > 50
     Perform 220-Headings
    EndIf

FIGURE 7.21(a) Pseudo code for the VSAM inventory update

Programming with VSAM Files

320-Set up-Print-Line
  1. Move master stock, order, reorder point, and description
     to detail line.
400-Update-Master
  1. Move transaction item number to record key field.
  2. If add item
        Perform 410-Add-Item
     Else
       If order item
            Perform 420-Order-Item
       Else
          If stock update
                Perform 430-Stock-Update
          Else
             If update item
                   Perform 440-Update-Item
             Else
                   Perform 450-Delete-Item
             Endif
410-Add-Item
  1. Move spaces to master record.
  2. Move transaction fields to master record.
  3. Move date to master activity date.
  4. Perform 520-Write-Master.
  5. If no key error
        Move 'record created' message to detail line
     Else
        Move 'record already exists' message to detail line
     Endif
  6. Perform 310-Print-Line.
420-Order-Item
  1. Perform 530-Read-Master.
  2. If key error
        Move 'record not found' message to detail line
        Perform 310-Print-Line
     Else
        Perform 425-Process-Order
     Endif
425-Process-Order
  1. Initialize backorder fields.
  2. Move fields to backorder record.
  3. If master stock quantity < transaction stock quantity
        Compute backorder quantity = trans − master
        Add backorder quantity to master order quantity
        Zero master stock quantity
        Move backorder quantity to backorder record
        Move backorder quantity to detail line
        Perform 560-Write-Backorder
     Else
        Subtract transaction stock quantity from master
        If master stock quantity <= reorder point
          Set backorder quantity to reorder point
          Move backorder quantity to detail line
          Add reorder point to order quantity
          Perform 560-Write-Backorder
        Endif
     Endif
  4. Perform 320-Set up-Print-Line.
  5. Move 'master revised' message to detail line.
  6. Perform 310-Print-Line.
  7. Perform 540-Rewrite-Master.

FIGURE 7.21(b)

430-Stock-Update
1. Perform 530-Read-Master.
2. If key error
　　Move 'record not found' message to detail line
　　Perform 310-Print-Line
　Else
　　Perform 435-Process-Stock
　EndIf

435-Process-Stock
1. Add transaction stock quantity to master stock quantity.
2. Subtract transaction stock quantity from order quantity.
3. Move date to activity date.
4. Perform 320-Set up-Print-Line
5. Move 'record revised' message to detail line.
6. Perform 310-Print-Line.
7. Perform 540-Rewrite-Master.

440-Update-Item
1. Perform 530-Read-Master.
2. If key error
　　Move 'record not found' message to detail line
　　Perform 310-Print-Line
　Else
　　Perform 445-Process-Update
　EndIf

445-Process-Update
1. Move date to activity date.
2. If transaction description is present
　　Move description to master
　Endif
3. If transaction unit cost is present
　　Move unit cost to master
　Endif
4. If transaction stock quantity is present
　　Move stock quantity to master
　Endif
5. If transaction order quantity is present
　　Move order quantity to master
　Endif
6. If transaction reorder point is present
　　Move reorder point to master
　Endif
7. Perform 320-Set up-Print-Line.
8. Move 'master revised' message to detail line.
9. Perform 310-Print-Line.
10. Perform 540-Rewrite-Master.

450-Delete-Item
1. Perform 530-Read-Master.
2. If key error
　　Move 'record not found' message to detail line
　　Perform 310-Print-Line
　Else
　　Perform 455-Process-Delete
　EndIf

455-Process-Delete
1. Perform 320-Set up-Print-Line.
2. Move 'record deleted' message to print line.
3. Perform 310-Print-Line.
4. Perform 550-Delete-Master.

510-Read
1. Read transaction
　　At end move 'yes' to Eof-Flag.

FIGURE 7.21(c)

520-Write-Master
1. Move 'no' to key error flag.
2. Write master record
   Invalid key move 'yes' to key error flag.

530-Read-Master
1. Move 'no' to key error flag.
2. Read master
   Invalid key move 'yes' to key error flag.

540-Rewrite-Master
1. Move 'no' to key error flag.
2. Rewrite master record
   Invalid key move 'yes' to key error flag.
3. If key error
   Move 'rewrite error' message to detail line
   Perform 310-Print-Line
   EndIf

550-Delete-Master
1. Move 'no' to key error flag.
2. Delete master
   Invalid key move 'yes' to key error flag.

560-Write-Backorder
1. Write backorder record.

600-Wrap-Up
1. Move spaces to detail line.
2. Move 'end of update' message to detail line.
3. Perform 310-Print-Line.

FIGURE 7.21(d)

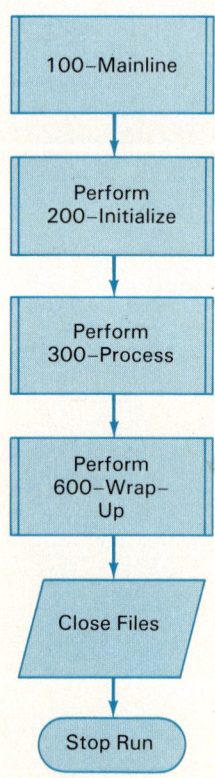

FIGURE 7.21(e)

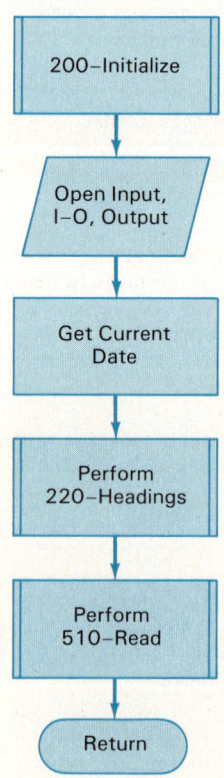

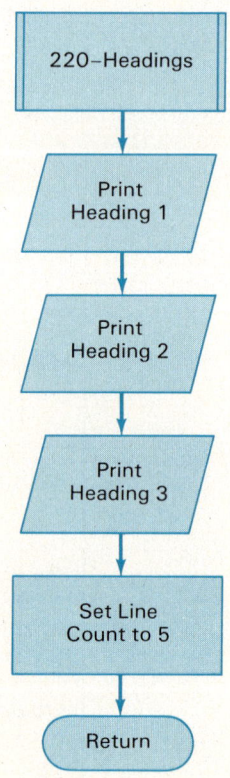

FIGURE 7.21(f)

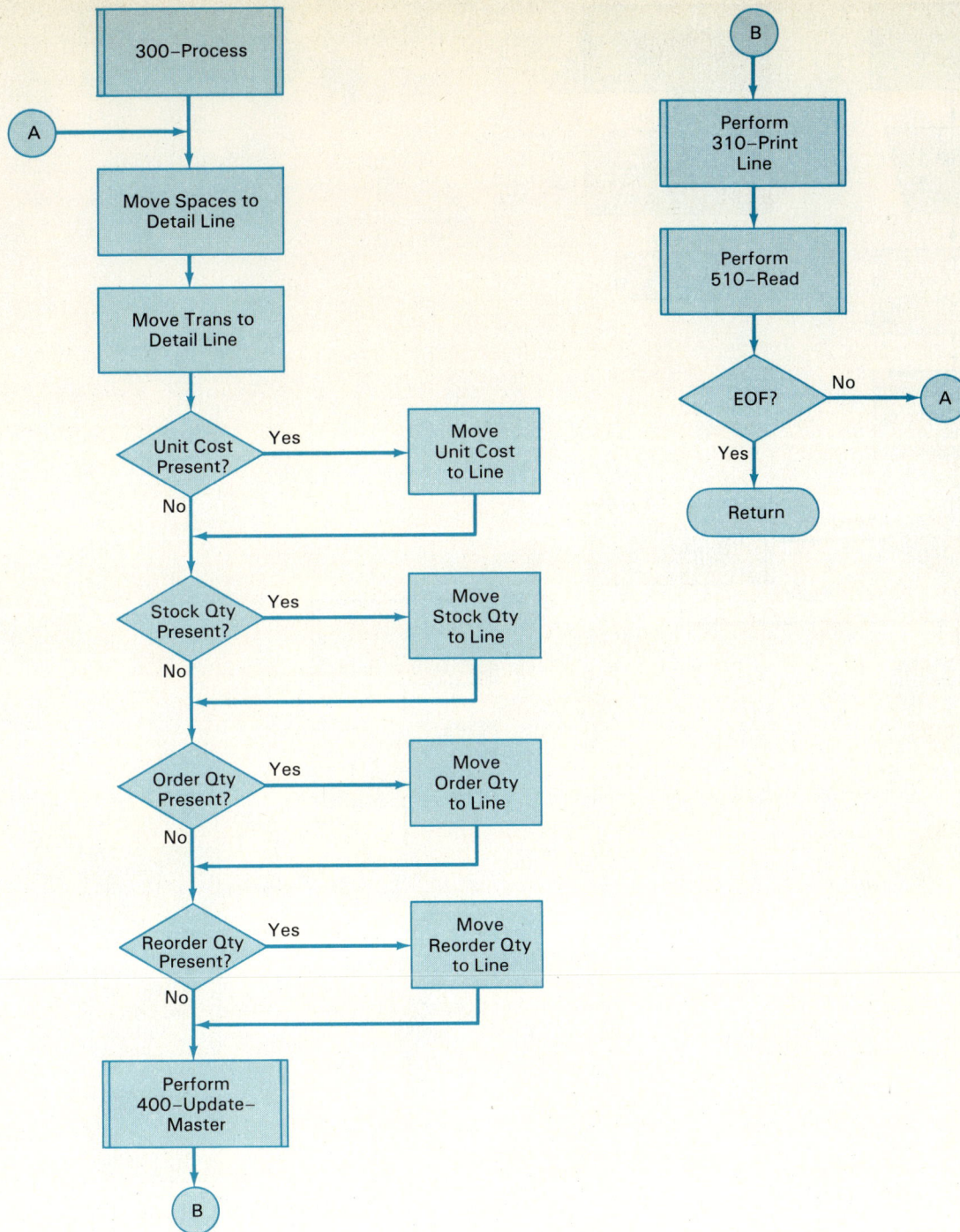

FIGURE 7.21(g)

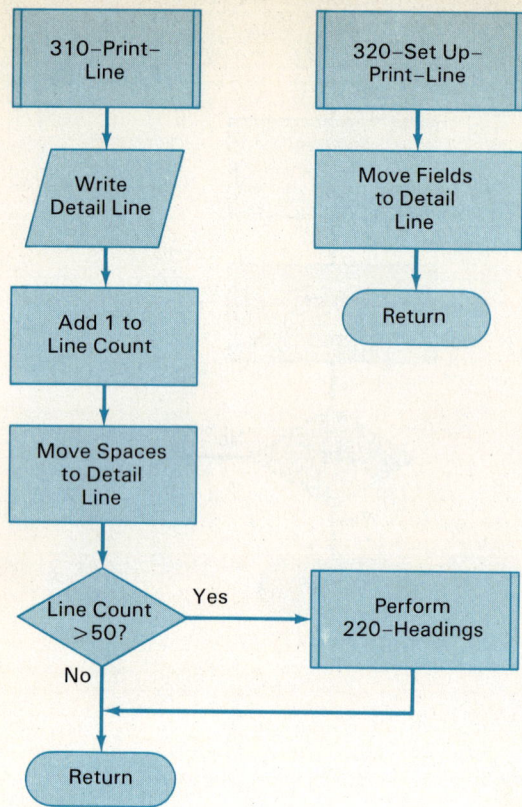

FIGURE 7.21(h)

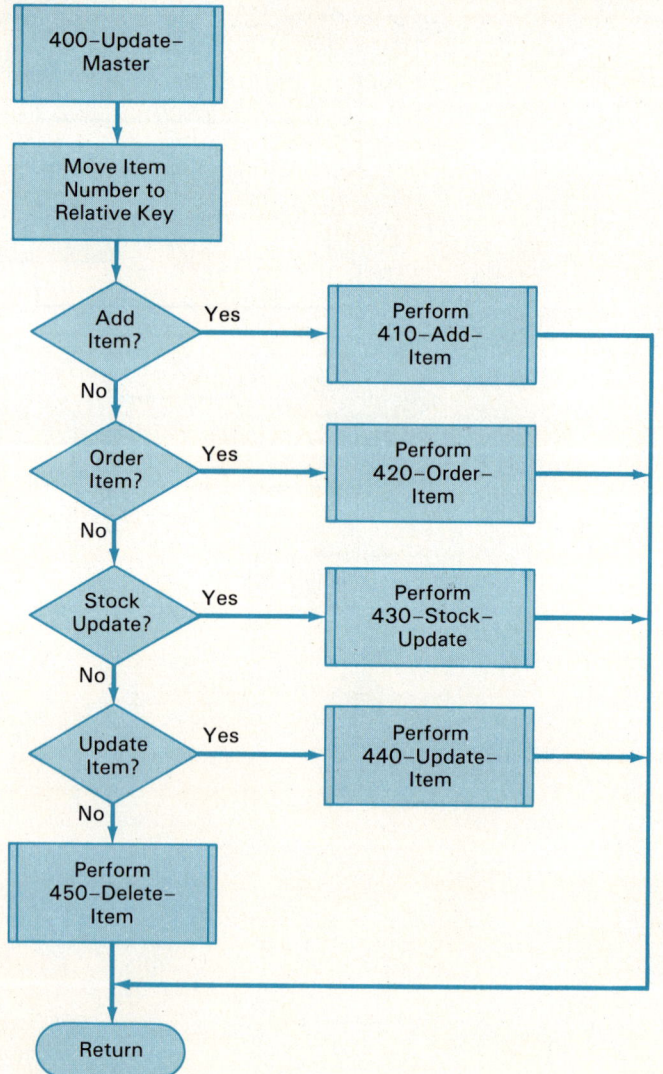

FIGURE 7.21(i)

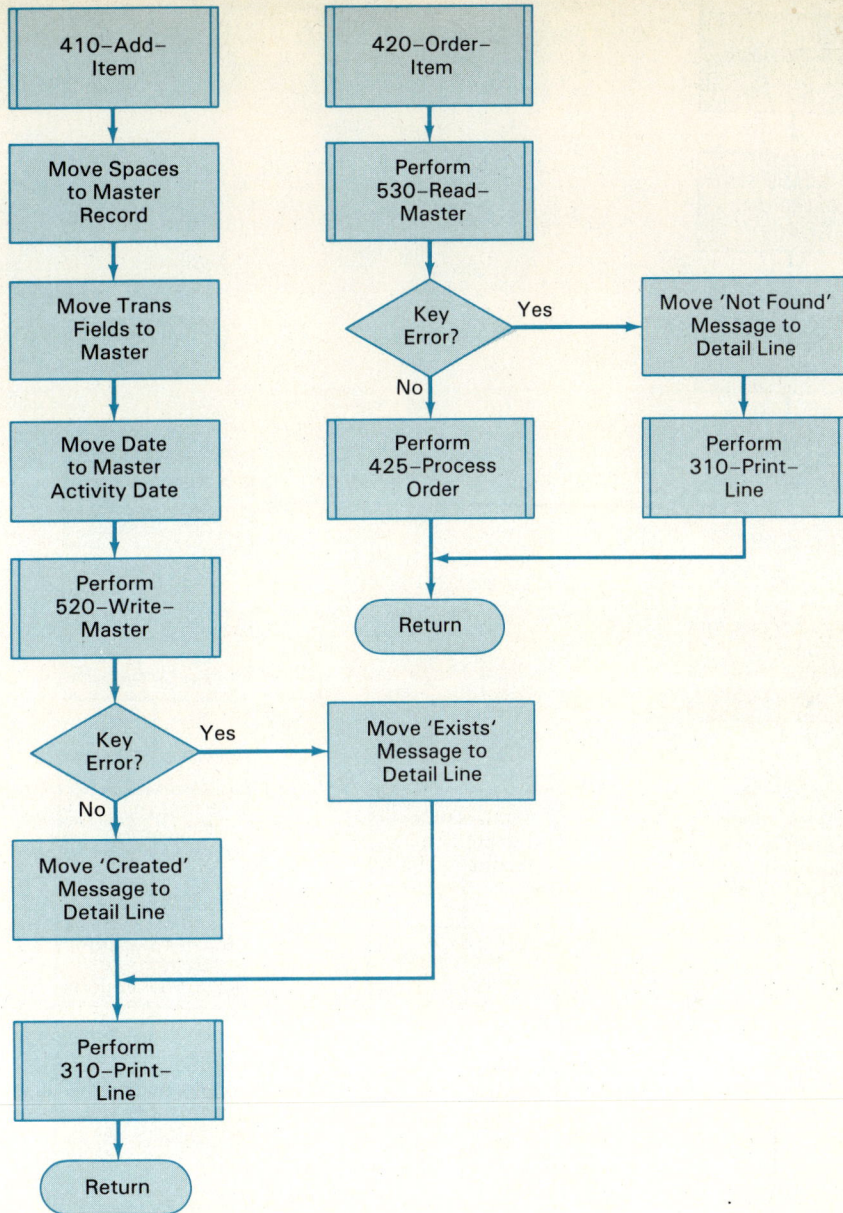

FIGURE 7.21(j)

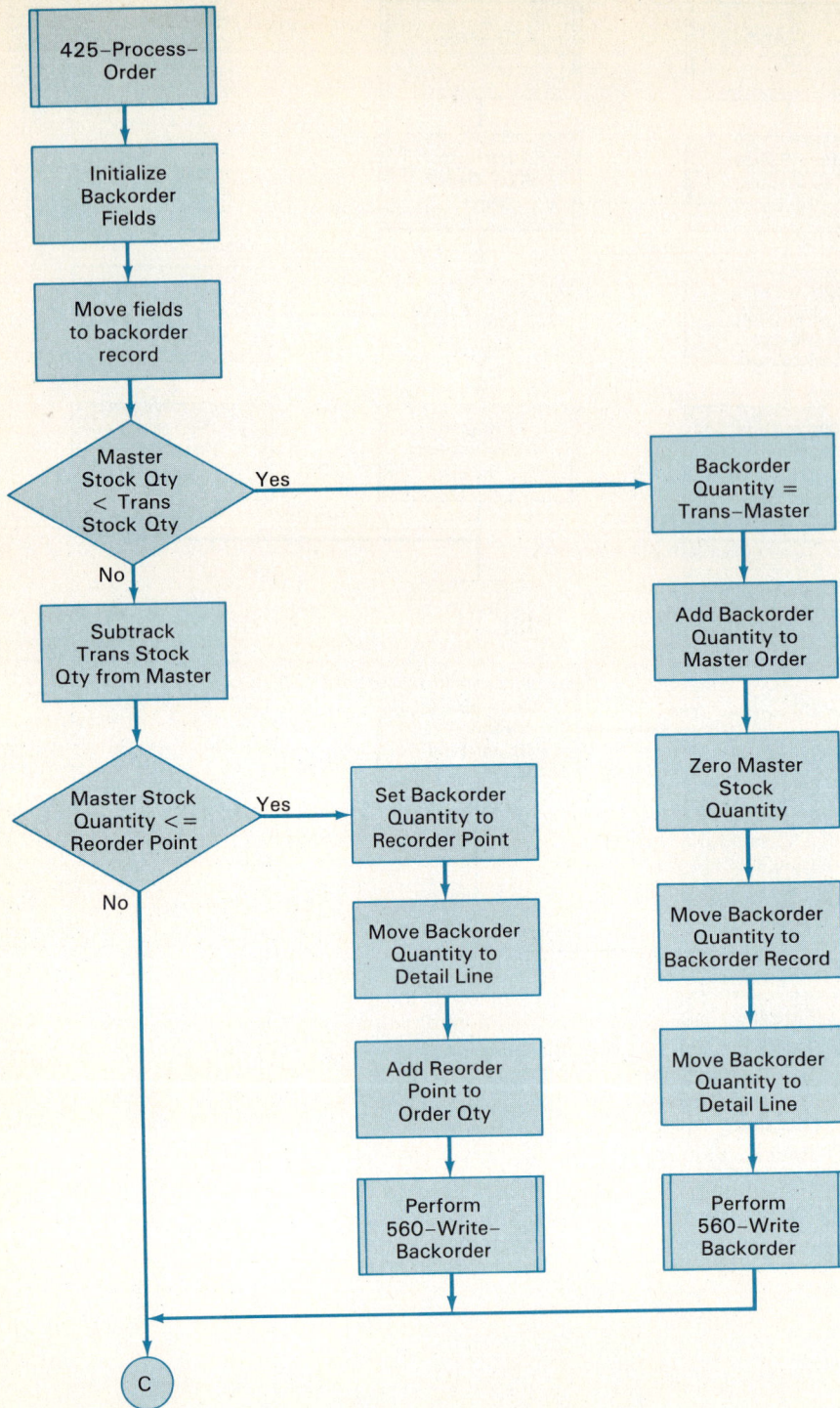

FIGURE 7.21(k)

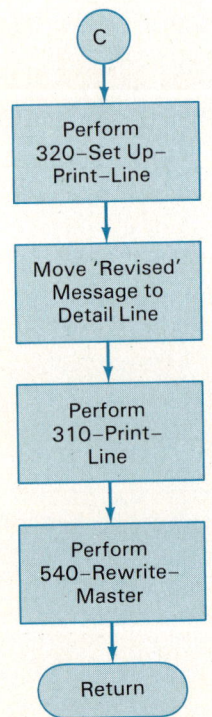

FIGURE 7.21(l)

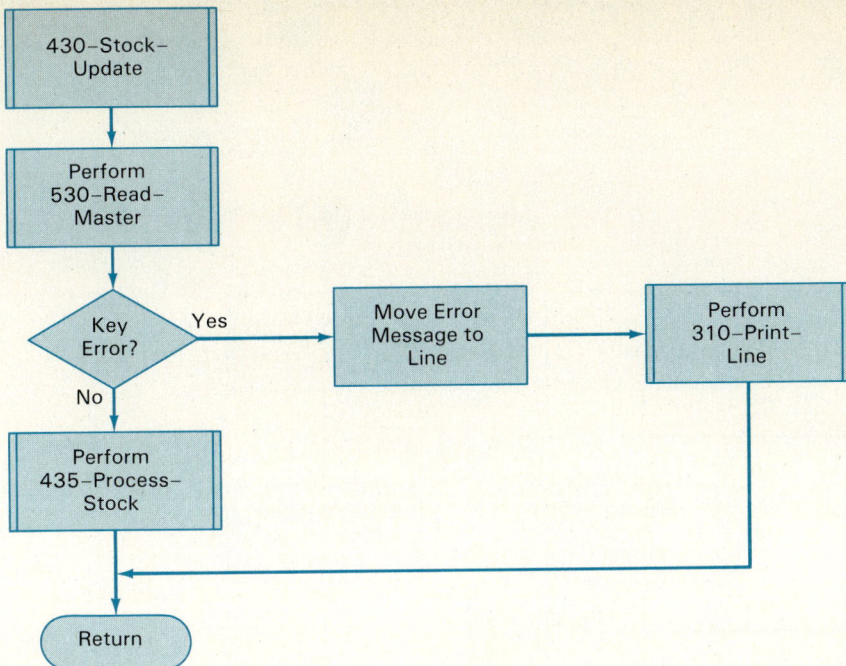

FIGURE 7.21(m)

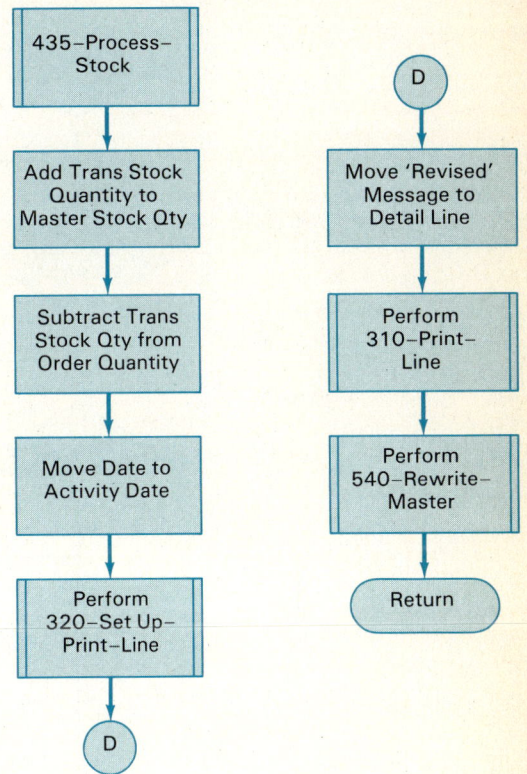

FIGURE 7.21(n)

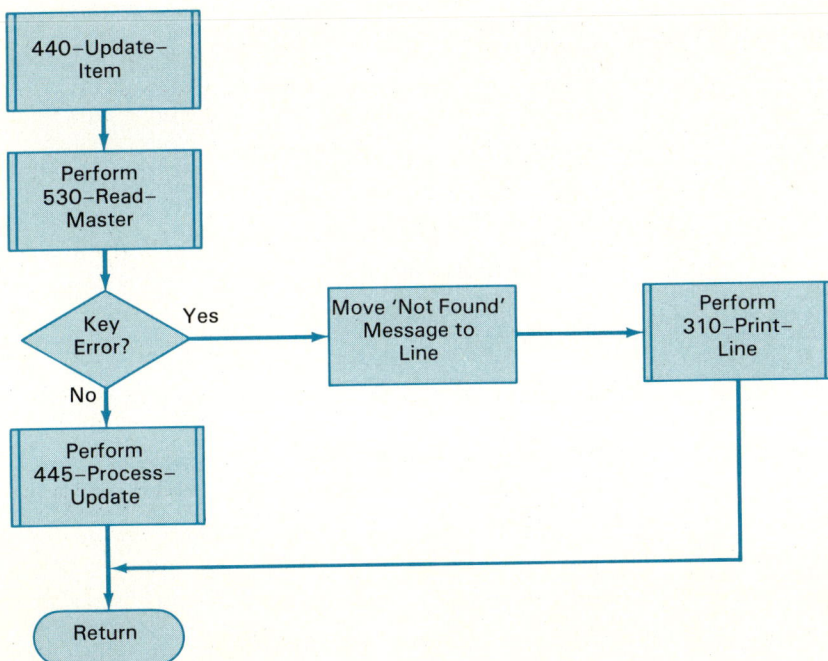

FIGURE 7.21(o)

Programming with VSAM Files

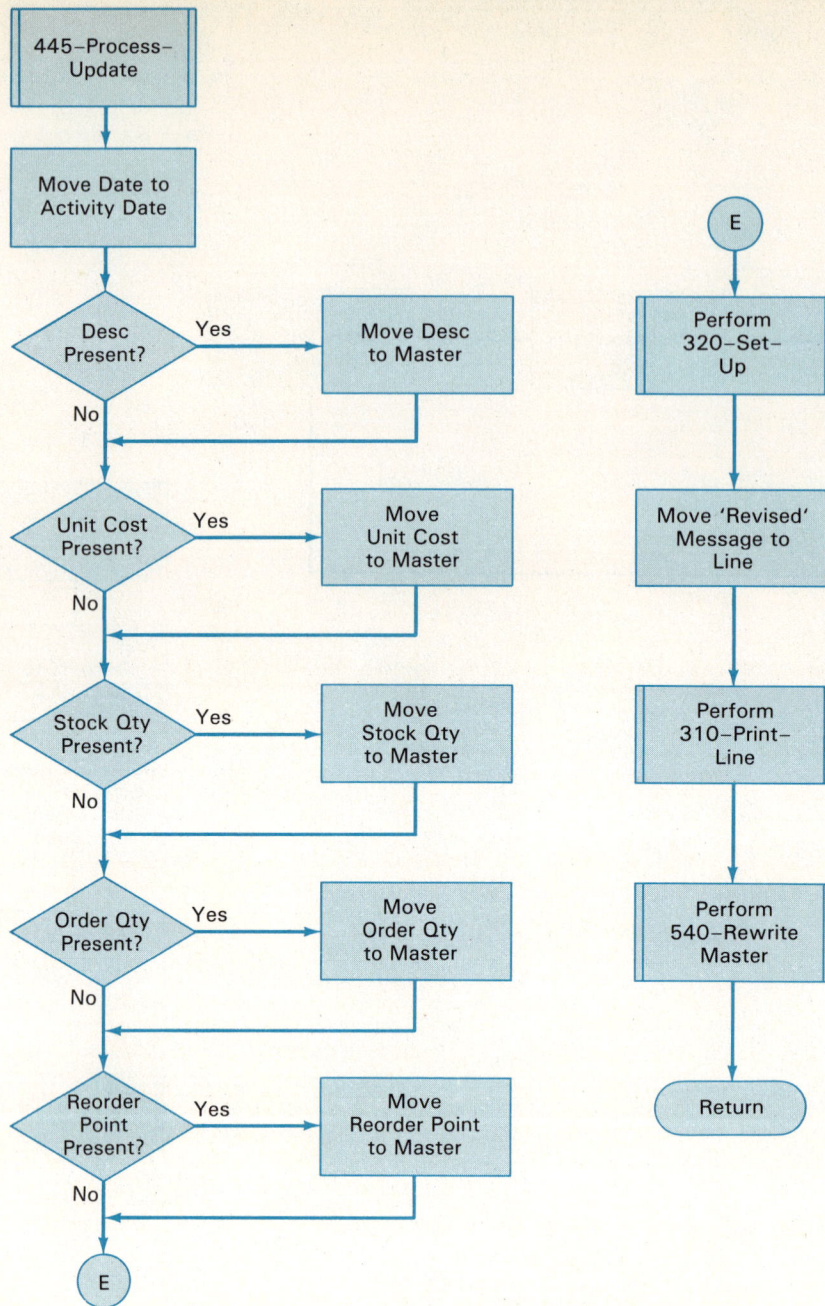

FIGURE 7.21(p)

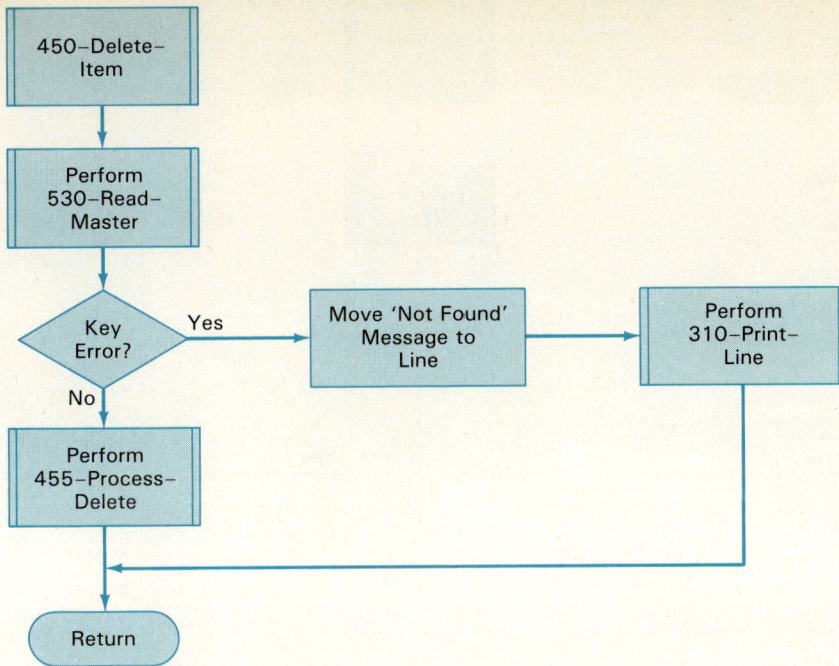

FIGURE 7.21(q)

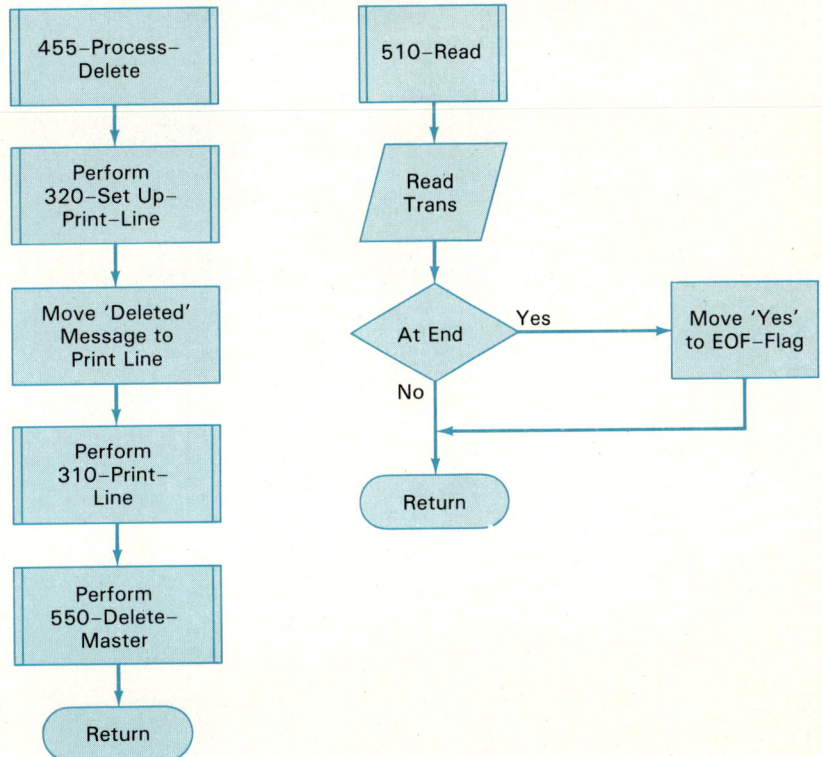

FIGURE 7.21(r)

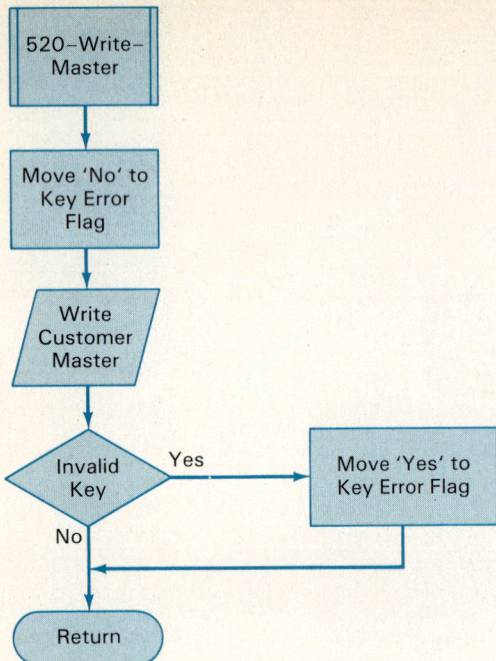

FIGURE 7.21(s)

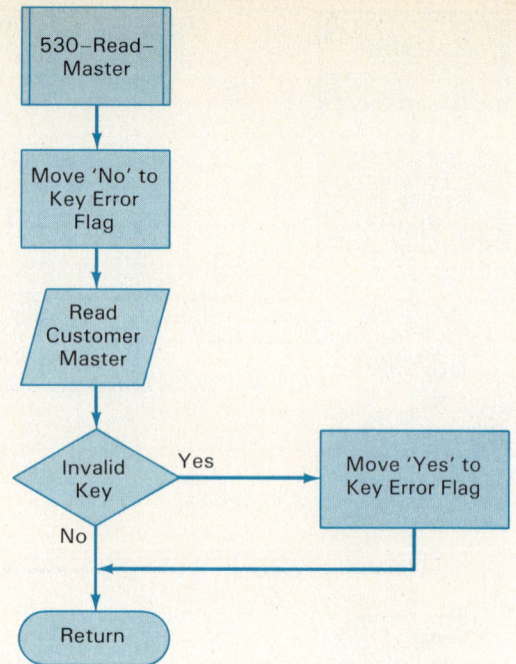

FIGURE 7.21(t)

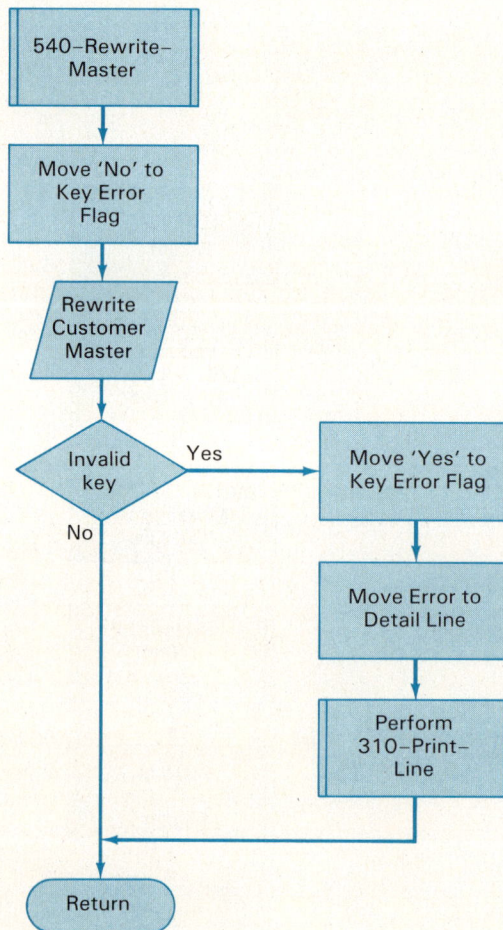

FIGURE 7.21(u)

Chapter 7

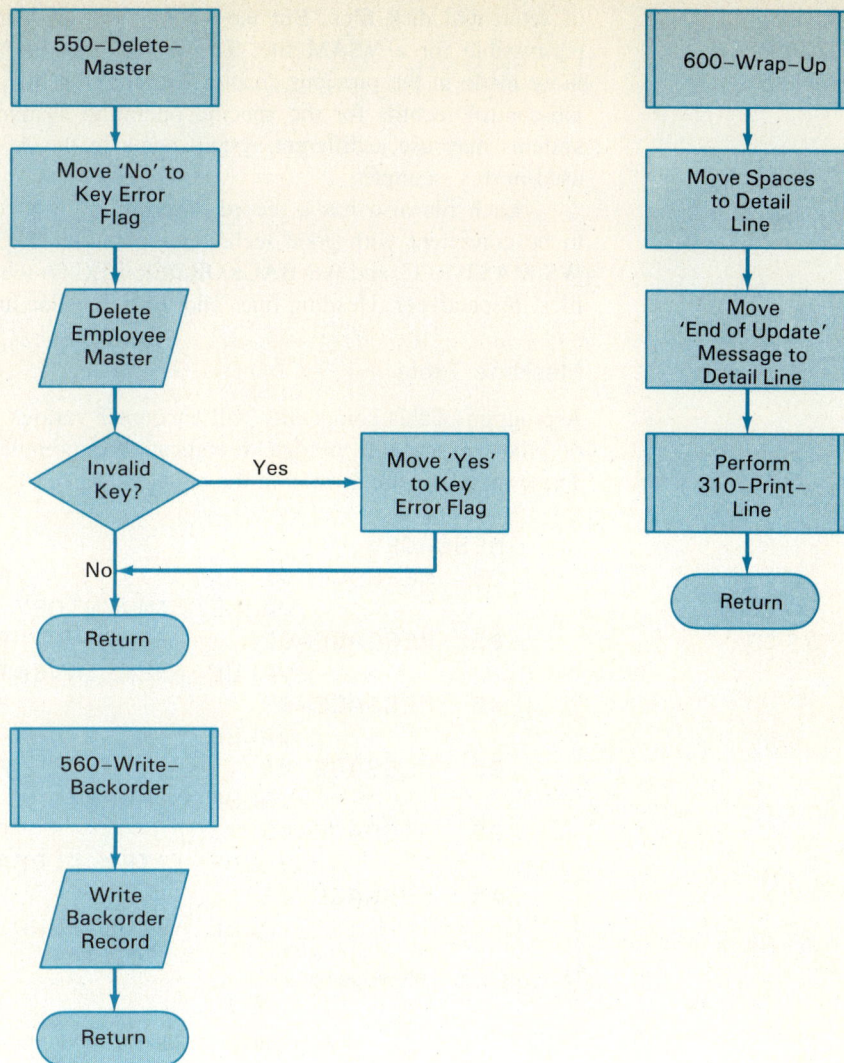

FIGURE 7.21(v)

PROGRAM CODING

Files

Four files are used by this program, and each requires a SELECT clause in the FILE-CONTROL paragraph. This is the first program we have written that uses more than two disk files, but this does not substantially change our approach. Each file is defined as shown in the following entries.

```
FILE-CONTROL.
    SELECT TRANSACTIONS      ASSIGN TO TRANS7.
    SELECT INVENTORY-MASTER ASSIGN TO MASTER7
            ORGANIZATION IS INDEXED
            ACCESS MODE IS RANDOM
            RECORD KEY IS MASTER-ITEM-NO.
    SELECT BACKORDER         ASSIGN TO BACK7.
    SELECT INVENTORY-REPORT ASSIGN TO PRINTER.
```

Each of these files has a corresponding FD entry in the FILE SECTION. Of these FDs, the transaction and backorder files include blocking factors for more efficient use of sequential disk files. But the VSAM master is not blocked, which would not be permissible for a VSAM file. The entries for the VSAM file are no different from those made in the previous chapter for an ISAM file. Any differences would be in the job-control records for the specific operating system used for the application. Some systems may use a different system name in the ASSIGN clause than the OS entries used in this example.

Each file also has a record description entry located in WORKING-STORAGE to be consistent with good techniques of style. These entries are WS-TRANS-REC, WS-MAST-REC, and WS-BACKORDER-REC for the transaction, master, and backorder files, respectively. Heading lines and the detail line are also described for the report.

Message Table

A program of this complexity will encounter various situations where an error message or other response is needed to indicate the completion of processing a transaction. These messages are located in the table shown in Figure 7.22.

```
01  MESSAGES.
    05  MESSAGE-01              PIC X(30)
            VALUE 'INVENTORY RECORD REVISED'.
    05  MESSAGE-02              PIC X(30)
            VALUE 'NEW INVENTORY RECORD CREATED'.
    05  MESSAGE-03              PIC X(30)
            VALUE 'INVENTORY RECORD DELETED'.
    05  MESSAGE-04              PIC X(30)
            VALUE 'INVENTORY RECORD NOT FOUND'.
    05  MESSAGE-05              PIC X(30)
            VALUE 'ITEM ALREADY EXISTS'.
    05  MESSAGE-06              PIC X(30)
            VALUE 'FILE REWRITE ERROR'.
```

FIGURE 7.22   Message table

100-MAINLINE   This paragraph is the top-level module that controls the major looping in the program. Although we are using four files, the transaction file is the source of all activity and so drives the logic of the loop. Each transaction must be processed until end of file is reached, at which point the program is terminated.

200-INITIALIZE   This paragraph opens the files, sets up the current date of the run, prints the first set of headings, and reads the first transaction record. Because this program uses four files, the OPEN statement must consider the way in which each file is to be used. The statement is written as follows.

```
OPEN INPUT  TRANSACTIONS
     I-O    INVENTORY-MASTER
     OUTPUT BACKORDER
            INVENTORY-REPORT.
```

Only the transaction file is used as input, whereas the master is used for both input and output and therefore is opened as I-O. The backoroder file and the report are both output files.

220-HEADINGS   This paragraph prints the headings at the top of each page of the report and updates the line count to reflect the beginning of the page.

300-PROCESS   Each transaction that is read is first processed by this paragraph. First, the transaction code, item, and description are moved to the detail line in preparation for the report. These fields will either always be present or are alphanumeric and thus can be moved without regard for their contents. For example, although the description field is not always required, it can always be moved to the detail line without causing a problem.

Next, the remaining transaction fields, unit cost, stock quantity, order quantity, and reorder point, are checked to see if they are present. This check is necessary because they are numeric fields, and if they are blank, a move to the edited picture in the detail line will cause a data error.

Now paragraph 400-UPDATE-MASTER is performed to apply the updating from the transaction to the appropriate master record.

Finally, a blank line is printed to get double spacing between transaction lines and the next transaction is read before the process loop continues.

310-PRINT-LINE Except for the headings, this paragraph is performed each time a line is printed. It is the responsibility for the performing program code to place the required data in the detail line before performing this paragraph.

320-SETUP-PRINT-LINE This paragraph is performed whenever fields are required from the master record for the report line. The fields stock quantity, order quantity, reorder point, and description are each moved from the master record to the detail line, assuming that a master record was previously read by the program.

400-UPDATE-MASTER By the time the program reaches this point in the logic, we know that a master record will be required for the processing. Therefore, the first step is to move the item number from the transaction to the record key field for the VSAM master file. This step is also necessary for adding a new record to the master, although strictly speaking a master is not required because it is being created; however, the key must still be established to create a new record.

Next, a series of nested IF statements is used to examine the transaction code (defined as 88-level entries) to determine the type of updating needed. As a result, one of five different update paragraphs is performed. These paragraphs all use a 4XX prefix in the paragraph name.

410-ADD-ITEM This paragraph will be performed whenever a new record is to be added to the master file. An assumption made here is that the record with the new item number will not currently be on the master file. The implication of this choice is that all the fields are set up in the master record in WORKING-STORAGE and then written to the master file. If for some reason the master already has a record with this key, a key error will result. In that case, an error message is produced; otherwise, a message indicates that the record was successfully added to the master.

An alternative way to approach this problem would be to first attempt a read of the master file. If a record is successfully read, you know that a new one cannot be created and an error message is produced. If a key error results, proceed to create the new record. Using this approach is actually somewhat more awkward to implement, which is why it is not used.

420-ORDER-ITEM and 425-PROCESS-ORDER These paragraphs function as a unit to process an order transaction. Paragraph 420 initiates a read of the master file, and if a record is successfully retrieved, paragraph 425 is performed. In the second paragraph the stock quantity is checked for a sufficient amount to fill the order. As explained earlier, in the pseudo code a backorder can be generated here for two reasons. One is due to insufficient stock and the other because the reorder point has been reached. The field WS-BACKORDER-QTY is used as a temporary field for calculating a backorder and moving the results to the backorder file and/or the report.

When all updating of the master, creating a backorder, and printing a detail line have been completed, the master record is rewritten by performing paragraph 540-RE-WRITE-MASTER.

430-STOCK-UPDATE and 435-PROCESS-STOCK   Again, two paragraphs are used here to apply a code 'S' transaction against the master. Like the previous pair of paragraphs used for processing an order, these follow a similar pattern. Paragraph 430 reads the master record and determines if a record is present on the file for updating.

When a record has been successfully accessed, paragraph 435 applies the update against the master record. This update requires adding the transaction quantity to the master's stock quantity and subtracting it from the order-quantity field. The activity date is updated, a detail line is printed, and the master record is rewritten on the master file.

440-UPDATE-ITEM and 445-PROCESS-DATE   An update transaction, code 'U', let's the user change any field, except the item number, in the master record. Paragraph 440 makes sure a record is available before paragraph 445 is performed to do the revision. The activity date is first updated, and then each field in the transaction is checked to see if it contains a value that will then be used to replace the value in the corresponding master field. After all changes have been made, the report line is printed, and the master record is rewritten to the master file.

450-DELETE-ITEM and 455-PROCESS-DELETE   To delete a record, that record is first read from the master. This process serves two purposes: (1) it determines if a record exists to be deleted and, (2) the master record provides the data for the report. Paragraph 450 takes care of determining if a record exists, and paragraph 455 controls the printing of the line and the deleting of the record from the master file.

5XX Paragraphs   All paragraphs beginning with a 5XX prefix are used to do a file operation. Each of these is a relatively simple paragraph that does an input or output operation against one of te files. Here are the paragraphs and their purpose.

```
510-READ              —reads a transaction record.
520-WRITE-MASTER      —writes a new record on the inventory
                         master file.
530-READ-MASTER       —reads a record from the inventory
                         master.
540-REWRITE-MASTER    —rewrites a revised master record.
550-DELETE-MASTER     —deletes an inventory master record.
560-WRITE-BACKORDER   —writes a record on the backorder file.
```

600-WRAP-UP   This final paragraph prints the 'end of update' message before the files are closed and the program terminated. The complete program is given in Figure 7.23.

```
IDENTIFICATION DIVISION.

PROGRAM-ID.
    INVENTORY.
*AUTHOR.
*    JOHNATHAN YOUNGMAN.
*INSTALLATION.
*    SALES UNLIMITED CORP.
*DATE-WRITTEN.
*    AUGUST 18.
*DATE-COMPILED.

*SECURITY.
*    NONE.
```

FIGURE 7.23(a)   Program to update the VSAM inventory file

```
ENVIRONMENT DIVISION.

CONFIGURATION SECTION.
SOURCE-COMPUTER.
    IBM-4381.
OBJECT-COMPUTER.
    IBM-4381.
SPECIAL-NAMES.
    C01 IS TO-TOP-OF-PAGE.

INPUT-OUTPUT SECTION.

FILE-CONTROL.
    SELECT TRANSACTIONS      ASSIGN TO TRANS7.
    SELECT INVENTORY-MASTER ASSIGN TO MASTER7
           ORGANIZATION IS INDEXED
           ACCESS MODE IS RANDOM
           RECORD KEY IS MASTER-ITEM-NO.
    SELECT BACKORDER         ASSIGN TO BACK7.
    SELECT INVENTORY-REPORT   ASSIGN TO PRINTER.

DATA DIVISION.

FILE SECTION.

FD  TRANSACTIONS
    BLOCK  CONTAINS 20 RECORDS
    RECORD CONTAINS 50 CHARACTERS
    LABEL RECORDS ARE STANDARD
    DATA RECORD IS TRANS-REC.
01  TRANS-REC.
    05  FILLER                  PIC X(50).

FD  INVENTORY-MASTER
    RECORD CONTAINS 50 CHARACTERS
    LABEL RECORDS ARE STANDARD
    DATA RECORD IS MASTER-REC.
01  MASTER-REC.
    05  FILLER                  PIC X(01).
    05  MASTER-ITEM-NO          PIC X(05).
    05  FILLER                  PIC X(44).

FD  BACKORDER
    BLOCK  CONTAINS 20 RECORDS
    RECORD CONTAINS 32 CHARACTERS
    LABEL RECORDS ARE STANDARD
    DATA RECORD IS BACKORDER-REC.
01  BACKORDER-REC.
    05  FILLER                  PIC X(32).

FD  INVENTORY-REPORT
    RECORD CONTAINS 133 CHARACTERS
    LABEL RECORDS ARE OMITTED
    DATA RECORD IS PRINT-REC.
01  PRINT-REC.
    05  PRINT-LINE              PIC X(133).

WORKING-STORAGE SECTION.

01  OTHER-ITEMS.
    05  EOF-FLAG                PIC X(03)    VALUE 'NO'.
        88  END-OF-FILE                      VALUE 'YES'.
    05  KEY-ERROR-FLAG          PIC X(03)    VALUE 'NO'.
        88  KEY-ERROR                        VALUE 'YES'.
        88  NO-KEY-ERROR                     VALUE 'NO'.
    05  WS-DATE                 PIC X(08).

01  TOTALS USAGE IS COMP-3.
    05  LINE-COUNT              PIC 9(03)    VALUE ZERO.
    05  WS-BACKORDER-QTY        PIC 9(03)    VALUE ZERO.
```

FIGURE 7.23(b)

```
01  MESSAGES.
    05  MESSAGE-01              PIC X(30)
            VALUE 'INVENTORY RECORD REVISED'.
    05  MESSAGE-02              PIC X(30)
            VALUE 'NEW INVENTORY RECORD CREATED'.
    05  MESSAGE-03              PIC X(30)
            VALUE 'INVENTORY RECORD DELETED'.
    05  MESSAGE-04              PIC X(30)
            VALUE 'INVENTORY RECORD NOT FOUND'.
    05  MESSAGE-05              PIC X(30)
            VALUE 'ITEM ALREADY EXISTS'.
    05  MESSAGE-06              PIC X(30)
            VALUE 'FILE REWRITE ERROR'.

01  WS-TRANS-REC.
    05  TRANS-CODE             PIC X(01).
        88  ADD-ITEM                    VALUE 'A'.
        88  ORDER-ITEM                  VALUE 'O'.
        88  STOCK-UPDATE                VALUE 'S'.
        88  UPDATE-ITEM                 VALUE 'U'.
        88  DELETE-ITEM                 VALUE 'D'.
    05  TRANS-ITEM-NO         PIC X(05).
    05  TRANS-DESCRIPTION     PIC X(15).
    05  TRANS-UNIT-COST       PIC 9(04)V99.
    05  TRANS-STOCK-QTY       PIC 9(03).
    05  TRANS-ORDER-QTY       PIC 9(03).
    05  TRANS-REORDER-POINT   PIC 9(03).
    05  TRANS-ACTIVITY-DATE   PIC X(08).
    05  FILLER               PIC X(06).

01  WS-MAST-REC.
    05  FILLER               PIC X(01).
    05  MAST-ITEM-NO         PIC X(05).
    05  MAST-DESCRIPTION     PIC X(15).
    05  MAST-UNIT-COST       PIC 9(04)V99.
    05  MAST-STOCK-QTY       PIC 9(03).
    05  MAST-ORDER-QTY       PIC 9(03).
    05  MAST-REORDER-POINT   PIC 9(03).
    05  MAST-ACTIVITY-DATE   PIC X(08).
    05  FILLER               PIC X(06).

01  WS-BACKORDER-REC.
    05  FILLER               PIC X(01).
    05  BACK-ITEM-NO         PIC X(05).
    05  BACK-DESCRIPTION     PIC X(15).
    05  BACK-STOCK-QTY       PIC 9(03).
    05  BACK-ACTIVITY-DATE   PIC X(08).

01  HEAD-1.
    05  FILLER               PIC X(45)   VALUE SPACES.
    05  FILLER               PIC X(16)
            VALUE 'INVENTORY REPORT'.

01  HEAD-2.
    05  FILLER               PIC X(01)   VALUE SPACES.
    05  FILLER               PIC X(45)
            VALUE 'TRANS  ITEM      DESCRIPTION           UNIT'.
    05  FILLER               PIC X(39)
            VALUE 'TRANSACTION     MASTER      REORDER'.
    05  FILLER               PIC X(20)
            VALUE 'BACKORDER   MESSAGES'.

01  HEAD-3.
    05  FILLER               PIC X(01)   VALUE SPACES.
    05  FILLER               PIC X(45)
            VALUE 'CODE     NO.                        COST'.
    05  FILLER               PIC X(39)
            VALUE 'STOCK  ORDER  STOCK  ORDER    POINT'.
    05  FILLER               PIC X(20)
            VALUE '   QTY'.
```

FIGURE 7.23(c)

```
01  DETAIL-LINE.
    05   FILLER                        PIC X(03)    VALUE SPACES.
    05   DET-CODE                      PIC X(01).
    05   FILLER                        PIC X(04)    VALUE SPACES.
    05   DET-ITEM-NO                   PIC 9(05).
    05   FILLER                        PIC X(04)    VALUE SPACES.
    05   DET-DESCRIPTION               PIC X(15).

    05   FILLER                        PIC X(04)    VALUE SPACES.
    05   DET-UNIT-COST                 PIC ZZZ9.99.
    05   FILLER                        PIC X(04)    VALUE SPACES.
    05   DET-TRN-STOCK-QTY             PIC ZZ9.
    05   FILLER                        PIC X(04)    VALUE SPACES.
    05   DET-TRN-ORDER-QTY             PIC ZZ9.
    05   FILLER                        PIC X(04)    VALUE SPACES.
    05   DET-MST-STOCK-QTY             PIC ZZ9.
    05   FILLER                        PIC X(04)    VALUE SPACES.
    05   DET-MST-ORDER-QTY             PIC ZZ9.
    05   FILLER                        PIC X(06)    VALUE SPACES.
    05   DET-REORDER-POINT             PIC ZZ9.
    05   FILLER                        PIC X(08)    VALUE SPACES.
    05   DET-BACKORDER-QTY             PIC ZZ9.
    05   FILLER                        PIC X(06)    VALUE SPACES.
    05   DET-MESSAGE                   PIC X(30).

PROCEDURE DIVISION.
100-MAINLINE.
    PERFORM 200-INITIALIZE.
    PERFORM 300-PROCESS
        UNTIL END-OF-FILE.
    PERFORM 600-WRAP-UP.
    CLOSE TRANSACTIONS
          INVENTORY-MASTER
          BACKORDER
          INVENTORY-REPORT.
    STOP RUN.

200-INITIALIZE.
    OPEN INPUT  TRANSACTIONS
         I-O    INVENTORY-MASTER
         OUTPUT BACKORDER
                INVENTORY-REPORT.
    MOVE CURRENT-DATE TO WS-DATE.
    PERFORM 220-HEADINGS.
    PERFORM 510-READ.

220-HEADINGS.
    WRITE PRINT-REC FROM HEAD-1
        AFTER ADVANCING TO-TOP-OF-PAGE.
    WRITE PRINT-REC FROM HEAD-2
        AFTER ADVANCING 2 LINES.
    WRITE PRINT-REC FROM HEAD-3
        AFTER ADVANCING 1 LINE.
    MOVE SPACES TO PRINT-REC.
    WRITE PRINT-REC
        AFTER ADVANCING 1 LINE.
    MOVE 5 TO LINE-COUNT.

300-PROCESS.
    MOVE SPACES                  TO DETAIL-LINE.
    MOVE TRANS-CODE              TO DET-CODE.
    MOVE TRANS-ITEM-NO           TO DET-ITEM-NO.
    MOVE TRANS-DESCRIPTION       TO DET-DESCRIPTION.
    IF TRANS-UNIT-COST IS NUMERIC
        MOVE TRANS-UNIT-COST     TO DET-UNIT-COST.
    IF TRANS-STOCK-QTY IS NUMERIC
        MOVE TRANS-STOCK-QTY     TO DET-TRN-STOCK-QTY.
    IF TRANS-ORDER-QTY IS NUMERIC
        MOVE TRANS-ORDER-QTY     TO DET-TRN-ORDER-QTY.
    IF TRANS-REORDER-POINT IS NUMERIC
        MOVE TRANS-REORDER-POINT TO DET-REORDER-POINT.
    PERFORM 400-UPDATE-MASTER.
    MOVE SPACES TO DETAIL-LINE.
    PERFORM 310-PRINT-LINE.
    PERFORM 510-READ.
```

FIGURE 7.23(d)

```
310-PRINT-LINE.
    WRITE PRINT-REC FROM DETAIL-LINE
        AFTER ADVANCING 1 LINE.
    ADD 1                       TO LINE-COUNT.
    MOVE SPACES                 TO DETAIL-LINE.
    IF LINE-COUNT IS GREATER THAN 50
        PERFORM 220-HEADINGS.


320-SETUP-PRINT-LINE.
    MOVE MAST-STOCK-QTY         TO DET-MST-STOCK-QTY.
    MOVE MAST-ORDER-QTY         TO DET-MST-ORDER-QTY.
    MOVE MAST-REORDER-POINT     TO DET-REORDER-POINT.
    MOVE MAST-DESCRIPTION       TO DET-DESCRIPTION.

400-UPDATE-MASTER.
    MOVE  TRANS-ITEM-NO    TO  MASTER-ITEM-NO.
    IF ADD-ITEM
        PERFORM 410-ADD-ITEM
    ELSE
        IF ORDER-ITEM
            PERFORM 420-ORDER-ITEM
        ELSE
            IF STOCK-UPDATE
                PERFORM 430-STOCK-UPDATE
            ELSE
                IF UPDATE-ITEM
                    PERFORM 440-UPDATE-ITEM
                ELSE
                    PERFORM 450-DELETE-ITEM.


410-ADD-ITEM.
    MOVE SPACES                 TO WS-MAST-REC.
    MOVE TRANS-ITEM-NO          TO MAST-ITEM-NO.
    MOVE TRANS-DESCRIPTION      TO MAST-DESCRIPTION.
    MOVE TRANS-UNIT-COST        TO MAST-UNIT-COST.
    MOVE TRANS-STOCK-QTY        TO MAST-STOCK-QTY.
    MOVE TRANS-ORDER-QTY        TO MAST-ORDER-QTY.
    MOVE TRANS-REORDER-POINT    TO MAST-REORDER-POINT.
    MOVE WS-DATE                TO MAST-ACTIVITY-DATE.
    PERFORM 520-WRITE-MASTER.
    IF NO-KEY-ERROR
        MOVE MESSAGE-02         TO DET-MESSAGE
    ELSE
        MOVE MESSAGE-05         TO DET-MESSAGE.
    PERFORM 310-PRINT-LINE.

420-ORDER-ITEM.
    PERFORM 530-READ-MASTER.
    IF KEY-ERROR
        MOVE MESSAGE-04         TO DET-MESSAGE
        PERFORM 310-PRINT-LINE
    ELSE
        PERFORM 425-PROCESS-ORDER.

425-PROCESS-ORDER.
    MOVE SPACES                 TO WS-BACKORDER-REC.
    MOVE ZEROS                  TO WS-BACKORDER-QTY.
    MOVE WS-DATE                TO MAST-ACTIVITY-DATE.
    MOVE WS-DATE                TO BACK-ACTIVITY-DATE.
    MOVE TRANS-ITEM-NO          TO BACK-ITEM-NO.
    MOVE MAST-DESCRIPTION       TO BACK-DESCRIPTION.
*
* CHECK FOR INSUFFICIENT STOCK
*
    IF MAST-STOCK-QTY IS LESS THAN TRANS-STOCK-QTY
        COMPUTE WS-BACKORDER-QTY = TRANS-STOCK-QTY -
                                   MAST-STOCK-QTY
        ADD WS-BACKORDER-QTY    TO MAST-ORDER-QTY
        MOVE ZEROS              TO MAST-STOCK-QTY
        MOVE WS-BACKORDER-QTY   TO BACK-STOCK-QTY
        MOVE WS-BACKORDER-QTY   TO DET-BACKORDER-QTY
        PERFORM 560-WRITE-BACKORDER
    ELSE
```

FIGURE 7.23(e)

```
*
* SUFFICIENT QUANTITY IS IN STOCK
*
          SUBTRACT TRANS-STOCK-QTY FROM MAST-STOCK-QTY
*
*     CHECK FOR STOCK AT OR BELOW REORDER POINT
*
          IF MAST-STOCK-QTY IS NOT GREATER THAN MAST-REORDER-POINT
              MOVE MAST-REORDER-POINT TO BACK-STOCK-QTY
              MOVE BACK-STOCK-QTY        TO DET-BACKORDER-QTY
              ADD MAST-REORDER-POINT   TO MAST-ORDER-QTY
              PERFORM 560-WRITE-BACKORDER.
      PERFORM 320-SETUP-PRINT-LINE.
      MOVE MESSAGE-01                  TO DET-MESSAGE.
      PERFORM 310-PRINT-LINE.
      PERFORM 540-REWRITE-MASTER.

430-STOCK-UPDATE.
      PERFORM 530-READ-MASTER.
      IF KEY-ERROR
          MOVE MESSAGE-04              TO DET-MESSAGE
          PERFORM 310-PRINT-LINE
      ELSE
          PERFORM 435-PROCESS-STOCK.

435-PROCESS-STOCK.
      ADD TRANS-STOCK-QTY         TO   MAST-STOCK-QTY.
      SUBTRACT TRANS-STOCK-QTY    FROM MAST-ORDER-QTY.
      MOVE WS-DATE                TO   MAST-ACTIVITY-DATE.
      PERFORM 320-SETUP-PRINT-LINE.
      MOVE MESSAGE-01                  TO   DET-MESSAGE.
      PERFORM 310-PRINT-LINE.
      PERFORM 540-REWRITE-MASTER.

440-UPDATE-ITEM.
      PERFORM 530-READ-MASTER.
      IF KEY-ERROR
          MOVE MESSAGE-04              TO DET-MESSAGE
          PERFORM 310-PRINT-LINE
      ELSE
          PERFORM 445-PROCESS-UPDATE.

445-PROCESS-UPDATE.
      MOVE WS-DATE                     TO   MAST-ACTIVITY-DATE.
      IF TRANS-DESCRIPTION IS NOT EQUAL TO SPACES
          MOVE TRANS-DESCRIPTION  TO MAST-DESCRIPTION.
      IF TRANS-UNIT-COST IS NUMERIC
          MOVE TRANS-UNIT-COST     TO MAST-UNIT-COST.
      IF TRANS-STOCK-QTY IS NUMERIC
          MOVE TRANS-STOCK-QTY     TO MAST-STOCK-QTY.
      IF TRANS-ORDER-QTY IS NUMERIC
          MOVE TRANS-ORDER-QTY     TO MAST-ORDER-QTY.
      IF TRANS-REORDER-POINT IS NUMERIC
          MOVE TRANS-REORDER-POINT TO MAST-REORDER-POINT.
      PERFORM 320-SETUP-PRINT-LINE.
      MOVE MESSAGE-01                  TO   DET-MESSAGE.
      PERFORM 310-PRINT-LINE.
      PERFORM 540-REWRITE-MASTER.

450-DELETE-ITEM.
      PERFORM 530-READ-MASTER.
      IF KEY-ERROR
          MOVE MESSAGE-04              TO DET-MESSAGE
          PERFORM 310-PRINT-LINE
      ELSE
          PERFORM 455-PROCESS-DELETE.

455-PROCESS-DELETE.
      PERFORM 320-SETUP-PRINT-LINE.
      MOVE MESSAGE-03                  TO   DET-MESSAGE.
      PERFORM 310-PRINT-LINE.
      PERFORM 550-DELETE-MASTER.
```

FIGURE 7.23(f)

```
510-READ.
    READ TRANSACTIONS INTO WS-TRANS-REC
        AT END MOVE 'YES' TO EOF-FLAG.

520-WRITE-MASTER.
    MOVE 'NO' TO KEY-ERROR-FLAG.
    WRITE MASTER-REC FROM WS-MAST-REC
        INVALID KEY MOVE 'YES' TO KEY-ERROR-FLAG.

530-READ-MASTER.
    MOVE 'NO' TO KEY-ERROR-FLAG.
    READ INVENTORY-MASTER INTO WS-MAST-REC
        INVALID KEY MOVE 'YES' TO KEY-ERROR-FLAG.

540-REWRITE-MASTER.
    MOVE 'NO' TO KEY-ERROR-FLAG.
    REWRITE MASTER-REC FROM WS-MAST-REC
        INVALID KEY MOVE 'YES' TO KEY-ERROR-FLAG.
    IF KEY-ERROR
        MOVE MESSAGE-06        TO DET-MESSAGE
        PERFORM 310-PRINT-LINE.

550-DELETE-MASTER.
    MOVE 'NO' TO KEY-ERROR-FLAG.
    DELETE INVENTORY-MASTER
        INVALID KEY MOVE 'YES' TO KEY-ERROR-FLAG.

560-WRITE-BACKORDER.
    WRITE BACKORDER-REC FROM WS-BACKORDER-REC.

600-WRAP-UP.
    MOVE SPACES                        TO DETAIL-LINE.
    MOVE '*** END OF FILE UPDATE ***' TO DET-MESSAGE.
    PERFORM 310-PRINT-LINE.
```

FIGURE 7.23(g)

DEBUGGING HINT: DUMPING A VSAM FILE

Completely debugging the update program will require frequent dumps of the VSAM inventory file. First, a dump is needed of the original VSAM master, and then after the update program is run, we will need to dump the file again to observe the changes made against it. If the dump shows that there were errors in the update, the master will need to be restored before correcting the program and doing another test run; otherwise, new errors will simply build on previous errors.

Figure 7.24 shows a program to dump the VSAM file. To read a VSAM file sequentially requires the SELECT clause to use the SEQUENTIAL mode, as follows:

```
SELECT INVENTORY-MASTER ASSIGN TO MASTER7
            ORGANIZATION IS INDEXED
            ACCESS MODE IS SEQUENTIAL
            RECORD KEY IS MASTER-ITEM-NO.
```

With this mode in use, the file will be opened as INPUT rather than I-O as used in the update program. The output file shown here is for the listing of the master file dump.

```
OPEN INPUT  INVENTORY-MASTER
            OUTPUT DUMP-INVENTORY.
```

The remainder of the program is written as a simple read and process loop that reads each record from the inventory file and prints it. Fields are not separated on this dump (Figure 7.25), as is the usual approach with such programs, but additional program code could be included to separate each field and provide editing with zero suppression and decimal insert as required.

```
IDENTIFICATION DIVISION.

PROGRAM-ID.
    DUMP-INVENTORY.
*AUTHOR.
*    JOHNATHAN YOUNGMAN.
*INSTALLATION.
*    SALES UNLIMITED CORP.
*DATE-WRITTEN.
*    AUGUST 27.
*DATE-COMPILED.

*SECURITY.
*    NONE.

ENVIRONMENT DIVISION.

CONFIGURATION SECTION.
SOURCE-COMPUTER.
    IBM-4381.
OBJECT-COMPUTER.
    IBM-4381.
SPECIAL-NAMES.
    C01 IS TO-TOP-OF-PAGE.

INPUT-OUTPUT SECTION.

FILE-CONTROL.
    SELECT INVENTORY-MASTER ASSIGN TO MASTER7
        ORGANIZATION IS INDEXED
        ACCESS MODE IS SEQUENTIAL
        RECORD KEY IS MASTER-ITEM-NO.
    SELECT DUMP-INVENTORY   ASSIGN TO PRINTER.

DATA DIVISION.

FILE SECTION.

FD  INVENTORY-MASTER
    RECORD CONTAINS 50 CHARACTERS
    LABEL RECORDS ARE STANDARD
    DATA RECORD IS MASTER-REC.
01  MASTER-REC.
    05  FILLER                  PIC X(01).
    05  MASTER-ITEM-NO          PIC X(05).
    05  FILLER                  PIC X(44).

FD  DUMP-INVENTORY
    RECORD CONTAINS 133 CHARACTERS
    LABEL RECORDS ARE OMITTED
    DATA RECORD IS PRINT-REC.
01  PRINT-REC.
    05  FILLER                  PIC X(001).
    05  PRINT-LINE              PIC X(132).

WORKING-STORAGE SECTION.

01  OTHER-ITEMS.
    05  EOF-FLAG                PIC X(03)   VALUE 'NO'.
        88  END-OF-FILE                     VALUE 'YES'.


01  HEAD-1.
    05  FILLER                  PIC X(12)   VALUE SPACES.
    05  FILLER                  PIC X(16)
            VALUE 'INVENTORY DUMP'.

PROCEDURE DIVISION.
100-MAINLINE.
    PERFORM 200-INITIALIZE.
    PERFORM 300-PROCESS
        UNTIL END-OF-FILE.
    CLOSE INVENTORY-MASTER
        DUMP-INVENTORY.
    STOP RUN.
```

FIGURE 7.24(a)   Program to dump the VSAM inventory file

```
200-INITIALIZE.
    OPEN INPUT  INVENTORY-MASTER
         OUTPUT DUMP-INVENTORY.
    PERFORM 220-HEADINGS.
    PERFORM 510-READ.

220-HEADINGS.
    WRITE PRINT-REC FROM HEAD-1
        AFTER ADVANCING TO-TOP-OF-PAGE.
    MOVE SPACES TO PRINT-REC.
    WRITE PRINT-REC
        AFTER ADVANCING 2 LINES.
    MOVE 3 TO LINE-COUNT.

300-PROCESS.
    MOVE MASTER-REC          TO PRINT-LINE.
    PERFORM 310-PRINT-LINE.
    PERFORM 510-READ.

310-PRINT-LINE.
    WRITE PRINT-REC FROM DETAIL-LINE
        AFTER ADVANCING 1 LINE.
    ADD 1                    TO LINE-COUNT.
    MOVE SPACES              TO DETAIL-LINE
    IF LINE-COUNT IS GREATER THAN 50
        PERFORM 220-HEADINGS.

510-READ.
    READ INVENTORY-MASTER
        AT END MOVE 'YES' TO EOF-FLAG.
```

FIGURE 7.24(b)

```
00230DISKETTE SS/DD  003895050010020
00231DISKETTE DD/DD  004195025000020
00235CARTRIDGE 1600  002795100020025
00300DISK FINDER     001995050000010
00310FLIP 'N' FILE   004295010020020
00850MAILER          000195100000050
01005HEAD CLEANER    000595040010020
01010PAPER 30 M      001595200050030
01011PAPER 40 M      001795150050030
01012PAPER 44 M      001995070020020
02100PLOTTER PEN     001395030010010
02120PLOTTER FILM    004895020000010
02300MAILING LABELS  006995060020025
02401RIBBON          000895200040050
02402RIBBON          000995140000050
02405RIBBON          001295045020050
03000MODEM CABLE     002195010020020
```

Activity date (blank)
Reorder point
Quantity on order
Quantity in stock
Description
Item number
Unit cost

FIGURE 7.25   Dump of the VSAM inventory master before updating

PROGRAM TESTING

Testing of the VSAM update will be done with the transactions listed in Figure 7.26.
Note the purpose for each transaction in the figure, which is an important consideration
for checking the effectiveness of the test. The comments to the right are not part of

each record, but rather are included to help the programmer devise an effective test run.

```
A00220DISKETTE SS/DD 002999000000030    add a new record
000231                         010      order qty of 10-backorder 20
000300                         030      order qty of 30-no backorder
S00310                         010      increase stock by 10
U00850MAILER           000219500000020  update fields in item 00850
D01005                                  delete record
001015                         050      no record found on master
002120                         030      reduce stock to 0-backorder 10
002401                         175      backorder 50
S03000                         020      increase stock by 20
```

FIGURE 7.26 Transaction file for the VSAM update

When reviewing the results of the test, it will be helpful to compare master fields before and after the update. Successful programmers frequently prepare a chart similar to the one in Figure 7.27, which shows the contents of important fields in selected records before and after the update. In this program, the fields for stock quantity, order quantity, and backorder amount (from the backorder file) are important values to track. It is also important to observe the contents of records that do not change as a result of the update and records that are either added to or deleted from the file.

Back-order	Item No.	Before Update Description	Unit Cost	Stk Qty	Ord Qty	After Update Description	Unit Cost	Stk Qty	Ord Qty
	00220	new record added to file				DISKETTE SS/DD	002999	000	000
020	00231	DISKETTE DD/DD	004195	025	000	DISKETTE DD/DD	004195	015	020
	00300	DISK FINDER	001995	050	000	DISK FINDER	001995	020	000
	00300	DISK FINDER	001995	050	000	DISK FINDER	004295	020	000
	00310	FLIP 'N' FILE	004295	010	020	FLIP 'N' FILE	000219	020	020
	00850	MAILER	000195	100	000	MAILER	000219	500	020
	01005	HEAD CLEANER	000595	040	010	record deleted			
010	02120	PLOTTER FILM	004895	020	000	PLOTTER FILM	004895	000	010
050	02401	RIBBON	000895	200	040	RIBBON	000895	025	090
	03000	MODEM CABLE	002195	010	020	MODEM CABLE	002195	030	000

FIGURE 7.27 Changes to the master resulting from the update

To complete the analysis of the test run of the VSAM update program, a copy of the report from the run is required and a dump of the master after updating and a dump of the backorder file. These listings are shown in Figures 7.28 to 7.30. A tall order for the programmer at this point is to check each entry in these listings and verify their accuracy. This is painstaking work, but it is one of the important aspects of programming. Small sets of test data, as used here, greatly simplify program testing and the checking of results. When satisfied that the program functions correctly with small amounts of carefully chosen data, larger quantities of records may be used to give the program a more lifelike test.

```
TRANS  ITEM   DESCRIPTION       UNIT   TRANSACTION     MASTER      REORDER  BACKORDER  MESSAGES
COSE   NO.                      COST   STOCK  ORDER  STOCK  ORDER  POINT      QTY

A      00220  DISKETTE SS/DD   29.99    0      0                    30                  NEW INVENTORY RECORD CREATED

O      00231  DISKETTE DD/DD           10            15     20      20         20       INVENTORY RECORD REVISED

O      00300  DISK FINDER              30            20     0       10                  INVENTORY RECORD REVISED

S      00310  FLIP  N FILE             10            20     10      20                  INVENTORY RECORD REVISED

U      00850  MAILER            2.19   500    0      500    0       20                  INVENTORY RECORD REVISED

D      01005  HEAD CLEANER                           40     10      20                  INVENTORY RECORD DELETED

O      01015                           50                                               INVENTORY RECORD NOT FOUND

O      02120  PLOTTER FILM             30            0      10      10         10       INVENTORY RECORD REVISED

O      02401  RIBBON                   175           25     90      50         50       INVENTORY RECORD REVISED

S      03000  MODEM CABLE              20            30     0       20                  INVENTORY RECORD REVISED
                                                                                        *** END OF FILE UPDATE ***
```

FIGURE 7.28   Inventory update report

```
00231DISKETTE DD/DD 02008/19/86
02120PLOTTER FILM   01008/19/86
02401RIBBON         05008/19/86
```

FIGURE 7.29   Backorder file dump.

```
              INVENTORY DUMP

00220DISKETTE SS/DD  0029990000003008/19/86
00230DISKETTE SS/DD  0038950500010020
00231DISKETTE DD/DD  0041950150200200 08/19/86
00235CARTRIDGE 1600  0027951000200025
00300DISK FINDER     0019950200000100 08/19/86
00310FLIP 'N' FILE   0042950200100200 08/19/86
00850MAILER          0002195000000200 08/19/86
01010PAPER 30 M      0015952000500030
01011PAPER 40M       0017951500500030
01012PAPER 44 M      0019950700200020
02122PLOTTER PEN     0013950300100010
02120PLOTTER FILM    0048950000100100 08/19/86
02300MAILING LABELS  0069950600200025
02401RIBBON          0008950250900500 08/19/86
02402RIBBON          0009951400000050
02405RIBBON          0012950450200050
03000MODEM CABLE     0021950300000200 08/19/86
```

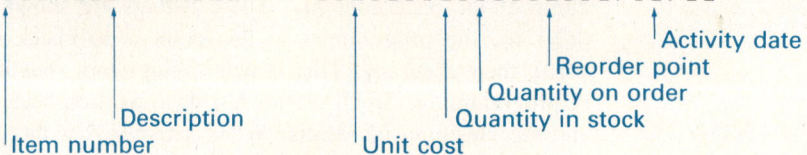

FIGURE 7.30   Updated inventory master dump

284   Chapter 7

VSAM files permit the addition and deletion of records without the need to do a file reorganization. A primary key field is used to uniquely identify each record in the file. Keys are not required to have consecutive values. VSAM also permits the use of an alternate key in addition to the primary one so that records may be accessed in more than one order. Composite keys may also be used that consist of the contents of several fields.

The VSAM file is defined in the SELECT clause, and, like ISAM, may assign several ALTERNATE AREAS for input/output buffers. ORGANIZATION IS INDEXED for VSAM, and ACCESS MODE may be SEQUENTIAL, RANDOM, or DYNAMIC. The SELECT clause must define a RECORD KEY field and may also have an ALTERNATE KEY entry. An FD for a VSAM file follows the rules that apply to other files, except that a BLOCK CONTAINS entry may not be used because VSAM determines its own optimum blocking.

VSAM files may be opened as INPUT, OUTPUT, or I-O. If the file is to be READ sequentially, a START statement may optionally be used to identify the record where reading is to begin. A sequential READ will also include an AT END clause todetect when end of file has occurred.

Random READ statements contain an INVALID KEY clause that is activated when no record is found for the key that was specified. WRITE is used to create a new record on the file and always contains an INVALID KEY clause, which is executed if a record with an equal key already exists. REWRITE is used when a record has been updated and needs to be rewritten on the file with the changes that have been made to it. A record is deleted from a VSAM file with the DELETE statement.

When a VSAM file is to be updated, the SELECT clause will identify an ACCESS MODE of RANDOM or DYNAMIC. The file will be opened as I-O and will be accessed using the READ, WRITE, and REWRITE statements as required.

A sequential use of the file would use an ACCESS MODE of SEQUENTIAL or DYNAMIC. This file is opened as INPUT and may use the START or READ statements for processing the file. An AT END clause would be used on the READ statement to detect end of file.

TERMS TO STUDY

ALTERNATE KEY	SEQUENTIAL
Backorder	Structure chart modules
Composite key	Top-down design
DYNAMIC	VSAM
Key	WITH DUPLICATES
RANDOM	

REVIEW QUESTIONS

TRUE/FALSE

1. VSAM files require periodic reorganization of the records to ensure efficient use of the file.

2. One way VSAM differs from ISAM is the availability of alternate keys with a VSAM file.

3. Each VSAM record requires a delete byte in the first position of the record.

4. When a group item containing three fields is used as a key, each field must be defined as the alternate key.

5. Normally, a key must be a unique value in the file for each record. However, this rule is not valid for the alternate key, which may contain duplicates.

6. The FD entry for a VSAM file may not specify blocked records.

7. The DELETE statement is used in the program to delete a record from the VSAM file.

8. To update a record on the VSAM file, it must first be read randomly from the file after a key has been provided.

9. To update a VSAM file, it must always be opened as INPUT by the program.

10. It is considered good style to use separate OPEN statements for each file used by the program.

11. Generally, a COBOL program may use any number of input or output files in an application.

12. An output file, such as the backorder file defined in this chapter, must always contain all the same fields as the input file that creates it.

FILL IN THE BLANKS

13. The letter V in VSAM means _____ .

14. The _____ statement removes a record permanently from a VSAM file.

15. In the following record, the group item _____ would be the record key name.

```
0 CLIENT-RECORD.
    05 CLIENT-NUMBER.
        10 REGION      PIC X(02).
        10 CLIENT      PIC X(05).
```

16. To update a VSAM file, the SELECT clause will contain the ACCESS MODE _____ .

17. When a VSAM file is to be read sequentially, it will be opened as _____ .

18. When updating is done to a VSAM file, it must be opened as _____ .

19. A _____ _____ value must be established before a record can be read randomly by the program.

20. The _____ statement may be used to position the file to the required record before it is read sequentially.

21. Complex structure charts can be more easily managed by dividing the chart into several _____ that represent a component of the problem.

22. If data from a VSAM record are required before it is deleted, a _____ statement will be necessary to access the record.

MULTIPLE CHOICE

23. Select a significant difference between ISAM and VSAM files.
    a. VSAM does not require a delete byte.
    b. ISAM requires occasional reorganization.
    c. VSAM may use an alternate key.
    d. All the above.
    e. None of the above.

24. Which statement is true when a composite of several fields is used as a VSAM key field?
    a. Each field is an alternate key.
    b. The group name is the record key.
    c. Only one field needs to be in sequence.
    d. Descending sequence of the fields is necessary.

25. Duplicate keys are acceptable in what situation?
    a. When an alternate key is used.   c. Anytime they occur.
    b. Only for the primary key.   d. Never.

26. One difference between the ISAM and VSAM SELECT clause is the possible use of the _____ entry for VSAM.
    a. ASSIGN   c. RECORD KEY
    b. ORGANIZATION   d. ALTERNATE RECORD

27. An update program will OPEN a VSAM file as:
    a. INPUT   c. I-O
    b. OUTPUT   d. UPDATE

28. Before a record from a VSAM file can be read directly into the program, what step is necessary?
    a. The file must be opened as I-O.   c. a and b.
    b. A key value must be moved to the record key field.   d. Neither a or b.

29. When a VSAM file is to be updated, what condition is necessary in the COBOL program?
    a. Transactions must be in key sequence.   d. All the above.
    b. Only the alternate key may be used.   e. None of the above.
    c. The VSAM file must be opened as OUTPUT.

30. When a VSAM file is used in an application:
    a. All files used by the program must be VSAM.
    b. Some files may be VSAM, but others may be sequential.
    c. The VSAM file must always be used as iNPUT.
    d. All the above.
    e. None of the above.

PROGRAMMING EXERCISES

1. Revise the inventory master update program in this chapter to make the backorder file a VSAM file. This file will contain only one record for each item on backorder, instead of a separate record each time a backorder is created in the current program. Consider the following program specifications as they apply to the new backorder file.

INPUT/OUTPUT RECORD DEFINITION				
File: Backorder file Record Length: 32 Sequence: Item number		File Type: VSAM Blocking Factor: N/A Access Method: Random		
COLUMNS	FIELD	TYPE	LENGTH	DECIMALS
1	Unused	A/N	1	
2–6	*Item number	N	5	
7–21	Description	A/N	15	
22–24	Backorder qty	N	3	
25–32	Date	N	8	
	*Primary key			

```
                        PROGRAMMING SPECIFICATIONS
PROGRAM NAME: Update Inventory Master            PROGRAM ID: INVENTORY
                    (revision 1.1)
PREPARED BY: Diane Quest                          DATE: Aug. 30, 1986
```

Program Description:

This specification represents a revision to the inventory master update program. Revisions are required to implement a VSAM backorder file.

Input File(s):

Transaction file

Inventory master file (I-O)

Backorder file (I-O)

Output File(s):

Inventory report

Program Requirements:

These requirements represent changes to an existing program. They should not be construed as a complete program definition.

1. When a backorder record is to be created, first check to see if a record exists on the backorder file for that item number. If a record exists, it will be updated to reflect the current backorder quantity. If no record exists, create a new one reflecting the backorder quantity that initiated the process.

2. A backorder is to be created for the same reasons as the current program. This order results because either the stock quantity reaches the reorder point or an order is received that exceeds the existing stock quantity.

3. If an existing backorder record is to be updated, the new quantity will be added to the current quantity on backorder file, thus creating an accumulation of backorder quantities.

4. When items are placed in stock (code 'S'), the new quantity will be subtracted from the backorder quantity for that item on the backorder file, in addition to the previously defined activities.

5. If the backorder quantity for an item on the backorder file has been reduced to zero, that record may be deleted from the file.

2. Write a program to update the customer aged balance file each month according to the following specifications. Design your month according to the following specifications. Design your own report for this application after becoming familar with the input and output and the program specifications.

INPUT/OUTPUT RECORD DEFINITION				
File: Aged balance file		File Type: VSAM		
Record Length: 55		Blocking Factor: N/A		
Sequence: Customer number		Access Method: Random & Seq.		
COLUMNS	FIELD	TYPE	LENGTH	DECIMALS
1	Unused	A/N	1	
2–7	*Customer number	N	6	
8–9	Branch	N	2	
10–24	Customer name	A/N	15	
25–29	Credit limit ($)	N	5	
30–35	Current amount	N	6	2
36–41	31–60 days due	N	6	2
42–47	61–90 days due	N	6	2
48–53	Over 90 days due	N	6	2
	*Primary key			

File: Transaction file
Record Length: 40
Sequence: N/A

File Type: Sequential disk
Blocking Factor: 10
Access Method: Sequential

COLUMNS	FIELD	TYPE	LENGTH	DECIMALS
1	Update code A—add record D—delete record P—purchase Y—payment G—age record	A/N	1	
2–7	Customer number	N	6	
8–9	Branch	N	2	
10–24	Customer name	A/N	15	
25–29	Credit limit ($)	N	5	
30–35	Amount	N	6	2

PROGRAMMING SPECIFICATIONS

PROGRAM NAME: Customer Balances
PREPARED BY: Diane Quest

PROGRAM ID: CUSTOMER7
DATE: Aug. 30, 1986

Program Description:
  This program updates the customer aged balance file by recording purchases, payments, and other updating, including aging the records at month end.
Input File(s):
  Transaction file
  Aged balance file (I-O)
Output File(s):
  Customer balance report
Program Requirements:
  1. Update the aged balance file by processing the transaction records.
  2. Print each transaction and identify the action taken during processing. If a code 'G' transaction is received, a complete customer listing will be produced at the end of other updating.
  3. Process each transaction according to the following specifications.
     A—This adds a new record to the master file. The amount field will not be used for this transaction, but other fields should be recorded in the new master record. Set the balance and other amount due fields to zero in the new master record.
     D—Delete the record with the equivalent customer number. The master record to be deleted must have zero for all amounts owing before a delete can be processed.
     P—A purchase adds the amount in the transaction to the current amount field in the master record. If the credit limit is exceeded, the customer record must be flagged in the report although the master will still reflect this new purchase.
     Y—When a payment is made, the amount is subtracted from the amount due field that is greater than zero. For example, if over 90 contains an amount, the payment is subtracted from this field. If over 90 is zero, then check 61–90, and so on.

     Several fields may be updated if the payment exceeds the amount owing in a given field. For example, assume the master fields contain the following values.

Current	31–60	61–90	Over 90
40	50	30	20

Programming with VSAM Files

PROGRAM NAME: Customer Balances   PROGRAM ID: CUSTOMER7
PREPARED BY: Diane Quest   DATE: Aug. 30, 1986

If a payment of $90 is made, $20 is deducted from over 90, $30 from 61–90, and $40 from 31–60, leaving the resulting values;

Current	31–60	61–90	Over 90
40	20	0	0

G—This transaction is always processed last, although it may appear anywhere in the transaction file. The best approach here is to set a flag in the program if a code 'G' is read and then do the processing after transaction end of file is reached.

Process a code 'G' by reading the master file sequentially and aging the customer balances in each record. Aging is accomplished by the following steps.

 Add the amount in 61–90 to over 90.
 Move the amount in 31–60 to 61–90.
 Move the amount in current amount to 31–60.
 Set the current amount to zero.

Produce a detail listing containing all customer records after the aging has occurred.

SUBPROGRAMS AND THE LINKAGE SECTION

WHY SUBPROGRAMS ARE NEEDED

Large-scale business programs frequently run into thousands of lines of code. Some on-line systems ultimately may consume tens of thousands of coding lines, thus representing a significant level of complexity and requiring the work of several programmers to complete the application. When programs reach this size and complexity, it is unreasonable to expect a single programmer to accomplish the task. Instead, the work is divided into modules written by separate individuals. In COBOL, these modules may be written as separate **subprograms,** which are then called as needed by a controlling main program (Figure 8.1).

Separate subprogram modules may also be tested independently, thus reducing the complexity of the testing environment. A subprogram may even call another subprogram to complete its operation. Each subprogram may be written and compiled separately, with additional (and temporary) driver code to supply any necessary data. The module is tested on its own first to discover any major bugs, which are corrected before the subprogram is used by the controlling program. Top-level subprograms are added first and additional testing is done before lower-level modules are used. This method is called top-down testing and obviously would be used only when major applications are developed.

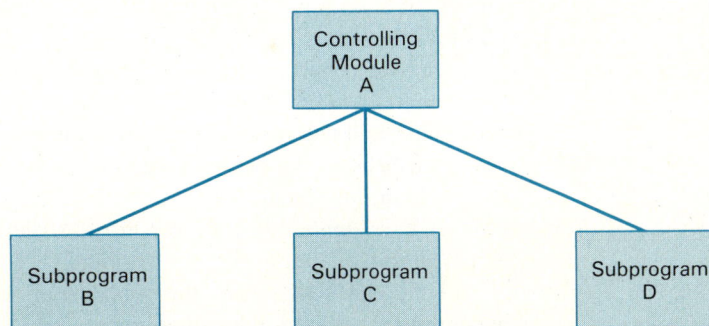

FIGURE 8.1   One program that uses several subprograms

Another use for subprograms is to avoid the duplication of code. Suppose a system frequently uses a procedure for calculating a federal tax amount. If several programs in the system require this procedure, the program code may need to be supplied in each of these programs. When a change is required to the tax procedure (which will invariably happen at least once a year), each program that contains this procedure will need to be changed.

Making the same change to several programs raises the possibility of making errors. One type of error can result from making the program change incorrectly in one or more of the programs. Thus some of the programs will end up working properly, while others will not. Another potential problem is that the change may be missed entirely in one or more of the programs, resulting in some programs representing current tax requirements, while others will be using out-of-date calculations. Clearly, neither of these situations will be acceptable to the business application.

The solution is to write a subprogram that does the federal tax calculation. Then each program that needs to determine the tax will call the subprogram, which does the necessary calculations and returns the result (Figure 8.2). Now if a change is needed to the tax calculations, only the subprogram will need to be changed. And, because each program calls the subprogram, the change will be reflected in every program in the same way.

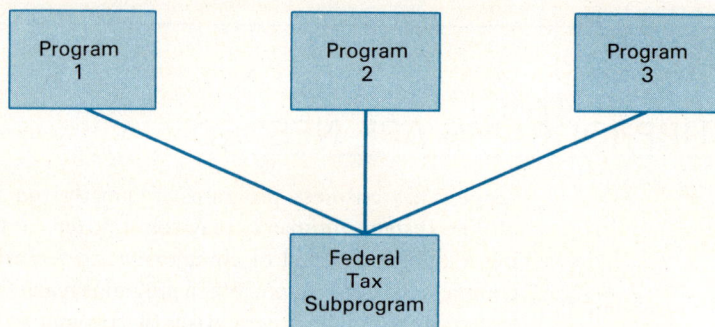

FIGURE 8.2   Several programs that each use the tax subprogram

THE CALLING PROGRAM
AND THE CALLED SUBPROGRAM

When subprograms are used, there must be a **main** (or top-level) **program** that is in charge of all activity. It is this calling program that activates a subprogram as it is needed. As shown in Figure 8.3, control is passed to the subprogram where the necessary processing is done. When this control is passed to the subprogram, some data are also supplied from the calling program, as represented by the line with the arrow pointing to the subprogram.

After the subprogram has been invoked, it may then do any necessary processing. At this point, the subprogram acts like an independent program and may have, if necessary, its own input and output files. When the subprogram is complete, control of the processing is returned back to the calling program. Returning control to the calling program may also result in data being supplied back to the calling program from the subprogram. These data are represented by the arrow pointing from the subprogram to the calling program in the diagram.

Figure 8.4 shows how the subprogram is called in COBOL and how data are transferred to and from the subprogram. The main program uses a **CALL** statement to invoke the suprogram and also to supply any data that the subprogram will need for its

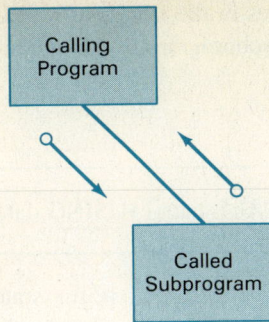

FIGURE 8.3 Relationship between the calling program and the subprogram

operation. These data arrive in the **LINKAGE SECTION** of the subprogram (actually this section is a section of memory that is shared between the main program and the subprogram and does not consist of additional memory requirements). The PROCEDURE DIVISION of the subprogram is now executed, and when the EXIT PROGRAM statement is reached, control is passed back to the calling program. Any data that the subprogram

- Calling Program

```
IDENTIFICATION DIVISION.
PROGRAM-ID
    MAINPROG.
    :
    :
WORKING-STORAGE SECTION.
    :
01   TAXABLE.
    :
01   PAYABLE.
    :
PROCEDURE DIVISION.
    :
    :
        CALL 'TAXCALC' USING TAXABLE PAYABLE.
    :
```

- Called Subprogram

```
IDENTIFICATION DIVISION.
PROGRAM-ID.
    TAXCALC.
    :
DATA DIVISION.
    :
LINKAGE SECTION.
01   SUPPLIED.
    :
01   RETURNED.
    :
PROCEDURE DIVISION USING SUPPLIED RETURNED.
    :
    :
    EXIT PROGRAM.
```

FIGURE 8.4 Calling a subprogram in COBOL

Subprograms and the LINKAGE SECTION

293

places in the LINKAGE SECTION are now available to the calling program as though the subprogram had returned values to the main program.

CALL STATEMENT

> CALL literal [USING data-name-1 [data-name-2] . . .]

The CALL is the statement used to pass control to a subprogram. The literal entry is the name of the subprogram being called and as a literal it must be enclosed in quotes. Some systems also permit the use of an identifier to supply the subprogram's name.

The USING clause supplies the data to the subprogram and also provides a place for data to be returned to the calling program. These data-name entries should be 01-level entries and not individual items within a record description (although some systems permit the use of an elementary item). These names must be found in the calling program's WORKING-STORAGE SECTION, but the corresponding fields in the subprogram may use a different name.

When the CALL is executed, the data contained in these data names are passed to the subprogram. The sequence of the fields in the CALL must correspond to the sequence in which they are received in the subprogram. The fields in the calling program must be initialized prior to reaching the CALL statement. Any number of data names may be specified, but using as few as possible will result in higher cohesion of the subprogram's code.

Example

```
        A   B
1   4   78  12                                                           72

    CALL 'TAXCALC' USING TAXABLE PAYABLE.
```

The subprogram named in this CALL is TAXCALC, which presumably will do some tax calculations for the calling program. Prior to issuing the CALL, the field TAXABLE must be set up with values that the subprogram will use. If the subprogram uses data in the identifier PAYABLE, then it must also be initialized. However, PAYABLE may be the field that returns values from the subroutine, in which case its value at the time of the CALL is not critical.

CALLED SUBPROGRAMS

> IDENTIFICATION DIVISION.
>
> PROGRAM-ID. program-name
>
> DATA DIVISION.
>
> [LINKAGE SECTION.
>
> [01   record-description-entry] . . .]
>
> PROCEDURE DIVISION
>
>   [USING data-name-1 [data-name-2] . . .] .
>
>   EXIT PROGRAM.

A called subprogram in COBOL is another COBOL program with a few important differences. The first item is to ensure that the PROGRAM-ID in the subprogram corresponds to the name used in the CALL of the calling program. This entry is the name that identifies the subprogram so that it can be accessed by other programs in the system.

```
      A    B
1   4  78   12                                                        72
        IDENTIFICATION DIVISION.
        PROGRAM-ID.
           TAXCALC.
```

LINKAGE SECTION

Each subprogram must contain a LINKAGE SECTION to identify the data passed between the calling program and the subprogram. In reality, the LINKAGE SECTION provides a connection between the memory space used in the calling program by the data names that were identified by the CALL statement. These data can then be referenced in the subprogram by using the names defined in the LINKAGE SECTION.

The LINKAGE SECTION follows the FILE and WORKING-STORAGE sections in the DATA DIVISION. Depending on the needs of the subprogram, it is possible that a FILE SECTION will not be necessary in the called subprogram. The LINKAGE

- Calling Program

```
        WORKING-STORAGE SECTION.
        01   CLASS-DATA.
             05 CLASS-NUMBER        PIC 9(06).
             05 CLASS-NAME          PIC X(20).
             05  CLASS-PERIOD-FROM  PIC 9(02).
             05 CLASS-PERIOD-TO     PIC 9(02).
             05 CLASS-DAY           PIC 9(02).
             05 CLASS-INSTRUCTOR    PIC X(12).
          :
        PROCEDURE DIVISION.
           CALL 'TIMETABLE' USING CLASS-DATA.
```

- Called Subprogram

```
        IDENTIFICATION DIVISION.
        PROGRAM-ID. TIMETABLE.
          :
        DATA DIVISION.
          :
        LINKAGE SECTION.
        01   LK-TIMETABLE-DATA.
             05 LK-NUMBER           PIC 9(06).
             05 LK-NAME             PIC X(20).
             05 LK-PERIOD-FROM      PIC 9(02).
             05 LK-PERIOD-TO        PIC 9(02).
             05 LK-DAY              PIC 9(02).
             05 LK-INSTRUCTOR       PIC X(12).
          :
        PROCEDURE DIVISION
             USING LK-TIMETABLE-DATA.
```

FIGURE 8.5 Relationship of the data between the calling program and the LINKAGE SECTION of the subprogram

SECTION contains record description entries that correspond to equivalent entries referenced by the CALL statement in the calling program. These entries may use different names, but the record lengths and data formats must be identical (Figure 8.5). Because no storage is allocated to data items in the LINKAGE SECTION, they may not contain a VALUE clause.

Other data may be needed for processing in the subprogram. These may be defined in either the FILE or WORKING-STORAGE sections, depending on how the data are used. Identifiers in WORKING-STORAGE should be initialized in the same manner as they would be if a program were being run for the first time. Thus totals and flags should be initialized in the usual manner. On a system where the subprogram occupies storage with the calling program, identifiers in the called subprogram must be initialized in the PROCEDURE DIVISION so that each time the subprogram is called initialization will take place.

USING IN THE PROCEDURE DIVISION

Another new entry in the subprogram is the **USING** clause that is part of the **PROCEDURE DIVISION** statement. This clause is required to identify the names of the data items that will be used in the LINKAGE SECTION. When there is more than one data item, the order of the names in the USING clause must correspond to the order they were used in the CALL statement of the calling program although the names may be different.

```
PROCEDURE DIVISION USING SUPPLIED RETURNED.
```

EXIT PROGRAM STATEMENT

When the subprogram has completed its processing, an **EXIT PROGRAM** statement must be executed. This statement causes the subprogram to be halted and control returned back to the calling program. If files were opened for use in the subprogram, they should be closed before returning to the calling program. Any data that have been moved to or changed in the LINKAGE SECTION will be passed back to the calling program when EXIT PROGRAM is executed. EXIT PROGRAM must be the last statement executed in the subprogram.

PROGRAMMING STYLE

- When the CALL statement requires a long list of names or the names themselves consist of many characters, place the USING clause on a second line indented four or more columns.

```
CALL 'FINDATA'
    USING CUSTOMER-NUMBER CONTRACT-NUMBER KEY-FLAG.
```

- Each item in the LINKAGE SECTION should be a separate record description entry. Of course, a single item may be a complete record containing many different fields. A prefix may also be used for each item in this section to identify the data source.

```
LINKAGE SECTION.
01   LK-CUSTOMER-NUMBER.
     05 LK-COUNTRY          PIC 9(02).
     05 LK-REGION           PIC 9(01).
     05 LK-CUSTOMER         PIC 9(06).
```

- As we discussed with the CALL, the PROCEDURE DIVISION entry may also be excessively long for one line. In the same manner as the CALL, place the USING clause on the next line with a four-column indent.

```
                    PROCEDURE DIVISION.
                        USING LK-CUSTOMER-NUMBER LK-LEGAL LK-FLAG.
```

ERROR CORRECTION

The program and subprogram in Figure 8.6 contain a number of errors that would prevent its successful compilation and execution. Here are a list of the errors and the steps needed to make the correction.

- Calling Program

```
        IDENTIFICATION DIVISION.
        PROGRAM-ID.
            VALIDATE.
            :
        DATA DIVISION.
        WORKING-STORAGE SECTION.

        01   WS-ORDER-REC USAGE COMP-3.
             05 WS-ORDER-NO        PIC 9(07).
             05 WS-ORDER-DATE      PIC 9(06).
             05 WS-ORDER-QTY       PIC 9(03).
             05 WS-ORDER-AMOUNT    PIC 9(05)V99.

        01   WS-FLAGS.
             05 WS-EOF-FLAG        PIC X.
             05 WS-KEY-FLAG        PIC X.

        PROCEDURE DIVISION.
            :
            CALL FILESRCH
                USING WS-ORDER-REC

            :
```

- Called Subprogram

```
        IDENTIFICATION DIVISION.
        PROGRAM-ID.
            SEARCH.
          :
        DATA DIVISION.
          :
        LINKAGE SECTION.

        01   LK-RECORD.
             05 LK-ORDER-NO        PIC 9(07).
             05 LK-ORDER-DATE      PIC 9(06).
             05 LK-ORDER-QTY       PIC 9(03).
             05 LK-ORDER-AMOUNT    PIC 9(05)V99.
             05 LK-DESCRIPTION     PIC X(15).

        01   LK-FLAGS.
             05 LK-EOF-FLAG        PIC X.
             05 LK-KEY-FLAG        PIC X.
             :
        PROCEDURE DIVISION
            USING LK-RECORD.
             :
            EXIT PROGRAM.
```

FIGURE 8.6 A program and called subprogram containing errors

1. In the calling program, the program name in the CALL statement should be contained in quotes because it must be a literal. A second error in the CALL is the missing second argument WS-FLAGS. This may not be obvious here until the contents of the subprogram are examined. Here is the corrected statement:

```
CALL 'FILESRCH'
     USING WS-ORDER-REC WS-FLAGS.
```

2. The file name used in the CALL does not match the name of the subprogram. These names should match in both programs. The correction is made to the subprogram as follows:

```
PROGRAM-ID.
     FILESRCH.
```

3. The USAGE of LK-RECORD in the LINKAGE SECTION of the subprogram does not agree with the COMP-3 usage in the calling program. Because the record in the LINKAGE SECTION occupies the same storage as the calling program's record, these USAGE clauses must agree. The subprogram entry is changed to the following:

```
LINKAGE SECTION.

01  LK-RECORD USAGE COMP-3.
```

4. The record in the LINKAGE SECTION contains a field called LK-DESCRIPTION, which was not defined in the calling program. Either the calling program missed this field or it should not be a part of the subprogram's LINKAGE SECTION. In this case, it is deleted from the LINKAGE SECTION entry.

```
LINKAGE SECTION.

01  LK-RECORD USAGE COMP-3.
     05 LK-ORDER-NO        PIC 9(07).
     05 LK-ORDER-DATE      PIC 9(06).
     05 LK-ORDER-QTY       PIC 9(03).
     05 LK-ORDER-AMOUNT    PIC 9(05)V99.
```

5. Although LK-FLAGS is defined in the LINKAGE SECTION, it is not defined as a parameter in the USING clause of the PROCEDURE DIVISION statement.

```
PROCEDURE DIVISION
     USING LK-RECORD LK-FLAGS.
```

Figure 8.7 shows these corrections included in the calling program and the subprogram.

• Calling Program

```
IDENTIFICATION DIVISION.
PROGRAM-ID.
     VALIDATE.
   :
WORKING-STORAGE SECTION.
```

```
01   WS-ORDER-REC USAGE COMP-3.
     05 WS-ORDER-NO        PIC 9(07).
     05 WS-ORDER-DATE      PIC 9(06).
     05 WS-ORDER-QTY       PIC 9(03).
     05 WS-ORDER-AMOUNT    PIC 9(05)V99.

01   WS-FLAGS.
     05 WS-EOF-FLAG        PIC X.
     05 WS-KEY-FLAG        PIC X.

PROCEDURE DIVISION.
     :
     CALL 'FILESRCH'
          USING WS-ORDER-REC WS-FLAGS.

     :
```

• Called Subprogram

```
         IDENTIFICATION DIVISION.
         PROGRAM-ID.
             FILESRCH.
             :
         DATA DIVISION.
             :
         LINKAGE SECTION.

             01   LK-RECORD USAGE COMP-3.
                  05 LK-ORDER-NO      PIC 9(07).
                  05 LK-ORDER-DATE    PIC 9(06).
                  05 LK-ORDER-QTY     PIC 9(03).
                  05 LK-ORDER-AMOUNT  PIC 9(05)V99.

             01   LK-FLAGS.
                  05 LK-EOF-FLAG      PIC X.
                  05 LK-KEY-FLAG      PIC X.
                  :
         PROCEDURE DIVISION
             USING LK-RECORD LK-FLAGS.
             :
             EXIT PROGRAM.
```

FIGURE 8.7   Corrected program code

TRAVEL DISCOUNTS: AN APPLICATION PROGRAM

We are to write a program that generates travel contracts for a travel agency. This application will use two programs. The main program will read the travel transactions and print the travel contracts with all the appropriate values.

To determine a discount percentage for the contract, the main program will call a subprogram that contains a table of discount rates. To find the correct rate, the transaction supplies a package key that is passed to the subprogram and used to find the matching table entry. The table also provides a description of the traveler's destination. Figure 8.8 shows the relationship between the main program and the subprogram in this application.

Figure 8.9 shows the system flowchart for this application. Note that only the main program is using input and output files, while the subprogram gets its data from the main program and returns the results through the LINKAGE SECTION. This solution is not to suggest that a subprogram cannot use files. Like any other program, it may

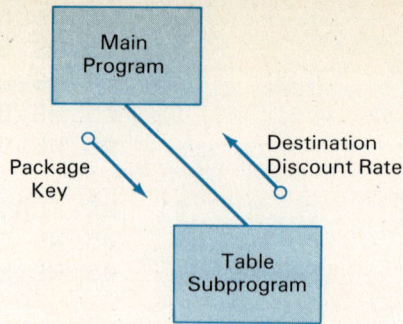

FIGURE 8.8 Relationship between the main travel program and its subprogram

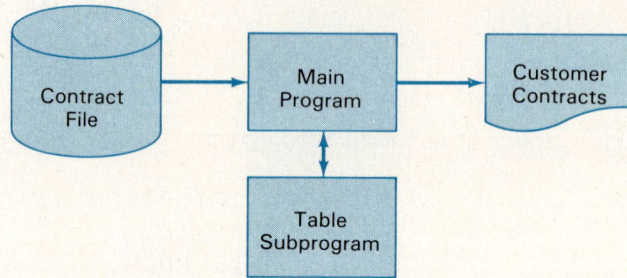

FIGURE 8.9 System flowchart for the travel discount application

have its own input and output files; but in this application there is no need for an input or output file in the table subprogram.

MAIN PROGRAM SPECIFICATIONS

Figure 8.10 shows the program specifications for the main program of this application. Because there is a main program and a subprogram, two sets of specifications are necessary. First, the specifications for the main program describe the operations to be done on the data from the input file. This description also indicates the need to call a subprogram to access the destination and discount rate required for the report. It is important here that the format for the data supplied by the call and the data to be returned be clearly identified.

PROGRAMMING SPECIFICATIONS   1 of 2

PROGRAM NAME: Travel Contracts   PROGRAM ID: TRAVEL8
PREPARED BY: Diane Quest   DATE: Sept. 4

Program Description:
    This program creates travel contracts for the agency's customers based on data accessed from a contract transaction file. By supplying a package key to the subprogram TABLE8, the discount rate and the trip's destination are provided.

Input File(s):
    Contract transaction file

Output File(s):
    Travel package contracts

Program Requirements:
    1. Read a transaction file of customer contracts.
    2. Supply the package key from each input record to the subprogram TABLE8, which will return a percentage discount rate and a descriptive destination. If the key does not match a table entry in the subprogram, a zero rate and a blank description will be returned.

FIGURE 8.10(a) Program specifications for the main travel contract program

3. The subprogram requires a record from the call in the following format as a single group item:

    1–2 Key value (supplied)

    3–17 Destination (returned from the subprogram)

    18–19 Rate (returned from the subprogram)

4. Print a package contract for each input record according to the output definition. Calculated values are determined as follows:

    a) Contract price is an input value.

    b) Discount rate (%) is returned from the subprogram.

    c) Discount amount = contract price × discount rate.

    d) Discounted price = contract price − discount amount.

    e) No. of tickets is an input value.

    f) Net price = no. of tickets × discounted price.

5. Each contract occupies a single output page.

FIGURE 8.10(b)

The subprogram specifications will be given after the main program is completely defined.

INPUT/OUTPUT DEFINITION: MAIN PROGRAM

Only the main program in this application uses input or output files. The subprogram does not require the use of a file for its operation. The travel contract program uses a transaction contract file (Figure 8.11), which supplies the basic data for each customer's contract. All this information is printed on the contract as it is read from the file. The report layout (Figure 8.12) shows most customer information in the top half of the contract and the financial data in the bottom half.

INPUT/OUTPUT RECORD DEFINITION				
File: Contract file	File Type: Disk			
Record Length: 90	Blocking Factor: 1			
Sequence: N/A	Access Method: Sequential			
COLUMNS	FIELD	TYPE	LENGTH	DECIMALS
1–3	Agency	A/N	3	
4–7	Customer number	N	4	
8–20	Name	A/N	13	
21–40	Address line 1	A/N	20	
41–60	Address line 2	A/N	20	
61–70	Phone number	N	10	
71–76	Contract price	N	6	2
77–78	No. of tickets	N	2	
79–80	Package key	N	2	
81–86	Date	N	6	

FIGURE 8.11   Input definition for the contract file

The package key, however, is used by the subprogram to supply a discount rate and a description of the destination. These values are also printed in the top part of the contract. The rate is then used by the main program for a series of calculations, as described in the specifications, which are then printed in the bottom section of the report.

```
          0         1         2         3         4         5         6         7
          1234567890123456789012345678901234567890123456789012345678901234567890123 45
```

```
                              PACKAGE  CONTRACT

      CUSTOMER NUMBER     AGENCY NUMBER      DATE      PACKAGE    DESTINATION

           9999               XXX         99/99/99       99      X-------------X


      NAME AND ADDRESS                    PHONE

      X-----------X                    999 999 9999
      X-------------------X
      X-------------------X


      CONTRACT       DISCOUNT     DISCOUNT     DISCOUNTED    NO. OF      NET
      PRICE             %          AMOUNT        PRICE       TICKETS    PRICE

       Z,ZZ9.99         Z9        Z,ZZ9.99     ZZ,ZZ9.99       Z9     ZZ,ZZ9.99
```

FIGURE 8.12   Printer layout for the customer contract

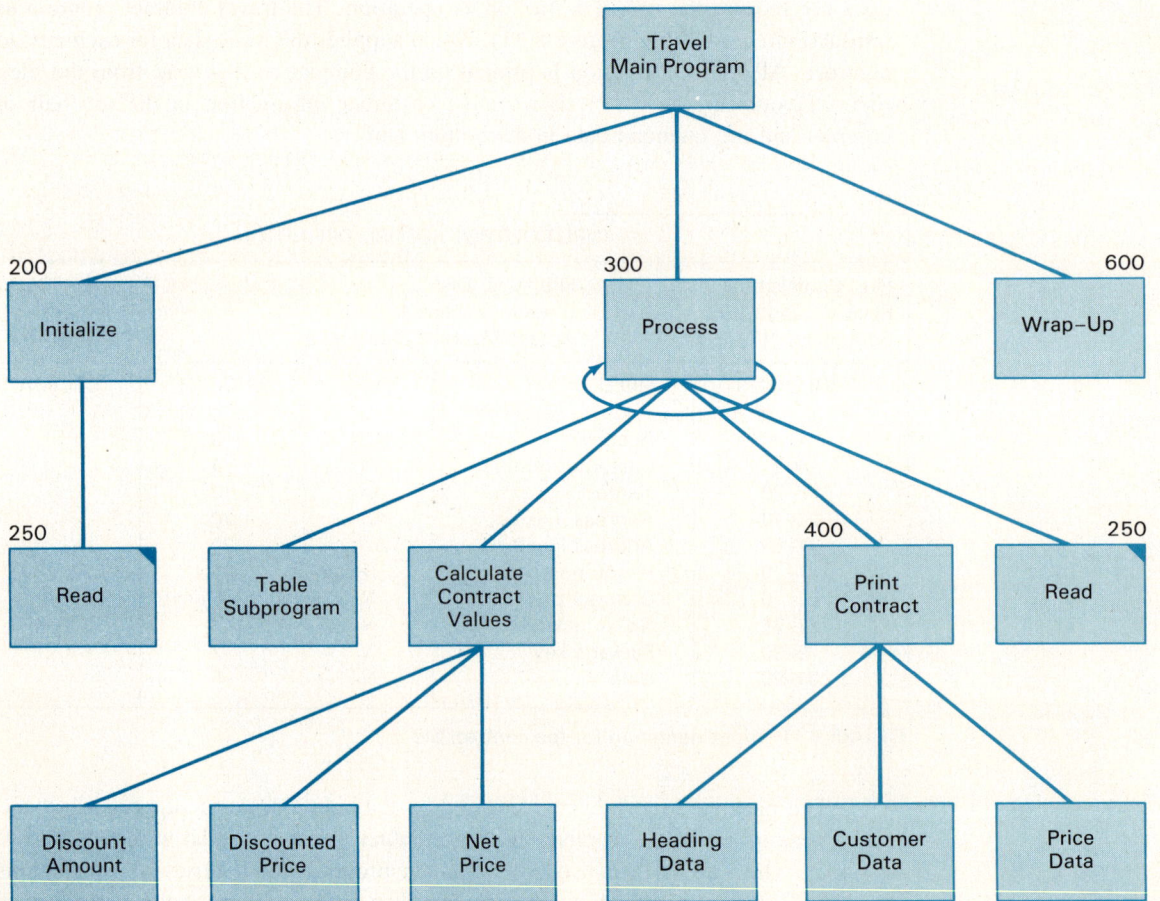

FIGURE 8.13   Structure chart for the travel contract program

STRUCTURE CHART: MAIN PROGRAM

Although this program uses a subprogram, it is not very complicated in itself. Basically, the structure (Figure 8.13) is a matter of reading a record, getting the discount rate and destination from the subprogram's table, doing a few calculations, and then printing the contract.

If the table were a part of this program, a module would be used in the structure chart to show where the table look-up occurred. This module might be expanded to show some lower-level components in the structure chart. However, in this application the module is a subprogram, and so all that is necessary is to show where it belongs in the scheme of things. The expansion of the module will then belong to the subprogram's structure chart and is not part of the main program.

PSEUDO CODE: MAIN PROGRAM

The code for the main program contains modules for initialization, a main process loop, and program wrap-up. In this sense, it follows the usual pattern of pseudo-code development. Because a subprogram is used, the pseudo code will use a Call statement to indicate the locations where the subprogram is called by the main program. This Call also specifies the field to be used by the subprogram with the Using entry as follows.

2. Call 'Table8' Using Comm-Fields

When the main program receives control back from the subprogram, the calculations are done for the contract. Three calculations are needed, which are based on the discount rate returned from the subprogram. These calculations are developed as follows:

3. Calculate discount amount = contract price × rate
4. Calculate discount price = contract price − discount amount
5. Calculate net price = discount price × no. of tickets

After these values have been determined, the module 400-Print-Contract is performed and the output is printed. Although the report is easy to produce, there are many different lines of output for each contract, thus requiring numerous moves and write statements. These steps can be summarized in the pseudo code and structured flowchart, as shown in Figure 8.14, and then developed more fully as the program code is written.

PROGRAM NAME: Travel Contracts		PROGRAM ID: TRAVEL8
PREPARED BY: Jonathan Youngman	DATE: Sept. 4	PAGE 1 of 1

100-Mainline
1. Perform 200-Initialize.
2. Perform 300-Process
   Until End of File.
3. Perform 600-Wrap-Up.
4. Stop Run.

200-Initialize
1. Open input and output files.
2. Perform 250-Read.

250-Read
1. Read Contract
   At end Move 'Yes' to Eof-Flag.

300-Process
1. Initialize Comm-Fields.
2. Call 'Table8' using Comm-Fields.
3. Calculate discount amount = contract price × rate.
4. Calculate discount price = contract price − discount amount.
5. Calculate net price = discount price × no. of tickets.
6. Perform 400-Print-Contract.
7. Perform 250-Read.

400-Print-Contract
1. Write Head-1
   After Advancing to top of page.
2. Write Head-2
   After Advancing 2 lines.
3. Move contract data to Detail-Line-1 area.
4. Write Detail-Line-1
   After advancing 2 lines.
5. Print 2 blank lines.
6. Write Head-3
   After advancing 1 line.
7. Move data to Detail-Line-2.
8. Write Detail-Line-2
   After advancing 2 lines.
9. Print Address-1.
10. Print Address-2.
11. Write Head-4
    After advancing 1 line.
12. Write Head-5
    After advancing 1 line.
13. Print contract pricing data.

600-Wrap-Up
1. Advance printer to new page.
2. Close files.

FIGURE 8.14(a)   Pseudo code for the main contract program

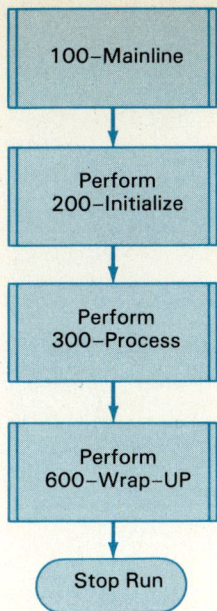

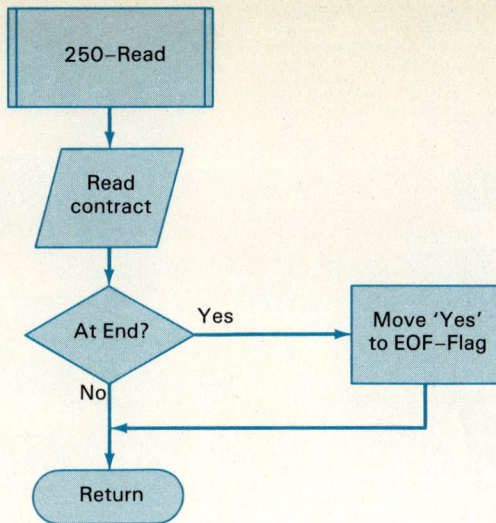

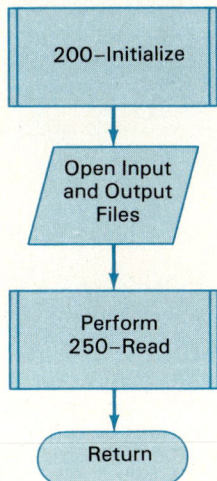

FIGURE 8.14(b)

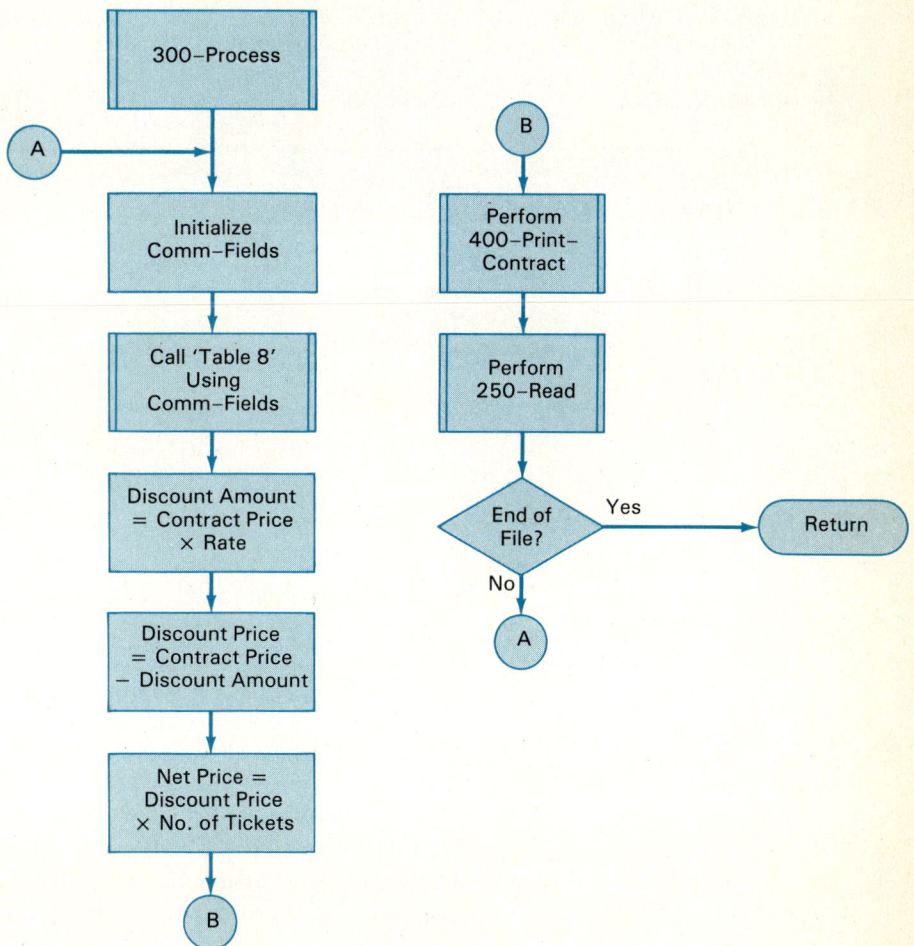

FIGURE 8.14(c)

Subprograms and the LINKAGE SECTION

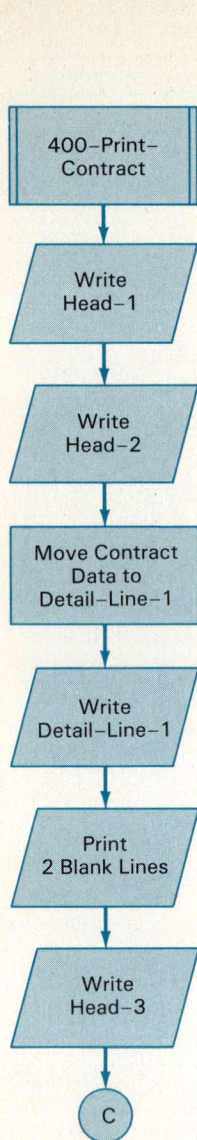

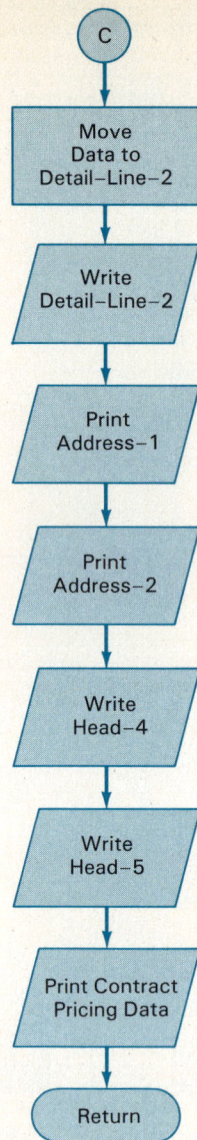

FIGURE 8.14(d)

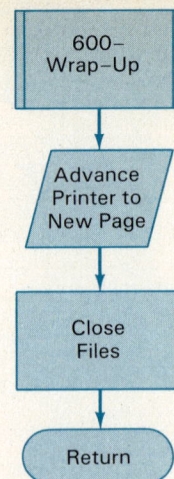

FIGURE 8.14(e)

SUBPROGRAM SPECIFICATIONS

The second set of specifications is for the subprogram (Figure 8.15). It is a program in its own right except that it is only used when called by another program. This particular subprogram does not have any input or output file, and so we need not look for these definitions. No files also means that the FILE SECTION will not be necessary in the COBOL subprogram.

The subprogram definition identifies the activities to be taken on the data and the data to be returned to the calling program. This specification is important, because it is possible in a large system that many programs could use this one subprogram, and this specification is the source of information for using the subprogram.

Program Description:

This subprogram receives a two-digit package key from the calling program. It returns a discount rate and a trip destination description after finding these items in a self-contained table.

Input File(s):

None

Output File(s):

None

Program Requirements:

1. This subprogram recrives a two-digit package key value from the calling program.
2. Look up the key in a table of values in the following format:

Key	Destination	Rate
21	MIAMI	10
23	MEXICO CITY	13
27	NASSAU	12
30	ST. VINCENT	15
31	SAN PEDRO	11
33	DALLAS	07
39	VIRGIN ISLANDS	10
40	MIAMI	10
45	RIO DE JANEIRO	20
47	CANARY ISLANDS	14
50	TAHITI	05
72	SAN DIEGO	12

where key is two digits
destination is 15 chars.
rate is two decimal digits.

3. Return the values for destination and rate to the calling program. The linkage section must follow the following format:
    1–2   Key value
    3–17 Destination
    18–19 Discount rate (2 decimal)
4. If a matching key is not found in the table, return a blank destination and a zero discount rate.

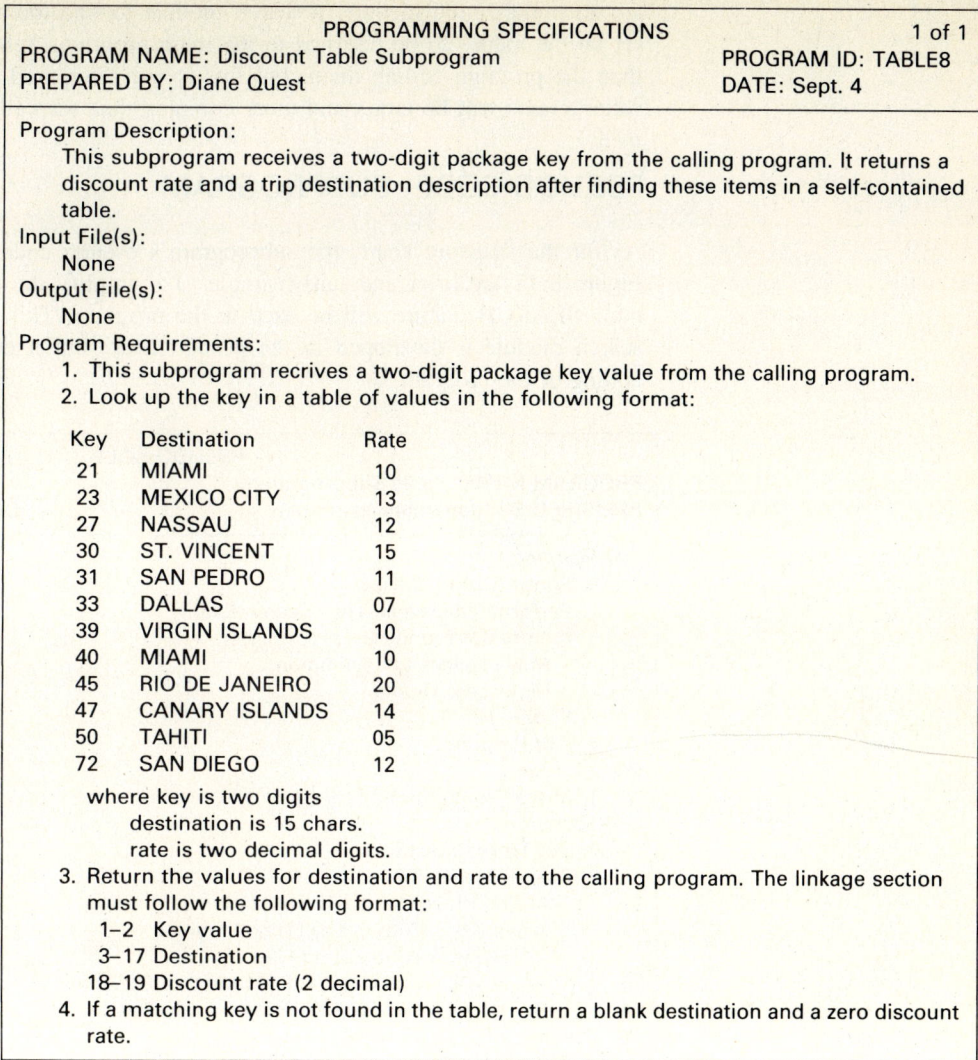

FIGURE 8.15   Program specifications for the table subprogram

STRUCTURE CHART: SUBPROGRAM

The main content of this subprogram is the table of values that is searched when the subprogram is called. Thus the activity in the program is quite direct and uncomplicated. As shown in Figure 8.16, there are three basic activities in the table subprogram. These

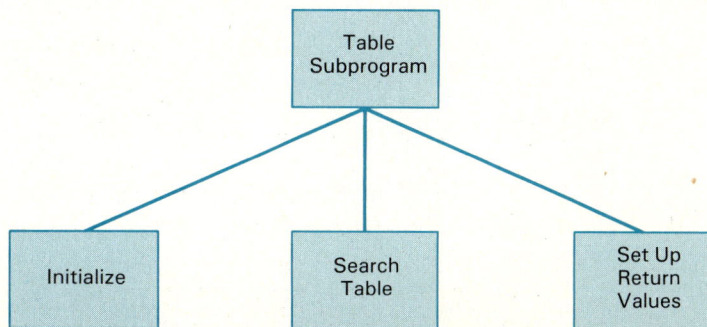

FIGURE 8.16   A structure chart for the discount table subprogram

are an initialization module, a search module to find the table entry, and a module to set up the values to be returned to the main program. Subprograms tend to be smaller than the program calling them, but this is not a required characteristic. In fact, some subprograms will be larger and more complex than the calling program.

PSEUDO CODE: SUBPROGRAM

As for the structure chart, the subprogram's pseudo code and structured flowchart in Figure 8.17 are brief and fairly simple. To simplify the use of a table, the COBOL table SEARCH feature will be used in the program. This decision affects the way the search module is developed in the pseudo code, but it does make for more efficient coding of the program.

PSEUDO CODE

PROGRAM NAME: Table Subprogram   PROGRAM ID: TABLE8
PREPARED BY: Jonathan Youngman   DATE: Sept. 4   PAGE 1 of 1

100-Mainline
   1. Perform 200-Initialize.
   2. Perform 300-Search Thru Search-Exit.
   3. If entry not found
       Move spaces to destination
       Move zero to rate
     Endif
   4. Exit Program.
200-Initialize
   1. Move 'No' to Found-Flag.
300-Search
   1. Set Travel-Index to 1.
   2. Search Travel-Table
       At End Move 'No' to Found-Flag
       When Key = Travel-Key (Travel-Index)
          Move 'Yes' to Found-Flag
          Move Travel-Dest (Travel-Index) to Destination
          Move Travel-Rate (Travel-Index) to Rate.
300-Search-Exit
   1. Exit.

FIGURE 8.17(a)   Pseudo code for the table subprogram

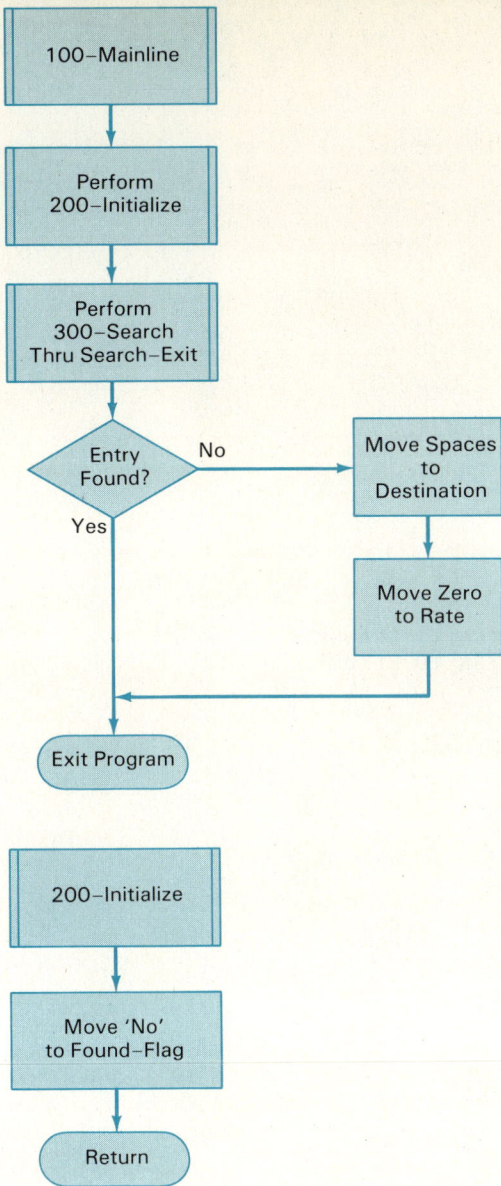

FIGURE 8.17(b)   Flowchart for the table subprogram

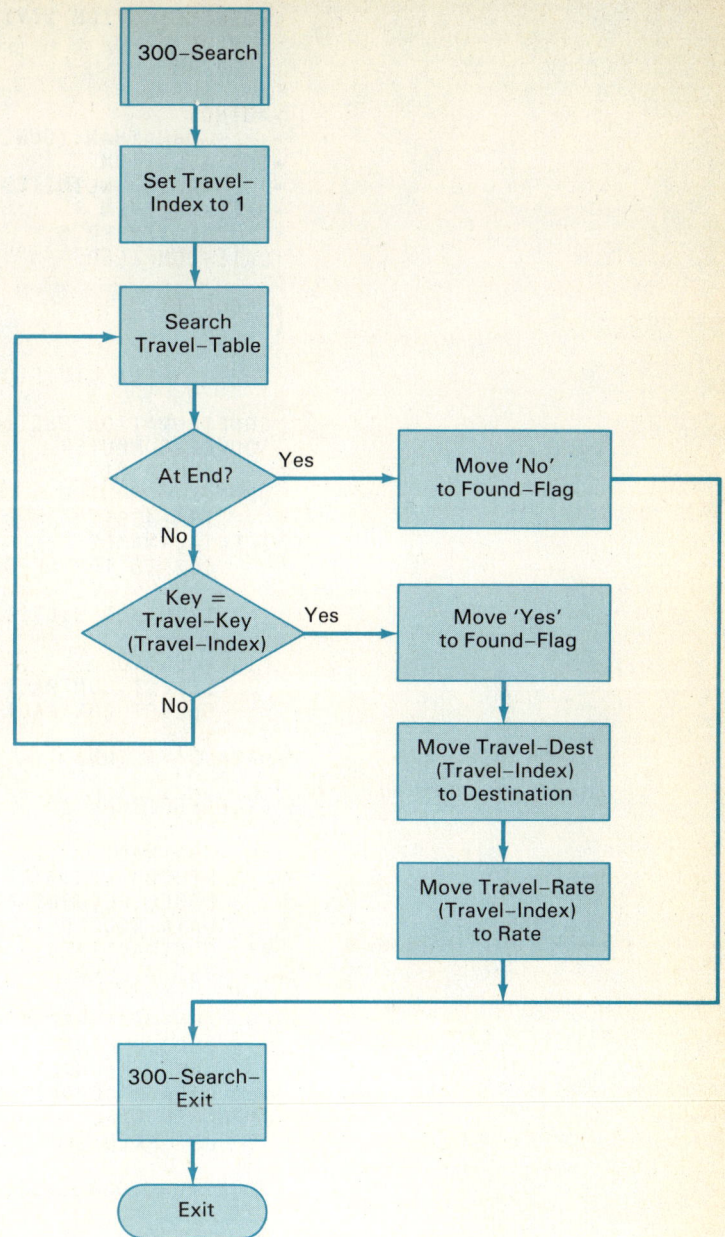

FIGURE 8.17(c)

PROGRAM CODING: MAIN PROGRAM

This program (Figure 8.18) begins with the usual entries made in the language based on previous coding experiences. Thus each division is coded like any other program with regard for input and output files, the need for WORKING-STORAGE identifiers for various calculations, and record descriptions for report lines and file formats.

Because we know by now that this program will be calling a subprogram, which in turn returns data to us here, an additional entry is made in WORKING-STORAGE for the data that are transferred to and from the subprogram. This entry is more a matter of style than of necessity, but it is used to group together all the data being communicated to and from the subprogram. We need to supply the subprogram with a key value representing the package key. The subprogram in turn sends back to us

```
        IDENTIFICATION DIVISION.

        PROGRAM-ID.
            TRAVEL8.
       *AUTHOR.
       *    JOHNATHAN YOUNGMAN.
       *INSTALLATION.
       *    SALES UNLIMITED CORP.
       *DATE-WRITTEN.
       *    SEPTEMBER 6.
       *DATE-COMPILED.

       *SECURITY.
       *    NONE.

        ENVIRONMENT DIVISION.

        CONFIGURATION SECTION.
        SOURCE-COMPUTER.
            IBM-4381.
        OBJECT-COMPUTER.
            IBM-4381.
        SPECIAL-NAMES.
            C01 IS TO-TOP-OF-PAGE.

        INPUT-OUTPUT SECTION.

        FILE-CONTROL.
            SELECT CONTRACT         ASSIGN TO TRANS8.
            SELECT CONTRACT-REPORT  ASSIGN TO REPORT.

        DATA DIVISION.

        FILE SECTION.

        FD  CONTRACT
            RECORD CONTAINS 90 CHARACTERS
            LABEL RECORDS ARE STANDARD
            DATA RECORD IS CONTRACT-REC.
        01  CONTRACT-REC.
            05  FILLER              PIC X(90).

        FD  CONTRACT-REPORT
            RECORD CONTAINS 133 CHARACTERS
            LABEL RECORDS ARE OMITTED
            DATA RECORD IS PRINT-REC.
        01  PRINT-REC.
            05  PRINT-LINE          PIC X(133).

        WORKING-STORAGE SECTION.

        01  OTHER-ITEMS.
            05  EOF-FLAG            PIC X(03)   VALUE 'NO'.
                88  END-OF-FILE                 VALUE 'YES'.

        01  COMM-FIELDS.
            05  COMM-KEY            PIC 9(02).
            05  COMM-DESTINATION    PIC X(15).
            05  COMM-RATE           PIC V99.

        01  CONTRACT-AMOUNTS.
            05  DISCOUNT-AMOUNT     PIC 9(04)V99.
            05  DISCOUNT-PRICE      PIC 9(05)V99.
            05  NET-PRICE           PIC 9(05)V99.
```

FIGURE 8.18(a) COBOL code for the main travel contract program

```
01  WS-CONTRACT-REC.
    05  AGENCY                    PIC X(03).
    05  CUSTOMER-NO               PIC 9(04).
    05  NAME                      PIC X(13).
    05  ADDRESS-01                PIC X(20).
    05  ADDRESS-02                PIC X(20).
    05  PHONE                     PIC 9(10).
    05  CONTRACT-PRICE            PIC 9(04)V99.
    05  TICKETS                   PIC 9(02).
    05  PACKAGE-KEY               PIC 9(02).
    05  DATE.
        10  CONTRACT-MONTH        PIC 99.
        10  CONTRACT-DAY          PIC 99.
        10  CONTRACT-YEAR         PIC 99.
    05  FILLER                    PIC X(04).

01  HEAD-1.
    05  FILLER                    PIC X(30)    VALUE SPACES.
    05  FILLER                    PIC X(16)
            VALUE 'PACKAGE CONTRACT'.

01  HEAD-2.
    05  FILLER                    PIC X(01)    VALUE SPACES.
    05  FILLER                    PIC X(48)
            VALUE 'CUSTOMER NUMBER  AGENCY NUMBER     DATE'.
    05  FILLER                    PIC X(22)
            VALUE 'PACKAGE      DESTINATION'.

01  HEAD-3.
    05  FILLER                    PIC X(01)    VALUE SPACES.
    05  FILLER                    PIC X(49)
            VALUE 'NAME AND ADDRESS                   PHONE'.

01  HEAD-4.
    05  FILLER                    PIC X(01)    VALUE SPACES.
    05  FILLER                    PIC X(37)
            VALUE 'CONTRACT    DISCOUNT     DISCOUNT'.
    05  FILLER                    PIC X(30)
            VALUE 'DISCOUNTED   NO. OF      NET'.

01  HEAD-5.
    05  FILLER                    PIC X(01)    VALUE SPACES.
    05  FILLER                    PIC X(37)
            VALUE ' PRICE            %        AMOUNT'.
    05  FILLER                    PIC X(32)
            VALUE '  PRICE        TICKETS     PRICE'.

01  DETAIL-LINE-1.
    05  FILLER                    PIC X(06)    VALUE SPACES.
    05  DET-CUSTOMER-NO           PIC 9(04).
    05  FILLER                    PIC X(14)    VALUE SPACES.
    05  DET-AGENCY                PIC X(03).
    05  FILLER                    PIC X(08)    VALUE SPACES.
    05  DET-DATE.
        10  DET-MONTH             PIC 99.
        10  FILLER                PIC X        VALUE '/'.
        10  DET-DAY               PIC 99.
        10  FILLER                PIC X        VALUE '/'.
        10  DET-YEAR              PIC 99.
    05  FILLER                    PIC X(08)    VALUE SPACES.
    05  DET-PACKAGE-KEY           PIC 99.
    05  FILLER                    PIC X(07)    VALUE SPACES.
    05  DET-DESTINATION           PIC X(15).

01  DETAIL-LINE-2.
    05  FILLER                    PIC X(01)    VALUE SPACES.
    05  DET-NAME                  PIC X(20).
    05  FILLER                    PIC X(08)    VALUE SPACES.
    05  DET-PHONE                 PIC 999B999B9999.
```

FIGURE 8.18(b)

```
01   DETAIL-LINE-3.
       05  FILLER                    PIC X(01)    VALUE SPACES.
       05  DET-CONTRACT-PRICE        PIC Z,ZZ9.99.
       05  FILLER                    PIC X(05)    VALUE SPACES.
       05  DET-RATE                  PIC ZZ.
       05  FILLER                    PIC X(09)    VALUE SPACES.
       05  DET-DISCOUNT-AMOUNT       PIC Z,ZZ9.99.
       05  FILLER                    PIC X(04)    VALUE SPACES.
       05  DET-DISCOUNT-PRICE        PIC ZZ,ZZ9.99.
       05  FILLER                    PIC X(06)    VALUE SPACES.
       05  DET-TICKETS               PIC Z9.
       05  FILLER                    PIC X(06)    VALUE SPACES.
       05  DET-NET-PRICE             PIC ZZ,ZZ9.99.

 PROCEDURE DIVISION.

 100-MAINLINE.
     PERFORM 200-INITIALIZE.
     PERFORM 300-PROCESS
         UNTIL END-OF-FILE.
     PERFORM 600-WRAP-UP.
     STOP RUN.

 200-INITIALIZE.
     OPEN INPUT  CONTRACT
          OUTPUT CONTRACT-REPORT.
     PERFORM 250-READ.

 250-READ.
     READ CONTRACT INTO WS-CONTRACT-REC
         AT END MOVE 'YES' TO EOF-FLAG.

 300-PROCESS.
     MOVE SPACES          TO COMM-FIELDS.
     MOVE PACKAGE-KEY     TO COMM-KEY.
     CALL 'TABLE8'
         USING COMM-FIELDS.
     MULTIPLY CONTRACT-PRICE BY COMM-RATE
         GIVING DISCOUNT-AMOUNT.
     SUBTRACT DISCOUNT-AMOUNT FROM CONTRACT-PRICE
         GIVING DISCOUNT-PRICE.
     MULTIPLY DISCOUNT-PRICE BY TICKETS
         GIVING NET-PRICE.
     PERFORM 400-PRINT-CONTRACT.
     PERFORM 250-READ.

 400-PRINT-CONTRACT.
     WRITE PRINT-REC FROM HEAD-1
         AFTER ADVANCING TO-TOP-OF-PAGE.
     WRITE PRINT-REC FROM HEAD-2
         AFTER ADVANCING 2 LINES.
     MOVE CUSTOMER-NO       TO DET-CUSTOMER-NO.
     MOVE AGENCY            TO DET-AGENCY.
     MOVE CONTRACT-MONTH    TO DET-MONTH.
     MOVE CONTRACT-DAY      TO DET-DAY.
     MOVE CONTRACT-YEAR     TO DET-YEAR.
     MOVE PACKAGE-KEY       TO DET-PACKAGE-KEY.
     MOVE COMM-DESTINATION  TO DET-DESTINATION.
     WRITE PRINT-REC FROM DETAIL-LINE-1
         AFTER ADVANCING 2 LINES.
     MOVE SPACES TO PRINT-REC.
     WRITE PRINT-REC
         AFTER ADVANCING 2 LINES.

     WRITE PRINT-REC FROM HEAD-3
         AFTER ADVANCING 1 LINE.
     MOVE NAME              TO DET-NAME.
     MOVE PHONE             TO DET-PHONE.
```

FIGURE 8.18(c)

```
        WRITE PRINT-REC FROM DETAIL-LINE-2
            AFTER ADVANCING 2 LINES.
        MOVE SPACES               TO DETAIL-LINE-2.
        MOVE ADDRESS-01           TO DET-NAME.
        WRITE PRINT-REC FROM DETAIL-LINE-2
            AFTER ADVANCING 2 LINES.
        MOVE SPACES               TO DETAIL-LINE-2.
        MOVE ADDRESS-02           TO DET-NAME.
        WRITE PRINT-REC
            AFTER ADVANCING 2 LINES.
        MOVE SPACES TO PRINT-REC.


        WRITE PRINT-REC FROM HEAD-4
            AFTER ADVANCING 1 LINE.
        WRITE PRINT-REC FROM HEAD-5
            AFTER ADVANCING 1 LINE.
        MOVE CONTRACT-PRICE       TO DET-CONTRACT-PRICE.
        MULTIPLY COMM-RATE BY 100
            GIVING DET-RATE.
        MOVE DISCOUNT-AMOUNT      TO DET-DISCOUNT-AMOUNT.
        MOVE DISCOUNT-PRICE       TO DET-DISCOUNT-PRICE.
        MOVE TICKETS              TO DET-TICKETS.
        MOVE NET-PRICE            TO DET-NET-PRICE.
        WRITE PRINT-REC FROM DETAIL-LINE-3
            AFTER ADVANCING 2 LINES.

    600-WRAP-UP.
        MOVE SPACES TO PRINT-REC.
        WRITE PRINT-REC
            AFTER ADVANCING TO-TOP-OF-PAGE.
        CLOSE CONTRACT
            CONTRACT-REPORT.
```

FIGURE 8.18(d)

values for the discount rate and the destination. These entries are defined as follows in the program:

```
    01  COMM-FIELDS.
        05  COMM-KEY              PIC 9(02).
        05  COMM-DESTINATION      PIC X(15).
        05  COMM-RATE             PIC V99.
```

The prefix COMM is used to indicate that these are communication fields; that is, they are being communicated to and from the subprogram. There is no standard practice for this prefix, so you may decide on some other descriptive term in your programs; but the point is to clearly identify entries that will be used by the CALL statement and the subprogram.

100-MAINLINE   The mainline logic controls the program's operation. It performs the initialization module, does the process loop until end of file is reached, and wraps up program execution with the final paragraph.

200-INITIALIZE   Initialize opens the input and output files and performs the first read statement.

250-READ   This paragraph reads each input record from the contract file and tests for the occurrence of end of file.

300-PROCESS   The process paragraph takes care of the processing of each input record. First, the fields that communicate with the subprogram are initialized, and then the CALL is issued to pass control to the table subprogram.

```
MOVE SPACES          TO COMM-FIELDS.
MOVE PACKAGE-KEY     TO COMM-KEY.
CALL 'TABLE8'
     USING COMM-FIELDS.
```

Notice that only the name of the group item is needed in the CALL and therefore only one name is supplied as an argument. The paragraph next calculates the values for the travel contract.

```
MULTIPLY CONTRACT-PRICE BY COMM-RATE
     GIVING DISCOUNT-AMOUNT.
SUBTRACT DISCOUNT-AMOUNT FROM CONTRACT-PRICE
     GIVING DISCOUNT-PRICE.
MULTIPLY DISCOUNT-PRICE BY TICKETS
     GIVING NET-PRICE.
```

Process finishes by performing the next paragraph (400-PRINT-CONTRACT) to print the contents of the customer's contract and then reads the next input record.

400-PRINT-CONTRACT   This paragraph is performed each time a contract page is to be printed. Although the paragraph is quite long, it is fundamentally simple. Basically, it consists of MOVE and WRITE statements to print each line of the report. Because there are many heading and detail lines in this report, a lot of these seemingly repetitious but necessary statements are used.

600-WRAP-UP   When all the input records have been read and each contract has been printed, this paragraph completes the program run. The printer is first advanced to a new page and then the files are closed. Program control returns from this paragraph to the mainline where the program is terminated.

PROGRAM CODING: SUBPROGRAM

The main purpose of the subprogram (Figure 8.19) is to look up the package key in a table and supply the calling program with a discount percentage and a destination. The

```
IDENTIFICATION DIVISION.

PROGRAM-ID.
    TABLE8.
*AUTHOR.
*    JOHNATHAN YOUNGMAN.
*INSTALLATION.
*    SALES UNLIMITED CORP.
*DATE-WRITTEN.
*    SEPTEMBER 6.
*DATE-COMPILED.

*SECURITY.
*    NONE.

ENVIRONMENT DIVISION.

CONFIGURATION SECTION.
SOURCE-COMPUTER.
    IBM-4381.
OBJECT-COMPUTER.
    IBM-4381.
```

FIGURE 8.19(a)   COBOL code for the table subprogram

```
DATA DIVISION.
WORKING-STORAGE SECTION.

01   OTHER-ITEMS.
     05   FOUND-FLAG              PIC X(03)   VALUE 'NO'.
          88   FOUND                          VALUE 'YES'.
          88   NOT-FOUND                      VALUE 'NO'.

01   TABLE-ENTRIES.
     05   FILLER     PIC X(19)   VALUE '21MIAMI          10'.
     05   FILLER     PIC X(19)   VALUE '23MEXICO CITY    13'.
     05   FILLER     PIC X(19)   VALUE '27NASSAU         12'.
     05   FILLER     PIC X(19)   VALUE '30ST. VINCENT    15'.
     05   FILLER     PIC X(19)   VALUE '31SAN PEDRO      11'.
     05   FILLER     PIC X(19)   VALUE '33DALLAS         07'.
     05   FILLER     PIC X(19)   VALUE '39VIRGIN ISLANDS 10'.
     05   FILLER     PIC X(19)   VALUE '40MIAMI          10'.
     05   FILLER     PIC X(19)   VALUE '45RIO DE JANEIRO 20'.
     05   FILLER     PIC X(19)   VALUE '47CANARY ISLANDS 14'.
     05   FILLER     PIC X(19)   VALUE '50TAHITI         05'.
     05   FILLER     PIC X(19)   VALUE '72SAN DIEGO      12'.
01   TABLE-ENTRIES-2 REDEFINES TABLE-ENTRIES.
     05   TRAVEL-TABLE OCCURS 12 TIMES
               INDEXED BY TRAVEL-INDEX.
          10   TRAVEL-KEY    PIC 99.
          10   TRAVEL-DEST   PIC X(15).
          10   TRAVEL-RATE   PIC V99.

LINKAGE SECTION.

01   LINK-FIELDS.
     05   LINK-KEY           PIC 9(02).
     05   LINK-DEST          PIC X(15).
     05   LINK-RATE          PIC V99.

PROCEDURE DIVISION USING LINK-FIELDS.

100-MAINLINE.
     PERFORM 200-INITIALIZE.
     PERFORM 300-SEARCH THRU 300-SEARCH-EXIT.
     IF NOT-FOUND
          MOVE SPACES TO LINK-DEST
          MOVE ZERO   TO LINK-RATE.
     EXIT PROGRAM.

200-INITIALIZE.
     MOVE 'NO' TO FOUND-FLAG.

300-SEARCH.
     SET TRAVEL-INDEX TO 1.
     SEARCH TRAVEL-TABLE
          AT END MOVE 'NO' TO FOUND-FLAG
          WHEN LINK-KEY = TRAVEL-KEY (TRAVEL-INDEX)
               MOVE 'YES' TO FOUND-FLAG
               MOVE TRAVEL-DEST (TRAVEL-INDEX) TO LINK-DEST
               MOVE TRAVEL-RATE (TRAVEL-INDEX) TO LINK-RATE.

300-SEARCH-EXIT.
     EXIT.
```

FIGURE 8.19(b)

table consists of these three values: a key, discount, and destination. Because we will be using the SEARCH feature, the table is set up as follows with an INDEX allocated to the table entries.

```
01   TABLE-ENTRIES.
     05   FILLER     PIC X(19)   VALUE '21MIAMI          10'.
     05   FILLER     PIC X(19)   VALUE '23MEXICO CITY    13'.
     05   FILLER     PIC X(19)   VALUE '27NASSAU         12'.
     05   FILLER     PIC X(19)   VALUE '30ST. VINCENT    15'.
```

```
05  FILLER        PIC X(19)    VALUE '31SAN PEDRO       11'.
05  FILLER        PIC X(19)    VALUE '33DALLAS          07'.
05  FILLER        PIC X(19)    VALUE '39VIRGIN ISLANDS 10'.
05  FILLER        PIC X(19)    VALUE '40MIAMI           10'.
05  FILLER        PIC X(19)    VALUE '45RIO DE JANEIRO 20'.
05  FILLER        PIC X(19)    VALUE '47CANARY ISLANDS 14'.
05  FILLER        PIC X(19)    VALUE '50TAHITI          05'.
05  FILLER        PIC X(19)    VALUE '72SAN DIEGO       12'.
01  TABLE-ENTRIES-2 REDEFINES TABLE-ENTRIES
    05  TRAVEL-TABLE OCCURS 12 TIMES
            INDEXED BY TRAVEL-INDEX.
        10  TRAVEL-KEY    PIC 99.
        10  TRAVEL-DEST   PIC X(15).
        10  TRAVEL-RATE   PIC V99.
```

Because this is a subprogram, a LINKAGE SECTION is necessary. The entries in this section must correspond to the argument(s) supplied in the CALL statement of the calling program, although the names of the fields may be different as in this case.

```
LINKAGE SECTION.

01  LINK-FIELDS.
    05  LINK-KEY          PIC 9(02).
    05  LINK-DEST         PIC X(15).
    05  LINK-RATE         PIC V99.
```

The PROCEDURE statement must make reference to the LINKAGE SECTION and is done so in the following fashion in this subprogram.

```
PROCEDURE DIVISION USING LINK-FIELDS.
```

100-MAINLINE   The mainline of the subprogram initializes the flags used in the program. Then the paragraph 300-SEARCH is performed to search the table for a matching key entry. If an entry was found, all is well; but if there was no matching entry, then the paragraph moves zero to the discount rate and spaces to the destination field. Finally, the EXIT PROGRAM statement is used to leave the subprogram and return to the calling program with the new data.

200-INITIALIZE   This paragraph takes care of initializing any fields that the subprogram is dependent on. In this application, only the FOUND-FLAG needs to be initialized, but in some applications initialization of fields can be an extensive operation.

300-SEARCH   This paragraph searches the table for a matching key entry. If an entry is not found, the value 'NO' is moved to the FOUND-FLAG. On finding a matching key, 'YES' is moved to the flag and the related discount value and destination are moved to the LINKAGE SECTION fields. Setting the flag in either case is important, because the program must either move the data that are found in the table to the linkage section or it must return a zero for the discount and spaces for the destination. Using the flag determines which action is to be taken. In some programs the flag is passed back to the calling program, but returning known data values is a preferred method.

PROGRAM TESTING

Testing a COBOL program that uses a subprogram requires some special considerations. Exactly what is required will depend on your system and any special software that might be in place for testing student programs. Usually, some additional job control statements will be necessary when a subprogram is used, but your instructor or computer center will be able to supply the necessary details.

Test data for this program are shown in Figure 8.20. When the program is run, there is no specific evidence that a subprogram is in use. The two programs will run together as a unit, and the report is printed in the same manner as expected from a single program. The output from this run is shown in Figure 8.21.

```
1203356J.L. SMITH    205 SPRING RD.    BELFOREST RI 23709  8012356701062500027011287
1203445G.T. WILSON  15 BELL COURT      TREMONT  SD  70110  2104926712120000150022787
1203546L.L. ABLE     210 TRADE ST.     WILMONT  PA  49122  4237768292050000312011587
1312300Q.B. BRAVO    1 FIRST ST.       CHICAGO  IL  23501  2014426380650950445020187
1312301R. TRAVELER  101 WEST AVE.      BURBANK  CA  41101  2052340000125000233021387
1504000D.C. LESSAC  410 BAY DR.        TORONTO  ONT M9S 2D4 4167678891240000250010287
```

FIGURE 8.20   Test data for the travel contract program

```
                          PACKAGE CONTRACT

CUSTOMER NUMBER    AGENCY NUMBER       DATE        PACKAGE    DESTINATION
     3356               120          01/12/87        27       NASSAU


NAME AND ADDRESS                PHONE

J.L. SMITH                      801 235 6701
205 SPRING RD.
BELFOREST RI 23709

CONTRACT       DISCOUNT      DISCOUNT       DISCOUNTED    NO. OF       NET
 PRICE            %           AMOUNT          PRICE       TICKETS     PRICE

 625.00          12           75.00          550.00         2       1,100.00
```

```
                          PACKAGE CONTRACT

CUSTOMER NUMBER    AGENCY NUMBER       DATE        PACKAGE    DESTINATION
     3445               120          02/27/87        50       TAHITI


NAME AND ADDRESS                PHONE

G.T. WILSON                     210 492 6712
15 BELL COURT
TREMONT SD 70110

CONTRACT       DISCOUNT      DISCOUNT       DISCOUNTED    NO. OF       NET
 PRICE            %           AMOUNT          PRICE       TICKETS     PRICE

1,200.00          5           60.00         1,140.00         1       1,140.00
```

FIGURE 8.21(a)   Contracts printed by the travel program

```
                          PACKAGE CONTRACT

   CUSTOMER NUMBER   AGENCY NUMBER      DATE        PACKAGE      DESTINATION
        3546              120        01/15/87         12


   NAME AND ADDRESS                    PHONE

   L.L. ABLE                       423 776 8292
   210 TRADE ST.
   WILMONT PA 49122

   CONTRACT       DISCOUNT      DISCOUNT      DISCOUNTED     NO. OF        NET
    PRICE            %           AMOUNT         PRICE        TICKETS      PRICE

    500.00                        0.00         500.00          3        1,500.00
```

```
                          PACKAGE CONTRACT

   CUSTOMER NUMBER   AGENCY NUMBER      DATE        PACKAGE      DESTINATION
        2300              131        02/01/87         45       RIO DE JANEIRO


   NAME AND ADDRESS                    PHONE

   Q.B. BRAVO                      201 444 2638
   1 FIRST ST.
   CHICAGO IL 23501

   CONTRACT       DISCOUNT      DISCOUNT      DISCOUNTED     NO. OF        NET
    PRICE            %           AMOUNT         PRICE        TICKETS      PRICE

    650.95          20           130.19        520.76          4        2,083.04
```

FIGURE 8.21(b)

```
                          PACKAGE CONTRACT

CUSTOMER NUMBER   AGENCY NUMBER      DATE         PACKAGE    DESTINATION
    2301               131         02/13/87         33       DALLAS


NAME AND ADDRESS                PHONE

R. TRAVELER                  205 234 0000
101 WEST AVE.
BURBANK CA 41101

CONTRACT      DISCOUNT      DISCOUNT      DISCOUNTED    NO. OF        NET
 PRICE           %          AMOUNT          PRICE      TICKETS      PRICE

1,250.00         7           87.50        1,162.50        2       2,325.00
```

```
                          PACKAGE CONTRACT

CUSTOMER NUMBER   AGENCY NUMBER      DATE         PACKAGE    DESTINATION
    4000               150         01/02/87         50       TAHITI


NAME AND ADDRESS                PHONE

D.C. LESSAC                  416 767 8891
410 BAY DR.
TORONTO ONT M9S 2D4

CONTRACT      DISCOUNT      DISCOUNT      DISCOUNTED    NO. OF        NET
 PRICE           %          AMOUNT          PRICE      TICKETS      PRICE

2,400.00         5          120.00        2,280.00        2       4,560.00
```

FIGURE 8.21(c)

SUMMARY

Subprograms are needed in large applications so that the work of several programmers may be combined in a single programming project. Subprograms may also be tested independently and then run as a system when module testing is complete. Using subprograms also helps to avoid the duplication of code and reduces the possibility of introducing errors when changes are made to the program.

The calling program invokes the subprogram with a CALL statement and passes data to the subprogram through the LINKAGE SECTION. The subprogram may also return data to the calling program through the LINKAGE SECTION fields common to both modules. The called subprogram returns to the calling program when the EXIT PROGRAM statement is reached.

The CALL statement that invokes the subprogram uses a literal to define the name of the subprogram. The USING clause identifies the fields containing data that are to be provided to the subprogram. These names will be found in the calling program's WORKING-STORAGE SECTION and will correspond to identifiers in the subprogram's LINKAGE SECTION, although the names may be different.

Each subprogram must contain a LINKAGE SECTION after the WORKING-STOR-AGE SECTION. Entries in the LINKAGE SECTION must correspond by position to entries in the USING clause of the CALL in the calling program. The entries may use different names, but data lengths and formats must be identical. The subprogram will also use the USING entry in the PROCEDURE DIVISION statement. This entry defines the fields that are used in the LINKAGE SECTION.

At the end of the subprogram is the EXIT PROGRAM statement, which returns control to the calling program. If the subprogram has opened any files for use, they should be closed before reaching the EXIT PROGRAM statement.

TERMS TO STUDY

CALL	Main program
EXIT PROGRAM	PROCEDURE DIVISION USING
LINKAGE SECTION	Subprogram

REVIEW QUESTIONS

TRUE/FALSE

1. Subprograms can be useful when they are used to break up a large program into a main program that calls one or more subprograms.

2. The subprogram must always be smaller in size than the main program.

3. Using subprograms will automatically reduce the number of errors made by the programmer.

4. Data are passed from the calling program to the subprogram. The subprogram may in turn return data to the calling program.

5. The CALL statement transfers control from the main program to the subprogram.

6. Both the calling program and the subprogram must use a LINKAGE SECTION as part of their DATA divisions.

7. The USING clause in the CALL statement identifies the subprogram to be called.

8. The RETURN statement is used in the subprogram to return control back to the calling program.

9. The LINKAGE SECTION supplies a link between the data in the main program that are to be used by the subprogram.

10. Only the PROCEDURE DIVISION of the calling program will have a USING clause.

FILL IN THE BLANK

11. The _____ statement is used to pass control from the main program to a subprogram.

12. Control will always be returned to the _____ program after a subprogram has completed execution.

13. In the statement

```
CALL 'QUERY' USING CUSTOMER-NO REGION-NO.
```

the entry 'QUERY' is the name of the _____ that is to be used by this program.

14. The names CUSTOMER-NO and REGION-NO in the previous question refer to _____ that are defined in the current program.

15. A subprogram must always have a _____ _____ to receive and return data from and to the calling program.

16. The _____ clause of the PROCEDURE DIVISION identifies the data that are received by the subprogram and data that are to be returned.

17. The statement _____ _____ is used to return control from the subprogram to the calling program.

18. A _____ SECTION may not be necessary in a subprogram.

MULTIPLE CHOICE

19. Which of the following statements are true of subprograms?
    a. A subprogram must be invoked by a calling program.
    b. There may be more than one subprogram used in an application.
    c. Data may be passed to and from the subprogram.
    d. a and b.
    e. a and c.
    f. a, b, and c.

20. What statement will contain both a program name and at least one identifier?
    a. CALL
    b. PERFORM
    c. PROCEDURE
    d. PROGRAM-ID

21. The USING clause in the CALL statement performs a specific purpose in the calling program. What is it?
    a. It identifies each subprogram that is used.
    b. It identifies data being passed to and from the subprogram.
    c. It is an optional entry that is seldom required.
    d. It identifies the address to return to after the subprogram has finished its operation.

22. The LINKAGE SECTION appears in what location?
    a. The DATA DIVISION.
    b. The subprogram.
    c. The main program.
    d. a and b.
    e. a and c.
    f. a, b, and c.

23. Select a statement that would correctly invoke the subprogram called BILLING that passes a customer record called CUST-RECORD and returns a flag called OK-FLAG.
    a. CALL BILLING (CUST-RECORD, OK-FLAG).
    b. CALL 'BILLING (CUST-RECORD, OK-FLAG)'.
    c. CALL 'BILLING' USING (CUST-RECORD OK-FLAG).
    d. CALL 'BILLING' USING CUST-RECORD OK-FLAG.

24. The PROCEDURE DIVISION USING statement will contain names that are identified in what statement or area?
    a. CALL statement.
    b. LINKAGE SECTION.
    c. WORKING-STORAGE SECTION.
    d. PROGRAM-ID.

1. Revise the discount program and the table subprogram to include the following changes: A new value in the table provides an airline code; this value is to be included on the contract report as shown in the revised layout. The destination on the report should show the entry (NOT IDENTIFIED) if no matching table entry was found by the subprogram. Otherwise, the actual destination will be shown.

PROGRAMMING SPECIFICATIONS	1 of 1
PROGRAM NAME: Discount Table Subprogram	PROGRAM ID: TABLE8
(revised specifications)	
PREPARED BY: Diane Quest	DATE: Sept. 12

Program Description:
   The subprogram is to be revised to include an airline code in the table.
Input File(s):
   None
Output File(s):
   None
Program Requirements:
   1. This subprogram receives a two-digit package key value from the calling program.
   2. Look up the key in a table of values in the following format.

Key	Destination	Rate	Airline
21	MIAMI	10	EASTERN
23	MEXICO CITY	13	TWA
27	NASSAU	12	NASSAU AIR
30	ST. VINCENT	15	AIR BAHAMA
31	SAN PEDRO	11	AIR JAMAICA
33	DALLAS	07	CONTINENTAL
39	VIRGIN ISLANDS	10	EASTERN
40	MIAMI	10	US AIR
45	RIO DE JANEIRO	20	UNITED
47	CANARY ISLANDS	14	AIR FRANCE
50	TAHITI	05	QUANTIS
72	SAN DIEGO	12	AMERICAN

```
  0         1         2         3         4         5         6         7
  1234567890123456789012345678901234567890123456789012345678901234567890123 45

                         PACKAGE CONTRACT

CUSTOMER NUMBER    AGENCY NUMBER       DATE        PACKAGE     DESTINATION
     9999               XXX          99/99/99         99       (NOT IDENTIFIED)


NAME AND ADDRESS                  PHONE             AIRLINE

X----------X               999 999 9999            X------------------X
X-----------------X
X-----------------X


CONTRACT       DISCOUNT       DISCOUNT       DISCOUNTED     NO. OF        NET
  PRICE           %            AMOUNT          PRICE        TICKETS      PRICE

 Z,ZZ9.99         Z9         Z,ZZ9.99       ZZ,ZZ9.99         Z9       ZZ,ZZ9.99
```

2. This exercise was originally presented in the first book of this series *Introduction to Structured COBOL and Program Design*. It has been revised here to include a subprogram as part of its requirements.

In the report, which you are to design, print all the input data and any error messages necessary to communicate to the user any problems that you found in the data. Also, print a value for taxable income if all input fields are numeric. Taxable income is found by subtracting federal pension, registered pension, personal deductions, medical, and charitable from the total earnings. Design the report format, prepare a structure chart and pseudo code, and write, test, and debug the main program and subprogram for this assignment.

PROGRAMMING SPECIFICATIONS	1 of 1
PROGRAM NAME: Income Tax Validation	PROGRAM ID: VALID8
PREPARED BY: Diane Quest	DATE: Sept. 13

Program Description:
   The income tax reporting file for the country of Iberia is to be validated and an edit report prepared according to the specifications given below.

Input File(s):
   Tax file

Output File(s):
   Validation report

Program Requirements:
   1. Read each input tax record and check each field for the presence of valid data.
   2. Error evaluation is based on the following criteria:
      a) All fields must contain only numeric data.
      b) Social insurance number must contain a valid modulus-11 check digit in the units position. This checking will be done in a called subprogram.
      c) Total earnings must not exceed $100,000.00 for this file. Higher earnings are handled in another system not described here.
   3. If all fields check out to be numeric, proceed with the following checks.
      a) Registered pension must not exceed federal pension.
      b) Personal deductions must not exceed 5% of total earnings.
      c) Charitable donations are not to exceed 30% of total earnings.
      d) The total of all deductions (federal pension, registered pension, tax, personal deductions, medical, and charitable) must not exceed total earnings.

INPUT/OUTPUT RECORD DEFINITION				
File: Tax reporting		File Type: Disk		
Sequence: Social insurance number		Blocking: 5		

COLUMNS	FIELD	TYPE	LENGTH	DECIMALS
1–9	Social ins. number	N	9	
10–17	Total earnings	N	8	2
18–22	Federal pension	N	5	2
23–27	Registered pension	N	5	2
28–34	Tax deducted	N	7	2
35–41	Personal deduction	N	7	2
42–48	Medical	N	7	2
49–55	Charitable	N	7	2

PROGRAM NAME: Modulus-11 Subprogram Check   PROGRAM ID: MODULUS
PREPARED BY: Diane Quest   DATE: Sept. 13

Program Description:

    This subprogram does a modulus-11 check on a field passed to it from the calling program. It is to be written to handle any field, not just the social insurance number used in this exercise.

Input File(s):

    None

Output File(s):

    None

Program Requirements:

    Receive a numeric field and check its contents to ensure that it contains a modulus-11 check digit. If the field checks out correctly, return a flag value of 'Yes'; otherwise, return a value 'NO'.

Computing a Modulus-11 Check Digit

for

Social Security Number 145683725

1. A factor is assigned to each digit of the number. The factor begins with 2 for the units position and is increased by 1 for each position until the factor of 7 is reached. Then the factor is repeated beginning with 2.

Number	1	4	5	6	8	3	7	2	5
Factor	4	3	2	7	6	5	4	3	2

2. Multiply each digit by its assigned factor.

Number	1	4	5	6	8	3	7	2	5
Factor	4	3	2	7	6	5	4	3	2
Product	4	12	10	42	48	15	28	6	10

3. Find the sum of the products.

$4 + 12 + 10 + 42 + 48 + 15 + 28 + 6 + 10 = 175$

4. Divide the sum by 11 to get a remainder.

$175 / 11 = 15$ Remainder 10

5. Subtract the remainder from 11 to get the check digit.

$11 - 10 = 1$

COBOL'S REPORT WRITER FEATURE

One objective of contemporary programming is to reduce the time it takes to write programs and to implement them error free. To achieve these objectives, most installations are using structured design and programming techniques. However, another way these objectives are being met is through the use of fourth-generation languages. These are **nonprocedural languages** that do not require writing the usual type of program logic that we have been accustomed to using. By using one of these languages, programmers become more productive and programs are implemented with lower error rates.

COBOL's report writer feature may be thought of as a type of fourth-generation language that is used within the context of a COBOL program. In reality, the report writer is not a fourth-generation language; in fact, it has preceded these languages by at least a decade. But it does have many of the characteristics of a nonprocedural language, which makes it a useful part of the programmer's repertoire.

TYPES OF REPORTS

The report writer feature provides an easy way to create traditional reports with headings, detail lines, and control break totals. By using report writer, the programmer need only supply the format of the report and the names of identifiers to be used in the DATA DIVISION and a few statements to generate the report in the PROCEDURE DIVISION. The COBOL program will generate all detail lines, accumulate totals, check for control breaks, print total lines, and reset the totals, without any direction from the programmer. While this may seem a bit mysterious, we will see that it all happens very naturally when a program is written with the report writer.

Reports created by the report writer look no different from a report printed in the usual manner. The report in Figure 9.1 was produced by a COBOL program using the report writer. This report contains many of the characteristics we would expect of any report. It has a report heading, page headings with a page number, detail lines consisting of input data, and calculated values. There is a control break on the region number field when a region total is printed, and a report total is given at the end.

```
                       SALES UNLIMITED CORPORATION

                     ITEM SALES REPORT                    PAGE NO.  1

    REGION       ITEM      DESCRIPTION       QUANTITY      UNIT          TOTAL
    NUMBER       NUMBER                                    COST          COST


      10         1234      LAMP                  5        16.99          84.95
      10         1234      LAMP                 12        16.99         203.88
      10         1975      KNIFE BLOCK          20        12.69         253.80
      10         2631      DOOR LOCK            10        18.49         184.90

                                             REGION TOTAL              727.53


      12         1234      LAMP                 20        16.99         339.80
      12         1809      TENNIS RACQUET        4        29.99         119.96
      12         1809      TENNIS RACQUET       10        29.99         299.90
      12         1975      KNIFE BLOCK          15        12.69         190.35
      12         2631      DOOR LOCK             6        18.49         110.94

                                             REGION TOTAL            1,060.95


      15         1234      LAMP                 15        16.99         254.85
      15         1809      TENNIS RACQUET        3        29.99          89.97
      15         1975      KNIFE BLOCK           8        12.69         101.52
      15         2631      DOOR LOCK            11        18.49         203.39

                                             REGION TOTAL              649.73


                                             REPORT TOTAL            2,438.21
```

FIGURE 9.1 Sales report created by a program using the report writer

Individual fields in the report, such as quantity, unit cost, and total cost, are edited with zero suppression and decimal insertion as required. Spacing between fields and between lines is also under the programmer's control through the report writer specifications.

Almost all the above characteristics are controlled by entries in the REPORT SECTION, which is part of the DATA DIVISION. These are all newly defined statements in COBOL, which will be identified in this chapter. A few additional statements are required in the PROCEDURE DIVISION to complete the use of the report writer.

A BRIEF LOOK AT A PROGRAM USING REPORT WRITER

The program in Figure 9.2 was used to create the sales report. There are several features to observe in the program for now, and then we will discuss in detail the various components of the report writer in COBOL. Much of the content of this program will appear different from previous programs, so let's take a quick tour through it.

The first difference to note is the use of the entry REPORT IS SALES-REPORT in the FD for the REPORT-FILE. This entry identifies the use of an RD in the REPORT SECTION. The REPORT SECTION is a new section that always follows the WORKING-STORAGE SECTION in the program.

An RD (report definition) identifies a specific report in the REPORT SECTION.

```
      IDENTIFICATION DIVISION.

      PROGRAM-ID.
          ITEM09.
     *AUTHOR.
     *    JONATHAN YOUNGMAN.
     *INSTALLATION.
     *    SALES UNLIMITED CORP.
     *DATE-WRITTEN.
     *    SEPTEMBER 15.
     *DATE-COMPILED.
     *    SEPTEMBER 15.
     *SECURITY.
     *    NONE.
     *REMARKS.
     *    THIS PROGRAM PRODUCES THE ITEM SALES REPORT.

      ENVIRONMENT DIVISION.

      CONFIGURATION SECTION.
      SOURCE-COMPUTER.
          IBM-4381.
      OBJECT-COMPUTER.
          IBM-4381.
      INPUT-OUTPUT SECTION.
      FILE-CONTROL.
          SELECT SALES-IN     ASSIGN TO SYS001-UT-3340-S-FILEA.
          SELECT REPORT-FILE ASSIGN TO SYS005-UR-1403-S.

      DATA DIVISION.

      FILE SECTION.

      FD  SALES-IN
          RECORD CONTAINS 80 CHARACTERS
          BLOCK CONTAINS 5 RECORDS
          LABEL RECORDS ARE OMITTED
          DATA RECORD IS SALES-REC.
      01  SALES-REC.
          05  FILLER                    PIC X(80).

      FD  REPORT-FILE
          RECORD CONTAINS 133 CHARACTERS
          LABEL RECORDS ARE OMITTED
          REPORT IS SALES-REPORT.

      WORKING-STORAGE SECTION.

      01  OTHER-DATA.
          05  EOF-FLAG               PIC 9          VALUE ZERO.
          05  TOTAL-COST             PIC 9(04)V99   VALUE ZERO.

      01  INPUT-RECORD.
          05  REGION-IN              PIC 9(02).
          05  ITEM-IN                PIC 9(04).
          05  DESCRIPTION-IN         PIC X(15).
          05  QUANTITY-IN            PIC 9(03).
          05  UNIT-COST-IN           PIC 9(03)V99.
          05  FILLER                 PIC X(11).

      REPORT SECTION.

      RD  SALES-REPORT
          CONTROLS ARE FINAL REGION-IN
          PAGE LIMIT IS 55 LINES
          HEADING 1
          FIRST DETAIL 8
          LAST DETAIL 48
          FOOTING 50.
```

FIGURE 9.2(a) A COBOL program using the report writer feature

```
01   TYPE IS REPORT HEADING.
     05   LINE NUMBER IS 1
          COLUMN NUMBER IS 25
          PICTURE IS X(27)
          VALUE IS 'SALES UNLIMITED CORPORATION'.

01   TYPE IS PAGE HEADING.
     05   LINE NUMBER IS 3.
          10   COLUMN NUMBER IS 30
               PICTURE IS X(17)
               VALUE IS 'ITEM SALES REPORT'.
          10   COLUMN NUMBER IS 66
               PICTURE IS X(08)
               VALUE IS 'PAGE NO.'.
          10   COLUMN NUMBER IS 75
               PICTURE IS Z9
               SOURCE PAGE-COUNTER.
     05   LINE NUMBER IS 5.
          10   COLUMN NUMBER IS 1
               PICTURE IS X(41)
               VALUE IS
               'REGION      ITEM        DESCRIPTION'.
          10   COLUMN NUMBER IS 41
               PICTURE IS X(35)
               VALUE IS
               'QUANTITY       UNIT            TOTAL'.

     05   LINE NUMBER IS 6.
          10   COLUMN NUMBER IS 1
               PICTURE IS X(16)
               VALUE IS 'NUMBER    NUMBER'.
          10   COLUMN NUMBER IS 56
               PICTURE IS X(20)
               VALUE IS 'COST            COST'.

01   DETAIL-LINE TYPE IS DETAIL
               LINE NUMBER IS PLUS 1.
     05   COLUMN IS 2
               PICTURE IS 9(02)
               SOURCE IS REGION-IN.
     05   COLUMN IS 11
               PICTURE IS 9(04)
               SOURCE IS ITEM-IN.
     05   COLUMN IS 21
               PICTURE IS X(15)
               SOURCE IS DESCRIPTION-IN.
     05   COLUMN IS 42
               PICTURE IS ZZ9
               SOURCE IS QUANTITY-IN.
     05   COLUMN IS 54
               PICTURE IS ZZ9.99
               SOURCE IS UNIT-COST-IN.
     05   COLUMN IS 68
               PICTURE IS Z,ZZ9.99
               SOURCE IS TOTAL-COST.

01   TYPE IS CONTROL FOOTING REGION-IN.
     05   LINE NUMBER IS PLUS 2.
          10   COLUMN IS 41
               PICTURE IS X(12)
               VALUE IS 'REGION TOTAL'.
          10   REGION-TOTAL
               COLUMN IS 67
               PICTURE IS ZZ,ZZ9.99
               SUM TOTAL-COST.

01   TYPE IS CONTROL FOOTING FINAL.
     05   LINE NUMBER IS PLUS 2.
          10   COLUMN IS 41
               PICTURE IS X(12)
               VALUE IS 'REPORT TOTAL'.
          10   COLUMN IS 67
               PICTURE IS ZZ,ZZ9.99
               SUM REGION-TOTAL.
```

FIGURE 9.2(b)

```
PROCEDURE DIVISION.

000-MAINLINE.
    PERFORM 100-INITIALIZE.
    PERFORM 300-PROCESS-SALES
        UNTIL EOF-FLAG = 1.
    PERFORM 400-WRAP-UP.
    STOP RUN.

100-INITIALIZE.
    OPEN INPUT  SALES-IN
         OUTPUT REPORT-FILE.
    INITIATE SALES-REPORT.
    PERFORM 200-READ-DATA.

200-READ-DATA.
    READ SALES-IN INTO INPUT-RECORD
        AT END MOVE 1 TO EOF-FLAG.

300-PROCESS-SALES.
    MULTIPLY QUANTITY-IN BY UNIT-COST-IN
        GIVING TOTAL-COST.
    GENERATE DETAIL-LINE.
    PERFORM 200-READ-DATA.

400-WRAP-UP.
    TERMINATE SALES-REPORT.
    CLOSE SALES-IN
          REPORT-FILE.
```

FIGURE 9.2(c)

It is possible to have more than one report, but we will restrict ourselves to one here. The RD identifies some basic characteristics of the report, such as the control break fields, the number of lines on the page, where the heading line is printed, and where the detail lines will begin and end.

Following the RD are a number of entries that look deceivingly like record description entries and in reality have many similar characteristics. The first line of each of these entries tells the report writer what type of line is being printed. For this report, the following types of lines are used:

Type	Use in the Report
REPORT HEADING	First heading in the report. Appears only on the first page.
PAGE HEADING	Next three heading lines, which will appear on each page of the report.
DETAIL	Describes the format and content of each detail line.
CONTROL FOOTING REGION-IN	Defines the total line to be printed when a region control break occurs.
CONTROL FOOTING FINAL	Defines the total line to print at the end of the report.

Each of these line types has certain specifications and options that are used to control the appearance and content of the output. Some commonly used entries are the following: COLUMN NUMBER, which defines the column at which a given field prints (no FILLER entries are needed here); LINE NUMBER, which defines the line or relative line number at which a line of output will be printed; PICTURE, which is written in the same way as it was for other printed output. Other keywords used are VALUE, which provides a literal value, SOURCE, which specifies the identifier that contains a value you want to print, and SUM, which identifies a total.

Finally, the PROCEDURE DIVISION contains three new statements, **INITIATE,**

GENERATE, and **TERMINATE,** that are used with the report writer feature. Notice from the program that the PROCEDURE DIVISION does not contain the usual logic required for report production. Some looping is necessary for reading the input file, but lacking is the code for most calculations, control break testing, moving fields, and writing print lines.

FD ENTRIES FOR THE REPORT FILE

```
DATA DIVISION.

FILE SECTION.
FD file-name
    BLOCK CONTAINS integer-1   RECORDS
    RECORD CONTAINS integer-2   CHARACTERS
    LABEL {RECORD IS    } {STANDARD}
          {RECORDS ARE}  {OMITTED }
    {REPORT IS  }
    {REPORTS ARE}      report-name-1      [report-name-2   . . .].
```

This FD entry should look familiar because it is the same as that used for other reports with one important difference. That difference is the REPORT IS entry. This entry refers to the name of the report that will be included as an RD in the REPORT SECTION. All other entries for this FD should be made in the same way as for any printed report. An FD entry for a report must not include a record description entry that is common for other FDs in the FILE SECTION.

The following FD was used in the sales report:

```
FD   REPORT-FILE
     RECORD CONTAINS 133 CHARACTERS
     LABEL RECORDS ARE OMITTED
     REPORT IS SALES-REPORT.
```

The file name REPORT-FILE refers to the file as described in the SELECT clause of the INPUT-OUTPUT SECTION. This file will be opened and closed in the usual way in the PROCEDURE DIVISION. The RECORD CONTAINS and LABEL RECORDS clauses are written in the expected manner for a report. Finally, the REPORT IS entry refers to the report SALES-REPORT, which will be described in the RD.

THE REPORT SECTION

```
REPORT SECTION.
RD report-name
    {CONTROL IS  } {data-name-1    [, data-name-2]   . . .            }
    {CONTROLS ARE} {FINAL   [, data-name-1   [, data-name-2]   . . .]}
    [PAGE [LIMIT IS   ] integer-1 [LINE ]
          [LIMITS ARE]           [LINES]
    [HEADING      integer-2]
    [FIRST DETAIL integer-3]              [LAST DETAIL   integer-4]
    [FOOTING integer-5]]    .
{report-group-description-entry}      . . .]      . . .]
```

The **REPORT SECTION** defines the specific details for the contents of the report. For each report (there may be more than one), there will be an RD entry followed by a series of report group description entries.

RD ENTRY

The **RD** (report description) entry identifies the control breaks that will be used in the report in the CONTROL clause. These entries are made from major to minor order. If a control total is required at the report end, the keyword **FINAL** will be the first entry, followed by the identifiers of other fields that identify control breaks. In the example program, the only control break occurs on the REGION-IN field, but a final break is also needed. Therefore, both FINAL and REGION-IN are specified as Figure 9.3 shows.

```
RD   SALES-REPORT
     CONTROLS ARE FINAL REGION-IN
     PAGE LIMIT IS 55 LINES
     HEADING 1
     FIRST DETAIL 8
     LAST DETAIL 48
     FOOTING 50.
```

FIGURE 9.3   An RD entry in the REPORT SECTION

The remainder of the RD entry defines the distribution of lines on the report. PAGE LIMIT indicates how many total lines are available on the page. HEADING indicates where the heading lines will begin. FIRST DETAIL and LAST DETAIL identify the range of lines that will be used for detail lines in the report, and FOOTING indicates the line where a page footer may begin if it is used. Figure 9.4 shows pictorially the allocation of these lines.

```
HEADING──────→              SALES UNLIMITED CORPORATION              ←REPORT HEADING

                         ITEM SALES REPORT              PAGE NO. 1 ┐
                                                                   │
               REGION   ITEM    DESCRIPTION   QUANTITY     UNIT    │ TOTAL   } PAGE HEADING
               NUMBER   NUMBER                             COST    │ COST
                                                                   ┘
FIRST DETAIL─→ 10       1234    LAMP             5       16.99      84.95   ←DETAIL LINE
               10       1234    LAMP            12       16.99     203.88
               10       1975    KNIFE BLOCK     20       12.69     253.80
               10       2631    DOOR LOCK       10       18.49     184.90

                                REGION TOTAL                       727.53   ←CONTROL FOOTING

               12       1234    LAMP            20       16.99     339.80
               12       1809    TENNIS RACQUET   4       29.99     119.96
               12       1809    TENNIS RACQUET  10       29.99     299.90
               12       1975    KNIFE BLOCK     15       12.69     190.35
               12       2631    DOOR LOCK        6       18.49     110.94

                                REGION TOTAL                     1,060.95

               15       1234    LAMP            15       16.99     254.85
               15       1809    TENNIS RACQUET   3       29.99      89.97
               15       1975    KNIFE BLOCK      8       12.69     101.52
               15       2631    DOOR LOCK       11       18.49     203.39

                                REGION TOTAL                       649.73   ←CONTROL FOOTING

LAST DETAIL──────→              REPORT TOTAL                     2,438.21   ←CONTROL FOOTING
                                                                             FINAL

FOOTING──────→
```

FIGURE 9.4   Report writer page format

REPORT GROUP DESCRIPTIONS

Following each RD will be a number of report group description entries. These entries look like record descriptions, but contain unique entries to define the format of each type of line in the report. Separate entries will be made for headings, detail lines, and control break footings. The first general format for these descriptions is as follows:

Format 1

```
Ø1      data-name-1

        ⎡                 ⎧integer-1         ⎫⎤
        ⎢LINE NUMBER IS   ⎨PLUS  integer-2   ⎬⎥
        ⎣                 ⎩NEXT PAGE         ⎭⎦

                         ⎧REPORT HEADING                      ⎫
                         ⎪PAGE HEADING                        ⎪
                         ⎪CONTROL HEADING  ⎧data-name-2⎫      ⎪
                         ⎪                 ⎨FINAL      ⎬      ⎪
        TYPE IS          ⎨                 ⎩           ⎭      ⎬
                         ⎪DETAIL                              ⎪
                         ⎪CONTROL FOOTING  ⎧data-name-3⎫      ⎪
                         ⎪                 ⎨FINAL      ⎬      ⎪
                         ⎪                 ⎩           ⎭      ⎪
                         ⎪PAGE FOOTING                        ⎪
                         ⎩REPORT FOOTING                      ⎭

        ⎡                 ⎧integer-3         ⎫⎤
        ⎢NEXT GROUP IS    ⎨PLUS  integer-4   ⎬⎥
        ⎣                 ⎩NEXT PAGE         ⎭⎦

        [ [USAGE IS]   DISPLAY]      .
```

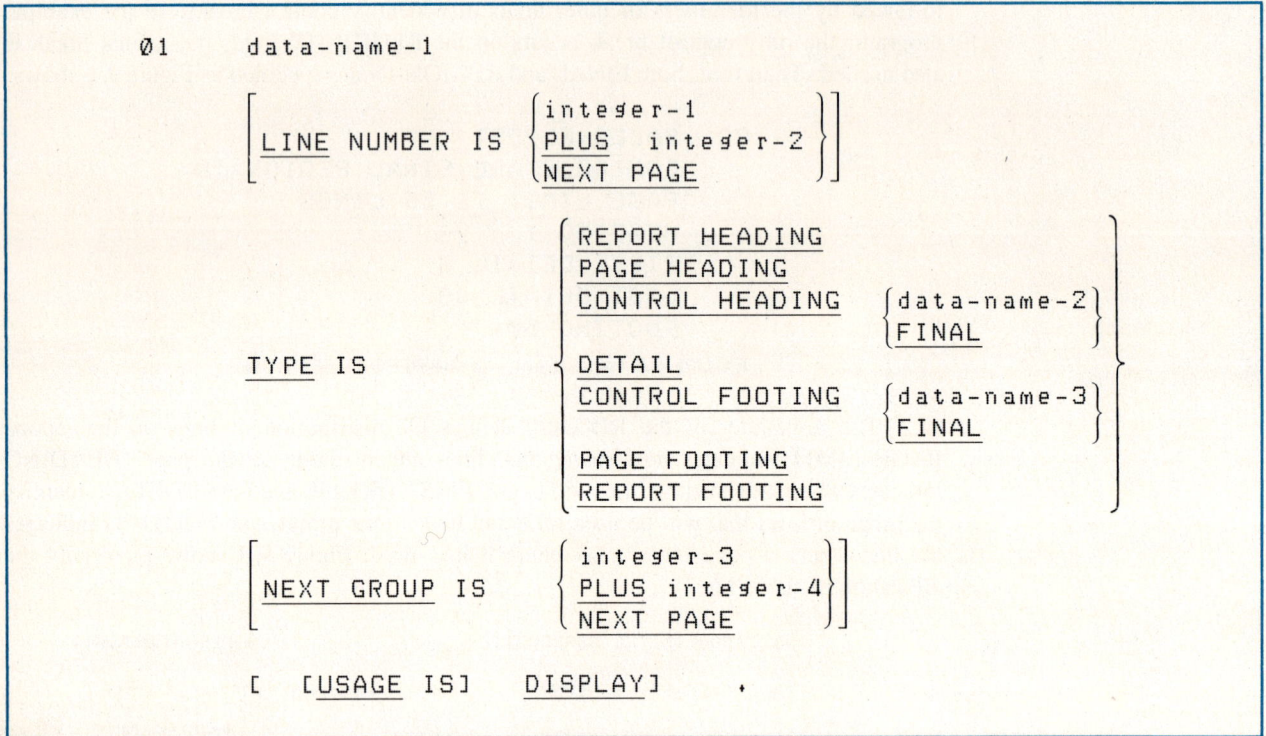

The LINE NUMBER clause indicates the line on which the output line will print. For heading lines, this entry will give a specific line number such as

```
                    LINE NUMBER IS 3
```

while detail and total lines will usually be given as a relative line number such as

```
                    LINE NUMBER PLUS 1.
```

The TYPE clause identifies the kind of line to be printed. There are several types of lines, ranging from a report heading and page heading to the detail and total lines. Each line will be defined separately. For example, the 01 entry for the page heading is written as follows:

```
        Ø1   TYPE IS REPORT HEADING.
```

An entry for the detail line could be

```
        Ø1   DETAIL-LINE TYPE IS DETAIL
                    LINE NUMBER IS PLUS 1.
```

The NEXT GROUP clause is used to identify the line spacing to use after the current line has been printed. This entry is typically used for a control footing (say, a control break on region) to start the next group of records (for the next region) on a new page or, if desired, after spacing several lines.

```
Ø1   TYPE IS CONTROL FOOTING REGION-IN
     NEXT GROUP NEXT PAGE.
```

Following the 01 entry, which defines the type of line, will be one or more entries with a higher-level number that define the format of the line. Two general formats (Figure 9.5) relate to the use of this line. While the options are numerous and may seem complex, they are actually quite easy to use.

Format 2

```
level-number     [data-name-1]

[                    ┌integer-1         ┐]
[LINE NUMBER IS  { PLUS   integer-2 }]
[                    └NEXT PAGE         ┘]
[[ USAGE IS ] DISPLAY ] .
```

Format 3

```
level-number     [data-name-1]

[BLANK WHEN ZERO]

[GROUP INDICATE]

[  ┌JUSTIFIED┐           ]
[  { JUST     }    RIGHT ]

[                    ┌integer-1         ┐]
[LINE NUMBER IS  { PLUS   integer-2 }]
[                    [NEXT PAGE]         ]

[COLUMN NUMBER IS integer-3]

┌PICTURE┐
{ PIC     }   IS  character-string
└       ┘

┌                                                        ┐
│ SOURCE IS identifier-1                                 │
│                                                        │
│ VALUE IS literal                                       │
│                                                        │
│ SUM identifier-2  [ , identifier-3 ]   ...             │
│    [UPON data-name-2  [ , data-name-3 ]   ... ]   ...  │
│                                                        │
│     ┌RESET ON ┌data-name-4┐┐                           │
│     └         └FINAL      ┘┘                           │
└                                                        ┘

[ [USAGE IS ] DISPLAY ] .
```

FIGURE 9.5   Formats 2 and 3 for report description entries

REPORT HEADINGS

The entry for a report heading uses some of these options, as shown in the following example:

```
01    TYPE IS REPORT HEADING.
      05   LINE NUMBER IS 1
           COLUMN NUMBER IS 25
           PICTURE IS X(27)
           VALUE IS 'SALES UNLIMITED CORPORATION'.
```

The 05-level number and associated entries use options from these two formats. The first entry LINE NUMBER indicates the line on which the heading is printed. The LINE NUMBER entry may appear on the 01 level or at a lower level (higher-level number). One reason for using LINE NUMBER on a 05 level is that it will apply only to the line defined by that entry. Headings, especially page headings, often consist of several lines, each of which is described by a 05 entry with its own line number.

The COLUMN NUMBER entry indicates the column number on the line at which the following PICTURE and VALUE clause contents will be printed. With report writer it is not necessary to use FILLER clauses to create spacing between fields.

PICTURE entries define the type of field (numeric, edited, alphanumeric, etc.), its length, and any special characteristics such as editing for numeric fields. Any PICTURE that might have previously been used for printed output in your programming may be used in the report writer.

The VALUE clause is used to supply a value for printing. Usually, this clause is used to define the literal values for headings as shown in the example.

PAGE HEADINGS

Figure 9.6 shows the entries for the page heading. In this program the heading consists of three lines, and so we use three 05 groups in the report description entry. Each 05 represents a separate page heading. Detail entries within each line of the page heading are made with the 10-level number entries. The actual numbers used here are not important, but the relationship between them is significant.

A new entry used in this heading is the SOURCE PAGE-COUNTER clause. The keyword **SOURCE** means that the program must get the value for this entry from some other location or source in the program. Often this source is an input field or a calculated value, but in this case it is the PAGE-COUNTER identifier. **PAGE-COUNTER** is a special register defined within the report writer, which is automatically updated each time a new page is printed. By using it in the SOURCE entry, the page number is included on the report.

```
Ø1  TYPE IS PAGE HEADING,
    Ø5  LINE NUMBER IS 3,
        1Ø  COLUMN NUMBER IS 3Ø
            PICTURE IS X(17)
            VALUE IS 'ITEM SALES REPORT',
        1Ø  COLUMN NUMBER IS 66
            PICTURE IS X(Ø8)
            VALUE IS 'PAGE NO,',
        1Ø  COLUMN NUMBER IS 75
            PICTURE IS Z9
            SOURCE PAGE-COUNTER,
    Ø5  LINE NUMBER IS 5,
        1Ø  COLUMN NUMBER IS 1
            PICTURE IS X(41)
            VALUE IS
            'REGION    ITEM        DESCRIPTION',
        1Ø  COLUMN NUMBER IS 41
            PICTURE IS X(35)
            VALUE IS
            'QUANTITY        UNIT          TOTAL',
    Ø5  LINE NUMBER IS 6,
        1Ø  COLUMN NUMBER IS 1
            PICTURE IS X(16)
            VALUE IS 'NUMBER   NUMBER',
        1Ø  COLUMN NUMBER IS 56
            PICTURE IS X(2Ø)
            VALUE IS 'COST          COST',
```

Output created

```
                    ITEM SALES REPORT                           PAGE NO,  1

REGION    ITEM       DESCRIPTION          QUANTITY        UNIT          TOTAL
NUMBER    NUMBER                                          COST          COST
```

FIGURE 9.6   A page heading in the report section

DETAIL LINE

The detail line in Figure 9.7 uses several new entries from the report description formats. First, the 01 level contains a name **DETAIL-LINE** that identifies the line. This name is necessary for a detail line because it is used in the PROCEDURE DIVISION by the GENERATE statement to identify the line to be printed.

```
01   DETAIL-LINE TYPE IS DETAIL
            LINE NUMBER IS PLUS 1.
      05   COLUMN IS 2
            PICTURE IS 9(02)
            SOURCE IS REGION-IN.
      05   COLUMN IS 11
            PICTURE IS 9(04)
            SOURCE IS ITEM-IN.
      05   COLUMN IS 21
            PICTURE IS X(15)
            SOURCE IS DESCRIPTION-IN.
      05   COLUMN IS 42
            PICTURE IS ZZ9
            SOURCE IS QUANTITY-IN.
      05   COLUMN IS 54
            PICTURE IS ZZ9.99
            SOURCE IS UNIT-COST-IN.
      05   COLUMN IS 68
            PICTURE IS Z,ZZ9.99
            SOURCE IS TOTAL-COST.
```

Output created
```
10      1234      LAMP              5        16.99           84.95
```

FIGURE 9.7   A detail line defined in the report section

This record also includes the entry

```
LINE NUMBER IS PLUS 1.
```

It indicates that each detail line will be printed one line below the previous line. In other words, the line counter is advanced one line each time a detail line is printed. This action creates single spacing. A value of PLUS 2 could be used to get double-spacing of the detail line.

This example also makes extensive use of the SOURCE clause to identify the values used on the line. Most of these values come from an input record, but a total cost comes from the result of a calculation that is stored in WORKING-STORAGE.

USING GROUP INDICATE ON A DETAIL LINE

When reports are created that contain control breaks, which includes the majority of reports, the control break field will be printed each time the line that contains it is printed. This was evident in the report produced for this example, where the region number was printed on each line. This is an unnecessary duplication of a value and would give a better appearance if only the first region number in the group were printed.

By using the **GROUP INDICATE** option on the line where this field is specified, the report writer will only print the region the first time. Subsequent prints will leave a blank space where the region goes. The entry in the program is made in the following manner:

```
01   DETAIL-LINE TYPE IS DETAIL
            LINE NUMBER IS PLUS 1.
      05   COLUMN IS 2 GROUP INDICATE
            PICTURE IS 9(02)
            SOURCE IS REGION-IN.
```

Figure 9.8 shows how the appearance of the report is affected by this entry. The first line for region 10 shows the region number, but subsequent lines do not. When the region changes, the new region, in this case 12, is printed, but the following is a blank. GROUP INDICATE may only be used on control break fields that are recorded in sequence.

```
              SALES  UNLIMITED  CORPORATION

                 ITEM  SALES  REPORT                PAGE NO.   1

 REGION     ITEM        DESCRIPTION      QUANTITY        UNIT       TOTAL
 NUMBER     NUMBER                                       COST       COST

   10       1234        LAMP                5          16.99        84.95
            1234        LAMP               12          16.99       203.88
            1975        KNIFE BLOCK        20          12.69       253.80
            2631        DOOR LOCK          10          18.49       184.90

                                     REGION  TOTAL                 727.53


   12       1234        LAMP               20          16.99       339.80
            1809        TENNIS RACQUET      4          29.99       119.96
            1809        TENNIS RACQUET     10          29.99       299.90
            1975        KNIFE BLOCK        15          12.69       190.35
            2631        DOOR LOCK           6          18.49       110.94

                                     REGION  TOTAL               1,060.95


   15       1234        LAMP               15          16.99       254.85
            1809        TENNIS RACQUET      3          29.99        89.97
            1975        KNIFE BLOCK         8          12.69       101.52
            2631        DOOR LOCK          11          18.49       203.39

                                     REGION  TOTAL                 649.73

                                     REPORT  TOTAL               2,438.21
```

FIGURE 9.8 Sales report using GROUP INDICATE on the region field

CONTROL BREAKS

Figure 9.9 shows the entry for a control footing line to create a total line for the change of region number. The record shows a TYPE of **CONTROL FOOTING** and specifies that the field REGION-IN will be checked for a changed value to create this line of output. Each level of a control break in a report requires a separate entry such as this one. If there were three levels of control breaks, there would be three separate CONTROL FOOTING report descriptions.

This report entry uses other entries that have been described already, including LINE NUMBER, COLUMN, PICTURE, and VALUE. A new entry used here is the keyword **SUM,** which identifies a field that is to be summed. Each record that has been processed and printed prior to this control break will have its TOTAL-COST

```
01   TYPE IS CONTROL FOOTING REGION-IN.
     05   LINE NUMBER IS PLUS 2.
          10   COLUMN IS 41
               PICTURE IS X(12)
               VALUE IS 'REGION TOTAL'.
          10   REGION-TOTAL
               COLUMN IS 67
               PICTURE IS ZZ,ZZ9.99
               SUM TOTAL-COST.
```

Output created

REGION TOTAL   727.53

FIGURE 9.9   Entry for a control break total line

amount added to a sum by the report writer. It is not necessary to identify a field for this sum; neither is it necessary to add a value to it. All this is handled by the report writer by simply specifying SUM TOTAL-COST.

The identifier name REGION-TOTAL for this level-10 entry gives a name to the sum so that it may be used in further calculations. We will see this name referenced in the final total line when it is accumulated for the final total.

FINAL TOTALS

A CONTROL FOOTING FINAL entry specifies that this line is to be printed when end of file has been reached and the report is to be terminated. Entries in this report description line (Figure 9.10) will be similar to those in a control break line. Significantly, an entry for at least one SUM will identify the field to represent a final total. Of course, several columns of numbers may have final totals in this line. In this example the entry SUM REGION-TOTAL refers to a total field in the REGION-IN control break line.

```
01   TYPE IS CONTROL FOOTING FINAL.
     05   LINE NUMBER IS PLUS 2.
          10   COLUMN IS 41
               PICTURE IS X(12)
               VALUE IS 'REPORT TOTAL'.
          10   COLUMN IS 67
               PICTURE IS ZZ,ZZ9.99
               SUM REGION-TOTAL.
```

Output created

REPORT TOTAL   2,438.21

FIGURE 9.10   Creating a final total line

PROCEDURE DIVISION STATEMENTS

Several statements are required in the procedure division to activate the report and write the contents (see Figure 9.11). Prior to the reading or processing of input records, input and output files, including the printer for the report, must be opened. Then the INITIATE statement for the report must be given.

```
PROCEDURE DIVISION.
000-MAINLINE.
    PERFORM 100-INITIALIZE.
    PERFORM 300-PROCESS-SALES
        UNTIL EOF-FLAG = 1.
    PERFORM 400-WRAP-UP.
    STOP RUN.

100-INITIALIZE.
    OPEN INPUT  SALES-IN
        OUTPUT REPORT-FILE.
    INITIATE SALES-REPORT.◄─────────────── Activate the report.
PERFORM 200-READ-DATA.

200-READ-DATA.
    READ SALES-IN INTO INPUT-RECORD
        AT END MOVE 1 TO EOF-FLAG.

300-PROCESS-SALES.
    MULTIPLY QUANTITY-IN BY UNIT-COST-IN
        GIVING TOTAL-COST.
    GENERATE DETAIL-LINE.◄────────────── Create a detail
    PERFORM 200-READ-DATA.                output line.

400-WRAP-UP.
    TERMINATE SALES-REPORT.◄──────────── Terminate the report.
    CLOSE SALES-IN
        REPORT-FILE.
```

FIGURE 9.11   INITIATE, GENERATE, and TERMINATE in the PROCEDURE DIVISION

INITIATE

> INITIATE report-name-1   [, report-name-2]   . . .

In the sample program the statement

```
                INITIATE SALES-REPORT.
```

is issued to begin the use of the SALES-REPORT. The name in the INITIATE statement refers to the RD name for the report. Using this statement causes all counters associated with the SUM clause to be initialized, control break fields to be set, and PAGE-COUNTER to be reset. During the processing of each record, the GENERATE statement will be used.

GENERATE

> GENERATE $\begin{Bmatrix} \text{data-name} \\ \text{report-name} \end{Bmatrix}$

The GENERATE statement causes a detail line to be generated. Thus, prior to issuing this statement, an input record must be read and available for reference by any SOURCE entries used by the detail line. Also, if values need to be calculated that are not a part of the input, such as TOTAL-COST in the previous example, then this amount must be calculated before issuing the GENERATE. GENERATE refers to the name of the detail line in the report for normal operation.

```
GENERATE DETAIL-LINE.
```

Finally, after all records have been processed and end of file has been reached on the input file, the report needs to be terminated.

TERMINATE

TERMINATE report-name-1   [, report-name-2]   . . .

TERMINATE completes the processing of the report. It causes the last control footings to be printed, including the final footing. If there is a report footing, it will also be printed at this time. After TERMINATE has been issued, the file used for the report must be closed with the usual CLOSE statement.

PROGRAM STYLE AND THE REPORT SECTION

Although the REPORT SECTION contains many new COBOL entries, the general nature and appearance of these entries have many similarities to other lines of COBOL code. Thus style considerations should be consistent with previous rules of style and not deviate from current practices. In the following material we will examine how these rules apply to the REPORT SECTION.

- In the RD, use a separate line for each entry and indent all entries after the first to a common column. This approach is consistent with the method for writing FD entries.

```
RD  PAYROLL-REPORT
    CONTROLS ARE FINAL DIVISION DEPARTMENT
    PAGE LIMIT IS 66 LINES
    HEADING 3
    FIRST DETAIL 8
    LAST DETAIL 55
    FOOTING 60.
```

- Write report description entries as you would record descriptions, using level numbers such as 01, 05, 10, and so on, to permit easy revision. Subsequent levels should be indented to reflect their level in the hierarchy. Each main entry should occupy a separate line.

```
01  TYPE IS REPORT HEADING.
    05  LINE NUMBER IS 3
        COLUMN NUMBER IS 35
        PICTURE IS X(14)
        VALUE IS 'PAYROLL REPORT'.
```

- When VALUE clauses are used, place the literal on a separate line. This practice will permit the use of longer literals and result in making fewer entries in the report description. Exceptionally short literals, such as 'PAGE NO.', may be written on the same line as the VALUE clause.

```
Ø5   LINE NUMBER IS 8.
        10   COLUMN NUMBER IS 1
             PICTURE IS X(39)
             VALUE IS
             'RATE      HOURS        JOB TYPE'.
        10   COLUMN NUMBER IS 41
             PICTURE IS X(35).
             VALUE IS
             'GROSS        FEDERAL      STATE   OTHER'.
```

WIDGET PRODUCTION REPORT: AN APPLICATION PROGRAM

This application will use the report writer feature in COBOL to produce the production report. This report utilizes many of the features available in report writer, including report and page headings, detail lines with group printing of control fields, and major, intermediate, and minor control breaks with several totals on each control footing line. In addition, the report will use various editing of output fields and page overflow after a division control break.

To tell whether an application is a candidate for the report writer, we need to look for the preceding characteristics. If the main output from the program is to be a report, then it is a likely candidate. Also, the report needs to follow the traditional format with headings, detail lines, and control break total lines. Although there is a reasonable amount of flexibility with the report writer, it is still quite restrictive as compared to writing all your own program code.

PROGRAM SPECIFICATIONS

Because this application is to use the report writer, it will be very much report oriented. The only output is a report that follows traditional lines. Although we will see all the specification and design documents, the report layout will be of the greatest significance when writing this program. Figure 9.12 supplies the specifications for the program.

PROGRAMMING SPECIFICATIONS   1 of 1
PROGRAM NAME: Widget Production Report   PROGRAM ID: REPORTW
PREPARED BY: Diane Quest   DATE: Sept. 15

Program Description:
    This program produces the widget production report from a file of production records.
    COBOL's report writer feature is to be used for this application.
Input File(s):
    Product file
Output File(s):
    Widget production report
Program Requirements:
    1. Read a file of production records by item within department within division sequence.
    2. Using the report writer, prepare a report containing each input record according to the
       following requirements:
       a) Single space each detail line.
       b) Double space total lines.
       c) Group-print the division and department fields.
       d) After a division control break, total line advance to a new page before printing the
          next detail line.
       e) Print a single asterisk (*) beside the minor total line, a double asterisk (**) beside
          the intermediate total, and a triple asterisk (***) beside the major total line.
    3. Material cost on the report is calculated by multiplying the input quantity by the unit
       material cost.
    4. Labor cost is the quantity multiplied by the unit labor cost.
    5. Production cost is the sum of material cost and labor cost.

FIGURE 9.12 Program specifications for the Widget production report

INPUT/OUTPUT DEFINITION

The input file to this program is described in Figure 9.13. It is a disk file with records stored in sequence on division, department, and item number, ranging from the major to the minor field. While it is customary to sequence-check input records, we will avoid this step to concentrate on using the report writer.

INPUT/OUTPUT RECORD DEFINITION				
File: Product file Record Length: 40 Sequence: Division (major) 　　　　　Department (intermediate) 　　　　　Item number (minor)		File Type: Disk Blocking Factor: 12 Access Method: Sequential		
COLUMNS	FIELD	TYPE	LENGTH	DECIMALS
1	Division	N	1	
2–3	Department	N	2	
4–7	Item number	N	4	
8–10	Quantity	N	3	
11–15	Unit material cost	N	5	2
16–19	Unit labor cost	N	4	2

FIGURE 9.13　Input definition for the production file.

Figure 9.14 shows the layout for the widget production report. The first line of the report will be a report heading and will appear only on the first page and not on subsequent pages. The other two heading lines are page headings and will be printed on the first page and at the top of each new page.

Detail lines, as shown, will group-indicate the control fields for division and department. Although item number is a sequence field, it is not group-printed because there will be no duplicate items within a department. The values for the fields material cost, labor cost, and production cost are calculated by the program before a detail line is printed.

There are three types of total lines to print. One is for department totals. This is

```
0         1         2         3         4         5         6         7         8         9
12345678901234567890123456789012345678901234567890123456789012345678901234567890123456789Ø


               WIDGET PRODUCTION REPORT


DIVISION     DEPT.        ITEM        QUANTITY     MATERIAL      LABOR         PRODUCTION
                          NUMBER      PRODUCED     COST          COST          COST

   9          99          9999        ZZ9          ZZ,ZZ9.99     ZZ,ZZ9.99     ZZ,ZZ9.99
                          9999        ZZ9          ZZ,ZZ9.99     ZZ,ZZ9.99     ZZ,ZZ9.99
                          9999        ZZ9          ZZ,ZZ9.99     ZZ,ZZ9.99     ZZ,ZZ9.99
                          9999        ZZ9          ZZ,ZZ9.99     ZZ,ZZ9.99     ZZ,ZZ9.99

          DEPARTMENT TOTALS                        ZZ,ZZ9.99     ZZ,ZZ9.99     ZZ,ZZ9.99   *

   9          99          9999        ZZ9          ZZ,ZZ9.99     ZZ,ZZ9.99     ZZ,ZZ9.99
                          9999        ZZ9          ZZ,ZZ9.99     ZZ,ZZ9.99     ZZ,ZZ9.99
                          9999        ZZ9          ZZ,ZZ9.99     ZZ,ZZ9.99     ZZ,ZZ9.99
                          9999        ZZ9          ZZ,ZZ9.99     ZZ,ZZ9.99     ZZ,ZZ9.99

         DEPARTMENT TOTALS                         ZZ,ZZ9.99     ZZ,ZZ9.99     ZZ,ZZ9.99   *
         DIVISION TOTALS                           ZZ,ZZ9.99     ZZ,ZZ9.99     ZZ,ZZ9.99   **
         COMPANY TOTALS                            ZZ,ZZ9.99     ZZ,ZZ9.99     ZZ,ZZ9.99   ***
```

FIGURE 9.14　Printer layout for the production report

the minor total and will have a single asterisk printed to the right of the line contents. The second total line is the intermediate total for the division. It will contain two asterisks to indicate its level. After a division total has been printed, the report is to eject to a new page if there are more data to be printed.

The final or company total line has three asterisks. The first two total lines can print any number of times, depending on the number of control breaks encountered in the data. The final total line will, of course, print only once at the end of the report.

STRUCTURE CHART

Programs using the report writer typically have a small amount of program logic because most of the coding will be done in the REPORT SECTION of the program. This characteristic is reflected in the structure chart, which is only used to show the hierarchy of modules in the program's PROCEDURE DIVISION. The chart in Figure 9.15 shows the top-down development, which breaks the problem into components of initialization, process, and final wrap-up. The report is initialized in the program initialization module and the first input record is read.

Processing is rather simple. Three calculations are necessary for each input record to get values for the material cost, labor cost, and production cost. The detail line is then generated and the next record is read. All the other work pertaining to creating the report is done by the report writer based on the report section code and is not reflected in the structure chart.

The wrap-up module will terminate the report and close the files.

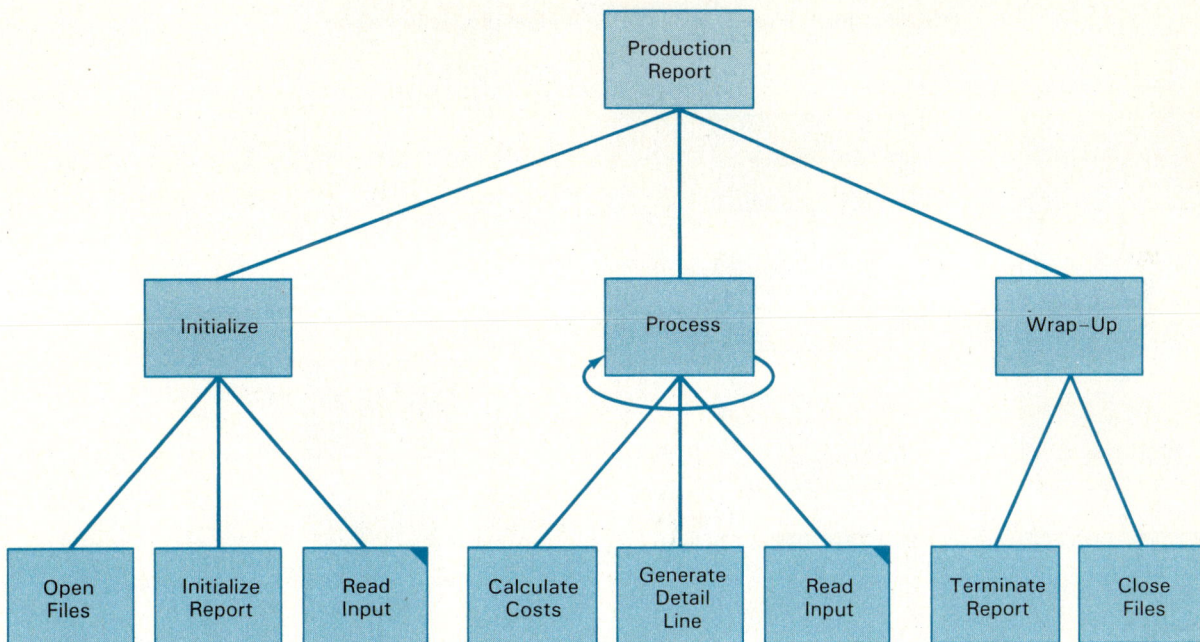

FIGURE 9.15 Structure chart for the production report program

PSEUDO CODE

Figure 9.16 gives the pseudo-code entries, followed by the structured flowchart, for this application. Like the structure chart, pseudo code for a program using the report writer will be brief and generally simple in nature. Any complexity will be due to calculations and analysis of data that might be needed prior to generating a detail line. Logic for the report details (headings, control breaks, page control, and so on) is taken

```
                            PSEUDO CODE
PROGRAM NAME: Widget Production Report        PROGRAM ID: REPORTW
PREPARED BY: Jonathan Youngman      DATE: Sept. 17      PAGE 1 of 1

100-Mainline
    1. Perform 200-Initialize.
    2. Perform 300-Process
            Until EOF.
    3. Perform 400-Wrap-Up.
    4. Stop Run
200-Initialize
    1. Open input and output files.
    2. Initialize production report.
    3. Perform 250-Read.
250-Read
    1. Read product file
        at end move 'yes' to EOF-Flag.
300-Process
    1. Multiply unit material cost by quantity
            giving material cost.
    2. Multiply unit labor cost by quantity
            giving labor cost.
    3. Add material cost and labor cost
            giving production cost.
    4. Generate print line.
    5. Perform 250-Read.
400-Wrap-Up
    1. Terminate production report.
    2. Close files.
```

FIGURE 9.16(a)   Pseudo code for the Widget production report

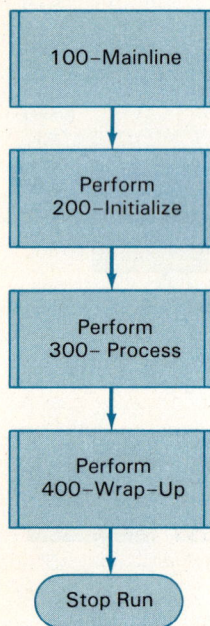

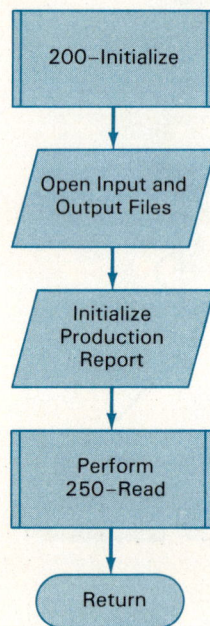

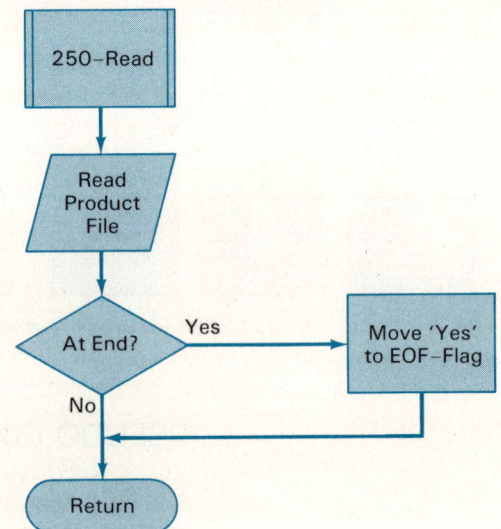

FIGURE 9.16(b)   Structured flowchart for the Widget production report

FIGURE 9.16(c)

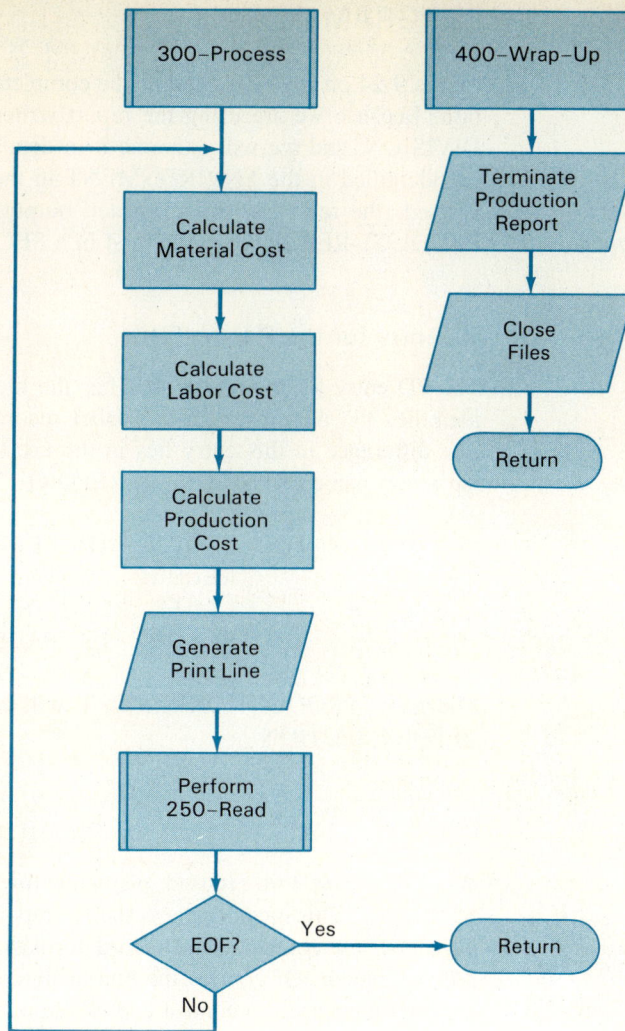

FIGURE 9.16(d)

care of by COBOL's REPORT SECTION code, for which there will be no pseudo code.

Important considerations in this code are the placement of the initiate, generate, and terminate statements. The report is initiated in paragraph 200-Initiate after the input and output files have been opened. The first input record is also read here in the usual manner of other programs that do sequential processing.

The paragraph 300-Process calculates the three cost values before the detail line is generated. This is an important sequence of events because the detail print line cannot be generated until all the values it contains are available. Notice that none of the data is moved to the print line; rather, the generate statement is simply issued to create the line. Although this is still pseudo code, this approach accurately portrays the identical steps followed in the program.

Finally, paragraph 400-Wrap-Up terminates the report. The terminate statement must precede the closing of the files because it is responsible for printing the last total lines and completing the content of the report. After the terminate is finished, the files are closed and the program itself is terminated.

PROGRAM CODING

Figure 9.24 on page 35 contains the complete program for the production report application. Because we are using the report writer, most of the code is found in the DATA DIVISION, and we will examine it in detail. First, note that the input and output files are identified in the ENVIRONMENT in the usual manner. Although the report writer is used, the report is still a printed output and thus the printer is needed. This file, PRODUCT-REPORT, is identified in a SELECT clause and also in an FD entry.

FD Entry for the Report File

The FD entry for the report specifies the file name used in the SELECT clause. It also identifies the record length and label records in the same manner as for any printer. The difference in this entry lies in the use of the REPORT IS clause, which identifies the report name PRODUCTION-REPORT.

```
FD   PRODUCT-REPORT
     RECORD CONTAINS 133 CHARACTERS
     LABEL RECORDS ARE OMITTED
     REPORT IS PRODUCTION-REPORT,
```

The name PRODUCTION-REPORT will be the name used for the SD entry in the REPORT SECTION.

WORKING-STORAGE and the Report Writer

When the report writer is used, many identifiers will not need to be defined in WORKING-STORAGE. This includes items such as report totals, previous fields for control variables, page and line counters, and record formats. What is left after this list is exhausted is not very much. Of course, the record description for the input record is necessary and also any flags used to control end of file on the input.

Other identifiers will be necessary when the program needs to do calculations to create some of the data necessary for the report. In this application, the material, labor, and production costs need to be calculated, and so identifiers for these fields are established in the program, as follows:

```
01   OTHER-DATA,
     05 EOF-FLAG                    PIC X(03) VALUE 'NO',
        88 END-OF-FILE                        VALUE 'YES',
     05 MATERIAL-COST               PIC 9(05)V99,
     05 LABOR-COST                  PIC 9(05)V99,
     05 PRODUCTION-COST             PIC 9(06)V99,
```

The REPORT SECTION

This section is where all the action is in this program. So let's take a detailed look at how the entries are made for this application and discuss the importance and use of the main components of the RD and report descriptions.

RD Entry   The RD (Figure 9.17) contains the same name used in the FD to identify the report. Its first entry is the CONTROLS ARE clause, which identifies the control breaks used for this report. Control totals are identified by the entries FINAL, PROD-DIV, and PROD-DEPT to indicate that a final total is needed, a division total, and a department total, respectively.

```
RD    PRODUCTION-REPORT
          CONTROLS ARE FINAL PROD-DIV PROD-DEPT
          PAGE LIMIT IS 55 LINES
          HEADING 1
          FIRST DETAIL 6
          LAST DETAIL 48
          FOOTING 50.
```

FIGURE 9.17   RD entry for the production report

Page specifications follow in the RD, indicating that the page can accept 55 lines. The headings begin at line 1, which is where the report heading will go. By placing the first detail line at line 6, one blank line is allowed between the last heading line and the first detail line. It is important to count these lines carefully on the printer layout sheet to ensure that the spacing between headings and detail is accurate. The last detail is placed at line 48 to permit space between it and a footer if it is used. Although this program does not produce a footer, this type of planning would make it easy for the programmer to include a footer as a later revision.

The REPORT HEADING   The heading 'WIDGET PRODUCTION REPORT' will be printed at the top of the first page of the report and so its TYPE is **REPORT HEADING** (Figure 9.18). It will be printed on line 1 in the column and using the picture indicated in the report description.

```
01    TYPE IS REPORT HEADING.
      05    LINE NUMBER IS 1
            COLUMN NUMBER IS 30
            PICTURE IS X(24)
            VALUE IS 'WIDGET PRODUCTION REPORT'.
```

FIGURE 9.18   Entry for the report heading

The PAGE HEADING   The page heading consists of two lines in the report and will print at the top of each page beginning on line 3. On the first page, it will be preceded by the report heading, but on subsequent pages will appear by itself.

The record description for this entry is shown in Figure 9.19. The TYPE clause

```
01    TYPE IS PAGE HEADING.
      05    LINE NUMBER IS 3.
            10    COLUMN NUMBER IS 1
                  PICTURE IS X(50)
                  VALUE IS
                  'DIVISION      DEPT.         ITEM           QUANTITY'.
            10    COLUMN NUMBER IS 50
                  PICTURE IS X(36)
                  VALUE IS
                  'MATERIAL       LABOR        PRODUCTION'.
      05    LINE NUMBER IS 4.
            10    COLUMN NUMBER IS 25
                  PICTURE IS X(39)
                  VALUE IS
                  'NUMBER       PRODUCED       COST'.
            10    COLUMN NUMBER IS 64
                  PICTURE IS X(20)
                  VALUE IS
                  'COST            COST'.
```

FIGURE 9.19   Page heading entries

defines it as a **PAGE HEADING.** Because there are two lines in this heading, two 05-level entries are made. The first describes the contents for LINE NUMBER 3 and the second for LINE NUMBER 4. Within each of these 05 levels are several 10-level entries that describe the literal values for the heading lines. These entries begin with a column number and are followed by a PICTURE and VALUE clause based on the contents of the report layout.

Creating the Detail Line The detail line in the report shows seven fields with group printing on the control fields division and department. Specific editing and positioning of each field are also shown on the layout. This information translates to the entries made in the detail line for the report writer shown in Figure 9.20.

```
01   PRINT-LINE TYPE IS DETAIL
                LINE NUMBER IS PLUS 1,
     05   COLUMN IS 5  GROUP INDICATE
                PICTURE IS 9
                SOURCE IS PROD-DIV,
     05   COLUMN IS 15 GROUP INDICATE
                PICTURE IS 9(02)
                SOURCE IS PROD-DEPT,
     05   COLUMN IS 26
                PICTURE IS 9(04)
                SOURCE IS PROD-ITEM,
     05   COLUMN IS 39
                PICTURE IS ZZ9
                SOURCE IS PROD-QUANTITY,
     05   COLUMN IS 49
                PICTURE IS ZZ,ZZ9.99
                SOURCE IS MATERIAL-COST,
     05   COLUMN IS 61
                PICTURE IS ZZ,ZZ9.99
                SOURCE IS LABOR-COST,
     05   COLUMN IS 75
                PICTURE IS ZZZ,ZZ9.99
                SOURCE IS PRODUCTION-COST,
```

FIGURE 9.20   Detail line entries

TYPE is DETAIL for this line, and the LINE NUMBER entry shows PLUS 1. This relative line number is important here because detail lines can be printed on a range of lines, in this case including lines 6 to 48 as specified in the RD entry.

Entries for the division and department include the GROUP INDICATE option so that only the first line of each group will print these data. Each field on the detail line is specified in a 05-level number entry. Each entry includes a COLUMN, PICTURE, and SOURCE to identify the location the value is to print on the line, its format, and where the data are to come from. SOURCE entries for the first four fields refer to identifier names in the input record of the production file. The last three entries for the costs refer to the WORKING-STORAGE value that is calculated before the detail line is generated.

DEPARTMENT TOTALS A CONTROL FOOTING entry is used to identify the department total line in Figure 9.21. The control field is PROD-DEPT for this entry, and whenever the report writer detects a new value in PROD-DEPT, it will print this total line. First, the line contains a label entry for the title 'DEPARTMENT TOTALS.' Following this entry are three entries for the totals on material, labor, and production costs. Each entry has a name to identify it so it may be used in the division total line. The names MINOR-MATERIAL, MINOR-LABOR, and MINOR-PRODUCTION are programmer chosen.

```
01   TYPE IS CONTROL FOOTING PROD-DEPT.          Control break
     05   LINE NUMBER IS PLUS 2.                  on department.
          10   COLUMN IS 8
               PICTURE IS X(18)

               VALUE IS 'DEPARTMENT TOTALS'.
          10   MINOR-MATERIAL
               COLUMN IS 49
               PICTURE IS ZZ,ZZ9.99
               SUM MATERIAL-COST.
          10   MINOR-LABOR                        Names of totals
               COLUMN IS 61                       to be used in
               PICTURE IS ZZ,ZZ9.99               the division
               SUM LABOR-COST.                    total line.
          10   MINOR-PRODUCTION
               COLUMN IS 75
               PICTURE IS ZZZ,ZZ9.99
               SUM PRODUCTION-COST.
          10   COLUMN IS 87
               PICTURE IS X(01)
               VALUE IS '*'.
```

FIGURE 9.21   Department total line entry

Each total uses the SUM option to indicate that the value printed here will be the sum of several values provided from the identifier specified. The sum in the MINOR-MATERIAL field will be the total of all values read between the previous control break and the current one on the field MATERIAL-COST. Each department total field follows this pattern.

The last entry in the total line provides a single asterisk (*) to print after the total production cost is printed. This asterisk identifies a minor total line and is simply supplied as a literal in the record description.

Division Totals   Developing the entry for the division total line follows the same procedure as used for the department total line. The main difference, as seen in Figure 9.22, is the use of the NEXT GROUP NEXT PAGE clause, which tells the report writer to

```
01   TYPE IS CONTROL FOOTING PROD-DIV             Control break
     LINE NUMBER IS PLUS 2 NEXT GROUP NEXT PAGE.  on division.
          10   COLUMN IS 8
               PICTURE IS X(16)
               VALUE IS 'DIVISION TOTALS'.
          10   INTER-MATERIAL                      Name of an intermediate
               COLUMN IS 49                        total.
               PICTURE IS ZZ,ZZ9.99
               SUM MINOR-MATERIAL.                 Sum of a minor total.
          10   INTER-LABOR
               COLUMN IS 61
               PICTURE IS ZZ,ZZ9.99
               SUM MINOR-LABOR.
          10   INTER-PRODUCTION
               COLUMN IS 75
               PICTURE IS ZZZ,ZZ9.99
               SUM MINOR-PRODUCTION.
          10   COLUMN IS 87
               PICTURE IS X(02)
               VALUE IS '**'.
```

FIGURE 9.22   Division total line entry

eject a new page after the division line has been printed. However, if there are no more data available, then the final total line would be printed without ejecting the page.

Each total in this line is identified using the names INTER-MATERIAL, INTER-LABOR, and INTER-PRODUCTION to indicate they are intermediate totals. Each total is the SUM of a minor total, using the names described in the section on department totals. The last entry prints two asterisks to indicate an intermediate total line required by the program specifications.

Creating the Final Total Line The last entry in the REPORT SECTION defines the FINAL total line (Figure 9.23). It follows the pattern established for the department and division total line. Notice that these entries proceed from minor to major total. The control for this line is FINAL because it does not depend on a specific field for a control break, but rather is produced after end of file has been reached. None of these fields is given a name as done for the department and division totals because the final totals are not used for further sums. The three asterisks at the end indicate a major total line.

```
Ø1   TYPE IS CONTROL FOOTING FINAL,          ◄──── Major control break.
     Ø5   LINE NUMBER IS PLUS 2,
          1Ø   COLUMN IS 8
               PICTURE IS X(15)
               VALUE IS 'COMPANY TOTALS',
          1Ø   COLUMN IS 49
               PICTURE IS ZZ,ZZ9,99
               SUM INTER-MATERIAL,          ◄──── Sum of an intermediate
          1Ø   COLUMN IS 61                         total.
               PICTURE IS ZZ,ZZ9,99
               SUM INTER-LABOR,
          1Ø   COLUMN IS 75
               PICTURE IS ZZZ,ZZ9,99
               SUM INTER-PRODUCTION,
          1Ø   COLUMN IS 87
               PICTURE IS X(Ø3)
               VALUE IS '***',               ◄──── Three asterisks indicate
                                                   a final total line.
```

FIGURE 9.23 Final total line entries

PROCEDURE DIVISION Entries

While writing the pseudo code, we saw that the program logic for this program was minimal because of the use of the report writer feature. This relative simplicity extends to the program code, which consists of a fairly short PROCEDURE DIVISION for this application.

100-MAINLINE The mainline for this program activates three modules that take care of most of the program's activity. These modules initialize the processing, process each input record, and do a final wrap-up of the program. In other words, this paragraph follows the basic format for the processing of a sequential file.

200-INITIALIZE The initialize module opens each input and output file prior to any other processing. Because we are using the report writer, the INITIALIZE statement is issued here to begin the reporting activity. Finally, the first input record is read before leaving the module.

250-READ This module reads a record from the production file.

300-PROCESS   The process module processes an individual record. First, it calculates each of the costs of production, including material cost, labor cost, and production cost. Then the report writer statement GENERATE is issued to create a detail PRINT-LINE as described in the report section of the program. Finally, the process module issues a read to get another input record before the process loop is repeated.

400-WRAP-UP   This paragraph is performed when all input records have been processed and all detail lines generated. The TERMINATE statement is issued here, which causes all remaining total lines, including the FINAL total line, to be printed. Then the files are closed and control returns to the mainline when the program itself is terminated.

Figure 9.24 gives the complete program for this application.

```
IDENTIFICATION DIVISION.

PROGRAM-ID.
    REPORTW.
*AUTHOR.
*    JOHNATHAN YOUNGMAN.
*INSTALLATION.
*    SALES UNLIMITED CORP.
*DATE-WRITTEN.
*    SEPT 23.
*DATE-COMPILED.
*
*SECURITY.
*    NONE.

ENVIRONMENT DIVISION.

CONFIGURATION SECTION.
SOURCE-COMPUTER.
    IBM-4381.
OBJECT-COMPUTER.
    IBM-4381.
SPECIAL-NAMES.
    C01 IS TO-TOP-OF-PAGE.

INPUT-OUTPUT SECTION.

FILE-CONTROL.
    SELECT PRODUCT            ASSIGN TO SYS001-UT-3340-FILEP.
    SELECT PRODUCT-REPORT   ASSIGN TO SYS005-UR-1403-S.

DATA DIVISION.

FILE SECTION.

FD   PRODUCT
     BLOCK CONTAINS 12 RECORDS
     RECORD CONTAINS 40 CHARACTERS
     LABEL RECORDS ARE STANDARD
     DATA RECORD IS PROD-RECORD.
01   PROD-RECORD.
     05   FILLER                PIC X(40).

FD   PRODUCT-REPORT
     RECORD CONTAINS 133 CHARACTERS
     LABEL RECORDS ARE OMITTED
     REPORT IS PRODUCTION-REPORT.

WORKING-STORAGE SECTION.

01   OTHER-DATA.
     05   EOF-FLAG              PIC X(03) VALUE 'NO'.
          88 END-OF-FILE                  VALUE 'YES'.
     05   MATERIAL-COST         PIC 9(05)V99.
     05   LABOR-COST            PIC 9(05)V99.
     05   PRODUCTION-COST       PIC 9(06)V99.
```

FIGURE 9.24(a)   Production report program code

```
01  WS-PROD-RECORD.
    05  PROD-DIV                PIC 9.
    05  PROD-DEPT               PIC 9(02).
    05  PROD-ITEM               PIC 9(04).
    05  PROD-QUANTITY           PIC 9(03).
    05  PROD-UNIT-MATERIAL      PIC 9(03)V99.
    05  PROD-UNIT-LABOR         PIC 9(02)V99.

REPORT SECTION.

RD  PRODUCTION-REPORT
    CONTROLS ARE FINAL PROD-DIV PROD-DEPT
    PAGE LIMIT IS 55 LINES
    HEADING 1
    FIRST DETAIL 6
    LAST DETAIL 48
    FOOTING 50.

01  TYPE IS REPORT HEADING.
    05  LINE NUMBER IS 1
        COLUMN NUMBER IS 30
        PICTURE IS X(24)
        VALUE IS 'WIDGET PRODUCTION REPORT'.

01  TYPE IS PAGE HEADING.
    05  LINE NUMBER IS 3.
        10  COLUMN NUMBER IS 1
            PICTURE IS X(50)
            VALUE IS
            'DIVISION      DEPT.        ITEM        QUANTITY'.
        10  COLUMN NUMBER IS 50
            PICTURE IS X(36)
            VALUE IS
            'MATERIAL       LABOR        PRODUCTION'.
    05  LINE NUMBER IS 4.
        10  COLUMN NUMBER IS 25
            PICTURE IS X(39)
            VALUE IS
            'NUMBER        PRODUCED        COST'.
        10  COLUMN NUMBER IS 64
            PICTURE IS X(20)
            VALUE IS
            'COST            COST'.

01  PRINT-LINE TYPE IS DETAIL
            LINE NUMBER IS PLUS 1.
    05  COLUMN IS 5  GROUP INDICATE
            PICTURE IS 9
            SOURCE IS PROD-DIV.
    05  COLUMN IS 15 GROUP INDICATE
            PICTURE IS 9(02)
            SOURCE IS PROD-DEPT.
    05  COLUMN IS 26
            PICTURE IS 9(04)
            SOURCE IS PROD-ITEM.
    05  COLUMN IS 39
            PICTURE IS ZZ9
            SOURCE IS PROD-QUANTITY.
    05  COLUMN IS 49
            PICTURE IS ZZ,ZZ9.99
            SOURCE IS MATERIAL-COST.
    05  COLUMN IS 61
            PICTURE IS ZZ,ZZ9.99
            SOURCE IS LABOR-COST.
    05  COLUMN IS 75
            PICTURE IS ZZZ,ZZ9.99
            SOURCE IS PRODUCTION-COST.

01  TYPE IS CONTROL FOOTING PROD-DEPT.
    05  LINE NUMBER IS PLUS 2.
        10  COLUMN IS 8
            PICTURE IS X(18)
            VALUE IS 'DEPARTMENT TOTALS'.
```

FIGURE 9.24(b)

```
               10    MINOR-MATERIAL
                     COLUMN IS 49
                     PICTURE IS ZZ,ZZ9.99
                     SUM MATERIAL-COST.
               10    MINOR-LABOR
                     COLUMN IS 61
                     PICTURE IS ZZ,ZZ9.99
                     SUM LABOR-COST.
               10    MINOR-PRODUCTION
                     COLUMN IS 75
                     PICTURE IS ZZZ,ZZ9.99
                     SUM PRODUCTION-COST.
               10    COLUMN IS 87
                     PICTURE IS X(01)
                     VALUE IS '*'.

        01   TYPE IS CONTROL FOOTING PROD-DIV
             LINE NUMBER IS PLUS 2 NEXT GROUP NEXT PAGE.
               10    COLUMN IS 8
                     PICTURE IS X(16)
                     VALUE IS 'DIVISION TOTALS'.
               10    INTER-MATERIAL
                     COLUMN IS 49
                     PICTURE IS ZZ,ZZ9.99
                     SUM MINOR-MATERIAL.
               10    INTER-LABOR
                     COLUMN IS 61
                     PICTURE IS ZZ,ZZ9.99
                     SUM MINOR-LABOR.
               10    INTER-PRODUCTION
                     COLUMN IS 75
                     PICTURE IS ZZZ,ZZ9.99
                     SUM MINOR-PRODUCTION.
               10    COLUMN IS 87
                     PICTURE IS X(02)
                     VALUE IS '**'.

        01   TYPE IS CONTROL FOOTING FINAL.
             05  LINE NUMBER IS PLUS 2.
               10    COLUMN IS 8
                     PICTURE IS X(15)
                     VALUE IS 'COMPANY TOTALS'.
               10    COLUMN IS 49
                     PICTURE IS ZZ,ZZ9.99
                     SUM INTER-MATERIAL.
               10    COLUMN IS 61
                     PICTURE IS ZZ,ZZ9.99
                     SUM INTER-LABOR.
               10    COLUMN IS 75
                     PICTURE IS ZZZ,ZZ9.99
                     SUM INTER-PRODUCTION.
               10    COLUMN IS 87
                     PICTURE IS X(03)
                     VALUE IS '***'.

   PROCEDURE DIVISION.

   100-MAINLINE.
       PERFORM 200-INITIALIZE.
       PERFORM 300-PROCESS
           UNTIL END-OF-FILE.
       PERFORM 400-WRAP-UP.
       STOP RUN.

   200-INITIALIZE.
       OPEN INPUT  PRODUCT
            OUTPUT PRODUCT-REPORT.
       INITIATE PRODUCTION-REPORT.
       PERFORM 250-READ.

   250-READ.
       READ PRODUCT INTO WS-PROD-RECORD
           AT END MOVE 'YES' TO EOF-FLAG.
```

FIGURE 9.24(c)

```
300-PROCESS.

    MULTIPLY PROD-UNIT-MATERIAL BY PROD-QUANTITY
        GIVING MATERIAL-COST.
    MULTIPLY PROD-UNIT-LABOR    BY PROD-QUANTITY
        GIVING LABOR-COST.
    ADD MATERIAL-COST LABOR-COST
        GIVING PRODUCTION-COST.
    GENERATE PRINT-LINE.
    PERFORM 250-READ.

400-WRAP-UP.
    TERMINATE PRODUCTION-REPORT.
    CLOSE PRODUCT
        PRODUCT-REPORT.
```

FIGURE 9.24(d)

PROGRAM TESTING

Testing a report writer program is no different from testing any other program that produces a report. The program is compiled and then run with a file of test data chosen for the specific purpose of testing each of the program's features. Figure 9.25 shows

Input values in the first record:

Quantity	Unit Material	Unit Labor
5	25.50	7.25

Calculated results:

Material Cost	Labor Cost	Production Cost
127.50	36.25	163.75

```
1101234005025500725
1101244010012000800
1201250025020100950
1201255012012571200
1201263100050001525
1201275050008501400
1211234005025500725
1211244010012000800
1211250025020100950
1211255012012571200
2111234005025500725
2111244010012000800
2131250025020100950
2131255012012571200
2131263100050001525
2131275050008501400
2132234003024501225
2191244010012000800
2191250025020100950
```

Item number
Department
Division

FIGURE 9.25 Test data for the production program

the data for this test. Records are created to produce a control break on several departments within a division and on several divisions. Within each department, several items are produced. In choosing the data values, it is important to ensure that all control breaks in the report are considered.

Other values are not quite as important, but it is still necessary to ensure that all calculations are done correctly and that these values are printed. In this program we will need to calculate the values for material cost by multiplying quantity by unit material cost. Labor cost is derived by multiplying quantity by unit labor cost. The production cost is the sum of these two results.

The output in Figure 9.26 can be used to confirm these results. Checking the printout shows the headings to be located as required. The first detail line confirms the values for the material, labor, and production costs. The input values and the results for the first record were as follows:

These values are correctly reflected in the report. Further examination shows that the report contains each input record and that the control breaks and control totals are all included. The page break at the end of a division is also reflected in the results. We can also confirm the line and field spacing on this output to ensure that it matches the output specifications. Finally, the flagging of total lines to show minor, intermediate, and major totals is done with the asterisks as required.

```
                          WIDGET PRODUCTION REPORT

   DIVISION      DEPT.       ITEM      QUANTITY     MATERIAL       LABOR      PRODUCTION
                            NUMBER     PRODUCED       COST         COST          COST

      1           10         1234          5         127.50        36.25        163.75
                             1244         10         120.00        80.00        200.00

            DEPARTMENT  TOTALS                        247.50       116.25        363.75  *

      1           20         1250         25         502.50       237.50        740.00
                             1255         12         150.84       144.00        294.84
                             1263        100       5,000.00     1,525.00      6,525.00
                             1275         50         425.00       700.00      1,125.00

            DEPARTMENT  TOTALS                      6,078.34     2,606.50      8,684.84  *

      1           21         1234          5         127.50        36.25        163.75
                             1244         10         120.00        80.00        200.00
                             1250         25         502.50       237.50        740.00
                             1255         12         150.84       144.00        294.84

            DEPARTMENT  TOTALS                        900.84       497.75      1,398.59  *

         DIVISION  TOTALS                           7,226.68     3,220.50     10,447.18  **
```

FIGURE 9.26(a)   Production report produced by the report writer program

DIVISION	DEPT.	ITEM NUMBER	QUANTITY PRODUCED	MATERIAL COST	LABOR COST	PRODUCTION COST
2	11	1234	5	127.50	36.25	163.75
		1244	10	120.00	80.00	200.00
	DEPARTMENT TOTALS			247.50	116.25	363.75 *
2	13	1250	25	502.50	237.50	740.00
		1255	12	150.84	144.00	294.84
		1263	100	5,000.00	1,525.00	6,525.00
		1275	50	425.00	700.00	1,125.00
		2234	3	73.50	36.75	110.25
	DEPARTMENT TOTALS			6,151.84	2,643.25	8,795.09 *
2	19	1244	10	120.00	80.00	200.00
		1250	25	502.50	237.50	740.00
	DEPARTMENT TOTALS			622.50	317.50	940.00 *
	DIVISION TOTALS			7,021.84	3,077.00	10,098.84 **
	COMPANY TOTALS			14,248.52	6,297.50	20,546.02 ***

FIGURE 9.26(b)

SUMMARY

COBOL's report writer provides many nonprocedural features to provide a relatively easy way to create reports with headings, detail lines, and control break totals. The FD used for a report will not contain the usual entries, but simply makes reference to the report's name as defined in the REPORT SECTION.

The REPORT SECTION follows the WORKING-STORAGE SECTION and contains numerous entries for defining the content and format of the report. The RD entry defines the name of the report, the control breaks (CONTROLS) that will be used, the length of the page (PAGE LIMITS), where the first (FIRST DETAIL) and last detail (LAST DETAIL) lines will go, and the line number for the footer (FOOTING).

Following the RD are a number of report description entries. These entries define the REPORT HEADING, PAGE HEADING, DETAIL line, CONTROL FOOTING, and the final CONTROL FOOTING.

The PROCEDURE DIVISION contains the INITIATE statement to begin the report and the GENERATE statement to issue individual lines within the report. The report writer automatically generates control breaks, total lines, and page overflow with headings as lines are generated. The report is completed by issuing the TERMINATE statement.

CONTROL FOOTING   PAGE HEADING
DETAIL-LINE   RD
FINAL   REPORT HEADING
GENERATE   REPORT SECTION
GROUP INDICATE   SOURCE
INITIATE   SUM
Nonprocedural language   TERMINATE
PAGE-COUNTER

REVIEW QUESTIONS

TRUE/FALSE

1. Because the report writer always prints, there is no need to define a printer with the SELECT clause.
2. The report writer has many similarities to a nonprocedural language and therefore does not require the use of any program logic in the PROCEDURE DIVISION.
3. The LINE NUMBER clause in a report heading line is used to identify the precise line on which the heading is printed.
4. The position of a field on the print line is indicated with the COLUMN entry.
5. The report writer may use any form of PICTURE clause that is normally used for other types of printed data.
6. The GROUP INDICATE clause is used to indicate that a specific group of data is to be kept together on one page of output.
7. The SOURCE clause identifies the location where the data are to be found for a specific field.
8. The CONTROL FOOTING clause must always include the name of a field or the keyword FINAL in the entry.
9. The INITIATE statement must always be issued prior to opening the report file.
10. The phrase LINE NUMBER PLUS 1 is used to indicate single spacing of a line.

FILL IN THE BLANKS

11. The keyword _____ in the PROCEDURE DIVISION is used to create a detail line.
12. The report writer RD entry is found in the _____ SECTION of the COBOL program.
13. In the entry CONTROLS ARE FINAL PLANT FLOOR the name FLOOR refers to a _____ control total field.
14. A report description entry for the line referred to by FLOOR in question 13 would use a TYPE entry of _____ _____.
15. The GROUP INDICATE clause on a field causes the _____ occurrence of the field's value to be printed.
16. An input field called QUANTITY is to be printed on a detail line. The _____ clause would be used to identify this field in the report description entry.

17. The _____ clause is used to define a field whose total of each record is to be accumulated and printed.

18. Group printing of control fields is accomplished by using the _____ _____ clause.

19. TYPE IS _____ _____ will be used to print a heading at the top of each page of the report.

20. TYPE IS _____ _____ _____ is used on a report description entry to print a total line at the end of the report.

21. The entry NEXT GROUP _____ _____ will cause the detail lines for the following group of records to start at the top of a new page.

MULTIPLE CHOICE

22. The name of a report is first identified in what part of the program?
   a. SELECT clause
   b. FD entry
   c. RD entry
   d. INITIATE statement

23. Which entry in the RD defines the number of lines available for printing on the report?
   a. PAGE LIMIT
   b. HEADING
   c. FIRST DETAIL
   d. LAST DETAIL
   e. c and d

24. What purpose does the HEADING entry in the RD serve?
   a. It specifies where the heading area begins.
   b. It defines the line number of the first heading.
   c. It defines the contents of the heading line.
   d. It is an optional entry that is seldom used.

25. If the REPORT HEADING is given a LINE NUMBER value of 1 and we want two blank lines between it and the PAGE HEADING, what LINE NUMBER will be used for the page heading entry?
   a. 1
   b. 2
   c. 3
   d. 4

26. A control break is required on the field ACCOUNT. Where will this field be named in the report writer entries?
   a. RD entry.
   b. TYPE IS CONTROL FOOTING entry.
   c. PAGE HEADING entry.
   d. a and b.
   e. All the above.
   f. None of the above.

27. A CONTROL FOOTING line is required when the field DEPT changes value. This line must have one blank line between the previous detail line and itself. Which entry would be used in the CONTROL FOOTING?
   a. LINE NUMBER IS 2.
   b. LINE NUMBER IS PLUS 2.
   c. LINE NUMBER IS PLUS 1.
   d. LINE NUMBER IS GROUP INDICATE.

28. A report program contains the entry

```
10 MINOR-AMOUNT
      COLUMN IS 8
      PICTURE IS ZZ,ZZ9.99
      SUM AMOUNT-PAID.
```

Which statement best describes the value that will be printed as a result of this entry?
   a. It will be the sum of the values in the field MINOR-AMOUNT.
   b. It will be the sum of values supplied by the field called AMOUNT-PAID.

    c. It will be a numeric value starting in column 8.

    d. a and b.

    e. b and c.

    f. a, b, and c.

29. Given the following partial entry, what would be the most effective method to get the value of the field TAX-PAID to print in this entry?

```
10 TAX-AMOUNT
       COLUMN IS 28
       PICTURE IS ZZ,ZZ9.99
```

    a. MOVE TAX-PAID TO TAX-AMOUNT.   c. SUM TAX-PAID.

    b. SOURCE IS TAX-PAID.   d. Any of the above.

30. A literal to be used as a heading or a descriptive entry on a line would be best entered with what clause?

    a. SOURCE   c. VALUE

    b. SUM   d. PICTURE

PROGRAMMING EXERCISES

1. Write a program using the report writer to read data in the format specified and create the following sales register report. There are no calculations for individual records, but a region total and a report total are required.

INPUT/OUTPUT RECORD DEFINITION					
File: Sales file Record Length: 40 Sequence: Region			File Type: Disk Blocking Factor: 12 Access Method: Sequential		
COLUMNS	FIELD	TYPE	LENGTH	DECIMALS	
1–2	Region	N	2		
3–6	Invoice number	N	4		
7–11	Customer number	N	5		
12–31	Customer name	A/N	20		
32–37	Amount purchased	N	6	2	

```
           0           1           2           3           4           5           6           7
           1234567890123456789012345678901234567890123456789012345678901234567890
```

```
                                       SALES REPORT


                                                                    PAGE NO, Z9

        REGION        INVOICE       CUSTOMER          CUSTOMER                  PURCHASE
        NUMBER        NUMBER        NUMBER              NAME                     AMOUNT


         99            9999          99999       X------------------X          Z,ZZ9.99

         99            9999          99999       X------------------X          Z,ZZ9.99

         99            9999          99999       X------------------X          Z,ZZ9.99

                      REGION TOTAL                                            ZZ,ZZ9.99

         99            9999          99999       X------------------X          Z,ZZ9.99

         99            9999          99999       X------------------X          Z,ZZ9.99

                      REGION TOTAL                                            ZZ,ZZ9.99

                      COMPANY TOTAL                                           ZZ,ZZ9.99
```

2. Write a program to produce the stock purchase report based on the output report format and the format of the input data. Each department must begin a new page on the report, and department number is to be group-printed. The stock amount is derived by multiplying the shares purchased by the price per share. Company contribution is always 5% of the stock amount and is the value by which the amount is reduced to get the amount payable. The price per share in the total line is the average price for that department. All other values are totals for the specific column under which the value is printed.

INPUT/OUTPUT RECORD DEFINITION				
File: Stock purchase file Record Length: 80 Sequence: Dept. (major) Employee (minor)		File Type: Disk Blocking Factor: 20 Access Method: Sequential		
COLUMNS	FIELD	TYPE	LENGTH	DECIMALS
1–3	Dept.	N	3	
4–8	Employee number	N	5	
9–28	Employee name	A/N	20	
29–30	No. of shares	N	2	
31–35	Price per share	N	5	2

```
         0         1         2         3         4         5         6         7         8         9
         1234567890123456789012345678901234567890123456789012345678901234567890123456789012345
```

```
                                    STOCK  PURCHASES                              PAGE NO. Z9


  DEPT.    EMPLOYEE   NAME                       SHARES      PRICE     PURCHASE      COMPANY      AMOUNT
  NUMBER   NUMBER                                PURCHASED    PER      AMOUNT        CONTRIB      PAYABLE
                                                            SHARE


  999      99999    X------------------X          Z9        ZZ9.99   Z,ZZ9.99       ZZ9.99     Z,ZZ9.99
           99999    X------------------X          Z9        ZZ9.99   Z,ZZ9.99       ZZ9.99     Z,ZZ9.99
           99999    X------------------X          Z9        ZZ9.99   Z,ZZ9.99       ZZ9.99     Z,ZZ9.99
           99999    X------------------X          Z9        ZZ9.99   Z,ZZ9.99       ZZ9.99     Z,ZZ9.99


                                                 ZZ9        ZZ9.99  ZZ,ZZ9.99     Z,ZZ9.99    ZZ,ZZ9.99



  999      99999    X------------------X          Z9        ZZ9.99   Z,ZZ9.99       ZZ9.99     Z,ZZ9.99
           99999    X------------------X          Z9        ZZ9.99   Z,ZZ9.99       ZZ9.99     Z,ZZ9.99
           99999    X------------------X          Z9        ZZ9.99   Z,ZZ9.99       ZZ9.99     Z,ZZ9.99
           99999    X------------------X          Z9        ZZ9.99   Z,ZZ9.99       ZZ9.99     Z,ZZ9.99


                                                 ZZ9        ZZ9.99  ZZ,ZZ9.99     Z,ZZ9.99    ZZ,ZZ9.99


                                                 ZZ9        ZZ9.99  ZZ,ZZ9.99     Z,ZZ9.99    ZZ,ZZ9.99
```

3. Create a report as specified in the layout from records contained in a VSAM payroll file. The file is organized with a key consisting of division, department, and employee number from major to minor. Read the file sequentially and produce the report as shown.

INPUT/OUTPUT RECORD DEFINITION				

File: Dept. payroll
Record Length: 80
Sequence: Division (major)
          Department (intermediate)
          Employee (minor)
		File Type: VSAM
		Blocking Factor: N/A
		Access Method: Sequential		

COLUMNS	FIELD	TYPE	LENGTH	DECIMALS
1	Division	N	1	
2–3	Department	N	2	
4–7	Employee number	N	4	
8–11	Gross pay	P	7	2
12–15	Federal tax	P	7	2
16–18	State tax	P	5	2
19–21	FICA	P	5	2
22–24	Medical	P	5	2
25–27	Other deductions	P	5	2
N—zoned decimal numeric field P—packed decimal numeric field				

```
         0         1         2         3         4         5         6         7         8         9
123456789012345678901234567890123456789012345678901234567890123456789012345678901234567890123456789012345
```

```
                              PAYROLL REPORT                           PAGE NO. Z9


 DIV. DEPT. EMP.      GROSS        FEDERAL       STATE      FICA      MEDICAL     OTHER       NET
 NO.  NO.  NUMBER      PAY          TAX           TAX                 AMOUNT      DED.        PAY


 9    99    9999    ZZ,ZZ9.99    ZZ,ZZ9.99    ZZ9.99    ZZ9.99     ZZ9.99     ZZ9.99    ZZ,ZZ9.99
            9999    ZZ,ZZ9.99    ZZ,ZZ9.99    ZZ9.99    ZZ9.99     ZZ9.99     ZZ9.99    ZZ,ZZ9.99
            9999    ZZ,ZZ9.99    ZZ,ZZ9.99    ZZ9.99    ZZ9.99     ZZ9.99     ZZ9.99    ZZ,ZZ9.99
            9999    ZZ,ZZ9.99    ZZ,ZZ9.99    ZZ9.99    ZZ9.99     ZZ9.99     ZZ9.99    ZZ,ZZ9.99

 DEPT TOTALS        ZZ,ZZ9.99    ZZ,ZZ9.99    ZZ9.99    ZZ9.99     ZZ9.99     ZZ9.99    ZZ,ZZ9.99

 9    99    9999    ZZ,ZZ9.99    ZZ,ZZ9.99    ZZ9.99    ZZ9.99     ZZ9.99     ZZ9.99    ZZ,ZZ9.99
            9999    ZZ,ZZ9.99    ZZ,ZZ9.99    ZZ9.99    ZZ9.99     ZZ9.99     ZZ9.99    ZZ,ZZ9.99
            9999    ZZ,ZZ9.99    ZZ,ZZ9.99    ZZ9.99    ZZ9.99     ZZ9.99     ZZ9.99    ZZ,ZZ9.99
            9999    ZZ,ZZ9.99    ZZ,ZZ9.99    ZZ9.99    ZZ9.99     ZZ9.99     ZZ9.99    ZZ,ZZ9.99

 DEPT TOTALS        ZZ,ZZ9.99    ZZ,ZZ9.99    ZZ9.99    ZZ9.99     ZZ9.99     ZZ9.99    ZZ,ZZ9.99

 DIVISION TOTALS    ZZ,ZZ9.99    ZZ,ZZ9.99    ZZ9.99    ZZ9.99     ZZ9.99     ZZ9.99    ZZ,ZZ9.99

 9    99    9999    ZZ,ZZ9.99    ZZ,ZZ9.99    ZZ9.99    ZZ9.99     ZZ9.99     ZZ9.99    ZZ,ZZ9.99
            9999    ZZ,ZZ9.99    ZZ,ZZ9.99    ZZ9.99    ZZ9.99     ZZ9.99     ZZ9.99    ZZ,ZZ9.99
            9999    ZZ,ZZ9.99    ZZ,ZZ9.99    ZZ9.99    ZZ9.99     ZZ9.99     ZZ9.99    ZZ,ZZ9.99
            9999    ZZ,ZZ9.99    ZZ,ZZ9.99    ZZ9.99    ZZ9.99     ZZ9.99     ZZ9.99    ZZ,ZZ9.99

 DEPT TOTALS        ZZ,ZZ9.99    ZZ,ZZ9.99    ZZ9.99    ZZ9.99     ZZ9.99     ZZ9.99    ZZ,ZZ9.99

 DIVISION TOTALS    ZZ,ZZ9.99    ZZ,ZZ9.99    ZZ9.99    ZZ9.99     ZZ9.99     ZZ9.99    ZZ,ZZ9.99

 COMPANY TOTALS     ZZ,ZZ9.99    ZZ,ZZ9.99    ZZ9.99    ZZ9.99     ZZ9.99     ZZ9.99    ZZ,ZZ9.99
```

10

CHARACTER MANIPULATION TECHNIQUES

Applications that use **nonnumeric data,** such as names, addresses, and descriptions, cannot usually use the computational variety of statements available to the COBOL programmer. Although these data can often be processed by using the MOVE and IF statements with some clever use of OCCURS and REDEFINES, there are times when these approaches are inadequate. This lack brings us to two unique statements in COBOL that are available in post-1968 versions of the language. These are the STRING and UNSTRING statements.

STRING STATEMENT

$$\underline{\text{STRING}} \left\{ \begin{array}{l} \text{identifier-1} \\ \text{literal-1} \end{array} \right\} \left[\begin{array}{l} \text{identifier-2} \\ \text{literal-2} \end{array} \right] \cdots \underline{\text{DELIMITED BY}} \left\{ \begin{array}{l} \text{identifier-3} \\ \text{literal-3} \\ \underline{\text{SIZE}} \end{array} \right\}$$

$$\left[\left\{ \begin{array}{l} \text{identifier-4} \\ \text{literal-4} \end{array} \right\} \left[\begin{array}{l} \text{identifier-5} \\ \text{literal-5} \end{array} \right] \cdots \underline{\text{DELIMITED BY}} \left\{ \begin{array}{l} \text{identifier-6} \\ \text{literal-6} \\ \underline{\text{SIZE}} \end{array} \right\} \right]$$

$$\underline{\text{INTO}} \text{ identifier-7 [WITH } \underline{\text{POINTER}} \text{ identifier-8]}$$
$$\text{[ON } \underline{\text{OVERFLOW}} \text{ imperative-statement]}$$

The **STRING** statement is used to combine data from two or more identifiers or literals into a single field. The effect of this operation is similar to doing concatenation in a language like BASIC, although STRING is more flexible and gives several options for its use.

In its simplest form, STRING combines the data from two identifiers into a single field. The example in Figure 10.1 shows the identifiers MONTH-A, DAY-A, and YEAR-A containing corresponding values. These fields are the sending fields because they supply the data. The STRING statement combines these values with the space to create a composite DATE-A field. DATE-A is the receiving field.

363

```
01 FIELDS.
    05 MONTH-A      PIC X(04) VALUE 'JAN,'.
    05 DAY-A        PIC X(02) VALUE '15'.
    05 YEAR-A       PIC X(04) VALUE '1987'.

01 DATE-A           PIC X(12) VALUE SPACES.

        :

PROCEDURE DIVISION.

        :
    STRING DAY-A DELIMITED BY SIZE
        ' ' DELIMITED BY SIZE
            MONTH-A DELIMITED BY SIZE
        ' ' DELIMITED BY SIZE
            YEAR-A DELIMITED BY SIZE
        INTO DATE-A.
```

```
┌───────┐   ┌──────┐   ┌──────┐
│ JAN,  │   │  15  │   │ 1987 │
└───────┘   └──────┘   └──────┘
 MONTH-A      DAY-A      YEAR-A
```

```
┌──────────────────┐
│  15 JAN, 1987    │
└──────────────────┘
      DATE-A
```

FIGURE 10.1   Using STRING to create a composite date

As shown in the example, a **string** may be represented by an identifier in the DATA DIVISION, such as DAY-A, or it may be a literal used directly in the statement itself. The use of a blank literal is quite common in the STRING statement to separate individual fields as they are combined in the receiving field.

DELIMITED BY ENTRY

The keywords **DELIMITED BY** are used to identify a character contained in the sending field that is used to terminate the sending of data. For example, if the field ADDRESS contained the string

```
'2475 CENTRAL AVE, BOSTON MA,'
```

and the STRING statement used the expression

```
ADDRESS DELIMITED BY ','
```

then only the values

```
2475 CENTRAL AVE
```

would be returned because the comma in the field is the **delimiter** that terminates the sending of the data.

The delimiter **SIZE** as used in the previous example indicates that all the characters in the field are to be sent and combined with other data in the receiving field. SIZE means that the size of the sending field determines the number of characters that are sent.

INTO ENTRY

The INTO clause in the STRING statement is always required as part of the statement. It defines the identifier where the data are to be combined as a result of the operation. Only an identifier name is permitted in this entry.

Unlike a MOVE statement, if this field is longer than the data that are supplied to it, the remaining positions will not be cleared to spaces. Therefore, if it is likely that the sending data will be shorter than the receiving field, it is necessary to move SPACES to the receiving field before the STRING statement is issued.

WITH POINTER OPTION

A pointer variable is permitted with the STRING statement to indicate where in the receiving field data are to begin. Without the use of **POINTER,** data will always begin in column or position 1 of the receiving field. When POSITION is used (see Figure 10.2), it defines a numeric identifier that may be DISPLAY, COMPUTATIONAL, or COMP-3. The size of the field must be large enough to represent the length of the receiving field plus one. This identifier must be initialized before using the STRING statement to a value of 1 or greater.

```
            A    B
    1   4   78   12                                                    72
───────────────────────────────────────────────────────────────────────
            01 FIELDS,
                05 NAME      PIC X(15) VALUE 'J.A. TRADER,   ',
                05 STREET    PIC X(15) VALUE '210 WATTS AVE,,',
                05 CITY      PIC X(15) VALUE 'STONEHILL',
                05 STATE     PIC X(10) VALUE 'MA, 21031',
                05 PTR-A     PIC 99    VALUE 0,

            01 DATA-1        PIC X(50) VALUE SPACES,

                :

            PROCEDURE DIVISION,

                :
                STRING NAME   DELIMITED BY ','
                       ' '    DELIMITED BY SIZE
                       STREET DELIMITED BY ','
                       ' '    DELIMITED BY SIZE
                       CITY   DELIMITED BY ','
                       ' '    DELIMITED BY SIZE
                       STATE  DELIMITED BY ','
                       INTO   DATA-1
                       WITH   POINTER PTR-A,
```

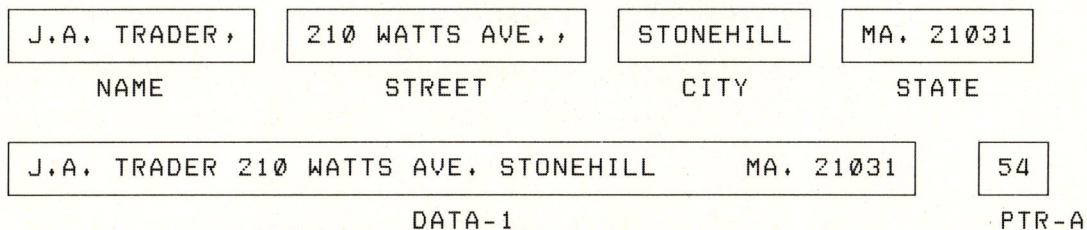

J.A. TRADER,	210 WATTS AVE,,	STONEHILL	MA, 21031
NAME	STREET	CITY	STATE

J.A. TRADER 210 WATTS AVE, STONEHILL MA, 21031	54
DATA-1	PTR-A

FIGURE 10.2 Using STRING with a POINTER option

As the string data are moved into the receiving field, the program will automatically update the pointer, and when the operation is complete, the POINTER identifier's value will indicate the position of the last character placed in the receiving field.

ON OVERFLOW OPTION

This optional entry, **OVERFLOW,** may be used when there is a chance of there being more data than the length of the receiving field. This option is used in the same way as the overflow statement in an arithmetic statement. With STRING, the overflow condition is activated when the position of a character being transferred to the receiving field exceeds the last position in the field. This is equivalent to the POINTER value exceeding the length of the field. When overflow occurs, whether or not the OVERFLOW option is used, the transmission of data to the receiving field will be terminated, which results in less data transfer than requested.

UNSTRING STATEMENT

UNSTRING identifier-1

$$\left[\underline{\text{DELIMITED BY}} \text{ [\underline{ALL}]} \begin{Bmatrix} \text{identifier-2} \\ \text{literal-1} \end{Bmatrix} \left[\underline{\text{OR}} \text{ [\underline{ALL}]} \begin{Bmatrix} \text{identifier-3} \\ \text{literal-2} \end{Bmatrix} \right] \dots \right]$$

  <u>INTO</u> identifier-4 [<u>DELIMITER</u> IN identifier-5] [<u>COUNT</u> IN identifier-6]

    identifier-7 [<u>DELIMITER</u> IN identifier-8] [<u>COUNT</u> IN identifier-9]] . . .

 [WITH <u>POINTER</u> identifier-10] [<u>TALLYING</u> IN identifier-11]

 [ON <u>OVERFLOW</u> imperative-statement]

Whereas STRING is used to combine several string values into a single string, **UNSTRING** does the opposite. It takes the contents of a single string and extracts separate portions of the string and assigns their values to other identifiers. The example in Figure 10.3 shows the identifier DATA-1 (sending field), containing name and address information. Each component of this string is separated from the other by a comma. Using the UNSTRING statement extracts the first part of the string up to the comma delimiter and allocates it to the identifier NAME (the receiving field). The next set of characters to the second comma delimiter is assigned to STREET, and so on, until all values have been allocated.

When using UNSTRING, only the characters up to the delimiter are transferred to the receiving field. Any unused positions in the receiving field are unaffected by the operation; thus it is normally necessary to initialize the receiving field to spaces before the UNSTRING is issued. It is the responsibility of the programmer to ensure there is adequate room in the receiving field to receive the length of data that is transmitted to it. A short receiving field will result in the truncation of characters.

DELIMITED BY OPTION

DELIMITED BY defines the character used to determine when transmission of data is to be terminated from the sending field. The entry

```
DELIMITED BY ','
```

will look for a comma in the sending field. Often spaces are used and could be detected with the entry

```
DELIMITED BY ' '
```

However, if two or more adjacent spaces are used, then each would be considered a delimiter, and the UNSTRING would transmit an empty string. This problem can be

```
        01 DATA-1              PIC X(50)
              VALUE ' J.A. TRADER, 210 WATTS AVE., STONEHILL, MA. 21031'.

        01 FIELDS.
              05 NAME           PIC X(15) VALUE SPACES.
              05 STREET         PIC X(15) VALUE SPACES.
              05 CITY           PIC X(15) VALUE SPACES.
              05 STATE          PIC X(10) VALUE SPACES.

              :

        PROCEDURE DIVISION.

              :

        UNSTRING DATA-1 DELIMITED BY ','
              INTO NAME
                   STREET
                   CITY
                   STATE.
```

```
| J.A. TRADER, 210 WATTS AVE., STONEHILL, MA. 21031 |
                          DATA-1
```

```
| J.A. TRADER |   | 210 WATTS AVE. |   | STONEHILL |   | MA. 21031 |
    NAME               STREET            CITY            STATE
```

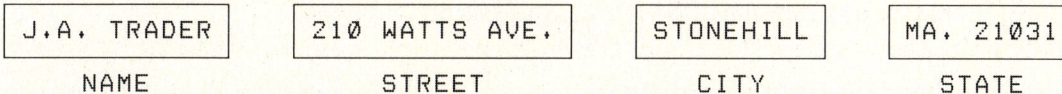

FIGURE 10.3 Using UNSTRING to extract name and address data

resolved by using the ALL option, which will ignore contiguous uses of the same delimiter.

```
                    DELIMITED BY ALL ' '
```

Sometimes a string may use several delimiters, such as the occasional comma and/or spaces. The DELIMITED option permits the use of the OR condition to define two or more different delimiters in the string. The presence of either delimiter will terminate the sending of data.

```
                DELIMITED BY ',' OR ALL ' '
```

DELIMITER IN OPTION

When the delimiter character that has terminated transmission of data needs to be stored, the DELIMITER IN option may be used. It is associated with the INTO clause and returns the delimiter character that stopped the transfer of data to the receiving field. The statement

```
        UNSTRING FIELD-IN DELIMITED BY ',' OR ALL ' '
              INTO NAME DELIMITER IN CHAR-IN.
```

will cause the characters in FIELD-IN up to the first comma or space to be transferred to the receiving field NAME. The delimiter that stopped the transfer, either a comma or a space, will be stored in the field CHAR-IN.

Character Manipulation Techniques

COUNT IN OPTION

This option also applies to the receiving field. It counts the number of characters transferred to the receiving field. COUNT IN must specify a numeric identifier with usage of DISPLAY, COMP, or COMP-3. This identifier must also be large enough to accommodate a count consistent with the size of the data transferred to the receiving field.

WITH POINTER OPTION

The POINTER option in the UNSTRING statement functions similarly to its use in the STRING statement. In UNSTRING it defines the starting position in the sending field where the data are to begin. It's starting value must be 1 or greater. As data are transferred, the program automatically updates this pointer to indicate the position of each character sent. When the UNSTRING statement is finished, the POINTER will contain the value of the position of the last character sent.

The identifier used for the pointer must be numeric and must be of a length to represent the maximum number of characters in the receiving field plus one.

TALLYING IN OPTION

Use the TALLYING option if it is necessary to count the number of receiving fields that get data from the UNSTRING statement. The identifier used is usually initialized to zero and must be a numeric field large enough to represent a count of the number of fields used. As data are transferred from the sending to receiving fields, TALLYING will count the number of fields that receive data, including any null strings because of adjacent delimiters. This option may be useful when all receiving fields are unlikely to receive data each time UNSTRING is executed.

ON OVERFLOW OPTION

As with the STRING statement, OVERFLOW may also be used in UNSTRING to indicate when there are unprocessed characters in the sending field. This action occurs when there are more data in the sending field than receiving fields to accept the data. Several reasons may exist for this occurrence. One may be the presence of too many delimiters in the sending field; another reason may be an inaccurate use of the DELIMITED BY option.

Example 1

Figure 10.4 shows the use of the POINTER option to indicate the position of the data from the sending field as they are extracted. This example also shows how UNSTRING may be used in a loop and that the POINTER variable permits the program to pick out successive characters from the sending field by retaining the position in the field each time through the loop.

Example 2

Figure 10.5 shows the use of the COUNT IN and TALLYING options. COUNT IN counts the number of characters transferred to the receiving field. In this example, the identifier COUNT-A is used in the option and is displayed each time a string is extracted. The count in this program includes the space that is the first character in each of the fields extracted from the sending string.

The TALLYING option is used to count the number of fields that receive data from the sending string. In this case, there is data for NAME each time through the loop, and so the value of COUNT-B for the tally is 4 when the process is complete.

```
      A   B
1  4  78  12                                             72
----------------------------------------------------------
       01 DATA-1            PIC X(50)
          VALUE ' J.A. TRADER, 210 WATTS AVE., STONEHILL, MA. 21031'.

       01 FIELDS.
          05 NAME           PIC X(15) VALUE SPACES.
          05 PTR-A          PIC 99    VALUE 1.
              :

       PROCEDURE DIVISION.

           PERFORM SELECT-WORD 4 TIMES.

              :

       SELECT-WORD.
           UNSTRING DATA-1 DELIMITED BY ','
               INTO NAME
               WITH POINTER PTR-A.

           DISPLAY PTR-A, NAME.
```

```
J.A. TRADER, 210 WATTS AVE., STONEHILL, MA. 21031
```

DATA-1

Display Results

Value in PTR-A	Value in NAME
14	J.A. TRADER
30	210 WATTS AVE.
41	STONEHILL
51	MA. 21031

FIGURE 10.4 Using a loop and a POINTER option in UNSTRING

```
        01 DATA-1             PIC X(50)
             VALUE ' J.A. TRADER, 210 WATTS AVE., STONEHILL, MA. 21031'.

        01 FIELDS.
             05 NAME          PIC X(15) VALUE SPACES.
             05 PTR-A         PIC 99    VALUE 1.
             05 COUNT-A       PIC 99    VALUE 0.
             05 COUNT-B       PIC 99    VALUE 0.

                  :

        PROCEDURE DIVISION.

             PERFORM SELECT-WORD 4 TIMES.
             DISPLAY COUNT-B.

                  :

        SELECT-WORD.
             UNSTRING DATA-1 DELIMITED BY ','
                  INTO NAME COUNT IN COUNT-A
                  WITH POINTER PTR-A
                  TALLYING IN COUNT-B.

             DISPLAY PTR-A, NAME, COUNT-A.
```

```
┌────────────────────────────────────────────────────────────┐
│ J.A. TRADER, 210 WATTS AVE., STONEHILL, MA. 21031            │
└────────────────────────────────────────────────────────────┘
                              DATA-1
```

Display Results

Value in PTR-A	Value in NAME	Value in COUNT-A
14	J.A. TRADER	12
30	210 WATTS AVE.	15
41	STONEHILL	10
51	MA. 21031	10

Value in COUNT-B		
4		

FIGURE 10.5 Using COUNT, POINTER, and TALLYING in UNSTRING

INSPECT STATEMENT

Format 1

```
INSPECT   data-name-1   TALLYING   data-name-2

     FOR ⎧⎧ALL      ⎫  ⎧data-name-3⎫⎫
         ⎨⎨LEADING  ⎬  ⎨literal-1   ⎬⎬
         ⎩ CHARACTERS ⎭  ⎩           ⎭⎭

     ⎡⎧BEFORE⎫            ⎧data-name-4⎫⎤
     ⎢⎨AFTER ⎬   INITIAL  ⎨literal-2   ⎬⎥
     ⎣⎩      ⎭            ⎩           ⎭⎦
```

Format 2

```
INSPECT   data-name-1   REPLACING

     CHARACTERS

         ⎧ALL     ⎫  ⎧data-name-2⎫
         ⎨LEADING ⎬  ⎨literal-1   ⎬
         ⎩FIRST   ⎭  ⎩           ⎭

     BY⎧data-name-3⎫ ⎡⎧BEFORE⎫          ⎧data-name-4⎫⎤
       ⎨literal-2   ⎬ ⎢⎨AFTER ⎬ INITIAL ⎨literal-3   ⎬⎥
       ⎩           ⎭ ⎣⎩      ⎭          ⎩           ⎭⎦
```

The **INSPECT** statement is available to 1974 and 1985 ANS COBOL users. INSPECT was covered in depth in the first book in this series and so we will only look at it briefly here. INSPECT is in two formats: Format 1 examines an identifier, from left to right, for the presence of a character and counts the number of occurrences of that character. Format 2 may be used to replace a specific character with another character.

Example 1 Use of Format 1

A field called ORDER-DATE must contain two slashes (/) for a valid date. Use INSPECT to determine the number of slash characters in the field.

```
      A    B
1   4  78  12                                                          72
         05   ORDER-DATE        PIC X(08).
              :
         05   COUNT2            PIC 9(01) VALUE ZERO.
              :

         INSPECT ORDER-DATE   TALLYING COUNT2
              FOR ALL '/'.
```

Sample values after INSPECT	ORDER-DATE	COUNT2
	02/12/86	2
	06/2/86/	3

Example 2 Format 1

Determine the number of characters that are in EMP-CODE before the first X is found.

```
        A    B
1   4   78   12                                                                    72
```

```
            Ø5   EMP-CODE        PIC X(Ø6).
                 :
            Ø5   COUNT4          PIC 9(Ø1) VALUE ZERO.
                 :

        INSPECT EMP-CODE  TALLYING COUNT4
            FOR CHARACTERS BEFORE INITIAL 'X'.
```

```
                Sample values       EMP-CODE        COUNT4
                after INSPECT     ┌─────────┐      ┌───┐
                                  │ 1S3XR6  │      │ 3 │
                                  └─────────┘      └───┘

                                  ┌─────────┐      ┌───┐
                                  │ W5F7G5  │      │ 6 │
                                  └─────────┘      └───┘
```

The second format of the INSPECT statement differs from the first in one way. Instead of tallying the number of occurrences of a character in data-name-1, it replaces the character with another. This feature allows you to patch up a field when a character occurs that is known to represent some other character. The REPLACING feature also permits the removal of a character by replacing it with a space or zero.

Example 3 Use of Format 2

Replace the first number sign (#) found with a dollar sign ($).

```
        A    B
1   4   78   12                                                                    72
```

```
            Ø5   DESCRIPTION     PIC X(1Ø).
                 :
                 :
        INSPECT DESCRIPTION REPLACING FIRST '#'
            BY '$'.
```

```
    Sample values       DESCRIPTION         DESCRIPTION
    after INSPECT         before              after

                      ┌───────────┐       ┌───────────┐
                      │ bb#456#890 │       │ bb$456#890 │
                      └───────────┘       └───────────┘

                      ┌───────────┐       ┌───────────┐
                      │ #1#2#3#4#5 │       │ $1#2#3#4#5 │
                      └───────────┘       └───────────┘
```

EXAMINE STATEMENT

```
EXAMINE    data-name-1    TALLYING    ┌ UNTIL FIRST ┐
                                      │ ALL         │
                                      └ LEADING     ┘
literal-1    REPLACING BY    literal-2
```

Format 2

```
EXAMINE    data-name-1    REPLACING

┌ ALL         ┐
│ LEADING     │
│ FIRST       │  literal-1    BY    literal-2
└ UNTIL FIRST ┘
```

The **EXAMINE** statement is available to 1968 users of ANS COBOL. If you are using this level of the COBOL compiler, then EXAMINE will be used instead of INSPECT. Essentially, EXAMINE offers the same features as the INSPECT statement with some minor variations. One difference is that format 1 of EXAMINE permits both the tallying of a specific character and its replacement in one statement. Another difference is the lack of the BEFORE or AFTER option that INSPECT provides.

When the TALLYING option is used in EXAMINE, a special counter called TALLY is used to record the count. Unlike the counter in the INSPECT, which the programmer provides, TALLY is built into the system and is automatically initialized to zero. TALLY's value may be used in expressions like any other identifier in the COBOL program, except that TALLY may not receive a value.

Example 1 Use of Format 1

Find the number of hyphens in the field ACCOUNT-NO.

```
      A    B
1  4  78   12                                                     72
              05   ACCOUNT-NO      PIC X(Ø7),
                     :
                     :
              EXAMINE ACCOUNT-NO TALLYING ALL '-',
```

```
Sample values          ACCOUNT-NO        TALLY
after EXAMINE
                       ┌──────────┐      ┌────┐
                       │ 23-4-33  │      │ Ø2 │
                       └──────────┘      └────┘

                       ┌──────────┐      ┌────┐
                       │ 1234567  │      │ ØØ │
                       └──────────┘      └────┘
```

Example 2 Use of Format 2

Replace all the characters that are in EMP-CODE before the first X is found with an asterisk (*).

```
            05   EMP-CODE           PIC X(06).
                   :
                   :
            EXAMINE EMP-CODE   REPLACING UNTIL FIRST 'X'
                 BY '*'.
```

```
Sample values          EMP-CODE           EMP-CODE
after EXAMINE          before             after

                      ┌────────┐         ┌────────┐
                      │ 1S3XR6 │         │ ***XR6 │
                      └────────┘         └────────┘

                      ┌────────┐         ┌────────┐
                      │ W5F7G5 │         │ W5F7G5 │
                      └────────┘         └────────┘
```

PERSONALIZED LETTERS: AN APPLICATION PROGRAM

Creating a personalized letter from a standard letter form is one application that uses the STRING and UNSTRING statements in COBOL. In this application, we are to prepare a series of personalized letters inviting potential customers to subscribe to a travel magazine. The program will contain data representing the form of the letter with appropriate empty spaces to insert the client's name and subscriber number. An input file will be used to provide the name and address data of each potential subscriber. These data are merged with the letter format to produce separate individualized letters for each customer on the file.

PROGRAM SPECIFICATIONS

The specifications for an application such as this will be rather brief because there is very little in the way of definition that can be said. While the program itself may be fairly challenging, its definition is quite simple and straightforward, as indicated in Figure 10.6.

PROGRAMMING SPECIFICATIONS

PROGRAM NAME: Travel Magazine Letter   PROGRAM ID: TRAVEL10
PREPARED BY: Diane Quest   DATE: Oct. 2, 1986

Program Description:
    This program produces personalized letters inviting customers to subscribe to Travel World Magazine.
Input File(s):
    Contract file
Output File(s):
    Personalized letters
Program Requirements:
    1. Read customer records from the contract file. This file was previously used for the travel contract report.
    2. For each input record, create a personalized letter based on the format described in the output definition.
    3. Create a subscriber number for each letter consisting of the three-character agency number, the first five letters of the customer's surname, and the last four digits of the phone number.
    4. Insert the customer's name and address in the appropriate position in the letter.
    5. Extract the customer's surname from the name field and insert it into the two locations provided in the letter.
    6. Print one letter per customer.

FIGURE 10.6   Program specifications for the personalized letter

INPUT/OUTPUT DEFINITION

The input file for this application is the contract file used for the travel application in Chapter 8. It is not unusual for a file to be used in several applications or for a company to purchase a mailing list that was used for other applications. In this case, the contract file contains fields such as contract price and number of tickets that were used in the previous application but are not essential to this one. Although the fields are defined here as part of the record format in Figure 10.7, they will not be processed by the program when creating the personalized letter.

    The output in Figure 10.8 shows the layout of the personalized letter. The lowercase names in parentheses, such as (name), are there to identify the contents of the field

INPUT/OUTPUT RECORD DEFINITION

File: Contract file
Record Length: 90
Sequence: N/A

File Type: Disk
Blocking Factor: 1
Access Method: Sequential

COLUMNS	FIELD	TYPE	LENGTH	DECIMALS
1–3	Agency	A/N	3	
4–7	Customer number	N	4	
8–20	Name	A/N	13	
21–40	Address line 1	A/N	20	
41–60	Address line 2	A/N	20	
61–70	Phone number	N	10	
71–76	Contract price	N	6	2
77–78	No. of tickets	N	2	
79–80	Package key	N	2	
81–86	Date	N	6	

FIGURE 10.7   Input record format for the personalized letter application.

```
        0         1         2         3         4         5         6         7
        123456789012345678901234567890123456789012345678901234567890123456789012345678901234567890

        PERSONALIZED SUBSCRIBER NUMBER: 120SMITH6701

        J.L. SMITH
        205 SPRING RD.
        BELFOREST RI 23709

        DEAR MR. SMITH:

        AS A LOYAL CUSTOMER OF NO-NAME TRAVEL AGENCY
        YOU HAVE BEEN SELECTED TO RECEIVE A SPECIAL
        SUBSCRIPTION RATE FOR TRAVEL WORLD MAGAZINE.
        FOR THE LOW PRICE OF ONLY $19.95 YOU WILL RECEIVE
        12 EXCITING ISSUES OF THE LATEST IN TRAVEL
        INFORMATION. THIS IS A ONE TIME OFFER AND IF YOU
        RESPOND TODAY A DIGITAL TRAVEL ALARM CLOCK WILL
        BE INCLUDED WITH YOUR FIRST ISSUE.

        I KNOW, MR. SMITH, THAT YOU WILL FIND TRAVEL
        WORLD TO BE AN ENJOYABLE MAGAZINE SO PLEASE
        RETURN THE ENCLOSED CARD FOR PROMPT SERVICE.

        SINCERELY,

        JANE R. LAWRENCE
        TRAVEL WORLD
```

FIGURE 10.8   Output definition for the subscriber letter

because headings are not used. This description will not be printed by the program but is only provided for reference purposes.

The subscriber number shown is an example of how the number would look after it has been developed from one set of input data. More will be said about this later. Finally, there are two locations in the letter where the surname appears. These data must be extracted from the customer names supplied by the input record.

STRUCTURE CHART

Figure 10.9 shows the structure chart for the application. This chart follows a customary pattern, with unique modules included as an expansion of the process box. These modules identify the need to provide program code to extract the customer data from the input record, create the letter from these data, and then print the letter. This problem is unique in the sense that a great number of modules is not used but some of the code they contain is reasonably complex. This complexity is not apparent from the structure chart, which after all is one of the reasons for using a structure chart—to reduce complexity in the early stages of program design. As we progress into the pseudo and then the program code, this complexity becomes more apparent.

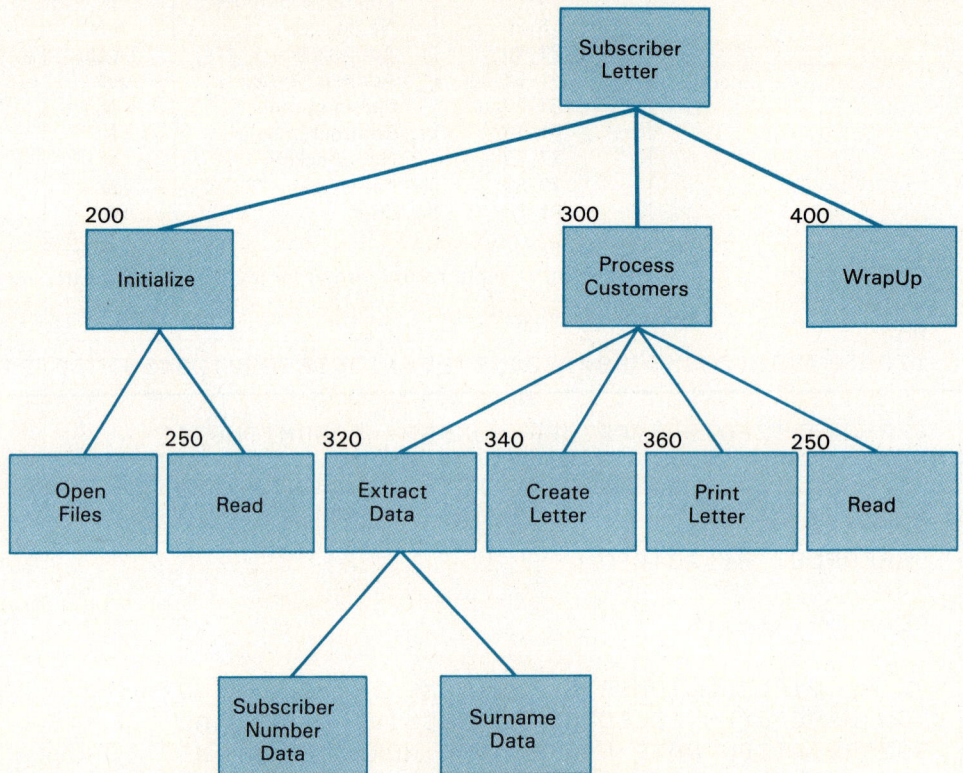

FIGURE 10.9   Structure chart for the subscriber letter application

PSEUDO CODE

Figure 10.10 shows the pseudo code and structured flowchart for developing the personalized letter program. There are two particularly important modules here that are keys to the program's development. These are 320-Extract-Data and 340-Create-Letter. Module 320-Extract-Data defines the necessary steps to extract each field or portion of a field needed to create the subscriber number. The pseudo code describes the steps required without going into all the detail of writing STRING and UNSTRING statements needed in the COBOL program. This paragraph also extracts the surname that is necessary for the personalized part of the letter.

The module 340-Create-Letter moves each line of the letter to a print line for printing. The decision made here is to store each line of the letter in an element of an array or table, and so this module moves all the variable data, such as the subscriber number, name, address, and surname, to their respective locations in the letter. Then paragraph 360-Print-Letter is performed repetitively to print each line of the letter from the array.

This process is repeated until each input record has been printed as a personalized letter. When end of file is reached, the program is terminated.

PSEUDO CODE

PROGRAM NAME: Travel Magazine Letter   PROGRAM ID: TRAVEL10

PREPARED BY: Jonathan Youngman   DATE: Oct. 3   PAGE 1 of 1

100-Mainline
1. Perform 200-Initialize.
2. Perform 300-Process
   Until EOF.
3. Perform 400-Wrap-Up.
4. Stop Run

200-Initialize
1. Open input and output files.
2. Perform 250-Read.

250-Read
1. Read contract
   at end move 'yes' to EOF-Flag.

300-Process
1. Perform 320-Extract-Data.
2. Perform 340-Create-Letter.
3. Write blank line from detail line
   after advancing to top of page.
4. Perform 360-Print-Letter
   Varying Subs-1 from 1 by 1
   Until Subs-1 > 25.
5. Perform 250-Read.

320-Extract-Data
1. Extract five letters from surname
2. Extract last four digits of phone number.
3. Create subscriber number.
4. Extract surname.

340-Create-Letter
1. Initialize PTR-S, PTR-1, PTR-2.
2. Place subscriber number in output line.
3. Move name and address to output.
4. Insert surname in Name-Line-01.
5. Insert surname in Name-Line-02.

360-Print-Letter
1. Move Letter-Line (Subs-1) to Detail-Line.
2. Write print-rec from Detail-Line
   after advancing 1 line.

400-Wrap-Up
1. Close files.

FIGURE 10.10(a) Pseudo code for the personalized travel letter

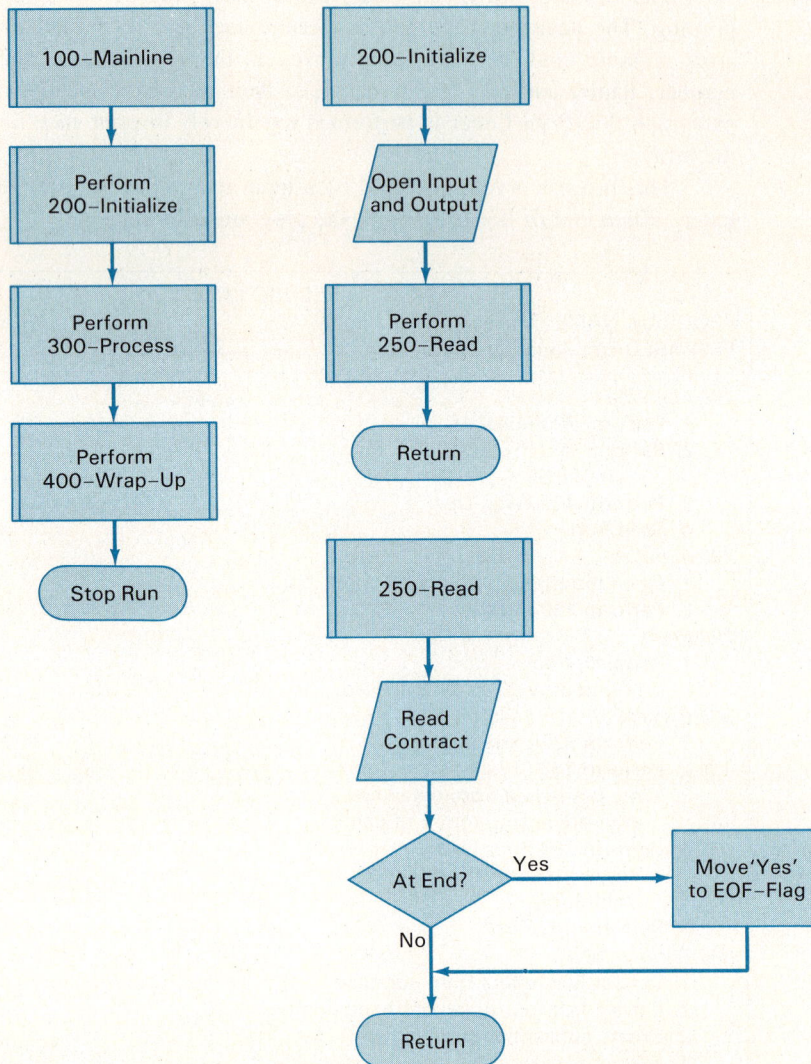

FIGURE 10.10(b) Flowchart for the personalized travel letter program

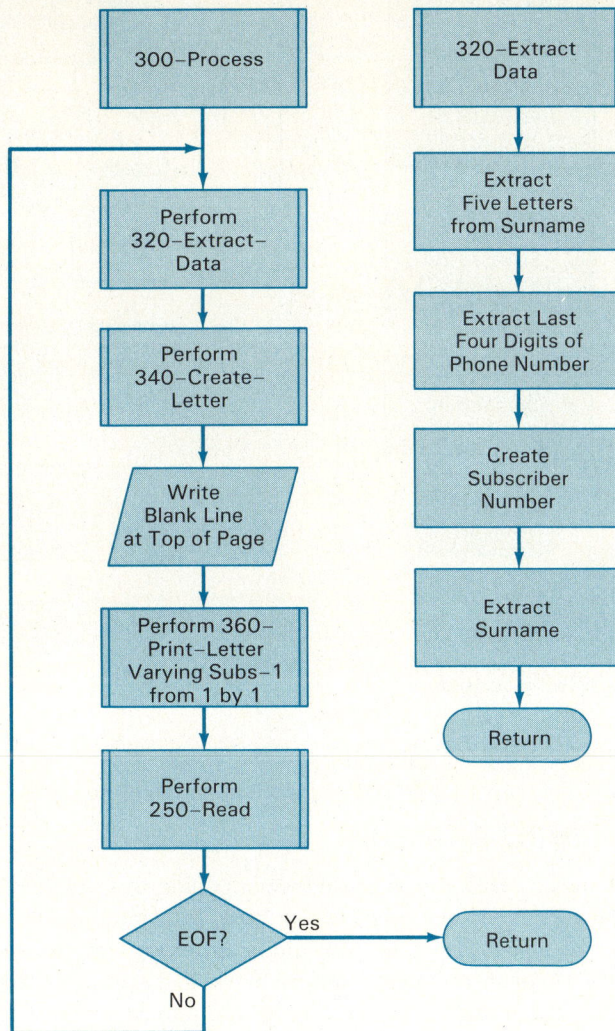

FIGURE 10.10(c)

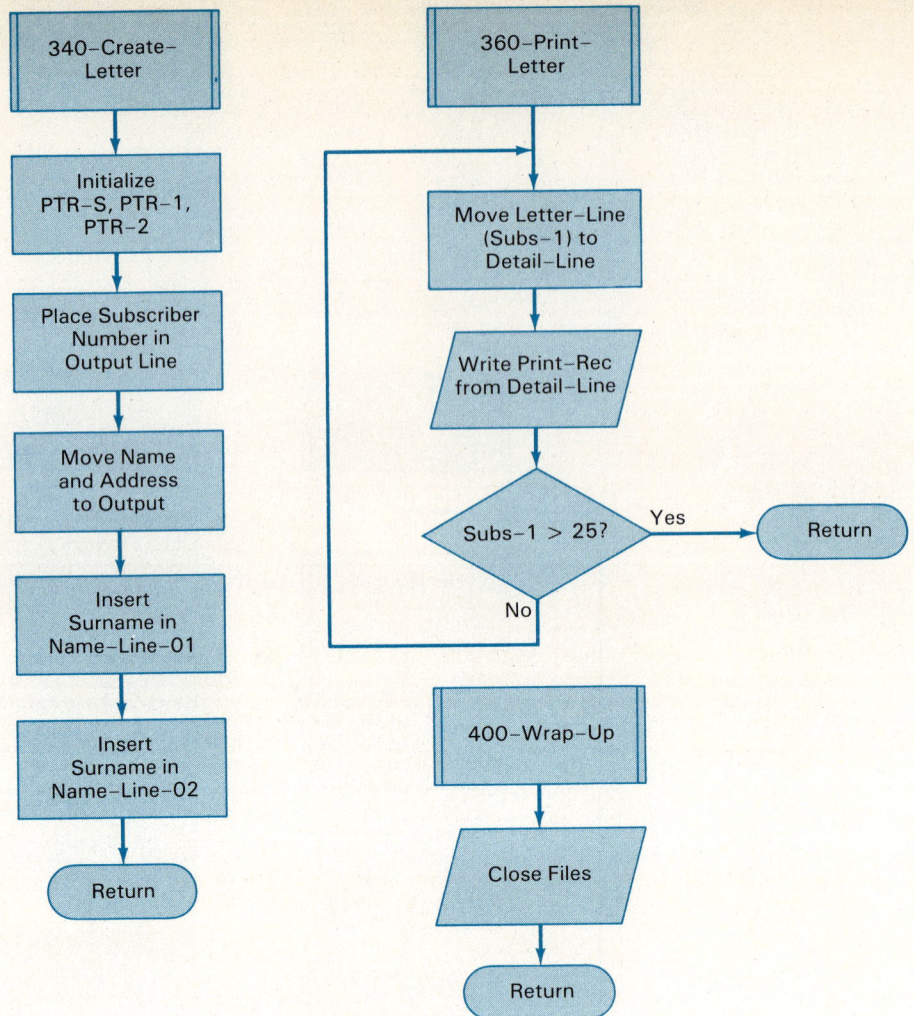

FIGURE 10.10(d)

PROGRAM CODING

WORKING-STORAGE

A major decision to be made when coding this program is to determine how the letter data are stored and ultimately printed. We could consider storing all of it consecutively in memory, but then there would be problems with the limit on the size of alphanumeric fields. Another possible approach would be to store the letter on a separate file and read it into this program as it is being printed. Clearly, this approach was not taken as suggested in the program specifications.

The approach finally used is to store each line of the letter as a separate FILLER entry. In the case of lines that need to have additional data inserted, an identifier is used rather than a FILLER. The names OUT-SUBSCRIBER, OUT-NAME, OUT-ADDRESS-01, OUT-ADDRESS-02, NAME-LINE-01, and NAME-LINE-02 are all examples of this usage. Figure 10.11 shows how this organization is created.

Blank lines in the letter are represented by a FILLER with a VALUE of SPACES. To simplify the printing of each line of the letter, the record LETTER-DATA is redefined as LETTER and the identifier LETTER-LINE is used with an OCCURS clause to create a table of entries. This approach will make it fairly easy to subscript each line of the letter and move it to the print area for printing.

```
Ø1  LETTER-DATA.
    Ø5  OUT-SUBSCRIBER            PIC X(65)
        VALUE 'PERSONALIZED SUBSCRIBER NUMBER:     '.
    Ø5  FILLER                    PIC X(65)
        VALUE SPACES.
    Ø5  OUT-NAME                  PIC X(65)
        VALUE SPACES.
    Ø5  OUT-ADDRESS-Ø1            PIC X(65)
        VALUE SPACES.
    Ø5  OUT-ADDRESS-Ø2            PIC X(65)
        VALUE SPACES.
    Ø5  FILLER                    PIC X(65)
        VALUE SPACES.
    Ø5  NAME-LINE-Ø1              PIC X(65)
        VALUE 'DEAR MR.           :'.
    Ø5  FILLER                    PIC X(65)
        VALUE SPACES.
    Ø5  FILLER                    PIC X(65)
        VALUE 'AS A LOYAL CUSTOMER OF NO-NAME TRAVEL AGENCY '.
    Ø5  FILLER                    PIC X(65)
        VALUE 'YOU HAVE BEEN SELECTED TO RECEIVE A SPECIAL '.
    Ø5  FILLER                    PIC X(65)
        VALUE 'SUBSCRIPTION RATE FOR TRAVEL WORLD MAGAZINE. '.
    Ø5  FILLER                    PIC X(65)
        VALUE 'FOR THE LOW PRICE OF ONLY $19.95 YOU WILL RECEIVE'.
    Ø5  FILLER                    PIC X(65)
        VALUE '12 EXCITING ISSUES OF THE LATEST IN TRAVEL'.
    Ø5  FILLER                    PIC X(65)
        VALUE 'INFORMATION. THIS IS A ONE TIME OFFER AND IF YOU '.
    Ø5  FILLER                    PIC X(65)
        VALUE 'RESPOND TODAY A DIGITAL TRAVEL ALARM CLOCK WILL '.
    Ø5  FILLER                    PIC X(65)
        VALUE 'BE INCLUDED WITH YOUR FIRST ISSUE. '.
    Ø5  FILLER                    PIC X(65)
        VALUE SPACES.
    Ø5  NAME-LINE-Ø2              PIC X(65)
        VALUE 'I KNOW, MR.          , THAT YOU WILL FIND TRAVEL'.
    Ø5  FILLER                    PIC X(65)
        VALUE 'WORLD TO BE AN ENJOYABLE MAGAZINE SO PLEASE '.
    Ø5  FILLER                    PIC X(65)
        VALUE 'RETURN THE ENCLOSED CARD FOR PROMPT SERVICE. '.
    Ø5  FILLER                    PIC X(65)
        VALUE SPACES.
    Ø5  FILLER                    PIC X(65)
        VALUE 'SINCERELY,'.
    Ø5  FILLER                    PIC X(65)
        VALUE SPACES.
    Ø5  FILLER                    PIC X(65)
        VALUE 'JANE R. LAWRENCE'.
    Ø5  FILLER                    PIC X(65)
        VALUE 'TRAVEL WORLD'.
Ø1  LETTER REDEFINES LETTER-DATA.
    Ø5  LETTER-LINE OCCURS 25 TIMES PIC X(65).
```

FIGURE 10.11 Defining the letter in WORKING-STORAGE

Take notice of how the lines that receive data are set up in the record. For example, NAME-LINE-01 contains the VALUE entry as follows:

```
05 NAME-LINE-01             PIC X(65)
   VALUE 'DEAR MR.           :'.
```

The space between the salutation (Mr.) and the semicolon will be used to receive the surname after it has been extracted from the input record. A similar approach is used where the surname is to appear on the body of the letter.

```
05 NAME-LINE-02             PIC X(65)
   VALUE 'I KNOW, MR.          , THAT YOU WILL FIND TRAVEL'.
```

The surname will be inserted into these lines by using the STRING statement in the PROCEDURE DIVISION.

Other entries are needed in WORKING-STORAGE to be used when extracting parts of the input fields. These components, such as the last four digits of phone number, the surname, and the last five characters of surname, are all needed in the letter for either the subscriber number or the reference to the customer's name. Figure 10.12 shows these entries in WORKING-STORAGE.

```
01  OTHER-ITEMS.
    05  EOF-FLAG              PIX X(03)     VALUE 'NO'.
        88  END-OF-FILE                     VALUE 'YES'.
    05  INITIALS              PIC X(05)     VALUE SPACES.
    05  SURNAME-FIVE          PIC X(05)     VALUE SPACES.
    05  PHONE-FOUR            PIC X(04)     VALUE SPACES.
    05  SUBSCRIBER-NUMBER     PIC X(12)     VALUE SPACES.
    05  SURNAME               PIC X(10).
    05  PTR-S                 PIC 9(02)     VALUE ZERO.
    05  PTR-1                 PIC 9(02)     VALUE ZERO.
    05  PTR-N                 PIC 9(02)     VALUE ZERO.
    05  SUBS-1                PIC 9(02)     VALUE ZERO.
```

FIGURE 10.12   Temporary fields in WORKING-STORAGE

The fields PTR-S, PTR-1, and PTR-2 are defined here also. PTR-1 is used to point to the position where the surname will go on NAME-LINE-01 and PTR-2 points to the position on NAME-LINE-02. PTR-S points to the position where the subscriber number is to be inserted on the output line. Each entry will be used in STRING statements and will be initialized in the PROCEDURE DIVISION because these pointers need to be reset each time a new value is combined with the field.

The last entry in this group is SUBS-1, which is defined for use as a subscript when referencing the current line of the letter to be printed.

100-MAINLINE   This paragraph follows what by now is a tradition in programming applications. It performs the initialization paragraph, specifies the main process loop, and performs the wrap-up paragraph before terminating the program.

200-INITIALIZE   Initialization in this program is a matter of opening the input and output files and performing the initial read paragraph to provide the name and address of the first customer.

250-READ   This paragraph reads each input record as required by the program.

300-PROCESS   This is the main process loop, which creates a personalized letter for each customer. The paragraph is executed for each input record that is read. First, paragraph 320-EXTRACT-DATA is performed to extract the values required from the input record. Next, paragraph 340-CREATE-LETTER is performed to insert all the needed data into the form letter.

Then a blank line is printed when the printer is advanced to a new page. The paragraph 360-PRINT-LETTER is then performed 25 times to print each of the 25 lines of the letter using the redefined subscripted fields. Finally, a new input record is read and the process is repeated.

320-EXTRACT-DATA This paragraph extracts the data from the input record that are necessary for use in the letter. First, the data for the subscriber number are extracted. To get the first five characters of the surname, an UNSTRING is used as follows:

```
UNSTRING NAME DELIMITED BY ALL ' '
    INTO INITIALS
        SURNAME-FIVE.
```

All characters up to the first blank space in NAME will be transferred into INITIALS. The remaining characters will go into SURNAME-FIVE. Because SURNAME-FIVE is only five characters in length, any additional characters will be truncated, leaving us with the first five. A shorter surname will result in spaces after the initial characters.

The four digits of phone number are extracted simply by using a REDEFINES in the input record that calls the last four positions of the number LAST-FOUR-DIGITS. These digits are moved with the statement

```
MOVE LAST-FOUR-DIGITS TO PHONE-FOUR.
```

Now the subscriber number can be created because we have fields for each of the parts. Using the STRING statement combines these separate parts into the one field called SUBSCRIBER-NUMBER, as follows:

```
STRING AGENCY        DELIMITED BY SIZE
       SURNAME-FIVE DELIMITED BY SIZE
       PHONE-FOUR    DELIMITED BY SIZE
       INTO SUBSCRIBER-NUMBER.
```

The next step is to extract the surname in its entirety for use in the letter. This procedure uses the STRING statement as before, but this time the field SURNAME is long enough to receive all the characters from the NAME field. First, SURNAME is initialized to SPACES and then the surname is extracted.

```
MOVE SPACES TO SURNAME.
UNSTRING NAME DELIMITED BY ALL ' '
    INTO INITIALS
        SURNAME.
```

340-CREATE-LETTER Creating the letter requires that the data unique to each potential subscriber be moved to the open spaces in the letter. First, the pointers to be used to specify the exact position within the fields must be initialized. This initialization is done with three moves, as follows:

```
MOVE 33 TO PTR-S.
MOVE 10 TO PTR-1.
MOVE 13 TO PTR-N.
```

Now the subscriber number can be moved to the line called OUT-SUBSCRIBER using PTR-S to identify the location within the field. The STRING statement is used for this move, as follows:

```
STRING SUBSCRIBER-NUMBER DELIMITED BY SIZE
      INTO OUT-SUBSCRIBER
      WITH POINTER PTR-S.
```

The name and address lines are moved to the appropriate letter fields in the normal manner with MOVE statements.

Finally, the paragraph inserts the surname into NAME-LINE-01 and NAME-LINE-02 using STRING statements and pointers PTR-1 and PTR-2, respectively.

```
STRING SURNAME DELIMITED BY SIZE
       INTO NAME-LINE-Ø1
       WITH POINTER PTR-1.
   STRING SURNAME DELIMITED BY SIZE
       INTO NAME-LINE-Ø2
       WITH POINTER PTR-N.
```

Preparing the data for the operation in the previous paragraph is an important part of getting the surname into the letter. It is this operation that results in the personalized letter we are seeking to create.

360-PRINT-LETTER   Now that the data have been merged into the letter format, the letter itself can be printed. This paragraph is contained in a loop that supplies a subscript SUBS-1 to move each line of the letter to the DETAIL-ENTRY of the detail line and print it. The steps for printing are very direct, as follows:

```
MOVE LETTER-LINE (SUBS-1) TO DETAIL-ENTRY.
WRITE PRINT-REC FROM DETAIL-LINE
      AFTER ADVANCING 1 LINE.
```

400-WRAP-UP   This paragraph completes the operation of the program by closing the files.

Figure 10.13 shows a complete program listing for this application.

```
IDENTIFICATION DIVISION.

PROGRAM-ID.
    SUBSCRIBE10.
*AUTHOR.
*    JOHNATHAN YOUNGMAN.
*INSTALLATION.
*    SALES UNLIMITED CORP.
*DATE-WRITTEN.
*    OCTOBER 1.
*DATE-COMPILED.

*SECURITY.
*    NONE.

ENVIRONMENT DIVISION.

CONFIGURATION SECTION.
SOURCE-COMPUTER.
    IBM-4381.
OBJECT-COMPUTER.
    IBM-4381.
SPECIAL-NAMES.
    C01 IS TO-TOP-OF-PAGE.

INPUT-OUTPUT SECTION.

FILE-CONTROL.
    SELECT CONTRACT    ASSIGN TO   TRANS10.
    SELECT SUB-LETTER  ASSIGN TO   REPORT.
```

FIGURE 10.13(a)   Program code for creating a personalized letter

```
DATA DIVISION.

FILE SECTION.

FD  CONTRACT
    RECORD CONTAINS 90 CHARACTERS
    LABEL RECORDS ARE STANDARD
    DATA RECORD IS CONTRACT-REC.
01  CONTRACT-REC.
    05  FILLER                      PIC X(90).

FD  SUB-LETTER
    RECORD CONTAINS 133 CHARACTERS
    LABEL RECORDS ARE OMITTED
    DATA RECORD IS PRINT-REC.
01  PRINT-REC.
    05  PRINT-LINE                  PIC X(133).

WORKING-STORAGE SECTION.

01  OTHER-ITEMS.
    05  EOF-FLAG                    PIC X(03)    VALUE 'NO'.
        88  END-OF-FILE                          VALUE 'YES'.
    05  INITIALS                    PIC X(05)    VALUE SPACES.
    05  SURNAME-FIVE                PIC X(05)    VALUE SPACES.
    05  PHONE-FOUR                  PIC X(04)    VALUE SPACES.
    05  SUBSCRIBER-NUMBER           PIC X(12)    VALUE SPACES.
    05  SURNAME                     PIC X(10).
    05  PTR-S                       PIC 9(02)    VALUE ZERO.
    05  PTR-1                       PIC 9(02)    VALUE ZERO.
    05  PTR-N                       PIC 9(02)    VALUE ZERO.
    05  SUBS-1                      PIC 9(02)    VALUE ZERO.

01  WS-CONTRACT-REC.
    05  AGENCY                      PIC X(03).
    05  CUSTOMER-NO                 PIC 9(04).
    05  NAME                        PIC X(13).
    05  ADDRESS-01                  PIC X(20).
    05  ADDRESS-02                  PIC X(20).
    05  PHONE                       PIC X(10).
    05  NEW-PHONE REDEFINES PHONE.
        10  FILLER                  PIC X(06).
        10  LAST-FOUR-DIGITS        PIC X(04).
    05  CONTRACT-PRICE              PIC 9(04)V99.
    05  TICKETS                     PIC 9(02).
    05  PACKAGE-KEY                 PIC 9(02).
    05  CONTRACT-DATE.
        10  CONTRACT-MONTH          PIC 99.
        10  CONTRACT-DAY            PIC 99.
        10  CONTRACT-YEAR           PIC 99.
    05  FILLER                      PIC X(04).

01  LETTER-DATA.
    05  OUT-SUBSCRIBER              PIC X(65)
        VALUE 'PERSONALIZED SUBSCRIBER NUMBER:      '.
    05  FILLER                      PIC X(65)
        VALUE SPACES.
    05  OUT-NAME                    PIC X(65)
        VALUE SPACES.
    05  OUT-ADDRESS-01              PIC X(65)
        VALUE SPACES.
    05  OUT-ADDRESS-02              PIC X(65)
        VALUE SPACES.
    05  FILLER                      PIC X(65)
        VALUE SPACES.
    05  NAME-LINE-01                PIC X(65)
        VALUE 'DEAR MR.           :'.
    05  FILLER                      PIC X(65)
        VALUE SPACES.
    05  FILLER                      PIC X(65)
        VALUE 'AS A LOYAL CUSTOMER OF NO-NAME TRAVEL AGENCY '.
    05  FILLER                      PIC X(65)
        VALUE 'YOU HAVE BEEN SELECTED TO RECEIVE A SPECIAL '.
```

FIGURE 10.13(b)

```
            05 FILLER                      PIC X(65)
               VALUE 'SUBSCRIPTION RATE FOR TRAVEL WORLD MAGAZINE. '.
            05 FILLER                      PIC X(65)
               VALUE 'FOR THE LOW PRICE OF ONLY $19.95 YOU WILL RECEIVE'.
            05 FILLER                      PIC X(65)
               VALUE '12 EXCITING ISSUES OF THE LATEST IN TRAVEL'.
            05 FILLER                      PIC X(65)
               VALUE 'INFORMATION. THIS IS A ONE TIME OFFER AND IF YOU '.
            05 FILLER                      PIC X(65)
               VALUE 'RESPOND TODAY A DIGITAL TRAVEL ALARM CLOCK WILL '.
            05 FILLER                      PIC X(65)
               VALUE 'BE INCLUDED WITH YOUR FIRST ISSUE. '.
            05 FILLER                      PIC X(65)
               VALUE SPACES.
            05 NAME-LINE-02                PIC X(65)
               VALUE 'I KNOW, MR.          , THAT YOU WILL FIND TRAVEL'.
            05 FILLER                      PIC X(65)
               VALUE 'WORLD TO BE AN ENJOYABLE MAGAZINE SO PLEASE '.
            05 FILLER                      PIC X(65)
               VALUE 'RETURN THE ENCLOSED CARD FOR PROMPT SERVICE. '.
            05 FILLER                      PIC X(65)
               VALUE SPACES.
            05 FILLER                      PIC X(65)
               VALUE 'SINCERELY,'.
            05 FILLER                      PIC X(65)
               VALUE SPACES.
            05 FILLER                      PIC X(65)
               VALUE 'JANE R. LAWRENCE'.
            05 FILLER                      PIC X(65)
               VALUE 'TRAVEL WORLD'.
        01 LETTER REDEFINES LETTER-DATA.
            05 LETTER-LINE OCCURS 25 TIMES PIC X(65).


        01 DETAIL-LINE.
            05 FILLER              PIC X(001)    VALUE SPACES.
            05 DETAIL-ENTRY        PIC X(132)    VALUE SPACES.

        PROCEDURE DIVISION.

        100-MAINLINE.
            PERFORM 200-INITIALIZE.
            PERFORM 300-PROCESS
                UNTIL END-OF-FILE.
            PERFORM 400-WRAP-UP.
            STOP RUN.

        200-INITIALIZE.
            OPEN INPUT   CONTRACT
                 OUTPUT SUB-LETTER.
            PERFORM 250-READ.

        250-READ.
            READ CONTRACT INTO WS-CONTRACT-REC
                AT END MOVE 'YES' TO EOF-FLAG.

        300-PROCESS.
            PERFORM 320-EXTRACT-DATA.
            PERFORM 340-CREATE-LETTER.
            MOVE SPACES TO DETAIL-LINE.
            WRITE PRINT-REC FROM DETAIL-LINE
                AFTER ADVANCING TO-TOP-OF-PAGE.
            PERFORM 360-PRINT-LETTER
                VARYING SUBS-1 FROM 1 BY 1
                UNTIL SUBS-1 IS GREATER THAN 25.
            PERFORM 250-READ.

        320-EXTRACT-DATA.
        *
        *    CREATE SUBSCRIBER NUMBER CONSISTING OF
        *    3 CHAR. AGENCY, 5 LETTERS FROM SURNAME,
        *    AND LAST 4 DIGITS OF PHONE NUMBER.
        *
```

FIGURE 10.13(c)

```
          UNSTRING NAME DELIMITED BY ALL ' '
              INTO INITIALS
                   SURNAME-FIVE.
          MOVE LAST-FOUR-DIGITS TO PHONE-FOUR.
          STRING AGENCY          DELIMITED BY SIZE
                 SURNAME-FIVE DELIMITED BY SIZE
                 PHONE-FOUR   DELIMITED BY SIZE
                 INTO SUBSCRIBER-NUMBER.
   *
   *      EXTRACT SURNAME
   *
          MOVE SPACES TO SURNAME.
          UNSTRING NAME DELIMITED BY ALL ' '
              INTO INITIALS
                   SURNAME.

   340-CREATE-LETTER.
          MOVE 33 TO PTR-S.
          MOVE 10 TO PTR-1.
          MOVE 13 TO PTR-N.
          STRING SUBSCRIBER-NUMBER DELIMITED BY SIZE
              INTO OUT-SUBSCRIBER
              WITH POINTER PTR-S.
          MOVE NAME         TO OUT-NAME.
          MOVE ADDRESS-01 TO OUT-ADDRESS-01.
          MOVE ADDRESS-02 TO OUT-ADDRESS-02.
          STRING SURNAME DELIMITED BY SIZE
              INTO NAME-LINE-01
              WITH POINTER PTR-1.
          STRING SURNAME DELIMITED BY SIZE
              INTO NAME-LINE-02
              WITH POINTER PTR-N.

   360-PRINT-LETTER.
          MOVE LETTER-LINE (SUBS-1) TO DETAIL-ENTRY.
          WRITE PRINT-REC FROM DETAIL-LINE
              AFTER ADVANCING 1 LINE.

   400-WRAP-UP.
          CLOSE CONTRACT
                SUB-LETTER.
```

FIGURE 10.13(d)

PROGRAM TESTING

To test this program, the same data that were used in the travel agency problem will be used (see Figure 10.14). Although this file contains more data than are necessary, only the required fields are actually used by the program. Having extra fields containing unused data is a normal situation in a business application, and this will not present any problems when testing the program.

```
1203356J.L. SMITH     205 SPRING RD.    BELFOREST RI 23709   80123567010625000227011287
1203445G.T. WILSON    15 BELL COURT     TREMONT SD   70110   21049267121200000150022787
1203546L.L. ABLE      210 TRADE ST.     WILMONT PA   49122   42377682920500000312011587
1312300Q.B. BRAVO     1 FIRST ST.       CHICAGO IL   23501   20144426380650950445020187
1312301R. TRAVELER    101 WEST AVE.     BURBANK CA   41101   20523400001250000233021387
1504000D.C. LESSAC    410 BAY DR.       TORONTO ONT M9S 2D4  41676788912400000250010287
```

FIGURE 10.14   Test data for the personalized letter application

Each input record results in a complete personalized letter in the output. A letter requires a complete page, and so the six-input record in our test file will create six letters. Figure 10.15 shows the letters. After reviewing the results, we may not be quite satisfied with the appearance of some of the lines. For example, the line containing

          DEAR MR. SMITH   :

leaves extra blank spaces between SMITH and the colon (:) that ends the line. This effect is a result of the name being shorter than the space provided. Of course, a name that requires the entire space will not have this problem, but most names are shorter than the length of this empty slot in the letter.

A similar problem occurs in the second personalized line.

```
I KNOW, MR. SMITH      THAT YOU WILL FIND TRAVEL
```

Again the space in the line allows for the maximum length of the name and, as a result, if the name is shorter, extra space will be shown. These are not major problems and you will be asked to find a solution in Programming Exercise 1 at the end of the chapter.

```
PERSONALIZED SUBSCRIBER NUMBER: 120SMITHG701

J.L.  SMITH
205 SPRING RD.
BELFOREST RI 23709

DEAR MR. SMITH      :

AS A LOYAL CUSTOMER OF NO-NAME TRAVEL AGENCY
YOU HAVE BEEN SELECTED TO RECEIVE A SPECIAL
SUBSCRIPTION RATE FOR TRAVEL WORLD MAGAZINE.
FOR THE LOW PRICE OF ONLY $19.95 YOU WILL RECEIVE
12 EXCITING ISSUES OF THE LATEST IN TRAVEL
INFORMATION. THIS IS A ONE TIME OFFER AND IF YOU
RESPOND TODAY A DIGITAL TRAVEL ALARM CLOCK WILL
BE INCLUDED WITH YOUR FIRST ISSUE.

I KNOW, MR. SMITH      THAT YOU WILL FIND TRAVEL
WORLD TO BE AN ENJOYABLE MAGAZINE SO PLEASE
RETURN THE ENCLOSED CARD FOR PROMPT SERVICE.

SINCERELY,

JANE R. LAWRENCE
TRAVEL WORLD
```

FIGURE 10.15(a) Personalized letter from the travel program

```
PERSONALIZED SUBSCRIBER NUMBER: 120WILSO6712

G.T. WILSON
15 BELL COURT
TREMONT SD  70110

DEAR MR. WILSON     :

AS A LOYAL CUSTOMER OF NO-NAME TRAVEL AGENCY
YOU HAVE BEEN SELECTED TO RECEIVE A SPECIAL
SUBSCRIPTION RATE FOR TRAVEL WORLD MAGAZINE.
FOR THE LOW PRICE OF ONLY $19.95 YOU WILL RECEIVE
12 EXCITING ISSUES OF THE LATEST IN TRAVEL
INFORMATION. THIS IS A ONE TIME OFFER AND IF YOU
RESPOND TODAY A DIGITAL TRAVEL ALARM CLOCK WILL
BE INCLUDED WITH YOUR FIRST ISSUE.

I KNOW, MR. WILSON     THAT YOU WILL FIND TRAVEL
WORLD TO BE AN ENJOYABLE MAGAZINE SO PLEASE
RETURN THE ENCLOSED CARD FOR PROMPT SERVICE.

SINCERELY,

JANE R. LAWRENCE
TRAVEL WORLD
```

FIGURE 10.15(b)

```
PERSONALIZED SUBSCRIBER NUMBER: 120ABLE 8292

L.L. ABLE
210 TRADE ST.
WILMONT PA  49122

DEAR MR. ABLE      :

AS A LOYAL CUSTOMER OF NO-NAME TRAVEL AGENCY
YOU HAVE BEEN SELECTED TO RECEIVE A SPECIAL
SUBSCRIPTION RATE FOR TRAVEL WORLD MAGAZINE.
FOR THE LOW PRICE OF ONLY $19.95 YOU WILL RECEIVE
12 EXCITING ISSUES OF THE LATEST IN TRAVEL
INFORMATION. THIS IS A ONE TIME OFFER AND IF YOU
RESPOND TODAY A DIGITAL TRAVEL ALARM CLOCK WILL
BE INCLUDED WITH YOUR FIRST ISSUE.

I KNOW, MR. ABLE       THAT YOU WILL FIND TRAVEL
WORLD TO BE AN ENJOYABLE MAGAZINE SO PLEASE
RETURN THE ENCLOSED CARD FOR PROMPT SERVICE.

SINCERELY,

JANE R. LAWRENCE
TRAVEL WORLD
```

FIGURE 10.15(c)

```
PERSONALIZED SUBSCRIBER NUMBER: 131BRAVO2638

Q.B. BRAVO
1 FIRST ST.
CHICAGO IL  23501

DEAR MR. BRAVO      :

AS A LOYAL CUSTOMER OF NO-NAME TRAVEL AGENCY
YOU HAVE BEEN SELECTED TO RECEIVE A SPECIAL
SUBSCRIPTION RATE FOR TRAVEL WORLD MAGAZINE.
FOR THE LOW PRICE OF ONLY $19.95 YOU WILL RECEIVE
12 EXCITING ISSUES OF THE LATEST IN TRAVEL
INFORMATION. THIS IS A ONE TIME OFFER AND IF YOU
RESPOND TODAY A DIGITAL TRAVEL ALARM CLOCK WILL
BE INCLUDED WITH YOUR FIRST ISSUE.

I KNOW, MR. BRAVO      THAT YOU WILL FIND TRAVEL
WORLD TO BE AN ENJOYABLE MAGAZINE SO PLEASE
RETURN THE ENCLOSED CARD FOR PROMPT SERVICE.

SINCERELY,

JANE R. LAWRENCE
TRAVEL WORLD
```

FIGURE 10.15(d)

```
PERSONALIZED SUBSCRIBER NUMBER: 131TRAVE0000

R. TRAVELER
101 WEST AVE.
BURBANK CA  41101

DEAR MR. TRAVELER  :

AS A LOYAL CUSTOMER OF NO-NAME TRAVEL AGENCY
YOU HAVE BEEN SELECTED TO RECEIVE A SPECIAL
SUBSCRIPTION RATE FOR TRAVEL WORLD MAGAZINE.
FOR THE LOW PRICE OF ONLY $19.95 YOU WILL RECEIVE
12 EXCITING ISSUES OF THE LATEST IN TRAVEL
INFORMATION. THIS IS A ONE TIME OFFER AND IF YOU
RESPOND TODAY A DIGITAL TRAVEL ALARM CLOCK WILL
BE INCLUDED WITH YOUR FIRST ISSUE.

I KNOW, MR. TRAVELER   THAT YOU WILL FIND TRAVEL
WORLD TO BE AN ENJOYABLE MAGAZINE SO PLEASE
RETURN THE ENCLOSED CARD FOR PROMPT SERVICE.

SINCERELY,

JANE R. LAWRENCE
TRAVEL WORLD
```

FIGURE 10.15(e)

```
PERSONALIZED SUBSCRIBER NUMBER: 150LESSA8891

D.C. LESSAC
410 BAY DR.
TORONTO ONT M9S 2D4

DEAR MR. LESSAC      :

AS A LOYAL CUSTOMER OF NO-NAME TRAVEL AGENCY
YOU HAVE BEEN SELECTED TO RECEIVE A SPECIAL
SUBSCRIPTION RATE FOR TRAVEL WORLD MAGAZINE.
FOR THE LOW PRICE OF ONLY $19.95 YOU WILL RECEIVE
12 EXCITING ISSUES OF THE LATEST IN TRAVEL
INFORMATION. THIS IS A ONE TIME OFFER AND IF YOU
RESPOND TODAY A DIGITAL TRAVEL ALARM CLOCK WILL
BE INCLUDED WITH YOUR FIRST ISSUE.

I KNOW, MR. LESSAC      THAT YOU WILL FIND TRAVEL
WORLD TO BE AN ENJOYABLE MAGAZINE SO PLEASE
RETURN THE ENCLOSED CARD FOR PROMPT SERVICE.

SINCERELY,

JANE R. LAWRENCE
TRAVEL WORLD
```

FIGURE 10.15(f)

SUMMARY

The STRING and UNSTRING statements are available to simplify the manipulation of alphanumeric data in a COBOL program. 1968 ANS COBOL users must use REDEFINES and OCCURS to achieve similar results.

The STRING statement is used to combine alphanumeric data from two or more identifiers or literals into a single field. The DELIMITED BY option may be used to terminate the transfer of data when the delimiter character is found in the sending field. The INTO clause defines the receiving field for the result of the operation. WITH POINTER may be used to define the starting location where data are to be transferred into the receiving field. ON OVERFLOW provides for an action to be taken if there are more data than the receiving field may accept.

The UNSTRING statement takes a single alphanumeric field and extracts parts of it, placing these parts into other identifiers. The DELIMITER option in this statement determines when the transfer of data from the sending field is to be terminated. The IN option permits the delimiter to be stored in a separate field as part of the UNSTRING operation. UNSTRING may also use a POINTER to determine the starting location of the data in the sending field.

INSPECT or EXAMINE (for 1968 ANS COBOL users) examines an identifier from left to right for the presence of a specific character. Format 1 counts the number of occurrences of the character and format 2 may be used to replace the character with another character.

Delimiter
DELIMITED BY
EXAMINE
INSPECT
Nonnumeric data
OVERFLOW

POINTER
SIZE
String
STRING
UNSTRING

REVIEW QUESTIONS

TRUE/FALSE

1. The STRING statement is used to extract a portion of a string from a nonnumeric field.

2. A delimiter is a character that can be used to detect the separation of two or more parts of a field, such as name from address.

3. The use of the POINTER option in the STRING statement is to indicate where the data are to begin in the receiving field.

4. A DELIMITED BY option in the UNSTRING statement identifies the location to store the delimiter in when it is found.

5. When using UNSTRING, a delimiter is identified to determine when the transfer of data from the receiving field is to stop.

6. The COUNT IN option is only used with the UNSTRING statement. It is not available for use with STRING.

7. The TALLYING option in the UNSTRING statement is useful to tally or count the number of characters transferred to the receiving fields.

8. INSPECT is a useful statement when a particular character in a field is to be replaced by another character.

MULTIPLE CHOICE

9. Which statement type is used to extract a portion of a field, such as the initials from a name field?
   - a. STRING
   - b. UNSTRING
   - c. INSPECT
   - d. All the above
   - e. None of the above

10. Which statement type is used to combine the contents of several fields to create one field?
    - a. STRING
    - b. UNSTRING
    - c. INSPECT
    - d. All the above
    - e. None of the above

11. Which statement type could be used most effectively to replace every comma in a field with a semicolon?
    - a. STRING
    - b. UNSTRING
    - c. INSPECT
    - d. All the above
    - e. None of the above

12. Select the statement that best expresses what the following STRING statement is doing:

```
STRING INITIALS DELIMITED BY SIZE
         ' ' DELIMITED BY SIZE
       SURNAME DELIMITED BY ','
       INTO FULL-NAME.
```

   a. INITIALS and SURNAME are combined in FULL-NAME separated by a blank.

   b. The first initial is selected from INITIALS.

   c. INITIALS must be the same SIZE as SURNAME to be selected.

   d. The SIZE of the field FULL-NAME must not exceed the total length of the initials and surname plus the blank.

13. What is the function of the POINTER option in the following statement?

```
STRING FIELD-1 DELIMITED BY ','
         ' ' DELIMITED BY SIZE
       FIELD-2 DELIMITED BY ','
         ' ' DELIMITED BY SIZE
       INTO FIELD-3
       WITH POINTER PTR-1.
```

   a. PTR-1 counts the number of characters moved to FIELD-3.

   b. PTR-1 controls the number of delimiters that are checked.

   c. PTR-1 determines when the data stop being inserted in FIELD-1.

   d. PTR-1 determines the starting position of the data going into FIELD-1.

14. Which statement best describes the operation of the following use of UNSTRING?

```
UNSTRING NAME DELIMITED BY ','
       INTO SALUTATION
            INITIALS
            SURNAME.
```

   a. The fields SALUTATION, INITIALS, and SURNAME are combined into NAME separated by commas.

   b. Commas will be used to separate the items in the field NAME.

   c. All characters between the first and second comma are stored in INITIALS.

   d. a and b.

   e. b and c.

   f. a, b, and c.

15. What is the purpose of the WITH POINTER option in the UNSTRING statement?

   a. It counts the number of characters in the receiving field.

   b. It defines the starting position in the sending field where the data are to begin.

   c. It points to the last field to receive data.

   d. It defines the number of fields that received data.

PROGRAMMING EXERCISES

1. Revise the personalized letter program in this chapter to eliminate the extra space after the surname in the letter. As a result, the letter to MR. SMITH should have the following appearance. Notice the use of a comma following the second entry containing MR. SMITH's name.

```
PERSONALIZED SUBSCRIBER NUMBER: 120SMITH6701

J.L. SMITH
205 SPRING RD.
BELFOREST RI 23709

DEAR MR. SMITH:

AS A LOYAL CUSTOMER OF NO-NAME TRAVEL AGENCY
YOU HAVE BEEN SELECTED TO RECEIVE A SPECIAL
SUBSCRIPTION RATE FOR TRAVEL WORLD MAGAZINE.
FOR THE LOW PRICE OF ONLY $19.95 YOU WILL RECEIVE
12 EXCITING ISSUES OF THE LATEST IN TRAVEL
INFORMATION. THIS IS A ONE TIME OFFER AND IF YOU
RESPOND TODAY A DIGITAL TRAVEL ALARM CLOCK WILL
BE INCLUDED WITH YOUR FIRST ISSUE.

I KNOW, MR. SMITH, THAT YOU WILL FIND TRAVEL
WORLD TO BE AN ENJOYABLE MAGAZINE SO PLEASE
RETURN THE ENCLOSED CARD FOR PROMPT SERVICE.

SINCERELY,

JANE R. LAWRENCE
TRAVEL WORLD
```

2. Using the same file as used for the personalized letter, create a receipt for the purchase of travel tickets. An important part of this receipt is the printing of the amount paid in words after reading it as a numeric value from the file. Also include the customer's name and address, showing initials, surname, street, city, state or province, and zip code as separate fields on the receipt. Notice that this is an international travel company and that Canadian postal codes use seven alphanumeric characters including a blank in the center position, while U.S. codes use five digits.

INPUT/OUTPUT RECORD DEFINITION				
File: Contract file		File Type: Disk		
Record Length: 90		Blocking Factor: 1		
Sequence: N/A		Access Method: Sequential		
COLUMNS	FIELD	TYPE	LENGTH	DECIMALS
1–3	Agency	A/N	3	
4–7	Customer number	N	4	
8–20	Name	A/N	13	
21–40	Address line 1	A/N	20	
41–60	Address line 2	A/N	20	
61–70	Phone number	N	10	
71–76	Contract price	N	6	2
77–78	No. of tickets	N	2	
79–80	Package key	N	2	
81–86	Date	N	6	

Sample test data:

```
1203356J.L. SMITH     205 SPRING RD.    BELFOREST RI 23709   8012356701062500022701287
1203445G.T. WILSON    15 BELL COURT     TREMONT SD   70110   2104926712120000015002787
1203546L.L. ABLE      210 TRADE ST.     WILMONT PA   49122   4237768292050000031201587
1312300Q.B. BRAVO     1 FIRST ST.       CHICAGO IL   23501   2014442638065095044502087
1312301R. TRAVELER    101 WEST AVE.     BURBANK CA   41101   2052340000125000023302187
1504000D.C. LESSAC    410 BAY DR.       TORONTO ONT  M9S 2D4 4167678891240000025001287
```

3. Create a KWIC (Key Word in Context) index for a list of titles so that they may be more readily referenced by subject. A keyword in this list is one that is not an article or preposition, such as a, an, the, to, of, and so on. Therefore, a table of these nonkeywords will need to be maintained. All other words will be considered keywords.

For example, if the following three titles were supplied,

- An Introduction to Computer Languages
- Computers and Society
- Concepts of Data Base

the following output would be generated as a KWIC index.

Concepts of Data	Base
An Introduction to	Computer Languages
	Computers and Society
	Concepts of Data Base
Concepts of	Data Base
An	Introduction to Computer Languages
An Introduction to Computer	Languages
Computers and	Society

In your output design, include headings on the report and list the author and publisher data with each title as it is listed in the KWIC index.

INPUT/OUTPUT RECORD DEFINITION				
File: Book title file Record Length: 100 Sequence: N/A		File Type: Disk Blocking Factor: 1 Access Method: Sequential		
COLUMNS	FIELD	TYPE	LENGTH	DECIMALS
1–20	Author	A/N	20	
21–40	Publisher	A/N	20	
41–100	Title	A/N	60	

INTERACTIVE COBOL PROGRAMMING

BATCH-PROCESSING SYSTEMS

COBOL was originally designed as a language for developing batch applications for information systems. Batch-oriented systems are those for which the transactions to be processed are all accumulated prior to processing. Typically, a transaction file is provided for the processing of the data, whether to update a master file or to produce a report. This **batch** of data is then processed at a scheduled time by the computer. Outputs are made available to the user or to other applications after the processing is complete.

In batch processing there may be considerable time delay from the time the transaction occurs until the results are made available. Although time delays are significant, they do not always present a serious problem. Applications such as monthly billing or weekly payroll are typically batch and actually use the computer resource most effectively by using a batch process. The batch method does permit the processing of large amounts of data at one time and, in so doing, makes the most efficient use of the hardware.

REMOTE JOB ENTRY (RJE)

Remote job entry is essentially like batch processing, except transactions are accumulated in a location physically remote from the computer. Remote could mean down the hall, on another floor in the same building, in another building, or even in another city or country. After the data are accumulated at the remote site, the file is transmitted to the computer where it is processed as a batch. Using this method, the data does not need to be physically transported to the computer center but may be sent by a communication line to the central site. Results are often transmitted back to the remote location after processing has been completed.

ON-LINE PROCESSING

An **on-line** system is one that receives its data directly from the environment that creates it. This might be from a terminal in an agent's office connected to an airline reservation system or from a terminal in the order department of a mail-order company. In an on-line system, each transaction is processed as it is received, and so there is little time delay from the time the transaction is entered on the terminal to the time the results are displayed. This delay may vary from a fraction of a second to several seconds, depending on the system's design and the number of users on the system.

USING AN ON-LINE SYSTEM

Most on-line systems use a display terminal with a keyboard to access the computer. A major use of this type of system is to make an **inquiry** or **query** into the current status of data such as a customer's record. For example, a customer may call the office regarding an order that was not received. The person handling the customer's request would respond to a **prompt** on the screen that asks for the customer's number (see Figure 11.1).

```
           CUSTOMER ORDERS




   CUSTOMER NUMBER           ? 1234
```

FIGURE 11.1 An inquiry about a customer's order is made by responding to a prompt on the screen

When the customer number has been typed and the Enter key pressed, the computer program reads a record from a file for that customer. The first part of the order record is then displayed on the screen, as shown in Figure 11.2. The customer may then be advised that items 220, 231, and 234 have been sent, but that item 233 is on backorder because it is temporarily out of stock. In this application, the backorder indicator is highlighted to draw attention to backorder items.

Also highlighted is the MORE indicator. This tells the user that another page of information is available. At the press of a key, the page is flipped and the next screen

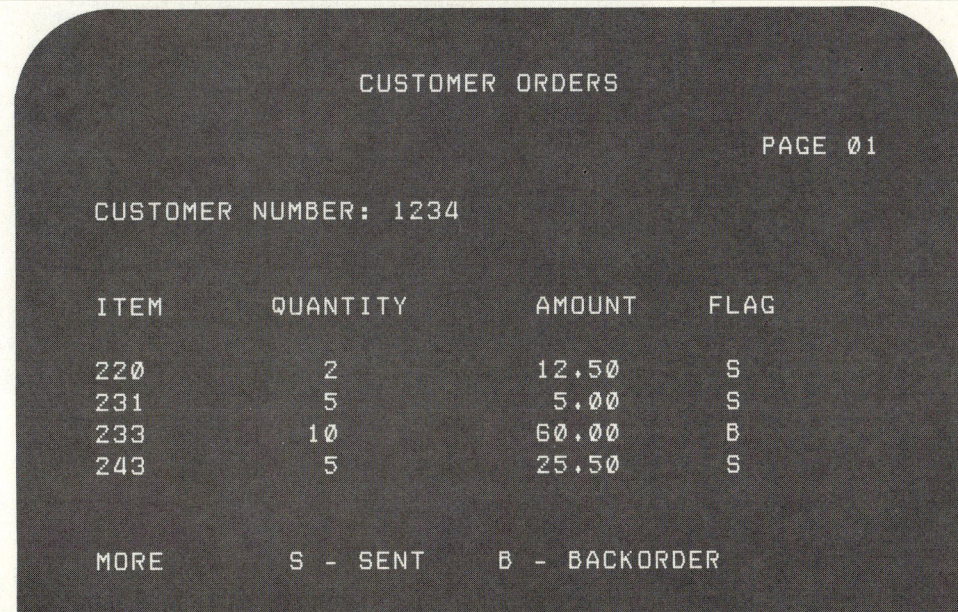

```
              CUSTOMER ORDERS

                                      PAGE 01

   CUSTOMER NUMBER: 1234


   ITEM         QUANTITY        AMOUNT     FLAG

   220             2            12.50       S
   231             5             5.00       S
   233            10            60.00       B
   243             5            25.50       S


   MORE         S - SENT     B - BACKORDER
```

FIGURE 11.2 The on-line program displays the first page of the customer record on the screen

is displayed (see Figure 11.3), which shows that item 310 is also on backorder. This time there is no MORE indicator, so we know that all pages for customer 1234 have been displayed.

Users can also be asked to respond to a **menu** of choices on the screen. Figure 11.4 shows a menu that might be used on an accounts receivable application to let the user select from several options available in the system. By typing the appropriate number, one of the choices would be made and the program would begin the type of processing selected.

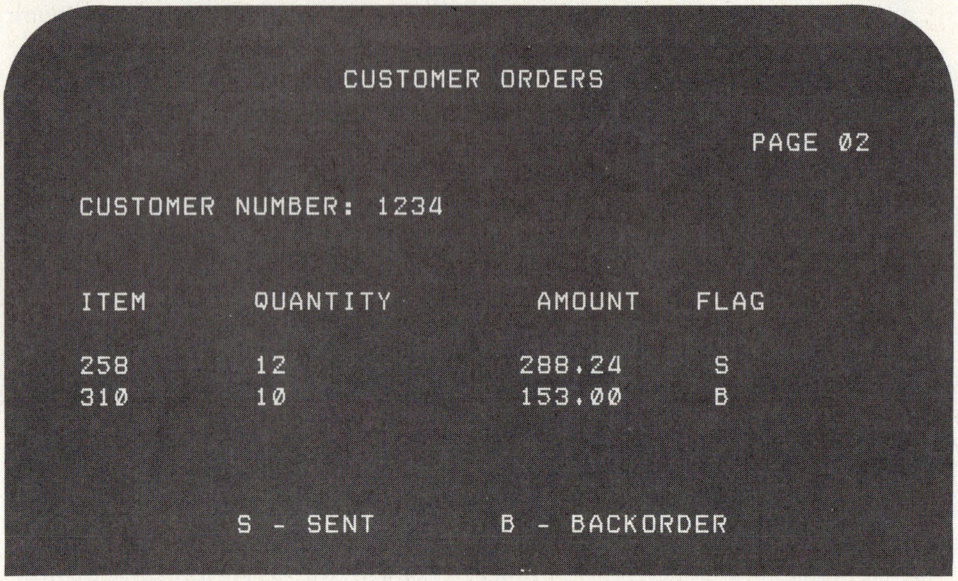

```
                    CUSTOMER ORDERS


                                            PAGE 02

       CUSTOMER NUMBER: 1234


       ITEM        QUANTITY          AMOUNT      FLAG

       258         12                288.24       S
       310         10                153.00       B



            S - SENT         B - BACKORDER
```

FIGURE 11.3 By pressing a key, the second page of the customer record is displayed

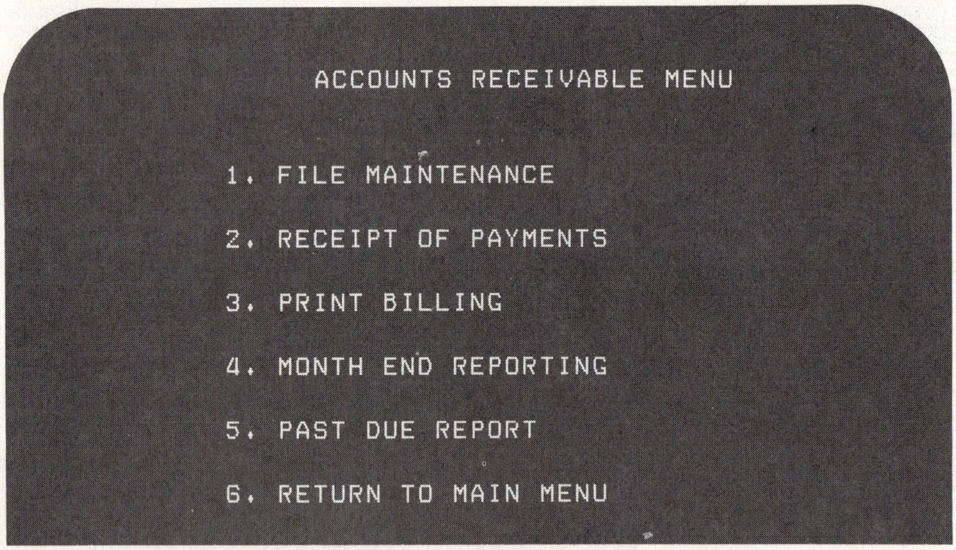

```
                 ACCOUNTS RECEIVABLE MENU


            1. FILE MAINTENANCE

            2. RECEIPT OF PAYMENTS

            3. PRINT BILLING

            4. MONTH END REPORTING

            5. PAST DUE REPORT

            6. RETURN TO MAIN MENU
```

FIGURE 11.4 Menu for an accounts receivable application.

COBOL ON MICRO
VERSUS MAINFRAME COMPUTERS

Since personal or microcomputers have reached the memory capacity of 64K and above with speeds to match, COBOL has become a possible language for use on these systems. However, COBOL has never become a major contender for use on personal computers and probably never will. A primary reason for this is that COBOL provides few capabilities for **interactive** processing, which is a typical need for personal computer applications. However, some COBOL compilers or interpreters have been produced for use on personal computers. Microsoft COBOL is one of the better known of these for business use, and WATCOM COBOL, from the University of Waterloo, is widely used in educational circles.

COBOL is by a wide margin the most widely used language on mainframe computers. For interactive applications, COBOL continues to be the main application language, although it is usually used with other software because of its inherent limitations for this use. This software is usually a **front-end** program that provides the program code for presenting screen formats and defining the type of user interaction; it can even do error checking on the data entered at the terminal. COBOL then provides the code for file access and other processing requirements in the application.

The most widely used front-end communications program with COBOL is IBM's Customer Information Control System (**CICS,** pronounced kicks) or more recently CICS/VS for use with DOS/VS or OS/VS operating systems. CICS provides the programming for terminal interaction, and COBOL provides the code for all other processing. Other competitive systems are Cullinane's IDMS/DC, Altergo Products' Shadow II, and Cincom Systems' Environ/1.

These software packages manage access to the system from all terminals that use it. The software recognizes a request from the terminal and causes data to be transmitted to the mainframe computer where they are processed. The communications packages may also check the transaction for errors and provide an appropriate response to the user of the system.

The front-end software may also format the transaction into a record that the COBOL program can accept and process. It may also receive the results of the processing and structure it for display on the screen at the user's location. Communications software also provides a scheduling facility for determining priorities of terminals, types of transactions, and the queuing of requests.

DISPLAY STATEMENT

DISPLAY $\begin{Bmatrix} \text{identifier-1} \\ \text{literal-1} \end{Bmatrix}$ $\begin{bmatrix} \text{identifier-2} \\ \text{literal-2} \end{bmatrix}$ . . . [UPON mnemonic-name]

The **DISPLAY** statement is usually used in COBOL on mainframe computers for low-volume output, such as for error messages or as an assist to the programmer when debugging the program. In the second case, the statement is only temporary and is removed from the program as soon as debugging is complete. DISPLAY may also create output on devices other than the printer. The most common of these is the operator CONSOLE, where messages may be communicated to the operator during program operation. These messages would be for problems such as exceeding the amount of space available in a VSAM file or not finding data in the file.

On personal computers the DISPLAY statement is used to display data on the screen. Most of the time, DISPLAY is used with ACCEPT on a personal computer, and acts in response to queries or requests entered by the user of the program. DISPLAY may also be used in this situation to place a menu of options on the screen or to supply a prompt to which the user responds.

When DISPLAY is used in the program, no file needs to be defined in the ENVIRONMENT or DATA divisions. For a given system, DISPLAY will default to a specific device. On a mainframe, this is usually the printer, and on a personal computer it is usually the screen. The UPON option may be specified to define a device other than the default device.

Data displayed may be either a literal or an identifier or any combination of these. An identifier may be an elementary item, group item, or an entire record. The length of the data should be considered when using DISPLAY to ensure that it does not exceed the line length of the device being used. Printers may be anywhere from 80 to 132 characters per line and a few may be wider. When displaying on a screen, data that exceed the length of a line will display on the following line.

Example 1 Use a DISPLAY statement to print the contents of the identifier NAME-IN preceded by a descriptive label.

```
DISPLAY 'NAME: ' NAME-IN.
```

Example 2 DISPLAY the contents of the CUSTOMER-RECORD.

```
DISPLAY CUSTOMER-RECORD.
```

Example 3 DISPLAY a message to the operator indicating job completion.

```
DISPLAY 'PAYROLL JOB 23 COMPLETED' UPON CONSOLE.
```

Example 4 When a mnemonic name is used in the DISPLAY statement, it must be defined in the SPECIAL-NAMES paragraph of the ENVIRONMENT DIVISION. The following shows a message displayed on a typewriter console.

```
ENVIRONMENT DIVISION.
    .
    .
    .
CONFIGURATION SECTION.
    .
    .
    .
SPECIAL-NAMES.
    CONSOLE IS TYPEWRITER.
    .
    .
    .
PROCEDURE DIVISION.
    .
    .
    .
DISPLAY 'VSAM FILE FULL' UPON TYPEWRITER.
```

ACCEPT STATEMENT

```
ACCEPT   identifier   [FROM mnemonic-name]
```

The **ACCEPT** statement is used to read low volumes of data into the program. Normally, ACCEPT is used to access data from the operator console or terminal keyboard, but it may be used to input data from other devices by defining an appropriate mnemonic name. Only one item of data may be received at a time, and this item will be stored in the identifier used in the statement. However, if the identifier is a group item, several items of data may be combined in one input operation. An example of this use is the entry of date, where the date includes six digits in the format YYMMDD for 1974 and 1985 ANS COBOL users.

When ACCEPT is used, the file it accesses must not be defined in either the ENVIRONMENT or DATA divisions. Rather, the default file is accessed unless the FROM option is used. On mainframe systems, the reader (SYSIPT) is often the default, whereas the keyboard usually is on personal computing interpreters.

Example 1 ACCEPT a date from the default system input device.

```
ACCEPT DATE-TODAY.
```

Example 2 ACCEPT a response of YES or NO from the user at the console typewriter. This example uses the SPECIAL-NAMES paragraph to define the TYPEWRITER, as explained for the DISPLAY statement.

```
SPECIAL-NAMES.
    CONSOLE IS TYPEWRITER.
        .
        .
        .
PROCEDURE DIVISION.
        .
        .
        .
    ACCEPT USER-RESPONSE FROM TYPEWRITER.
```

Example 3 Give the user three options and then accept the value chosen.

```
DISPLAY 'ENTER A LETTER TO SELECT AN OPTION'.
DISPLAY ' '.
DISPLAY 'A - ADD RECORD TO MASTER'.
DISPLAY ' '.
DISPLAY 'R - REVISE A MASTER RECORD'.
DISPLAY ' '.
DISPLAY 'U - DELETE A MASTER RECORD'.
DISPLAY ' '.
ACCEPT OPTION-SELECTED.
```

PROGRAMMING STYLE WITH DISPLAY AND ACCEPT

- When coding a long DISPLAY statement, it is best to break it into several statements instead of using a continuation line. Keep in mind that this approach will produce as many output lines as DISPLAY statements.

  Instead of using

```
DISPLAY ACCOUNT-NUMBER REGION CUSTOMER-NAME
-          CUSTOMER-ADDRESS.
```

use

```
DISPLAY ACCOUNT-NUMBER REGION.
DISPLAY CUSTOMER-NAME.
DISPLAY CUSTOMER-ADDRESS.
```

- In some situations, splitting the data into two or more lines may be unavoidable. Some improvement may be achieved by using an identifier instead of placing a message in the DISPLAY statement.

  Instead of using

```
DISPLAY 'THERE IS AN OVERDUE PAYMENT AGAINST THE ACCOUNT
        'NUMBER:' ACCOUNT-IN.
```

use

```
DISPLAY MESSAGE-01 ACCOUNT-IN.
```

INTERACTIVE UPDATE OF THE EMPLOYEE MASTER FILE: AN APPLICATION PROGRAM

In Chapter 5, we wrote an application program to update an employee master that had been stored as a relative file. This update was written as a batch program, and all the updating transactions were processed against the master in a single run of the program. Now we will write a program to update this file interactively, using a terminal for the transactions. Figure 11-5 shows the system flowchart for this program. A terminal will be used to provide the requests for activity against the master file. The result of any processing will either appear on the screen, as in the case of a query against a master record, or will result in updating of the master file when certain data are entered at the terminal.

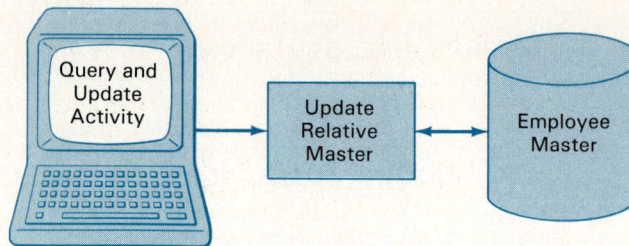

FIGURE 11.5   System flowchart for interactive access to a relative master file

PROGRAM SPECIFICATIONS

Program specifications for the interactive update program are supplied in Figure 11.6. These are similar to those given for the relative update program in Chapter 5 with adjustments included because of the interactive nature of this implementation. Instead of reading a transaction file sequentially, this program will respond to inquiries entered at a terminal after displaying a menu of options that the user may choose from. Depending on the option chosen, a variety of activities may occur, ranging from a display of data from the master file to a complete updating of the master record.

PROGRAMMING SPECIFICATIONS

PROGRAM NAME: Employee Master Update   PROGRAM ID: UPDATE11
PREPARED BY: Diane Quest   DATE: Oct. 20, 1986

Program Description:
   The program defined here updates the relative record employee master file interactively
   from a user's terminal.
Input File(s):
   Terminal keyboard
Input/Output File(s):
   Relative employee master file
Output File(s):
   Display screen
Program Requirements:
   1. Display a menu of choices on the screen giving the following options:
      1 Add a new employee record to the master.
      2 Revise an existing record.
      3 Delete an employee record.
      4 Query an employee record.
      5 Exit from the application.

FIGURE 11.6(a)   Program specifications for updating the relative employee master

PROGRAM NAME: Employee Master Update	PROGRAM ID: UPDATE11
PREPARED BY: Diane Quest	DATE: Oct. 20, 1986

2. Because the master contains a delete code in the first byte of the record, it is necessary to test for this code. A value of 9 indicates the record has been previously deleted and should not be considered currently active. To delete an active record, move a 9 to this field and rewrite the master record.

3. Print a message for each error found. Some likely errors that may occur during the update are:
   a) A master record cannot be found.
   b) A master already exists for a new add to the file.
   c) A key error occurs on a rewrite. This indicates a system problem but it should not be ignored.

4. Also print a message for successful processing of each transaction, including the following:
   a) When the master record is revised.
   b) When a new master record is created.
   c) When a master record has been deleted.

5. An add to the master (a 1 option from the menu) requires prompting the user for each field and then creating a master record after each field has been entered.

6. Updates (a 2 option on the menu) occur to a field when the user identifies that field for updating. See the menus to follow, which identify how the user selects a field for updating by typing the first letter of the field name.

7. A query requires the master record to be accessed and its data displayed on the screen. No updating occurs with a query operation.

8. Check for an invalid key on the master, and if one occurs, print an appropriate error message. The exception to this is when an invalid key occurs for a new record to be added. In this case the record can be written to the master.

FIGURE 11.6(b)

INPUT/OUTPUT DEFINITION

The inputs and outputs to and from this program are not as clearly separated from each other as is the case with most of our programs. In this application, two major devices are used to supply the input and output. The first of these is the employee master file, which is a relative input/output file (see Figure 11.7). It provides master records as input to the program and acts as an output when either new records are created or existing records are revised and rewritten to the master.

The second device used is the terminal, which also acts an an input/output device.

INPUT/OUTPUT RECORD DEFINITION

File: Employee master	File Type: Relative disk
Record Length: 60	Blocking Factor: 1
Sequence: Employee number	Access Method: Sequential

COLUMNS	FIELD	TYPE	LENGTH	DECIMALS
1	Delete byte*	A/N	1	
2–5	Employee number**	N	4	
6–25	Name	A/N	20	
26–28	Current dept.	A/N	3	
29–31	Previous dept.	A/N	3	
32–35	Year employed	A/N	4	
36–41	Birth date	A/N	6	
42	Education code	A/N	1	
43–44	Job code	A/N	2	
45–52	Income	N	8	2

 * The delete byte is necessary only on 1968 ANS COBOL.
** Relative key field.

FIGURE 11.7   Definition for the employee master file

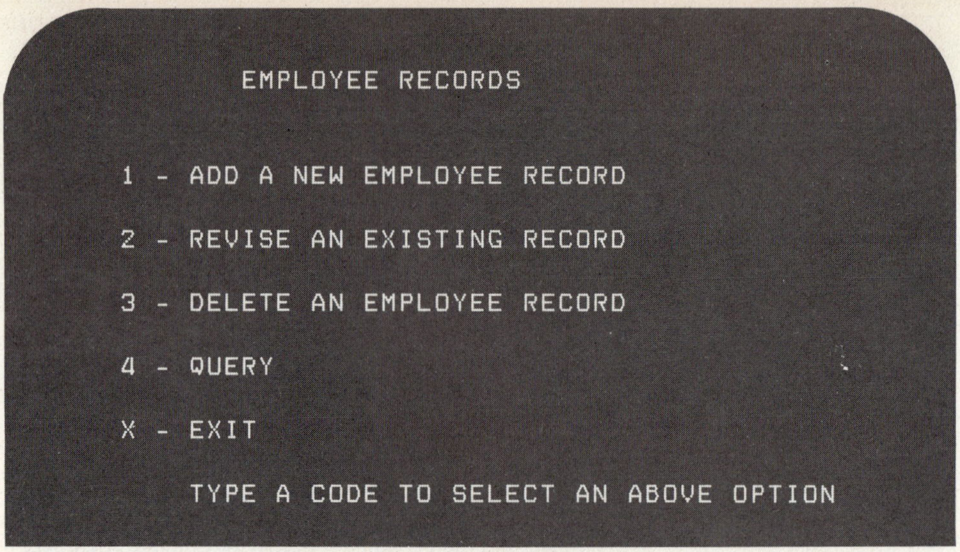

```
                EMPLOYEE RECORDS


    1 - ADD A NEW EMPLOYEE RECORD

    2 - REVISE AN EXISTING RECORD

    3 - DELETE AN EMPLOYEE RECORD

    4 - QUERY

    X - EXIT

        TYPE A CODE TO SELECT AN ABOVE OPTION
```

FIGURE 11.8 Main menu for the employee records program

When menus, prompts, or data are displayed, the screen is an output from the program. But when the user responds to a prompt by typing a character or an employee number, the keyboard provides input to the program. Because there are a variety of requirements in this program, several screen definitions are required.

Figure 11.8 shows the top-level menu, which the user will see when the program first begins. One of several options are selected from this menu by typing a value of 1 to 4 or the value X to terminate the program. When an option has been selected, one of the four screens is displayed (see Figures 11-9 to 11-12).

When a new employee is to be added to the file, the screen in Figure 11.9 is displayed. First, the user is asked for the employee number, and the program will use

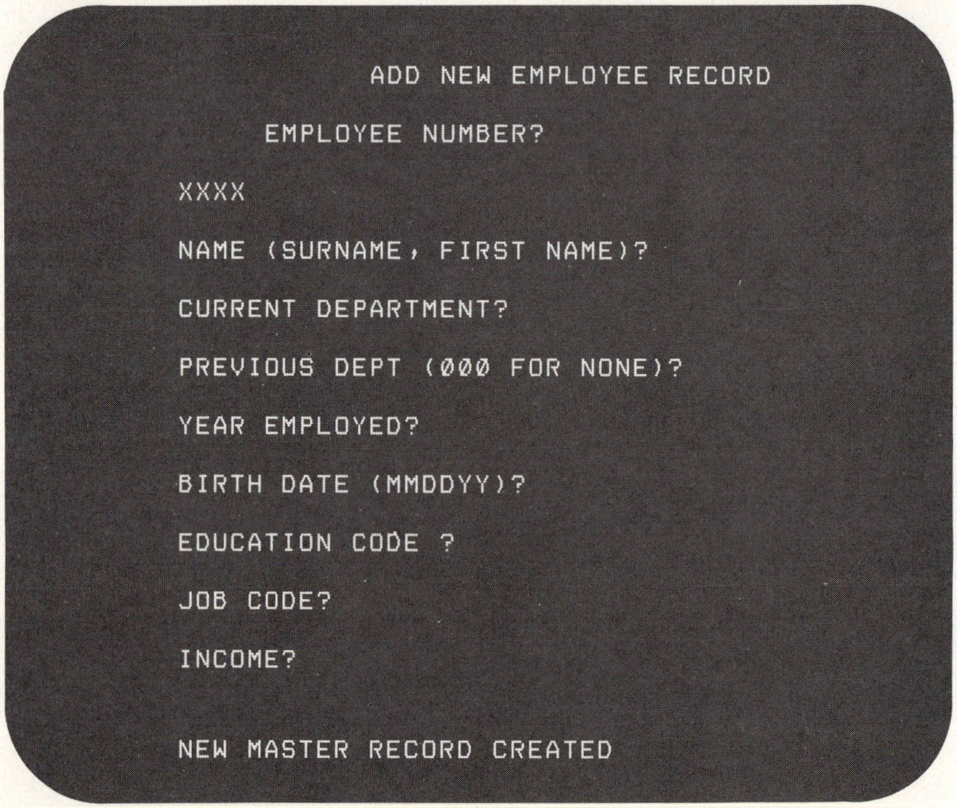

```
            ADD NEW EMPLOYEE RECORD

        EMPLOYEE NUMBER?

    XXXX

    NAME (SURNAME, FIRST NAME)?

    CURRENT DEPARTMENT?

    PREVIOUS DEPT (000 FOR NONE)?

    YEAR EMPLOYED?

    BIRTH DATE (MMDDYY)?

    EDUCATION CODE ?

    JOB CODE?

    INCOME?


    NEW MASTER RECORD CREATED
```

FIGURE 11.9 Screen display for adding a new master record

```
            REVISE EMPLOYEE RECORD

      EMPLOYEE NUMBER?
XXXX

TYPE FIRST LETTER OF FIELD TO BE REVISED.

NAME, CURR-DEPT, PREV-DEPT, YEAR-EMPL, BIRTH-DATE,
EDUCATION, JOB, INCOME, QUIT

N
CURRENT NAME X-----------X
X-----------X


MASTER RECORD REVISED
```

FIGURE 11.10 Screen display for revising a master record

this number to check if the employee already exists on the file. If the employee record does not exist, an error message is displayed; otherwise, the user is prompted for each of the input fields. Although the screen layout shows all the prompts, the program will display them one at a time and wait for the user's response before displaying the next prompt. This approach keeps screen clutter to a minimum and helps the user to concentrate on one entry at a time.

Figure 11.10 shows the screen layout for a revision to an employee record. Again, the user is first asked for the employee number, and if a matching record is not found on the master file, an error message is displayed and the program returns to the main menu. For a matching record, the screen will ask the user to indicate which field is to be revised. Because one or more fields may be changed, a message is displayed giving the names of each field and asking the user to type the first letter of the name (Lotus 1-2-3 style) to indicate the field to be changed. This method requires us to use names on the screen that have a unique first letter so that a choice may be made. The last choice is Quit, which will be selected to indicate that updating is complete.

When a choice is made, the program displays the current contents of that field and waits for the user to type the new field contents. Then a second choice may be made, and so on, until all necessary fields have been revised. When Q is entered to quit the revise operation, the program will then rewrite the revised record on the master file.

When the delete option is selected from the main menu, the screen in Figure 11.11 is displayed. This is the simplest of the screens to design because all the program

```
                DELETE EMPLOYEE RECORD

        EMPLOYEE NUMBER?

      XXXX

      MASTER RECORD DELETED
```

FIGURE 11.11 Screen display for deleting a record

Interactive COBOL Programming

```
                    EMPLOYEE RECORD QUERY

          EMPLOYEE NUMBER?

     0003

     NAME X-------------X              INCOME 99999V99

     DEPT XXX    PREVIOUS XXX

     YEAR EMPLOYED XXXX

     BIRTH DATE  XXXXXX

     EDUCATION  X

     JOB CODE   XX

     PRESS RETURN TO CONTINUE
```

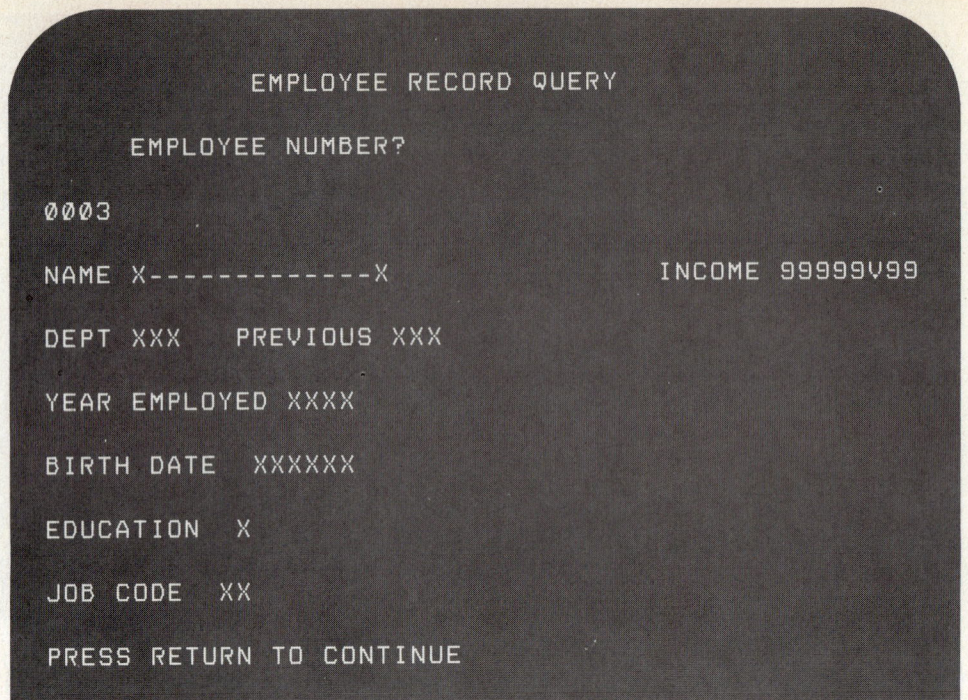

FIGURE 11.12   Query screen format

needs to know is the employee number of the record to be deleted. If a record exists for that employee, it will be deleted. Otherwise, an error message is displayed and the program will return to the main menu.

The fourth type of screen display is for an employee record query (see Figure 11.12). This option permits the user to view the employee's record, but does not give any updating options. It might be considered equivalent to producing a report in a batch application that shows this record. The user is prompted for the employee number and then the contents of the record are displayed on the screen. A message, PRESS RETURN TO CONTINUE, is displayed at the end of the screen. This message causes the program to wait for the user to read the screen contents and then to press the return key to indicate that the data shown are no longer needed on the screen, and the program returns to the main menu for the next instruction.

STRUCTURE CHART

Developing a structure chart for an interactive program is similar to other applications except that this program does not have a transaction file. Instead, the source of all updating activity comes from the terminal as the user types it. It might help to think of the terminal input as a transaction in planning the solution, because it is the type of entry made at the terminal that determines what action is taken by the program. So, in a sense, the terminal does provide the transaction.

Another component of the solution to think about is the use of a menu or a prompt that the program displays on the screen for the user to read and respond to. This is a form of output, but because of its detailed nature it will not appear initially on the structure chart, but will come later in the detailed top-down development.

The top level of the structure chart is as follows:

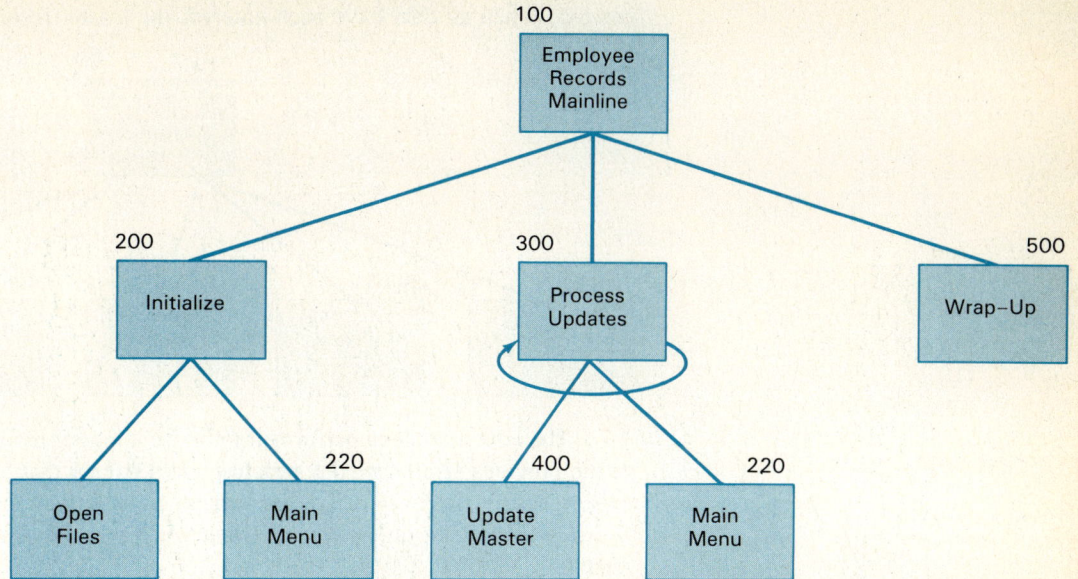

One significant part of this structure chart is the use of the entry 220 Main Menu. It is equivalent to the reading of a transaction in a batch application. But in this case the main menu gives the user the options, one of which is then selected to determine the processing that is to be done. This solution is not to suggest that all interactive programs will follow the pattern of processing a sequential transaction file, just as all batch programs are not necessarily transaction driven.

When the user has selected an option, the module 400 Update Master will determine where the processing is to occur. Because there are four possible processes, this module is refined as follows:

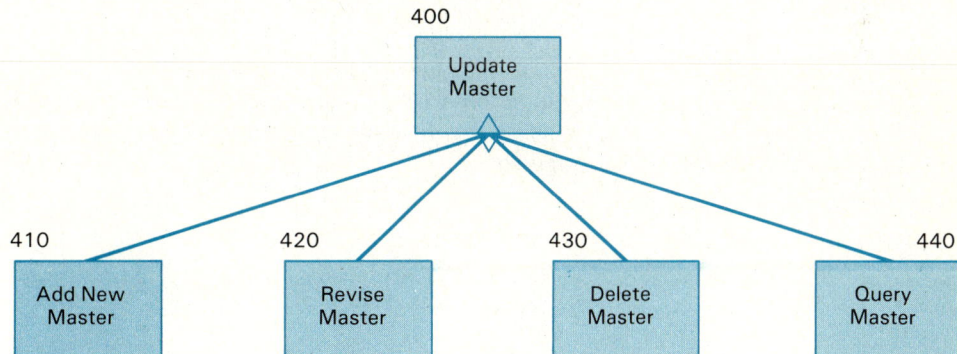

As the menu for the employee records suggests, these four processes are selective. Depending on the choice made by the user, one of these modules will be selected by the program and the appropriate processing done.

The first update module adds a new record to the master file. First, the program needs to get an employee number from the user, which identifies the key of the record to be created. The master is then read to ensure that a record does not already exist for that employee. If there is a current record (signified by the presence of a delete code), an error message is displayed on the screen and the program will then return to the display of the main menu. Otherwise, the delete code is cleared and the user is prompted for each field required in the master record. The record is created as these data are entered. When all data have been entered, the master record is rewritten on the file.

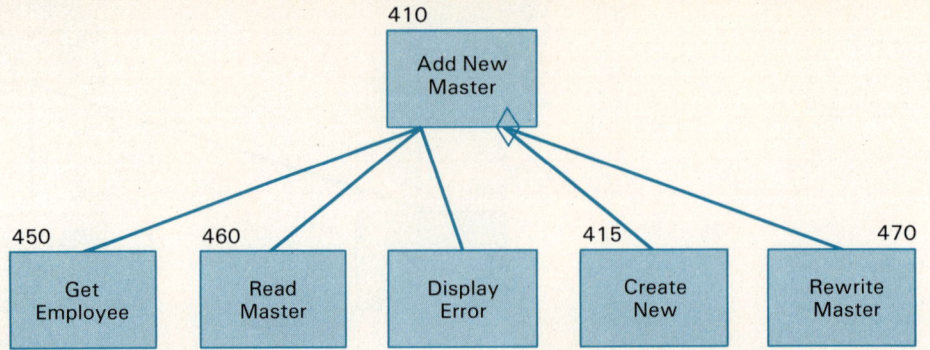

```
                              410
                         ┌──────────┐
                         │ Add New  │◇
                         │  Master  │
                         └──────────┘
        ┌──────────┬──────────┼──────────┬──────────┐
  450   │    460   │          │    415   │    470    │
┌──────────┐ ┌──────────┐ ┌──────────┐ ┌──────────┐ ┌──────────┐
│   Get    │ │   Read   │ │ Display  │ │  Create  │ │ Rewrite  │
│ Employee │ │  Master  │ │  Error   │ │   New    │ │  Master  │
└──────────┘ └──────────┘ └──────────┘ └──────────┘ └──────────┘
```

The next module is performed to revise a master record. The steps here are similar to the previous section of the structure chart except that a module is used to revise an existing master in this case, rather than to create a new record. Naturally, a number of details will need to be developed when we get to the pseudo code. Here is the revise module.

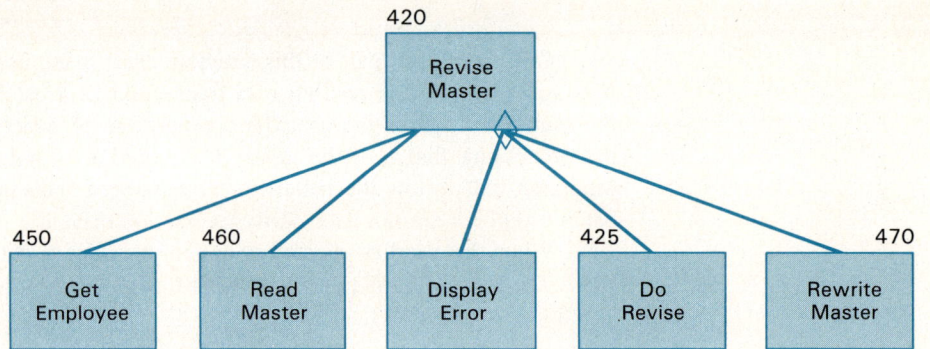

```
                              420
                         ┌──────────┐
                         │  Revise  │◇
                         │  Master  │
                         └──────────┘
        ┌──────────┬──────────┼──────────┬──────────┐
  450   │    460   │          │    425   │    470    │
┌──────────┐ ┌──────────┐ ┌──────────┐ ┌──────────┐ ┌──────────┐
│   Get    │ │   Read   │ │ Display  │ │    Do    │ │ Rewrite  │
│ Employee │ │  Master  │ │  Error   │ │  Revise  │ │  Master  │
└──────────┘ └──────────┘ └──────────┘ └──────────┘ └──────────┘
```

The next module to develop is used to delete an employee record from the master file. As for the other modules, an employee number must first be accessed from the terminal user. Then the master record can be read and, if it is present, it is deleted by setting the delete code. A missing record, meaning that the delete code indicates it is already deleted, will result in an error message, as the following part of the structure chart suggests:

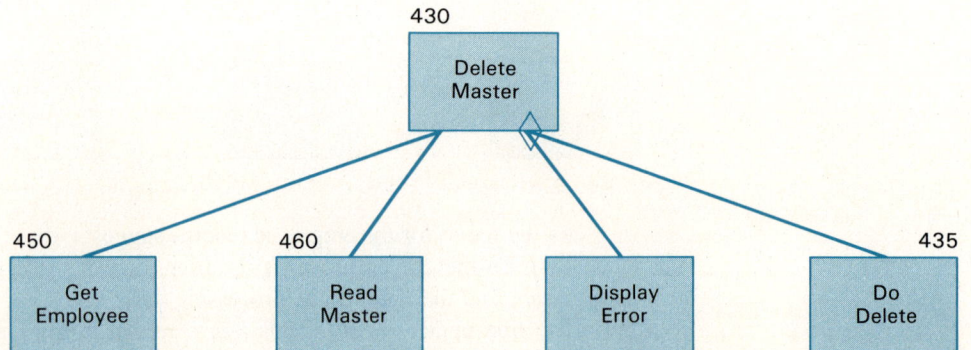

```
                              430
                         ┌──────────┐
                         │  Delete  │◇
                         │  Master  │
                         └──────────┘
        ┌──────────────┼──────────────┬──────────────┐
  450   │        460   │              │        435    │
┌──────────┐    ┌──────────┐    ┌──────────┐    ┌──────────┐
│   Get    │    │   Read   │    │ Display  │    │    Do    │
│ Employee │    │  Master  │    │  Error   │    │  Delete  │
└──────────┘    └──────────┘    └──────────┘    └──────────┘
```

The final module to develop is the query. It will be used when the person at the terminal wants to see the contents of an employee record but does not need to update that record. Of course, they could query the record and then issue another selection from the main menu to do a revise or delete of the same record. This module follows the same steps as used for the revise module, except the record is displayed on the screen when it is successfully accessed from the file. Because no changes are made to the file in a query, there is no need to rewrite the master record when the module is finished.

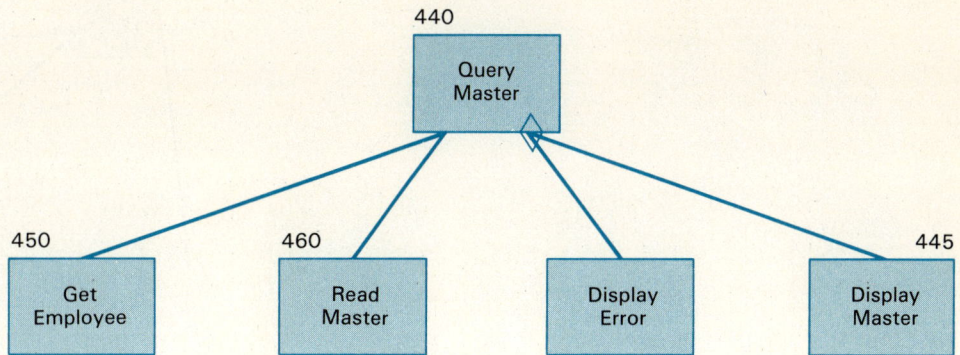

Figure 11.13 shows the complete structure chart for this problem. You might want to compare it to the chart developed in Chapter 5 when the application was batch. The main differences relate to the use of the transaction file and the printer for a report. In this interactive solution, the printer is not used and so all messages and data are displayed on the screen.

PSEUDO CODE

The pseudo code in Figure 11.14 on pages 413 to 415, followed by the structured flowchart, is developed on the basis of a user responding to a menu of options. This menu is displayed in module 220 as follows:

```
220-Main-Menu
        1. Display main menu options
            1 - Add a new employee record
            2 - Revise an existing record
            3 - Delete an employee record
            4 - Query
            X - Exit
        2. Accept code.
```

When the user enters a code of 1, 2, 3, 4, or X, it will then be examined by the logic in paragraphs 300 and 400. In 300 only the exit (X) is tested, as follows:

```
300-Process
        1. If not an exit code
                Perform 400-Update-Master
                Perform 220-Main-Menu
            EndIf
```

If it is entered, the program leaves the paragraph and returns to the top level, where the master file is closed and the program terminated.

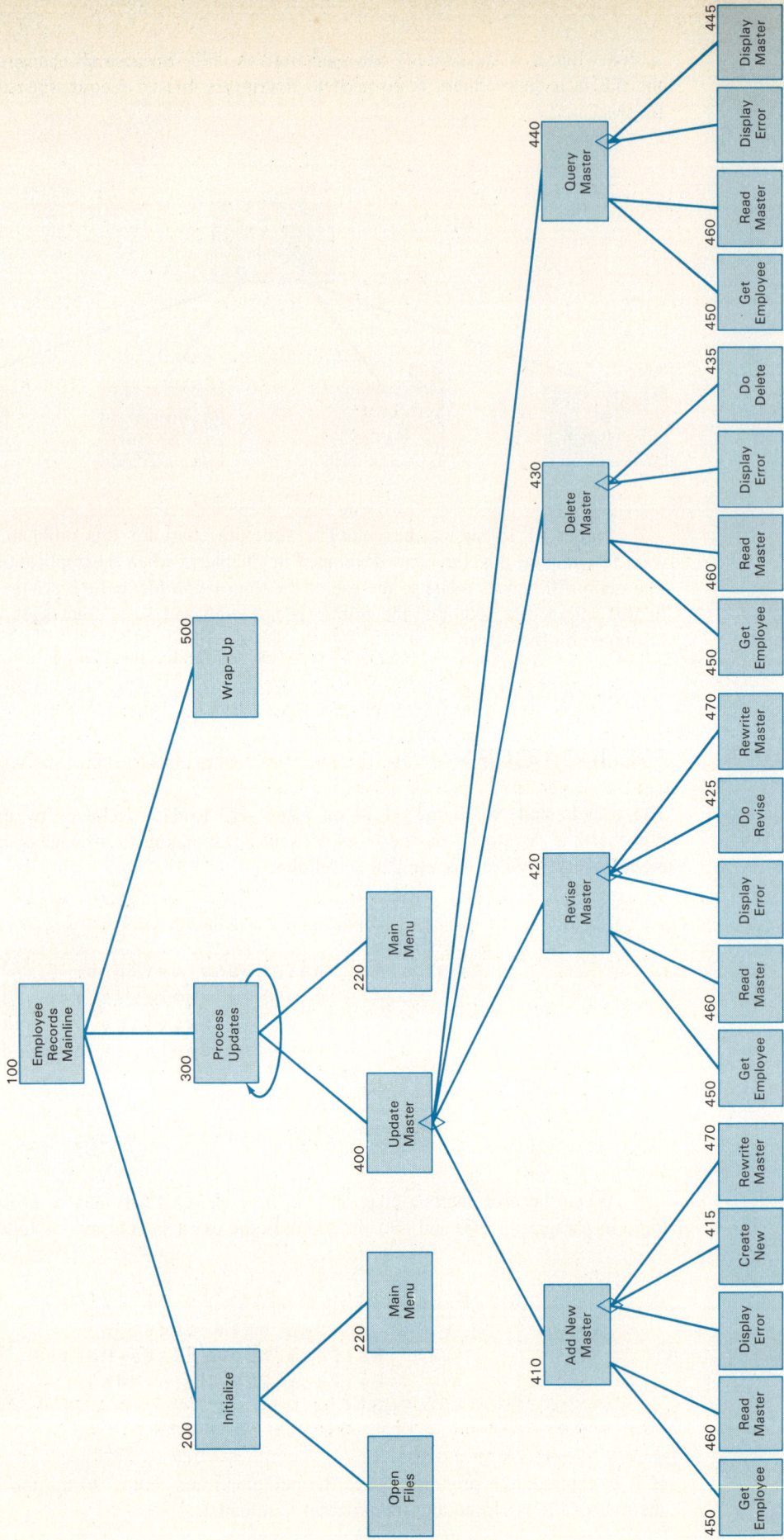

FIGURE 11.13   Structure chart for the interactive update

All other codes are checked by paragraph 400, which performs the appropriate module depending on the code entered. Paragraph 400 is a series of nested If's, as follows:

```
400-Update-Master
       1. If add transaction
             Perform 410-New-Master
         Else
          If revise transaction
                Perform 420-Revise-Master
           Else
            If delete transaction
                  Perform 430-Delete-Master
             Else
              If query
                    Perform 440-Query-Master
              EndIf
            EndIf
          EndIf
        EndIf
```

The four paragraphs identified here, 410, 420, 430, and 440, each follow similar patterns. An identifying header is displayed on the screen and the user is asked for an account number by performing 450-Get-Employee. This number identifies either the record to be accessed from the master or the account of a new record to be created. In each case the master is read using paragraph 460-Read-Master. Then appropriate action is taken, depending on the code entered by the user and whether a master record was found or a key error occurred during the read.

Adding a New Record

Paragraph 410-New-Master is performed to create a new master record. This action requires an access of the master and a check of the delete code. Only previously deleted records are eligible for use as a new record. The new record is created in paragraph 415-Create-New, which prompts the user for each field and then accepts the new data, which are entered into the master record. Here are the entries for the first two master fields:

```
415-Create-New

       1. Clear master delete code.

       2. Display name prompt.

       3. Accept name.

       4. Display current dept prompt.

       5. Accept current dept.
```

Each subsequent field is prompted for in the same manner and the data accepted from the user. When all data have been entered, the master record is rewritten, which in effect creates a new record.

Revising a Master Record

Paragraph 420-Revise-Master processes the revision against a master record. First, the record is retrieved from the file and then paragraph 425-Do-Revise is performed. The paragraph displays a message telling the user how to select a field for revision by typing the first letter of the field name.

```
425-Do-Revise

    1. Display fields to update prompt.

    2. Move spaces to response.

    3. Perform 426-Revise to 426-Revise-Exit
         Until Response = 'Q'.
```

A key to this activity is the use of paragraph 426-Revise, which is performed in a loop. This loop permits the user to select more than one field for revision by continuing to type a first letter. By checking for each letter, the paragraph selects the field for revision, displays its current contents so the user can see what is being changed, and accepts the new data for the field. Here are the statements in paragraph 426 for revising the first two fields in the record:

```
426-Revise

    1. If name
         Display name
         Accept new name
       End If

    2. If current dept
         Display current dept
         Accept new current dept
       End If
```

Finally, by typing a Q for quit, the loop is terminated and paragraph 420 rewrites the master with the changes.

Deleting a Master Record

Paragraphs 430-Delete-Master and 435-Do-Delete take care of the deleting process. The master to be deleted is identified by the account number entered by the user. That record is then read, and if it is not already flagged with a delete code, a value of 9 is moved to the delete flag and the record is rewritten. The presence of the flag on the record indicates it has been deleted, although the physical record still exists on the file.

Master Record Query

Paragraphs 440-Query-Master and 445-Display-Master process a request for a query. The master record is read by paragraph 440 and then the contents are displayed on the screen in paragraph 445. At the end of paragraph 445 is an instruction to press return to continue. This statement uses a display and an accept. By issuing an accept, the program will wait for the user to make a response. Because no specific data are required, the user can simply press the return key and the program will continue.

```
445-Display-Master

     1. Display master record contents.

     2. Display 'press return to continue'.

     3. Accept response.
```

Figure 11.14 shows the complete pseudo-code solution.

PSEUDO CODE

PROGRAM NAME: Employee Records Update   PROGRAM ID: UPDATE11
PREPARED BY: Jonathan Youngman   DATE: Oct 23   PAGE 1 of 3

```
100-Mainline
     1. Perform 200-Initialize.
     2. Perform 300-Process
          Until menu exit.
     3. Perform 500-End-of-Update.
     4. Close files.
     5. Stop run.
200-Initialize
     1. Open files.
     2. Perform 220-Main-Menu.
220-Main-Menu
     1. Display main menu options
          1—Add a new employee record
          2—Revise an existing record
          3—Delete an employee record
          4—Query
          X—Exit
     2. Accept code.
300-Process
     1. If not an exit code
          Perform 400-Update-Master
          Perform 220-Main-Menu
        Endif
400-Update-Master
     1. If add transaction
          Perform 410-New-Master
        Else
        If revise transaction
             Perform 420-Revise-Master
        Else
            If delete transaction
                 Perform 430-Delete-Master
            Else
                If query
                     Perform 440-Query-Master
                Endif
            Endif
        Endif
     Endif
```

FIGURE 11.14(a) Pseudo code for the interactive employee update program

410-New-Master
1. Display header.
2. Perform 450-Get-Employee.
3. Perform 460-Read-Master.
4. If no key error
    Display error message
  Else
    Perform 415-Create-New
    Perform 470-Rewrite-Master
  EndIf

415-Create-New
1. Clear master delete code.
2. Display name prompt.
3. Accept name.
4. Display current dept prompt.
5. Accept current dept.
6. Display previous dept prompt.
7. Accept previous dept.
8. Display year employed prompt.
9. Accept year employed.
10. Display birth date prompt.
11. Accept birth date.
12. Display education code prompt.
13. Accept education code.
14. Display income prompt.
15. Accept income.

420-Revise-Master
1. Display header.
2. Perform 450-Get-Employee.
3. Perform 460-Read-Master.
4. If key error
    Display error message
  Else
    Perform 425-Do-Revise
    Perform 470-Rewrite-Master
    Display message
  End If

425-Do-Revise
1. Display fields to update prompt.
2. Accept response from user.
3. Perform 426-Revise to 426-Revise-Exit
    Until Response = "Q."

426-Revise
1. Accept response from user.
2. If name
    Display name
    Accept new name
  End If
3. If current dept
    Display current dept
    Accept new current dept
  End If
4. If previous dept
    Display previous dept
    Accept new previous dept
  End If
5. If year employed
    Display year employed
    Accept new year employed
  End If

FIGURE 11.14(b)

6. If birth date
    Display birth date
    Accept new birth date
  End If
7. If education code
    Display education code
    Accept new education code
  End If
8. If job code
    Display job code
    Accept new job code
  End If
9. If income
    Display income
    Accept new income
  End If
10. Accept response from user.

430-Delete-Master
1. Display header.
2. Perform 450-Get-Employee.
3. Perform 460-Read-Master.
4. If key error
    Display error message
  Else
    Perform 435-Do-Delete
  End If

435-Do-Delete
1. Move '9' to master delete code.
2. Perform 470-Rewrite-Master.
3. Display message.

440-Query
1. Display header.
2. Perform 450-Get-Employee.
3. Perform 460-Read-Master.
4. If key error
    Display error message
  Else
    Perform 445-Display-Master
  End If

445-Display-Master
1. Display master record contents.
2. Display 'press return to continue.'
3. Accept response.

450-Get-Employee
1. Display 'Employee Number?' prompt.
2. Accept employee number.
3. Move employee number to trans employee number.

460-Read-Master
1. Read Employee Master
    Invalid key move 'yes' to key error flag.
2. If Master delete code = '9'
    Move 'yes' to key error flag
  End If

470-Rewrite-Master
1. Rewrite Employee Master
    Invalid key Display error message.

500-End-Of-Update
1. Display *end of update* message.

FIGURE 11.14(c)

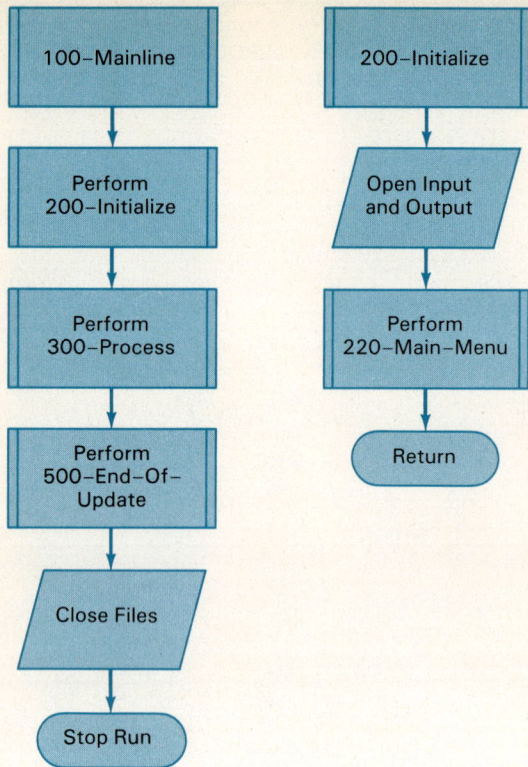

FIGURE 11.14(d)

Flowchart for the interactive employee update program

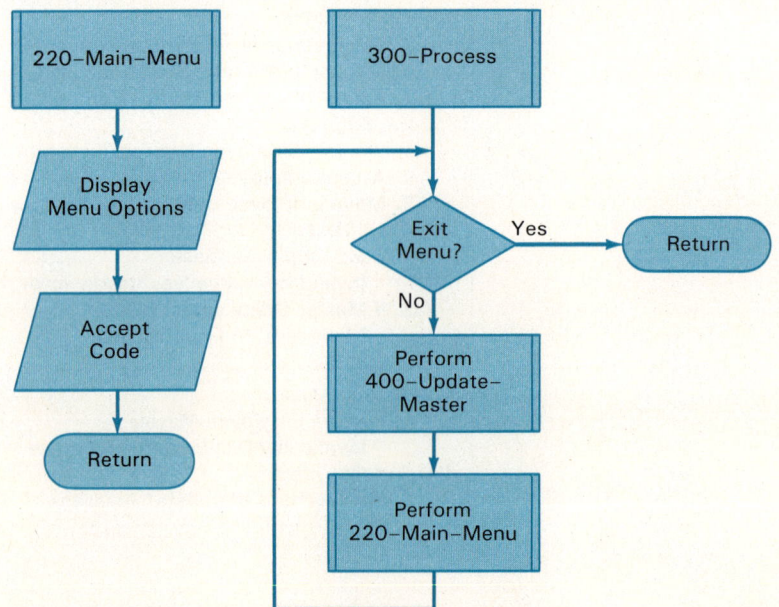

FIGURE 11.14(e)

Chapter 11

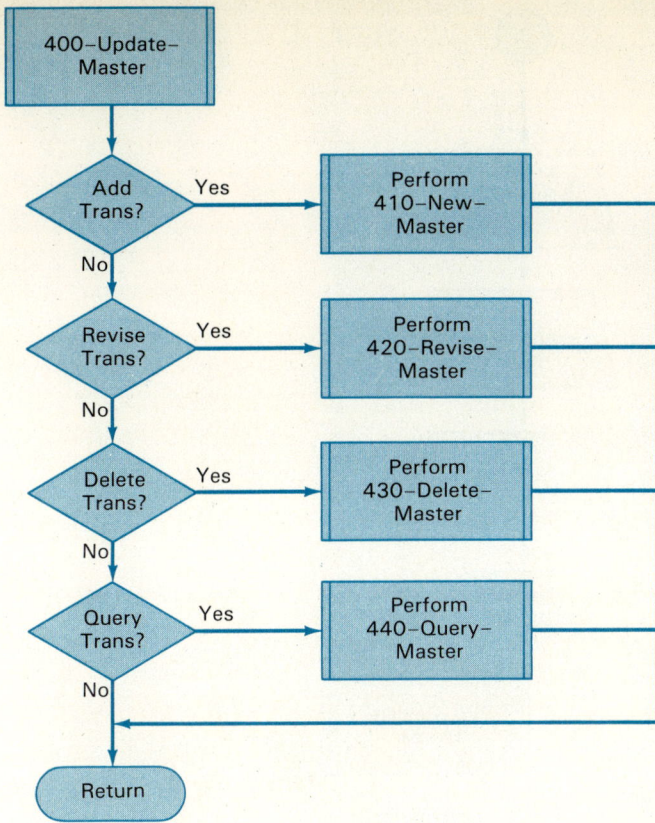

FIGURE 11.14(f)

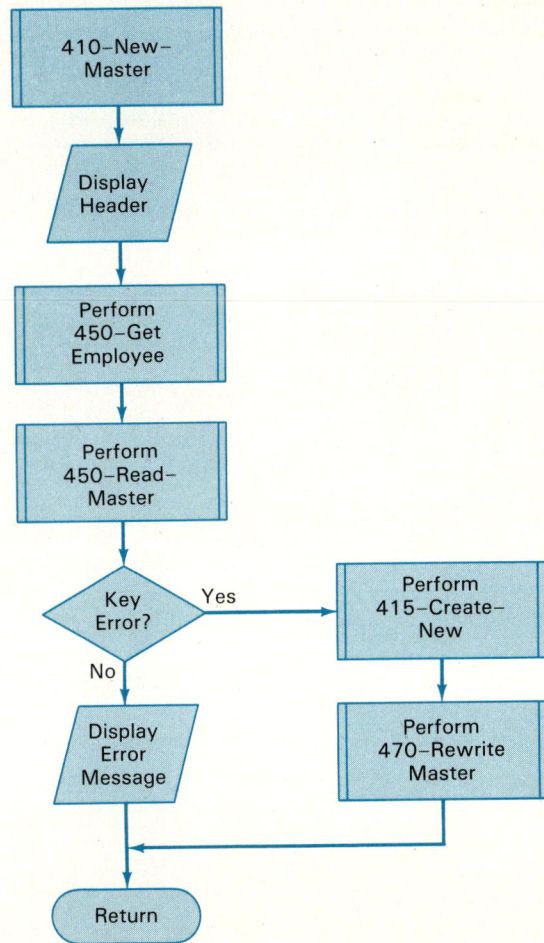

FIGURE 11.14(g)

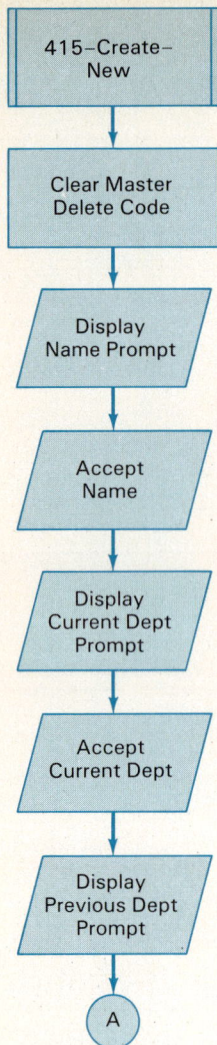

FIGURE 11.14(h)

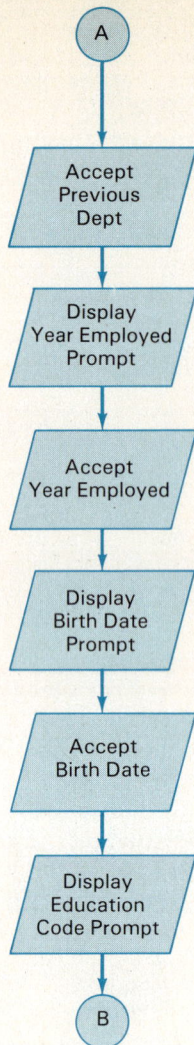

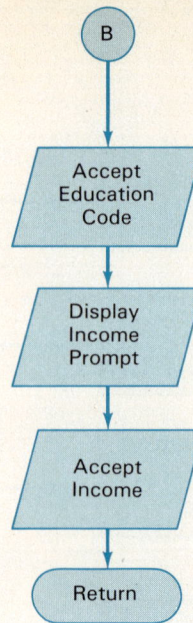

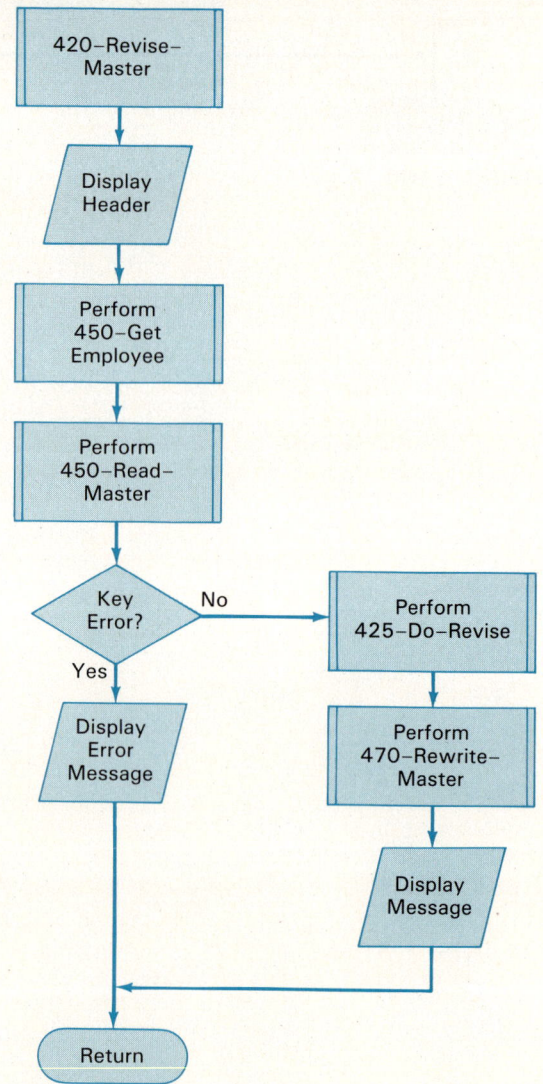

FIGURE 11.14(i)

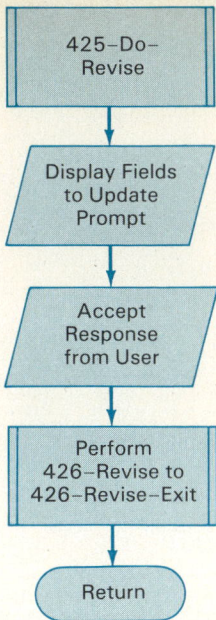

FIGURE 11.14(j)

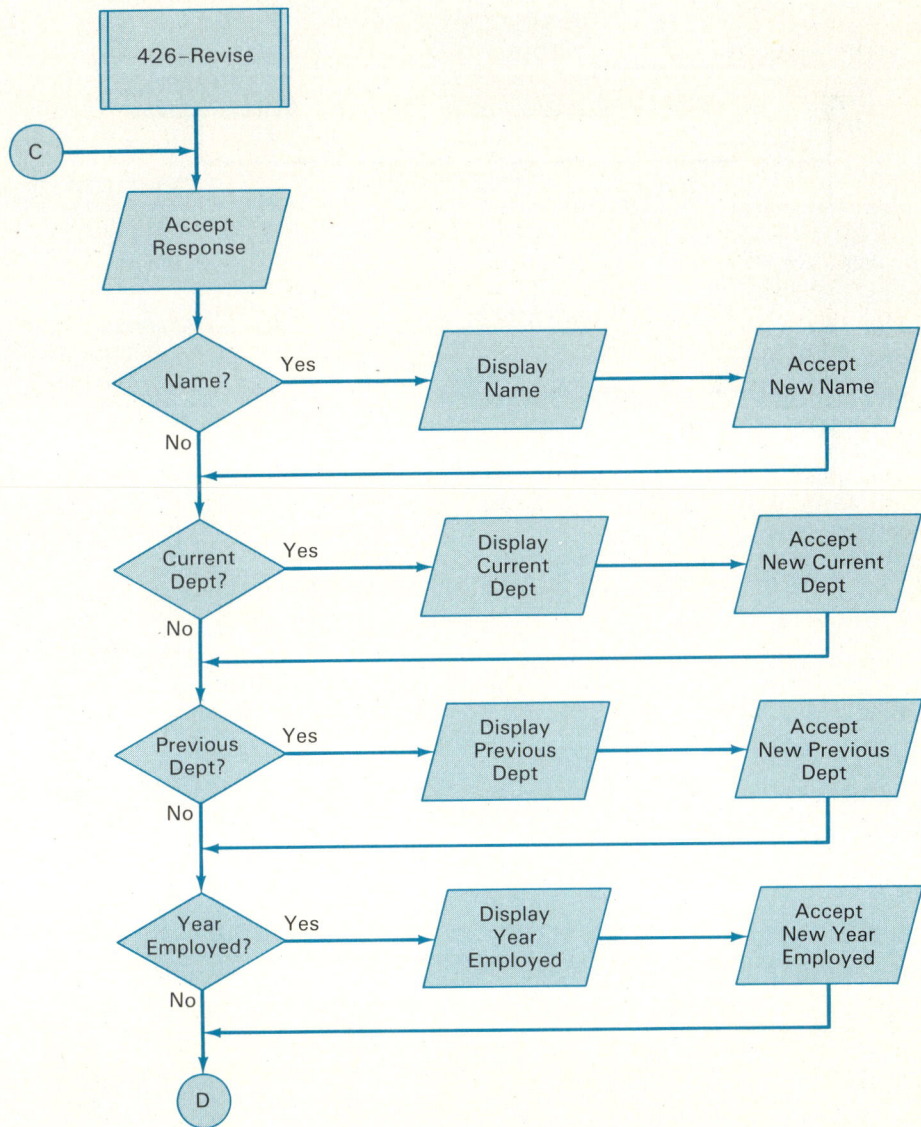

FIGURE 11.14(k)

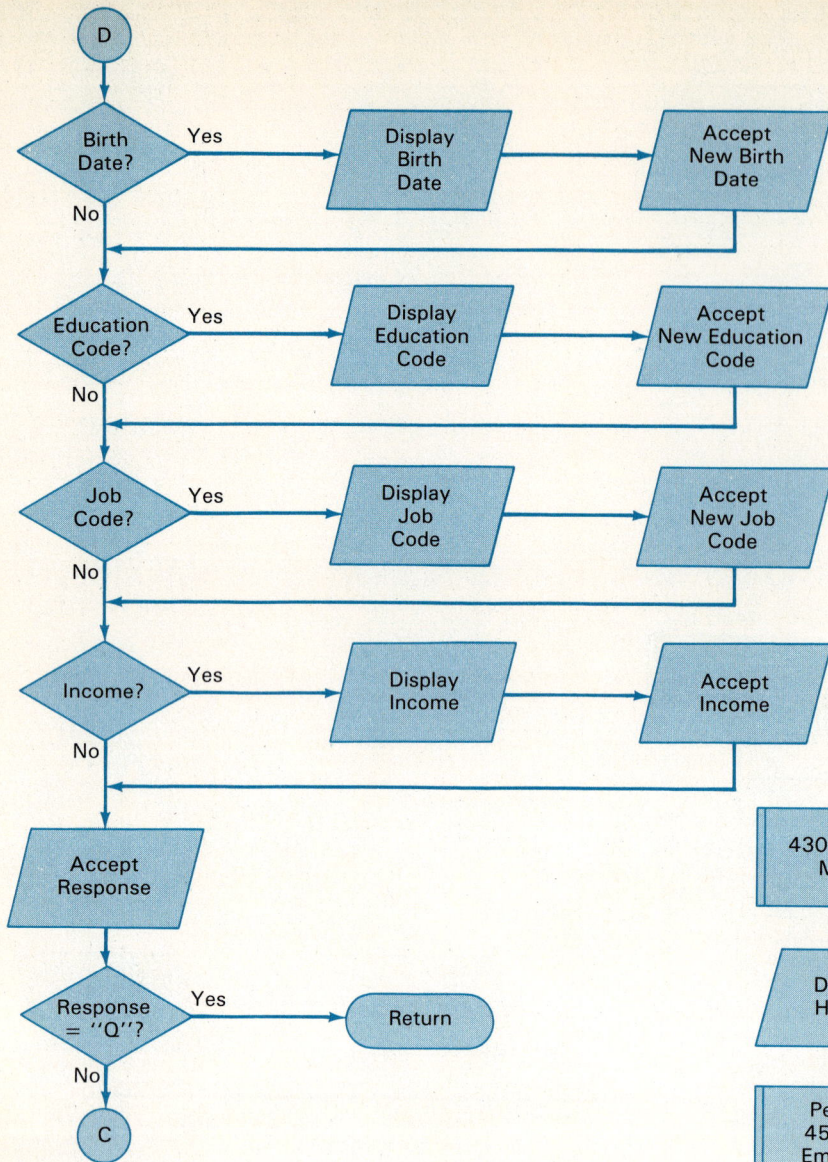

FIGURE 11.14(l)

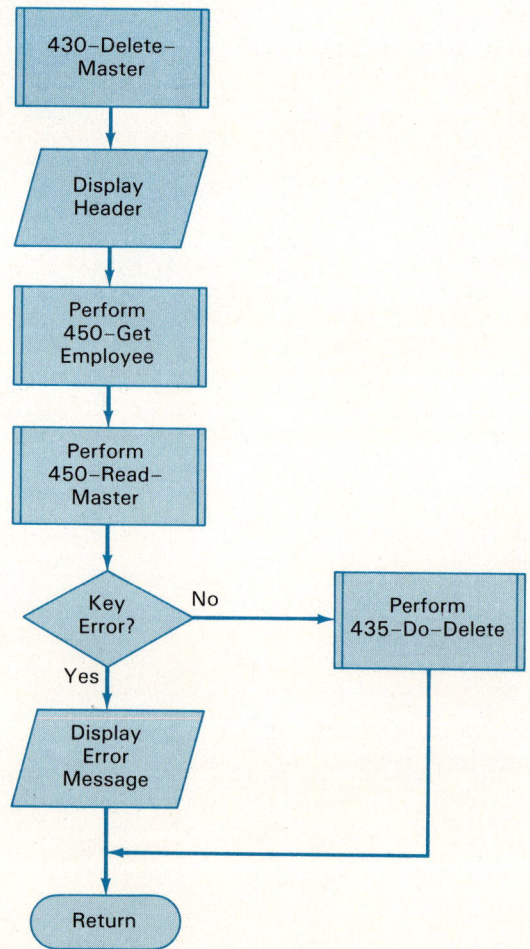

FIGURE 11.14(m)

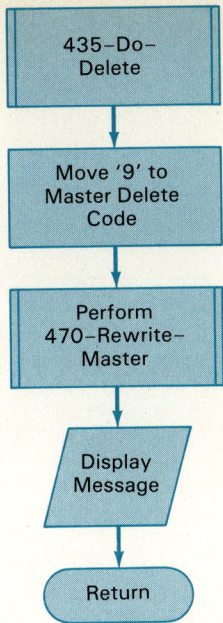

FIGURE 11.14(n)

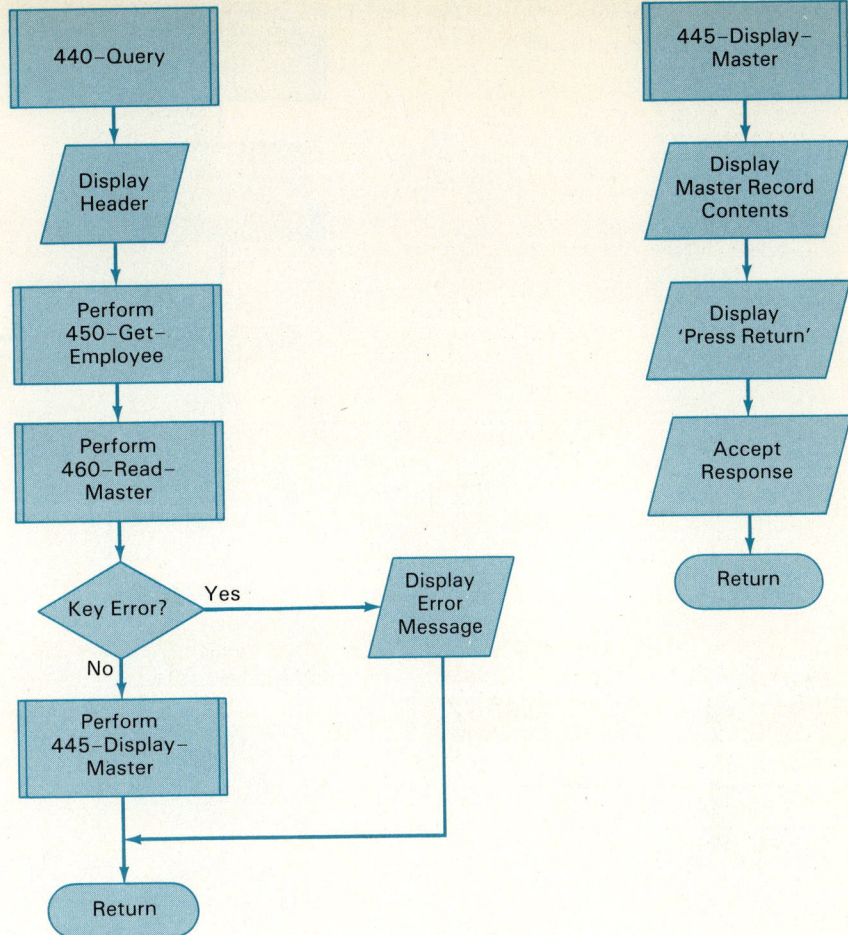

FIGURE 11.14(o)

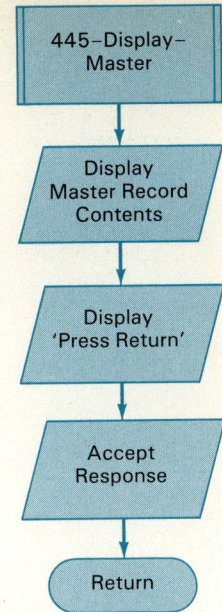

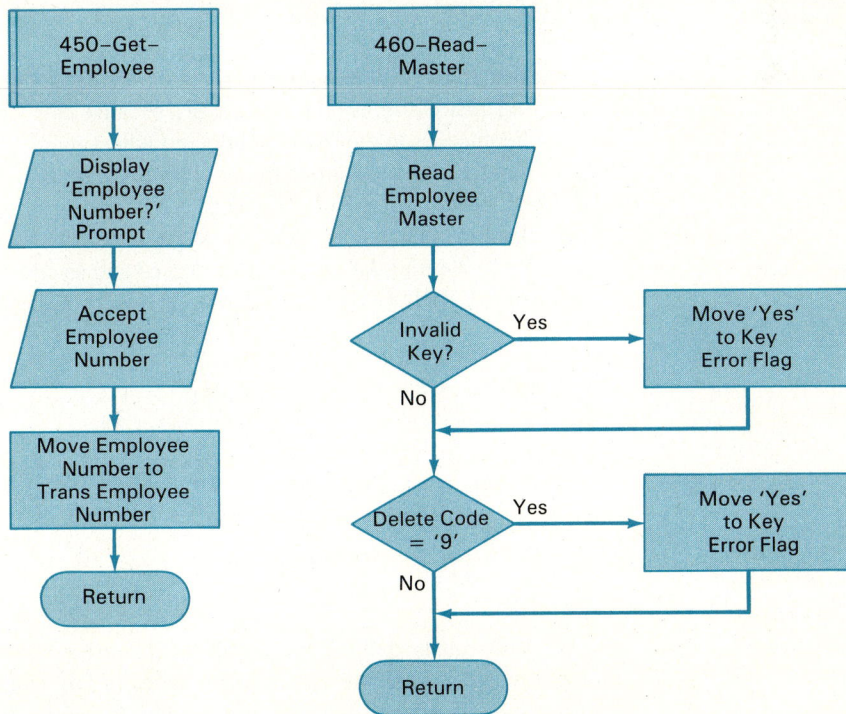

FIGURE 11.14(p)

Interactive COBOL Programming

421

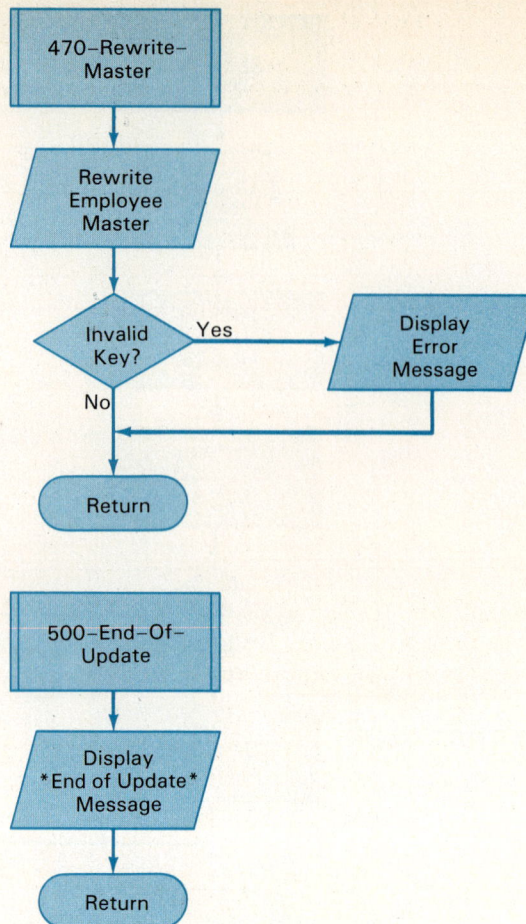

FIGURE 11.14(q)

PROGRAM CODING

If the program for this application is compared to the one written in Chapter 5, you will find many similarities. However, because this update is done interactively, there are differences, some of them subtle and others more obvious, but all important. Because a terminal is used for input rather than a transaction file, there is no usual concept of processing until end of file. Instead, the user determines when the application is to end by indicating that the program is to be terminated. As a result, although there is no transaction, similar data are being accessed and so codes will be necessary. The following entry in WORKING-STORAGE will receive these codes:

```
01   WS-TRANS-REC.
     05   TRANS-EMPLOYEE-NO       PIC X(04).
     05   TRANS-CODE              PIC X(01).
          88  ADD-TRANS                            VALUE '1'.
          88  REVISE-TRANS                         VALUE '2'.
          88  DELETE-TRANS                         VALUE '3'.
          88  QUERY-TRANS                          VALUE '4'.
          88  EXIT-TRANS                           VALUE 'X'.
```

The values defined in the 88-level entries correspond to the values the user is asked to enter from the menu on the screen. The value X is used when the use of the program is complete and the user wishes to terminate the run. We will examine the menu used in paragraph 220.

100-MAINLINE This top-level paragraph performs the initialization paragraph, does the process loop until a request to exit is received from the user, and finally wraps up the processing before terminating the program.

200-INITIALIZE This paragraph opens the employee master as an I-O file for updating or query activities. It then performs paragraph 220 to display the main menu.

220-MAIN-MENU The main-menu paragraph displays the menu from which all other activity branches. The menu offers a choice of activities, which the user can select by typing the appropriate character.

```
DISPLAY '          EMPLOYEE RECORDS'.
DISPLAY ' '.
DISPLAY '1 - ADD A NEW EMPLOYEE RECORD'.
DISPLAY ' '.
DISPLAY '2 - REVISE AN EXISTING RECORD'.
DISPLAY ' '.
DISPLAY '3 - DELETE AN EMPLOYEE RECORD'.
DISPLAY ' '.
DISPLAY '4 - QUERY'.
DISPLAY ' '.
DISPLAY 'X - EXIT'.
DISPLAY ' '.
DISPLAY '    TYPE A CODE TO SELECT AN ABOVE OPTION'
DISPLAY ' '.
ACCEPT TRANS-CODE.
```

The character entered is accepted into TRANS-CODE, which may then be tested by the program for the appropriate module to be performed.

300-PROCESS This paragraph is the main process loop. Each time it is performed the code is checked to see if exit was specified. If it was entered, the paragraph exits to the top level and the program will be terminated. If any other code has been selected by the user, the paragraph 400-UPDATE-MASTER is performed to determine the type of updating to be done. When updating is complete, the program executes 220-MAIN-MENU again to repeat the process.

400-UPDATE-MASTER This paragraph tests the selection made from the main menu and performs the appropriate paragraph, depending on the choice made. Four possible activities can stem from this paragraph: create a new master record, revise a record, delete a master record, and do a query. Any other choice would cause the program to loop back and redisplay the main menu.

410-NEW-MASTER Paragraph 410 is performed when a new master record is to be created. First, the paragraph identifies itself with a message on the screen and then the user is prompted to enter the employee number of the new employee. Because the entry of an employee number is a common requirement, paragraph 450-GET-EMPLOYEE is used to prompt the user and accept the employee number.

Next, a master record is read for this employee number. Ideally, a key error should be detected here, because with the relative file only previously deleted records are eligible to be used to create a new record. So if a key error is found, the new record is created by paragraph 415-CREATE-NEW and written to the master file by paragraph 470-REWRITE-MASTER.

415-CREATE-NEW This paragraph accepts data for a new master record. First, it clears the master delete code field and then moves the employee number previously read to the master record. Next, each field required for the master is requested from the master. The prompt is used, giving the name of the field, and then the data are accepted into the master field. For example, the name field is processed as follows:

```
DISPLAY 'NAME (SURNAME, FIRST NAME)?',
ACCEPT MAST-NAME,
```

The remaining fields in the master are handled in the same manner as name.

420-REVISE-MASTER After getting the employee number and the corresponding master record, this paragraph proceeds to perform paragraph 425-DO-REVISE, which, as the name suggests, revises the master record. Then paragraph 470-REWRITE-MASTER is executed to record the changes on the master file.

425-DO-REVISE Paragraph 425 prompts the user for the field to be revised in the master record. This prompt indicates that the first letter of the field is to be typed to identify the field, as follows:

```
425-DO-REVISE,
    DISPLAY 'TYPE FIRST LETTER OF FIELD TO BE REVISED,',
    DISPLAY ' ',
    DISPLAY 'NAME, CURR-DEPT, PREV-DEPT, YEAR-EMPL, BIRTH-DATE,',
    DISPLAY 'EDUCATION, JOB, INCOME, QUIT',
    DISPLAY ' ',
```

Because it is critical that the user identify the field correctly, each name is displayed in the prompt to ensure that when the first letter is typed it will correctly identify the field. Next, the response is accepted and paragraph 426-REVISE is performed where the response character is examined and the appropriate field is revised. This paragraph is written in a loop so that several fields may be revised before leaving this area of the program.

426-REVISE When this paragraph is performed, it first selects the field to be revised based on the code entered by the user. That field's current value is then displayed so that the user can see what is being revised. Then the new value is accepted and entered into the master field. For example, the name field is revised as follows:

```
IF RESPONSE = 'N'
    DISPLAY 'CURRENT NAME ' MAST-NAME
    ACCEPT MAST-NAME,
```

430-DELETE-MASTER This paragraph gets the employee number and the master record to be deleted. If an active record is found, paragraph 435-DO-DELETE is performed to do the actual delete operation.

435-DO-DELETE This paragraph deletes a master record by moving a 9 to the master delete code and rewriting the master.

440-QUERY-MASTER This paragraph will be performed when a query request has been issued for a master record. The employee number is first accepted from the user, and then the master record is read. Finally, paragraph 445-DISPLAY-MASTER is performed to display the contents of the master file on the screen.

445-DISPLAY-MASTER This paragraph displays the contents of the master record on the screen. Each field is identified with a descriptive label and lines are double-spaced for readability. At the end of the paragraph, an ACCEPT statement is used to temporarily stop the program to give the user time to read the data on the screen. Pressing return will cause the program execution to continue.

450-GET-EMPLOYEE This paragraph prompts the user to enter an employee number, accepts that number, and moves it to the relative key field.

460-READ-MASTER Read master does as the name suggests. It also checks for a key error, which can also be determined by the presence of the delete flag in a record that was otherwise correctly read.

470-REWRITE-MASTER A master record is rewritten here whenever a change has been made to the record contents. With a relative file, a rewrite is necessary after creating a new record, revising a record, and deleting a record.

The complete program is shown in Figure 11.15.

```
IDENTIFICATION DIVISION.

PROGRAM-ID.
    UPDATE11.
*AUTHOR.
*    JOHNATHAN YOUNGMAN.
*INSTALLATION.
*    SALES UNLIMITED CORP.
*DATE-WRITTEN.
*    OCT 18.
*DATE-COMPILED.

*SECURITY.
*    NONE.

ENVIRONMENT DIVISION.

CONFIGURATION SECTION.
SOURCE-COMPUTER.
    IBM-PC.
OBJECT-COMPUTER.
    IBM-PC.

INPUT-OUTPUT SECTION.

FILE-CONTROL.
    SELECT EMPLOYEE-MASTER  ASSIGN TO 'MASTER'
            ORGANIZATION IS RELATIVE
            ACCESS IS RANDOM
            RELATIVE KEY IS WS-EMPLOYEE-NO.

DATA DIVISION.

FILE SECTION.

FD  EMPLOYEE-MASTER
    RECORD CONTAINS 60 CHARACTERS
    LABEL RECORDS ARE STANDARD
    DATA RECORD IS MASTER-REC.
01  MASTER-REC.
    05  FILLER                  PIC X(60).

WORKING-STORAGE SECTION.

01  OTHER-ITEMS.
    05  WS-EMPLOYEE-NO          PIC 9(04).
    05  KEY-ERROR-FLAG          PIC X(03)    VALUE 'NO'.
        88  KEY-ERROR                        VALUE 'YES'.
    05  RESPONSE                PIC X.
```

FIGURE 11.15(a)   Program code for the interactive update

```
01  MESSAGES.
    05  MESSAGE-01              PIC X(25)
            VALUE 'MASTER RECORD REVISED'.
    05  MESSAGE-02              PIC X(25)
            VALUE 'NEW MASTER RECORD CREATED'.
    05  MESSAGE-03              PIC X(25)
            VALUE 'MASTER RECORD DELETED'.
    05  MESSAGE-04              PIC X(25)
            VALUE 'MASTER RECORD NOT FOUND'.
    05  MESSAGE-05              PIC X(25)
            VALUE 'NON-NUMERIC EMPLOYEE NO.'.
    05  MESSAGE-06              PIC X(25)
            VALUE 'MASTER REWRITE ERROR'.
    05  MESSAGE-07              PIC X(25)
            VALUE 'MASTER ALREADY EXISTS'.

01  WS-TRANS-REC.
    05  TRANS-EMPLOYEE-NO       PIC X(04).
    05  TRANS-CODE              PIC X(01).
            88  ADD-TRANS                       VALUE '1'.
            88  REVISE-TRANS                    VALUE '2'.
            88  DELETE-TRANS                    VALUE '3'.
            88  QUERY-TRANS                     VALUE '4'.
            88  EXIT-TRANS                      VALUE 'X'.

01  WS-MAST-REC.
    05  MAST-DELETE             PIC X(01).
    05  MAST-EMPLOYEE-NO        PIC X(04).
    05  MAST-NAME               PIC X(20).
    05  MAST-CURRENT-DEPT       PIC X(03).
    05  MAST-PREV-DEPT          PIC X(03).
    05  MAST-YEAR-EMPLOYED      PIC X(04).
    05  MAST-BIRTH-DATE.
        10  MAST-MONTH          PIC X(02).
        10  MAST-DAY            PIC X(02).
        10  MAST-YEAR           PIC X(02).
    05  MAST-EDUCATION          PIC X(01).
    05  MAST-JOB-CODE           PIC X(02).
    05  MAST-INCOME             PIC 9(06)V99.
    05  FILLER                  PIC X(08).

PROCEDURE DIVISION.

100-MAINLINE.
    PERFORM 200-INITIALIZE.
    PERFORM 300-PROCESS
        UNTIL EXIT-TRANS.
    PERFORM 500-END-OF-UPDATE.
    CLOSE EMPLOYEE-MASTER.
    STOP RUN.

200-INITIALIZE.
    OPEN I-O EMPLOYEE-MASTER.
    PERFORM 220-MAIN-MENU.

220-MAIN-MENU.
    DISPLAY '       EMPLOYEE RECORDS'.
    DISPLAY ' '.
    DISPLAY '1 - ADD A NEW EMPLOYEE RECORD'.
    DISPLAY ' '.
    DISPLAY '2 - REVISE AN EXISTING RECORD'.
    DISPLAY ' '.
    DISPLAY '3 - DELETE AN EMPLOYEE RECORD'.
    DISPLAY ' '.
    DISPLAY '4 - QUERY'.
    DISPLAY ' '.
    DISPLAY 'X - EXIT'.
    DISPLAY ' '.
    DISPLAY '    TYPE A CODE TO SELECT AN ABOVE OPTION'
    DISPLAY ' '.
    ACCEPT TRANS-CODE.
```

FIGURE 11.15(b)

```
300-PROCESS.
    IF NOT EXIT-TRANS
        PERFORM 400-UPDATE-MASTER
        PERFORM 220-MAIN-MENU.

400-UPDATE-MASTER.
    IF ADD-TRANS
        PERFORM 410-NEW-MASTER
    ELSE
        IF REVISE-TRANS
            PERFORM 420-REVISE-MASTER
        ELSE
            IF DELETE-TRANS
                PERFORM 430-DELETE-MASTER
            ELSE
                IF QUERY-TRANS
                    PERFORM 440-QUERY-MASTER.

410-NEW-MASTER.
    DISPLAY '                ADD NEW EMPLOYEE RECORD'.
    DISPLAY ' '.
    PERFORM 450-GET-EMPLOYEE.
    PERFORM 460-READ-MASTER.
    IF NOT KEY-ERROR
        DISPLAY '**ERROR** ' MESSAGE-07
    ELSE
        PERFORM 415-CREATE-NEW
        PERFORM 470-REWRITE-MASTER
        DISPLAY MESSAGE-02.

415-CREATE-NEW.

    MOVE   SPACES                    TO  MAST-DELETE.
    MOVE   TRANS-EMPLOYEE-NO         TO  MAST-EMPLOYEE-NO.
    DISPLAY 'NAME (SURNAME, FIRST NAME)?'.
    ACCEPT MAST-NAME.
    DISPLAY 'CURRENT DEPARTMENT? '.
    ACCEPT MAST-CURRENT-DEPT.
    DISPLAY 'PREVIOUS DEPT (000 FOR NONE)? '.
    ACCEPT MAST-PREV-DEPT.
    DISPLAY 'YEAR EMPLOYED? '.
    ACCEPT MAST-YEAR-EMPLOYED.
    DISPLAY 'BIRTH DATE (MMDDYY)? '.
    ACCEPT MAST-BIRTH-DATE.
    DISPLAY 'EDUCATION CODE? '.
    ACCEPT MAST-EDUCATION.
    DISPLAY 'JOB CODE? '.
    ACCEPT MAST-JOB-CODE.
    DISPLAY 'INCOME? '.
    ACCEPT MAST-INCOME.

420-REVISE-MASTER.
    DISPLAY '                REVISE EMPLOYEE RECORD'.
    DISPLAY ' '.
    PERFORM 450-GET-EMPLOYEE.
    PERFORM 460-READ-MASTER.
    IF KEY-ERROR
        DISPLAY '**ERROR** ' MESSAGE-04
    ELSE
        PERFORM 425-DO-REVISE
        PERFORM 470-REWRITE-MASTER
        DISPLAY MESSAGE-01.

425-DO-REVISE.
    DISPLAY 'TYPE FIRST LETTER OF FIELD TO BE REVISED.'.
    DISPLAY ' '.
    DISPLAY 'NAME, CURR-DEPT, PREV-DEPT, YEAR-EMPL, BIRTH-DATE,'.
    DISPLAY 'EDUCATION, JOB, INCOME, QUIT'.
    DISPLAY ' '.
    ACCEPT RESPONSE.
    PERFORM 426-REVISE THRU 426-REVISE-EXIT
        UNTIL RESPONSE = 'Q'.
```

FIGURE 11.15(c)

```
426-REVISE.
    IF RESPONSE = 'N'
        DISPLAY 'CURRENT NAME ' MAST-NAME
        ACCEPT MAST-NAME.
    IF RESPONSE = 'C'
        DISPLAY 'CURRENT DEPT ' MAST-CURRENT-DEPT
        ACCEPT MAST-CURRENT-DEPT.
    IF RESPONSE = 'P'
        DISPLAY 'PREVIOUS DEPT ' MAST-PREV-DEPT
        ACCEPT MAST-PREV-DEPT.
    IF RESPONSE = 'Y'
        DISPLAY 'YEAR EMPLOYED ' MAST-YEAR-EMPLOYED
        ACCEPT MAST-YEAR-EMPLOYED.
    IF RESPONSE = 'B'
        DISPLAY 'BIRTH DATE (MMDDYY) ' MAST-BIRTH-DATE
        ACCEPT MAST-BIRTH-DATE.
    IF RESPONSE = 'E'
        DISPLAY 'EDUCATION CODE ' MAST-EDUCATION
        ACCEPT MAST-EDUCATION.
    IF RESPONSE = 'J'
        DISPLAY 'JOB CODE ' MAST-JOB-CODE
        ACCEPT MAST-JOB-CODE.
    IF RESPONSE = 'I'
        DISPLAY 'INCOME ' MAST-INCOME
        ACCEPT MAST-INCOME.
    ACCEPT RESPONSE.

430-DELETE-MASTER.
    DISPLAY '           DELETE EMPLOYEE RECORD'.
    DISPLAY ' '.
    PERFORM 450-GET-EMPLOYEE.
    PERFORM 460-READ-MASTER.
    IF KEY-ERROR
        DISPLAY MESSAGE-04
    ELSE
        PERFORM 435-DO-DELETE.

435-DO-DELETE.
    MOVE '9'                 TO MAST-DELETE.
    PERFORM 470-REWRITE-MASTER.
    DISPLAY MESSAGE-03.

440-QUERY-MASTER.
    DISPLAY '           EMPLOYEE RECORD QUERY'.
    DISPLAY ' '.
    PERFORM 450-GET-EMPLOYEE.
    PERFORM 460-READ-MASTER.
    IF KEY-ERROR
        DISPLAY '**ERROR** ' MESSAGE-04
    ELSE
        PERFORM 445-DISPLAY-MASTER.

445-DISPLAY-MASTER.
    DISPLAY 'NAME ' MAST-NAME '   INCOME ' MAST-INCOME.
    DISPLAY ' '.
    DISPLAY 'DEPT ' MAST-CURRENT-DEPT ' PREVIOUS ' MAST-PREV-DEPT.
    DISPLAY ' '.
    DISPLAY 'YEAR EMPLOYED ' MAST-YEAR-EMPLOYED.
    DISPLAY ' '.
    DISPLAY 'BIRTH DATE ' MAST-BIRTH-DATE.
    DISPLAY ' '.
    DISPLAY 'EDUCATION ' MAST-EDUCATION.
    DISPLAY ' '.
    DISPLAY 'JOB CODE ' MAST-JOB-CODE.
    DISPLAY ' '.
    DISPLAY 'PRESS RETURN TO CONTINUE'.
    ACCEPT RESPONSE.

450-GET-EMPLOYEE.
    DISPLAY '     EMPLOYEE NUMBER?'.
    DISPLAY ' '.
    ACCEPT WS-EMPLOYEE-NO.
    MOVE WS-EMPLOYEE-NO TO TRANS-EMPLOYEE-NO.
```

FIGURE 11.15(d)

```
460-READ-MASTER.
    READ EMPLOYEE-MASTER INTO WS-MAST-REC
        INVALID KEY MOVE 'YES' TO KEY-ERROR-FLAG.
    IF MAST-DELETE IS EQUAL TO '9'
        MOVE 'YES' TO KEY-ERROR-FLAG.

470-REWRITE-MASTER.
    REWRITE MASTER-REC FROM WS-MAST-REC
        INVALID KEY DISPLAY '**REWRITE ERROR** ' MESSAGE-06.

500-END-OF-UPDATE.
    DISPLAY ' '.
    DISPLAY '*** END OF FILE UPDATE ***'.
```
FIGURE 11.15(e)

PROGRAM TESTING

Testing an interactive program requires as much foresight and planning as a batch program. In this application, a master file is required (see Figure 11.16), which can be created in the manner discussed in Chapter 5. Although there is no transaction file, some thought needs to be given to the entries that will be made at the terminal to test the program. These should be written down so that a record can be made of each activity and the result when that entry is made interactively. This written document will prove useful both during the test and after, when it may be necessary to do some program debugging.

EMPLOYEE MASTER FILE DUMP

```
0001Falcon, Lloyd          140    1950032532342042500000
0002Carney, Jim            130    1963040444435035600000
0003Chambers, JK           130    1965071543342042130000
0004Gallagher, Angelo      120    1966111145326031500000
0005Ellis, Mike            140    1968010546223025900000
0006Dawson, Mary           140    1972123055327030100000
0007Arbor, Noel            105    1974040153223027334587
0008DaCosta, Michael       105    1975062957545052750000
0009Eagle, Wilfred         190    1977051831114023400000
0010Assad, James           110    1978091846325029453000
0011Baird, Joan            105    1983101159221016800000
0012Gallagher, Pat         115    1983123162221016800000
0013Baird, Joan            105    1983010162221016800000
0014Cantoone, Phil         120    1984082754437012400000
0015Harris, Jim            105    1984032156421016700000
```

FIGURE 11.16 Dump of the master file before the update

The easiest type of activity to test is the query, and so the results in Figures 11.17 and 11.18 show what happens when a query is requested for employee number 0003. First, the main menu is displayed, the code for a query (code 4) is selected, and the second screen is shown, where the employee number is entered and the record's data are displayed.

After each activity is complete, the program will again display the main menu, but for sake of space we will not show it here each time. Figure 11.19 shows the screen when a record is revised. In the first example, only one field is revised for record 0001 and then a Q is entered to complete the revision. In Figure 11.20, each field for employee number 0006 is revised to ensure that the revision is functional for every field the program is intended to revise.

Figure 11.21 shows an add of a new record to the file. Because the master contains only active records, no new records may be added. If record 0006 had been previously deleted, an add operation would be acceptable. Instead, the program produces an error message, which is the correct action in this situation.

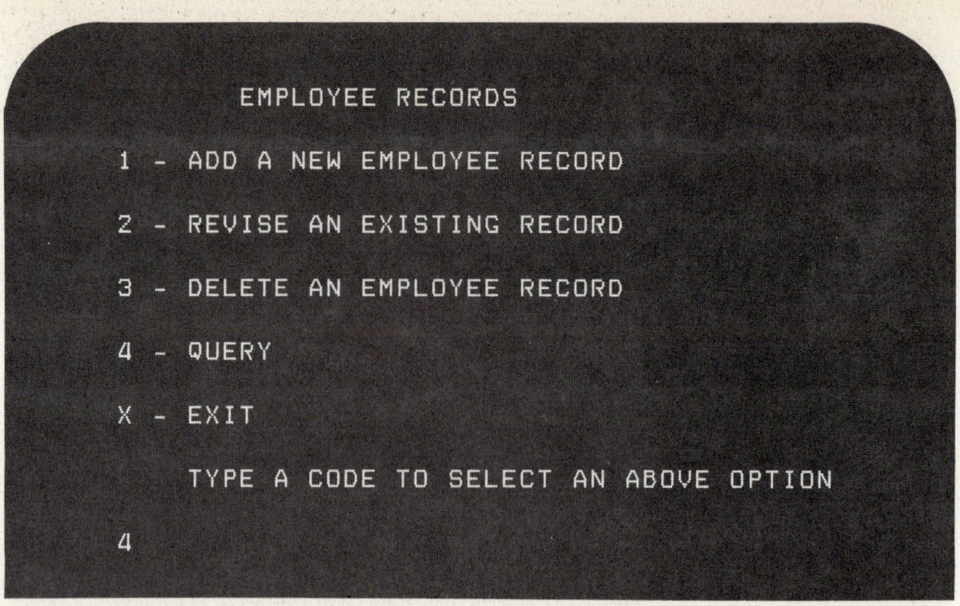

FIGURE 11.17   Display of the main menu during program testing.

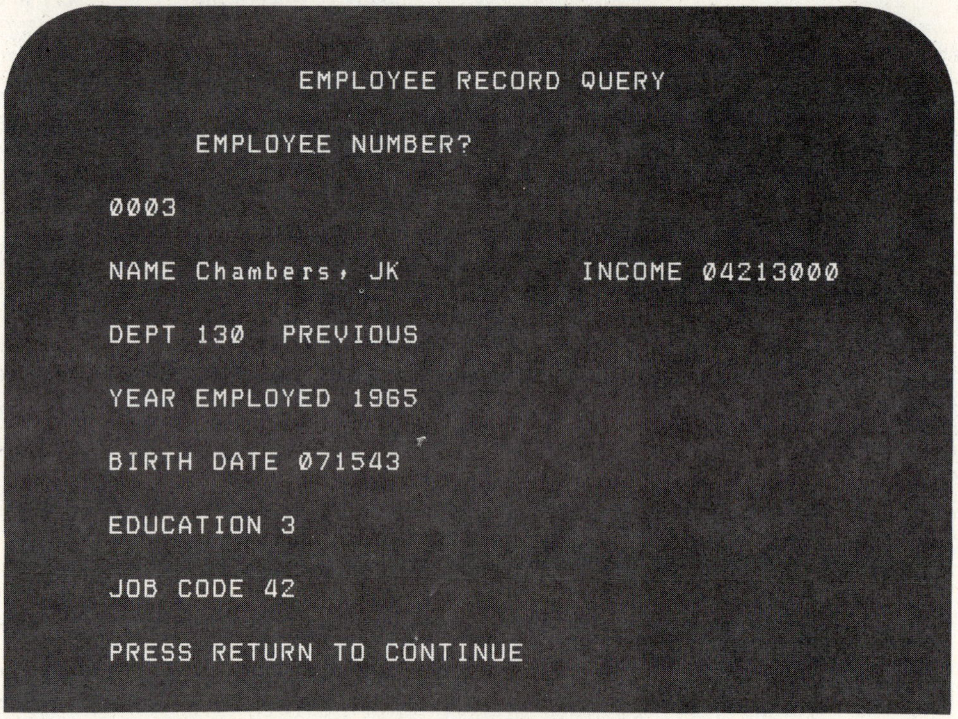

FIGURE 11.18   Screen display for a query on employee 0003

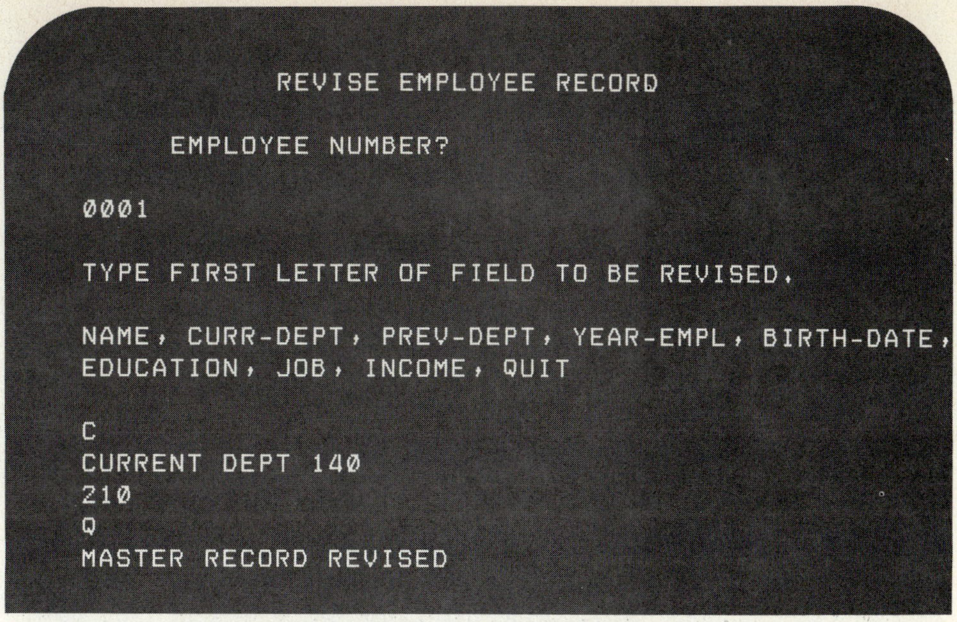

```
                    REVISE EMPLOYEE RECORD

        EMPLOYEE NUMBER?

0001

TYPE FIRST LETTER OF FIELD TO BE REVISED.

NAME, CURR-DEPT, PREV-DEPT, YEAR-EMPL, BIRTH-DATE,
EDUCATION, JOB, INCOME, QUIT

C
CURRENT DEPT 140
210
Q
MASTER RECORD REVISED
```

FIGURE 11.19   Revising the current department field in record 0001

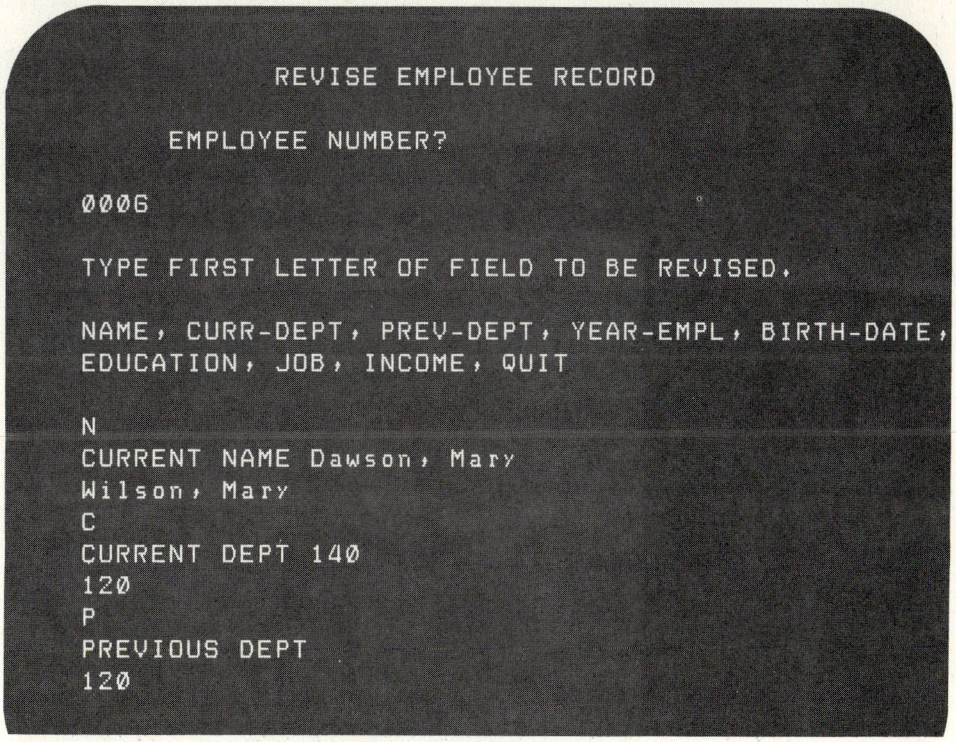

```
                    REVISE EMPLOYEE RECORD

        EMPLOYEE NUMBER?

0006

TYPE FIRST LETTER OF FIELD TO BE REVISED.

NAME, CURR-DEPT, PREV-DEPT, YEAR-EMPL, BIRTH-DATE,
EDUCATION, JOB, INCOME, QUIT

N
CURRENT NAME Dawson, Mary
Wilson, Mary
C
CURRENT DEPT 140
120
P
PREVIOUS DEPT
120
```

FIGURE 11.20(a)   Screen display when all fields are revised in a record

```
Y
YEAR EMPLOYED 1972
1982
B
BIRTH DATE (MMDDYY) 123055
102461
E
EDUCATION CODE 3
5
J
JOB CODE 27
23
I
INCOME 3010000
3250000
Q
MASTER RECORD REVISED
```

FIGURE 11.20(b)   Screen display when all fields are revised in a record

```
            ADD NEW EMPLOYEE RECORD

    EMPLOYEE NUMBER?

0006
**ERROR** MASTER ALREADY EXISTS
```

FIGURE 11.21   Screen display for an attempt to add an existing record

The screen for deleting a record is shown in Figure 11.22. When a delete occurs, only the employee number is displayed. In some cases, it might be desirable to display the contents of the record before completing the delete.

Notice that some of the fields displayed have a minimum of readability. For instance, when income is displayed, it does not contain a decimal point. Birth date does not delimit the month, day, and year with slashes. This can be rectified by moving the field to an edited picture before displaying it on the screen. Similarly, when a field such as income is entered, it could be typed without leading zeros and with a decimal

```
            DELETE EMPLOYEE RECORD

    EMPLOYEE NUMBER?

0012

MASTER RECORD DELETED
```

FIGURE 11.22   Screen display for deleting an existing record

point, which is a more natural method. But then the program would need to reconstruct the data so that they are correctly formed for the income field in the master record. Obviously, COBOL is not designed to relieve the program of this burden. However, other software, such as CICS, do simplify this type of data communication between the user and the application program.

SUMMARY

In batch-processing systems, the transactions to be processed are all accumulated prior to processing and then processed as a batch. Remote job entry (RJE) is like batch, except transactions are accumulated at a location physically remote from the computer. They are then transmitted over a communication line to the computer, where batch processing is done.

On-line processing receives data directly from the environment where they are created and processes the data immediately without waiting for other transactions to be accumulated. An on-line system generally uses a terminal that communicates directly with the computer system. The user can make a direct inquiry and the program will immediately read data from a file and display a response on the screen. On-line systems typically present a menu of choices for the user to select from.

On-line systems may use COBOL for the processing and file-retrieval operations required by the system, but usually some other front-end communications program is used to control the terminal operation, recognize a request, and check for errors. Software such as CICS (IBM's Customer Information Control System) IDMS/DC, Shadow II, and Environ/1 are all available for this purpose.

The DISPLAY statement is used in COBOL for low-volume output or for program debugging. DISPLAY may also be used to create output on the CONSOLE or terminal and therefore be used for user communication. DISPLAY is typically used for this purpose on personal computers that use COBOL.

DISPLAY does not require a file to be defined in the ENVIRONMENT or DATA divisions of the program. Data to be displayed may be either a literal or identifier or a combination of these.

ACCEPT is used to read or input low volumes of data from the operator CONSOLE or keyboard. Like DISPLAY, the ACCEPT statement does not require a file definition in the ENVIRONMENT or DATA divisions. ACCEPT may be used to read the user's response from a terminal.

Writing interactive programs in this chapter requires the use of DISPLAY to prompt the user. One form of prompt is to simply ask the user a question, which is then answered by typing in data such as a name or account number. These data are read by the ACCEPT statement. Another way to interact with the user is to display a menu using a series of DISPLAY statements. The user then makes a choice, usually by typing a single letter or number to indicate the selection made from the menu. This choice is also read by using an ACCEPT statement.

TERMS TO STUDY

ACCEPT	Interactive
Batch	Menu
CICS	On line
DISPLAY	Prompt
Front end	Query
Inquiry	Remote job entry

TRUE/FALSE QUESTIONS

1. In a batch system the transactions for a given application are accumulated together for processing.
2. One advantage of a batch system is that time delays are kept to a minimum.
3. The term RJE means remote job execution.
4. An on-line system receives the data directly from the user without waiting for them to be accumulated.
5. A prompt is only needed for users that do not fully understand the system.
6. A menu offers the user of an on-line system a selection of options available in the program.
7. COBOL is often used on personal or microcomputers because of its strengths for interactive processing.
8. IBM's Customer Information Control System (CICS) is often used as a front-end communications program with COBOL.
9. The only purpose of DISPLAY is to display information on the computer's screen.
10. ACCEPT may be used to get small amounts of input data without the need to define a file.

FILL IN THE BLANKS

11. In _____-oriented systems, the transactions to be processed are all accumulated prior to processing.
12. An _____ system is one that receives the data directly from the environment that creates it.
13. A _____ is often used on a display screen to offer the user a series of choices that are available in the system.
14. When the system asks the user a question for which a response must be typed, the question is called a _____.
15. When COBOL is used for interactive applications on mainframe computers, a _____ program such as CICS is usually used with it.
16. The _____ statement may be used to write data on the operator console or the printer.
17. The _____ statement is used for low-volume input from SYSIPT or a console keyboard.

MULTIPLE CHOICE

18. What type of process most effectively uses the computer's resources for applications such as weekly payroll or monthly billing?
    a. Batch
    b. On-line
    c. CICS
    d. None of the above
19. What type of process usually has the longest time delay for processing transactions?
    a. Batch
    b. On-line
    c. CICS
    d. None of the above
20. What type of process usually has the shortest time delay for processing transactions?
    a. Batch
    b. On-line
    c. CICS
    d. None of the above

21. What is the term used for data that are entered into the computer from a distant location?
    a. Batch
    b. On-line
    c. Remote job entry
    d. None of the above

22. What type of device is used for communication with the computer on most on-line business systems?
    a. Tape drive
    b. Disk drive
    c. Terminal
    d. Telephone

23. What is the term for a question, such as "Enter customer number," that the computer asks the user?
    a. Enter or return
    b. Display
    c. Accept
    d. Prompt

24. What does the term menu refer to?
    a. Something you read in a restaurant.
    b. A series of choices displayed on the screen.
    c. a and b.
    d. Neither a nor b.

25. Which of the following is often used with COBOL to develop an effective on-line program with extensive communications capabilities?
    a. IBM's CICS.
    b. Cullinane's IDMS/DC.
    c. Cincom Systems' Environ/1.
    d. All the above.
    e. None of the above.

PROGRAMMING EXERCISES

1. The employee record program in this chapter requires some improvements, so for this exercise implement the changes from the following specifications.

PROGRAMMING SPECIFICATIONS

PROGRAM NAME: Employee Master Update (revision)   PROGRAM ID: UPDATE11
PREPARED BY: Diane Quest   DATE: Nov. 1, 1986

Program Description:
    Include these modifications to the program for the new release. Files used are unchanged from the original program.
Program Requirements:
    1. When a query is done to an existing master, offer the user a chance to revise or delete the master before returning to the main menu.
    2. Modify the paragraph 450-GET-EMPLOYEE so that the user may enter the employee number without the need to type leading zeros.
    3. Whenever birth date is displayed, separate the month, day, and year with slashes (10/15/87). Similarly, display income with a decimal point and suppress leading zeros.
    4. When processing a revision, display the first letter prompt after each entry has been made. Also, permit the user to make no entry if the wrong field was selected. If no entry is made, the contents of the field should remain unchanged.

---

2. Write an interactive program to prepare a record of payments for a loan or mortgage based on the following formula:

$$\text{Payment} = \text{principal} * \frac{\text{interest}}{1 - (1 + \text{interest})^{-n}}$$

where principal is the amount of the loan, interest is the rate per period (n), and n is the number of periods.

Assuming that terms are expressed in years, begin by prompting the user for this input, as shown in the following screen format:

```
          PRINCIPAL?            10000

          ANNUAL INTEREST?      0.10
          PAYMENTS/YEAR?          12
          TERM IN YEARS?           5
```

Next compute and display the rate per period, the number of periods per year, and the payment. The screen should have the following appearance when this step is complete.

```
          PRINCIPAL             10000

          ANNUAL INTEREST        0.10
          PAYMENTS/YEAR            12
          TERM IN YEARS            5
          RATE PER PERIOD    0.00833
          PERIODS/YEAR            60

          PAYMENT            $212.47
```

Finally, display a schedule of payments showing the following values. When the screen is full, wait temporarily until the user indicates to continue or to quit. The first and last screens for the values entered are as follows:

```
                  PAYMENT SCHEDULE

MONTH    PRINCIPAL        PAYMENT       INTEREST   NEW PRINCIPAL

  1     10000.00         212.47         83.33        9870.86
  2      9870.86         212.47         82.26        9740.65
  3      9740.65         212.47         81.17        9609.35
  4      9609.35         212.47         80.08        9476.96
  5      9476.96         212.47         78.97        9343.46
  6      9343.46         212.47         77.86        9208.85
  7      9208.85         212.47         76.74        9073.12
  8      9073.12         212.47         75.61        8936.26
  9      8936.26         212.47         74.47        8798.26
 10      8798.26         212.47         73.32        8659.11
 11      8659.11         212.47         72.16        8518.80
 12      8518.80         212.47         70.99        8377.32
 13      8377.32         212.47         69.81        8234.66
 14      8234.66         212.47         68.62        8090.81
 15      8090.81         212.47         67.42        7945.76
 16      7945.76         212.47         66.21        7799.51
 17      7799.51         212.47         65.00        7652.03
 18      7652.03         212.47         63.77        7503.33

PRESS RETURN - TO CONTINUE    Q - TO QUIT
```

```
                    PAYMENT SCHEDULE

   MONTH    PRINCIPAL       PAYMENT         INTEREST    NEW PRINCIPAL

    54       1438.93        212.47            11.99        1238.45
    55       1238.45        212.47            10.32        1036.30
    56       1036.30        212.47             8.64         832.47
    57        832.47        212.47             6.94         626.93
    58        626.93        212.47             5.22         419.69
    59        419.69        212.47             3.50         210.71
    60        210.71        212.47             1.76           .00

   PRESS RETURN - TO CONTINUE     Q - TO QUIT
```

3. Using the file of publication titles from Programming Exercise 3, page 395, Chapter 10, write an interactive program that provides the user with several options, as described next. Design your own menus and prompts for this application.

   a. List the data for books containing a specific keyword. For example, if the keyword PASCAL were entered, all books containing PASCAL in the title would be listed. Allow for multiple keywords, such as DATA BASE.

   b. List books by a specific author. Author names are stored with the surname first, followed by given names, and initials. Allow for wild-card searches so that if the author's full name is not known or the spelling is uncertain, then a partial key can be entered. For example, entering PETER* would list books by PETER, D., PETER, J., PETERS, J., and PETERSON, L.

   c. Provide an option so that a KWIC index may be printed by requesting it from the screen interactively, but printing it on the printer in the usual manner. This option should be limited to selection just prior to terminating the program. Because the terminal will be unavailable for use while this index is being created and printed, display an occasional message so that the user will know that the program is still active. For example, while creating the KWIC index, a message could be displayed every 100 records. Then another message could indicate when printing has begun and when it is ended.

INPUT/OUTPUT RECORD DEFINITION				
File: Book title file Record Length: 100 Sequence: N/A		File Type: Disk Blocking Factor: 1 Access Method: Sequential		
COLUMNS	FIELD	TYPE	LENGTH	DECIMALS
1–20	Author	A/N	20	
21–40	Publisher	A/N	20	
41–100	Title	A/N	60	

APPENDIX A

SORT/MERGE STATEMENTS

SORT STATEMENT AND RELATED ENTRIES

File-oriented programs typically require data to be ordered in a specific sequence for successful execution of the program. This is particularly true of batch programs using transaction files or master files for report generation. A file may be in one sequence for a given application, but may need to be resequenced for a different use. A sales file may be in sequence by salesperson, which is fine if the application is to generate commission checks. But when the file is to be used to produce a summary of the sales for each item sold, then an item number sequence would be more appropriate.

Another need for the same file could be to list the sales of each item within the different regions where it is sold. This need requires the file to be in item-within-region sequence. So you can see that the same data that were used to produce the commission checks for each salesperson may also be sorted into different sequences to produce different reports.

With the SORT feature, the COBOL programmer may code a sort directly into the program and sort an input file as a part of the program specifications. This is a handy feature because it does not require a separate utility program to be run prior to running the COBOL program. A second advantage of the COBOL SORT is that it permits preprocessing of the file prior to sorting or postprocessing after it is sorted.

ENVIRONMENT DIVISION.

   [INPUT-OUTPUT SECTION.
   FILE-CONTROL.
      SELECT sort-file-name ASSIGN TO system-name.]

```
DATA DIVISION.

FILE SECTION.
SD  sort-file-name

      [RECORD CONTAINS [integer-2 TO] integer-3 CHARACTERS]
      [DATA  {RECORD IS    }
             {RECORDS ARE  }     data-name-1 [data-name-2]. . .].
  01    data-name
```

```
PROCEDURE DIVISION.
      SORT sort-file-name ON {ASCENDING }  KEY data-name-1 [data-name-2] . . .
                             {DESCENDING}

            [ ON {ASCENDING } KEY data-name-3 [data-name-4] . . . ] . . .
                 {DESCENDING}

      {INPUT PROCEDURE IS section-name-1 }
      {USING file-name-1 [file-name-3] . . . }

      {OUTPUT PROCEDURE IS section-name-2 }
      {GIVING file-name-2 }
```

Using the SORT feature affects three areas of the COBOL program. A SELECT clause in the ENVIRONMENT DIVISION is needed to identify a work file used for sorting. Second, this same work file is defined in the FILE SECTION of the DATA DIVISION with a Sort Description (SD) entry. Finally, the sort itself is defined in the PROCEDURE DIVISION with the SORT statement.

SELECT CLAUSE

Each program that uses the SORT requires a work file to be defined for sorting. The SORT statement copies the file to be sorted into this work file where the sort is done. When the sort is completed, the newly sequenced records are in the work file, which is then copied to the output file. Although the work file is only temporary, it must be defined for the sort.

All files, including the sort's work file, are first defined by a SELECT clause. Normally, this file will be a disk file with a system name that corresponds to the rules for system names in the computer you are using. An entry for an IBM OS/VS system might be as follows:

```
     A  B
1  4 78 12                                                              72
─────────────────────────────────────────────────────────────────────────
     ENVIRONMENT DIVISION.
     INPUT-OUTPUT SECTION.
     FILE-CONTROL.
         SELECT WORK-FILE ASSIGN TO UT-S-SORTWORK.
```

SD STATEMENT

Each program that does a sort will require an SD entry to define the sort work file. This is the same file that was identified by the SELECT clause. Options in the SD are similar to the FD entry, except that a BLOCK CONTAINS clause is not available.

Because the defaults in the SD will automatically assign the correct record length and data record, a simple entry with a record as follows would satisfy COBOL's requirements:

```
    A   B
1   4   78  12                                                          72
────────────────────────────────────────────────────────────────────────
        SD   WORK-FILE.
        01   SORT-RECORD.
             05 ACCOUNT-NUMBER   PIC 9(07).
             05 FILLER           PIC X(93).
```

THE SORT STATEMENT

The final statement needed to do a sort is the SORT statement itself, which will be located in the PROCEDURE DIVISION. SORT is an executable statement like any other COBOL statement in the PROCEDURE DIVISION. It is not executed until the program reaches the statement, just like a READ or a COMPUTE is only executed when the program reaches their location in the program.

For example, take the following SORT statement:

```
    A   B
1   4   78  12                                                          72
────────────────────────────────────────────────────────────────────────
        SORT WORK-FILE
            ON ASCENDING KEY   ACCOUNT-NUMBER
            USING   ACCOUNTS-FILE
            GIVING SORTED-ACCOUNTS-FILE.
```

The file name WORK-FILE refers to the file identified earlier in the SELECT and SD statements. This file is used by the program for doing the sort and is not to be confused with the file that needs to be sorted.

ASCENDING KEY refers to the field in the record that determines the sequence from the lowest to the highest value. DESCENDING KEY would choose to sort from the highest to the lowest value. In this example, the file is to be sorted in account number sequence and so the field ACCOUNT-NUMBER is identified.

The USING clause identifies the file (ACCOUNTS-FILE) containing the data to be sorted. GIVING tells the sort where to place the output (in the SORTED-ACCOUNTS-FILE) after the sort is complete.

Although not evident from the SORT statement, the SORT causes the USING file to be copied to the WORK-FILE (sort file). The WORK-FILE is then used by the sort to reorder the records into the sequence specified by the SORT statement. When the records have been sorted into the desired order, the GIVING file is created as an output from the sort.

Another SORT statement to sort a sales file into department within region follows. When two or more fields are required in the sort specifications, the first entry in the SORT statement defines the major sequence. In this example, region is the major sequence. Each additional KEY entry proceeds from major to minor, so the department number is the minor sequence in this example.

```
    A   B
1   4   78  12                                                          72
────────────────────────────────────────────────────────────────────────
        SORT WORK-FILE
            ON ASCENDING KEY   REGION-NUMBER
            ON ASCENDING KEY   DEPARTMENT-NUMBER
            USING   SALES-FILE
            GIVING SORTED-SALES-FILE.
```

A COMPLETE SORT PROGRAM

A COBOL program that does nothing except sort the ACCOUNTS-FILE is given next. This file is a sequential disk file containing 100-byte records in random order. Output from the sort is to be a SORTED-ACCOUNTS-FILE, which will contain the records in account number sequence. A WORK-FILE is to be used to do the sort.

The FILE CONTROL paragraph describes each of these files and allocates them to the disk name and device on which they are located. The FILE SECTION in the DATA DIVISION defines the FD and SD for these files. Notice from this program that the input file (ACCOUNTS-FILE) and the output (SORTED-ACCOUNTS-FILE) do not have any field descriptions except for a FILLER, which defines the length of the record.

However, the SD contains a record description that defines the ACCOUNT-NUMBER field. This field is necessary for the sort to define the KEY field. The remainder of the record for the SD is a FILLER also. This does not mean there are no data in the record, but rather that the remaining 93 bytes of the record do not need to be referenced by this program.

Finally, the PROCEDURE DIVISION contains the SORT statement. This statement, as in earlier examples, defines the sort file (WORK-FILE), the file to use (ACCOUNTS-FILE), and the file to be given (SORTED-ACCOUNTS-FILE) as a result of the sort. The SORT also defines the sort KEY to be ACCOUNT-NUMBER. Notice there is no need to open or close the files because the SORT takes care of all file activities.

```
IDENTIFICATION DIVISION.
PROGRAM-ID.
    SORT.
*AUTHOR.
*    DON CASSEL.
*INSTALLATION.
*    HUMBER COLLEGE.
*DATE-WRITTEN.
*    NOVEMBER 5.
*DATE-COMPILED.
*    NOVEMBER 5.
*REMARKS.
*    DEMONSTRATE THE SORT FEATURE.

ENVIRONMENT DIVISION.
CONFIGURATION SECTION.
SOURCE-COMPUTER.
    IBM-370.
OBJECT-COMPUTER.
    IBM-370.
INPUT-OUTPUT SECTION.
FILE-CONTROL.
    SELECT ACCOUNTS-FILE        ASSIGN TO UT-3380-S-DISK1.
    SELECT WORK-FILE            ASSIGN TO UT-3380-SORTWORK.
    SELECT SORTED-ACCOUNTS-FILE ASSIGN TO UT-3380-S-DISK2.
```

```
DATA DIVISION.
FILE SECTION.
FD   ACCOUNTS-FILE
     RECORD CONTAINS 100 CHARACTERS
     LABEL RECORDS ARE STANDARD
     DATA RECORD IS ACCOUNTS-RECORD.
01   ACCOUNTS-RECORD.
     05  FILLER                    PIC X(100).


SD   WORK-FILE.
01   SORT-RECORD.
     05 ACCOUNT-NUMBER  PIC 9(07).
     05 FILLER          PIC X(93).


FD   SORTED-ACCOUNTS-FILE
     RECORD CONTAINS 100 CHARACTERS
     LABEL RECORDS ARE STANDARD
     DATA RECORD IS SORTED-ACCOUNTS-RECORD.
01   SORTED-ACCOUNTS-RECORD.
     05  FILLER                    PIC X(100).


PROCEDURE DIVISION
000-SORT-ACCOUNTS.
     SORT WORK-FILE
          ON ASCENDING KEY  ACCOUNT-NUMBER
          USING  ACCOUNTS-FILE
          GIVING SORTED-ACCOUNTS-FILE.
     STOP RUN.
```

USING AN INPUT PROCEDURE AND RELEASE STATEMENT

> RELEASE   record-name   [FROM identifier]

Sorts may define additional processing to be done on the file prior to the sort operation. Several reasons for this may exist. Perhaps only certain records in the input file are to be selected for the sort; others are simply to be ignored. Another reason can be to validate the input data to ensure the sort receives only valid records. Another may require preprocessing of the input to do some calculations before the sort is done. Whatever the reason, preprocessing of the file may be defined by using the INPUT PROCEDURE option of the SORT statement instead of the USING option. This INPUT PROCEDURE must be defined as a SECTION name.

When an INPUT PROCEDURE is used by the SORT, a statement is required to tell the SORT that you are finished with the preprocessing of a record. By using the RELEASE statement, the record is released to the SORT from your INPUT PROCEDURE. The RELEASE always refers to a record-name, which is the record associated with the sort file. A FROM option is available to be used to obtain another source for the record, such as WORKING-STORAGE.

```
        000-SORT-ACCOUNTS SECTION.
            OPEN INPUT ACCOUNTS-FILE.
            SORT WORK-FILE
                ON ASCENDING KEY  ACCOUNT-NUMBER
                INPUT PROCEDURE 200-VALIDATE-INPUT
                GIVING SORTED-ACCOUNTS-FILE.
            CLOSE ACCOUNTS-FILE.
            STOP RUN.

        200-VALIDATE-INPUT SECTION.

        210-INITIALIZE.
            PERFORM 220-READ-ACCOUNT.
            PERFORM 230-VALIDATE
                UNTIL EOF-FLAG = 1.
            GO TO 250-SORT-ACCOUNTS-EXIT.

            :

        250-SORT-ACCOUNTS-EXIT.
            EXIT.
```

USING AN OUTPUT PROCEDURE AND RETURN STATEMENT

RETURN sort-file-name   [INTO identifier]

    AT END   imperative-statement

OUTPUT PROCEDUREs are the converse of INPUT. Whereas an INPUT PROCE-DURE allows for preprocessing of the file before sorting, the OUTPUT PROCEDURE permits postprocessing of the records after they have been sorted. This use of the SORT option can be helpful when the sorted records are to be printed. Because the GIVING file cannot be a printer, an OUTPUT PROCEDURE may be defined to create a printed report from the SORT.

The RETURN statement is used in the OUTPUT PROCEDURE to access a record from the sort file and make it available to the program in the sort's input record area. The RETURN functions like a READ statement, because each time it is executed a new record is made available in the input record area. Like a READ, the RETURN statement must check for end of file. Therefore, it has an AT END clause. The only difference between a READ and the RETURN is that a RETURN is used for accessing records from a sort file.

WRITING A PROGRAM WITH AN OUTPUT PROCEDURE

An OUTPUT PROCEDURE also uses a SECTION in the program, and so the discussion about sections for the INPUT PROCEDURE also applies here. All code in the program will be organized into sections, with one of these sections being the OUTPUT PROCE-DURE.

Any files to be used by the OUTPUT PROCEDURE must be opened prior to issuing the SORT statement. After the SORT is finished, the program then closes these files. In the code that follows, the printer is opened prior to giving the SORT command.

```
PROCEDURE DIVISION,

000-SORT-ACCOUNTS SECTION,

    OPEN OUTPUT REPORT-FILE,
    SORT WORK-FILE
        ON ASCENDING KEY  ACCOUNT-NUMBER
        USING ACCOUNTS-FILE
        OUTPUT PROCEDURE 300-PRINT-REPORT,
    CLOSE REPORT-FILE,
    STOP RUN,

300-PRINT-REPORT SECTION,

310-INITIALIZE,
    PERFORM 320-GET-RECORD,
    PERFORM 330-PRINT-RECORDS
        UNTIL EOF-FLAG = 1,
    GO TO 350-PRINT-REPORT-EXIT,

320-GET-RECORD,
    RETURN WORK-FILE
        AT END MOVE 1 TO EOF-FLAG,

330-PRINT-RECORDS,
    MOVE SORT-RECORD TO LINE-OUT,
    WRITE PRINT-LINE
        AFTER ADVANCING 1 LINE,
    PERFORM 320-GET-RECORD,

350-PRINT-REPORT-EXIT,
    EXIT,
```

MERGE STATEMENT AND RELATED ENTRIES

ENVIRONMENT DIVISION.

[INPUT-OUTPUT SECTION.

FILE-CONTROL.
    SELECT merge-file-name ASSIGN TO system-name.]

DATA DIVISION.

FILE SECTION.

SD merge-file-name

    [RECORD CONTAINS [integer-2 TO] integer-3 CHARACTERS]

    [DATA $\begin{Bmatrix} \text{RECORD IS} \\ \text{RECORDS ARE} \end{Bmatrix}$ data-name-1 [data-name-2]. . .].

01 data-name.

```
PROCEDURE DIVISION.

    MERGE merge-file-name ON {ASCENDING / DESCENDING} KEY data-name-1 [data-name-2] . . .

                [ON {ASCENDING / DESCENDING} KEY data-name-3 [data-name-4] . . . ] . . .

        USING file-name-1 [file-name-3] . . .

        {OUTPUT PROCEDURE IS section-name-1}
        {GIVING file-name-2                 }
```

A MERGE (ANS COBOL 1974 and 1985) uses a concept similar to the SORT except that with the merge operation the contents of two or more files are combined to create a single file. MERGE uses a SELECT clause, an SD, and a MERGE statement in a manner similar to writing a SORT. The main difference is that MERGE requires two or more files in the USING clause. Another difference is that an INPUT PROCEDURE is not available for the programmer's use; however, an OUTPUT PROCEDURE may be specified. Entries in the ASCENDING or DESCENDING KEY, USING, GIVING, and OUTPUT PROCEDURE are the same as discussed for the SORT.

The following MERGE statement is written to merge the contents of the files FIRST-QTR-ACCOUNTS and SECOND-QTR-ACCOUNTS to create a merged file ACCOUNTS-FILE.

```
      A   B
1   4 78  12                                                                          72
─────────────────────────────────────────────────────────────────────────────────────
        MERGE WORK-FILE
            ON ASCENDING KEY  ACCOUNT-NUMBER
            USING  FIRST-QTR-ACCOUNTS  SECOND-QTR-ACCOUNTS
            GIVING ACCOUNTS-FILE
```

The following program merges the contents of two files and creates a third containing the contents of the two input files.

```
      IDENTIFICATION DIVISION.

      PROGRAM-ID
          MERGE.
     *AUTHOR.
     *    DON CASSEL.
     *INSTALLATION.
     *    HUMBER COLLEGE.
     *DATE-WRITTEN.
     *    NOVEMBER 5.
     *DATE-COMPILED.
     *    NOVEMBER 5.
     *REMARKS.
     *    DEMONSTRATE THE MERGE FEATURE.
```

```
ENVIRONMENT DIVISION.

CONFIGURATION SECTION.

SOURCE-COMPUTER.
    IBM-370.
OBJECT-COMPUTER.
    IBM-370.

INPUT-OUTPUT SECTION.
FILE-CONTROL.
    SELECT FIRST-QTR-ACCOUNTS     ASSIGN TO UT-3380-S-DISK1.
    SELECT SECOND-QTR-ACCOUNTS    ASSIGN TO UT-3380-S-DISK2.
    SELECT WORK-FILE              ASSIGN TO UT-3380-SORTWORK.
    SELECT ACCOUNTS-FILE          ASSIGN TO UT-3380-S-DISK3.

DATA DIVISION.

FILE SECTION.

FD  FIRST-QTR-ACCOUNTS
    RECORD CONTAINS 100 CHARACTERS
    LABEL RECORDS ARE STANDARD
    DATA RECORD IS ACCOUNTS-RECORD-1.
01  ACCOUNTS-RECORD-1.
    05  FILLER                    PIC X(100).

FD  SECOND-QTR-ACCOUNTS
    RECORD CONTAINS 100 CHARACTERS
    LABEL RECORDS ARE STANDARD
    DATA RECORD IS ACCOUNTS-RECORD-2.
01  ACCOUNTS-RECORD-2.
    05  FILLER                    PIC X(100).

SD  WORK-FILE.
01  MERGE-RECORD.
    05 ACCOUNT-NUMBER  PIC 9(07).
    05 FILLER          PIC X(93).

FD  ACCOUNTS-FILE
    RECORD CONTAINS 100 CHARACTERS
    LABEL RECORDS ARE STANDARD
    DATA RECORD IS ACCOUNTS-RECORD-3.
01  ACCOUNTS-RECORD-3.
    05  FILLER                    PIC X(100).

PROCEDURE DIVISION.

000-MERGE-ACCOUNTS.
    MERGE WORK-FILE
        ON ASCENDING KEY  ACCOUNT-NUMBER
        USING  FIRST-QTR-ACCOUNTS  SECOND-QTR-ACCOUNTS
        GIVING ACCOUNTS-FILE.
    STOP RUN.
```

COBOL'S TABLE-HANDLING FEATURE

INDEXED BY CLAUSE

OCCURS integer   TIMES

  [INDEXED BY   index-name-1 [index-name-2] . . .]

The INDEXED BY clause is available in the OCCURS clause to associate an index name with a table. An index is very similar in concept to a subscript and is usually used in the same way. Indexes are more efficient than subscripts, especially when larger tables are used. But there are some important differences between an index and a subscript.

The first difference is that an index does not require a separate definition in the DATA DIVISION, unlike the subscript, which does require a definition. Indexes do not have a PICTURE clause nor are they given a value. The following example shows a DATA DIVISION entry that contains an OCCURS clause with an INDEX entry:

```
      A   B
1   4  78  12                                                           72


      01   POLICY-TABLE REDEFINES POLICY-TABLE-VALUES,
           05 POLICY-ENTRIES          OCCURS 100 TIMES
                                      INDEXED BY PC-INDEX,
              10 POLICY-CODE          PIC 9(04),
              10 POLICY-RATE          PIC 9(04)V99,
```

The second difference between a subscript and a table is that an index uses displacement values, whereas a subscript uses positional values. If each entry in the table were 10 bytes in length, the index would be increased beginning at zero in increments of 10 for each element of the table. A subscript, on the other hand, is increased in increments of 1 for each element in the table. Although this may seem like an awkward feature of

447

an index, it is a characteristic that seldom affects the way we write programs. Fortunately, COBOL worries about the displacement, so usually we can still think in terms of positions within the array, as we did with subscripts.

Another way indexes differ from subscripts is that they are adjusted by the SET statement. An index cannot be manipulated by the MOVE statement. Neither can it be used in an arithmetic statement such as an ADD or SUBTRACT. The alternative is the SET statement, which may be used to initialize, increase, or decrease the index.

THE SET STATEMENT

Format 1

$$\underline{\text{SET}} \left\{ \begin{array}{l} \text{index-name-1 [index-name-2]} \dots \\ \text{identifier-1} \quad \text{[identifier-2]} \dots \end{array} \right\} \underline{\text{TO}} \left\{ \begin{array}{l} \text{index-name-3} \\ \text{identifier-3} \\ \text{literal-1} \end{array} \right\}$$

Format 2

$$\underline{\text{SET}} \text{ index-name-4 [index-name-5]} \dots \left\{ \begin{array}{l} \underline{\text{UP BY}} \\ \underline{\text{DOWN BY}} \end{array} \right\} \left\{ \begin{array}{l} \text{identifier-4} \\ \text{literal-2} \end{array} \right\}$$

The SET statement is used to initialize an index to increase or decrease its value. SET is used in the PROCEDURE DIVISION and is an executable statement like a MOVE or ADD statement. Values that are given to an index refer to the occurrence value of the table. COBOL automatically translates the occurrence value to a displacement value. So when a statement such as

```
      A    B
1  4  78   12                                                              72

      SET PC-INDEX TO 1.
```

is used, the index PC-INDEX is set to represent element 1 of the table. An index may also be set to the value of a second index. If this second index (RATE-INDEX) has been set by some previous operation, PC-INDEX can be given its value with the following statement:

```
      A    B
1  4  78   12                                                              72

      SET PC-INDEX TO RATE-INDEX.
```

An index's value may be increased or decreased by the SET statement. The following statement increases PC-INDEX by 1, which is similar to adding 1 to a subscript.

```
      A    B
1  4  78   12                                                              72

      SET PC-INDEX UP BY 1.
```

To reduce the index's value by 1, use the following statement:

                    SET PC-INDEX DOWN BY 1.

THE SEARCH STATEMENT

Format 1

$$\begin{array}{l}
\underline{SEARCH}\quad identifier\text{-}1\quad \left[\underline{VARYING}\quad \begin{Bmatrix} identifier\text{-}2 \\ index\text{-}name\text{-}1 \end{Bmatrix}\right] \\[2ex]
\qquad [\underline{AT}\ \underline{END}\quad imperative\text{-}statement\text{-}1] \\[2ex]
\qquad \underline{WHEN}\quad condition\text{-}1\quad \begin{Bmatrix} imperative\text{-}statement\text{-}2 \\ \underline{NEXT\ SENTENCE} \end{Bmatrix} \\[2ex]
\qquad \underline{WHEN}\quad condition\text{-}2\quad \left.\begin{Bmatrix} imperative\text{-}statement\text{-}3 \\ \underline{NEXT\ SENTENCE} \end{Bmatrix}\right]\ \ldots
\end{array}$$

The SEARCH statement is used for searching sequenced keyed tables. The statement comes in two formats; the first does a serial search of the table, and the second format, SEARCH ALL, performs a binary search. Using the SEARCH statement simplifies table search because the programmer is not required to write a PERFORM loop to vary a subscript. SEARCH uses the index associated with the table in the DATA DIVISION to reference the location of entries within the table.

SEARCH also eliminates the need for complex logic to find the entry in the table or to take special action if the entry is not found. So SEARCH can be used to reduce program complexity and thus greatly diminish the possibility of errors in table-handling logic.

The SEARCH statement contains two clauses for its use. One is the AT END clause, which is executed only when no matching key entry is found within the table. The second clause is the WHEN clause. WHEN is followed by a conditional expression that is used to identify a match within the table. When this condition is satisfied, the search is ended and the action following the WHEN clause is taken by the program.

More than one WHEN clause may be used if there are different conditions to satisfy the search. Any WHEN condition that is satisfied will end the search and the actions associated with that WHEN clause will be taken. Actions on any other WHEN clause in the SEARCH statement will not be executed.

The VARYING clause may also be used when a second index for the current table or a second table is to be varied.

Prior to using the SEARCH statement, the index must be set to 1. The SET statement is then used with the SEARCH statement as shown in the next example. POLICY-TABLE is used for this serial search. Note the use of a performed paragraph to do this search.

When the paragraph is first entered, the index PC-INDEX is set to 1 prior to initiating the search. Then the SEARCH statement is given. It provides for setting a flag if the end of the table is reached without getting a match. Alternatively, the WHEN condition defines the condition for getting a match in the table. If this condition is found to be true, the SEARCH executes the WHEN clause's action, which sets the flag. After returning from the table search paragraph, the flag is tested and appropriate action taken.

     A   B
1 4 78 12   72
```

```
01   POLICY-TABLE REDEFINES POLICY-TABLE-VALUES.
     05 POLICY-ENTRIES          OCCURS 100 TIMES
                                INDEXED BY PC-INDEX.
         10 POLICY-CODE         PIC 9(04).
         10 POLICY-RATE         PIC 9(04)V99.

                 :
                 :


     PERFORM 500-SEARCH-POLICY-TABLE.
     IF POLICY-CODE-FLAG-ON
         MOVE POLICY-RATE (PC-INDEX) TO NEW-RATE
     ELSE
         DISPLAY 'POLICY CODE NOT FOUND'.

                 :

500-SEARCH-POLICY-TABLE.
   SET PC-INDEX TO 1.
   SEARCH POLICY-ENTRIES
       AT END MOVE 'NO' TO POLICY-CODE-FLAG
       WHEN CODE-IN IS EQUAL TO POLICY-CODE (PC-INDEX)
           MOVE 'YES' TO POLICY-CODE-FLAG.
```

The next example shows a table in COBOL code using the SEARCH statement to find the correct product entry.

PRODUCT-IN

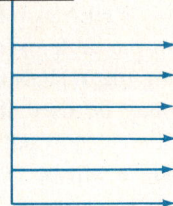

	PRODUCT-TABLE	
	PRODUCT-NUMBER	DISCOUNT-RATE
1	1285	.07
2	1450	.12
3	1554	.10
4	1800	.08
5	2035	.11
= 6	2130	.10
7	2285	.20
8	3500	.12
9	5905	.05
10	6650	.15
```

```
     01    PRODUCT-ENTRIES.
           05 FILLER      PIC X(06)       VALUE '128507'.
           05 FILLER      PIC X(06)       VALUE '145012'.
           05 FILLER      PIC X(06)       VALUE '155410'.
           05 FILLER      PIC X(06)       VALUE '180008'.
           05 FILLER      PIC X(06)       VALUE '203511'.
           05 FILLER      PIC X(06)       VALUE '213010'.
           05 FILLER      PIC X(06)       VALUE '228520'.
           05 FILLER      PIC X(06)       VALUE '350012'.
           05 FILLER      PIC X(06)       VALUE '590505'.
           05 FILLER      PIC X(06)       VALUE '665015'.
     01    PRODUCT-ENTRIES-2 REDEFINES PRODUCT-ENTRIES.
           05 PRODUCT-TABLE OCCURS 10 TIMES
                              INDEXED BY PR-INDEX.
               10 PRODUCT-NUMBER   PIC 9(04).
               10 DISCOUNT-RATE    PIC V99.
                   :
                   :
           PERFORM 300-SEARCH-PRODUCT-TABLE.
           IF FOUND = 'YES'
               DISPLAY DISCOUNT-RATE (PR-INDEX)
           ELSE
               DISPLAY '**NOT FOUND**'.
                   :
                   :
     300-SEARCH-PRODUCT-TABLE.
           SET PR-INDEX TO 1.
           SEARCH PRODUCT-TABLE
               AT END MOVE 'NO' TO FOUND
               WHEN PRODUCT-IN IS EQUAL TO PRODUCT-NUMBER (PR-INDEX)
                   MOVE 'YES' TO FOUND
                   MOVE DISCOUNT-RATE (PR-INDEX) TO HOLD-RATE.
```

SEARCH ALL

Format 2

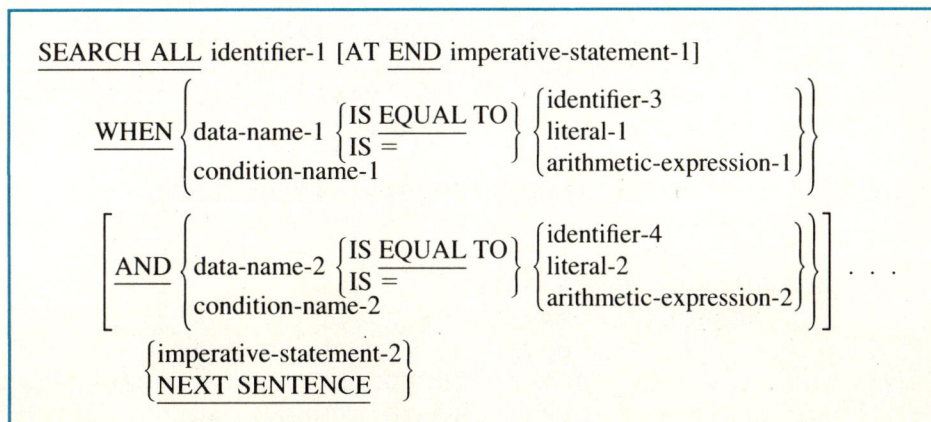

The keyword ALL in the SEARCH statement indicates that a binary search is to be done. A binary search requires the table to be in sequence, either ascending or descending, and the KEY clause must be used with the OCCURS clause in the table. The KEY clause defines the field to be used as a key in the table and whether the table is in ascending or descending sequence. It is the programmer's responsibility to ensure that the table is in the order specified.

OCCURS integer TIMES

$$\left[\begin{Bmatrix} \text{ASCENDING} \\ \text{DESCENDING} \end{Bmatrix} \text{KEY IS} \quad \text{data-name-2 [data-name-3]} \ldots \right] \ldots$$

[INDEXED BY index-name-1 [index-name-2] . . .]

To use a SEARCH ALL, the table must first be defined with a key and index. A SET statement is not necessary with the ALL option because the binary search sets its own index. Like a serial search, an AT END phrase is specified to identify action to be taken if the key is not found in the table. There is only one WHEN clause available, but multiple conditions may be specified by using the AND operator. Only the EQUAL TO condition is permitted with a SEARCH ALL statement.

An example of a table and the SEARCH ALL statement is given next. This table contains three entries for each element: a part number, its description, and its location. The field PART-NUMBER is the key to the table and, as the DATA DIVISION entries show, the table is in ascending sequence on this part number. The index PART-INDEX is attached to the table.

In the PROCEDURE DIVISION, the SEARCH ALL statement is used to search the table for a part number that is equal to an input part number. If it is found, a 'YES' value is moved to the FOUND-FLAG. If the entire table is searched without getting an equal comparison, the AT END option is executed and 'NO' is moved to the FOUND-FLAG.

```
      A   B
1   4  78  12                                                           72
─────────────────────────────────────────────────────────────────────────
      01    PARTS-TABLE-INPUT.
            05 PARTS-TABLE OCCURS 1000 TIMES
                    ASCENDING KEY IS PART-NUMBER
                    INDEXED BY PART-INDEX.
                10 PART-NUMBER      PIC 9(07).
                10 DESCRIPTION      PIC X(15).
                10 LOCATION         PIC X(06).
                    :
                    :
            PERFORM 400-SEARCH-PARTS-TABLE.
            IF FOUND-FLAG = 'YES'
                MOVE DESCRIPTION (PART-INDEX) TO PART-OUT
                MOVE LOCATION (PART-INDEX) TO LOCATION-OUT
            ELSE
                MOVE '**NOT FOUND**' TO MESSAGE-OUT.
                    :
                    :
      400-SEARCH-PARTS-TABLE.
            SEARCH ALL PARTS-TABLE
                AT END MOVE 'NO' TO FOUND-FLAG
                WHEN PART-IN IS EQUAL TO PART-NUMBER (PART-INDEX)
                    MOVE 'YES' TO FOUND-FLAG.
```

APPENDIX C

EBCDIC AND ASCII CONVERSION TABLES

Decimal	Hexadecimal	Binary	EBDCIC	ASCII
0	00	0000 0000	NUL	NUL
1	01	0000 0001	SOH	SOH
2	02	0000 0010	STX	STX
3	03	0000 0011	ETX	ETX
4	04	0000 0100	SEL	EOT
5	05	0000 0101	HT	ENQ
6	06	0000 0110	RNL	ACK
7	07	0000 0111	DEL	BEL
8	08	0000 1000	GE	BS
9	09	0000 1001	SPS	HT
10	0A	0000 1010	RPT	LF
11	0B	0000 1011	VT	VT
12	0C	0000 1100	FF	FF
13	0D	0000 1101	CR	CR
14	0E	0000 1110	SO	SO
15	0F	0000 1111	SI	SI
16	10	0001 0000	DLE	DLE
17	11	0001 0001	DC1	DC1
18	12	0001 0010	DC2	DC2
19	13	0001 0011	DC3	DC3
20	14	0001 0100	RES	DC4
21	15	0001 0101	NL	NAK
22	16	0001 0110	BS	SYN
23	17	0001 0111	POC	ETB
24	18	0001 1000	CAN	CAN
25	19	0001 1001	EM	EM
26	1A	0001 1010	UBS	SUB
27	1B	0001 1011	CU1	ESC
28	1C	0001 1100	IFS	FS
29	1D	0001 1101	IGS	GS
30	1E	0001 1110	IRS	RS
31	1F	0001 1111	ITB	US

Decimal	Hexadecimal	Binary	EBDCIC	ASCII
32	20	0010 0000	DS	SP
33	21	0010 0001	SOS	!
34	22	0010 0010	FS	''
35	23	0010 0011	WUS	#
36	24	0010 0100	BYP	$
37	25	0010 0101	LF	%
38	26	0010 0110	ETB	&
39	27	0010 0111	ESC	'
40	28	0010 1000	SA	(
41	29	0010 1001	SFE	)
42	2A	0010 1010	SM	*
43	2B	0010 1011	CSP	+
44	2C	0010 1100	MFA	`
45	2D	0010 1101	ENQ	-
46	2E	0010 1110	ACK	.
47	2F	0010 1111	BEL	/
48	30	0011 0000		0
49	31	0011 0001		1
50	32	0011 0010	SYN	2
51	33	0011 0011	IR	3
52	34	0011 0100	PP	4
53	35	0011 0101	TRN	5
54	36	0011 0110	NBS	6
55	37	0011 0111	EOT	7
56	38	0011 1000	SBS	8
57	39	0011 1001	IT	9
58	3A	0011 1010	RFF	:
59	3B	0011 1011	CU3	;
60	3C	0011 1100	DC4	<
61	3D	0011 1101	NAK	=
62	3E	0011 1110		>
63	3F	0011 1111	SUB	?
64	40	0100 0000	space	@
65	41	0100 0001		A
66	42	0100 0010		B
67	43	0100 0011		C
68	44	0100 0100		D
69	45	0100 0101		E
70	46	0100 0110		F
71	47	0100 0111		G
72	48	0100 1000		H
73	49	0100 1001		I
74	4A	0100 1010		J
75	4B	0100 1011	.	K
76	4C	0100 1100	<	L
77	4D	0100 1101	(	M
78	4E	0100 1110	+	N
79	4F	0100 1111			O
80	50	0101 0000	&	P
81	51	0101 0001		Q
82	52	0101 0010		R
83	53	0101 0011		S
84	54	0101 0100		T
85	55	0101 0101		U
86	56	0101 0110		V
87	57	0101 0111		W
88	58	0101 1000		X
89	59	0101 1001		Y
90	5A	0101 1010	!	Z
91	5B	0101 1011	$	[

Decimal	Hexadecimal	Binary	EBDCIC	ASCII
92	5C	0101 1100	*	/
93	5D	0101 1101	)	]
94	5E	0101 1110	;	
95	5F	0101 1111		
96	60	0110 0000	-	
97	61	0110 0001	/	a
98	62	0110 0010		b
99	63	0110 0011		c
100	64	0110 0100		d
101	65	0110 0101		e
102	66	0110 0110		f
103	67	0110 0111		g
104	68	0110 1000		h
105	69	0110 1001		i
106	6A	0110 1010	|	j
107	6B	0110 1011	,	k
108	6C	0110 1100	%	l
109	6D	0110 1101	_	m
110	6E	0110 1110	>	n
111	6F	0110 1111	?	o
112	70	0111 0000		p
113	71	0111 0001		q
114	72	0111 0010		r
115	73	0111 0011		s
116	74	0111 0100		t
117	75	0111 0101		u
118	76	0111 0110		v
119	77	0111 0111		w
120	78	0111 1000		x
121	79	0111 1001	`	y
122	7A	0111 1010	:	z
123	7B	0111 1011	#	{
124	7C	0111 1100	@	|
125	7D	0111 1101	'	}
126	7E	0111 1110	=	~
127	7F	0111 1111	"	DEL
128	80	1000 0000		
129	81	1000 0001	a	
130	82	1000 0010	b	
131	83	1000 0011	c	
132	84	1000 0100	d	
133	85	1000 0101	e	
134	86	1000 0110	f	
135	87	1000 0111	g	
136	88	1000 1000	h	
137	89	1000 1001	i	
138	8A	1000 1010		
139	8B	1000 1011		
140	8C	1000 1100		
141	8D	1000 1101		
142	8E	1000 1110		
143	8F	1000 1111		
144	90	1001 0000		
145	91	1001 0001	j	
146	92	1001 0010	k	
147	93	1001 0011	l	
148	94	1001 0100	m	
149	95	1001 0101	n	
150	96	1001 0110	o	
151	97	1001 0111	p	

Decimal	Hexadecimal	Binary	EBDCIC	ASCII
152	98	1001 1000	q	
153	99	1001 1001	r	
154	9A	1001 1010		
155	9B	1001 1011		
156	9C	1001 1100		
157	9D	1001 1101		
158	9E	1001 1110		
159	9F	1001 1111		
160	A0	1010 0000		
161	A1	1010 0001	~	
162	A2	1010 0010	s	
163	A3	1010 0011	t	
164	A4	1010 0100	u	
165	A5	1010 0101	v	
166	A6	1010 0110	w	
167	A7	1010 0111	x	
168	A8	1010 1000	y	
169	A9	1010 1001	z	
170	AA	1010 1010		
171	AB	1010 1011		
172	AC	1010 1100		
173	AD	1010 1101		
174	AE	1010 1110		
175	AF	1010 1111		
176	B0	1011 0000		
177	B1	1011 0001		
178	B2	1011 0010		
179	B3	1011 0011		
180	B4	1011 0100		
181	B5	1011 0101		
182	B6	1011 0110		
183	B7	1011 0111		
184	B8	1011 1000		
185	B9	1011 1001		
186	BA	1011 1010		
187	BB	1011 1011		
188	BC	1011 1100		
189	BD	1011 1101		
190	BE	1011 1110		
191	BF	1011 1111		
192	C0	1100 0000	{	
193	C1	1100 0001	A	
194	C2	1100 0010	B	
195	C3	1100 0011	C	
196	C4	1100 0100	D	
197	C5	1100 0101	E	
198	C6	1100 0110	F	
199	C7	1100 0111	G	
200	C8	1100 1000	H	
201	C9	1100 1001	I	
202	CA	1100 1010		
203	CB	1100 1011		
204	CC	1100 1100		
205	CD	1100 1101		
206	CE	1100 1110		
207	CF	1100 1111		
208	D0	1101 0000		
209	D1	1101 0001	J	
210	D2	1101 0010	K	
211	D3	1101 0011	L	

Decimal	Hexadecimal	Binary	EBDCIC	ASCII
212	D4	1101 0100	M	
213	D5	1101 0101	N	
214	D6	1101 0110	O	
215	D7	1101 0111	P	
216	D8	1101 1000	Q	
217	D9	1101 1001	R	
218	DA	1101 1010		
219	DB	1101 1011		
220	DC	1101 1100		
221	DD	1101 1101		
222	DE	1101 1110		
223	DF	1101 1111		
224	E0	1110 0000	\	
225	E1	1110 0001		
226	E2	1110 0010	S	
227	E3	1110 0011	T	
228	E4	1110 0100	U	
229	E5	1110 0101	V	
230	E6	1110 0110	W	
231	E7	1110 0111	X	
232	E8	1110 1000	Y	
233	E9	1110 1001	Z	
234	EA	1110 1010		
235	EB	1110 1011		
236	EC	1110 1100		
237	ED	1110 1101		
238	EE	1110 1110		
239	EF	1110 1111		
240	F0	1111 0000	0	
241	F1	1111 0001	1	
242	F2	1111 0010	2	
243	F3	1111 0011	3	
244	F4	1111 0100	4	
245	F5	1111 0101	5	
246	F6	1111 0110	6	
247	F7	1111 0111	7	
248	F8	1111 1000	8	
249	F9	1111 1001	9	
250	FA	1111 1010			
251	FB	1111 1011		
252	FC	1111 1100		
253	FD	1111 1101		
254	FE	1111 1110		
255	FF	1111 1111	EO	

APPENDIX D

COBOL RESERVED WORDS

Each COBOL compiler reserves a number of keywords that are for use by the language and cannot be used for other purposes in the program. The list usually includes most of the ANS COBOL words, plus any additional words used by the specific compiler.

Words listed here are from the 1974 and 1985 ANS standard COBOL. Words flagged with a single asterisk (*) are only applicable to 1985 ANS COBOL.

ACCEPT	BEFORE	COMMUNICATION
ACCESS	BINARY*	COMP
ADD	BLANK	COMPUTATIONAL
ADVANCING	BLOCK	COMPUTE
AFTER	BOTTOM	CONFIGURATION
ALL	BY	CONTAINS
ALPHABET*		CONTENT*
ALPHABETIC	CALL	CONTINUE*
ALPHABETIC-LOWER*	CANCEL	CONTROL
ALPHABETIC-UPPER*	CD	CONTROLS
ALPHANUMERIC*	CF	CONVERTING*
ALPHANUMERIC-EDITED*	CH	COPY
ALSO	CHARACTER	CORR
ALTER	CHARACTERS	CORRESPONDING
ALTERNATE	CLASS*	COUNT
AND	CLOCK-UNITS	CURRENCY
ANY	CLOSE	
ARE	COBOL	DATA
AREA	CODE	DATE
AREAS	CODE-SET	DATE-COMPILED
ASCENDING	COLLATING	DATE-WRITTEN
ASSIGN	COLUMN	DAY
AT	COMMA	DAY-OF-WEEK*
AUTHOR	COMMON	DE

458

DEBUG-CONTENTS	EVALUATE*	LEFT
DEBUG-ITEM	EVERY	LENGTH
DEBUG-LINE	EXCEPTION	LESS
DEBUG-NAME	EXIT	LIMIT
DEBUG-SUB-1	EXTEND	LIMITS
DEBUG-SUB-2	EXTERNAL*	LINAGE
DEBUG-SUB-3		LINAGE-COUNTER
DEBUGGING	FALSE*	LINE
DECIMAL-POINT	FD	LINE-COUNTER
DECLARATIVES	FILE	LINES
DELETE	FILE-CONTROL	LINKAGE
DELIMITED	FILLER	LOCK
DELIMITER	FINAL	LOW-VALUE
DEPENDING	FIRST	LOW-VALUES
DESCENDING	FOOTING	
DESTINATION	FOR	MEMORY
DETAIL	FROM	MERGE
DISABLE		MESSAGE
DISPLAY	GENERATE	MODE
DIVIDE	GIVING	MODULES
DIVISION	GLOBAL*	MOVE
DOWN	GO	MULTIPLE
DUPLICATES	GREATER	MULTIPLY
DYNAMIC	GROUP	
		NATIVE
EGI	HEADING	NEGATIVE
ELSE	HIGH-VALUE	NEXT
EMI	HIGH-VALUES	NO
ENABLE		NOT
END	IDENTIFICATION	NUMBER
END-ADD*	IF	NUMERIC
END-CALL*	IN	NUMERIC-EDITED
END-COMPUTE*	INDEX	
END-DELETE*	INDEXED	OBJECT-COMPUTER
END-DIVIDE*	INDICATE	OCCURS
END-EVALUATE*	INITIAL	OF
END-IF*	INITIALIZE*	OFF
END-MULTIPLY*	INITIATE	OMITTED
END-OF-PAGE	INPUT	ON
END-PERFORM*	INPUT-OUTPUT	OPEN
END-READ*	INSPECT	OPTIONAL
END-RECEIVE*	INSTALLATION	OR
END-RETURN*	INTO	ORDER*
END-REWRITE*	INVALID	ORGANIZATION
END-SEARCH*	I-O	OTHER*
END-START*	I-O-CONTROL	OUTPUT
END-STRING*	IS	OVERFLOW
END-SUBTRACT*		
END-UNSTRING*	JUST	PACKED-DECIMAL*
END-WRITE*	JUSTIFIED	PADDING*
ENTER		PAGE
ENVIRONMENT	KEY	PAGE-COUNTER
EOP		PERFORM
EQUAL	LABEL	PF
ERROR	LAST	PH
ESI	LEADING	PIC

PICTURE	RH	TABLE
PLUS	RIGHT	TALLYING
POINTER	ROUNDED	TAPE
POSITION	RUN	TERMINAL
POSITIVE		TERMINATE
PRINTING	SAME	TEST*
PROCEDURE	SD	TEXT
PROCEDURES	SEARCH	THAN
PROCEED	SECTION	THEN*
PROGRAM	SECURITY	THROUGH
PROGRAM-ID	SEGMENT	THRU
PURGE*	SEGMENT-LIMIT	TIME
	SELECT	TIMES
QUEUE	SEND	TO
QUOTE	SENTENCE	TOP
QUOTES	SEPARATE	TRAILING
	SEQUENCE	TRUE*
RANDOM	SEQUENTIAL	TYPE
RD	SET	
READ	SIGN	UNIT
RECEIVE	SIZE	UNSTRING
RECORD	SORT	UNTIL
RECORDS	SORT-MERGE	UP
REDEFINES	SOURCE	UPON
REEL	SOURCE-COMPUTER	USAGE
REFERENCE	SPACE	USE
REFERENCES*	SPACES	USING
RELATIVE	SPECIAL-NAMES	
RELEASE	STANDARD	VALUE
REMAINDER	STANDARD-1	VALUES
REMOVAL	STANDARD-2*	VARYING
RENAMES	START	
REPLACE*	STATUS	WHEN
REPLACING	STOP	WITH
REPORT	STRING	WORDS
REPORTING	SUB-QUEUE-1	WORKING-STORAGE
REPORTS	SUB-QUEUE-2	WRITE
RERUN	SUB-QUEUE-3	
RESERVE	SUBTRACT	ZERO
RESET	SUM	ZEROES
RETURN	SUPPRESS	ZEROS
REWIND	SYMBOLIC	
REWRITE	SYNC	
RF	SYNCHRONIZED	

COBOL FORMAT NOTATION

This appendix contains the general language formats of the American National Standard (ANS) COBOL. Because it is a complete appendix not all of these statements or options are discussed in this book.

General Format for IDENTIFICATION DIVISION

```
IDENTIFICATION DIVISION.

PROGRAM-ID. program-name.

[AUTHOR. [comment-entry] . . . ]

[INSTALLATION. [comment-entry] . . . ]

[DATE-WRITTEN. [comment-entry] . . . ]

[DATE-COMPILED. [comment-entry] . . . ]

[SECURITY. [comment-entry] . . . ]
```

General Format for ENVIRONMENT DIVISION

```
ENVIRONMENT DIVISION.

CONFIGURATION SECTION.

SOURCE-COMPUTER.   computer-name [WITH DEBUGGING MODE].

OBJECT-COMPUTER.   computer-name

                                      ⎧ WORDS      ⎫
    [ , MEMORY SIZE integer           ⎨ CHARACTERS ⎬ ]
                                      ⎩ MODULES    ⎭

    [ , PROGRAM COLLATING SEQUENCE IS alphabet-name]

    [ , SEGMENT-LIMIT IS segment-number].

[SPECIAL-NAMES.   [ , implementor-name

     IS mnemonic-name [ , ON STATUS IS condition-name-1  [ , OFF STATUS IS condition-name-2]]
     IS mnemonic-name [ , OFF STATUS IS condition-name-2 [ , ON STATUS IS condition-name-1]]

     ...

     ON STATUS IS condition-name-1  [ , OFF STATUS IS condition-name-2]
     OFF STATUS IS condition-name-2 [ , ON STATUS IS condition-name-1]

                              ⎧ STANDARD-1         ⎫
     [ , alphabet-name IS     ⎨ NATIVE             ⎬
                              ⎩ implementor-name   ⎭

                    ⎧ THROUGH ⎫
         literal-1  ⎨ THRU    ⎬ literal-2  [ , ALSO literal-3 [ , ALSO literal-4] ...]
                    ⎩         ⎭

                    ⎧ THROUGH ⎫
         literal-5  ⎨ THRU    ⎬ literal-6
                    ⎩         ⎭          ... [ , ALSO literal-7 [ , ALSO literal-8] ...]

     ...

     [ , CURRENCY SIGN IS literal-9]
     [ , DECIMAL-POINT IS COMMA ] . ]
```

```
[INPUT-OUTPUT SECTION.

FILE-CONTROL.

    {file-control-entry} ...

[I-O-CONTROL.

    [ ; RERUN [ ON  [ {file-name-1}        ] ]
                    [ {implementor-name}   ]

              EVERY   { [END OF] {REEL}            }
                      {          {UNIT} OF file-name-2 } ...
                      { integer-1 RECORDS            }
                      { integer-2 CLOCK-UNITS        }
                      { condition-name              }

    [ ; SAME [ RECORD     ] AREA FOR file-name-3  { , file-name-4} ...  ] ...
             [ SORT       ]
             [ SORT-MERGE ]

    [ ; MULTIPLE FILE TAPE CONTAINS file-name-5 [ POSITION integer-3]
        [, file-name-6 [POSITION integer-4]]  ... ]].
```

General Format for FILE-CONTROL Entry

Format 1

```
SELECT [OPTIONAL] file-name

    ASSIGN TO implementor-name-1 [, implementor-name 2] ...

    [ ; RESERVE integer-1  [ AREA  ] ]
                           [ AREAS ]

    [; ORGANIZATION IS SEQUENTIAL]

    [; ACCESS MODE IS SEQUENTIAL]

    [; FILE STATUS IS data-name-1] .
```

Format 2

```
SELECT    file-name

    ASSIGN TO implementor-name-1  [, implementor-name-2] ...

    [; RESERVE integer-1 [ AREA  ] ]
                         [ AREAS ]

    ; ORGANIZATION IS RELATIVE

    [                   { SEQUENTIAL  [, RELATIVE KEY IS data-name-1] }   ]
    [ ; ACCESS MODE IS  { { RANDOM  }                                 }   ]
    [                   { { DYNAMIC }  , RELATIVE KEY IS data-name-1  }   ]

    [ ; FILE STATUS IS data-name-2] .
```

Format 3

```
SELECT    file-name

    ASSIGN TO implementor-name-1  [, implementor-name-2] ...

    [; RESERVE integer-1 [ AREA  ] ]
                         [ AREAS ]

    ; ORGANIZATION IS INDEXED

    [                   { SEQUENTIAL } ]
    [ ; ACCESS MODE IS  { RANDOM     } ]
    [                   { DYNAMIC    } ]

    ; RECORD KEY IS data-name-1

    [; ALTERNATE RECORD KEY IS data-name-2 [WITH DUPLICATES]] ...

    [; FILE STATUS IS data-name-1] .
```

Format 4

```
SELECT file-name ASSIGN TO implementor-name-1 [, implementor-name-2] ...
```

```
DATA DIVISION.

[FILE SECTION.

[FD file-name

    [; BLOCK CONTAINS [integer-1] TO integer-2 {RECORDS   }]
                                               {CHARACTERS}

    [; RECORD CONTAINS [integer-3 TO] integer-4 CHARACTERS]

    ; LABEL {RECORD IS  } {STANDARD}
            {RECORDS ARE} {OMITTED }

    VALUE OF implementor-name-1 IS {data-name-1}
                                   {literal-1  }

        [, implementor-name-2 IS {data-name-2}] ...
                                 {literal-2  }

    ; DATA {RECORD IS  } data-name-3 [, data-name-4] ...
           {RECORDS ARE}

    ; LINAGE IS {data-name-5} LINES [, WITH FOOTING AT {data-name-6}]
                {integer-5  }                          {integer-6  }

        [, LINES AT TOP {data-name-7}] [, LINES AT BOTTOM {data-name-8}]
                        {integer-7  }                     {integer-8  }

    [; CODE-SET IS alphabet-name]

    ; {REPORT IS  } report-name-1 [, report-name-2] ... .
      {REPORTS ARE}

[record-description-entry] ... ] ...]
```

```
[SD file-name
    [; RECORD CONTAINS [integer-1 TO] integer-2 CHARACTERS]

       ⎡   ⎧ RECORD IS   ⎫                              ⎤
       ⎢ ; ⎨             ⎬ data-name-1  [, data-name-2] ... ⎥ .
       ⎣   ⎩ RECORDS ARE ⎭                              ⎦

    {record-description entry} ... ] ... ]


[WORKING-STORAGE SECTION.

    ⎡ 77-level-description-entry ⎤
    ⎢                            ⎥ ...
    ⎣ record-description-entry   ⎦


[LINKAGE SECTION.

    ⎡ 77-level-description-entry ⎤
    ⎢                            ⎥ ...
    ⎣ record-description-entry   ⎦


[COMMUNICATION SECTION.

    [communication-description-entry
    [record-description-entry] ... ] ... ]


[REPORT SECTION.

[RD report-name
    [; CODE literal-1]

       ⎡   ⎧ CONTROL IS   ⎫ ⎧ data-name-1  [, data-name-2]                          ⎫ ⎤
       ⎢ ; ⎨              ⎬ ⎨                                                        ⎬ ⎥
       ⎣   ⎩ CONTROLS ARE ⎭ ⎩ FINAL [, data-name-1] , data-name-2] ...]             ⎭ ⎦

       ⎡   PAGE ⎡ LIMIT IS  ⎤ integer-1 ⎡ LINE  ⎤ [, HEADING integer-2]             ⎤
       ⎢ ;      ⎣ LIMITS ARE⎦           ⎣ LINES ⎦                                    ⎥
       ⎣                                                                             ⎦

       [, FIRST DETAIL integer-3]   [, LAST DETAIL integer-4]

       [, FOOTING integer-5]] .

    {report-group-description-entry} ... ] ... ]
```

General Format for Data Description Entry

Format 1

```
level-number    { data-name-1 }
                { FILLER      }

[; REDEFINES data-name-2]

[; {PICTURE} IS character-string]
   {PIC    }

[; [USAGE IS] {COMPUTATIONAL}]
              {COMP         }
              {DISPLAY      }
              {INDEX        }

[; [SIGN IS] {LEADING } [SEPARATE CHARACTER]]
             {TRAILING}

[; OCCURS {integer-1 TO integer-2 TIMES DEPENDING ON data-name-3}
          {integer-2 TIMES                                      }

   [{ASCENDING } KEY IS data-name-4 [, data-name-5] ...] ...
    {DESCENDING}

   [INDEXED by index-name-1 [, index-name-2] ...]]

[; {SYNCHRONIZED} [LEFT ]]
   {SYNCHRONIZED} [RIGHT]

[; {JUSTIFIED} RIGHT]
   {JUST     }

[; BLANK WHEN ZERO]

[; VALUE IS literal].
```

Format 2

```
66  data-name-1; RENAMES data-name-2 [{THROUGH} data-name-3].
                                      {THRU   }
```

467

Format 3

```
88  condition-name;  ⎧ VALUE IS  ⎫  literal-1  ⎡ ⎧ THROUGH ⎫  literal-2 ⎤
                      ⎨          ⎬             ⎢ ⎨         ⎬            ⎥
                      ⎩ VALUES ARE ⎭           ⎣ ⎩ THRU    ⎭           ⎦

    ⎡ , literal-3  ⎡ ⎧ THROUGH ⎫  literal-4 ⎤ ⎤  ... .
    ⎣             ⎣ ⎨         ⎬            ⎦ ⎦
                    ⎩ THRU    ⎭
```

General Format for Communication Description Entry

Format 1

```
CD  cd-name;

    ⎡[; SYMBOLIC QUEUE IS data-name-1]

    [ ; SYMBOLIC SUB-QUEUE-1 IS data-name-2]

    [ ; SYMBOLIC SUB-QUEUE-2 IS data-name-3]

    [ ; SYMBOLIC SUB-QUEUE-3 IS data-name-4]

    [ ; MESSAGE DATE IS data-name-5]

    [ ; MESSAGE TIME IS data-name-6]

    [ ; SYMBOLIC SOURCE IS data-name-7]

    [ ; TEXT LENGTH IS data-name-8]

    [ ; END KEY IS data-name-9]

    [ ; STATUS KEY IS data-name-10]

    [ ; MESSAGE COUNT IS data-name-11]⎤
    [data-name-1, data-name-2, ..., data-name-11]

FOR [INITIAL] INPUT
```

468

Format 2

```
CD cd-name;  FOR OUTPUT

    [; DESTINATION COUNT IS data-name-1]

    [; TEXT LENGTH IS data-name-2]

    [; STATUS KEY IS data-name-3]

    [; DESTINATION TABLE OCCURS integer-2 TIMES

        [; INDEXED BY index-name-1  [, index-name-2]... ]]

    [; ERROR KEY IS data-name-4]

    [; SYMBOLIC DESTINATION IS data-name-5] .
```

General Format for Report Group Description Entry

Format 1

```
01 [ data-name-1]

    [ ; LINE NUMBER IS  ⎰ integer-1  [ON NEXT PAGE] ⎱ ]
                        ⎱ PLUS integer-2            ⎰

    [ ; NEXT GROUP IS  ⎧ integer-3      ⎫ ]
                       ⎨ PLUS integer-4 ⎬
                       ⎩ NEXT PAGE      ⎭

    [ ; TYPE IS  ⎧ REPORT HEADING                  ⎫ ]
                 ⎪ RH                              ⎪
                 ⎪ PAGE HEADING                    ⎪
                 ⎪ PH                              ⎪
                 ⎪ CONTROL HEADING  ⎰ data-name-2 ⎱⎪
                 ⎪ CH               ⎱ FINAL       ⎰⎪
                 ⎨ DETAIL                          ⎬
                 ⎪ DE                              ⎪
                 ⎪ CONTROL FOOTING  ⎰ data-name-3 ⎱⎪
                 ⎪ CF               ⎱ FINAL       ⎰⎪
                 ⎪ PAGE FOOTING                    ⎪
                 ⎪ PF                              ⎪
                 ⎪ REPORT FOOTING                  ⎪
                 ⎩ RF                              ⎭

    [ ; [USAGE IS]  DISPLAY].
```

Format 2

```
level-number  [data-name-1]

   [; LINE NUMBER IS  {integer-1  [ON NEXT PAGE]} ]
                      {PLUS integer-2           }

   [; [USAGE IS]  DISPLAY ].
```

Format 3

```
level-number  [data-name-1]

[; BLANK WHEN ZERO]

[; GROUP INDICATE]

[;  {JUSTIFIED}  RIGHT ]
    {JUST     }

[; LINE NUMBER IS  {integer-1  [on NEXT PAGE]} ]
                   {PLUS integer-2           }

[; COLUMN NUMBER IS integer-3]

;  {PICTURE}  IS  character-string
   {PIC    }

; SOURCE IS identifier-1

; VALUE IS literal

{; SUM identifier-2 [, identifier-3] ...

     [UPON data-name-2 [, data-name-3] ...] ...

     [RESET on  {data-name-4} ] }
                {FINAL      }

[;  [USAGE IS]  DISPLAY] .
```

Format 1

```
ACCEPT identifier [FROM mnemonic-name]

ACCEPT identifier FROM  {DATE }
                        {DAY  }
                        {TIME }

ACCEPT cd-name MESSAGE COUNT

ADD  {identifier-1}  [, identifier-2]  ...  TO  identifier-m  [ROUNDED]
     {literal-1   }  [, literal-2   ]

     [, identifier-n  [ROUNDED]]  ...  [ON SIZE ERROR imperative-statement]

ADD  {identifier-1}  {identifier-2}  [, identifier-3]  ...
     {literal-1   }  {literal-2   }  [, literal-3   ]

     GIVING identifier-m  [ROUNDED]  identifier-n  [ROUNDED]]  ...

     [; ON SIZE ERROR imperative-statement]

ADD  {CORRESPONDING}  identifier-1 TO identifier-2  [ROUNDED]
     {CORR         }

     [; on SIZE ERROR imperative-statement]

ALTER procedure-name-1 TO [PROCEED TO] procedure-name-2
     [, procedure-name-3 TO [PROCEED TO] procedure-name-4]  ...

CALL {identifier-1}  [USING data-name-1  [, data-name-2]  ...]
     {literal-1   }

     [; ON OVERFLOW imperative-statement]

CANCEL  {identifier-1}  [, identifier-2]  ...
        {literal-1   }  [, literal-2   ]
```

```
CLOSE file-name-1   ⎡⎧REEL⎫ ⎡WITH NO REWIND⎤⎤
                    ⎢⎨    ⎬ ⎢              ⎥⎥
                    ⎢⎩UNIT⎭ ⎣ FOR REMOVAL  ⎦⎥
                    ⎢                       ⎥
                    ⎢      ⎧NO REWIND⎫      ⎥
                    ⎢ WITH ⎨         ⎬      ⎥
                    ⎣      ⎩  LOCK   ⎭      ⎦

          ⎡            ⎡⎧REEL⎫ ⎡WITH NO REWIND⎤⎤            ⎤
          ⎢, file-name-2⎢⎨    ⎬ ⎢              ⎥⎥  . . .    ⎥
          ⎢            ⎢⎩UNIT⎭ ⎣ FOR REMOVAL  ⎦⎥            ⎥
          ⎢            ⎢                       ⎥            ⎥
          ⎢            ⎢      ⎧NO REWIND⎫      ⎥            ⎥
          ⎢            ⎢ WITH ⎨         ⎬      ⎥            ⎥
          ⎣            ⎣      ⎩  LOCK   ⎭      ⎦            ⎦


CLOSE file-name-1 [WITH LOCK]   [, file-name-2  [WITH LOCK]] . . .


COMPUTE identifier-1 [ROUNDED] [, identifier-2  [ROUNDED]] . . .
        = arithmetic-expression [; ON SIZE ERROR imperative-statement]


DELETE file-name RECORD  [; INVALID KEY imperative-statement]


          ⎧INPUT ⎫                        ⎧identifier-1⎫
DISABLE   ⎨      ⎬ cd-name  WITH KEY       ⎨           ⎬
          ⎩OUTPUT⎭                        ⎩literal-1   ⎭


         ⎧identifier-1⎫ ⎡ ⎧identifier-2⎫⎤
DISPLAY  ⎨           ⎬ ⎢, ⎨           ⎬⎥ . . .  [UPON mnemonic-name]
         ⎩literal-1   ⎭ ⎣ ⎩literal-2   ⎭⎦


        ⎧identifier-1⎫
DIVIDE  ⎨           ⎬ INTO identifier-2  [ROUNDED]
        ⎩literal-1   ⎭

        [, identifier-3 [ROUNDED]] . . .[; ON SIZE ERROR imperative-statement]


        ⎧identifier-1⎫      ⎧identifier-2⎫
DIVIDE  ⎨           ⎬ INTO ⎨           ⎬ GIVING identifier-3  [ROUNDED]
        ⎩literal-1   ⎭      ⎩literal-2   ⎭

        [, identifier-4 [ROUNDED]] . . . [; ON SIZE ERROR imperative-statement]


        ⎧identifier-1⎫    ⎧identifier-2⎫
DIVIDE  ⎨           ⎬ BY ⎨           ⎬ GIVING identifier-3  [ROUNDED]
        ⎩literal-1   ⎭    ⎩literal-2   ⎭

        [, identifier-4 [ROUNDED]] . . .  [; ON SIZE ERROR imperative-statement]
```

472

```
DIVIDE  {identifier-1 / literal-1}  INTO  {identifier-2 / literal-2}  GIVING identifier-3  [ROUNDED]
        [REMAINDER identifier-4]  [; ON SIZE ERROR imperative-statement]

DIVIDE  {identifier-1 / literal-1}  BY  {identifier-2 / literal-2}  GIVING identifier-3  [ROUNDED]
        [REMAINDER identifier-4]  [; ON SIZE ERROR imperative-statement]

ENABLE  {INPUT [TERMINAL] / OUTPUT}  cd-name  WITH KEY  {identifier-1 / literal-1}

ENTER language-name [routine-name] .

EXIT [PROGRAM] .

GENERATE  {data-name / report-name}

GO TO [procedure-name-1]

GO TO procedure-name-1  [, procedure-name-2]  . . .  , procedure-name-n
      DEPENDING ON identifier

IF condition;  {statement-1 / NEXT SENTENCE}  {; ELSE statement-2 / ; ELSE NEXT SENTENCE}

INITIATE report-name-1  [, report-name-2]  . . .

INSPECT identifier-1 TALLYING
        , identifier-2 FOR  , {ALL / LEADING / CHARACTERS}  {identifier-3 / literal-1}
        [{BEFORE / AFTER} INITIAL {identifier-4 / literal-2}]  . . .  . . .
```

```
INSPECT identifier-1 REPLACING

    ⎰CHARACTERS BY ⎱identifier-6⎰ ⎡⎰BEFORE⎱ INITIAL ⎰identifier-7⎱⎤
    ⎱          ⎰literal-4 ⎰ ⎣⎰AFTER ⎱         ⎰literal-5 ⎰⎦

    ⎧ALL    ⎫ ⎡  ⎰identifier-5⎱    ⎰identifier-6⎱ ⎡⎰BEFORE⎱ INITIAL ⎰identifier-7⎱⎤   ⎤
    ⎨LEADING⎬ ⎢, ⎰literal-3 ⎰ BY ⎰literal-4 ⎰ ⎣⎰AFTER ⎱         ⎰literal-5 ⎰⎦ ...⎥ ...
    ⎩FIRST  ⎭ ⎣                                                                    ⎦


INSPECT identifier-1 TALLYING

    ⎡                 ⎰⎰ALL    ⎱ ⎰identifier-3⎱⎱                                          ⎤
    ⎢, identifier-2 FOR ⎨⎰LEADING⎰ ⎰literal-1 ⎰⎬ [⎰BEFORE⎱ INITIAL ⎰identifier-4⎱] ...⎥ ...
    ⎣                 ⎩CHARACTERS              ⎭  ⎰AFTER ⎱         ⎰literal-2 ⎰     ⎦


REPLACING

    ⎰CHARACTERS BY ⎱identifier-6⎰ ⎡⎰BEFORE⎱ INITIAL ⎰identifier-7⎱⎤
    ⎱          ⎰literal-4 ⎰ ⎣⎰AFTER ⎱         ⎰literal-5 ⎰⎦

    ⎧ALL    ⎫ ⎡  ⎰identifier-5⎱    ⎰identifier-6⎱ ⎡⎰BEFORE⎱ INITIAL ⎰identifier-7⎱⎤   ⎤
    ⎨LEADING⎬ ⎢, ⎰literal-3 ⎰ BY ⎰literal-4 ⎰ ⎣⎰AFTER ⎱         ⎰literal-5 ⎰⎦ ...⎥ ...
    ⎩FIRST  ⎭ ⎣                                                                    ⎦


MERGE file-name-1 ON ⎰ASCENDING ⎱ KEY data-name-1 [data-name-2] ...
                     ⎱DESCENDING⎰

                [ON ⎰ASCENDING ⎱ KEY data-name-3 [data-name-4] ...] ...
                    ⎱DESCENDING⎰

    [COLLATING SEQUENCE IS alphabet-name]

    USING file-name 2, file-name-3 [, file-name-4] ...

    ⎰OUTPUT PROCEDURE IS section-name-1 [⎰THROUGH⎱ section-name-2]⎱
    ⎱                                    ⎰THRU  ⎰               ⎰
    ⎰GIVING file-name-5                                          ⎰


MOVE ⎰identifier-1⎱ TO identifier-2 [, identifier-3] ...
     ⎱literal    ⎰

MOVE ⎰CORRESPONDING⎱ identifier-1 TO identifier-2
     ⎱CORR         ⎰
```

```
MULTIPLY {identifier-1}  BY  identifier-2   [ROUNDED]
         {literal-1  }
    [, identifier-3 [ROUNDED]] ... [; ON SIZE ERROR imperative-statement]


MULTIPLY {identifier-1}  BY  {identifier-2}  GIVING identifier-3  [ROUNDED]
         {literal-1  }       {literal-2  }
    [, identifier-4 [ROUNDED]] ... [; ON SIZE ERROR imperative-statement]


OPEN  { INPUT file-name-1 [REVERSED         ] [, file-name-2 [REVERSED         ]] ... } ...
                          [WITH NO REWIND]                   [WITH NO REWIND]
        OUTPUT file-name-3 [WITH NO REWIND] [, file-name-4 [WITH NO REWIND]] ...
        I-O file-name-5 [, file-name-6] ...
        EXTEND file-name-7 [, file-name-8] ...


OPEN  { INPUT  file-name-1 [, file-name-2] ... } ...
        OUTPUT file-name-3 [, file-name-4] ...
        I-O    file-name-5 [, file-name-6] ...


PERFORM procedure-name-1 [{THRU   } procedure-name-2]
                          {THROUGH}

PERFORM procedure-name-1 [{THRU   } procedure-name-2] {identifier-1} TIMES
                          {THROUGH}                   {integer-1   }

PERFORM procedure-name-1 [{THRU   } procedure-name-2] UNTIL condition-1
                          {THROUGH}
```

```
PERFORM procedure-name-1  [ { THRU    } procedure-name-2 ]
                            { THROUGH }

        VARYING { index-name-1  } FROM { index-name-2 }  UNTIL  condition-1
                { identifier-2  }      { literal-1    }
                                       { identifier-3 }

        BY { literal-4    }
           { identifier-3 }

      [ AFTER { index-name-3  } FROM { index-name-4 }
              { identifier-5  }      { literal-3    }
                                     { identifier-6 }

        BY { literal-4    }  UNTIL  condition-2
           { identifier-7 }

      [ AFTER { index-name-5  } FROM { index-name-6 }
              { identifier-8  }      { literal-5    }
                                     { identifier-9 }

        BY { literal-6     }  UNTIL  condition-3 ] ]
           { identifier-10 }


READ file-name RECORD [INTO identifier]  [; AT END imperative-statement]


READ file-name [NEXT] RECORD  [INTO identifier]

     [; AT END imperative-statement]


READ file-name RECORD  [INTO identifier]  [; INVALID KEY imperative-statement]


READ file-name RECORD  [INTO identifier]

     [; KEY IS data-name]
     [; INVALID KEY imperative-statement]


RECEIVE cd-name  { MESSAGE }  INTO  identifier-1  [; NO DATA imperative-statement]
                 { SEGMENT }


     RELEASE record-name  [FROM identifier]
```

```
RETURN file-name RECORD [INTO identifier]   ; AT END imperative-statement

REWRITE record-name [FROM identifier]

REWRITE record-name [FROM identifier] [; INVALID KEY imperative-statement]

SEARCH identifier-1 [VARYING {identifier-2      }] [; AT END imperative-statement-1]
                             {index-name-1      }

    ; WHEN condition-1 {imperative-statement-2}
                       {NEXT SENTENCE         }

   [; WHEN condition-2 {imperative-statement-3}] ...
                       {NEXT SENTENCE         }

SEARCH ALL identifier-1  [; AT END imperative-statement-1]

    WHEN {data-name-1 {IS EQUAL TO} {identifier-3           }}
         {            {IS =       } {literal-1              }}
         {                         {arithmetic-expression-1}}
         {condition-name-1                                  }

        [AND {data-name-2 {IS EQUAL TO} {identifier-4           }}] ...
             {            {IS =       } {literal-2              }}
             {                         {arithmetic-expression-2}}
             {condition-name-2                                  }

        {imperative-statement-2}
        {NEXT SENTENCE         }

SEND cd-name FROM identifier-1

SEND cd-name [FROM identifier-1] {WITH identifier-2}
                                 {WITH ESI         }
                                 {WITH EMI         }
                                 {WITH EGI         }

   [{BEFORE} ADVANCING {{identifier-3} {LINE }}]
    {AFTER } {          {integer     } {LINES}}
             {          {mnemonic-name        }}
             {          {PAGE                 }}
```

477

```
SET {index-name-1  [, index-name-2] ...}  TO  {index-name-3}
    {identifier-1  [, identifier-2] ...}       {identifier-3}
                                               {literal-1  }


SET index-name-4 [, index-name-5]... {UP BY  } {identifier-4}
                                     {DOWN BY} {integer-2  }


SORT file-name-1 ON {ASCENDING } KEY data-name-1 [, data-name-2] ...
                    {DESCENDING}

          [ON {ASCENDING } KEY data-name-3 [, data-name-4] ...] ...
              {DESCENDING}

     [COLLATING SEQUENCE IS alphabet-name]

     INPUT PROCEDURE IS section-name-1 [{THROUGH} section-name-2]
                                        {THRU   }

     USING file-name-2 [, file-name-3] ...

     OUTPUT PROCEDURE IS section-name-3 [{THROUGH} section-name-4]
                                         {THRU   }

     GIVING file-name-4


START file-name [KEY {IS EQUAL TO     } data-name]
                     {IS =            }
                     {IS GREATER THAN }
                     {IS >            }
                     {IS NOT LESS THAN}
                     {IS NOT <        }

     [; INVALID KEY imperative-statement]


STOP {RUN    }
     {literal }
```

```
STRING  {identifier-1}  [, identifier-2]  ...  DELIMITED BY  {identifier-3}
        {literal-1}     [, literal-2]                        {literal-3}
                                                             {SIZE}

        [, {identifier-4}  [, identifier-5]  ...  DELIMITED BY  {identifier-6}] ...
           {literal-4}     [, literal-5]                        {literal-6}
                                                               {SIZE}

     INTO identifier-7 [WITH POINTER identifier-8]

     [; ON OVERFLOW imperative-statement]


SUBTRACT  {identifier-1}  [, identifier-2]  ...  FROM identifier-m [ROUNDED]
          {literal-1}     [, literal-2]

     [, identifier-n [ROUNDED]] ...  [; ON SIZE ERROR imperative-statement]


SUBTRACT  {identifier-1}  [, identifier-2]  ...  FROM  {identifier-m}
          {literal-1}     [, literal-2]                {literal-m}

     GIVING identifier-n [ROUNDED] [, identifier-o  [ROUNDED]] ...

     [; ON SIZE ERROR imperative-statement]


SUBTRACT  {CORRESPONDING}  identifier-1  FROM  identifier-2  [ROUNDED]
          {CORR}

     [; ON SIZE ERROR imperative-statement]


SUPPRESS PRINTING


TERMINATE report-name-1  [, report-name-2 ] ...


UNSTRING identifier-1

     [DELIMITED BY [ALL]  {identifier-2}  [, OR [ALL]  {identifier-3}] ...
                          {literal-1}                  {literal-2}

     INTO identifier-4  [, DELIMITER IN identifier-5] [, COUNT IN identifier-6]

     [, identifier-7  [, DELIMITER IN identifier-8] [, COUNT IN identifier-9]] ...

     [WITH POINTER identifier-10] [TALLYING IN identifier-11]

     [; ON OVERFLOW imperative-statement]
```

479

$$\text{\underline{USE} AFTER STANDARD} \begin{Bmatrix} \text{EXCEPTION} \\ \text{\underline{ERROR}} \end{Bmatrix} \text{PROCEDURE \underline{ON}} \begin{Bmatrix} \text{file-name-1 [, file-name-2] ...} \\ \text{INPUT} \\ \text{\underline{OUTPUT}} \\ \text{\underline{I-O}} \\ \text{EXTEND} \end{Bmatrix}.$$

$$\text{\underline{USE} AFTER STANDARD} \begin{Bmatrix} \text{EXCEPTION} \\ \text{\underline{ERROR}} \end{Bmatrix} \text{PROCEDURE \underline{ON}} \begin{Bmatrix} \text{file-name-1 [, file-name-2] ...} \\ \text{INPUT} \\ \text{\underline{OUTPUT}} \\ \text{\underline{I-O}} \end{Bmatrix}.$$

USE BEFORE REPORTING identifier

$$\text{\underline{USE} FOR DEBUGGING ON} \begin{Bmatrix} \text{cd-name-1} \\ \text{[ALL REFERENCES OF] identifier-1} \\ \text{file-name-1} \\ \text{procedure-name-1} \\ \text{\underline{ALL PROCEDURES}} \end{Bmatrix} \left[, \begin{Bmatrix} \text{cd-name-2} \\ \text{[ALL REFERENCES OF] identifier-2} \\ \text{file-name-2} \\ \text{procedure-name-2} \\ \text{\underline{ALL PROCEDURES}} \end{Bmatrix} \right] \ldots.$$

$$\text{\underline{WRITE} record-name [\underline{FROM} identifier-1]} \left[\begin{Bmatrix} \text{\underline{BEFORE}} \\ \text{\underline{AFTER}} \end{Bmatrix} \text{ADVANCING} \begin{Bmatrix} \begin{Bmatrix} \text{identifier-2} \\ \text{integer} \end{Bmatrix} \begin{Bmatrix} \text{LINE} \\ \text{LINES} \end{Bmatrix} \\ \begin{Bmatrix} \text{mnemonic-name} \\ \text{PAGE} \end{Bmatrix} \end{Bmatrix} \right] \left[\text{; AT} \begin{Bmatrix} \text{END-OF-PAGE} \\ \text{EOP} \end{Bmatrix} \text{imperative-statement} \right]$$

$$\text{\underline{WRITE} record-name [\underline{FROM} identifier-1] [; \underline{INVALID KEY} imperative-statement]}$$

480

General Format for Conditions

Relation Condition

```
identifier-1        IS [NOT] GREATER THAN      identifier-2
literal-1           IS [NOT] >                  literal-2
arithmetic-expression-1  IS [NOT] LESS THAN    arithmetic-expression-2
index-name-1        IS [NOT] <                  index-name-2
                    IS [NOT] EQUAL TO
                    IS [NOT] =
```

Class Condition

```
identifier IS [NOT]  NUMERIC
                     ALPHABETIC
```

Sign Condition

```
arithmetic-expression IS [NOT]  POSITIVE
                                NEGATIVE
                                ZERO
```

Condition-Name Condition

```
condition-name
```

Switch-Status Condition

```
condition-name
```

Negated Simple Condition

```
NOT simple-condition
```

Combined Condition

```
condition  AND   condition  ...
           OR
```

Abbreviated Combined Relation Condition

```
relation-condition  AND   [NOT] [relational-operator] object  ...
                    OR
```

481

Miscellaneous Formats

Qualification

```
{ data-name-1     }  [ {OF}              ]
{ condition-name  }  [ {IN} data-name-2  ] ...

paragraph-name  [ {OF} section-name ]
                [ {IN}             ]

text-name  [ {OF} library-name ]
           [ {IN}             ]
```

Subscripting

```
{ data-name      } (subscript-1  [, subscript-2  [, subscript-3]])
{ condition-name }
```

Indexing

```
{ data-name      } ( { index-name-1 }  [ {+} literal-2 ]
{ condition-name }   { literal-1    }  [ {-}          ]

                     { index-name-2 }  [ {+} literal-4 ]    [ , { index-name-3 }  [ {+} literal-6 ] ] )
                     { literal-3    }  [ {-}          ]        { literal-5    }  [ {-}          ]
```

Identifier: Format 1

```
data-name-1  [ {OF} data-name-2 ] ... [(subscript-1  [, subscript-2
             [ {IN}             ]

[, subscript-3])]
```

Identifier: Format 2

```
data-name-1  [ {OF}              ]
             [ {IN} data-name-2  ] ....  [ ( { index-name-1 }  [ {+} literal-2 ]
                                             { literal-1    }  [ {-}          ]

{ index-name-2 }  [ {+} literal-4 ]    [ , { index-name-3 }  [ {+} literal-6 ] ] )
{ literal-3    }  [ {-}          ]        { literal-5    }  [ {-}          ]
```

General Format for COPY Statement

```
COPY text-name  [ {OF / IN} library-name ]

    [ REPLACING  { ==pseudo-text-1==    BY   ==pseudo-text-2==  } ... ]
               ┌                  ┐      ┌                  ┐
               |  ==pseudo-text-1==|      |  ==pseudo-text-2==|
               |  identifier-1    |      |  identifier-2    |
               |  literal-1       |      |  literal-2       |
               |  word-1          |      |  word-2          |
               └                  ┘      └                  ┘
```

483

INDEX